THE POLITICS OF FOOD

Geoffrey Cannon

CENTURY
LONDON · MELBOURNE · AUCKLAND · JOHANNESBURG

First published in 1987 by Century Hutchinson Ltd
Brookmount House, 62-65 Chandos Place
London WC2N 4NW

Century Hutchinson Australia Pty Ltd
PO Box 496, 16-22 Church Street, Hawthorn, Victoria 3122,
Australia

Century Hutchinson New Zealand Ltd
PO Box 40-086, 32-34 View Road, Glenfield, Auckland 10, New
Zealand

Century Hutchinson South Africa (Pty) Ltd
PO Box 337, Bergvlei, South Africa

Photoset in North Wales by
Derek Doyle & Associates, Mold, Clwyd
Printed and bound in Great Britain by
Richard Clay Ltd, Bungay, Suffolk

British Library Cataloguing in Publication Data

Cannon, Geoffrey
    The politics of food : the secret world
    of Whitehall and the food giants which
    threaten your health.
    1. Food industry and trade—Political
    aspects—Great Britain   2. Beverage
    industry—Political aspects—Great
    Britain
    I. Title
    338.4'7641'0941   HD9011.5

ISBN 0-7126-1210-6

CONTENTS

Acknowledgements

I have relied on many writers and researchers whose work, much of which is published in scientific journals, is acknowledged in the references printed at the back of this book.

I have learned much from many people in government, science and industry, in Britain and elsewhere, some acknowledged here. While responsibility for this book and the judgements in it are mine, my thanks for guidance in its preparation or for supply of information go to Dr Keith Ball, Dr Walter Barker, Professor Norman Blacklock, Sir Richard Body MP, Dr Jeremy Bray MP, Dr John Brown, Professor Derek Bryce-Smith, Dr Denis Burkitt, Dr David Buss, Professor Neville Butler, Peter Campbell, Professor Kenneth Carroll, Professor John Catford, Simon Coombs MP, Professor Michael Crawford, Dr John Cummings, Sir David Cuthbertson, Dr Stephen Davies, Libby Day, Anne Dillon, Professor Sir Richard Doll, Wendy Doyle, Professor John Durnin, Dr Peter Elwood, Lord Ennals, John Forsyth, Dr John Garrow, Dr Oliver Gillie, Doris Grant, Salle Gray, Peter Greaves, Barbara Griggs, Allan Hackett, Geoffrey Harrington, Dr Kenneth Heaton, Professor Mark Hegsted, Dorothy Hollingsworth, Dr David Horrobin, Dr Elwyn Hughes, Dr Sandra Hunt, Dr Michael Jacobson, Professor Philip James, Sir Geoffrey Johnson Smith MP, Sir Francis Avery Jones, Dr Tim Lang, Professor Barry Lewis, Dr Alan Long, Alistair Mackie, Professor Thomas McKeown, Dr Donald McLaren, Michael Meadowcroft MP, Dianna Melrose, Dr Erik Millstone, Professor Jerry Morris, Dr Brian Nicholls, Professor Michael Oliver, Professor Ralph

Paffenbarger, John Patten MP, Dr Andrew Prentice, Lord Rea, Dr Sheldon Reiser, John Rivers, David Roberts, Professor Geoffrey Rose, Andrew Roth, Margaret Sanderson, Barry Sheerman MP, Professor Aubrey Sheiham, Dr Helena Sheiham, Dr Derek Shrimpton, Dr Hugh Sinclair, Professor Alwyn Smith, Professor Richard Smithells, Dr David Snodin, Professor John Soothill, Dr David Southgate, Professor Jeremiah Stamler, Don Steele, Dr Hugh Trowell, Professor Stewart Truswell, Dr Richard Turner, Professor A.J. Vlitos, Caroline Walker, David Walker, Troth Wells, Jack Winkler, Professor Arvid Wretlind, Arthur Wynn, Margaret Wynn, Dr Walter Yellowlees, Professor John Yudkin.

Some of the research on which this book was based was done in the course of preparing features for The Sunday Times, The Times, The Observer, The Daily Telegraph, the British Medical Journal, New Scientist, New Health and She. Thanks, therefore, to Don Berry, Magnus Linklater, Nicholas Wapshott, Colin Tudge, Felicity Lawrence, Joyce Hopkirk and Hilary Smith. Gail Rebuck of Century-Hutchinson commissioned the book, Victoria Huxley and Christopher Pick edited it, Susan Lamb spoke on its behalf, and my agent, Deborah Rogers, made the arrangements. Thanks to them: and also to Nicola Dunn, Carole Hobson and Adriana Luba; Stephen Gee and Geoffrey Robertson; and, above all, to Caroline Walker.

April 1987

INTRODUCTION

In the Soup

Bold ideas, unjustified anticipations, and speculative thought, are our only means for interpreting nature ... We must hazard them to win our prize. Those among us who are unwilling to expose their ideas to the hazard of refutation do not take part in the scientific game.

Karl Popper, The Logic of Scientific Discovery,[1] 1934

The health of a population depends on the way in which political actions condition the milieu and create those circumstances which favour self-reliance, autonomy and dignity for all, particularly the weaker.

Ivan Illich, Medical Nemesis,[2] 1977

Michael Heath, The Sunday Times, 1983

1

British food is a joke, an old joke; but nobody now is laughing. British food is just about the worst in the Western world, it's true, but so is British health. Since 1983, everybody in Britain who reads newspapers and watches television has been told again and again that bad health is caused by bad food. And so we are no longer amused by British food: we are appalled.

What has gone wrong? Why is British food and health so bad? When did the rot set in, and who is responsible? How can we – consumers and citizens, whoever else we are – transform the quality of the British food supply, and thus the national health? These are all political questions, and are the reasons why I decided to write The Politics of Food. But first, a personal story.

GET FRESH, GET TETRAPACK

I enjoy milk, but years ago decided to stop drinking a lot of fat with my milk. Those were the days of The Sunday Times Book of Body Maintenance,[3] first published in 1978, which explained why saturated fats (as in cows' milk) are bad for health and that low-fat food tastes better. So I said to my milkman: 'low-fat milk, please'.

'Certainly', he said, and started to deliver milk with a different coloured top. It had no cream on the top and tasted the same as the silver-top milk. It seemed that switching to healthier food was easy. Boasting about my new awareness some time later, I pointed out the new bottle to a friend, who laughed and told me that I was drinking red-top homogenized milk, with exactly the same amount of fat in it as silver-top, but dispersed throughout the bottle. More than half the calories in silver-top and red-top milk are from highly saturated fats.

So I said to my milkman: 'this isn't low-fat milk. Can I have low-fat milk, please.' 'What's the matter with what I've been giving you?' he asked, unpleased. After all, it had no cream on the top. 'It's fine,' I said, 'except that what I want is low-fat milk.'

'OK,' he said, and started to deliver milk in a funny thin bottle with a metal cap. This relic of the 1960s looked like the type of bottle turpentine comes in from corner ironmongers, and I had to search in the back of a kitchen drawer for an old-style opener to wrench the cap off. The bottle looked weird, and getting into it was a feat. Worse, the milk tasted awful, like highly diluted condensed milk. It seemed that switching to healthier food was a penance. Making the most of my new sense of virtue some time later, I pointed out the new bottle to my friend. More laughter. This was sterilized milk, with exactly the same amount of fat in it as silver-top and red-top. The only essential difference was the disgusting taste.

'This isn't low-fat milk,' I said to my milkman. 'Yes it is,' he said. 'No it isn't,' I said, and being well-informed now, explained the difference between silver-top, red-top and metal-top milk, and said that what I wanted was skimmed milk. 'No call for it, squire,' he said. So I cancelled my order and started to buy skimmed milk at the local shop. This was ultra-heat-treated (UHT) milk, in packets you needed a bread knife to open. It tasted faintly chemical, I thought, and I started to go off the whole idea of milk.

One day in 1984, I saw my old milkman in the street. 'I've got skimmed milk now,' he said. He had, too: litre packs which also had to be sawed open. 'It's going very well,' he said, sounding surprised. 'Jolly good,' I said and gave him a regular order.

A week later I got nothing but silver-top for a week, and refused to pay for it. This made the milkman very sad, and he explained that the skimmed milk supplied to his yard had 'sell-by' dates only a day after the first day of delivery; it just wasn't worth his while picking them up. So that was why my skimmed milk had been going off! I supposed that the milkman was doing his best, and settled down to a routine of skimmed milk most of the time and silver-top (with the cream poured off) occasionally. The *Sunday Times* book was right, too. After a while full-fat milk tastes disgusting – so greasy!

By the summer of 1985, according to a feature in the *Observer*, sales of low-fat (semi-skimmed and skimmed) milk in Britain had increased in one year from 4 per cent to 13 per cent of total milk sales.[4,5] A new campaign by the advertising agency Allen Brady and Marsh was planned to emphasize the nutritional value of milk:[4]

The campaign will carry on the tradition of 'Gotta Lotta Bottle' and 'Get Fresh, Get Bottle' theme, but will give more information as to the composition of the six basic types of milk on the market – pasteurised, homogenised, sterilised, skimmed, semi-skimmed and Channel Islands.

And, indeed, in the same issue of the *Observer* there appeared a double-page colour advertisement, paid for by the National Dairy Council and devised by Allen Brady and Marsh.[6] It claimed that all types of milk are wonderfully, uniquely healthy:

> Every pint of silver-top is only 3.8 per cent fat. Which, when you think about it, leaves a whole 96.2 per cent of the pint that isn't.

Well, that's one way of putting it. The advertisement did not mention that about 90 per cent of milk is water; or, as my friend had told me a couple of years before, that 3.8 per cent by *weight* of fat means that over half the *calories* of full-fat milk are from highly saturated fats. The advertisement also did not mention h**rt d*s**s*; nor did it refer to the fact that my skimmed milk was coming in packs, not bottles. I suppose 'Everybody's Body Needs Cardboard' or 'Get Fresh, Get Tetrapack' are not ringing copy lines.

On 2 August 1985, my milkman delivered two pint bottles of fresh milk. Not skimmed, which is what I wanted, but semi-skimmed: red and white stripy top. (Skimmed is blue and white stripy top.) So, for the first time ever, I had succeeded in getting fresh and getting bottle, and not getting full-fat milk, from the milkman. One of the pints had a red, yellow and brown label stamped indelibly on the front. This label said, in big letters: 'COOL 'EM. MARS. COOL AND DELICIOUS STRAIGHT FROM THE FRIDGE' and underneath, in small letters, 'Advertisement'. On the back there was a picture of a Mars Bar and, again, 'COOL AND DELICIOUS STRAIGHT FROM THE FRIDGE' with, underneath in small letters, 'Please rinse and return to your milkman.'

Why didn't my milkman know the difference between homogenized, sterilized and skimmed milk? Indeed, why had I shared his ignorance, in common with 94 per cent of British women polled on the subject in 1984?[5] Why had deliveries of low-fat milk been erratic, and why, when it was delivered, was the milk often on the point of going bad? Why did it take four years for me to get the milk I wanted? And why, when it arrived conveniently bottled and fresh (although still not skimmed), had the bottle been turned into an advertisement for Mars Bars? It seemed to me that the dairy industry did not want to satisfy consumer demand for low-fat milk. Was I right to suspect this? *The Politics of Food* has been written to answer such questions.

THE NEW, IMPROVED,
LOW-SUGAR SAUSAGE

Discussion and argument about food, health and disease has now become part of a national debate. But the message has changed.

From the 1940s to the 1970s, the story was that everybody should be sure to eat enough good food. 'Just the stuff to give the troops,' my mother used to tell me, spoon poised in front of my infant lips . 'Don't forget the starving millions,' teachers urged me over dinner at primary school. What was meant by 'good food' was food high in protein, energy, and the vitamins and minerals everybody has heard of – vitamins A, B, C, D, calcium and iron.[7]

In the 1980s, as you will have noticed, the story is that everybody should take care to eat less bad food. What is meant by 'bad food' is food heavy in saturated fats, fats generally, 'empty' calories, processed sugars, salt and chemical additives.[8,9] Sections of the food industry have now decided that there are marketing opportunities in this message. In 1984, the Milk Marketing Board made semi-skimmed and skimmed milk nationally available for the first time, which was how my milkman came to tell me that I could, after all, stop him and buy some, and why the *Observer* and many other newspapers started carrying advertisements explaining that full-fat milk (which the Dairy Trades Federation prefers to call 'whole milk')[10] bulges with calcium, and that skimmed milk also bulges with calcium.

How can the old message about protein and energy be

reconciled with the new message about saturated fats, fats, empty calories, processed sugars, salt and additives? In the case of sausages, with great difficulty, you might think. Here, though, is one of the most ingenious marketing campaigns of our time. 'A leading sausage manufacturer has now announced a radical programme of reform,' read a press release from Walls, a Unilever subsidiary, in early 1985: 'super sausage launched'.[11]

50% LESS FAT. NOW 50% OF THE PRICE. OUR NEW SAUSAGES ARE THE LEANEST WE'VE EVER MADE. THAT'S SAYING SOMETHING

This was the wording in the subsequent £15,000 'special offer' advertisement[12] in Womans Own.

No artificial flavouring – they don't need it. Less sugar, less salt – the flavour's superb.

Boots the Chemist launched a campaign to increase its share of the baby food market with a £30,000 advertisement in Radio Times in April 1985.[13] After saying that one in every ten babies is estimated to react badly to cows' milk, with eczema as one result, the copywriter pressed on:

Then there's the 'No Added Preservatives' clause which speaks for itself. Along with flavourings and colourings, these additives add no nutrition whatever to your food ... Finally, and perhaps most predictably, we take a pretty dim view of sugar. It only supplies calories and is of no other nutritional value. It can give a baby a sweet tooth even before he's got any. And then rot them when he has.

'People need to be told of the need to change their regular eating habits,' said David Malpas, Managing Director (Trading) of Tesco, at a press conference held at the Café Royal in January 1985 to launch a major initiative.[14]

IF YOU'RE WATCHING WHAT YOU EAT LOOK FOR OUR LABELS

was the headline in Tesco advertisements in the national press. The copy ran:[15]

Most doctors agree we should choose a diet which reduces the amount of fat, salt and sugar we eat and increases the amount of fibre.

Malpas pledged that by May 1986 all 1400 Tesco own-label foods would carry details of the percentages of fat, added sugar and added salt they contain. Malpas said:

> This will start a major public debate. This is the first serious attempt on a really wide scale to come clean and tell people exactly what is in the pack. Never mind about what the government may do one day. We are the people who have the duty and the responsibility to respond, so we say – get on with it.

In their stores, Tesco proudly presented the launched products with their new health claims such as 'LOW FAT', 'NO ADDED SUGAR', 'REDUCED CALORIE' and 'LOW SALT'. Would a Tesco 'economy' sausage qualify for these labels in time? Tim Mason, head of the Tesco project team on healthy eating, agreed that no, it wouldn't.[16,17]

At the end of May 1986 Tesco announced a massive 51 per cent rise in its annual profits, which reached an all-time high of £122,900,000 for the year 1985-86.

The headline in the *Guardian*'s financial pages ran:[18]

JOY AT TESCO AS NEW 'QUALITY' IMAGE EMERGES

What did the government think of Tesco's own-brand labelling initiative? Not a lot, it seemed. A fortnight before Tesco's record results were announced, Mrs Peggy Fenner, then junior minister at Agriculture, Fisheries and Food (MAFF), addressed the Annual General Meeting of the Coronary Prevention Group (CPG). In common with Tesco, other supermarket chains, and every health and consumer organization with an informed view on the subject, the CPG had found that what we the consumers want to know is just how much sugars and salt, fats and saturated fats, the food we eat contains. And what we want is clear labelling to that effect, using visual symbols (like a globule of fat) and/or a simple HIGH MEDIUM LOW system.[19] Simple. Useful.

But 'there is no clear consensus of medical evidence'[20] on sugars and salt, Mrs Fenner said. The Government would say 'no' to symbols, which 'tended to offer only selected nutrients' (which is of course the whole idea). A senior civil servant from MAFF, also present at the meeting, told me privately that anybody who wanted clear graphic labelling of the fats, saturated fats, sugars and salt content of foods was wasting time talking to the British government: these things, he said, are settled in Brussels, headquarters of the European Community. Why does the British government continue to thwart our desire to choose good food? Is there a war going on, with government and giant food manufacturers on one side and consumers and retailers on the other? If so, why? Are we pawns in a game being played by bureaucrats in Brussels? *The Politics of Food* has been written to answer such questions.

NUTRITION GAINS SEX APPEAL

A Gallup poll conducted in autumn 1984[21] destroyed the myth that British shoppers are not interested in healthy food. Three-quarters of the 900 women interviewed said that they were concerned about eating healthily. The chief health worry is cancer; the chief food worry is additives, followed closely by calories, then fat, salt and sugar. Only 29 per cent thought that there is enough information on food labels. Concern was spread evenly across income groups, age groups and region: for instance, 77 per cent of London women and 76 per cent of Scottish women were 'very concerned' or 'fairly concerned' about eating healthily; and only 27 per cent of the low 'DE' income group women thought that food labels were adequate, much the same as the figure of 25 per cent for the high 'AB' group. Significantly, nearly one in eight of the people initially contacted by Gallup were excluded from the poll because ill-health requires them to eat special foods.

In June 1985 the British Market Research Bureau produced a report on attitudes to labelling, jointly commissioned by the Ministry of Agriculture (MAFF), the Consumers' Association, and the National Consumer Council. Of the 820 people polled nationwide in this representative survey, over one in five were eating special foods because of diet-related disease.[22,23] The detailed figures were as follows:

Diet to control high blood pressure	5 per cent
Diet to control heart disease	5 per cent
Avoiding a food allergy	5 per cent
Diabetic diet	3 per cent
Other medical/doctor's recommendation	4 per cent

If the additional 14 per cent following slimming diets are included, a total of 36 per cent of the poll – over one third – ate special food in order to counteract the effect of their 'normal' diet.

Sutcliffe, Britain's third largest catering company, which serves 3 million meals and snacks a week,[24] launched its 'Eat Fit' campaign in early 1985. The Sutcliffe training manual for catering staff said that:[25]

> We may yearn for chocolate, chips, luncheon meat, sausage rolls and fizzy drinks, but if we do make this our permanent diet, we are likely to end up overweight, listless, spotty, breathless and toothless.

Glossy booklets freely available in their canteens explained that:[26]

> Dietary guidelines are recommendations for the whole population with a view to modifying eating habits to prevent certain diseases and promote good health. They recommend changes in the proportions of dietary fibre, fat, salt and sugar in the diet.

Home-cooking tips were also given:

> When you make fruit crumble use oats and wholemeal flour and half the amount of fat and less sugar. In whipping up fruit mousse or fools use yoghurt mixed up with or instead of cream.

Tesco agreed. Its *Guide to Healthy Eating*[27] stated that:

> At the moment we include in our diet too many foods with a high saturated fat, sugar or salt content.

By 1987 twelve million copies of this glossy free booklet and associated leaflets had been picked up by Tesco shoppers,[17] and demand was not slackening.

Before 1984, television, radio, newspapers and magazines weren't very interested in food and health. 'Food' meant shopping, cooking, eating out or gourmandising. 'Health' (as in 'National Health Service') meant disease. 'Food and health' might rate a corner of a woman's page in a newspaper, with a feature on Handy Hints for the Housebound or something along those lines. 'Nutrition' was a fringe, 'soft' subject too, suggesting meals on wheels, or 'home economics': worthy but, in the judgement of the media people who set the news agenda, boring.

But now food and health (which is to say, nutrition) are on the agenda. This is because food is a political issue. The whole concept of nutrition has changed: once it was boring, but now it is interesting. This list shows our contrasting perceptions of nutrition.

Nutrition: 1983 Boring	Nutrition: 1987 Interesting
Vitamin C	Coal-tar dyes
Meals on wheels	Official Secrets Act
Slimming	Heart disease
School meals	Schoolburgers
Asian rickets	Spina bifida
Salads	Sugars
Health Education Council	British Nutrition Foundation
Scurvy	Western diseases
Nut cutlets	Sausages
F-plan	NACNE

The list on the left does contain subjects of great and absorbing interest to individuals and to groups of people. The *F-Plan Diet* sold millions of copies, to take one example. But news editors do not reckon that the 'boring' topics are of general interest: they are not 'sexy'. The only slimming story that hit the headlines before 1984 was the one about the American diet doctor who was shot by his mistress. By contrast, since 1984 the media have been on the rampage about sausages and coal-tar dyes, to take two examples. These and innumerable other stories about food have essentially the same message, which is not only that we are suffering from British food, but also that we are being poisoned. This is what gives the stories their 'bite' or 'edge', in news editors' words. Is there any truth in these stories? This is a question which prompted me to write *The Politics of Food*.

NORMAL? BALANCED? VARIED?

What lies behind the headlines? And what lies behind the press conferences and other special events that generate the headlines? As a writer with a special interest in food and health, I have been watching what the food manufacturers have been up to throughout the 1980s. I have attended conferences, read the food trade magazines and the business pages, and talked to people from industry and government.

My findings are set out in the six chapters of this book and in the three subsequent Documents.

Talk to a manufacturer of highly processed food – 'asparagus' 'soup', say, dyed with brilliant blue FCF (133 – no 'E' number) and he (it's almost always a man) won't make any great nutritional claims for the product. People like it, otherwise it wouldn't sell, he'll say. It's a free country. Besides – and here comes the line agreed by all food technologists – there's no such thing as junk food, only a junk diet. In a 'normal', 'varied' diet, one food is balanced by another, is the story. 'Asparagus' 'soup' provides calories, from its fats and sugars; other food provides, well, other things. Vitamins. Protein. Things like that. Everybody's entitled to a little treat once in a while. Don't be such a fuss-pot.

The idea behind this line, beloved by government and industry representatives, is that the normal diet is balanced and varied, supplying all the nourishment your body needs, and that the odd cup of brilliant blue soup, or the odd chocolate éclair, never did anybody any harm. Empty calories from saturated fats and/or processed sugars are just part of the 'balance'. Indeed, sugary or fatty foods restore 'lost' energy, or help you play, or aid recovery. Any food advertised as a source of energy is a source of calories and little if anything else, of course.

The myth that we live with, is that Britain is a healthy nation. You only have to walk down the street to realise that this is indeed a myth. And it is not only middle-aged and old people who look and obviously are in bad health. Children and young people are also evidently tired and often plainly unwell.

Every breeder knows that fragile animals are liable to pass on their weakness to the next generation. There is good reason to believe that the same is true of people, and that the children of badly fed parents and grandparents are more vulnerable to the constellation of diseases caused by bad food. That is to say, we in Britain may well be breeding not a rising generation, but a falling generation. Evidence now crowding into the leading medical journals is showing that highly processed food, drained of nourishment, can and does have a calamitous effect on vulnerable people at all stages of life.

Just as the propaganda of the manufacturers of highly processed food, seen in context, makes a pattern, so do the findings of well-conducted dietary surveys of British people. News of two of these surveys, of the food eaten by British children of 11 and 14,[28] and by 15 to 25-year-olds,[29] hit the headlines in 1985 and 1986. They had been commissioned by Government and their findings then obscured or suppressed because of the appalling story they told. I put these reports in context, in chapter 1.

Insofar as Britain has any national policy on food and health, this has in recent decades been nodded through Parliament by our elected representatives. Such policies as we have, are agreed by government officials and their masters in MAFF and the DHSS who pick and choose the convenient bits from Officially Secret expert advisory committee reports. These committees are dominated by middle-aged men from science, industry and government. Their recommendations may be rewritten, delayed, obscured, suppressed, or ignored by government.

Consumers have at best token representation on these expert advisory committees, whose reports in recent years have made recommendations on such topics as the amount of fat that can go into a sausage,[30] the amount of water that can be added to bacon,[31] and why orange drinks may contain no oranges.[32] Other such reports have agreed that white bread is good food,[33] that the coal-tar dye tartrazine (E102) is a necessary and safe chemical additive,[34] and that industry can go ahead and bombard food with gamma rays.[35] Why should these committees be covered by the Official Secrets

Act, have an agenda set by government officials, minimise consumer representation and be aloof from public debate on our food and our health? An explanation was given on BBC Television in April 1986 by Professor Frank Curtis who in 1987 is Chairman of the Food Advisory Committee, the central expert committee working to MAFF:[36]

> I must emphasise that a great deal of the work is really quite technical, so I hope I don't sound too arrogant about this, but it really is quite a technical discussion, and this is not to discount the advantage of, you know, the common man's advice, but certainly to say it needs to be a limited proportion.

'Quite technical' sounds like 'you wouldn't understand'. Why are sausages saturated in fat? Why does frying bacon spit in your eye? Why are 'fruit' drinks often no fruit, all sugars, colours and flavours? Why does so much of the food in the shops look like chemistry sets? Very technical. Don't worry. Trust the experts.

SECRETS OF SUGARS
AND CHEMICAL ADDITIVES

Like other professional elite groups – lawyers and journalists, for instance – doctors and scientists are often accused of arrogance and irresponsibility, and sometimes the accusation is just. Generally speaking, 'experts' like people to take their words on trust. If we have blind faith in experts they are likely to despise us as lesser creatures. Members of government advisory committees work hard and in good faith. But their work is crucially impeded by a secrecy which, over the years, has taken advantage of our ignorance and indifference as consumers and citizens, which has been shared by our elected representatives in Parliament.

But academics and experts from industry and government charged with making recommendations about food and health cannot reasonably be blamed for getting things wrong if you, I and the MPs who legislate on our behalf, neither know nor care about what they are getting up to. Like trust, democracy is two-way traffic.

The Politics of Food is designed to give you the information you need, to make the right choices and judgements as individuals, members of families, and as voters. Chapters 3 to 5, on Sugars, Additives, and Vitamins and Minerals, are detailed case histories of three aspects of modern food. The most significant fact about sugars, in the context of this book, is that in 1987 Britain has no policy, no view, about sugars and health. Yet processed sugars supply calories and no nourishment whatsoever, as everybody knows; and, as I show, average consumption of sugars in Britain today is around a hundred pounds a year, amounting to one-fifth of total calorie intake. Moreover, two-thirds of the sugars eaten in Britain now are 'hidden' in manufactured food, much of which is a confection of processed fats, starches, and sugars, tarted up with chemical additives. So why has government overlooked sugars, until 1987?

I start chapter 4 by showing that expert advisory government committees have been worried about coal-tar dyes in food, in the 1920s, the 1950s, the 1960s, the 1970s, and the late 1980s. The story put about by government and industry representatives that all permitted additives are agreed to be safe, is untrue.

Facts about the dangers of certain additives have been kept from us. Likewise, facts about the vital necessity of certain vitamins and minerals have been kept from us. The British food supply is short of nourishment and, in particular, is deficient in vitamins and minerals often destroyed in the manufacture of highly processed food. But in Britain, more than any other Western country, government and industry, with the support of food science and technology, is agreed on a policy of cheapened food, which is making us ill.

'The Mystery of the Disappearing (Spinal) Column', one section within chapter 5, tells the story of the obscuring of good scientific evidence that lack of a key B vitamin, lost in processed food, is an important cause of birth defects, notably spina bifida. Why are British women of child-bearing age almost certain to be short of this vitamin?

CLEAN, SAFE – AND UNHEALTHY

As with the cholera and typhoid epidemics of Victorian days, and the childhood rickets and malnutrition still rampant in the 1930s, most of the diseases we suffer and die from today are fundamentally not a medical problem but a public health problem,[37] with profound implications for government, science and industry, as well as for ourselves and our families. And the key issue is food.

Between the 1950s and the early 1980s, food and health became a dead issue in Britain. We have been encouraged to have blind faith in drugs and surgery, and to assume that our food is dull and boring, but wholesome, and to take less interest in the quality of our food, than in the quality of petrol we put in our cars. But it is literally true that, weight for weight, rats, dogs, cows and apes, in the laboratory, home, farm and zoo, are given food whose quality is higher than the average British human diet[38,39] and generally much higher than the standards for humans officially laid down by the Department of Health.[40]

In the 1930s, John Boyd Orr wrote his classic study 'Food Health and Income',[41] and said, of children in the poorer half of the population:

> If children of the three social groups were reared like young farm stock, giving them a diet below the requirements for health would be financially unsound. Unfortunately, the health and fitness of the rising generation are not marketable commodities which can be assessed in terms of money.

Boyd Orr was proved wrong in one respect. The government of his day listened to him and others, because young men and women were needed to fight and work in the looming second World War. Our belief that British food is wholesome, is a faded memory of the wartime days when the Ministry of Food was given great powers to direct farmers and the food industry to grow, produce, process, distribute, cook and sell good wholesome food, and when such food was protected by investment and subsidy.[42]

Those days are gone. The Ministry of Food was folded into the Ministry of Agriculture and Fisheries in 1955 and became dominated by trade. The Ministry of Health coupled with Social Services in 1968 and became overwhelmed by what is in truth the National Illness Service, itself dominated by high technology medicine. By the 1970s food and health was off the political agenda.[43]

In the 1970s knowledgeable people in government, science and industry knew that insofar as Britain has a food and health policy, it derives from ideas of the nineteenth and early twentieth century, many of which are unhelpful, irrelevant, misleading, outdated, or just plain wrong. Unfortunately, the British food and farming industries were – and are – built from these theories. In solving one set of public health problems, politicians and their scientific and industrial advisors created new problems. The British food supply, as we know and suffer it now, did not evolve naturally. It is not any result of 'consumer demand'. The British food supply has arguably been more mucked about and manipulated than the food supply of any other country in the developed world. It is clean, safe in the sense of being relatively free from microbial contamination, but demonstrably grossly unhealthy.

FOOD IS A POLITICAL ISSUE

Any public health problem must necessarily be a political issue, and in good times, a political opportunity. In the nineteenth century, it took statesmanship to build the British sewage system. Anybody concerned with public health in Britain today is, however, faced with what may prove to be an intractable problem, which is: there is no evident vested interest in good health. In the cold gloom of short-term economics, which is as good as we generally get nowadays, a healthy citizen is a wretched proposition.

Food manufacturers do not want to poison the population: of course not. Corpses do not eat. The problem is that generally speaking, it is not whole, fresh food, but highly processed food with its 'added value', that makes the money. From the business point of view, a potato is small potatoes. Better, is a chip. Better still, is a crisp. Best of all, is a Crunchy Waffle.*

Decisions made by politicians are not taken in a vacuum, and the senior scientists who advise government do not work in ivory towers. The network of communication between industry, science and government in Britain is complex, and policy in a modern democracy is made after pressure and counter-pressure. But key decisions that determine the quality of the British food supply, and therefore the quality of the food purchased and eaten by the people of Britain, are covered by the Official Secrets Act, and made by closed circles of powerful people in government, science and industry. This is the subject of Chapter 6.

After the main text of the book, Document B shows that a majority of the scientists who advise government on food policy, work for or have links with industry and/or government. Document A shows the links between 250 MPs in office on 1 January 1987, and the food industry. People with public responsibilities are charged to make decisions uninfluenced by their interests. To show links between scientists, politicians and industry, is not to say that those links are abused. But here they are. Document C presents the medical and scientific evidence linking typical British food with 65 diseases.

The main chapter and the Documents are 'closely referenced', and all the references appear together at the back of the book. The references are there, of course, to enable anybody with a special interest in any of the themes of this book to consult the sources I have used. I have often been asked, as I have prepared this book: 'what are your sources?' or 'where did you get that from?' The references are the answer.

'The Politics of Food' includes plenty of bad news. What is the good news? The concluding chapter includes an outline of a programme for reform: how the next British government can ensure a healthy food supply, fit for human consumption.

* KP Foods, a subsidiary of United Biscuits, announced the launch of Crunchy Waffles, potato pieces cut into a lattice shape with salt, or cheese and onion, or salt and vinegar flavour, in March 1985. They were 'rolled out nationally with a £2 million support package'.[44]

Food and health, and public health generally, are not party political issues. In 1985 the Labour Party issued 'Food Policy: a Priority for Labour'[45] following the advice of Walter Bodner, Professor Philip James and Dr Hugh Trowell. Current Government policy is 'chaotic, pointless, perverse and out of date' declared front-bench spokesman Dr Jeremy Bray, introducing the Labour good food plan.[46] Later in the year the Liberal Party Assembly passed a Resolution on 'Food and Health', stating that the Ministry of Agriculture, Fisheries and Food has 'a duty to encourage the production of food which is healthy.'[47] In 1986 Sir Richard Body became Chairman of the Parliamentary Select Committee on Agriculture: a remarkable move, for Sir Richard, whose family have been farmers for 300 years, represents those Conservative legislators who, true to the traditions of their party, are also conservationists, and who hate a chemicalized agriculture and food supply.[48]

Consumers are also citizens. You have a voice. Nothing will change until politicians are sure that there are votes in good food and good health. Now is your time to speak out.

Part One

CHAPTER 1

What We Eat Now: Britain is the Sick Man, Woman and Child of Europe

Four out of five children are now eating more fat than the Government itself believes people should eat ... If children continue to eat the same sort of food, we can pretty confidently predict that we will continue in Britain to have the highest heart disease rate in the world. Indeed one might predict that the heart attack rate will go up.

Professor Philip James, The Threatened Generation,[1] 1986

'Fresh'. This word is used in a variety of different ways, sometimes in combination with another word. Examples drawn to our attention are 'dew fresh', 'farm fresh', 'freshly harvested', 'garden fresh', 'kitchen fresh', 'ocean fresh', 'oven fresh', 'sea fresh', 'sun fresh'. Whilst these phrases are intended to have an emotive effect, they have no real meaning.

Ministry of Agriculture, Fisheries & Food,
Food Standards Committee Second Report on
Claims and Misleading Descriptions[2], 1980

Breakfast   Corn flakes, sugar, milk, two slices white toast, butter, marmalade, cup of tea, sugar, milk
Mid-morning   Cup of tea, sugar, milk
Lunch   Heinz vegetable soup, cup of tea, sugar, milk, two digestive biscuits
Afternoon   Cup of tea, sugar, milk
Evening   Fish fingers, peas, mash, cup cake, cup of tea, sugar, milk
Later   Horlicks, sugar
Meals of 76-year-old Manchester man, Jam Tomorrow?[3], 1984

What do people in Britain eat nowadays? Judging from the food columns in the posh papers, we do pretty well. Here's Drew Smith of the *Good Food Guide* writing in the *Guardian* on the revival of English cookery:[4]

> Typical of both the old English cookery and its revival are a 'hunter's pot' of marinaded venison and wild duck served with herb scones and pickled damsons.

That's a lunch Mr Smith enjoyed in a country restaurant. At the Hilton in London's Park Lane he did even better:

> Here it is possible to eat some of the finest ham (now there's another thing that has gone out of vogue) brought on a plate partly covered with a sauce of sour cream and chopped watercress and a splurge of nutmeggy mashed potato. By way of canapes the pastry cases are filled with smoked eel and horseradish.

In the *Sunday Times*, just by way of contrast, Antonio Carluccio tells the readers about British mushroom-hunting:[5]

> I have probably picked about four tons of mushrooms in my lifetime. The majority are used for Autumn delicacies in the restaurant in Neal Street which I run. I preserve some in oil and freeze others at home to provide friends with a treat during the long winter months.

Signor Carluccio provides recipes for *porcini trifolati*, *quaglie con i pinaroli*, and other treats.

That's for up-market people. In the same week, the popular women's magazines laid on some delicious choices. To coincide with a new healthy food series on BBC2, *Woman*[6] included recipes for Filleted Grilled Fish with Spring Onions and Ginger (from Madhur Jaffrey), Green Risotto (Antonio Carluccio again) and, to finish off, Fruit Salad on a Red Wine Jelly (Lyn Hall and Anton Mosimann of *Cuisine Naturelle*).

'Old-fashioned favourites just like Grandma used to make,' was the cover promise of *Woman's Realm*;[7] and inside, Christine France followed the Drew Smith line:

How many delicious dishes come from an English country kitchen? Farmhouse loaf and rabbit pie, Cider Chicken, Hot Berry Pud and Plum Chutney ... So even if you're a townie born and bred why not try some rural recipes from the homely heart of England?

Woman's Own[8] had a colour display of nine ways with a baked potato: Tandoori Topper, Prawn Mayonnaise, Kidney and Bacon, Ham 'n' Egg, Ratatouille, Cheese and Chive, Cool as Cucumber, Le Crunch, and Hot and Chilli.

MILKY BAR AND ANGEL CAKE KIDS

Advertisements in the same magazine matched this cornucopia. Woman readers could choose between protein from Batchelor's Bean Cuisine ('Tropical Beanfeast ... sets the bongos banging all right')[9] and Scotch beef with the Foodmark for 'British food quality' ('Best Scotch Beef. The very name is evocative of a uniquely British tradition'.)[10] Woman's Own carried other ads, for Batchelor's savoury rice ('everywhere people are falling over themselves to get at our tantalisingly tasty Batchelor's Savoury Rice')[11] and Mattesons' salads – 'Make every day a Mmm day' with the bright new packs ('crunch', 'smooth', 'fresh', 'crisp', 'elegant', 'creamy').[12] And Weetabix suggested that 'healthy eating is a thing of the past', explaining:[13]

> All recent interest in healthy eating and high-fibre has come as no surprise to us at Weetabix. We've been producing our famous breakfast cereal for fifty years, and it's always been good for you.

Homely Woman's Realm included ads for Sarson's pickling malt vinegar ('four easy steps to perfect pickled onions'),[14] made an offer of the St Ivel Book of Sandwiches, showed 'how to turn your kid into the Milky Bar Kid' with £7.99 and three wrappers,[15] included a recipe for Chicken with Cream and Cashew Sauce for 'Some Enchanted Evening','when there's just the two of you', and, on the handcraft pages, showed how to make plaited napkin rings and a decorative sheaf of corn from modelling clay made of bread dough.[15]

Food manufacturers such as Batchelor's and Mattesons

know what sells foods. They ought to, for together with Wall's, Birds Eye, John West, Lipton, Brooke Bond, MacFisheries and the margarine giant Van den Berghs and Jurgens (Krona, Flora, etc.), Batchelor's and Mattesons belong to the biggest food company in the world: Unilever, employer of 280,000 people in seventy countries,[16] and far and away the biggest advertiser in Britain, with a total spend of £48,406,000 on its foods in 1984.[17]

An archaeologist from the year 2500 who discovered copies of the *Sunday Times Magazine*, *Woman* and all the rest buried for posterity might imagine that, as the British approached the year 2000, they were eating pickled damsons, porcini trifolati, kidney and bacon jacket potatoes, Scotch beef and Weetabix – just as our notions about 'Old English cookery' of the year 1500 are based on lists of feasts set down by monks and other advertising copywriters of the day. But if you want to get an idea of what the British diet is like, don't look at the advertisements. Take a look instead at the contents of the supermarket trolleys in front of you and behind you in the check-out queue; and while you are at it, look at the contents of your own trolley too.

However, the only methodical and reliable way of finding out what people are eating is through dietary surveys, in which representative groups of people are asked to record what they eat. The day's food of an old Manchester man, listed on the first page of this chapter, was recorded by the Food Policy Unit of Manchester Polytechnic in its report *Jam Tomorrow?*[3] as reasonably typical of the food eaten by 1000 people on low incomes in the North of England in the 1980s. Everything in this man's daily diet can be purchased at small corner grocery shops in tins, packages and bottles. He ate nothing fresh at all, unless you count pasteurized milk as fresh.

And here, from the beginning of life, is what a twenty-five-month-old child in West Glamorgan ate one day in 1984, as recorded by the Child Development Programme at the University of Bristol; the most substantial recent investigation into the food and health of little children.[18]

Breakfast   Cornflakes, milk, cup of tea
Mid-morning   Cadbury Creme Egg, Milky Bar

Lunch   Baked potato, slice white bread and butter
Afternoon   Ice cream, two slices Angel Cake, two digestive
   biscuits
Evening   Chips, two slices white bread and butter, cup of
   coffee

After monitoring 1000 families, whose development for three years was supported and guided by health visitors and other professionals, the researchers reported:[18]

Although official pronouncements state that the only real nutritional problem in Britain is one of obesity, in fact the Project interviewers' experience has shown that there are many malnourished children in the Project samples, some of whom suffer continual illnesses, which are treated by strong drugs or hospitalization. In turn the repeated illnesses can lead to delayed development. Continuously sick children lose their curiosity and desire to learn.

The child whose daily diet is cited here was one of eighty-two two-year-olds chosen at random from council-house estates in West Glamorgan. Is this diet typical of what little children from lower social groups eat in Britain today? The answer is 'no'. The child belonged to an 'intervention group', whose mothers were given guidance on good food by health visitors: hence the baked potato, the one item of fresh food, and the digestive biscuits, recommended as useful sources of fibre. The potato and drink aside, however, the child's daily food is made up entirely of highly saturated fats, processed starches and sugars, salt and additives.

A BLIGHT ON YOUNG LIVES

I asked Dr Walter Barker, Director of the Child Development Programme, for his views. Among the 1000 children, he said:[19]

We noticed a tremendous amount of minor recurring illness, like diarrhoea and chest infection, that just shouldn't be there. The link between diet and chronic illness in children is a very close one.

He instanced a mother whose eighteen-month-old girl had been on six courses of antibiotics; the child ate nothing but biscuits, with tea to drink. 'A high sugar intake in infancy predicts a lot of illnesses later in life,' was Barker's opinion:[19]

> The brain is still developing in the first two years of life. Most of the children from poor households, and many of the better-off children, were eating a poor diet, high in sugars and low in whole foods. This can lead to retarded brain growth after weaning. The children will never reach their full potential.

Professor Neville Butler, also from Bristol University, reported on the food habits of ten-year-old children of all social classes at a week-end conference on 'Nutrition and the Prevention of Degeneration' held in Oxford in September 1984.[20] The National Child Health and Education Study, in which 15,000 children born between 5 and 11 April 1970 are observed, shows that two-thirds of the children 'never' or 'hardly ever' eat brown bread or fish while over seven out of ten eat chocolate 'nearly every day' or 'quite often'. (Total annual UK confectionery sales are almost twice annual UK bread sales.) Comparing the 1970 study with two earlier ones, of children born in 1946 and 1958, Dr Butler showed that the rate of childhood insulin-dependent diabetes has increased six-fold in the last twenty-five years. 'The refined sugar story is almost certain to be linked with this', he told me.

Childhood diabetes is not a common affliction. Nevertheless, a six-fold increase is highly significant, and it is most unlikely to be a chance finding. Childhood eczema, on the other hand, is very common. In December 1984 in the *Lancet*,[21] Dr Brent Taylor of St Mary's Hospital Medical School, London, with co-workers, using the same three national child health studies, showed that in the last twenty-five years the rate of eczema in children under seven years old has more than doubled. One in twenty children born in 1946 suffered from eczema; the rate for children born in 1970 was one in eight. What's more, if anything eczema is a middle-class affliction, to which breast-feeding offers no special protection. How can this be? The reason may be allergic reaction to food additives:[21]

The diet of the general population has changed considerably since the 1939-45 war; constituents such as processed food might not easily be rendered harmless in the maternal digestive system and may be absorbed relatively intact to cross as allergens in breast-milk.

That is to say, highly processed foods contain chemical additives that do the mother no evident harm, but, after she digests them, may pass into her breast-milk and damage the fragile and immature immune system of her baby. Does this mean that babies could be better off drinking formula milk? No:[21]

The overall increase in eczema even in non-breastfed children suggests there may be a more general environmental influence now operating. If some chemical or chemicals are the cause, agricultural pollution may have resulted in the substance or substances appearing in cows' milk used for infant formulae.

A conference on food and health was held at the Royal Society of Medicine on 11 December 1984,[22] three months after Professor Butler had reported his findings, and ten days after the report in the *Lancet* by Dr Taylor. Dr Roger Skinner, then head of the Nutrition Unit at the DHSS (Department of Health and Social Security), was one of the speakers. I asked him if he was taking an interest in the increase in childhood diabetes and the epidemic of childhood eczema. His answer? 'No.'

In September 1985 Dr Michael Wadsworth, a colleague of Professor Butler and Dr Taylor at Bristol, presented findings at a conference of the British Society for Population Studies, held at the University of Sussex. 'CHILDREN "HEALTHIER 35 YEARS AGO" '[23] was the *Guardian* headline. In the *Times* it ran, 'TODAY'S CHILDREN FATTER, SICKER AND MORE DISTURBED'.[24] As well as steep rises in eczema and insulin-dependent diabetes, Dr Wadsworth reported a doubling of obesity and a trebling of asthma in young children between the 1946 and the 1970 studies. It may be, Dr Wadsworth suggested, that doctors today are better at spotting disease than doctors a generation ago. Alternatively, increased disease may, he suggested, be caused at least in part by agrichemicals (eczema), sweets (diabetes) and pollution (asthma):[24]

There have been enormous increases in hospital care for children. Admissions have doubled for pre-school children during a period when one would have thought they would be getting fitter.

Common sense suggests that the quality of food and health is a function of class and money: that the working class and the poor eat worse food and have worse health than people with comfortable middle-class jobs. Common sense, confirmed by DHSS findings,[25] is correct.[26] It is also true that the quality of food and of health varies according to region: people in Scotland, Wales, Northern Ireland and the north of England have less money, experience greater unemployment, eat more highly processed food, and suffer worse health.[27,28] The book-reading classes may therefore believe that bad food and bad health is not their problem, apart from the odd touch of eczema. Such a belief is wrong. This book is not just about other people.

What about older children? Allen Hackett of Newcastle University, with co-workers, has studied the food habits of 405 eleven-to thirteen-year-olds from Northumberland.[29,30] 'There is a problem with obesity; it seems to be developing in early adolescence,' Hackett told me, when I asked him to comment on the significance of his studies. Yet the energy intake of schoolchildren has been falling for decades,[31] and the boys and girls of all social classes studied by Hackett had a calorie intake well below the level recommended by the DHSS. Most of the children were short of vitamin A and iron by DHSS standards, and their fibre intake was 'pretty miserable'. Worse yet, two-fifths of the calories the children consumed came from fats (much highly processed and thus highly saturated) and one-fifth from processed sugars (much, like the fats, from snack food). One in ten of the children consumed a quarter of their calories in the form of processed sugars.

'ROW OVER TEENAGE DIET REPORT'

In early 1986 I heard a rumour that the government was stalling publication of a report it had commissioned on the food eaten by schoolchildren, because its findings were so appalling. A search of *Hansard*, the official record of parliamentary proceedings, showed that the report certainly existed, and that the Prime Minister herself had some interest in its outcome. On 21 February 1984 Robert Adley, Conservative MP for Christchurch, asked the Prime Minister:[32]

if she is satisfied with the co-ordination between the Department of Education and Science and the Department of Health and Social Security concerning risks to schoolchildren of heart disease and the composition of school meals.

Mrs Thatcher replied:[32]

Yes, the two Departments have collaborated in arranging a dietary survey of schoolchildren which takes account of their nutritional intake from school meals. The fieldwork for the survey was completed last year and a report is expected later this year [1984].

On 17 December 1984 Dr Gordon Brown, Labour MP for Dunfermline East, who had evidently noticed that the year was wearing on, asked the Secretary of State for Social Services[33]

when he expects to publish the results of the dietary survey of schoolchildren referred to by the Prime Minister on 21 February.

There seemed to have been some delay. John Patten, then junior minister at the DHSS, replied[33]

I understand that preliminary findings from the dietary survey of schoolchildren are expected to be available in spring 1985.

On 19 March 1985, a couple of days before the first day of spring, Derek Fatchett, Labour MP for Leeds Central, Tony Lloyd, Labour MP for Stretford, and Robert Adley returned to the theme, and interrogated Robert Dunn, a junior minister at the Department of Education. Mr Dunn replied:[34]

I am aware of the concern felt by many about the link between diet and disease. The Department of Health and Social Security has commissioned a survey of the diet of schoolchildren. It is hoped that the results will be published in the very near future.

Nine months later, on 30 January 1986, Dr John Marek, Labour MP for Wrexham, tried again, asking the Prime Minister[35]

> if she will ask the Office of Population Censuses and Surveys to publish an interim report of the dietary survey of school-children in 1983 as soon as possible.

Interim report? It seemed that Dr Marek had some inside information about possible jiggery-pokery involving the DHSS, the Department of Education, the Office of Population Surveys and Censuses, and apparently the Prime Minister herself, who was taking personal responsibility for the survey, now three years old, which had not yet seen the light of day. Mrs Thatcher replied:[35]

> The survey was commissioned by the Department of Health and Social Security and my Right Hon. friend the Secretary of State is currently considering whether to publish an interim report.

Why should Mrs Thatcher herself reply to Parliamentary Questions about the food eaten by schoolchildren? She is a food technologist by training,[36] true, and therefore may be the only politician in the history of the world to have a sentimental attachment to food additives. But Dr Bernard Dixon gave a more plausible clue in a story about Mrs Thatcher published in *New Scientist* in February 1986.[37]

Fifteen years earlier, when she was Secretary of State for Education and Science, she earned her first nickname, Thatcher the Milk Snatcher, when the government withdrew free school milk for seven- to eleven-year-olds, without assessing the possible health consequences. 'The action had provoked weighty criticism from paediatricians and nutritionists throughout the country,' wrote Dr Dixon. In particular, *New Scientist*, of which he was then editor, published a survey which

> showed that the daily diet of 68 per cent of youngsters aged 10 to 13 were already inadequate when measured against recommended standards. Measurements of two specific nutrients, riboflavin and calcium, indicated that the proportion of malnourished children in certain social groups would rise dramatically if they no longer received the milk. But, of course,

the consequent ill effects would be long term ... They were unlikely to worry politicians thinking of the more immediate future.

In 1971, when Dr Dixon was Chairman of the Association of British Science Writers (ABSW), Mrs Thatcher accepted an invitation to speak at an ABSW luncheon at the Dorchester Hotel. The journalists present asked her about her policy towards the nourishment of schoolchildren:

There followed a dreadful series of exchanges, as one journalist after another raised different aspects of the school milk issue and was treated with near contempt by the minister. Nobody but she, it seemed, really understood what this was all about. All of her medical and scientific critics were wrong. And the rest was media mischief.

In 1980 Mrs Thatcher's government took a more radical decision about schoolchildren's food:[38]

Prior to 1980 the meals provided by schools in Britain had to conform to prescribed nutritional standards. The 1980 Education Act released Local Authorities from this requirement and left them free to decide the form, content and price of meals.

This time, Mrs Thatcher was rather more cautious, and was prepared to listen to the advice of experts, albeit after the decision to privatize school meals had been taken:[38]

In the debate on this Act, Ministers agreed that the effect of the new school arrangements and the proposals of the Bill would be monitored.

The matter was referred to the Chief Medical Officer at the DHSS, and as a result the panel of the official government advisory Committee on Medical Aspects of Food Policy (COMA) concerned with Nutritional Surveillance agreed to oversee a survey of the food eaten by a representative sample of eleven- to fourteen-year-old British schoolchildren. The survey, of 3285 boys and girls, was carried out between January and June 1983. So the survey existed, all right, and two and a half years later, in early 1986, its publication had indeed been put off, according to Parliamentary questions, at least three times.

In February 1986 a leaked copy of the draft report came into my hands. It was, so the first page said,[39] 'designed to examine the contribution of school meals to the overall diet'. One passage leapt off the page:

> Because of the large quantity of chips, cakes and biscuits consumed by these schoolchildren, the consumption of most other food items was correspondingly reduced. The evaluation of the dependence on just three types of food for a significant proportion of the total daily intakes of nutrients is beyond the scope of this report and will require further analysis and interpretation.

What did Mrs Molly Disselduff, the chief compiler of the report, think? In 1986 she retired from her work at the DHSS. After taking legal advice, she explained that she had signed the Official Secrets Act and was bound by it to the grave.[40] What does the report show? Tables at the back listed intakes of various nutrients, measured against the official DHSS 'Recommended Daily Amount'.[41]

Just to take one example, most British children today are short of iron. Children consuming below the official recommended level are as follows. For eleven-year-olds: boys 81 per cent, girls 95 per cent; fourteen-year-olds, boys 53 per cent, girls 77 per cent. Below two-thirds of the recommended level the figures are as follows: eleven-year-olds, boys 20 per cent, girls 40 per cent; fourteen-year-olds, boys 8 per cent, girls 33 per cent. The consequences of iron deficiency are serious, as two articles in the *British Medical Journal* in April 1986 made clear:[42,43]

> There is now substantial evidence that iron deficiency has an adverse effect on brain function .... Several studies have shown that iron deficiency in children, with or without anaemia, is associated with abnormalities of behaviour and mental performance which improve with treatment with iron ... Children with iron deficiency anaemia scored less well than other children in tests of mental development and ... the iron deficient children were more tense and fearful but otherwise less responsive.

In early April 1986 the report hit the headlines of the national newspapers. On 3 April the *Daily Telegraph*'s headline and introductory story ran:[44]

> ROW OVER TEENAGE DIET REPORT. A so-far unpublished report commissioned by the Government from its nutritional advisors

at the Department of Health shows that Britain's overweight teenagers are consuming masses of fatty and sugary foods. Independent dietitians say the report shows that children are storing up future health problems by eating the wrong food in their developing years but the report is noticeably silent on the possible consequences of teenagers' high fat, high sugar and low fibre choice of food.

The next day, the *Guardian* reported a development:[45]

SURVEY ON 'CHIPS AND BISCUITS' DIET TO BE RELEASED. The leaked report showing that schoolchildren's diet consists largely of crisps, chips and biscuits, is to be published ....A date has yet to be fixed, but it became clear that Mr Norman Fowler now realizes that he cannot keep the report buried for much longer.

Behind the scenes, members of the main Committee on Medical Aspects of Food Policy (COMA), who like Mrs Disselduff signed the Official Secrets Act,[46] were restless. A preliminary copy of the report was handed out at the six-monthly COMA meeting in December 1984. A complete draft was circulated in April 1985 and discussed at the subsequent COMA meeting in June 1985.

At that meeting, COMA member Dr John Garrow pointed out that children's school meals evidently contained more fat than the meals they ate at home. Together with Dr John Cummings and Professor John Durnin, both also members of the main COMA committee, Dr Garrow asked for the report to be published. On 4 April 1986 a story in the *Times* said that the DHSS 'yesterday denied suppressing the report'.[47]

On 10 April 1986 the DHSS issued a press release[48] announcing the 'publication of a preliminary survey'. Was there a press conference? No, there was not. Were journalists and other interested parties sent copies of the 'preliminary report'? No, they were not. Instead journalists attending another conference at the DHSS on the same day (on the subject of food safety) were given the press release, and, after insistent requests, photocopies of the report were handed out. Mr Ray Whitney, then junior Health Minister, said in the press release:

The preliminary results are encouraging and show that our children enjoy adequate nutrition.

Overleaf some other points were made. These included:

On average children's nutrient intakes were above the DHSS recommendations.

Children were heavier and taller than expected.

One child in three ate more fat than the experts would like.

Virtually all the children ate a lot of chips, crisps, cakes and biscuits.

Children need more education about healthy eating.

Granada Television's *World in Action* broadcast a special programme, called 'The Threatened Generation', on the report on 14 April 1986.[49] This is how it started:

Four days ago the Government released results of the biggest postwar survey of the kind of food children now eat in Britain. It involved more than three thousand youngsters and took three years to produce. But the only way to get the report last week was to fetch it from the Department of Health. £650,000 of research emerged as a sheaf of duplicated paper stapled between makeshift covers.

And the interesting passage about 'the large quantity of chips, cakes and biscuits' in the draft report was missing. Would the members of the COMA committee, bound to the grave by the Official Secrets Act, talk to Granada? A team turned up at Dr Cummings's offices at the Dunn Clinical Nutrition Centre at Cambridge to find him in prolonged telephone conversation with a DHSS official, who was reminding him that the report was Officially Secret.[40] Once the report was published, Dr Cummings decided to speak his mind. He said, as broadcast:[1]

This report shows quite clearly that the diet these children are eating, if we are to believe current nutritional guidelines, is likely to leave them open to developing heart disease and cancer .... This is the sort of diet which has been condemned both in this country and in many countries in the world as the one likely to lead in later life to a whole variety of ill-health.

Dr John Garrow also decided to speak out publicly. He said, as broadcast:[1]

The proportion of obese children is increasing, and that is worrying, because the evidence is that the younger you become obese and the longer you have been obese the more likely you are to develop diabetes and high blood pressure.

Dr Cummings is an internationally renowned authority on diseases of the gut and on the benefits of dietary fibre.[50] He continued:

> Diets ... low in fibre have been associated with a number of bowel diseases, particularly things like constipation, appendicitis, haemorrhoids or piles as they're commonly known; with diverticular disease and perhaps more important, with bowel cancer, which is the second commonest cancer in the Western world. And if you look more broadly, this sort of diet is also associated with the development of non-bowel disease, like gall stones, diabetes and overweight, so the whole range of important diseases common in the Western world are associated with this type of diet.

By which he meant, of course, the food British schoolchildren are eating right now, as you read this book.

Professor Philip James also spoke out. Professor James is best known as the chief compiler of the NACNE report[51] on dietary goals, originally commissioned under the government's aegis, delayed for over two years, eventually published in late 1983, and then disowned by government. I have told the NACNE story in another book.[52] Professor James is also a member of the central Ministry of Agriculture Food Advisory Committee and, more to the point, a member of the COMA panel whose report in 1984 on *Diet and Cardiovascular Disease** recommended that national consumption of fats and saturated fats be cut. (This recommendation was accepted by government,[53] and it is therefore official policy to cut some fats out of British food.)

Professor James made it clear that Mr Whitney's estimate that one in three schoolchildren are eating more fat than the fussy old experts 'would like', was rubbish. He said, as broadcast:[1]

> We're not talking about an ideal fat intake, we're talking about a practical immediate guideline that should be implemented; yet four out of five children are not eating that sort of food.

* Britain is not short of advisory committees, nor is it short of expert advisors. At this point you may be feeling somewhat overwhelmed with the names of professors and committees. Help is at hand. Document B, 'Two Hundred and Forty-Six Advisors: Government, Science and the Food Industry' lists members of COMA, FAC and other relevant official advisory committees, with their affiliations. This Document is a useful guide to who is who and what is what, in the corridors and committee rooms of the secret world of food and health policy. See also Chapters 5 and 6.

What exactly was the matter with the food schoolchildren are eating now?

> This type of diet is precisely what one would expect from a country with the highest risk of heart disease in the world, and clearly the type of food they are getting at school is even worse than the food they are getting at home .... I think if the children continue to eat the same sort of food, we can pretty confidently predict that we will continue in Britain to have the highest heart disease rate in the world. Indeed one might predict that the heart attack rate will go up.

The interviewer asked Professor James to confirm the point. 'Even higher than it is now?' 'Even higher than it is now,' said Dr James. 'It really ought to be seen in that context.'

Caroline Walker, a nutritionist (and author with me of *The Food Scandal*)[52] combed through the 'preliminary report' and worked out what food children are eating, month by month. She appeared on screen in front of a mound of 4½lb of chips, 8¼lb of biscuits and cakes, 13 pints of full-fat milk and 9 pints of soft drinks. 'Each of these cans might contain anything between five to seven or eight teaspoons of sugar,' she said.

> So that is an enormous amount of sugar .... What we have is not only a fatty kind of diet, but also a very sugary kind of diet.

What about fresh vegetables and fruit? 'I practically had to get out a microscope to find them,' she said. Why had the report been delayed? She was in no doubt:[1]

> I think it's quite obvious why this report has been delayed. Because the results are an embarrassment. Because what it clearly shows to anybody who has a training in nutrition ... is that children are eating highly processed unhealthy food. It shows that we are storing up an enormous problem for ourselves as a nation.

World In Action asked Ray Whitney why the report had been delayed and what he thought about its findings. The transcript of the programme quotes him as follows:[1]

I really am a bit puzzled by your line of questioning, particularly as you say, er the report itself erm is not er exciting in your terms. It's reassuring in what it says about the nutrition intake of our children.

Was the report published only because of the pressure put on government after it had been leaked?

Certainly not, we have always indicated er that we're studying the report and er a number of times er we've said it was in course of preparation.

Was the DHSS worried about the findings of the report?

The contents of the survey and the report are very encouraging .... One in three are probably having too much – or were then – having too much unsaturated fat* or too much salt in their food. It's something we need to improve .... A report which shows that the children studied are taller and heavier than people expected and the standards that apply, what can be embarrassing about that.

In his press release[48] Mr Whitney said that the report's findings would continue to be analysed until 1988 and that a final report would be published thereafter. By that time, he suggested, any problem might have gone away.

THE PRIVATIZATION OF PUBLIC HEALTH

In July 1986 the Government's proposal to abolish free school meals for between 500,000 and 650,000 children from poor families, was passed by the House of Lords. On 16 July the *Times* reported[54]

The Government succeeded in pushing through proposals last night to scrap free school meals for 650,000 children from low-pay families. Furious activity by the Whips behind the scenes prevented the Government suffering its fourth defeat in the House of Lords .... Conservative peers were pulled in to support the Government – some coming straight from a Buckingham Palace garden party.

* Mr Whitney meant 'saturated fat'. He was at the time new in his job as minister at the DHSS responsible for public health. On 10 September 1986 he was replaced in Mrs Thatcher's reshuffle.

Sir Douglas Black, ex-Chief Scientist at the Department of Health, later President of the Royal College of Physicians and the British Medical Association, and in 1987 Chairman of the BMA Board of Education and Science, wrote to the *Guardian*. 'MR FOWLER DRAWS UP A DIET FOR DISASTER' was the headline:[55]

> The removal of free school meals is bound to increase the intake of sugar, salt, and fat, and reduce essential nutrients, especially iron, putting children's health at risk now and in the future .... This constitutes too great a risk for the nation's children. The Government should abandon the proposal.

In a big feature published by the *Star* the same day[56] – 'FIGHT TO KEEP FREE SCHOOL NOSH' – Professor James agreed with Sir Douglas:

> The health of thousands of children would be 'gravely damaged' by the Government's proposal. Children would switch to eating junk food – leading to obesity and heart disease later in life.

Sir Douglas Black's and Professor James's views were published the day before the Conservative Lords were ferried over from their Buckingham Palace garden party.

On 25 July 1986 Buckingham (the county, not the Palace) voted to abolish its school meal service in both primary and secondary schools: a new first.[57] Fifteen years after her first moves as Secretary for Education, Mrs Thatcher's policy to privatize public health was in top gear.

This was not the first time that a recent report on the food eaten by young people was commissioned by government and then buried.

In 1982 MAFF (Ministry of Agriculture, Fisheries and Food) carried out a representative national survey of the eating habits of 1000 young people aged fifteen to twenty-five. Dr David Buss, head of the Nutrition Unit at the Ministry, was able to present some of the survey's findings in the middle of 1983:[58]

> When asked to name the foods they [young people] liked best, chips, hamburgers, sausages, yoghurt, breakfast cereals and sweets were found to top the list. Foods the young people disliked most were those they described as 'soggy' or 'slimy'.

Into this category came offal, custard and gravy, canned fruit, and most vegetables (which presumably were the over-cooked variety). Anything with an 'artificial flavour' was also disliked .... Greasy foods, sweets, biscuits and butter were generally considered to be 'bad for you' by this age group, but most of them ate the 'bad' foods all the same.

But it was only in 1985, three years after the survey, that its results were published. Was *Dietary Habits of 15 to 25-Year-Olds* published by HMSO and thus made available to the public over the counter of the HMSO bookshops? No, it was not. Was a press conference called to announce its findings, enabling specialist journalists to question Dr Buss and his colleagues and let everybody know what young people are eating nowadays? There was no press conference. Instead the report was privatized and discreetly published as a special edition of the journal *Human Nutrition: Applied Nutrition*,[59] available on subscription from the publisher John Libbey, or else at a special price of £10.00 for its sixty-eight pages. This device made it appear to be not a MAFF report but a private survey carried out by 'Bull, N.' (Nicola Bull, a colleague of Dr Buss). Likewise, the report on the food eaten by schoolchildren is officially recorded not as a DHSS document but by 'Wenlock, R., Disselduff M., Skinner R., Knight I.'. (Robert Wenlock was also a colleague of Dr Buss and in 1986 succeeded Roger Skinner as acting head of the Nutrition Unit at the DHSS. Dr Skinner is now working on AIDS. Ian Knight works for the Office of Population Censuses and Surveys.) Somebody without special knowledge might assume that the £650,000 survey had been carried out by the team as a private project. Clever.

What did this survey, of food eaten by fifteen- to twenty-five-year-olds, find?:[59]

> The diets and attitudes towards food of older adolescents have not been studied and it is important for their future health that young adults adopt balanced eating habits.

And, as written up, the survey, as this quotation shows, was in many respects impenetrable. For example, Dr Barker, Professor Butler, and Mr Hackett all have found that children typically eat a lot of processed sugars, with damaging effects. So how much sugars do fifteen- to twenty-five-year-olds eat? The Ministry survey is silent on this central question. Like the survey of food eaten by eleven- and fourteen-year-olds, it gives no data on sugars, only on carbohydrates.

What it does show is that young people are consuming somewhat more fat than the general population. In all age groups, young men and young women consume more calories from fats than from carbohydrates (starches and sugars taken together). And fibre intake is below the national average, a sure sign of high consumption of processed starches, as well as sugars, and of low consumption of whole cereal, fresh fruit and vegetables. The report said:[59]

> There is some concern about 'junk' foods and the chemicals used in processed foods. While acknowledging that they are 'fattening', chips, sweets, some fizzy drinks and biscuits are popular for their taste and convenience value.

In other words, people tend to buy what is offered to them. One in twenty young people say they are allergic to some foods (4 per cent of the young men, 7 per cent of the women).

Taken together, consumption of chocolate, other confectionery, crisps and other savoury snacks, biscuits, desserts, cakes and jam amounts to 4½ ounces a day, or over 8½lb a month. At four ounces a day, bread consumption is lower, and also below the national average. Butter, margarine and cheese, all high in saturated fats, together contribute more calories a day (270 calories, about an eighth of total calories) than bread (237 calories). These figures and comparisons have to be deduced from tables printed at the back of the report. Its text is full of remarks such as:

> Men and women living in the south of England. This group had the lowest average consumption of soup.

And:

> Men and women living in the Midlands. This group had neither the lowest nor the highest average consumption in any food group.

Gripping stuff!

What about fresh fruit and vegetables? Average consumption of vegetables is 7 ounces a day, of which chips makes up 2 ounces a day (which equals 4 lb a month). Chips and chocolate together contribute more calories a day than bread. After potatoes, a total of 3 ounces of vegetables a day are eaten, mainly peas, baked beans, carrots, tomatoes and cabbage. This is the equivalent of a couple of carrots, or one tomato, or one onion a day.

On fruit, the report says:

> Apples accounted for almost a third of fruit consumption, followed by citrus fruits and bananas.

But it omits to mention in the main text what the total average consumption of fruit actually is. The tables at the back give an average figure of 2 ounces a day. This comes to about 25 to 30 calories a day, compared with a figure three times higher, 75 to 90 calories a day, from soft drinks. Two ounces a day is the equivalent of half a small apple, or four segments of orange, or half a banana.

Young people in Britain in the 1980s have almost stopped eating fresh vegetables and fruit. These pitiful statistics are well below the British average national figures for all age groups.[27]

Why was *Dietary Habits of 15 to 25-Year-Olds* so discreetly published? Interviewed for *New Health* magazine, nutritionist Caroline Walker socked it to them once again:[60]

> It is no wonder that the Government has tried to bury the devastating results of its own survey. They show that the national food supply continues to deteriorate. This is because the food in the shops is becoming more and more highly processed.

One sure test of how much fresh food people are eating is to ascertain its folic acid content. Folic acid is a B vitamin, so-called because it is found in the foliage of green vegetables and in whole grain, fruit and other fresh food.[61] Like all vitamins and many trace elements, folic acid is an essential nutrient, not made in the body, which we therefore need to consume in food. In the USA the recommended daily intake of folic acid for men and non-pregnant women is 400 micrograms (mcg) a day.[62] A lower recommendation, 300 mcg a day, has recently been issued by MAFF.[63] The table below, which I have compiled, shows recommended and actual intakes of folic acid a day.

Folic acid: recommended and actual intakes in Britain (mcg a day)

| Recommendation | | UK intake all ages | UK men | | | UK women | | |
USA	UK (MAFF)		15–18	19–21	22–25	15–18	19–21	22–25
400	300	213	153	179	186	125	116	133

The higher the amount of folic acid people consume, the more fresh food they are eating. These figures show that on average young men in Britain today consume little more than half the British recommended amount. Young women consume even less: the lowest average, 116 mcgs a day for nineteen- to twenty-one-year-old women, is not much more than one third the recommended amount. So around half the nineteen- to twenty-one-year-old women in Britain today are likely to consume even less.

HAVING A BABY ON FIZZY DRINKS

Whole fresh food, and plenty of it, is vital when the body is growing, and most of all for pregnant women. There is compelling evidence that lack of vitamins and minerals found in fresh food, notably folic acid, is a major cause of foetal defects, the best known of which is spina bifida.[64,65] As with many essential nutrients, extra folic acid is needed in pregnancy. The US recommendation is 800 mcg a day:[62] six times higher than the average nineteen- to twenty-one-year-old woman in Britain is consuming now.

Here is what one pregnant woman in Hackney, a deprived inner-city area, ate one day, as reported in 1982 by Wendy Doyle and Professor Michael Crawford of the Nuffield Laboratories of Medicine, London:[66]

Breakfast   Nothing
Mid-day   Slice white bread and Stork, cup of tea, chocolate
   digestives
Afternoon   Birds Eye strawberry mousse, Rowntree Nutty Bar
Evening   Cornish pasty, chips fried in lard, Coca Cola, slice
   white bread
Later   Coffee, Pregaday pill (supplement including folic acid)

This diet includes nothing whole or fresh at all. Strawberries, nuts and potatoes have been processed into mousse, Nutty Bar, pasty and chips. The only rich source of nourishment is the Pregaday pill. In a study of 100 pregnant women, Doyle and Crawford compared the quality of the food eaten in Hackney and that of middle-class Hampstead.[67,68] Judged by current standards, they found that the Hackney mothers were not getting enough to eat, and that much of their food had little value:

> The nutritional deficits in the lower socio-economic group may not necessarily be due to lack of money but rather lack of appreciation of the importance of nutrition. The choice of food was not always related to cost: take-away foods, fizzy drinks and confectionery were eaten more regularly by the Hackney mothers. They may not attach a high priority to their food when they have more pressing problems.

The Hackney diet was liable to harm the health of babies. It was severely short of folic acid, unless supplements were taken, and also of many other nutrients, notably the essential fats crucial to the development of the nervous system, including the brain. A substantial number of the babies born to the Hackney women in the study were of low birth weight.

Wendy Doyle also quoted an American study[69] to me:

> Under-nutrition during the period of rapid brain growth may be looked upon as a serious drain on social resources even in an affluent society. We look forward to the day when normal development of the child's brain will be considered its birth right.

In other words, can Britain afford mothers so badly fed that their babies are born retarded?

Hackney is the most impoverished borough in London, and the Hampstead mothers ate better food. But in some respects the diet of the two groups of women was more remarkable for its similarities than for its differences. The Hampstead mothers were also very short of folic acid (unless supplemented), of the fibre and essential fats contained in whole foods, and also of a number of minerals that they and their growing babies needed.[68,70]

BRITAIN ON THE SLICED BREADLINE

Millions of people in Britain today cannot pay for enough good food to eat. What kind of food is eaten by people on the sliced breadline? In November 1984 the findings of *Jam Tomorrow?*,[3] were described by Christopher Driver, ex-editor of *The Good Food Guide*, in *New Society*,[71] as follows:

> Not only is a significant minority in Britain now eating very badly indeed, but the choices forced upon them are reopening questions about the national diet scarcely asked since 1939.

Here is what a 37-year-old unemployed man with a wife and two children under 11 ate one day, as reported in *Jam Tomorrow?*:

> *Breakfast* Cup of tea, sugar, milk
> *Mid-morning* Two custard cream biscuits, cup of tea, sugar, milk
> *Lunch* Nothing
> *Afternoon* Egg, chips, peas, two slices white bread, margarine, cup of tea, sugar, milk
> *Evening* Cup of tea, sugar, milk
> *Later* Crisps, cup of tea, sugar, milk

Impoverished people are not indifferent to the quality of food. People interviewed for *Jam Tomorrow?* widely disliked, and even feared chemical additives:[3]

> 'Label read like doctors prescription.' 'Frozen chicken filled with water and chemicals.' 'Long "sell-by" dates such as boxed cakes, pies etc.' 'Too many additives and not enough basic food.' 'X topping – reads like an essay in organic chemistry.'

How does Britain compare with other poor countries of Europe? In August 1985 Ian Jack compared the quality of life in Liverpool and Turin, following the football disaster at Belgium's Heysel Stadium in which Liverpool supporters were blamed for the deaths of over thirty Juventus fans. In a long feature in the *Sunday Times Magazine*,[72] what most impressed Jack was the contrast between the food in the two cities. In Turin pastas and meats were in abundance. And:

> Enough meat? Step this way to the fruit and vegetable market where out of their boxes come tumbling the fresh Sicilian lemon and the Tuscan tomato, the smooth nectarines and the furry peach, dark aubergines and bright pepper, the wild mushroom and the mysterious fig.

And Liverpool?:

> I thought of Liverpool's Kwik-Save supermarket where the Giro folk queue every fortnight with their trolleys full of wrapped bread and economy-sized bottles of orange squash; and other, smaller shops meshed against vandals where ... the customer is confronted with the usual jumble of Embassy Tipped, Bounty bars and tinned beans, the sustenance of lower English life.

Jack talked to an Italian family, with a husband in work, earning the equivalent of £7,000 a year, married with two children:

> That night they would sit down to some tuna and salami, green salad and tomato salad, cheese and fruit, wine. For breakfast they'd taken biscuits and milk. For lunch, pasta al burro, veal cutlets, more salad, more cheese, more fruit.

In Liverpool Jack met a single mother with one baby living in a council flat:

> She confined herself to the local chip-shop and the corner store that drew the steel shutters after six. We met her climbing the stairs with a bag of chips, grease shining through the paper, destined for the baby, who would only eat them cold.

Official figures show that over three times as much fresh vegetables and fruit is eaten in Italy as in Britain.[73] Over twice as much fresh fruit is eaten in Austria, France, Switzerland and West Germany as in Britain, and up to and more than three times as much in Spain and Portugal and Italy.

Can adults get by on poor food? A team from the School of Hygiene and Tropical Medicine at London University has for some years been examining the links between social class and death from heart disease. The senior member of the team is Professor Geoffrey Rose, chairman of a World Health Organization expert panel on heart disease prevention which reported in 1982.[74]

Four years earlier, in the British Medical Journal,[75] Dr Rose, with co-workers, wrote that death from heart disease should not be regarded as a 'disease of affluence'. Since the 1950s deaths from heart disease in all age-groups from thirty-five to forty-four years old upwards were most common in lower-class (IV and V) men. Was this solely because of smoking? It seemed unlikely. What about diet?:

> The worsening mortality of classes IV and V correlated with relatively more smoking, a higher consumption of sugar, and a lower consumption of wholemeal bread.

In 1984, the same team reported on social-class differences in deaths from all causes,[76] based on a study over ten years of more than 17,000 civil servants. Men in the lowest Civil Service grades experienced a death rate from all causes three times higher than men in the highest grades. One reason could be relatively bad food eaten since birth:

> a relative lack of specific items such as vitamin A, fibre, vitamin C, trace elements, and potassium which may be related to specific cancers, stroke and high blood pressure.

Research into why people from low social and income groups suffer so much from disease 'is an urgent task of public health'.[76]

Why are people admitted to hospital? Their diagnosed illness may not be their only medical problem. In a signed editorial in the British Medical Journal in 1984,[77] Professor Arnold Bender, recently of London University, demanded an improvement in the quality of hospital food:

Illness, drug treatment, poor appetite and the possibility of monotonous and unattractive food may all help to explain a report from the United States that half of all hospital patients are suffering from some degree of malnutrition .... Between 5 and 10 per cent literally die of starvation.

In May 1984 a Portsmouth study showed that the local hospital food was grossly deficient in whole food and equally grossly heavy in fats.[78] But the much maligned hospital food in Britain may well often be less bad than the food the patients eat at home. In 1979 Dr Christopher Schorah found that the vitamin C levels of 115 post-surgical patients[79]

were well below those in a younger population and were also lower than subjects of a similar age outside hospital. Indeed, the values overlapped the range found in clinical scurvy.

A leading article in the *Lancet* in 1983[80] reported that over two-fifths of people admitted to hospitals were suffering at least some degree of malnutrition. The consequences included wasting, apathy, infection and failure of wounds to heal.

What, then, is the true cause of the diseases from which these people are suffering? Fate? As a rule hospitals do not take account of the fact that patients are admitted suffering from bad food as well as from the diagnosed illness. In hospital, trauma, ranging from fear to surgery, greatly increases the body's need for nourishment.[81] As a rule, hospitals take no account of this fact, either.

Babies, children, adolescents, young adults, pregnant women, poor people, the elderly, hospital patients: these are examples of groups in the population most at risk of illness that can be directly attributed to a specific dietary deficiency. Any underlying vulnerability, such as a relatively fragile immune system, an unusual requirement for a specific nutrient, a system weakened by many years of bad food, or mental or physical trauma, is particularly likely to lead to illness among these 'at risk' groups, in a form that can be diagnosed by a physician. For example, up to one in seven people over seventy in Britain is estimated to be so deficient in folic acid that the ill-effects (a severe form of anaemia) can readily be diagnosed.[51]

VICTORIAN FOOD: WORSE, OR BETTER THAN NOW?

But what about the majority of people in Britain who are not 'at risk'? Is British food in general really so very bad? After all, 'everybody knows' that the food we eat now is altogether superior to the food people ate in Victorian days or in the 1930s. Indeed, our general sense of confidence in the state of our health is based on the notion of progress: that every day in every way things are getting better and better. Are they?

The quality of today's food can be put in historical perspective. In 1863 Dr Edward Smith, a fellow of the Royal Society, surveyed the diet of 51 agricultural families in Wales.[82,83] His work was so meticulous that Dr Elwyn Hughes of the University of Wales in Cardiff has been able to reconstruct this Victorian diet with confidence[84] and feed it to mice.[85] In his study, Dr Hughes fed another group of mice with modern Welsh food. These developed high blood cholesterol (an indication of heart disease) and died younger than the first group. Hughes's conclusion was that the food eaten in 1863 had 'greater life-span potential than that currently consumed in Wales'.

In 1863, Welsh agricultural families ate plenty of food: their relatively active life meant that they needed 500 to 750 more calories a day than adults need now.[86] The staples of their diet were rough bread and potatoes, together with small amounts of meat, fish, butter, cheese and sugar, and a mixture of low-fat and full-fat skimmed milk and buttermilk. It was common to keep pigs and hens, although bacon and eggs were eaten only occasionally, as a treat. Dr Hughes noted that the 1863 diet was short of vitamin C, which depended on the quality of the potatoes eaten, but discovered contemporary travellers' tales of *Diod criafol*, a cordial made from the berries of the mountain ash and drunk by the common people. Hughes re-formulated *Diod criafol* and found it to be rich in vitamin C – rather like blackcurrant 'health' drinks today, but without the added sugars and colours. 'People might be well advised to go back to the agricultural diet,' Dr Hughes told me.[87]

What about other nutrients? Dr Hughes calculated that the 1863 diet contained more protein (with less animal protein), more iron and more vitamin D than the average British diet today, and about the same amount of calcium. The comparison of folic acid intake was of special interest. Generally speaking, people living in Wales today take in well below the estimated national average of 213 mcgs a day[88] and massively below the recommended international level for pregnant women.[62] Correspondingly, the rate of spina bifida and other foetal defects is very high. Hughes found that the 1863 diet contained 476 micrograms of folic acid: less than ideal, perhaps, for pregnant women, but three times the amount a woman in Wales is likely to consume in the 1980s.

Starvation and gross malnutrition were common in early Victorian Britain among the urban poor and in the countryside.[89] Matters were made worse later in the century when steel roller mills and the relaxation of taxes made white bread and white sugar, drained or empty of nourishment, staple foods for the working classes.[90,91] But Dr Hughes's new analysis of Smith's data shows that when people had enough to eat, over a century ago, a rustic diet was not only very nourishing but in vital respects was superior to British food in the 1980s.

WHAT ABOUT THE 1930s WORKERS?

A rustic diet does not appeal to a modern palate, and the way of life of mid-Victorian agricultural labourers is as foreign to people in Britain today as the way of life and diet of rural people in India or Africa. Life in Britain fifty years ago, however, is well within the memory of older people today. What did people eat two generations ago? And, specifically, what about the workers of the 1930s? We have been brought up to believe that people's health, at least in the lower social classes, suffered not only because of the effects of mass unemployment but also because of poor-quality food.

This is largely the result of one man's work. In the 1930s, John Boyd Orr was head of the Rowett Research Institute in

Aberdeen; later he became head of the Food and Agriculture Organization (FAO). In 1935 he was commissioned by the government, with support from the food industry, to investigate the quality of the national diet. He wrote:

> Everybody is agreed that while it is economically desirable to make agriculture prosperous, it is equally desirable to ensure that the food supply of the nation is sufficient for health, and is available at a price within the reach of the poorest.

His findings were first published in 1936 in his book *Food Health and Income*. In the second edition, brought out the following year, he wrote:[92]

> The diet of nearly one half of the population, though sufficient to satisfy hunger, is deficient for health. This seemed to come as a shock to people who had previously given no thought to the subject.

Boyd Orr made himself unpopular by insisting that what he meant by 'health' was not merely the absence of disease, but a positive, optimum health: 'a state of well-being such that no improvement can be effected by a change in the diet.' Boyd Orr's philosophy is that of the World Health Organization today.[93]

In the preface to his book Boyd Orr stated that:

> The adoption of a standard of diet lower than the optimum is uneconomic. It leads to a great amount of preventable disease and ill-health which lay a heavy financial burden on the State ... It is probable that an enquiry would show that the cost of bringing a diet adequate for health within the purchasing power of the poorest would be less than the cost of treating the disease and ill-health that could thereby be prevented.

Boyd Orr became one of the principal architects of a new public health policy, which acknowledged that food and health in the 1930s needed radical reform. This would require 'economic statesmanship of the highest order'. Boyd Orr's findings became a key instrument of national policy. That is why we have heard about the pre-war national diet.

So how does the working-class diet of the 1930s compare with the food supply of the 1980s? To find out requires reliable and comparable data from both periods, and also fairly sophisticated computation. Modern data is readily available: the National Food Survey, conducted on a continuous basis by MAFF[27], is a mine of information on the food typically eaten in Britain today.

But what about the data from the 1930s? Boyd Orr's conclusions were published in his book. But where were the raw data, the meticulous dietary surveys that had been compiled? Caroline Walker and I contacted Professor Philip James, now a successor of Boyd Orr as Director of the Rowett Institute. Had any of the old work survived? Indeed it had: the 1930s data remained locked in cupboards in Aberdeen, much of it untouched for over forty years. Here, written up in longhand on specially designed eight-page forms, were the weekly weighed intakes of families from all over Britain.

What we had uncovered was not material from the 1935 survey, but from the later Carnegie survey, conducted in 1938-39.[94] Here was the 'dietary study' of a railway porter (goods) from Liverpool, whose wife's occupation was listed as 'lactating'. Here was an electric cable jointer from Aberdeen; a shepherd from Hadd's Crofts; a postman from Bethnal Green; a farm labourer and a porter on the LNER, both from Cambridge; and a miner with a wife and family of six children aged from four to seventeen living in Portobello, Edinburgh.

In 1939 (week ending 26 April) this miner's family, as well as plenty of bread, baps, scones, oats, potatoes, some chips and sugar, ate an egg a day; liver, mince, meat pies, mutton and fried fish; plenty of milk; carrots, turnips, beans, peas, leeks, marrow; oranges, rhubarb, pineapple and salads; and Peggy, the six-year-old, had school milk and dinners. A miner's family today would be glad to eat food of this quality.

In the Rowett cupboards we found not only the dietary studies of individual families but also the analyses of the nationwide surveys of different social groups. We selected the analysis of the food eaten in 1938-39 by 365 families (2027 people) in social group III, within the poorer half of the population. We then coded these data, together with the data for the national diet published by MAFF in 1984,[27] and fed all the information into a computer at the Nuffield Laboratories of Medicine which is specially programmed to provide a complete nutritional analysis of food.

It was evident from the raw data we had examined that working-class families half a century ago ate a lot of animal fats, white flour and processed sugars. Consequently, their food was short of fibre and various vitamins and minerals by any standard.[41] In the last fifty years the pattern of food consumption has changed,[95] and the food in the shops today looks very different. But when we extracted the analyses from the computer, we found that changes for the better since the 1930s have been more or less matched by changes for the worse.

Today's food supply contains more fibre than in 1938-39, but less vitamin C, calcium and iron.[41,96] We consume somewhat more polyunsaturated, essential fats than our grandparents' generation did; but, overall, 1980s food is fattier. The food supply today contains roughly 40 per cent of its calories in the form of fats;[97] in 1938-39 working-class food only 29.4 per cent of total calories was fats.* This finding was of special interest, given that the recommendation of the NACNE report,[51] 'that average intake of fats be cut to 30 per cent,' has been criticized as being unrealistic, unpalatable and un-British.[98]

Only two conclusions are possible. If 'nutrition in Britain is generally good',[41] which is the last official word on the subject, then it was generally good before the war as well, and the government at that time had no need to demand, as it did, immediate and urgent reform from the food industry and the farmers. If, on the other hand, the pre-war politicians were right to be scandalized by Boyd Orr's findings, then Britain is now suffering from a largely unrecognized public health problem of great and uncalculated gravity.

---

* National average consumption of total fats just before the Second World War has been calculated as only marginally lower than it is today, and it is generally supposed that the national diet only contained 30 per cent of calories as fats much earlier in the century.[95] But the Carnegie figures cited here are for working-class families, who consumed large quantities of bread and potatoes and comparatively small amounts of total fats. A high-fat diet was a sign of prosperity fifty years ago. It looks as if the middle classes in 1938-39 were consuming well over 40 per cent of calories as fats. This may help to explain the phenomenal rise of death from heart disease, notably among the middle classes, after the war.

THE SICK MAN, WOMAN
AND CHILD OF EUROPE

While I was analysing the Boyd Orr data in December 1984, the *British Medical Journal* published a report 'On the State of the Public Ill-Health',[28] by Professor John Catford, who with co-workers had compared data on premature death in the United Kingdom with countries in the EEC and Scandinavia.

Until then, statistics had showed that the rate of death from heart disease in Britain was the highest in the world, with the sole exception of Finland. Professor Catford demonstrated that the present position is even worse. Concentrating on premature deaths of men and women aged fifty-five to sixty-four, he found that rates of premature death from heart disease in both men and women are now higher in Scotland and Northern Ireland than in Finland, and that:

> In populations of equivalent size, for every ten women aged 55-64 dying of heart disease in Scotland and Northern Ireland, seven will die in England and Wales, five in Denmark, Belgium, Germany and Greece, and four or fewer in France, the Netherlands, Norway and Sweden.

What about middle-aged men?

> For every ten men aged 55-64 dying of heart disease in Scotland or Northern Ireland eight will die in England and Wales, six in Belgium, Germany, the Netherlands and Sweden, and four in France and Greece.

These chilling statistics destroy the myth that heart attacks are nature's way of carrying off otherwise spritely men in their 70s, and thus protecting them from senility.[99]

Dr Catford's data show that the rate of premature death from heart disease in Britain is now the highest in the developed world. But the explosive feature of the report was not so much the statistics of heart disease as the revelation that premature rates of death from all causes are now also highest in the UK, with Scotland, Northern Ireland and Wales generally worst of all. It may be, Catford suggested, that the public and politicians 'have been lulled into a false sense of security about the nation's health'. His conclusion was that:[28]

> public awareness should be raised urgently so that politicians and the political parties will respond quickly.

WESTERN FOOD AND
WESTERN DISEASES

Catford's findings should have come as no surprise to scientists. In 1973 Dr Denis Burkitt, working in partnership with Dr Hugh Trowell, proposed in the prestigious Crookshank Lecture, later printed in the *British Medical Journal*,[100] that a large number of non-infectious diseases, notably those of the heart and blood vessels (the cardiovascular system) and of the gut (the alimentary tract), have a common dietary cause. In 1956 Dr Hugh Sinclair had made a comparably wide claim in a letter to the *Lancet*,[101] the second of the two leading British general medical weeklies. In 1974 Surgeon-Captain T.L. Cleave published *The Saccharine Disease*,[102] which proposed that various diseases now known as 'Western Diseases'[103],[104] have a common dietary cause and should be seen as one 'master' disease with different manifestations.

Burkitt and Trowell concentrated on lack of dietary fibre, as contained in whole foods. Sinclair emphasized the lack of essential fats, lost in processed foods. Cleave, who died in 1983, was convinced that the chief dietary villain is processed sugars. Together with the multitude of research workers who incriminate saturated fats as the chief dietary cause of heart disease and as a major contributory cause of some common cancers, Burkitt, Trowell, Sinclair and Cleave are all proposing the same thesis, with different emphases. The causes of the diseases most of us suffer and die from in the West are staring us in the face – staring us squarely in the face three times a day. We smoke, we drink too much, we don't exercise regularly, we suffer a form of stress perhaps better termed 'frustration', we live in a contaminated environment; but, above all, we eat the wrong food.

Since the early 1960s, the work of Burkitt, Trowell, Sinclair, Cleave and others has galvanized medical research throughout the world. In Britain, leading physicians are convinced of the essential truth of the thesis. These include Sir Richard Doll, who jointly identified the causal connection between cigarettes and lung cancer; Sir Douglas Black, who is also Past President of the Royal College of Physicians in London; Sir Francis Avery Jones, the distinguished gastroenterologist; and Professor Thomas McKeown, advisor to the World Health Organization on global food and health policy.

Despite the support of these distinguished and influential men, the thesis that British food is a major public health problem was obscured until 1983, when the Health Education Council issued 'A discussion paper for proposals for nutritional guidelines for health education in Britain', better known as the 'NACNE Report'.[51]

Written in medical language for a professional audience, NACNE confirmed what citizens in the USA[105,106] and elsewhere[107,108] had learned years before: that Western food is the main single cause of a large number of non-infectious diseases, beginning with the biggest Western killer, heart disease. This thesis is furiously resisted by that section of the food manufacturing industry whose profits depend on foods made of saturated fats, processed starches and/or sugars, salt and/or additives. Hundreds of millions of pounds are being spent every year in an attempt to persuade us that the highly processed food on sale in the shops is good for our health.[109]

'THE GOVERNMENT MUST FACE ITS DUTY'

By 1986 experts all over the Western world had been agreeing for twenty years. In the last 150 years, and particularly over the last two or three generations, the food supply in Western countries has gone wrong, and this has had a deadly effect on the health of people in middle and old age. The recommendations of 65 of these reports are summarised overleaf.

Sixty-five expert reports on food and health, 1965–1987. Summary of recommendations.

	Everybody[a]		High Risk[a]		Total	
	Yes	No	Yes	No	Yes	No
Total calories (less)	4	1	29	0	33	1
Total fats (less)	55	1	4	0	59	1
Saturated fats (less)	52	0	3	0	55	0
Polyunsaturated fats (more)	35	3	3	0	38	3
Cholesterol (less)	31	2	3	0	34	2
Sugars (less)	42	0	8	0	50	0
Starch/complex carbohydrate (more)	38	0	1	0	39	0
Fibre (more)	32	0	1	0	33	0
Salt (less)	34	2	2	0	36	2
Vitamins (more)	15	0	0	0	15	0
Minerals (more)	14	0	0	0	14	0
Alcohol (less)	24	0	7	0	31	0
Exercise (more)	31	0	9	0	40	0
Smoking (less/no)	26	0	0	0	26	0
Wholegrain cereal (more)	40[b]	0	0	0	40[b]	0
Wholegrain bread (more)	35[c]	0	0	0	35[c]	0
Potatoes (more)	20	0	0	0	20	0
Vegetables (more)	42	0	1	0	43	0
Fruit (more)	42	0	1	0	43	0
Fish (more)	27	2	1	0	28	2
Lean meat (more)	31	0	0	0	31	0
Poultry (more)	25	0	1	0	26	0
Cakes/Biscuits (less)	20	0	2	0	22	0
Confectionery/Chocolate (less)	20	0	4	0	24	0
Soft drinks (less)	17	0	3	0	20	0
Fatty meat/Meat products (less)	32	0	2	0	34	0
Full-fat milk (less)	33	3	0	0	33	3
Butter (less)	34	0	1	0	35	0
Cheese/other dairy (less)	18	0	2	0	20	0
Eggs (or egg yolks) (less)	19	4	1	0	20	4

[a] 'Everybody' means the recommendation is for everybody in the population. 'High risk' means the recommendation is only for people with medical problems (obesity, clinical evidence of heart disease, etc).
[b] Of which 8 do not specify wholegrain.
[c] Of which 5 do not specify wholegrain.
References for this table from author.

It takes a lot to move the British medical establishment, but once moved it is a formidable force. In 1986 the leading representatives of the British medical profession made up their minds and agreed that food and health are political issues.

In March 1986 the British Medical Association's Board of Science and Education published *Diet, Nutrition and Health*.[110] Its conclusions are much the same as those of the McGovern report[105] and NACNE:[51] more fibre, fewer fats, saturated fats, processed sugars and salt. And goals are set. It also has a positive message:

> Rather than recommending people to eat less fat, sugar and salt and more fibre, it would be better to state this advice positively by emphasising the advantages of an increase in consumption of fresh fruit and vegetables, wholemeal and other bread and cereals generally.

The British Medical Association knows why the British government has blocked change:

> The Ministry of Agriculture, Fisheries and Food will wish to support the food industry .... Present policies artificially raise consumption of either potentially harmful products, such as sugar, whole fat milk and butter, or less healthy products such as white bread. Future policies should take public health factors into account.

Just as it did fifty years ago, in Boyd Orr's time, the BMA calls on the twelve government departments with some interest in food to unite and agree policies designed to ensure a healthy food supply. Food labelling and nutrition education, says the BMA, are side issues. The central issues are food composition and, above all, a commitment to better food and better public health.

On 23 August 1986 the *Lancet* published a leading article[111] which provoked news stories in the *Times*[112] and the *Daily Mirror*.[113] The headlines read:

BRITAIN NEEDS A FOOD AND HEALTH POLICY: THE GOVERNMENT MUST FACE ITS DUTY

MINISTERS ACCUSED OF FAILING IN FIGHT AGAINST BAD-DIET DEATHS

BRITONS 'EAT WORSE THAN DOGS'

The *Times* wrote:

> A strongly worded editorial in the *Lancet* accuses ministers and
> officials of delaying or disowning important reports by food and
> health experts and thus playing into the hands of vested
> interests in the food industry.

The *Lancet* reviewed the fate of the NACNE report
('demoted', 'disowned') and revealed that government had
put pressure on the Health Education Council to restrict the
number printed. It criticized the COMA report on *Diet and
Cardiovascular Disease*[97] ('its advice contained ambiguities')
and blamed government for making no attempt to curb
sugars and the sugar industry. It noted that one
government-backed booklet for the general public on how to
prevent heart disease[114] 'had suffered from further
government interference, this time over dairy products' and
had only been published after the Chairman of the
committee producing the booklet had threatened to resign. It
pointed out that a Health Education Council *Guide to
Healthy Eating* published in 1986,[115] whose
recommendations agreed with those of NACNE, McGovern
and the BMA, had 'no launch by press conference, lest, it
seemed, a public demand arose that could not be met'. And it
referred to the scandalous behaviour of government in the
case of the report on the food eaten by eleven- and
fourteen-year-old schoolchildren.

The tone of the editorial was cool outrage. A leader writer
on the *Daily Mirror* was inspired.[116] Britain is:

> A country eating itself into an early grave .... The diet of
> millions is all wrong. Wrong because the hard-up don't have
> enough cash for food which gives a balanced diet. Wrong
> because many others don't know what to eat to keep healthy ....
> You don't have to be a fruit and nut-case to agree with the
> medical mags. To see the government's doing little .... Even a
> nation of pet-lovers mustn't feed man's best friend better than
> man himself.

In 1982, Sir Richard Doll was chosen to give the keynote
Harveian Oration to his peers in the medical profession.[117]
Sir Richard, who has been Regius Professor of Medicine at
Oxford, said:

Whether the object is to avoid cancer, coronary heart disease, hypertension, diabetes, diverticular disease, duodenal ulcer, or constipation, there is broad agreement among research workers that the type of diet that is least likely to cause disease is one that provides a high proportion of calories in whole grain cereals, vegetables and fruit; provides most of its animal protein in fish and poultry; limits the intake of fats and, if oils are to be used, gives preference to liquid vegetable oils; include very few dairy products, eggs, and little refined sugar.

In 1984, in the course of preparing three features for *The Times* on the national diet, I asked Sir Richard if he had changed his view. 'I would strengthen that statement now,' he told me. 'The evidence is even stronger now than it was two years ago.' And on heart disease he said:[118]

We are pretty confident now that heart disease can be prevented; and not much is being done about it, in this country. A lot is being done in America, Australia and other countries, and there the rates of death are going down.

In the words of Professor Jerry Morris, chairman of the NACNE committee,[119] 'an extraordinary strength of medical and scientific opinion' throughout the world states that the food typically eaten today in Britain is the main single cause of the diseases we mostly suffer and die from, whether these be deadly, such as heart disease, stroke or cancers; disabling, such as diabetes, ulcers or gallstones; or debilitating, such as tooth decay, constipation or overweight.

'It looks as if you can't eat anything,' people sometimes say to me, gloomily or defiantly. But the reality, never stated in government reports, is simplicity itself. The problem is highly processed food.

Ten years and more later than in the USA, food, health and disease have now become part of the national debate in Britain. Politicians and editors are becoming aware of the issues. Policy in government, science and industry is just beginning to change, in belated response to the demands of voters, parents and consumers, who have found out for themselves that the food in the shops is, in time, enough to make them and their families sick. Why has it all taken so long, in Britain? Why is Britain the sick man – and woman and child – of Europe? That is what the rest of this book is about.

CHAPTER 2

The Latest Word on Food: Stuffed

Ingredients: Sugar, wheatflour, animal and vegetable fats, whole egg, glucose syrup, chocolate flavour coating (sugar, vegetable fat, whey powder, fat reduced cocoa powder, wheatflour, emulsifier E322, flavouring), skimmed milk powder, rice flour, salt; colours E102, E122, chocolate brown HT, E142; egg white, flavouring, preservative E202; emulsifiers E471, E477; modified starch.

Label of fondant fancies, 1986

Ingredients: Modified starch, dried glucose syrup, salt; flavour enhancers monosodium glutamate, sodium 5-ribonucleotide; dextrose, vegetable fat, tomato powder, hydrolysed vegetable protein, yeast extract, dried oxtail, onion powder, spices, flavouring; colours E150, E124, E102; caseinate, acidity regulator E460; emulsifiers E471, E472(b); antioxidant E320.

Label of oxtail soup, 1986

Ingredients: Sugar, modified starch, starch, skimmed milk powder, hydrogenated vegetable oil, whey powder, caseinates, salt, emulsifier E471; colours E102, E110, E127; flavourings.

Label of custard mix, 1986

61

Cake, soup and custard. We know these as different foods, eaten at different times of the day, one sweet, one savoury, one bland, and all part of the 'normal, balanced, varied diet' that we are told is more than enough for good health. But look at the ingredients labels on the previous page, typical of what appears on hundreds of popular branded and own-label items stocked by every supermarket.

Taken together, the 'fondant fancies', 'oxtail soup', and 'custard mix' include, in different guises, fats six times, starches seven times, sugars six times, sodium five times, and more than twenty-five additives. (Flavours do not have to be listed separately.)

Once upon a time custard was made with eggs. Here are the ingredients in Bee Nilson's classic of plain cookery, *The Penguin Cookery Book*.[1]

> Flour (two tablespoons), an egg, sugar (one tablespoon), milk (a pint), salt, flavouring to taste.

What happened to the egg in todays 'custard'? It has been displaced by a sophisticated combination of hydrogenated fat (oil converted into hard, saturated fat), caseinates (a 'whipping aid'[2] derived from skimmed milk with chemical acids and alkalis) and glyceryl monostearate (made from fats or glycerine as an emulsifier to bind fats and water).

TECHNOLOGICAL GRUEL

There is nothing new about 'custard' without eggs, in Britain. What about oxtail soup? Here are the ingredients from another standard cook-book, Marika Hanbury-Tenison's *Soups and Hors d'Oeuvres*.[3] The list is in descending order of weight, like the lists of ingredients on the labels of processed food.

> Stock, oxtail, shin beef, onion, carrots, turnip, celery, eggs, bacon fat, sherry, herbs, pepper, salt.

That is to say, oxtail soup, like many soups, is made from a harmonious stock, together with the main ingredient that gives it its name, plus vegetables, some enriching items (which can be left out) and seasoning.

What happened to the oxtail in today's 'oxtail soup'? It is eleventh in the list of ingredients. It has been displaced by processed 'modified' starch (a 'bulking aid');[2] glucose syrup (derived from corn starch, for flavour and more bulk); and a clever balance of sodium compounds to 'enhance' the flavour not just of the dustings of oxtail, onion and tomato powder, but also of the chemical flavourings designed to taste like oxtail but which need an extra punch from glutamates. Without such 'enhancement' the soup would taste of what it is: a technological version of the gruel served up in Victorian workhouses and Soviet prison camps. Gruel is pale grey, the colour of cardboard. Hence the addition of the dark brown caramel (E150) together with a subtle touch of the red and yellow coal-tar dyes ponceau 4R (E124) and tartrazine (E102).

Food technology in Britain can do more, much more, than make 'custard' without egg and 'oxtail soup' with next to no oxtail. Replace oxtail and vegetable powders with fat-reduced cocoa powder, caramel with chocolate brown HT, emulsifier E472(b) with emulsifiers E322 and E477 and lo!, with egg and a few technological tweaks, 'oxtail soup' becomes 'fondant fancies'.

Measured by value, four-fifths of the food supply in Britain today is processed,[4] and an increasing amount is highly processed by any definition. In the shop and in the mouth, highly processed foods look, smell, taste and feel different. But in the vat and in the gut, they amount to much the same thing: processed fats, starches and sugars, disguised by additives as real food.

Take a biscuit. Consumption of biscuits in Britain is the third highest in the world (after Finland and the Netherlands).[5] On average every single person in Britain eats $2\frac{1}{2}$ pounds of biscuits a month. In 1985 642,000 tonnes of biscuits were made in Britain, valued at £897,748,000. 'And our consumption is some 200,000 tonnes more than France, the next largest European producer,' boasted Mr Clive Snowden of the Cake and Biscuit Alliance in April 1986.[5] 'Long may this situation continue!'

Here is the ingredients list of a plain biscuit:

Ingredients: Flour, hydrogenated vegetable oil and animal fat, sugar, cane syrup, salt.

Fats are hardened and made saturated by the process of hydrogenation not because food manufacturers want to poison the population, but because hard fats keep: they are a good commodity. In the case of biscuits, hydrogenation stops the dreaded 'seepage' of fats, thereby preventing stained packets, promoting shelf life,[6] and allowing a packet of biscuits purchased on 8 July 1986 to be stamped 'best before 15.11.86'.

The contents of another British favourite, Swiss roll, have moved on from the days of Mrs Beeton to those of Mrs Thatcher. Every cook knows that Swiss roll is a sponge cake, made from flour, sugar and eggs, spread with a filling and then rolled. Before she entered politics, Mrs Thatcher was a food scientist, working for Lyons in their Cadby Hall factory in Hammersmith, West London.[7] One of her tasks was to devise Swiss roll fillings.

Although Swiss rolls nowadays have an impressively long shelf life, it is not suggested that Mrs Thatcher was personally responsible for devising this item, found in 1985:

> Ingredients: Black cherry flavour filling (sugar, gelling agent E440a, citric acid acidity regulator E330, flavouring, colours E122, E132); wheatflour, sugar, whole egg, butter, invert sugar syrup, marshmallow (glucose syrup, sugar, starch, albumen, citric acid); emulsifiers E470, E471; skimmed milk powder, animal and vegetable fats, glycerine, salt; colours E102, E110; preservative E202.

'Black cherry flavour' means that the roll contains no cherries, black or any other colour. If it did, the label would say 'black cherry flavoured'.[8] Instead, two coal-tar dyes, the red carmoisine, also known as azorubine (E122), and the blue indigo carmine (E132), are used, together with citric acid, pectin and unmentioned flavours, to recreate cherries out of processed sugars. An account of the effect of coal-tar dyes on vulnerable people is given in Chapter 4.

At this point you may be thinking: 'but I don't eat this stuff'. Maybe not. It is true that better-off people, who tend to buy books, eat somewhat more whole, fresh food than poor people.[9] But if you buy food, take another look at the labels of the tins and packets you put into your supermarket trolley. If you don't buy food, look at the labels of the products on your kitchen shelves and in your refrigerator. And take a close look at the labels of the 'fun' foods heavily advertised on television at times when children are watching as just the stuff for your kids, or the children of your family or friends.

SCRUMPTIOUS, OR STRANGELY CHEMICAL

What has the food manufacturing industry been up to lately? Newspaper readers, and indeed the journalists who write the stories, may have been getting the impression that everybody − or at least everybody else − has by now switched to a healthy, high-fibre diet low in fats, sugars, salt and additives. In the middle of 1986 Sainsbury's, the biggest food retailing giant of them all, announced annual profits of £208,500,000,[10] and chose five items for a new advertising campaign.[11] Vitapint ('less than half the fat of normal milk but with all the goodness') was puffed, together with 'Cheese 11% fat' ('half the fat of Edam'). Unsweetened Swiss-style Muesli was offered ('there is one sweetener, however − the price.') Wholemeal bread at 42p for 800g was labelled 'HIGH fibre NO artificial preservatives'. And finally ('better and different'): parsnip, spinach and carrot mousse. The slogan remained 'GOOD FOOD COSTS LESS AT SAINSBURY'S', but the meaning of 'good' had changed.

Television is certainly switched on to the story of high fibre and low fats, sugars, salt and additives. On 7 October 1985 Granada's *World in Action* broadcast 'The Great Food Scandal', which showed why and how the NACNE report on dietary goals for Britain had been suppressed between 1981 and 1983. The next two nights, 8 and 9 October, were taken up with 'Good Enough To Eat?', a two-part Thames Television documentary on food additives and pesticides. And for six months in 1985 and 1986 BBC Television ran a 'Food and Health Campaign', which included two series of *O'Donnell Investigates* on healthy food and the politics of food; *The Taste of Health*, a healthy cooking series; and two BBC1 series at the early evening peak viewing time, *You Are*

What You Eat, and *Go For It!*. Most of these programmes and series enjoyed twice the expected audience.[12,13] Supporting booklets were produced: 'Good Enough To Eat?'[14] was requested by 35,000 viewers,[12] while *Eat Your Way To Health*[15] and *You Are What You Eat*,[16] which accompanied two of the BBC TV series, were requested by 250,000 viewers.[13]

These, though, are stories about the new enthusiasm for healthy food shared by the food retailing industry, the media, and us, the consumers. What about the food manufacturing industry? I have been reading the trade papers and the business pages: and they tell a different story.

Confectionery is where a lot of food manufacturing action is. The new food smash-hit of 1984 was Cadbury-Schweppes's aerated chocolate bar, Wispa. John Moody, new product development controller at Cadbury's, set the scene in *Campaign*, the magazine of the advertising industry.

> With UK retail sales reaching a staggering £2,332 million last year, confectionery remains by far Britain's biggest packaged food market. It is bigger than bread (£1,500 million), three times the size of tea and coffee (£750 million) and nearly six times the size of another British staple, breakfast cereal (£400 million). Britain has the highest per capita confectionery consumption in the world.

After an investment of £15 million, including £6 million spent on a television advertising campaign featuring the stars of *Hi-de-Hi*, *Yes Minister* and *It Ain't Half Hot Mum*, Cadbury's was turning out 500,000 Wispas a week by January 1985. Business news journalists were suitably impressed, and tried some in-house consumer testing:[18]

> Judgements at the *Sunday Times* ranged from 'scrumptious' to 'strangely chemical in taste', though significantly the verdict among children who tried the bar was almost unanimously favourable.

Wispa has a long way to go, though, to catch up with the British market leader. About three million Mars Bars are eaten[19] every day, which comes to over 1,000,000,000 a year.

Mars Limited also spends more money on advertising: at £33,938,000 a year in 1983, Mars was second only to Unilever in the all-industry league, with Cadbury-Schweppes eighth, spending £23,548,000.[20] In 1984 four chocolate confectionery firms, Mars, Nestlé, Cadbury-Schweppes and Rowntree Mackintosh, were among the top ten British advertisers[21] and the total advertising spend on sugar and chocolate confectionery in 1985 was £85,237,000.[22]

THE GREAT BRITISH FUN BUN

Most people eat confectionery; everybody eats bread. For thirty years the big British bakers (which is to say, Allied Bakeries and Ranks Hovis McDougall, who between them in 1987 own 70 per cent of the British wrapped bread market)[23] have been trying to persuade the population that white bread is good for you. A breakthrough came in April 1985. The Health Education Council (HEC), whose budget for nutrition education was then, at £142,000[24], about 0.5 per cent or one two-hundredth of Mars' annual advertising budget, announced that it was prepared to give the seal of approval to all types of bread: sliced white, as well as brown, high-fibre, and wholemeal.[25]

This followed the publication in 1981 of a COMA report, the first and foremost recommendation of which was that 'the consumption of bread, whether it be white, brown or wholemeal, should be promoted.'[26] It also closely followed the announcement in March 1985 that Allied Bakeries, the makers of Sunblest bread, had put £200,000 into the Great British Fun Run, an HEC-sponsored event that took place in May–June 1985.

Was there any connection between the announcement in March that Allied Bakeries was funding the Fun Run and the announcement in April that the HEC was smiling upon Sunblest bread? Bluntly, was the HEC seal of approval for sale? Of course not, said HEC representatives; the two events had nothing to do with each other. Mother's Pride and the other breads made by Ranks Hovis McDougall were equally entitled to the HEC endorsement.

Allinson's bread is one product made by Allied Bakeries, which has 40 per cent of the £826 million British wrapped bread market. Mike Dowell, the product manager of Allinson's bread, explained his enthusiasm for the Fun Run:[27]

> From our point of view, the major reason we are in it is that there will be a number of health fairs around the country. This will get us out to consumers, the housewives and the local people, and will help us to identify the brand in the health area.

Twenty-eight other companies announced sports sponsorship projects in March 1985. Cigarette and alcohol companies have long been in the business of giving their products a healthy image through sports. But the biggest new sponsor of all was Nabisco, the American-based biscuit, snack and confectionery giant, which put $35 million into tennis.[28]

In celebration of its partnership with the Health Education Council, Allied Bakeries made a special item: not a cake, but a 'Great British Fun Bun'.

Throughout the month of the Fun Run, health fairs were held around Britain. One attraction was the Allied Bakeries tent, which contained rows of home computers whose print-out headline promised 'BEATING HEART DISEASE with ALLINSON HEALTH EDUCATION COUNCIL'.[29] In return for basic information such as your age, sex, weight and build, the computer told you:

> To enhance your diet eat:
> Allinson wholemeal bread
> Allinson stoneground bread
> Allinson stoneground rolls
> Allinson snack rolls
> Vitbe Hi-Bran bread
> Vitbe Hi-Bran bread rolls

As an experiment, I asked the computer about 'Jill' (5 feet 3 inches, 13 stone and 'muscular'); and 'Bill' (6 feet 10 inches, 7 stone 7lb and 'sedentary'). Jill was advised to lose 61 pounds, Bill was advised to gain 98 pounds.

How? Well, remarkably enough, the Allied Bakeries way

to lose weight, or to gain it, was the same way as to beat heart disease:

To enhance your diet eat:
Allinson wholemeal bread
Allinson stoneground bread
Allinson stoneground rolls
Allinson snack rolls
Vitbe Hi-Bran bread
Vitbe Hi-Bran bread rolls

RATS AT THE SUGAR BUREAU

On 24 April 1985 a meeting was arranged at 52 Cadogan Square, in one of the most fashionable parts of London, by an organization named 'Diet and Health', whose invitation explained that 'much research and debate has focused on the implications of diet on health' (true enough) and that

> these discussion meetings are provided in an effort to put research into perspective for the medical journalist.

Before I worked on a national newspaper, I thought that journalists went out in search of stories. Some do, of course. But usually it's stories that seek out journalists. Or rather, 'stories': publicity seeking the legitimacy of publication. Stephen Pile, the humorous columnist of the *Sunday Times*, gave a telling example in his feature 'How They Scotched the Great Auk Story', published in May 1986.[30] A public relations firm had persuaded 'most of Fleet Street' up to the Orkneys in search of a Great Auk. On arrival it turned out that there were, of course, no auks, but only bottles of whisky to be publicized.

> Some brave soul suggested that we ring our newspapers and tell them what had happened. 'What,' said one 'you mean the truth option?' 'We can't do that,' said another. 'Once you start telling the truth there is no saying where it will end.'

Stephen Pile quoted a survey which claimed that the number of journalists using public relations handouts as a basis for 'news' 'stories' had gone up from 37 per cent in 1982 to 67 per cent in 1986. And, likewise, almost twice as many journalists now see public relations material as 'factual'. Readers say, 'it must be true. I read it in the papers.' Increasingly, journalists say, 'it must be true. I read it in a PR handout.'

So from whose perspective were we being invited to meet 'Diet and Health'? I knew the phrase, as the name of a newsletter produced by Kingsway Public Relations for the Butter Information Council. It carried headlines such as 'HEART DISEASE STUDY FAILS TO IMPLICATE DIETARY FAT' and 'ISRAELI EXPERIENCE SHOWS STRESS MORE IMPORTANT THAN DIET'; and the accompanying 'news-sheets' ran long features explaining that margarine is terrible stuff.[31] But the meeting on 24 April was on the subject of 'Dental Caries'. Could it be that this first meeting of 'Diet and Health' would tell the medical press that butter is just the stuff to bung up your cavities?

Half was explained in the small print:[32]

> These meetings have been sponsored by the Sugar Bureau as part of their continuing information service to the Medical and Scientific Press.

And the telephone number given was indeed that of Kingsway Public Relations. 'Diet and Health' had extended its brief! Well, in for a penny, in for a pound; and, true enough, there's nothing inconsistent in saying that butter is terrific stuff and that sugar is terrific stuff as well. The address of the meeting was explained as we members of the Medical and Scientific Press (nice, the capital letters) waited in the splendid lobby at 52 Cadogan Square. Two workmen walked past us, carrying a carpet on which was chalked 'TATE AND LYLE BEDROOM'. We were in the central London pad of one of the two firms (the other being British Sugar) that fund the Sugar Bureau, and support the World Sugar Research Organization.

The speaker for the day was Professor Martin Curzon of the University of Leeds, a specialist in the effects of the element strontium on tooth decay, who, stated Graham Somerville of the Sugar Bureau, is not retained by the sugar industry. Dr Curzon described experiments in which rats were given seventeen snacks a day of foods carefully chosen by the researchers from local supermarkets. One batch of rats ate nothing but cup cakes, another bread alone, another chips with nothing else, another sucrose, and so forth. (They were also fed a balanced diet by tube directly into their stomachs.)

The finding was that sucrose rotted the rodents' teeth, of course. But in one test of 'buccal caries induction potential' raisins and bananas scored highest. Dr Curzon, who earlier in his career was head of the Eskimo Tooth Decay Research Station on Baffin Island,[33] pointed out that sticky starchy food, including processed snacks such as chips and white bread, was also rotten stuff as far as rats were concerned. Can we learn anything from experiments on rats? Yes: parents can be sure that rats fed bananas 17 times a day are liable to get buccal caries induction potential.

Dr Curzon quoted with approval the view of Dr Trevor Grenby of Guys Hospital that, as a generality and bananas aside, 'the more highly processed a food, the more cariogenic'. Or to be more specific, sticky foods as well as sugary food rots teeth. For instance, Dr Curzon found that, while All-Bran contains more added sugars than cornflakes, it is less rotten for rats' teeth.[34] He also found that wholemeal bread is fine, whereas sticky glutinous white bread can get stuck into teeth and thus cause cavities.

What was the Sugar Bureau driving at? An accompanying information pack, sent to doctors and dentists and to the press, and also given out at Cadogan Square, explained:[35]

> An increase in the level of dental caries has for many years been totally ascribed to an increase in sugar consumption. Yet at the same time changes in the extraction rate of flour and of the use of white bread also occurred.

Aha! In other words, sugar is terrible stuff, but white bread is pretty awful also. This is what is known as protecting the product by spreading a little misery around – for, after all, if everything rots your teeth, you might as well enjoy yourself and stick to sugar.

Dr Curzon's point, which does have some clinical backing, is that, while of course it is true that sugars rot teeth, sugary sticky snacks are catastrophic; and sticky food, especially if snacked, can also be bad news, even if it isn't very sugary. That isn't perhaps quite how the Sugar Bureau would put it. However, despite all these efforts, the Health Education Council gave its seal of approval to every variety of glutinous white bread. I asked Dr Curzon what snacks he recommended. He said cheese, and also yoghurt.[33]

BOOBS FROM THE BUTTER COUNCIL

So, that was the 'Diet and Health' people 'putting sugar in perspective' on 24 April 1985. Three weeks before, on 3 April, 'Diet and Health'[36] was putting the 'diet debate in perspective' on behalf of the Butter Information Council. At a press screening just up the road from Cadogan Square in Knightsbridge, BIC chairman James Morton welcomed us back to butter by means of a film called 'Facts on Fat', presented by TV personality Cliff Michelmore. As the accompanying booklet explained,[37] the BIC, too, was interested in spreading the gloom. Calories? If you think (proposed the BIC) that butter is bulging with calories, just compare 0.3 ounces of butter with an avocado plus oil, or a half a pound of moussaka, or a rump steak, or a quarter-pound lemon meringue pie! Fat? If you think that butter is soaked with fat, just compare bread, cheese and 0.3 ounces of butter with fish, chips and a dirty great blob of mayonnaise, or a pork pie and potato crisps! Breakfast? Did you know that if you were to stop eating fried bacon, fried egg, fried mushrooms and fried bread and grill the bacon and mushrooms and poach the egg, you can have two slices of toast – and butter – rather than one, and yet, eat fewer calories and less fat?

What did the BIC have to say to the earnest seeker after truth? Its phrases are somewhat omnipurpose defences. Try substituting 'sugar' for 'fat' in the following phrases from *Facts on Fat*. 'Fat is a vital ingredient of our diet. It provides energy in a concentrated form ... and that's what powers the human being .... Of particular importance, fat makes our food palatable and tasty .... It does not matter whether the source of the calories is fat, protein or carbohydrates .... On the same diet, some put on weight, others do not ...' and so forth. Is animal fat bad for us? 'This is a complex subject.' Won't we benefit from cutting down on fat? 'To make any real change in the balance of fats in our diet, revolutionary, and not simple, changes in our eating habits would be needed.'[37] Between the third quarter of 1983 and the corresponding period in 1984, sales of butter dropped 14 per cent.[38]

For the punter, the BIC had a simpler message to spearhead its 'multi-million pound spend'[36] (£2,873,200 in 1985):[22] its 'girl in a wet shirt' advertisement, breasts evidently bared to the sky. (Was this a new concept in advertising – saturation uncoverage?) Over her bare buttocks (the bottom line?) was the message for the waiting world, 'Butter has no more calories than margarine.' The advertisement did not say what the model had for breakfast.

The 'wet shirt' campaign drew a comment from a *Guardian* reader in July 1985:[39]

> Now that the 'butter lobby' has recommenced its absurd poster campaign, seemingly covering every bus shelter in the land, I am left once again trying to discover any possible connection between butter and near-naked young girls on beaches. The only link that comes to mind is that they both cause coronaries in middle-aged men. The line of wisdom that accompanies this picture 'Butter contains no more calories than margarine' is probably as relevant as stating that cyanide contains no more calories than salt.

PUFFS ABOVE AND BELOW THE LINE

In 1985 a quarter of all television advertising (judged by cost) was for food, and the total amount of money spent by the food industry in Britain on advertising was just under half a billion pounds: £483,824,000, to be exact, of which over four-fifths (84 per cent) is spent on television.[40] Media Expenditure Analysis Limited (MEAL) figures show that the biggest spending fourteen categories of food advertiser were unchanged between 1980 and 1985. Coffee and tea aside, the top ten spenders in 1985 were:[41]

The top ten spenders

Chocolate confectionery	£67,999,000
Ready-to-eat breakfast cereals	£45,057,000

Potato crisps and snacks	£26,317,000
Sauces, pickles, salad cream	£22,073,000
Frozen ready-to-eat meals	£19,737,000
Margarine	£17,401,000
Fresh and frozen meat and poultry	£16,460,000
Milk and milk products	£14,433,000
Sugar confectionery	£13,751,000

Some good food is represented in these product categories. Wholegrain breakfast cereals (Weetabix and Shredded Wheat) spent £7,797,000 between them in 1985.[22] Some of the eight Kellogg's products in the top 40 spenders are light in added sugars. A market newcomer, Nestlés Lean Cuisine, spent £2,289,000 on its up-market instant meals.[22] Fresh meat is nourishing. And so on. But if every single product represented in the Top Ten list were poured into ten thousand concrete-mixers, rotated for as long as it would take to turn them into slurry, and a sample chemically analysed, my guess is that about three-fifths (60 per cent) of the calories in this richly advertised cornucopia would prove to be made up of fats (maybe 40 per cent) and added sugars (maybe 20 per cent); and that, of the fats, about half would be saturated.

This is not a fanciful guess. It is much the same as the percentage of fats, saturated fats and added sugars in the national food supply.[42] It's what the industry manufactures and advertises and distributes; and it's what we buy and eat. What about fresh vegetables and fruit? The Health Education Council advertised these, out of its £142,000 annual nutrition education budget, and it's up to us to remember their value. In 1984 national average daily consumption of fresh vegetables and fruit in the home was:[9]

Potatoes	5¼ ounces
All other fresh vegetables	3 ounces
Fresh fruit	2½ ounces

This is the equivalent of one potato, a couple of carrots and half an apple a day.

Much of the most effective promotion of food is done 'below-the-line', by ways and means not meant to be obvious as advertisements. Journalists and readers should be aware that most of the 'news' that puts fats, sugars, and highly-processed foods in a good light is shaped by public relations companies employed by industry, or by organizations themselves created by industry to protect its interests. Thus, Unilever subsidiary Van den Berghs and Jurgens employ the PR firm Burson Marsteller, which invented the 'Flora Project for Heart Disease Prevention'. Every year, this invites plane-loads of medical journalists on trips abroad to see how heart disease can be prevented by polyunsaturated fats (Flora margarine, for example). I myself enjoyed a week in 1984 at a conference of the American Heart Association held at Tampa courtesy of Burson Marsteller, which enabled me to observe that Florida had become Flora with an added 'id'.

Allied Bakeries, makers of Sunblest as well as Allinson's bread, is represented by Public Relations Council, which was taken over in 1986 by Kingsway Public Relations (a subsidiary of Saatchi and Saatchi), the firm whose 'Diet and Health' 'news-sheets' beat the drums for sugar (the Sugar Bureau) and butter (the Butter Information Council). Early in 1986 the Salt Data Centre was 'set up to collect all scientific and medical information for the purpose of reviewing the literature on salt and its role in hypertension and health'.[43] The centre is funded by the Salt Manufacturing Association, which notably includes Ranks Hovis McDougall, makers of Mother's Pride and also of most of the salt we eat (and spread on the roads in winter).[44] The address of the Salt Data Centre is 10 Doughty Street, London WCI – the same as Kingsway PR. And in April 1986 the contract for the 'below-the-line' campaign funded by the Food and Drink Federation* to put in the good word for the chemical food additives used by the manufacturers whose

---

* The food industry is represented by many organisations, known in the trade by their initials. Sometimes these change. In 1984 the two key giant food manufacturers' organisations were the Food Manufacturers Federation (FMF) and the Food and Drink Industries Council (FDIC). In 1985 the FDIC turned itself into the Food and Drink Federation (FDF). In 1986 the FMF and FDF merged, the new body becoming the FDF. The FDIC, the FMF and the FDF all had and have essentially the same job: to protect the interests of British manufacturers of processed food in Whitehall, Westminster and Brussels. If you read 'a food industry spokesman said ...' in your newspaper, the chances are that the voice is that of the FDF: which is to say, of the giant food manufacturers, not of the food industry as a whole. (And see Chapter 6.)

interests it represents was given, with a certain inevitability, to Kingsway, whose portfolio in 1986 therefore included sugar, butter, white bread, salt and additives.

BUNFIGHT AT THE OK ABATTOIR

As somebody reared on cold cut sandwiches, I'd always thought of meat, like bread, as wholesome, unprocessed food. Images of food and eating often hark back to a supposedly simple past. The ruling classes, once upon a time, ate the Roast Beef of Old England; the working classes sang of boiled beef and carrots.

But in June 1984 the COMA report on *Diet and Cardiovascular Disease*[45] recommended that, to reduce the risk of heart attacks, people in Britain should consume quite a lot less solid, saturated fats. It also stated that:

> The major sources of saturated fatty acids are milk and cream (approximately one-fifth), meat and meat products (approximately one quarter), butter, margarines and cheese (approximately one-third) and cooking fats and oils (approximately one-tenth).

A few weeks after COMA reported, Professor Arnold Bender, recently retired from London University, addressed the meat trade at a conference, 'Meat and Meat Hygiene: Towards the 21st Century'. Dr Bender made his audience very sad, by saying[46]

> Fat is one of the main contributors to modern diseases. Forty two per cent of our diet is fat and a quarter of total fat is from meat .... It looks as if the public is starting to take notice. The meat industry is in for a shock.

And he pointed out that Mrs Bender was able to buy lean English lamb in Paris – but not in Britain. In response, John Locke, chairman of the Bacon and Meat Manufacturers Association, said that Professor Bender's ideas 'would devastate the industry and have serious commercial repercussions'.

'SHOWDOWN!' was the headline in the *Meat Trades Journal* at the end of June 1984.[47] The story began:

One of the world's top nutritionists has joined forces with the Meat Promotion Executive in a bid to kick the health lobby's arguments into touch.

This expert was Derek Miller, a colleague of Professor Bender. Professor Bender and Mr Miller were in 1984 two of the most influential nutritionists in Britain. The week before the report in the *Meat Trades Journal*, they had appeared side by side, in a double-page colour advertisement for Ranks Hovis McDougall's 'Windmill High-Fibre white' bread.[48] The advertisement claimed that

> of all the criticisms levelled at white bread, perhaps the only serious one is that it contains a very low level of dietary fibre.

So Windmill had been bulked up with fibre — from peas. 'Many people reject nutritionists' advice to eat wholemeal bread,' was Dr Bender's endorsement. 'Now for them there is a white loaf which contains all the fibre of wholemeal.' Mr Miller spoke warmly of Windmill also:

> For dedicated white bread eaters who want more fibre, there can be no better alternative. It tastes good *and* has the merits of wholemeal.

On the issue of meat, however, Professor Bender and Mr Miller found themselves opposed. 'You can't imagine a meal without meat, or another protein food like fish,' said Mr Miller, as quoted in the *Meat Trades Journal*.[47] 'I personally am all in favour of having a go at the vegetarian lobby.' But the chairman of the Meat Promotion Executive (MPE), Jim Munday, urged caution, being:[49]

> wary of a 'head-on' approach for fear of starting a massive confrontation out of which the trade can only be the loser.

But after Professor Bender's speech, the *Meat Trades Journal*'s editorial writer lost his patience:[50]

> As we sleep, people with much influence are pulling us to shreds. It is time to give Mr Miller his head. If anyone can knock these cock-eyed theories off the pages of the national press and off the nation's television screens he can .... We need Derek Miller to quieten Prof. Bender.

Between the third quarter of 1983 and the corresponding period in 1984 sales of carcass meat dropped by 8 per cent; bacon and ham also fell by 8 per cent; sausages dropped by 10 per cent; and sausage rolls and meat pies plummeted by 24 per cent.[38] In May 1985 the trade paper headline was 'BANG GOES THE MPE':[51] the Meat Promotion Executive had been scrapped. The bunfight at the OK abattoir between Mr Miller (who died in 1986) and Professor Bender never took place.

In April 1985 the *Meat Trades Journal* was on another tack. 'CANCER PREVENTION: NEW HOPE IN MEAT' was the headline: 'fewer tumours found in mice given beef diet.'[52] The reporter, Fred A'Court, quoted Dr Michael Pariza of the University of Wisconsin as saying that he had given a group of mice cancer-causing agents and had fed some of them 1 or 2 ounces of beef as well: the beefed-up mice had developed only half the number of tumours suffered by the mice that had to make do with poison alone. What was the protective factor in beef?

> Exactly what the 'something' is, remains a mystery .... The substance is being referred to in scientific circles as a mutagenesis modulator.

The same issue of the *Journal* announced that 13 May – 10 June 1985 was 'Pork Pie Month'. A previous issue[53] had announced a £400,000 multi-media campaign, with an eight-page supplement in *TV Times*, and

> with the pork pie man motif developed one stage further from last year, there will be the addition of a Son of Pork Pie Man, helping to consolidate the family appeal.

And (yes, this is true!), the *Journal* continued:

> In addition to information on pork pies, serving suggestions, and a children's page, the supplement will include a knitting pattern for a Pork Pie Man doll.

Fascinating stuff, the food industry trade journals. Here was another headline: 'REAL MEAT' COULD BE FUTURE GROWTH AREA. Geoffrey Harrington, Director of Planning at the Meat and Livestock Commission, had been speaking at a 'Meat International' conference in London.[54]

Mr Harrington explained that 'real meat' – the meat equivalent of real ale or real bread – would find a big market with the growing body of health-conscious consumers. The market would demand a totally natural product with no growth promoters or feed additives during the production stage and none of the common processing techniques such as massaging, tumbling, reforming or grinding .... Concern about residues, additives and unnatural practices during meat processing would gather pace in the future.

Good grief! What was Mr Harrington referring to? The April 1985 issue of *Meat Industry* gave an idea. 'For total control of injection on all bone-in and boneless products,' read one advertisement, with a colour picture showing a joint being injected with chemicals from scores of steel needles. 'When standards must be high only the best is good enough,' was the headline of another advertisement, for the 'Wolfking C250/300: a Truly Universal Grinder'.[55] Another advertisement for food processing equipment, with the tag 'when only the best will do', offered 'cutters, fillers, brine injectors, vacuum massagers and tenderisers'.

THE SALT WATER CURE

The firm supplying the brine injectors was aptly named 'J.C. Wetter'. A report from the Shropshire Trading Standards Office on *The Debasement of Food*[56] explains the background.

> Unfortunately with the assistance of modern technology, not even the meat itself, the basic raw material forming part of the staple diet of the population, is free from debasement or adulteration. As one manufacturer of the relevant trade equipment for use by meat producers so succinctly put it ... 'The Golden Water Tap Technique – Why sell meat when you can sell water?'

It is not suggested that the manufacturer cited was connected with J.C. Wetter, nor that there is anything illicit about the injection of meat with brine, or with water and polyphosphates. In the nineteenth century food manufacturers were fined and threatened with imprisonment if they debased their products. Today, the debasement of food is enshrined in law.[57,58]

Meat is expensive. Meat plus water is more profitable. The process of adding water is one of 'adding value'. Consumers are sometimes confused by the term 'added value', imagining that it refers to a product made more valuable. In a way that is exactly what the phrase does mean. But it refers to value added from the manufacturer's point of view. The Shropshire Trading Standards officers came across a couple of cases where the manufacturer had gone too far: a 'Traditional Gammon Ham' and an 'Old Fashioned Ham' had been found to contain 20 per cent and 13 per cent added water respectively. 'In the former case a "leg" of ham weighing 10 lb would have contained 2 lb of water.' Is this what the customer wants?[56]

> It is suggested by the trade that the consumer 'demands' the 'more succulent' product that the process imparts. If that is the case, then the extreme trade resistance to declaring the presence of the added water in the product to allow the housewife to make a more informed choice between the watered ham and the non-watered variety, still widely available, is difficult to understand.

The same report also discussed reformed meat. This is not meat that has mended its ways, but bits and pieces from the tumbler and massager, from different animals, crushed together with moulds 'and bound together on cooking into an apparently solid shape'.[56] Another term for this process is 'restructuring'. The resulting product has the same relationship to meat as chipboard has to wood.

Another process is 'mechanically recovered meat'. This enables the manufacturer to recover the bits of meat and gristle left on the bone after butchering, by crushing the bone and pressing the remains against a fine sieve, or by intense centrifugal force. This process of mechanical recovery can be used with fish and also with poultry. A case of 'chicken mince' is described:[56]

> It in fact consisted of chicken necks and stripped chicken carcasses, which were then crushed and placed in a centrifuge. A quantity of water was then added and the resulting slurry was centrifuged to remove the bone. Further ingredients and even

more water were then added. Not only did the end product contain 48% of added water but the Public Analyst found 'very little muscle tissue present, a high proportion of connective tissue, and traces of feather fragments.

In itself, the process of restructuring 'ham' and mechanically recovering 'chicken mince' is completely legal. In the cases cited the manufacturers had gone too far. The problem for reputable traders is that if the competition pumps meat, poultry or fish full of water, polyphosphates and other chemicals, and is able to sell the cheaper product with its 'added value' as the real thing, then the old-fashioned 'meat is meat' manufacturer has to choose between a financial beating, or joining in.

But what if the consumer is able to tell the difference? What happens when, for example, sausage manufacturers have to declare by law the fat content of a banger in percentage points? This is when Wall's starts to advertise its premium 'low-fat' sausages as containing 'less sugar, less salt'. Less added value, more value. The *Meat Trades Journal*[54] reported Geoffrey Harrington's explanation:

> Mr Harrington described 'real meat' as the antithesis of modern convenient processed meat. 'Value will be added by doing as little as possible.'

Let's get that quite clear. With a little bit of luck, and if consumers shout and scream loud and clear enough, in future the meat trade may be willing to breed, process and sell meat which is made solely of meat.

The *Meat Trades Journal* gave Derek Dickinson, Chairman of the Institute of Meat, a column to philosophize on the theme of 'DISPATCH THE SCAREMONGERS' in July 1984.[59]

> While I agree that the meat trade must not be complacent in the face of hostile and potentially damaging criticism, nor should it over-react. We must place some faith in the common sense of our customers. They are not the easily led fools that some think.

Or, to put it another way, you can lead the housewife to the water-filled 'Old Fashioned Ham' but you can't make her buy and eat. Hopefully.

In July 1986 Mr Wim Kok, Managing Director of

Mattesons Wall's, announced the closure of three Wall's factories, including two that made sausages in Southall (London) and Dyce (Scotland). '2,000 SAUSAGE JOBS CUT BLAMED ON MEDIA', said the *Times*.[60] According to the *Guardian*,[61] Mr Kok said that 'sausages have been under fire from adverse publicity, and understandably so.' But, he added, sausages in moderation could still form part of a healthy diet.

IN THE BEST POSSIBLE TASTE

What is healthy food? Everybody knows that wholegrain cereal and fresh vegetables and fruit are good food.[62] After all, that is how processed food is advertised and promoted, if Government regulations allow (which they usually do). Here is a breakfast cereal containing (large letters on the front) 'whole wheat'. What does the label (small letters) say?

Ingredients: Wheat, sugar, honey, glucose syrup, colours E102, E110.

This is a children's favourite. It contains 56.5 per cent sugars, so if the label listed 'sugars' it would read 'Sugars 56.5%, wheat 41%, water 2%, colours E102 and E110'. A really helpful label would remind the buyer that the colours are the coal-tar ('azo') dyes tartrazine and sunset yellow.

Fruit and vegetables? We all know that fruit and vegetables are good for us. Here is the list of ingredients from a packet of 'soup' decorated with a photograph of a little smiling boy peering into a tomato-coloured soup, on a tomato-coloured packet. This (you've guessed it!) is 'tomato' 'soup'.

Ingredients: Sugar, tomato powder, maltodextrin, food starch, vegetable fat, salt, flavour enhancer monosodium glutamate, onion powder, flavourings, malic acid E296; colours E102, E124; antioxidants E320, E321.

With water added, the texture, appearance and flavour of tomato are created by starch, coal-tar dyes (the yellow tartrazine, E102, and the red ponceau 4R, E124), and unspecified flavours boosted with monosodium glutamate, plus the main single ingredient, sugar.

Since food technology can create the illusion of tomato with chemicals, sweeteners and 'bulking aids', why use tomato powder in this 'tomato' 'soup' at all? The answer is that, by law, such a soup would have to be labelled 'tomato flavour soup'.[8] This would sadden the marketing managers of the packet-soup industry, so, until the price of tomatoes goes up, tomato powder will be added along with the processed sugars, starch and fats.

Another useful tip for the consumer is that if a product contains no natural ingredients (vegetables or fruit, for example) but only artificial flavours, colours and so forth, then it is forbidden to show a picture of that natural ingredient.[8] So you can be pretty sure that if a packet of 'soup' has a picture of a cup of soup, or of an attractive person drinking a cup of soup, on the front, the soup contains no vegetables, or at best only an eencee weencee bit of vegetable powder. Likewise with fruit. Here are the ingredients of a 'banana flavour milk shake drink'. The product comes in a banana-coloured package:

> Ingredients: Sugar, skim milk powder, flavouring, colours E102, E110; vitamins C, B2, A, B1.

The directions tell mothers to add the powder in the packet to half a pint of milk and whisk. Prepared as directed, the shake contains 'generous amounts of protein and calcium' – not just from the skim milk powder, but from the added milk! However, the shake does not contain any banana. And here is a packet of mandarin yoghurt flavour Angel Delight, for the kiddies' teatime:

> Ingredients: Sugar, hydrogenated vegetable oil, modified starch; emulsifiers E477, E322; flavourings, lactose, caseinate, fumaric acid; gelling agents E339, E450a; whey powder, stabiliser E440a; colours E110, E160a; antioxidant E320.

Turning from the front to the back of the packet, what do we find? A picture of a glass full of mandarin oranges, with angel delight on top. This is made legitimate by the legend 'recipe idea' on the picture: for the accompanying recipe is for mandarin oranges (purchased separately, of course) plus the sugar, hydrogenated vegetable oil, modified starch etc., etc. poured on top.

So much for vegetable and fruit products. What about meat? While meat has taken a battering on health grounds, largely because of its fat content,[63] white meat like chicken has a healthy image. Here is a packet of 'chicken' (big letters on the front of the packet) 'soup'. In small letters on the back?

Ingredients: Modified starch, dried glucose syrup, vegetable fat, dextrose; flavour enhancers, monosodium glutamate, sodium 5-ribonucleotide; salt, dried chicken, flavouring, onion powder, caseinate, acidity regulator E340, spices; emulsifiers E471, E472(b); colours E150, E102; antioxidants E320, E310.

This is an interesting food label to anybody knowledgeable about food law and food science. Four of the additives are not permitted in food 'intended' for babies and young children. These are monosodium glutamate or MSG (621 – it has no 'E' number), sodium 5-ribonuclueotide (635 – again, no 'E' number), propyl gallate (E310), and butylated hydroxyanisole or BHA (E320).

There is no mention of this fact on the packet of this and a wide range of similar handy snack foods, so any mother who thinks she might warm up her toddler with a quick cup of soup is on her own.

Notice also that 'chicken' is eighth on the list of ingredients, which are always in descending order of quantity, just as 'oxtail' is eleventh on the list of ingredients of 'oxtail soup' reproduced at the beginning of this chapter.

Many of the lead lines currently on sale in our supermarkets appear to be rich in wholegrain cereal, fresh vegetables or fruit, or fresh meat, while in truth they are highly processed products, not whole, not fresh, and drained of goodness. I call this counterfeit food. Everybody knows that good food is the food that mother – or grandmother – used to make. Hence the dimpled grannies, the rose cottages and the cobbled streets used to advertise technological food on television. Here are a couple of quaint food labels. First 'traditional recipe' (in Olde English Teashoppe typeface) 'chocolate sponge mix', in a red, white and blue packet:

Ingredients: Flour, sugar, fat reduced cocoa, raising agents (sodium bicarbonate, sodium aluminium phosphate, (acidic) E341, skimmed milk powder, dried glucose syrup; emulsifiers E471, E472, E477; caramel, salt, stabiliser E466.

Second, 'Memory Lane' jam tarts, advertised with a cameo portrait of a moustachioed Victorian paterfamilias, plus wife and two scrubbed children, in ruffs and velvet. 'We haven't forgotten how a good cake should taste,' is the slogan:

Ingredients: Wheatflour, sugar, glucose syrup, animal and vegetable fats, apples, gelling agent (liquid pectin), apricots, raspberries, blackcurrants, salt, citric acid, acidity regulator E331, flavours, colours E102, E110, E122, E123, E124, E132.

Advertising aside, these products are not really different from other brands of chocolate sponge mix or jam tart. And true, one has some cocoa, along with the sodium aluminium phosphate; and the other has some fruit, albeit tarted up with tartrazine, sunset yellow (E110), and other azo dyes azorubine (E122), amaranth (E123), ponceau 4R (E124) and indigo carmine (E132). But these are not the chocolate sponges and jam tarts that grandmother used to make. Derek Cooper, presenter of BBC Radio 4's *Food Programme*, gave the recipe for the technological sophistication of food in Britain today as a[64]

basic mix of sugars, starches and fats; throw in your colourings and flavourings, and there's a raspberry trifle, or a strawberry pudding. And you can have the illusion of eating the real thing, just by adding water or milk to a packet of powder.

In Britain the food flavour industry is itself worth about £70 million a year.[65] Nine-tenths of all chemical food additives are flavours, which are subject to no regulation whatsoever.[66] The true value of flavours is incalculably higher, though: for flavours, together with colours, other additives and sugars, are the means used by the food manufacturing industry to create the illusion of good food.

What is this counterfeiting worth to the industry as a whole? Richard Seal of Lucas Ingredients, writing in the trade magazine *Food Manufacture*, said this in August 1985:[65]

Flavourings penetrate every aspect of the food and drink industry .... One commentator has suggested that if flavours were banned from foodstuffs, half the food industry would disappear.

In March 1986 an International Symposium of Flavourists was held at the University of Reading. Two of its three sponsors were Cadbury-Schweppes and Tate & Lyle, both of whose industrial research laboratories are on the Reading campus, within the Department of Food Science.[67] The *Food Programme* interviewed Dr Mike Rhodes of the Food Research Institute of Norwich. Dr Rhodes explained that Britain is the world leader in the technology of food flavours:[68]

Overall there's more work done in the food flavour area, in plant cell culture, in the UK, than elsewhere.

Ranks Hovis McDougall does not just make bread and salt. One of the firm's subsidiaries is RHM Ingredients Supplies Ltd, whose advertisement in *Food Manufacture* in February 1985 read:[69]

In total confidence, they can create any flavour profile you can imagine. And many you can't.

Twenty-eight choices were listed on the double-page spread. These included Ansdell's Quiche Mix, Speedemix Sausage Roll Mix, Newtint Pork Seasoning, Francis's Special Black Pudding Mix and Lane's Farmhouse Sausage Seasoning.

Here we have everything necessary to go from original concept to finished product in one purpose-built, self-contained environment. To man this centre, some of the most experienced food technologists and flavourists in the business.

The headline was 'All done in the best possible taste'.

DREADFUL SECRETS

I have Michael Jopling, MP, Minister of Agriculture, Fisheries and Food, to thank for the title of this book. In July 1984, just after *The Food Scandal*, which I wrote with Caroline Walker, was published, the Government advisory

COMA committee report on 'Diet and Cardiovascular Disease'[45] was welcomed by Mr Jopling (or, rather, by his press-release writers) as follows:[70]

> This report will, I hope, knock on the head stories – so much more exciting than the truth – that the Government has suppressed evidence on the link between diet and health.

(or, rather, 'diet and disease'). He went on:

> The report is also a useful antidote to the extremists who appear to want to make our traditional eating habits into some sort of political scandal.

I thought I knew whom Mr Jopling had in mind. At much the same time his colleagues at the DHSS had circulated a confidential document explaining the purpose of COMA.[71] I was not supposed to see it. One section was headed 'MEDIA INTEREST IN THE EFFECT OF DIET ON HEALTH'. It started off:

> There is strong and growing media attention to diet and health and the many theories that are being propounded in this field. Much of the publicity is intensely critical of DHSS, MAFF and of the food industry, centring upon the allegations that Government, MAFF, the Health Departments and food manufacturers are collaborating so as to suppress the facts about diet and health in order to safeguard the industry's profits. During the week beginning Monday 11 June 'The Times' published a series of large feature articles under the general heading of 'The Food Scandal'. This series encapsulated virtually all the serious criticisms of the Government's and the Health Department's attitude to food and health [by which I think the writer meant 'food and disease']. These 'Times' articles follow slighter but similar recent articles in the 'Sunday Times'. They are the work of a freelance journalist, Geoffrey Cannon. He makes claims about the casual [sic] relationship between diet ...

at which point my copy of the document tantalisingly breaks off. I have a feeling, though, that the next two words were 'and health'; meaning 'and disease'.

I started to write this book after Caroline Walker and I had completed the expanded and updated paperback version of The Food Scandal in April 1985. The same month, the

London Food Commission was launched with £1 million funding provided by Ken Livingstone's GLC. Dr Tim Lang, the Director of the Food Commission, declared:[72]

> I want the debate, which properly has started with concern about health, to move to the production and distribution of food. In order to understand the effect of food and health, we need to understand everything that goes on in the food system before the food is eaten.

And the first issue of *London Food News*[73] announced a programme of Food Commission initiatives, including reports on food labelling,[74] food additives,[75] food irradiation,[76] pesticide residues in food,[77] and the impact of poverty on food,[78] all of which were duly published in 1985 and 1986.

Interest in British food and public health, dormant for a generation, jerked into wakefulness in the mid-1980s. Every periodical, from the *News of the World* to the *British Medical Journal*, showed an interest. In December 1985 the Food Additives Campaign Team, FACT for short, was launched at the House of Commons with support from MPs from the main political parties, following a series of features on chemical food additives that appeared in *New Health* over a six-month period. These led to two books published in 1986, *Food Additives* by Dr Erik Millstone,[79] and *Food Additives: Your Complete Survival Guide*,[80] written by some of the people (including myself) instrumental in setting up FACT and edited by Felicity Lawrence, then Editor of *New Health*.

The day after its launch, Derek Cooper of the *Food Programme* described FACT as:[81]

> a broad cross-section of organizations concerned about the way we eat, from the National Federation of Women's Institutes to the Bakers' Union.

This was because FACT was, and is, a means for consumer organizations to focus their concerns about chemical food additives. By the middle of 1986 the number of supporting organizations had grown to 27, and included the British Dietetic Association, the Campaign for Freedom of Information, The American Center for Science in the Public

Interest, the General, Municipal, Boilermakers and Allied Trades Union, the Health Visitors' Association, the Hyperactive Children's Support Group, the London Food Commission, and MPs from all the major parties.

> Never since the Dig for Victory campaign in the 1939-45 war has Britain experienced such public awareness as it now displays of the importance of food to health.

So declared the *Lancet* in a leading article published in August 1986.[82] And, as in Victorian days, in 1986 food and health became a political issue, seen in Parliament as a possible vote-winner – or a vote-loser.

The news that expert advice such as that in COMA reports to Government on food and health was – and still is – covered by the Official Secrets Act amazed the nation. 'GIVE THIS SECRECY THE BIRD!', proclaimed Sir Woodrow Wyatt, in his 'Voice of Reason' column in the *News of the World*.[83] What was the purpose of the Official Secrets Act? This was Sir Woodrow's characteristically colourful view:

> That's so manufacturers can keep their dreadful secrets of how they diddle us. But we don't want secrecy. We want the utmost publicity. That's the only way to force the Government to stop manufacturers poisoning and deluding us to increase their profits.

> Six months later Professor Geoffrey Rose, who had served on the COMA committee on *Diet and Cardiovascular Disease*, announced that he had resigned from another advisory committee, on Radioactive Waste Management; among his reasons was what he believed to be the Government's abuse of the Official Secrets Act.[84,85]

THE FOOD EMPIRE STRIKES BACK

One way and another, by 1985 I had become a participant in, rather than an observer of, the national debate on food, health and disease in Britain. I was – and am – convinced that British food is unbalanced and a major cause of many of the diseases from which we suffer and die. By 1986 the dietary goals of the NACNE report, that for good health everybody should reduce their consumption of fats, especially saturated fats, added sugars and salt by specified amounts, was supported by the British Dietetic Association,[86] the Health Education Council,[87] and by the British Medical Association in its report *Diet, Nutrition and Health*.[88]

For over a generation, government, science and industry in Britain has been united in the view that everything in the garden, farm and supermarket is lovely; or at least safe, clean and plentiful. People who favoured whole fresh food have been officially dismissed as faddists, or as the 'compost-grown school'.[89] By 1986 representatives of government, food science and technology, and the food-manufacturing industry, had discovered to their consternation that they were opposed by an alliance of consumers, environmentalists, the medical establishment, legislators, and the food retailing and catering industry.

At first, the food-manufacturing industry and its apologists seemed to think that its critics were fortune-hunters. Tim Fortescue, ex-Director General of the Food and Drink Industries Council (later the FDF), addressed himself to the subject of 'Nutrition: a New Challenge for the Food Industries of the World'[90] at the International Congress of Nutrition held at Brighton in August 1985 and, off the cuff, referred to 'a lot of money made by journalists of various kinds' who write rude remarks about British food. On 26 February 1986 Don Angel, Chairman of Birds Eye-Wall's, another Unilever subsidiary, announced that his firm was kicking various chemical additives out of its foods as a result of 'food zealots' spreading panic among the population:[91]

> There now seem to be a lot of people with aspirations to become rich and famous as critics of the food industry.

I was in the audience at Brighton, to Mr Fortescue's obvious surprise, and offered to meet him afterwards to exchange bank balances; since when, Mr Angel's allegation aside, the view that those who speak up for healthy food are only in it for the money, a version of 'where there's muck, there's brass', seems to have fallen out of favour. Instead, a new idea has emerged, designed to make the flesh creep.

In October 1985 Alan F. Hume, Director of Food and

Cosmetic Colours for the Williams division of Morton Thiakol, manufacturers of tartrazine, wrote on behalf of the Chemical Industries Association (CIA) to all the major supermarkets in Britain. Referring to the London Food Commission, Mr Hume said:[92]

> We understand that this Commission is largely funded by the GLC, as is at least one of the most vocal 'experts' on this subject. This suggests to us that the underlying aims of these people may not be all they appear to be.

Professor David Conning, a toxicologist who became Director-General of the food industry-funded British Nutrition Foundation* in 1985, had this to say in an interview for the *Sunday Times*[93] also published in October 1985:

> There are a number of interests operating whose concern is not public health, but to use data to attack the food industry or to gain some party political point or to undermine the confidence that people have in the country's institutions.

Reds under the bread! The Sugar Bureau developed these Dark Thoughts, curiously enough also in October 1985, in a 'news bulletin' headed[94] 'FOOD LENINISTS ATTACKED AT SUGAR CONFERENCE'. Issued by Kingsway Public Relations on behalf of 'Putting Sugar in Perspective', the Bulletin quoted 'top food writer' Digby Anderson as saying:

> Health education about diet should not be confused with Food Leninism .... A lobby has emerged demanding other policies. The Government should tax food products the food Leninists decree unhealthy and ban their advertisement, and also ordain how food should be labelled and push propaganda to persuade people to eat differently. Neither Government nor Food Leninists have the knowledge to invoke such proposals.

In March 1986 the Snack, Nut and Crisp Manufacturers

---

* The British Nutrition Foundation (BNF) is a controversial organisation, typically British in its ambiguity, whose influence on British food policy is comparable with that of the Food and Drink Federation (FDF) and its predecessors. The BNF was set up in 1967, as a forum for senior people from science, government and the food industry. While being wholly funded by the food industry, the BNF's stated aim is to spread the 'scientific' and 'objective' word about food and health; and its internal committees include many distinguished scientists. However, the views of the BNF are invariably sympathetic with those of the food manufacturing industry. (And see chapter 6, and Document B).

Association (SNACMA) promoted crisps as an 'ideal snack' at a press conference, and achieved the headline 'CRISPS: APPLE OF A DIETICIAN'S EYE' in the *Sunday Times*.[95] The 'dietician' was Professor Donald Naismith, head of the Department of Nutrition at King's College, London University, and a consultant of SNACMA.[96] He had this to say of some of the critics of the food-manufacturing industry:[97]

> Others have resorted to the tactics of the terrorist, holding to ransom the minds of the British public by generating doubts and fears about food in the hope of forcing government and the food manufacturers to bend to their uninformed opinions and half-baked hypotheses. Snack foods have been particularly maligned.

Professor Naismith was, it seems, thinking of the London Food Commission; for his colleague at King's, Dr Tom Sanders, was asked in February 1986 what he thought of its report on pesticides in food, written by Pete Snell.[77] Instead of making any comment on the science in the report, Dr Sanders said of the LFC:[98]

> They have been termed by a colleague as food terrorists. That is, they hold the Government to ransom, by making all sorts of wild claims .... Then they force the Government into taking some sort of action on the basis of a bandwaggon-type lobby.

Pete Snell, a qualified food scientist and a mild man, has not been known to stick a loaf of wholemeal bread into Mrs Thatcher's ribs, saying 'hands off the tiller of the Ship of State, or else I'll fill you full of insoluble fibre!' The idea that because it was originally funded by the GLC, the London Food Commission is a modern version of the Gunpowder Plot, was developed in a letter written to a GLC official by the chairman of the Abbotsbury Residents' Association (London W14 8EQ), curiously enough also in February 1986:[99]

> London Food Commission. I am concerned about the activities of this organization. It is being used, very effectively, to promote left-wing propaganda and uses the alleged deficiencies of the national diet as a stalking horse to attack the Government and the free enterprise system. It has achieved considerable success in penetrating such respectable bodies as the British Dietetic Association and the British Medical Association.

Was the Abbotsbury Resident suggesting that the BDA or the BMA were being ravished with spears of broccoli and sticks of rhubarb? He was in a position to know. He signed himself Professor R.J.L. Allen, without mentioning that in 1986 he was President of the British Dietetic Association, former Head of Research at Beecham, Vice-President and ex-Chairman of the British Nutrition Foundation, and a member of various committees of the Food and Drink Federation.

In 1985 and 1986, critics of the food manufacturing industry were called food activists, food faddists, food extremists, food zealots, food Fascists, food Leninists, food lentilists, food terrorists and food rapists. In July 1985, James Erlichman of the *Guardian*, intrigued by these imaginative accusations, wrote a story headed 'FOOD FIRMS PUT BITE ON "FADDISTS" WHO ARE RUINING THEIR FIGURES'.[100] He was impressed by the 'intense and expensive public relations campaign designed to discredit the health claims against their products made by the activists', and by the Kingsway PR operation:

> What is not usually clear is how many thousands (or millions) of pounds each client is spending to counter the 'food terrorists'. Kingsway says that it charges clients a consultancy fee of £64 per man-hour of time.

This is not of course to suggest that Professor Naismith, Dr Sanders, Professor Allen, or indeed any other person mentioned here, has expressed anything other than their sincere views.

But why, in 1987, do food manufacturers obstinately resist the call from experts and consumers alike for healthy food? Why the high-powered campaigns to beat the drum for saturated fats and processed sugars? Why fight? Why not switch to manufacturing nourishing food?

REDS, BLUES – AND GREENS

The notion that criticisms of British food manufacturers, and of British food, amount to revolutionary Socialist conspiracy is of course paranoid fantasy. Food and public

health are indeed political issues. But like many of the issues
that now concern us as citizens, they are not a party political
issue. Some of the fiercest opponents of chemicalized food in
the House of Commons are MPs who believe that
'Conservative' and 'conservation' are connected not just by
an accident of language, and who do not see food
technologists as pillars of society. There again, Labour MPs
with sugar refineries or cake and biscuits factories in their
constituencies who are told that what the workers want is a
thumping tax on sugars are not always known either for the
sweetness or the reason of their replies.

The fight for healthy food in Britain is led by people who
are politically the opposite colour to red: green. And in their
own parties both Conservative and Labour legislators are
learning to enjoy their greens.

The food industry as a whole is not accustomed to
criticism. Ever since the Second World War, food
manufacturers have been praised for supplying safe and
clean, cheap and plentiful food to a grateful population.
People in banking, circuses, oil, telecommunications and
trusses know that they are in business. People in
boil-in-a-bag beefburgers, bread, fat, tea and Instant Whip
fancy themselves as philanthropists.

The fact is, however, that there always has been, and
always will be, a potential conflict of interest between food
manufacturers and consumers. This has nothing to do with
morality. Manufacturers will always make what they can sell
and, being in business, ordinarily have no special interest in
whether the product is good or bad for the health of the
customer. Indeed, the food industry as a whole has good
reason to wish its customers long life, and a hearty and
healthy appetite. The underlying problem, for manufacturer
and consumer alike, is that good food goes bad. All whole,
fresh food is perishable, by reason of the life in it. By
contrast, generally speaking the best commodities are the
worst foods: they do not support life. Manufacturers will
always tend to make foods from good commodities, simply
because these good commodities are better for business.

Saturated fats, processed starches and sugars, and salt
have one quality in common: they are all good commodities.
Unsaturated oils are volatile and become rancid; turned into

solid, saturated fats by the process of hydrogenation, they become stable. Wholegrain flour goes rancid because of the unsaturated oils in the germ of the grain discarded in the manufacture of white flour, which therefore keeps much longer. Contained in fruit, natural sugars come as part of a wet, fibrous package which rots quickly; processed sugars, stripped of all nourishment, are therefore the best commodity of all and, like salt, are themselves preservatives.

But it is the goodness in whole, fresh food – cereals, vegetables, fruit, flesh – that nourishes us. The more highly processed food is, the worse it is likely to be for our health, simply because saturated fats, processed starches and sugars, and salt, together with chemical additives, are the staples used to make highly processed food. Take another look at the ingredients of fondant fancies, 'oxtail soup' and custard mix introducing this chapter. And next time you are in a supermarket, take a look at the ingredients of any packaged lead line.

But why should British food and health be any different from the food and health of any other industrialized country? The reasons lie within British history.

Britain has the bad luck to have been the first industrialized nation. In a couple of generations the peasantry was destroyed, the cities were crammed with factory workers supplied with the first crude mass-produced food, suffering general conditions of life worse than any in Britain for perhaps 500 years.[101] In the nineteenth century Britain became the world centre for sugar-refining and the manufacture of jam, biscuits and confectionery. These cheap staples, together with lard, white bread and some salted meat, ruined the health of the working classes who, by then, had lost touch with the earth and its fruits. Except at times of general famine, the health of people in Europe never deteriorated to such an extent. In Europe staple foods were, and are, less highly processed, small farmers retain peasant traditions, and the links between city and country life survive. By the 1930s the fact that bad food, drained of nourishment, was a major cause of the wretched health of the working classes in Britain was well known to scientists.[102]

Britain's second misfortune was an outcome of the Second

World War. At the time, government was understandably fearful of blockade by enemy submarines and the consequent starvation of the civilian population. Also, men had to be made fit to fight. So a national food policy was invented.[103] Government, science and industry combined in an experiment designed to manipulate the national food supply. It had two aims: first, to make Britain self-sufficient in agriculture; second, to feed the entire nation with food reckoned to be adequate for growth and health. This excellent wartime policy worked. Everybody had enough cheap food to eat. Supplies of bread increased, and the 'National Loaf' was brown. Supplies of animal fats from meat and butter decreased, as did sugar. Public health improved.[104]

The result was that everybody, not just the working classes, was trained to think of food as fuel, and to accept and eat, gratefully, whatever was supplied. The wartime policy of plenty of cheap food at all costs was endorsed by the post-war government. Unfortunately the result was that everybody longed for an end to austerity, and associated peacetime with a land flowing with white bread and sugar, fat, sweets and cheap meat which, from the 1950s, is what everybody got, in abundance.[105] This is recent history. I was born in 1940. Aged six, I was living in the East End of London, and well remember two everyday treats: bread and dripping, plus salt; and bread and marge, plus sugar. Aged twelve, I was living in North London, and well remember when sweets came off the ration: I thought that freedom from rationing meant that sweets were free, and had a disappointment that day.

People in government, science and industry today are not responsible for the British food supply of the eighteenth or nineteenth centuries, or of the 1930s and 1950s. But everybody in Britain in the 1980s is living with the consequences of an Industrial Revolution and a wartime food policy that created a food supply unlike that of any other country in the world.

The conflict of interests between food manufacturers and consumers, inherent in the commercial and chemical facts of food-processing, is minimized when people know the difference between good and bad food, value good food, are prepared to pay for it, and are able to make informed choices in a free market.

But for over 150 years most British people have not chosen their food: they have been supplied with what it has suited industry to manufacture. In recent years, the collaboration of government, science and industry in a gigantic experiment designed to make Britain self-sufficient in cheap food has created a food system where the decisions are taken by the supplier, not by the consumer. The British food chain is supply-led, not demand-led.[106] Now that Britain is subject to the Common Agricultural Policy, the task of industry is to get rid of gigantic overproduction of fats and sugars. In 1985, the meat, butter and milk industries had a Euromountain, slick and lake weighing 2,341,000 tonnes to get rid of.[107] Every year Europe produces 3,000,000 tonnes more sugar than the market wants.[108]

What happens to this excess fat and sugar? It is dumped on developing countries in the name of aid. Nationally, the plan is to pour sweet fat down British throats. Hence the multi-million pound above-the-line and below-the-line advertising and publicity campaigns. Good health goes against the economic grain. Consumer sovereignty is an illusion.

The production of cheap staple foods in Britain is concentrated in the hands of fewer firms than in any other country in the industrialized world. Most of the biscuits, bread, breakfast cereals, cakes, chocolate confectionery, ice-cream, margarine, milk, pot snacks, ready meals, savoury snacks, soft drinks, soups and sugar manufactured or processed in Britain are made, in each case, by two or at the most three firms.[109,110] Unilever, as the biggest food production company in the world,[111] dominates the margarine, ice-cream, ready meals, and meat products markets, and is big in chemical additives too. Since the war the British agrichemicals industry has been dominated by ICI.[112] In 1987 Unilever and ICI each declared annual profits exceeding £1,000,000,000.[113,114] In turn, five firms own a majority of the food retailing market.[108] The titanic multi-billion pound take-over battles involving food firms in 1985 and 1986 concentrated even more production in the hands of colossal international conglomerate companies. And most of them are geared to produce unhealthy food.

The result has been good for big business, but not for the food industry as a whole. Overall, food production is not a particularly profitable business in Britain.[109] On 25 February 1986 Robert Tyrrell, head of the Henley Centre for Forecasting, addressed a conference of the Food and Drink Federation.[115] He pointed out that the proportion of total consumer spending on food has been falling rapidly recently in Britain, at a time when real incomes have risen very little. By contrast, in Europe consumers are continuing to spend the same proportion of their incomes on food. A chart produced by Tyrrell showed:[115]

> a continuing decline in the proportion of spending on food from around 17 per cent of consumer spending in 1980 to around $13\frac{1}{2}$ per cent in 1990. In effect this is a damning indictment of British food manufacturers and retailers!

Exclamation mark or no, this forecast is no joke, either to the food industry or to us, the consumers. It shows that the food industry is dominated by manufacturers of highly processed food who are producing cheapened food, that we, the consumers, do not value, and, increasingly, do not want.

CHAPTER 3

Sugars: The Amazing Vanishing Conference

In Britain the consumption of sugar per head is higher than in most other countries and, apart from its effect on dental caries, sugar is an unnecessary source of energy in a community with such a widespread problem of overweight. A halving of the average sugar consumption per head of the population would increase the nutrient/energy density of the diet.

Royal College of Physicians, Report on Obesity,[1] 1983

Tate and Lyle's managing director, Mr Neil Shaw, said yesterday that the company was now drawing up a big advertising campaign to trumpet the virtues of sugar. It will draw heavily on a recent government study which targeted fats and cigarette smoking as the real hazards to healthy living. British doctors prepared to speak up in defence of sugar will be enlisted in the campaign, Mr Shaw added.

'Tate & Lyle in £35 million US expansion', *Guardian*[2], 1984

Ingredients: Filling: Sugar, cheese powder, modified starch, whey powder, skimmed milk powder, dried glucose syrup, vegetable fat, lactose, dextrose, caseinate; emulsifiers E450a, E341, E471 (a) (b); flavouring, salt; colours E102, E124; stabiliser E401, butter, fat. Biscuit crumb: Wheatflour, sugar, animal and vegetable fat (with antioxidant E320), golden syrup, salt, colour E102.

Label of cheesecake mix, 1985

Two speakers from Britain were billed to address the final session of a two-day conference held at the Maharani Hotel in Durban, on 22-23 March 1983. The host was Dick Ridgway, Chairman of the South Africa Sugar Association. The occasion was the twelfth annual meeting of the World Sugar Research Organization (WSRO). Bill Sprague, Chairman of the WSRO and former Chairman of the Sugar Association of America, had opened the proceedings on the first day thus:[3]

> None of us have to stand back and take it when our product is accused of causing heart disease, diabetes, obesity, etc. In fact, we are now prepared to fight back with facts based on good scientific research. However, we are still on the defensive, and I would hope that, as members of the WSRO, we could start figuring out ways of going on the offensive. For instance, the UK is considering sending the WSRO bulletin to all of the doctors and dentists in the UK.

'Finally' said Mr Sprague, 'I feel that WSRO allows the top people in the Sugar World to meet and get to know each other.'

The first British guest of the WSRO to speak on the afternoon of the 23rd was Professor Ian Macdonald. In 1987 Dr Macdonald is Professor of Applied Physiology at Guys Hospital, London; he is Chairman of the food industry-funded British Nutrition Foundation (BNF) and he has been a member of the Food Advisory Committee, the chief expert committee that advises MAFF on food and health. 'I should like to emphasise that I hold no brief for or against sucrose,' he said:[4]

> Life span in Western communities is longer than in the Third World .... The Third World does not live long enough to get coronary artery disease or diabetes or even cancer .... I suspect that even the militants of the anti-sucrose left are having to shift their ground on the part played by sucrose in the causation of diabetes and of coronary heart disease.

Professor A.J. (Chuck) Vlitos was the second British guest speaker. At the time he was Visiting Professor at the Department of Nutrition at King's College, London, and also at Reading University;[5] Head of Research at Tate & Lyle, whose research laboratories, you will recall, are on the campus at Reading University;[6] Tate & Lyle's representative as an Industrial Governor of the BNF;[7] and about to become Director-General of the WSRO, a job he still holds in 1987. His presentation was a rallying call:[8]

> The myth which claims that the sucrose in fruits is 'wholesome' while so-called 'refined sugar' is 'evil' will remain with us for many years to come. We must, in return, not only defend our product, but continue to seek sound scientific data which will assist our various sugar associations in promoting sucrose for its positive characteristics.

In the audience were Mr Neil Shaw, who in 1987 is chairman of Tate & Lyle,[9] and Michael Shersby, Conservative MP for Uxbridge, who is Director-General of the Sugar Bureau,[10] the promotional arm of the British sugar industry. Mr Shaw spoke of his work for the sugar industry in Canada, and specifically of a film made with the help of Professor Fredrick Stare of Harvard University, which:[11]

> contains expert views from authorities in the US on obesity, CHD [coronary heart disease], caries and so forth, and it is seen every day in our sugar museum in Toronto. It is approved by the educational authorities and every child over fourteen sees it .... I think we have to spend a lot of money getting the facts to the consumer.

Mr Shersby agreed. 'I should like to say that we in Britain have now got fairly advanced plans. We are now able to speak with conviction when we are criticized by some doctors.'[11]

THE HIDDEN AGENDA

The speaker between Professors Macdonald and Vlitos was Professor John Reid, Deputy Principal of the University of Cape Town. His talk, on 'The Life Cycle of Funding Committees, and the Basis of Committee Decisions' was more interesting than its title suggests.

Professor Reid explained how best to fund scientists in order 'to improve and communicate scientific information on the uses of sugar'.[12] 'What produces maximum benefit in relation to the cost?' he asked – evidently on behalf of the

World Sugar Research Organization rather than the University of Cape Town. Is it best to support a promising scientist or a promising research proposal?:[12]

> If you have located a person whom you have confidence in as a research worker and as one who will keep your needs in mind and not just use your money – then to go on supporting him is much cheaper than assembling panels of experts to vet in great detail the research proposal, engaging in negotiation to alter here and improve there.

How precise should the requirements of the funding organization – in this case the sugar industry – be? Professor Reid recommended casting a wide net:

> Let us take the case of dental caries. Should one say to the research fraternity at large – caries is the problem, let's hear from you? Or immunization against caries is the name of the game: let's have the proposals. I am a believer in one side of this: the side that does not specify but leaves it open. That way you actually enlist the services of the whole research fraternity in determining where the likely pay off projects are to be located. You can apply your own criteria at a later stage of the process of deciding who and what to support.

He emphasized the value of funding researchers who work in a 'prestigious place', bearing in mind the 'superior back-up facilities' and that 'better people are generally to be found in better places'. He then said:

> There is a hidden agenda in the research support business. Those who accept your support are often perceived to be less likely to give you a bad scientific press. They may come up with the results that cause you problems, but they will put them in a context in a way that leaves you happier than had they emanated from someone not receiving your support. My own observation and comment is that this hidden effect is powerful – more powerful certainly than we care to state loudly, either from the point of view of the honour in science or in industry. It takes a lot to bite the hand that feeds you: a muzzle is a good insurance against unwelcome bites.

Finally, the sugar industry should guard against seeming to be 'thoughtless, and therefore heartless':

> Just as the glow of virtue surrounding all sugar may be heightened by showing that packing it into wounds does good, which is relevant to the use of .000001 per cent of sugar, so the dark cloud spreads to the product from the image of an exploitative mercenary antisocial industry.

It cannot be assumed that any of the senior scientists from Britain and South Africa who enjoyed the hospitality of the South Africa Sugar Association at the Maharani Hotel see things the same way as Professor Reid. Many scientists, including those whose work is funded by the sugar industry, believe that their work and their judgement is not affected by the source of their research funds. On 27 March 1984 I visited Professor Vlitos for lunch at the WSRO offices in central London, and he kindly gave me the proceedings of WSRO conferences held between 1979 and 1983, including the one in Durban. He also gave me a copy of WSRO *Special Bulletin no. 1*, which lists 'recent research projects sponsored by members of the World Sugar Research Organization – a global effort'.[13] More of this later.

FEWER PACKETS OF SUGAR – OFFICIAL

What's the story about sugar in Britain? For one thing, you may have got the impression that we are all eating less sugar nowadays. 'A HEALTHY TREND IN OUR EATING HABITS' read a headline in the *Daily Mail* in June 1983.[14] Another edition of the same day's paper was even more enthusiastic: 'BRITAIN IS TUCKING INTO FITNESS'.[14] The story continued:

> The average Briton is following the advice of nutrition experts .... Sugar sales continue to decline – now down by nearly one-third on 1973 figures.

The *Daily Telegraph* carried a similar story on the same day.[15]

This flurry of evidently good news was repeated in October 1984. ' "HEALTHY TREND" IN FOOD SALES' was the *Telegraph*'s headline:[16]

Britons are buying more skimmed milk, wholemeal bread, poultry and fresh fruit, and fewer dairy products, sugar, eggs and red meat .... This suggests that as a nation we are becoming more health conscious and responding to campaigns to cut down on food that can lead to heart disease.

On the same day, the *Mail* claimed that ' "DANGER" MEAT GETS THE COLD SHOULDER',[17] the *Mirror* announced that 'OAT CUISINE IS IN';[18] and the *Sun* said that ' "GOOD HEALTH" FOOD IS TOP OF THE MENU':[19]

health-conscious Britons are eating less of the foods thought to cause heart attacks – dairy products, sugar and red meat.

The source of these stories is the Ministry of Agriculture, Fisheries and Food (MAFF) which, four times a year, sends newspapers quarterly summaries of its National Food Survey, together with a couple of pages of commentary to guide journalists without the time, skill or inclination to work out the meaning of the statistics by themselves. The head of the National Food Survey at MAFF is Dr David Buss.

Thus, in June 1983 the press release said:[20]

Sugar continued its downward trend in the first quarter of 1983. The recorded average of 9.81 oz per person per week represents a fall of nearly a third since the first quarter of 1973.

And in October 1984: 'Consumption of sugar was lower than a year ago.'[21] MAFF also publishes an annual report of the National Food Survey. In 1984 the report for the year 1982 said that 'the long-term downward trend in the consumption of sugar continued.'[22] In 1986, the report for 1984 said:[23]

The long-term downward trend in the purchases of sugar continued with the average for 1984 falling to 9.15 oz per person per week.

The NACNE report in 1983[24] and the COMA report in 1984[25] said much the same thing: not surprisingly, since both reports took their figures from MAFF, supplemented, in the case of NACNE, by a personal conversation between a senior member of the committee and a senior civil servant from MAFF.

THE BEST THING SINCE SLICED BREAD?

Government and science are telling the same story, and the press is repeating it: consumption of sugar in Britain is dropping, hardly 'gradually', but at a rate of maybe 20 per cent a decade or more. Correspondingly, expert medical reports in the last decade have taken an increasingly relaxed view of sugar. For example, COMA has reported twice on diet and heart disease; in 1974[26] and again in 1984.[25] The orthodox medical view is that sugar is a cause of overweight and obesity and that overweight people are more likely to suffer heart attacks. It follows that, even if sugar is not a direct cause of heart disease, it may be an indirect cause. Both COMA reports reflected this orthodox view. The 1974 report said:[26]

> Sucrose is widely available, and a cheap, palatable and concentrated source of food energy; it can easily be consumed beyond satiety in a way that is unlikely to occur with other sources of food energy. The panel believes a reduction in the incidence of obesity to be desirable ... and that a continued fall in the intake of sucrose would assist in achieving this aim.

That diabetics are more likely to suffer from heart attacks was not mentioned in COMA 1974, and only in passing in COMA 1984, which took a softer line on sugars:

> Sugars and foods containing them are appreciable sources of food energy and may contribute to obesity ... Certain foods containing these sugars may also contribute saturated fatty acids (eg cakes, biscuits) .... The panel notes that restriction of intake of these sugars has been recommended on other health grounds (eg dental caries).

And the recommendation was:

> The Panel recommends that intake of simple sugars (sucrose, glucose and fructose) should not be increased further.

There are three reasons for this change of line. First, the evidence against saturated fats has overwhelmed all but the most hardened doubters in the last ten years. Second, Professor John Yudkin, retired head of the Department of Nutrition at London University, who maintains that sugars are a direct cause of heart disease, was a member of the 1974 panel but was not invited to serve on the 1984 panel; this may have led the panel members to play down the significance of sugars. Third, the 1984 panel evidently believed that any public health problem caused by sugars is vanishing.

By his own reckoning, Professor Yudkin has maintained since 1957 that sugars are likely to be a more important cause of heart disease than dietary fats.[27] He has also been an advisor to the dairy industry and to margarine manufacturers Unilever, and has spoken at public meetings organized by and on behalf of the Butter Information Council.[27] Is his scientific judgement affected by his links with industry? Certainly not, he says. First, he has also been an advisor to Ranks Hovis McDougall, Heinz and other food manufacturers.[28] And second, on his own behalf and that of fellow scientists, he says:[29]

> The barons of the food industry are often accused of plying us with foods while ignoring their nutritional qualities and their effects on our health. What they should do, we are told, is to seek the advice of nutritionists. Yet when they do so, we are told that we must always suspect what the nutritionists say since they are likely to have been suborned by the food industry .... There are many honest food manufacturers, and many honest nutritionists. The latter can be recognized by the fact that the views they express publicly are the same that they express to their scientific peers in the ivory towers of academia.

According to the WSRO's *Special Bulletin no 1*,[13] Professor Harry Keen, a colleague of Professor Ian Macdonald at Guys Hospital and also a member of the 1974 COMA panel, was funded by the sugar industry for a ten-year project on 'Sugar Intake, Diabetes, Atherosclerosis and Obesity' between 1974 and 1983. Professor Keen, an authority on diabetes, was also funded by the WSRO for a two-year project with the same title, beginning in 1981; and for a third project on the 'Role of Sucrose in the Cause of Diabetes Mellitus in Man' for one year beginning in 1977. In 1987 Professor Keen remains a member of the main COMA committee, and was also a member of the 1984 COMA panel which produced the report on *Diet and Cardiovascular Disease*.[25]

Two fellow-members of the 1984 COMA panel were Dr Jim Mann of Oxford University, whom 'Special Bulletin no 1' lists as funded by the WSRO for a two-year project on 'High Carbohydrate Diets in Diabetes', beginning in 1981 and identified as 'active' when the bulletin was published in October 1983; and Professor John Durnin of Glasgow University, who on 9 May 1986 spoke at a public meeting organized by and on behalf of the Sugar Bureau,[31] as Professor Keen had done on 15 May 1985.[31] 'SWEET NEWS – SUGAR DOES NOT MAKE YOU FAT', announced the Sugar Bureau[30] in a press release promoting Professor Durnin's views. He also had this to say:[32]

> I hold no brief for the sugar industry. I get no grants from them for research. I am not in their pay. Apart from the social consequences, I really do not care too much, as a nutritionist, whether or not people eat more, less or the same amount of sugar. I am interested only in the evidence which would suggest that sugar intake is a decisive factor in obesity. The evidence is clearly not there.

Does it matter that industry funds a great deal of scientific research, and that many scientists advise industry? The subject is sensitive. It would certainly be absurd to claim that the work of every scientist funded by industry should be doubted or dismissed. On the other hand, as Professor Reid's talk to the WSRO at Durban makes clear, to claim that industry never influences the work it pays for is equally absurd. Much depends on the scientist and the industry. Individual cases are unlikely to be significant. But a pattern of patronage, involving a major foodstuff of doubtful value and scientists who are national policy-makers on food and health, is likely to be significant, and is certainly a matter of public interest and concern. The scientists themselves may be unaware of the place their research occupies in the industry's strategy.

A year after his stay in Durban, Michael Shersby was delighted with COMA 1984. 'COMA REPORT CLEARS SUGAR FROM CHD IMPLICATION,' read a Sugar Bureau press release issued four days after the report itself.[33] Mr Shersby agreed that obesity should be avoided by a 'combination of appropriate food intake and exercise'. But the Bureau maintained that COMA

> has exonerated sugar consumption as a contributory factor to heart disease. After a two year deliberation ... the Committee has concluded that the UK population's present average level of consumption of sugars can be maintained.

Neil Shaw, then Managing Director of Tate & Lyle, was even more enthusiastic. As reported in the *Observer*:[34]

> Shaw disputes some medical claims about the perils of sugar, preferring to draw attention to this month's Department of Health report 'saying that present consumption was about right'. What it did say was that the 'intake of simple sugars should not be increased further'. But why shouldn't he sweeten the pill a little?

Interviewed by the *Guardian*, in December 1984, Mr Shaw was yet more bullish; as can be seen from the quotation introducing this chapter.[2] Moreover, Shaw went on to tell the reporter that Tate & Lyle had discovered a new sweetener with indigestible calories: 'It tastes sweet but it goes right through you,' he explained.

So in July 1984 Mr Shersby was saying that sugars have nothing to do with heart disease, and in December 1984 Mr Shaw was saying that sugars are altogether good stuff. In February 1985 the industry went over the top. 'Medical research is confirming sugar's nutritional value,' chorused Alfred Derde of Tate & Lyle and Peter Gibbs of British Sugar in a supplement to the trade paper the *Grocer*[35] paid for by the Sugar Bureau (chairman, Mr Gibbs, funded by Tate & Lyle and British Sugar). The academic voice in the supplement was that of Professor Vincent Marks, consultant chemical pathologist at St Luke's Hospital, Guildford, who wrote:

> Of the many authoritative committees that have issued reports and recommendations on diet and its role in the causation of disease, none has incriminated sugar.*

---

* This is not so. The current DHSS publication, *Eating for Health*[36] links sugars with tooth decay, obesity and (indirectly) heart disease; and some fifty independent expert reports worldwide have identified sugars as a public health problem and recommended that their consumption be cut. (See Chapter 1)

So science, government and industry seems to be in harmony on the subject of sugar, at least as far as its role in heart disease is concerned. Certainly, everybody seems to agree that sugar is a diminishing ingredient in the national diet. This assumption enables the industry to take the line that sugar is not a public health problem, but even if it was, the problem is solving itself – a line designed to melt the hardest opponents of sugar. Hence, too, 'BRITAIN IS TUCKING INTO FITNESS', 'A HEALTHY TREND IN OUR EATING HABITS' and similar newspaper headlines. Thank goodness for that! Nothing to worry about!

MORE PACKETS OF SUGAR – FACT

Funnily enough, though, the industry itself does not claim that the consumption of sugars (notice the plural) is falling: not at all. Here is Robert Haslam, then chairman of Tate & Lyle, boasting about 'RECORD PROFITS AND DIVIDEND AFTER FIVE YEARS' PROGRESS' in the financial pages at the beginning of 1984: 'the total UK market has not declined during the year.'[37] And here is Graham Somerville, Mr Shersby's deputy at the Sugar Bureau, writing in the *Lancet* at the end of 1984[38] on sales to industry (disappearance data), since the late 1960s in the USA and Australia:

> as in the UK, total consumption of refined sugars (as judged by disappearance) has remained static in both countries over this period.

It is always interesting to discover what the industry is saying in its internal discussions. In 1979 the World Sugar Research Organisation (also supported by Tate & Lyle and British Sugar) held its annual conference at the Hilton Hotel, Caracas, Venezuela. One of the speakers was John Beckett, then Chief Executive of the British Sugar Corporation, as British Sugar was then called. Mr Beckett had this to say:[39]

> The consumption of retail sugar that was sold over the counter to housewives in the United Kingdom in 1955 was 1,700,000 tons, by 1970 it had fallen to 1,250,000 and by 1978 to 1,000,000.

This is why MAFF continues to tell the press that sugar consumption is dropping. What MAFF is referring to is not what you or I might think of as sugar, but solely packet sugar purchased 'over the counter' for consumption 'at home'.[40] The figure does not even include sugar purchased wholesale for catering use and refers only to sucrose, not to glucose, dextrose, syrups and other forms of sugar. So MAFF's 1983 figure of 9.81 oz per person per week, (31.9 lb, 14.5kg, a year) refers solely to sugar consumed at home; likewise the 1984 total of 9.15 oz a week (29.7 lb, 13.5 kg, a year).

What, then, about sugar 'hidden' in processed foods? Mr Beckett continued to be helpful:

> In those same dates the sale of industrial sugars to the food industry and elsewhere have risen from 1,000,000 tons in 1955 to 1,400,000 tons in 1970 and remained at 1,400,000 tons in 1978. So that the total sales of sugar were 2,700,000 in 1955, 2,650,000 in 1970, and 2,400,000 in 1978.

In 1985, sales of industrial sugar (sucrose) to industry were stated in Parliament to be 1,400,000 tonnes a year, all used by the food industry (bar 25,000 tonnes).[41] Because the tonne is marginally greater than the ton, the net figure for sales to the food industry remains at Mr Beckett's figure of 1,400,000 tons.

This is why the NACNE and COMA reports refer to a drop in sucrose consumption (although their figures do not tally with those of Mr Beckett). It is also the reason why Mr Somerville stated that consumption of sugars (notice the plural) has remained static. For, as Mr Beckett explained, sales of glucose rose from 150,000 tons in 1955, to 225,000 tons in 1970 and 450,000 tons in 1978. So, added to sucrose:[39]

> sales of natural sweeteners were 2,850,000 [tons] in 1955, 2,875,000 in 1970, and 2,850,000 in 1978. It is quite extraordinary that over a 23 year period the sales of natural sweeteners have been almost absolutely stable.

Later in the day in Caracas, Mr Shersby made the same point. 'Any reduction in sucrose consumption has been caused by an increase in glucose consumption.'[39]

So when MAFF and the newspapers refer to 'sugar' they mean 'sugar purchased in packets for household consumption', although it is doubtful whether either journalists or their readers understand this definition. When NACNE and COMA (and other expert medical committees) refer to 'sugar' they mean 'sucrose'. But when industry uses the correct term 'sugars', to refer to sugar in all its processed forms – glucose, dextrose, syrups etc., as well as sucrose – it turns out that consumption of sugars is not falling at all. As fast as consumers stop buying packet sugar (sucrose), manufacturers put sugars (sucrose, glucose, etc.) back into processed foods. The result can be seen by looking at food labels and counting just how often the different forms of processed sugar appear.

Take the label from a packet of cheesecake mix, introducing this chapter. This packet contains 'sugar' (sucrose) twice, dried glucose syrup, lactose (milk sugar), dextrose (another form of glucose) and golden syrup (basically sugar and water). What the label does not list is 'total added sugars'. Nor can we discover the percentage of total calories (or of weight) supplied by all added sugars. This is information that the food manufacturing industry does not want to appear on food labels.

So just how much processed sugars do we eat? Since 1978 the UK population has been static, at about 56.25 million people. Given the industry's statement that total consumption of sugars has also been static, it follows that the total of sugars moving into consumption is about 113.5 pounds per person per year. This is higher than the amount actually eaten; both industry[42] and government[43] estimate that 10 per cent is wasted. So the average amount of processed sugars every man, woman and child actually eats is, in round figures, 100 lb a year, or just under 2lb a week.

The most meaningful way of expressing this figure is as a percentage of total calories. Allowing for the energy value of sucrose and glucose,[44] 100 lb of processed sugars a year works out at 487 calories a day. What percentage this is of total calories depends, of course, on who you are. The DHSS estimates that 'moderately active' eighteen- to sixty-five-year-old men consume 2950 calories a day,[45] of which 487 calories of sugars are 16.5 per cent. On the other hand, eighteen- to fifty-five-year-old women in 'most occupations' are estimated to consume 2200 calories a day, of which 487 calories are 22.1 per cent. For 'sedentary' women over fifty-five on 2000 calories a day, the figure is 24.3 per cent.*

These figures do not take into account the minority of very active adults. Nor do they allow for elderly people, young children, or the sick. Furthermore, an ageing and increasingly sedentary population is eating less food nowadays.[22,23] All in all, it is safe to say that processed sugars supply about 20 per cent of total calorie intake in the UK. And since the population as a whole is tending to become less active, any public health problem caused by sugars can only continue to increase.

What, then, is the matter with refined sugars – sucrose, glucose, glucose syrup, dextrose, fructose, invert sugar, syrup, golden syrup, corn syrup, and all the other sugars and syrups added to our food?

CUBE AID

As an industry concerned like any other to protect its interests, the sugar industry has five advantages.

○ *Tradition*. The sugar trade is now in its sixth century of prosperity. In 1598, Queen Elizabeth's black teeth were judged to be 'a defect the English seem subject to, from their too great use of sugar';[47] and it was written in 1633 that the immoderate use of sweetmeats (which only the well-off could afford) 'and also of sweet confections and sugar-plummes ... rotteth the teeth, maketh them look black.'[48]

○ *Geography*. Originally the third side of the slave triangle that helped to make England the richest nation on earth, and which established the fortunes of Bristol and

---

* New work strongly suggests that official figures for the energy expenditure of average healthy people in Britain today are both unreliable and over-estimated. A group of non-pregnant women leading normal lives was studied at the Dunn Clinical Nutrition Centre at Cambridge[46] and found to be in energy balance at 1991 calories a day – which means that, if they consumed more than 2000 calories a day, they would be liable to gain fat. The average sugars consumption of 487 calories a day is 24.46 per cent of 1991 calories.

Liverpool, sugar has always been a world trade. Sugar cane and sugar beet remain profitable cash crops, attractive both to farmers and factory-owners in developed countries and in the Third World.[7] New fortunes are there for the making as non-western countries are Coca-colonized.

○ *Unity*. The worldwide interests of the sugar industry are indivisible. In sharp contrast, for instance, the fats and oils industry is divided against itself. In London the interests of butter are spread about by Kingsway Public Relations, of soft margarine by the global PR giant Burson Marsteller. If you want a sheaf of bad news about margarine or butter you need only lift the telephone. The sugar and chemical sweetener industries do plot against each other, but discreetly.

○ *Versatility*. Because sugars combine with hardened, saturated fats, and with processed starches, to make them palatable, they are popular with all food processors. Sir Derrick Holden-Brown, Chairman of Allied Lyons and President of the Food and Drink Federation until 1987, has said of sugar that he had seen 'the vital role it plays in brewing, distilling and soft drink manufacture, as well as being a sweetener, preservative, bulking agent and texture provider.'[35]

○ *Profitability*. Sugar is an ideal commodity. According to Mr Shersby:[35] 'One of the wonders of sugar is that it can still be eaten unheated or uncooked after many years' storage.' It remains the cheapest form of calories. It is uniform, stable, compact, does not rot, and packs and travels well. In these respects it is as close as a food can be to metal. It can be turned into detergent, and into fuel for animals and cars.[7]

In his book *Sweetness and Power*,[49] published in 1985, Sidney Mintz writes:

Probably no single food commodity in the world market has been subjected to so much politicking as sugar .... Sucrose was a source of bureaucratic, as well as mercantile and industrial, wealth. Once the magnitude of its market and potential market was grasped, maintaining control over it became important. Sugar led all else in dramatising the tremendous power concealed in mass consumption.

Slavery has now been replaced by more subtle forms of colonization, but the world power of the sugar industry has not faded. For example, sugar planting and refining has become a key part of the African operation of the British-based multinational Lonrho.[50] The sugar industry estimates that world consumption of sugar is currently just over 100 million tons a year,[42] and that the industry employs close to a million people, many of them in the developing, tropical world.[51] The industry warns those who seek to cut consumption of sugars that sugar dominates the economies of countries such as 'Mauritius, Fiji, Swaziland, Guyana, Barbados, etc. It is highly unlikely that another crop can readily replace sugarcane in these nations' or 'could provide the employment which is necessary to support the economies of these nations'.[51] Take three lumps, not one, and help to feed the starving millions. Cube Aid!

'GAIN EQUAL TIME ON TV ...'

How does the sugar industry operate in order to protect its interests (apart, that is, from funding academic research)? A planning document produced for the Sugar Association of America by the public relations consultants Carl Byoir and Associates has come into my hands.[52] It reads in part:

> III. Objectives/Short-term. Reach the following target audiences with the scientific facts concerning sugar and enlist their aid in educating the consuming public: A. The medical community; B. Nutritional professionals; C. Sugar-using industries; D. The media; E. Government health officials.

This is followed by 'Strategy' and a nineteen-point 'Execution' plan. Some of these points are:

> C. Enlist the counsel of leading medical experts .... E. Let qualified medical experts speak for the industry, regardless of potential negatives .... 7. Distribute literature to food editors and science writers .... 8. Respond to all public criticisms of sugar; send literature .... 12. Organise two national mailings to doctors 1. Heart disease. 2. Obesity .... 13. Gain equal time on TV by offering up medical experts .... 17. Work regularly with

newspapers, wire services and magazines, providing background, short takes, and filler, as well as assisting in the preparation of feature articles .... 18. Maintain contact with key federal government health officials and regularly provide pertinent information regarding sugar and health .... 19. Attend conventions of professional dietitians, food technologists, home economists and various user-industry groups.

Before I show how the sugar industry in Britain has recently made friends and influenced people, some points need to be made. First, any industry has the job of protecting and promoting itself. Second, it is normal for political decisions in a society such as ours to be made following pressure and counter-pressure; it is not the responsibility of the sugar industry to counter its own pressure. Third, it is common practice for industry to fund research and pay consultants, and research into some areas of human nutrition depends on money from industry. Indeed, entire academic departments of food and agriculture in Britain are supported by industry, a tendency that is increasing, especially since it is government policy to reduce independent funding of research into food and to increase funding from industry.[53] Fourth, being paid by industry is not in itself disreputable or illegitimate. Politicians or scientists in receipt of industry funds have the responsibility to act objectively when the need arises.

All that said – and it applies to everything in this chapter and indeed in this book – it is not well known just how influential the British sugar industry is.

As well as being Director-General of the Sugar Bureau, Michael Shersby MP is Chairman of the Conservative backbench committee on Food and Drink, and is a member of the Council of the Food and Drink Federation, the food manufacturers' trade organization. The Vice-Chairman of the Conservative Food and Drink committee is Conal Gregory MP, author of *Beers of Britain*. The previous Vice-Chairman was Colin Moynihan MP. Mr Moynihan is consultant to Tate & Lyle and Vice-Chairman of Ridgways Tea, which Tate & Lyle owns.[10] In 1985 he was Parliamentary Private Secretary (PPS) to Kenneth Clarke, then a Minister in the Department of Health. Could this have had any significance? David Watson-James, of the

British Dental Association (BDA), thought that it did. The BDA's policy is to press the Department of Health to recommend a tax on sugars, as 'disease-causing, both dental and otherwise'.[54] In early 1985 the relevant Minister was Kenneth Clarke. As Mr Watson-James said, 'one of the first people he will speak to is Colin Moynihan – a member of the sugar lobby'.[54] In September 1985 Clarke became a Cabinet Minister at the Department of Employment, taking Moynihan with him.

The power the sugar industry exercises in Parliament today is not blatant as it was in the eighteenth and nineteenth centuries, when the 'West India interest' in the Commons 'represented a solid phalanx'[55] that succeeded in pushing rum down the throats of the navy and, later, sugar and jam down the throats of the working classes, and through its power in the market created the British sweet tooth.[49] That job has been accomplished. Today, the job is to maintain sugar's market position and to hold consumption as close as possible to the target for developed countries of 50 kg a person a year.

'Two Hundred and Forty Six Politicians and the Food Industry' (Document B) shows that in 1987 at least twenty MPs have direct connections either with the sugar industry or with the section of the food manufacturing industry that uses large amounts of sugars. Some of these MPs are known to be less active on behalf of the industry than others with a previous history in industry or who have industry interests in their constituency. The total number of such MPs, including those with constituency interests, is at least sixty-four.

SWEET NOTHINGS ABOUT
HEALTH EDUCATION

In 1978, the Health Education Council, which was funded by the DHSS, gave a grant to Allison Quick, Helena Sheiham and Aubrey Sheiham, to investigate the sugar industry and in particular 'the information the public receives about sugar'. Aubrey Sheiham is now Professor of Community

Dental Health at University College, London.

The 561-page report, *Sweet Nothings*,[56] completed in November 1980, reviewed the information issued by industry, educators and government agencies on sugars and health. It also examined the evidence linking sugars with tooth decay, overweight and obesity, diabetes and heart disease, and found that in all these conditions industry pressure had obscured the scientific evidence against sugars. The report queried the role of the Mars Dental Education Fund and of the Cocoa, Chocolate and Confectionery Alliance (CCCA) in funding both research into tooth decay and also educational material published by the General Dental Council (GDC):

> The CCCA produced the GDC's catalogue of educational aids and helped to sponsor a film made for the GDC – rather like the Distiller's Association funding Alcoholics Anonymous.

Sweet Nothings also found that advice to parents on how to feed their children, issued both by commercial interests and by health educators, was often wrong. In particular, it lumped sugars and starches together as 'carbohydrates':[56]

> Current nutritional thinking suggests that the average British diet could well be improved by a substantial *increase* in consumption of starches and a substantial *decrease* in sugar consumption [original italics]. Surely it is not unreasonable to expect health education material to reflect this view.

Examples of the 'carbohydrate confusion' and of the condemnation of starchy foods were given from pamphlets produced by the Flour Advisory Bureau, Beecham Foods, The British Medical Association, Boots, the Health Visitors Association, the National Dairy Council, Heinz, The Dairy Produce Advisory Service, and the British Dietetic Association. *Sweet Nothings* concluded:

> All in all, the pamphlets do little to dispel, and much to reinforce, some very common misconceptions about carbohydrates in general and the difference between starches and sugar in particular.

Copies of the report were sent to DHSS officials and to members of the HEC Council; and another copy was lodged in the HEC library.

The original plan had been to produce a few hundred copies of *Sweet Nothings*, or of an abridged version, as an HEC monograph intended for a professional readership. This happened from time to time to HEC-funded research of interest to health educators. But shortly after *Sweet Nothings* was completed, Alistair Mackie, the Director-General of the HEC, left his job, abruptly, after a series of rows with the DHSS, who felt he was too hostile to the giant food manufacturers. The attitude to *Sweet Nothings* changed. It became disliked and was seen as 'propaganda' and 'journalistic'. Both these accusations are in a sense true: the report does include severe criticism of the sugar and associated industries, and it is also a good read (while being furnished with 426 references). Nobody in government or the HEC to whom I have spoken has been keen to go on record about the fate of *Sweet Nothings*. But it is safe to say that DHSS officials did not clamour for its publication. It has never been published, although anybody with the time and money to spare can photocopy the original.

LUMPS STICK IN SAATCHI'S THROAT

At this time, the HEC's advertising agency was Saatchi and Saatchi, whose anti-smoking 'pregnant man' advertisement had been a great hit. Between 1981 and 1983 the HEC went rather quiet on the subject of food, health and the national diet. This was the time when the NACNE report was the subject of animated 'exchanges of view' between the HEC, the food industry-funded British Nutrition Foundation and the DHSS, and was redrafted following pressure from the food industry.[57]

However, in the beginning of 1983 the HEC was discussing plans with Saatchi and Saatchi for an advertising campaign to encourage a healthier national diet. Four full-page advertisements in the national press were devised, entitled 'What shook 100 million Americans into eating less salt'; 'Why thin people should be as worried about fatty foods as fat people'; 'If you're overweight, try eating more bread and potatoes'; and 'Sugar. How many lumps does your body really need?'. Jeremy Sinclair, creative director of Saatchi

and Saatchi, art director Digby Atkinson and copywriter
Christopher Waite prepared the advertisements,[58] as part of
the HEC's 'Look After Yourself' campaign.

Each advertisement ended with the same message:

> We believe you have a right to receive totally unbiased advice
> about your diet. The only thing we are interested in selling you
> is better health.

The sugar advertisement was designed to convey some
fundamental points to the general public. These included:

○ Sugar contains no nourishment. It only contains calories.
  The last thing that a sedentary body needs is calories
  without nourishment.
○ All types of processed sugars, lumps or grains, brown or
  white, come to the same thing from the health point of
  view: they are all empty calories.
○ Sugar is liable to make you fat. Overweight people are
  more likely to develop high blood pressure and eventually
  have a heart attack.
○ Sugar rots teeth. 'A sweet tooth can become no tooth at
  all.' The very worst thing for children is eating or
  drinking sweet foods between meals.
○ Sweet foods contain a lot of sugar. 'Cola contains as much
  as 10 lumps per can!' So do many savoury foods. 'Tomato
  ketchup ... is 20% sugar by weight.'

Copies of the four advertisements were sent to the DHSS.
There was no enthusiasm for the sugar advertisement. Views
were exchanged. New drafts were written. In early 1983 the
fat, starch and salt advertisements appeared. The sugar
advertisement has never been published. Why?

As with *Sweet Nothings*, nobody with whom I have
discussed the advertisement has wanted to be quoted. It is,
however, safe to say that DHSS officials could not have
objected to the final draft of the advertisement on scientific
grounds, for the Department's own booklet, *Eating for
Health*,[36] available to anyone who visits an HMSO bookshop
with £2.25 to spare, takes an very similar view of sugar.

In June 1984 Saatchi and Saatchi won the Design and Art
Direction silver award for the most outstanding public
service campaign for their 'Look After Yourself' series for

the HEC. And lo and behold, the trade magazine *Campaign* reproduced the suppressed sugar advertisement in a 1.5 by 2 inch miniature version.[59] This must be the first time that an award-winning national public-service campaign advertisement can only be read with the aid of a magnifying glass.

In May 1984 British Sugar announced, in the words of its marketing and sales director Peter Gibbs (who has been, you will recall, Chairman of the Sugar Bureau) 'the biggest ever advertising campaign by a sugar manufacturer'.[60,61]

> The multi-media campaign is based on the theme that sugar is fundamental to taste enjoyment and is an essential ingredient in a healthy, active life.

Symmetrically enough, the '£2 million sales push'[60] was 'rolled out' in June 1984. The advertising agency employed by British Sugar was Saatchi and Saatchi.

Before then, Alistair Mackie, the former Director General of the HEC, had provided a postscript, in a letter to the *Sunday Times* in July 1983. Referring to Michael Shersby, Mr Mackie wrote that[62]

> the HEC's educational forays under my direction had upset him – and his counterparts rooting for fat, meat and sliced bread .... The suppressions and evasions of complaisant ministers, a supine Department of Health and powerful lobbyists are winning the day; and the food industry seems set to continue what a Reith lecturer called its enormous success in ruining our diet and consequently our health.

Next time you hear the suggestion that the public is confused about food and health, remember the story of Saatchi and Saatchi and the suppressed sugar advertisement. In November 1986 the Health Education Council was abolished and replaced by a 'Special Health Authority' directly controlled by government.[63]

CHEMICAL SWEETENER WARS

The greatest threat to a food product comes when a substitute is developed with advantages of its own. Although anybody who is accustomed to a food and enjoys it is unlikely to want to go without, they may well be prepared to switch to an alternative. So, while people continue to spread fats on bread, they have largely switched from butter to margarine. Margarine is cheaper and more spreadable than butter, and it is now widely believed that butter is bad for health.

Similarly, for many years the great threat to sugar has been from chemicals with the sweetness but without the calories of sugar. The best known of these are saccharin and cyclamates. The wars between the sugar industry and the manufacturers of chemical sweeteners began at the beginning of the century.[64] Tests on laboratory animals suggest that both saccharin and cyclamates are possible causes of cancers.[65] Currently cyclamates are banned in both the USA and the UK, whereas saccharin may be sold.[65,66] However, in the USA sachets of saccharin must carry this warning:

USE OF THIS PRODUCT MAY BE HAZARDOUS TO YOUR HEALTH. THIS PRODUCT CONTAINS SACCHARIN WHICH HAS BEEN DETERMINED TO CAUSE CANCER IN LABORATORY ANIMALS.

Despite all of its power, the sugar industry cannot win every battle: the demand for 'diet' products is too great. 'Diet Coke' using saccharin was introduced in 1982. In 1983 250 million cases were sold, and Brian G. Dyson, the US President of Coca-Cola, described it as 'the fastest growing major soft drink in history'.[67] Nevertheless, Coca-Cola remained the biggest single user of sugar in the world; 'regular' Coke sold 1.53 billion cases in 1983, as the leader of the world's soft drinks industry, worth £70 billion a year.[68]

In 1983 aspartame, a new chemical sweetener, developed by the American drug company G.D. Searle, posed a new threat to the sugar industry. Although it had been in existence for several years, it was only approved as safe for general use in the USA in June 1983[69] and in Britain in September 1983.[70] The report in the *Times* headed 'NEW CHEMICAL SWEETENERS SET TO CHALLENGE SUGAR AND SACCHARIN MONOPOLIES', began:

An unprecedented commercial battle for the sweet tooth of Britain's slimmers will start after next week's government approval of new substitutes for sugar. It is likely to be a dirty fight with allegations about the health risks of the rival products.

The *Wall Street Journal* predicted sales of aspartame worth $1 billion by 1985 and gave this forecast:[71]

The growth of low calorie sweeteners, led by aspartame, is expected to slash world sugar production by 10% over the next 15 years.

CRAVING THE CARBOHYDRATES

Between 3 and 9 September 1983 the medical correspondent of the *Guardian*, Andrew Veitch, published a run of features whose headlines tell the story:[72]

MEDICAL DOUBTS SOUR LAUNCH OF NEW SWEETENER
MP SEEKS SWEETENER BAN
TOO MUCH PHENYLALANINE IN YOUR CUP OF COFFEE
SWEETENER LAUNCH GOES ON DESPITE INVESTIGATION

By the end of the week aspartame had been linked with migraine, insomnia, blood pressure problems, obesity, and severe brain damage in adults and unborn children. In Britain aspartame 'could constitute a health hazard for more than a million people'.[72]

The chief scientific source for these horror stories was Professor Richard Wurtman of the Massachusetts Institute of Technology (MIT) who, said Veitch 'has done most of the independent work on the biochemical effects of aspartame'. Professor Wurtman said that aspartame tends to make dieters fat:

Unless of course, they satisfy what he calls a craving for carbohydrates by eating more aspartame – which in turn creates more craving. He has a case to prove his point: a woman who was taking 30 packets of aspartame sweetener a day. She happened to be related to a professor at Harvard who phoned Wurtman to ask what she should do about it because she couldn't sleep. Wurtman helped reduce her intake to 10 packets a day.

In 1984 the *Daily Mail* serialized extracts from *The Carbohydrate Craver's Diet*[73] by Judith Wurtman, which became known popularly as the 'liquorice all-sort diet' because of its enthusiasm for sugary snacks as a slimming aid. Judith Wurtman is a professional associate, and the wife, of Professor Richard Wurtman.

Following its clearance in the USA, G.D. Searle gambled all on aspartame, on which their patent runs out in 1992. A new plant costing over $100 million was built in Augusta, Georgia, near Atlanta, Georgia, home of Coca-Cola. Searle had less than ten years to establish its brand name 'Nutra-Sweet' as the 'Hoover' or 'Xerox' of aspartame for ever. What better than cans of Coke with 'Now with Nutrasweet' stamped on them? In July 1983 Searle and Coca-Cola signed a contract. As reported in the *Wall Street Journal*, Searle had to keep its very powerful neighbour sweet.[71] An expert witness said:

> I certainly wouldn't want to be in Searle's position of trying to tell Coke or Pepsi what to do .... That's something like pushing an elephant. You're in trouble if the elephant ever decides to push back.

Coca-Cola wanted aspartame; and also wanted it all ways. 'Regular' sugared Coke was the priority,[74] while saccharin continued to be used, together with aspartame, in Diet Coke.

DR ALI AKBAR'S INVITATION

Early in 1983 Dr Ali Akbar, Medical Director of G.D. Searle in Britain, visited a number of leading doctors, one by one and privately, to invite them to participate in an all-day 'International Seminar' on 'Dietary Carbohydrate and Disease'. It was an ambitious affair: as well as people from Searle's headquarters in Skokie, Illinois, Dr Sheldon Reiser (from the US Department of Agriculture's Nutrition Research Center in Beltsville, Maryland) and Professor Aharon Cohen (from Hadassah University Hospital, Jerusalem) were also invited to speak on sugar, diabetes and heart disease.

Everything was organized for the seminar to take place at the Hilton Hotel, Stratford-upon-Avon, on 10 November 1983, two months after aspartame had been officially cleared for use in the UK as a sugar substitute. Programmes and abstracts of the presentations were printed. The first expert to speak, after some introductory remarks by Professor John Yudkin, would be Dr Kenneth Heaton, a gastroenterologist who had been secretary of the Royal College of Physicians' working party on *Medical Aspects of Dietary Fibre*, whose 1980 report[75] inspired Audrey Eyton's *F-Plan Diet* and the fibre boom, and who in 1987 is chairman of the Royal Society of Medicine's Forum on Food and Health.

Dr Heaton's interests extend beyond fibre to foods devoid of fibre, notably processed sugars, and to gallstones, which he believes can be caused by refined sugar.[76] But his presentation at the G.D. Searle seminar was on a commoner complaint; overweight and obesity. The sugar industry has always maintained that processed sugars do not make you fat and that 'a calorie is a calorie' – indeed, that sugars can and should be part of a slimming regime.[77] However, Dr Heaton was to present the results of a study in which volunteers were fed either a whole-food diet or else a 'refined' diet with typical amounts of processed starches and sugars included. Dr Heaton's conclusion was:[78]

> Fibre-free sugars trick man into taking in more energy than he needs .... It is concluded that, to avoid overweight as well as to avoid dental disease, sugar should be chewed or eschewed. To paraphrase the Anglican wedding service 'What nature has joined together, let no man put asunder'.

Dr John Garrow, an authority on obesity, and later chairman of the JACNE Committee (see Chapter 6), was billed to speak after Dr Heaton. He was also unenthusiastic about sugar:[78]

> Sugar has been stigmatised as a particularly damaging component of the diet in causing obesity (as well as other ailments with which I am not concerned). There is moderately strong evidence for this point of view.

SUGARS, DIABETES AND HEART DISEASE

The papers to be given by Professor Cohen and Dr Reiser in the afternoon session at Stratford were liable to cause the greatest stir. The policy of the Sugar Bureau in Britain,[77,79] in accordance with international sugar industry policy,[52] is to accept that sugars are one cause of tooth decay but to deny that sugar itself causes obesity. On diabetes and heart disease, the industry line is that 'sugar does not cause diabetes' and that 'sugar does not cause heart disease'.[77]

However, since the early 1970s Dr Reiser has been studying the effects of sugars on animals and on human volunteers in laboratory conditions, and has confirmed the findings that Professor John Yudkin made in the 1960s.[80] Dr Reiser finds that processed sugars can indeed raise the levels of blood glucose, insulin, cholesterol and uric acid, and also blood triglycerides. All these changes in 'blood profile' are known to increase the risk not only of heart disease but also of diabetes.[81,82] But Dr Reiser's most important finding is that about one in five or six people react much more dramatically. When these 'sugar-sensitive' people are given no more than the national average amount of sugars – about 18 per cent of total calories – their blood profile changes in such a way as to increase their risk of diabetes and/or heart disease. At Stratford, he planned to say that:[78]

> The consumption of sucrose by those individuals described as carbohydrate-sensitive produces greater increases in metabolism risk factors than it does in the general population.

Earlier in the day at Stratford Professor Barry Lewis of St Thomas's Hospital, London, was due to conclude:[78]

> It is appropriate to restrict sucrose in a coronary heart disease prevention diet because of its role as an energy source and because carbohydrate foods that provide fibre and vitamins are clearly preferable.

It is normal practice for drug and food companies to fund and organize conferences whose theme, as elaborated by the chosen speakers, will turn out to be of advantage to the company's product. Business is business. Nor, of course, does this practice of itself bring the integrity of the speakers into question. As planned, G.D. Searle's seminar on 'Dietary Carbohydrate and Disease' was all set to become a landmark in the understanding of the role of sugars in disease, as well as a spur to the company's profits.

So why, about ten days before it was due to take place, did Michael Pearce of the medical division of Searle in High Wycombe ring up the British speakers and say 'I'm terribly sorry. It's all off'? I tried to find out. Mr Pearce was unavailable: he had gone on holiday. Dr Ali Akbar did not want to comment. Dr Reiser had no idea, when I telephoned him in Maryland; not only had he not received a formal invitation, he hadn't been told of the cancellation either. Had Searle and Coca-Cola discussed the conference? The decision to cancel was taken not in High Wycombe but in the USA. Denise Ertell, a representative of Searle at their headquarters in Skokie, also could not enlighten me, although she did tell me that there was talk of a replacement conference: 'We may broaden the approach, and look at sweeteners as a whole.'

THE MULTIFACTORIAL
AETIOLOGY CHORUS

As Professor John Reid explained at the 1983 WSRO conference in South Africa already mentioned,[12] one of the WSRO's functions is to fund scientific research; target areas include tooth decay, overweight and obesity, diabetes and heart disease. Rationally enough, the sugar industry is most likely to fund research from scientists whose views are consistent with its aims; and the results of such research may well be publicized.

One further subject for WSRO research funding is sugar's use as a form of bandage to help to heal wounds. For example, the WSRO has funded research by Professor Sydney Selwyn of the Department of Medical Microbiology, Westminster Medical School, on 'Experimental Studies on the Effects of Granulated Sugar on Micro-Organisms Pathogenic to Man';[13] he reported on his findings at the Durban conference.[83] And Marsh Midda of the Dental School at the University of Bristol has received funds for a video on 'Dental Caries' suitable for schools and other institutions.[13]

In summer 1984, I wrote a series of features for the *Times* broadly on the same theme as this book;[84] the articles appeared simultaneously with my previous book *The Food Scandal*, co-written with Caroline Walker.[57] Professor Vlitos wrote a witty reply:[85]

> When an author is given three full pages in the *Times* to review his own book one wonders whether the food industry, as it is accused by Geoffrey Cannon, is really quite as influential as he is!

He did not identify himself as Director-General of the WSRO. Mr Midda, who does not believe that sugars are the chief cause of tooth decay, also wrote to the *Times*:[86]

> The recent articles in which Geoffrey Cannon reviews his own book require some comment on scientific fact .... Current concepts on caries research show undeniably that caries is a multifactorial disease in which the dietary factor is only one of the aetiological agents.

Nor was Professor Selwyn, who also replied to my *Times* features, impressed by epidemiological evidence against sugar. He omitted to make the same joke as Professor Vlitos and Mr Midda, but did say:[86]

> It is possible to claim that the steady increase in life expectancy during the past century has been due to the parallel rise in the consumption of refined sugar.

Professor Selwyn objected to my 'tirade against the food industry', and emphasized what he believes is the multifactorial nature of Western diseases:

> Our evaluation of the complex factors in the causation of chronic diseases is in no way facilitated by the rehearsal of a personal campaign which is being conducted against one particular industry.

Curiously enough, Sidney Selwyn's little joke about sugars being the key to long life was repeated by Professor Macdonald in his British Nutrition Foundation (BNF) Annual Lecture in 1984,[87] the year before he became Chairman of the BNF:

> In fact if one wanted to be mischievous one could manipulate data to show how sucrose is associated with increased life span.

This jest was accompanied by big graphs showing the rise in British sugar consumption and life expectancy at birth, in 1770, 1870 and 1970.*

Sugar is a world trade, and the WSRO *Special Bulletin*[13] details research funded by the sugar industry in Australia, Canada, Europe, Argentina and the USA.

This includes work done by Professor Stewart Truswell in Australia (a three year project begun in 1982), Professor Wurtman in the USA (a three year project ended in 1979), Dr A.R.P. Walker in South Africa (a study of sugar, tooth decay, obesity, glucose tolerance and heart disease, begun in 1972); Dr P.J. Nestel in Australia (sugar and heart disease), Dr David Kritchevsky in the USA (a study of refined carbohydrates and heart disease, begun in 1968); and Professor Kelly West in the USA (sugar, obesity, diabetes and heart disease in native Americans), as well as Professor Keen and Dr Mann. These senior scientists have a world reputation as authorities in their fields, are currently or have been advisors to governments in their own or other countries, and have written or contributed to standard textbooks on food, health and disease.

The most publicized case of a scientist whose views chime with those of the sugar industry is Fredrick Stare, now retired as Professor of Nutrition at Harvard, who for many years has repeated his view that sugars in the amount typically consumed in the USA, Britain and other Western countries are not a health problem.[89] Professor Stare has never made a secret of the fact that the food industry funded his department at Harvard. In 1951 he said:[90]

> The food industries, the Sugar Foundation, the Nutrition Foundation, and a number of food companies as individual companies have certainly done a lot to support basic nutrition, and a lot in helping to support our department.

According to a report published by the Center for Science

---

* Professor Macdonald continued to enjoy his joke. On 18 August 1986, Reuters put out a story from Australia, picked up in Britain by the *Daily Telegraph*. The headline was, 'SCIENTIST SAYS SUGAR MAY PROLONG LIFE'.[88] On tour, Professor Macdonald had stated that 'people lived longer in countries where sugar consumption was high'. He was also reported as saying that 'sugar could sometimes help relieve stress', that 'it was difficult to eat too much sugar at any one time' and that 'apart from dental decay, there was no evidence that it was harmful to health.'

in the Public Interest, the food industry provided about $2 million to Harvard between 1971 and 1974. Donors included the Sugar Association, Coca-Cola, Kelloggs and the International Sugar Research Foundation (now re-named the WSRO).[91]

The Sugar Association, the US equivalent of the Sugar Bureau in Britain, 'fostered the organization' of a body of doctors and dentists called the 'Food and Nutrition Advisory Council' (FNAC) in the USA. Under the direction of Professor Stare, the FNAC organized a series of papers on sugar that showed it to be a 'safe food'.[52] These were published in the *World Review of Nutrition and Dietetics*, whose circulation was increased by an order for 25,000 copies from the sugar industry, which distributed the reprints to health professionals.[52] By such means does the sugar industry give scientific findings favourable to its cause an almighty boost. But no vested interest broadcasts the evidence that sugars, consumed in typical quantities, are a menace to public health.

'MUESLI BELT SHOCK HORROR DRAMA'

As spelled out by Carl Byoir and Associates, the 'Objectives/Short-term' for the sugar industry include enlisting the aid of 'A. The medical community; B. Nutritional professionals'.[52] Here is one way this is done in Australia, a major producer of cane sugar. *Sugar Nutrition Abstracts* is regularly sent to nutritionists and dietitians. One item in the February 1985 issue was headed 'TOO MUCH OF A GOOD THING CAN BE DANGEROUS'.[92] 'Is more of a good thing better? Not necessarily,' the story continues. Water-soluble vitamins B and C can be toxic in very high doses, it says. Gobbling niacin (B3) can result in 'acute gouty arthritis'. Overdosing on vitamin C can 'acidify urine, precipitate urate and oxalate and cause' – wait for this – 'nephrolithiasis'. And popping pyridoxine (B6) can lead to 'severe sensory nerve damage'.

The references are, of course, to the abuse of megavitamin pills. Only good and no possible harm can come from vitamins in whole food, bizarre diets aside. But a reader of

Sugar Nutrition Abstracts with a short attention span might just get the impression that the way to avoid arthritis, nephrothingummybob and severe sensory nerve damage is to throw the wholegrain bread, broccoli and oranges in the bin and pig out on good old reliable chocolate fudge sundae.

Virtually all publicity for the sugar industry in Britain and the USA is 'below the line'; organized by public relations companies. *Sweet Nothings*[57] reviewed the activities of the Sugar Bureau during the 1970s. In spring 1985, Kingsway Public Relations staged an evidently low-key series of presentations on 'Diet and Health' on behalf of its clients, the Sugar Bureau.[31] I have already mentioned the session on 24 April, when Professor Martin Curzon spoke. The next meeting was on 15 May, with Professor Harry Keen.

Dr Keen questioned the now orthodox view that diabetics should avoid added sugars,[93,94] and cited with approval a study published in the *Lancet* the previous year whose conclusion was that 'reasonable liberalisation of sugar intake might have a positive effect on diabetes control'[95] − a view furiously disputed in the *Lancet*'s correspondence columns by Dr Heaton and others.[96] Dr Keen acknowledged that opinion on sugars and diabetes is divided about 50/50, displaying a 'league table' of experts who believe that sugars are an important cause of adult-onset diabetes and of those who, like himself, do not consider sugars especially important.[97] The 'no' list included a number of scientists funded by the sugar industry: himself, Dr Mann, Professor Stare, Professor Truswell, Dr Walker, and his colleague at Guys, Professor R.J. Jarrett.[13,90,98] The sugar industry is indeed resourceful in supporting the work of scientists whose views are harmonious with its interests.

The third speaker in the series of spring presentations was Professor Vincent Marks, who three months previously had published his views in the Sugar Bureau's supplement to the *Grocer*.[35] This time he spoke on 'Diet and Behaviour'. 'The Diet Scandal − or are we being conned?' read the invitation.[31] Dr Marks condemned the opposition to sugar as 'a sensationalist bandwagon based on nothing more than anecdotal, incorrectly interpreted data'. The Sugar Bureau handed out glossy wallets stuffed with briefing papers on 'dental caries', 'diabetes', 'diet and behaviour' and 'obesity' (big letters), all subtitled 'putting sugar in perspective' (small letters)[99] at these and other meetings, and has been distributing them to journalists and health professionals ever since. An enquirer was told:[100]

> The information contained in this report is drawn from an extensive scientific and medical database covering independent international research. This database is kept constantly up-to-date.

Vincent Marks continued to speak at meetings organized by the sugar industry in 1985 and 1986. On 21 August 1985 he was on a Sugar Bureau platform at the XIII International Congress of Nutrition at Brighton, together with Dr J. Jewell of Cadbury-Schweppes and Professor Jarrett.[101] Was sugar a cause of any disease? 'Yes', he said: hereditary fructose intolerance (a 'very rare disease'); sucrose intolerance ('very rare'); and glucose/galactose intolerance ('exceedingly rare'). Dental caries was 'an infectious disease of the teeth' and in any case 'less and less common'.[102] As he spoke, that week's copy of *Newsweek* was rapidly selling out in Brighton. Its cover story was headlined 'WARNING. SWEET FOODS MAY BE DANGEROUS TO YOUR HEALTH'.[103] The Sugar Bureau delegation was no doubt unpleased.

Two months later Dr Marks was billed by the Sugar Bureau as 'a top food scientist'[104] on a platform shared with Marsh Midda. 'FOOD LENINISTS ATTACKED AT SUGAR CONFERENCE' was the press handout headline. 'There is no direct evidence that any food contributes to, let alone causes, any serious disease or death,' said Dr Marks, adding that 'there is now a problem of scientific misinformation being spread by people without expert knowledge.'

On 27 May Dr Marks was on a sugar industry platform again, this time at the invitation of Professor Vlitos and the World Sugar Research Organization. His fellow speakers included Professor Curzon, Professor Durnin (of whom more later) and Professor Don Naismith (whose views on food terrorists and crisps have already been recounted). Dr David Buss and Robert Wenlock, the chief nutritionists at MAFF and the DHSS, were also on the platform.[105] Michael Shersby MP was one of the thirty-five representatives of the sugar industry, and the Sugar Bureau one of the 138 organizations (from Reuters and the *Financial Times*, to the Universities of Birmingham, Bradford, Cambridge, Glasgow, Leeds, Reading and Surrey, to Saatchi and Saatchi, Snackfood Manufacturing and Marketing, the British Nutrition Foundation and Unilever) that had accepted the invitation to attend.[106]

At the top of the bill was Dr Alan Forbes of the American Food and Drug Administration (FDA), whom the WSRO had brought over from Washington to summarize the preliminary findings of an FDA report on sugar. These included the comment that:[107]

> There is no conclusive evidence that dietary sugars are an independent risk factor for coronary heart disease in the general population.

The Sugar Bureau translated this view into: 'there is no evidence to link sugar with ... heart disease.'[108] But, as it turned out, Dr Marks stole the show with a phrase of his own invention that national newspaper editors found irresistible: 'muesli belt malnutrition'.

The posh and the pop papers alike loved the story, which a fascinated Press Association reported to all the national news rooms. Here are the headlines:

MALNUTRITION RISK FOR FOOD FADDISTS' CHILDREN (*Daily Telegraph*)[109]
PROFESSOR SCOLDS 'MUESLI-BELT PARENTS' (*Times*)[110]
'MIDDLE CLASS FOOD FADS HARM CHILDREN' (*Daily Mail*)[111]
FOOD FAD THREAT TO CHILDREN'S HEALTH (*Daily Express*)[112]
KIDS STARVE ON HEALTH FOODS (*Daily Mirror*)[113]
EXPERT RAPS THE 'MUESLI MENACE' (*Today*)[114]

What did Dr Marks actually say? Quoted in the *Times*:

> Many children are suffering from 'muesli-belt malnutrition' which could cause stunted growth and weight loss.

In the *Daily Telegraph*:

> Children who suffer from this modern form of malnutrition are taken to paediatricians who tell their parents to feed them properly. This means letting the kids enjoy things like sweets and so-called junk foods .... They need these sugars and fat to grow properly.

The next day *Today* ran a rapturous leader.[115]

> You can recognise them by their sickly pallor and the look of longing in their eyes. They live in places like Hampstead and Islington, and are often to be seen pressing their noses against the windows of sweetshops and McDonalds. They are the forgotten children, victims of health-foodism, sufferers from muesli belt malnutrition. But now they have a saviour. The courageous Professor Vincent Marks .... There is now every chance that the neglected children of food faddism can look forward to a normal, greasy-mouthed, chocolate-spattered existence.

Dr Marks warmed to his theme in a follow-up interview for the *Daily Telegraph* in a Paddington pub.[116]

> 'We're in danger of producing a generation of anorexics,' he told me, knocking back a pint of best bitter and waving around a chunk of ghostly white, so-called French bread .... 'We see children who are eating too many oranges because their parents know that oranges are good for you. In moderation they are, but oranges and tomatoes turn your blood yellow if you eat too many of them, and some of these children look yellow.'

What did the Sugar Bureau think about all this? The *Daily Express*'s follow-up story ran:[117]

> 'We would go along with what he is saying', said a Sugar Bureau spokesman. 'We are aware of his work and he may have spoken at our events. But there is no direct connection between us. We do not fund his research.'

By now the newspapers were noticing the fact that the story came from the WSRO conference, and that the British Medical Association had described Dr Marks' statements as 'indefensible and irresponsible'.[117] Patricia Clough of the *Times* asked a pertinent question. Where were these children?[118]

> Professor Marks told the *Times* yesterday he had 'personally seen at least one' child with such malnutrition, as had every paediatrician he had spoken to.

And what had the parents of at least one child given him

and/or her to eat? Muesli, as part of a low-sugar, low-fat diet? Or a bizarre diet? Dr Marks is not, as far as I know, on record as having answered this question.

SWEET TALK AT THE NUTRITION FOUNDATION

On 19 November 1984 Simon Coombs, Conservative MP for Swindon, asked the Department of Health (DHSS) to set up a COMA committee[119]

> to review the effect of sugars such as sucrose, glucose, maltose, fructose and caramel, on health, and to make recommendations on desirable levels of intake for the whole UK population.

His request was refused.

On 4 June 1985 Annie Cushing of the consumer group Advice and Information on Sugar wrote from the London Hospital Dental School to Dr Donald Acheson, Chief Medical Officer at the DHSS, effectively repeating Simon Coombs' request. Refusing her request[120] Jeremy Metters of the DHSS wrote:

> As you may know, the British Nutrition Foundation has set up a Task Force on Sugar ... consisting of various medical, dental, dietetic and food science experts, with observers from the DHSS and Ministry of Agriculture, Fisheries and Food. Its report should be ready for publication early in 1986 and will no doubt be of interest to groups such as the one you represent.

I asked John Patten, then DHSS Minister responsible for public health, for an explanation. He replied on 1 August 1985. 'I must first reiterate that it is to COMA that the Government looks for scientific advice on diet and health,' he told me[121] – as he was bound to, since this was the reason he had already given, in Parliament and elsewhere,[122] to justify disowning the NACNE report. He went on to say:

> For the moment we have decided to await the report of the BNF Task Force on sugars before considering any action.

So the Department of Health (meaning, the government) disowned the NACNE report, compiled by people with no connection with the food industry, by saying that only

COMA reports count; and then, without exactly owning the food industry-funded British Nutrition Foundation (BNF) Task Force, recognized it. Moreover, a decision to send 'observers' to meetings indicates quasi-official status: observers watch, and also listen, speak, report back, and, on occasion, leak.

At the second meeting of the Task Force, on 2 May 1984, held as always at the BNF's headquarters, Professor Albert Neuberger, then President of the BNF, made a statement:[123]

> The Foundation, although financed by the food industry, should in no way have its scientific judgement affected by the commercial interests of the food industry. He concluded that if the judicial function of the Task Force is to be successfully carried out then it is of utmost importance that complete confidentiality should be observed.

Some time later all the Task Force documents came into my hands: two box files filled with successive drafts of chapters of the report, correspondence, minutes of the meetings, and memoranda from interested parties like Tate & Lyle and Mars.

The BNF has no official standing with government in Britain. But in the absence of any COMA report on sugars, the Task Force report would be used by the DHSS and MAFF as the most up-to-date scientific review of sugar and health. The BNF's ambition is to achieve quasi-official status for itself and for its statements and reports.

All BNF statements and reports are friendly to the food manufacturing industry, or at least are accommodated comfortably within industry policy. The story of the Task Force sugars report shows why.

The Task Force's original terms of reference[123] included the following:

> Explore the choices and constraints on eating habits and food manufacture if less sugar and syrups were consumed.

The minutes of the first meeting of the Task Force, on 15 February 1984,[123] record the following amendment:

> 'Less sugar and syrups' should also be replaced by 'if a change in consumption of sugars were recommended' so as not to presuppose a recommendation for less rather than more sugar being consumed.

Any recommendation that people should eat more sugars would be a world first!

On 1 March 1985, Elizabeth Morse, Executive Secretary to the Task Force, produced a list of twelve recommendations made in Britain (five), Ireland, the USA, Canada, Australia, Sweden, Norway and France on dietary goals, all of which unanimously recommended a cut in consumption of sugars.[124] Ms Morse's paper was rejected for publication in the Task Force's report.

At the meeting on 2 May, Professor Neuberger, although he was not the Chairman of the meeting, explained on behalf of the BNF that:[123]

> Some people will have definite ideas and some will have legitimate commercial interests and it is important that both sides of the argument should be represented.

So, who were the lions and who were the Christians in this contest?

A full list of members of the Task Force, and their interests, is included in Document B. The neutral Chairman was Sir Cyril Clarke, ex-President of the Royal College of Physicians. The full-time employees of the sugar industry were Professor Vlitos and Dr George Greener, Director of Research at Mars Confectionery. Professor Neuberger and Sir Alan Marre represented the BNF, as its President and Chairman at that time. Sir Alan Marre did not attend any meetings. Food science was represented by Professor John Hawthorn of Strathclyde University, who agreed to draft jointly with Dr Greener the first and third chapters of the report, 'What are Sugars and Syrups?' and 'The Role of Sugars in Food and Drink'. The second chapter, 'Production of Sugars and Syrups', was to be drafted by Professor Vlitos.

During the eighth meeting of the Task Force on 7 June 1985,[123] it was proposed that the report should have two main sections. The chapters by Dr Greener, Professor Vlitos and Professor Hawthorn, together with another drafted by Dr David Booth of the University of Birmingham on appetite and liking for sugars, would form the first section. The second would open with a chapter on 'Physiology and Metabolism of Sugars' by Professor Ian Macdonald, who certainly does have 'definite ideas' about sugars. In his BNF

Annual Lecture in 1984 before he succeeded Sir Alan Marre as Chairman of the BNF in 1985, he said:[87]

There is no doubt that sucrose does have deleterious effects, most notably on the teeth, but the hard evidence that suggests it is causative in numerous other diseases of man does not exist.

Initially[123] four chapters were proposed on sugars and diseases. These were on diabetes, by Dr David Pyke of King's College Hospital; epidemiology (meaning, mostly, sugars and heart disease) by Dr Tom Meade, a colleague of Dr Garrow at Northwick Park Hospital, Harrow; energy metabolism (meaning obesity) by Dr Garrow; and dental health (meaning tooth decay) by Professor Michael Edgar of the University of Liverpool Dental School.

The three other members of the Task Force were Professor A.B. Foster and Dame Elizabeth Ackroyd, (neither of whom attended any meetings) and Margaret Sanderson, a community dietitian, whose task was to provide practical advice for health workers. The report itself was originally aimed at 'The *Times* readership'.[123]

From the start every Task Force meeting was attended by up to four BNF staff. These were Dr Derek Shrimpton, Director-General in 1984; Dr Richard Cottrell, Science Director; Elizabeth Morse; and the minutes secretary, Alexandra MacColl, who was also the Director-General's secretary. After the fifth meeting on 30 November 1984, Dr Shrimpton no longer attended, having quit the BNF after disagreements with his colleagues on the issue of the BNF's dependence on the food industry.[125] He was replaced by Professor David Conning. The government observers were Dr Shirley Fine and Mr P. Vidler from the DHSS, and Dr David Buss from MAFF.

... SHALL COME FORTH SWEETNESS

Tins of Tate & Lyle syrup show a picture of a lion with the motto 'Out Of The Strong Shall Come Forth Sweetness'. The lions of the Task Force certainly included Hawthorn and Macdonald as well as Greener and Vlitos: their four chapters said nothing likely to caramelize the sugar industry.

Nor were the lions mauled by the Christians; drafts of chapters helpful to the industry were accepted with little demur. Sugars and starches are carbohydrates, and carbohydrates 'are a necessary part of the human diet,'[126] said Greener and Hawthorn. Also, 'the sucrose contained in strawberries and carrots is the same as sucrose extracted from sugar-cane or sugar-beet.'[127] And it seems that humanity owes its very existence to sugars:

> Pleasure and Variety. This can best be appreciated by trying to imagine a world in which sugars did not exist, or in which their consumption was forbidden. In the latter case, the human race, as we know it could hardly survive in that breast milk, fruit and vegetables would be forbidden. If sugars did not exist it is possible that the human race might never even have evolved.

Thank the Lord for sugars! What about over-eating?

> The appetite for sweetness, as of all things, is normally self-limiting; like any appetite it is open to abuse.

This means that if you are normal sugars will not make you fat, but if you are greedy any food, including sugars of course, can make you fat.

Where are sugars found in food? Various examples of the sugar content of foods expressed as a percentage of total energy ('dry weight') were given: 52 per cent in skimmed milk, 86.5 per cent in apples, 52.9 per cent in carrots, 98 per cent in jam, 70.9 per cent in brown ale, 16.9 per cent in shortbread, 48 per cent in tomato soup.[127]

Professor Hawthorn and Dr Greener did not list the sugars content of a Mars Bar (65.8 per cent), cola drinks (100 per cent), sweets (100 per cent), or, come to that, processed sugars in any form (100 per cent).[44] They made no distinction between naturally occurring sugars and processed sugars. Indeed, the Task Force report makes no explicit reference to the fact that whole food with naturally occurring sugars is more nourishing than processed food containing added sugars (not to mention saturated fats, salt and additives).

Professor Vlitos reminded the Task Force that the sugar industry employs up to a million people all round the world, notably in impoverished countries that need the foreign exchange.[51]

So much for the lions. What about the Christians? The minutes of the Task Force's meetings record that Dr Booth thought there wasn't much point in encouraging the population to consume less sugars and that in any case there wasn't much evidence to show that sugars are a problem, apart from tooth decay.[128] (The line that health education is a waste of time is also popular with the sugar industry.) Dr Pyke, quoting his own previously published work, saw adult-onset diabetes as an inherited condition: 'dietary factors − whether total energy or type of food consumed − are of little importance.' And in the treatment of diabetes 'there is a common supposition that sugar itself is bad for diabetics. This is not so.'[129]

There is general agreement among scientists that added sugars are an important cause of overweight and obesity, and that the most sensible way to lose excess body fat is to reduce consumption of foods that supply calories but little or no nourishment − saturated fats, added sugars and alcohol. There is also general agreement that sucrose and other added sugars are the essential cause of tooth decay. Any expert report that proposed otherwise would have a credibility problem. So the two Christians left writing chapters for the report were Dr Garrow and Professor Edgar.

The views of Dr Garrow and Professor Edgar on sugars and health differ from those of the sugar industry. But it is a matter of record that the Sugar Association funded a research project of which Dr Garrow was co-author in 1982;[130] the Association's planning strategy has already been summarized[52]. Professor Edgar's research has been funded by the Cocoa, Chocolate and Confectionery Alliance[131] (and still was in 1986),[132] by Mars,[133] by the WSRO[13] and, as with Dr Garrow, by the Sugar Association.[131]

Tate & Lyle and Mars confectionery personnel produced lengthy memoranda challenging the views of Dr Garrow and Professor Edgar. The conclusion of Dr Garrow's temperate chapter on obesity[134] was that eating sugar

in some circumstances probably leads to overeating and obesity. It is logical to advise overweight people to reduce their intake of sugar, since this effects a decrease in energy intake without an associated decrease in important nutrients.

This is the only reference in the entire Task Force report (as published) to the fact that sugars contain all calories, no nourishment.

In due course a paper from Tate & Lyle arrived.[135] Obesity is a very, very complicated subject, it said. (This line can appeal to scientists looking for research grants.) 'Because of the multifaceted nature of obesity, it is unwise to isolate variables such as sugar consumption,' said Tate & Lyle.

By this time, Dr Garrow, who is also the leading English authority on obesity, had become wise to the ways of the food industry as Chairman of the NACNE committee. He refused to re-write his chapters. An apology came from Professor R.C. Righelato of Tate & Lyle. 'I am grateful to Professor Garrow for bringing our attention to the error in our paper on obesity', he wrote.[136] But Dr (not Professor) Garrow was unmoved.

FLUORIDE DEFICIENCY
AND ALL THAT ROT

In the first draft of his chapter,[137] Professor Edgar made the following points. Sugars, and sucrose in particular, are the essential cause of tooth decay; starchy foods have an insignificant role; snacking of sticky sugary foods has a calamitous effect on teeth; fluoride is effective, but only up to a point; and industry and educators should continue to find ways to reduce sugar manufacture and consumption.

Dr Greener, the man from Mars and an energetic member of the Task Force, did not care for this line. For sugar, read 'fermentable carbohydrate', he said, in a detailed reply to Professor Edgar.[138] Commenting on another point, Dr Greener wrote:

p 8 para 2 line 1. 'Sucrose eaten frequently is highly cariogenic'. This is true but it is not the whole truth. We should say something like '... fermentable carbohydrates eaten frequently are highly cariogenic. We cannot be certain whether sugars are worse than starch in this respect.'

'Avoid constant nibbling' was the message favoured by Dr Greener. Earlier Dr Greener had mounted another detailed attack on Professor Edgar[138] supported by a long paper from Mars, which repeated the worldwide sugar industry line; all carbohydrates can cause tooth decay. 'As nearly all foods contain some fermentable carbohydrate, they are all potentially involved in the caries process' – which means that you have a choice: starve or rot. Mars quoted an American health educator: 'our efforts to control the abusive use of sugars, although admirable, are unrealistic in most instances.'

The sugar industry line on obesity, remember,[30,52,77,79,99,107] is to look you in the eye and say, 'sugars can cause obesity. But so can all other foods. Obesity is caused by greed.' The line on tooth decay is to be equally forthright and frank and say, 'sugars can cause tooth decay. But so can all carbohydrates. Tooth decay is caused by food. Sticky food between meals is a problem, but the solution is toothbrushing and fluoride. Scarce tax-payers' money should not be spent on futile health education.'

The memo from Mars said:[139]

the ecological concept of the disease is very important, in order to maintain a balanced perspective in the role that the various agents play in the ecological triad of the disease.'

Lucky for their profits that they don't try to sell Mars Bars with language like that! What this means is that for a tooth to decay, you need a tooth and bacteria as well as sugars. This is like saying that for a car crash you need a pedestrian and a car as well as a drunk driver. Here is the high spot in this memo:

Some researchers have therefore referred to dental caries as a flouride [sic] deficiency disease.

This is like saying that depression is a Valium deficiency disease. Members of the Task Force complained about the Tate & Lyle submissions. 'The Task Force was under no obligation to accept them,' said Sir Cyril Clarke.[123]

By 21 May 1985 Professor Edgar had made further modifications to his chapter. Links between sucrose consumption and tooth decay 'is impressive' became 'sugar intake is only weakly correlated with the incidence of caries'. Eating sticky sweets between meals causes 'very high levels of caries' became 'a higher incidence of caries'. 'The evidence strongly suggests that starch contributes very little to caries' was altered to 'most studies indicate that the potential cariogenicity of starch is of a lower order than that of sucrose'.[137]

New passages were inserted. Should sugar consumption be cut?[137]

> It is not unreasonable to question its possible role in future attempts to eliminate the residue of dental caries in the developed world.

This is, I think, bad English for saying that there may be little point in eating less sugar. Or, as Elizabeth Morse put it in a draft conclusion to the report:[124]

> If you are a slim adult with good teeth (or dentures) then it probably does not matter how much sugar you eat.

Professor Edgar, who is not a health educator, incorporated another suggestion from industry[139] into his chapter:

> While the more cariogenic foods almost all contain sugar, labelling of prepared foods with percentage sugar content data is unlikely to be helpful as far as preventing dental caries is concerned as, in certain contexts, a small amount of sugars can be as cariogenic as larger quantities.

This is a key point of the sugar industry's policy. Having confined the discussion of sugars and health to tooth decay, the industry goes on to argue that to label foods with their sugars content would lull the population into a false sense of security and would actually be misleading, since any problem is caused by carbohydrate, not sugars. This audacious line means that the sugars content of processed food should remain a mystery to consumers, not for the sake of industry but for the sake of public health!

On 17 February 1986 Simon Coombs MP again asked for a COMA report, this time on sugars and dental health. 'I have no such plans at present,' replied the then Health Minister, Barney Hayhoe.[140] On 13 May Mr Coombs persisted, this time making the request of the then junior Agriculture Minister Peggy Fenner at the Annual General Meeting of the Coronary Prevention Group. This was a matter for the Department of Health, she replied: [141]

> My Department has not medical expertise. If the Department of Health feels there is a case, I've no doubt they will do it. We have to rely on the expertise of the experts.

CRUNCH POINTS

In early 1986, the experts round the BNF Task Force table were having to deal with Margaret Sanderson, former Chair of the British Dietetic Association Community Dietitian's Group and a formidably knowledgeable specialist on sugars who is committed to 'the need to reduce sugar consumption in the UK ... by 50 per cent'. [143]

The first draft of her paper, 'Sugars in the Diet: Practical Aspects', was circulated in January 1986. It caused a stir. She said: [144]

> Extracted or refined sugars such as glucose, fructose, and sucrose, contribute nothing to the diet apart from calories.

She gave a practical example, of two ways in which a twelve-year-old boy might consume one-fifth of his daily energy requirement:

Choice 1	Choice 2
3 oz boiled sweets	1 slice of fruit cake
1 glass fizzy drink (eg cola)	1 glass of fruit juice
3 cups of tea with 2 teaspoons sugar	1 slice wholemeal bread and butter/ margarine
	3 cups of tea (no sugar)

The first choice contains 120 grams and 480 calories all from added sugars: no fibre, no vitamins, virtually no nourishment. The second choice, which has 10 grams of added sugars, is rich in vitamin C and iron, and provides a fair source of fibre and other nutrients. Citing Swedish, Dutch and US recommendations, together with those of the

Royal College of Physicians in its report on obesity,[1] Ms Sanderson recommended that the consumption of added sugars should be halved, by eleven teaspoons of sugars a day. And she provided a ready reckoner showing the sugars content of many common manufactured foods, including, among numerous other brands of confectionery, 'Mars. 1 bar. 9 teaspoons of sugar'.

This was Professor Vlitos' response:[145]

I have read Ms Sanderson's paper with interest, but I cannot accept it in its present form, nor would I have my name associated with the Task Force Report if her chapter is reproduced as it stands .... It is unrealistic to advise the public to give up its sweet taste as Ms Sanderson urges it to do. I do think that she should keep in mind that with the exception of aspartame (which has problems of its own!) both saccharin and cyclamate are recognised carcinogens in several countries.

Dr Greener went to the top, with a letter to Sir Cyril Clarke, copied to Richard Cottrell, Science Director of the BNF. 'I find this paper unacceptable,' he wrote:

This paper infers that energy is not in itself valuable in the diet. This is nonsense when one considers that the greatest primary nutritional need in the world is energy .... the only health risk associated with the frequent consumption of sugars is dental caries.

Dr Booth went over the top, accusing Ms Sanderson of having a 'professed aim of eliminating sucrose and syrups from people's diets'. Lists of foods with their sugars content are 'irresponsible', he said; without alternative choices, 'you are misleading professionals and scaring and confusing the public to no benefit to them'.[147]

Dr Garrow was not having any of this:[148]

Dr Greener rightly says that there is no evidence that sugar is a unique cause of obesity. I do not think anyone suggested it was. Similarly we could say that alcohol is not a unique cause of road accidents, smoking is not a unique cause of lung cancer and high winds are not a unique cause of trees falling over. We can all think of teetotallers who have road accidents, non-smokers who have lung cancer and trees that fall over on a calm day when a lorry runs into them. Nevertheless, I think we would all agree that alcohol, smoking and high winds could reasonably be classified as contributing to road accidents, lung cancer and fallen trees respectively. Likewise, I think it is fair to say on the evidence that the consumption of sugars contributes to obesity.

At this point the new Director-General of the BNF, Professor David Conning, who was not a member of the Task Force, took an initiative and redrafted Ms Sanderson's paper. The statement that sugars 'predispose to dental caries and obesity. Obesity, in turn, predisposes to other diseases such as hypertension, non insulin-dependent diabetes and gallstones'[144] was changed to 'sugars may have a role in causation of obesity and dental caries.'[149] How best should overweight people reduce? 'Sugars are therefore prime candidates for reduction. Alcohol and fats are also candidates,'[144] became a recommendation to cut ' "energy dense" components of the diet such as carbohydrate, fat and alcohol'.[149] And Dr Conning, who does not agree with national dietary guidelines, added a thought of his own:[149]

In practice there seems to be little justification for an interventionist approach to reduce sugars consumption in relation to the disease processes in which excess sugar consumption may play a role.

Supported by Dr Garrow and Professor Edgar, Ms Sanderson demanded that most of Dr Conning's thoughts be omitted from her chapter, which they were, in successive drafts circulated in February, April and July 1986.[144]

As time went on the draft chapters became knocked into a shape which suited the BNF, the sugar manufacturing industry and the Ministry of Agriculture. At the twelfth meeting of the Task Force, held on 29 January 1986, which neither Dr Meade nor Dr Greener attended,[123] it was agreed that Dr Meade's chapter be chopped up. The first section became a new chapter called 'Consumption of Sugars', revised by Dr Buss. Dr Cottrell of the BNF did a four-page whistle-stop review of sugars and Crohn's disease (no 'firm information'), cancers ('no adequate evidence'), gall stones ('neither study throws much light on the predisposing factors'), and stones in the urinary tract ('this finding has not yet been confirmed independently' and no 'clear evidence').[150]

The first submission to the Task Force on sugars and heart

disease was written in 1984 by Dr David Snodin of the Tate & Lyle research laboratories.[6] 'The data do not support a causal link between refined sucrose consumption and CHD [coronary heart disease],' he concluded.[151] The final draft of Dr Meade's two-page chapter accepts the connection between sugars and heart disease through obesity, but concludes that 'sugar consumption is not of over-riding aetiological importance.'[152] Dr Snodin and Dr Meade agree that the view that sugars cause heart disease is, in the words of Dr Snodin, 'essentially the work of one man, John Yudkin'.[151] All other work linking sugars with heart disease was ignored.

A STICKY END

What was Professor David Conning, the new Director-General of the BNF, to do, in the spring of 1986? One way or the other, it looked as if two members of the Task Force would resign, or at least resort to a minority report, that expedient so detested by believers in the indivisibility of science. Professor Vlitos and Dr Greener would protest if the report recommended a general cut in the consumption of sugars; Dr Garrow and Ms Sanderson would protest if it did not.

Eight founder members of the BNF had a special interest in the Task Force.[153,154] These were Berisfords, British Sugar and Tate & Lyle (with Tate & Lyle, British Sugar, which is owned by Berisfords, has a virtual duopoly of British sugar production); Cadbury-Schweppes, Coca-Cola and Beecham, who between them make most of the sugared drinks sold in Britain; and Mars and Rowntree Mackintosh, who with Cadbury-Schweppes dominate the British sugar and chocolate confectionery market. These firms would be sorry to see yet another expert report recommending a halving of sugars consumption – and therefore production.

But would anybody outside the food-manufacturing industry take an expert report seriously that did not recommend a cut in consumption? The sugar industry matters to the BNF. But so does the medical establishment, represented among others on the BNF's governing body by

Sir Douglas Black, ex-President of both the Royal College of Physicians and the BMA, and Chairman of the BMA Board of Science and Education whose report recommending a halving of sugars consumption appeared in March 1986.[155] More to the point, what would government think? At about this time Dr Conning was interviewed by Dr Michael O'Donnell for the last in a series of four BBC TV programmes in the BBC 'Food and Health Campaign' season. The programme in question, 'Calling the Tune', was scheduled for transmission on 29 April. Dr O'Donnell asked Dr Conning if the BNF was independent. Dr Conning replied:[156]

It would be ridiculous to say that the Foundation is totally independent in the sense that it's totally dependent on industry money. But the important thing, as I say, is that it was set up to access nutritional information in as impartial a manner as possible.

Dr O'Donnell was quizzical:[156]

Before the Department of Health decides where it stands on sugar and health it's looking to the Task Force for guidance – a Task Force set up by the BNF, which is almost totally funded by the sugar and sweet industry and other big food companies.

This is something of an overstatement. On paper the sugar, confectionery, chocolate and soft drinks industries do not dominate BNF funding. But 'Calling The Tune' had got the drift. It would certainly be fair to say that Mars and Tate & Lyle were taking a livelier interest in the Task Force than, say, the Eggs Authority or *Slimming* magazine (to name two other BNF sponsors), which had not sent submissions on sugars to Sir Cyril Clarke. So what was Dr Conning to do? In April 1986 he himself drafted the 'Conclusions and Recommendations' of the report,[157] partly from suggestions made by the members of the Task Force; and added some of his own views, in particular about journalists.

Professional communicators need to keep in mind the extent of their influence and accept their responsibility to ensure that the public are not misled either deliberately or inadvertently.

He then called a press conference for 25 April – four days before transmission of the BBC TV programme – to announce the 'Conclusions and Recommendations', together with another ticking off for the press:[158]

> Communicators and the media are singled out for particular attention in a plea to avoid further confusing the public by the deliberate or accidental dissemination of incomplete, unproven or inconclusive information on matters which affect the diet.

The message that Dr Conning wanted to get across to the public, through the media, was this:

> The plain facts with regard to sugars, syrups and sometimes starches, is that they are primarily sources of energy which – if used too frequently – present a risk to teeth and possibly to weight gain. These are valuable and good dietary components if used in an intelligent, moderate way.

The last sentence in Dr Conning's draft[157] was omitted from the published recommendations.[159] However, journalists from the national and medical press who attended the press conference were altogether more interested in the fact that members of the Task Force, notably Sir Cyril Clarke, had not been told about the press conference,[160] and that Dr Conning's recommendations had been released before the report itself had been agreed. As Dr Conning suspected, copies of the Task Force's proceedings had been leaked, and some senior medical correspondents were well informed. So there were, after all, no headlines saying 'TOP DOC RAPS PRESS, SAYS SUGARS VALUABLE AND GOOD DIETARY COMPONENTS'. Instead, these were the headlines in the *Daily Telegraph*, the *Guardian* and the *Lancet* respectively:[161,162,163]

DOCTORS IN ROW OVER 'DILUTED' SUGAR REPORT
SUGAR INQUIRY REPORT RELEASED WITHOUT EVIDENCE
A CURIOUS PRESS CONFERENCE

'The mood of the journalists in the press conference was hostile,' reported the *Lancet*. The general feeling was that Dr Conning was disseminating information that was unproven and inconclusive if only because it was incomplete. What about Margaret Sanderson's chapter? Dr Conning said that it was on its way. Dr Conning was asked whether, in his opinion, the evidence was that it doesn't matter if people eat ten, twenty, thirty, forty or fifty kilograms of sugar a year.[164] 'That's exactly what I'm saying,' he replied.

'In the event, the BNF has plainly sacrificed the goodwill of some of its advisors and gained nothing in the process,' concluded the *Lancet*. A reader of the *Daily Telegraph* commented on the sugar wars:[165]

> On each occasion this issue comes to the fore a very fierce exchange occurs between the politically strong and very wealthy sugar industry on one side, and representatives of those who spend their working lives treating the effects of sugar-related diseases on the other .... Surely the open conflict that exists between the sugar lobby and the health profession should be put to rest once and for all by the setting-up of a Chief Medical Officer's Committee of inquiry into sugar and health.

A few weeks later, on Friday 20 June, Dr Donald Acheson (now Sir Donald), Chief Medical Officer at the DHSS, held the regular six-monthly meeting of COMA. Sugar was on the Officially Secret agenda. Government policy, to await publication of the BNF report 'before considering any action',[121] was reviewed. Could the government take 'Sugars and Syrups' on board? Or, given the rubbishing its recommendations had already had, was a COMA panel necessary after all? Dr Acheson decided to set up a COMA panel 'to examine the effect of sugars in the diet'.[166] The persistence above all of one Conservative MP, Simon Coombs, had paid off. After two and a half years, the Task Force report was, at least for a while, kicked into touch. On 10 September 1986 Barney Hayhoe and Peggy Fenner were dropped in Mrs Thatcher's autumn reshuffle.

COCA-COLONIALISM

The British baking industry maintains that white sliced bread is the best thing since mother's milk, but it is now making more wholegrain bread. The British dairy industry maintains that full-fat cow's milk is the best thing since sliced bread, but at the same time it is distributing more low-fat milk. Up to a point, the British bread and dairy industries can respond to pressure and manufacture more nourishing products. In terms of public health, the problem is not bread, but white bread; not so much milk, as full-fat milk. Sugar, though, is a different story. As with alcohol, the healthy alternative to sugar is less sugar, and the best choice is no sugar. So while the bread and dairy industries can switch products, the sugar industry will fight to maintain average consumption in Britain and other Western countries at about 100 pounds for every man, woman and child, every year.

In 1986 Neil Shaw, Chairman of Tate & Lyle, remained ebullient. In April, his company bid just under £500 million for Berisford's and thus for British Sugar.[167] This would turn a virtual duopoly into a monopoly of the British sugar market. Shaw's audacious argument was that the Mono- polies Commission should consider sugar as a European, not a British, commodity. 'With their considerable political clout – Lord Jellicoe, ex-Cabinet Minister, is on the board – they hope to get Government approval,' explained the *Sunday Times*.[167] In a later *Sunday Times* story, Mr Shaw posed with his hand over the head of a large model of the patriotic Mr Cube, sword and shield held high; the headline was 'THREAT TO SUGAR JOBS AS BID WAR BOILS OVER'.[9] Mr Shaw indicated that if the Monopolies Commission blocked his bid for British Sugar, Tate & Lyle might well abandon its sugar refineries in Britain, with the loss of 3000 jobs in east London and near Glasgow.

Shaw's policy of enlisting 'doctors prepared to speak up in defence of sugar'[2] continued. In April the story was 'JUNK FOOD "ADDS SPICE TO YOUR LIFE" ' (*Daily Express*),[168] 'THE JUNK FOOD WAY TO KEEP IN GOOD HEALTH' (*Today*),[169] and 'WARNING: FOOD FADDISTS ARE BAD FOR YOUR HEALTH' (*Guardian*).[170] In its story the *Daily Telegraph* explained:[171]

> Dr Elizabeth Whelan, founder of the non profit-making American Council on Science and Health and a holder of impressive degrees from Harvard and Yale Universities, is making it her life's work to debunk the food faddists.

Dr Whelan had been brought over from the USA by the Sugar Bureau, whose staff took her round a week of interviews with the British media. What did she think of sugar?[171]

> There's no proof that sugar adversely affects behaviour, causes cravings or obesity, or is associated with diabetes or heart disease.

Were these stories all got up by the journalists? Not exactly: 'It's all a myth created by food extremists,' she said, adding 'sugar doesn't necessarily cause tooth decay .... we've got worked up over nothing.'[171]

What are Dr Whelan's origins? The annual report for 1984-85 of the American Council on Science and Health (ACSH) shows that it has some affinity with the BNF. Over 200 industrial sponsors are listed, including Bobs Candies, the California and Hawaiian Sugar Company, Coca-Cola (twice), the Hawaiian Sugar Planters' Association, the Hershey Fund, the Holly Sugar Corporation, the National Soft Drink Association, Nestlé (four times), Pepsico, the Sugar Association, and the United States Sugar Association.[172] Dr Whelan herself worked as a research associate for Professor Fredrick Stare at Harvard, and Dr Stare is on the board of ACSH.[173] I asked Dr Whelan about the sources of her funding. She replied that in 1986 funding from the food industry had fallen from 18 to 8 per cent, while petrochemical companies contributed 25 per cent. Most ACSH funding, she said, was from foundations:[174]

> who support the free enterprise system. They don't want society to be changed for health reasons when there's no good scientific reason to back such change.

The British press asked no questions about Dr Whelan's origins.

The interests of the sugar industry are indivisible and worldwide. It operates more like the tobacco and drugs industries than the rest of the food industry. In some respects, its position in Britain and other western countries can be compared with that of the cigarette industry a generation ago. Nothing good can be said of sugar, from the health point of view; but national and international economies depend on sugar. The difference between sugar and tobacco is that the evidence against sugar on health grounds continues to be disputed. Senior people in the industry no doubt still believe that sugar is a good food. In the 1980s, it is inconceivable that a director of a tobacco firm could preside over medical research. But in 1982 Lord Jellicoe moved from being Chairman of Tate & Lyle to the Medical Research Council. In 1986 he is Chairman of the Medical Research Council, and on Neil Shaw's board of directors.[175] Should the Chairman of the MRC be an employee of the sugar industry? As far as I know, until now the question has never been asked.

Like the tobacco industry, the sugar industry does not expect increased sales in Britain. The British food supply is as sweetened as it will ever be. The industry's policy of maintaining production of sugars in Britain at about 50 kilograms a year, and therefore consumption at about 100 lb a year,[42] was fulfilled a generation ago: Britain has been saturated for over thirty years. Nothing will change nationally unless a British government decides to cut the amount of sugars entering the food supply. As long as sugars get a good press, that will never happen.

Worldwide, the annual consumption of sugars of just over 100 million tonnes[42] is increasing by about 2 per cent,[7] which means that on average, every year, every mouth on earth is swallowing almost 50 lb of sugar.[42] The target is the Third World and, most of all, the East. The Chinese eat less than 10 lb of sugar a year. The name of the world game is Coca-Colonialism. Bob Beeby, President of Pepsico International, explains:[176]

There's Coke and there's Pepsi, and no one can come into the game and hope to win. We're only just beginning overseas. We are in Russia with fifteen plants. China has a population of 1.2 billion; India has 711 million ... you know what I'm saying. It's all out there.

CHAPTER 4

Additives: The Dirty Dozen Dyes and Other Stories

When consumer representatives talk to the food industry about additives, they are made to feel alarmist and irresponsible, if they suggest there is the slightest degree of risk. Civil servants often point out that no one has ever been known to have suffered any harm, either in the short – or the long term, from an additive.
Daphne Grose, Royal Society of Health Journal,[1] 1977

We are at present carrying out a full review of additives in foods described either directly or by implication as specially prepared for infants or young children and we shall be issuing a full report on this Review in due course. It is, however, our opinion that a case of need has not been demonstrated for the use of added colouring matter in these foods .... Moreover, the Committee on Toxicity has recommended in its report that colouring matters should not be used in such foods and we recommend therefore that the use of added colouring matter in food described either directly or by implication as having been specially prepared for infants or young children should be prohibited.
Ministry of Agriculture, Fisheries and Food,
Interim Report on the Review of the Colouring Matter
in Food Regulations 1973[2], 1979

Ingredients: Raspberry flavour jelly crystals: sugar, gelling agents E410, E407, E340, potassium chloride; adipic acid, acidity regulator E336, flavourings, stabiliser E466, artificial sweetener (sodium saccharin), colour E123. Raspberry flavour custard powder: starch, salt, flavourings, colours E124, E122. Sponge, with preservatives E202, colours E102, E110. Decorations with colours E110, E132, E123, E127. Topping mix: hydrogenated vegetable oil, whey powder, sugar, emulsifiers E477, E332, modified starch, lactose, caseinate, stabiliser E466, flavourings, colours E102, E110, E160a, antioxidant E320.
Label of trifle, 1986

The Ministry of Agriculture, Fisheries and Food is known in the official Whitehall jargon as the 'sponsor' of the food industry;[3] and thus it was that Mrs Peggy Fenner, then junior Agriculture Minister, went to Brighton to open the eighth Fast Food Fair on 11 November 1985. She had some good news for the assembly.[4]

> By and large, the products of your industry compare well with other food products and represent valuable sources of protein, vitamins and minerals to customers who might otherwise forego them. There are no such things as good or bad foods – only good or bad diets.

Derek Cooper, who presents BBC Radio 4's *Food Programme*, went to the sixth Fast Food Fair for the *Observer*, and did not like what he saw:[5]

> The product development men have at their disposal one of the most advanced technologies of any industry. Dream up a new fantasy food and the chemists will engineer it into reality. Anything edible can be rendered instant, converted into powder or granule form. There is no feeling of shame in applying the words 'home style' to a sachet of chemicals .... Any number of flavourings, preservatives, antioxidants, emulsifiers, dyes, colours, bleaches, humectants, anti-caking agents, surfectants, stabilisers, sequestrants, moisteners, non-nutritive sweeteners, thickeners and thinners can be used to enhance the product.

Mrs Fenner gave Mr Cooper and his ilk a slap on the wrist, and for good measure added some words of reassurance in her role as 'sponsor' of fun food:[4]

> A good deal of attention has recently been focused by the media on additives in food .... I would like to take this opportunity to reassure anyone worried by the recent publicity that all permitted additives are safe.

MR JOPLING TAKES THE BISCUIT

A couple of weeks previously, on 25 October, Michael Jopling, Mrs Fenner's boss, addressed the joint annual lunch of the Cake and Biscuit Alliance (CBA) and the Cocoa, Chocolate and Confectionery Alliance (CCCA) in London. The CBA and the CCCA have been nicknamed the Sweet Fat

Alliances, Sweet FA for short. This is misleading, for the British cake, biscuit, chocolate and confectionery trades rely on chemical food additives just as much as on saturated fats and processed sugars. Here, for instance, are some secrets of the British 'chocolate' biscuit, as disclosed by the industry magazine *Food Manufacture* in January 1985:[6]

Chocolate milk and sometimes very dark biscuits do not have true chocolate shades when using caramel colours .... In milk, caramel colours have almost a 'muddy' appearance, but this can be overcome by the addition of approximately 0.01% by weight of amaranth giving reddish chocolate shades. By the addition of a small amount of blue and yellow to this mixture a more typical chocolate shade can be achieved.

Mr Jopling did not, as far as I know, have 'chocolate' biscuits for his joint lunch. And he even wondered if his hosts would be willing to say 'when' a little sooner while adding dyes to their products:[7]

There is no point in over-colouring. It would be sensible to see whether a reduction in the amount of colours used would still satisfy consumer demand.[9]

Are dyes and colours safe, as used in food? Although he has the same team of speechwriters as Mrs Fenner, Mr Jopling was a little more cautious:

It is of course impossible to state that anything, even so-called natural food is totally safe, but we can take the most rigorous steps to ensure that all permitted additives are screened for safety before approval .... None are permitted until their safety has been checked by the Committee on Toxicity and the need for them assessed by the Food Advisory Committee.

These ministerial words were provoked by two Thames Television programmes on food additives and contaminants called *Good Enough To Eat?*, broadcast on 8 and 9 October 1985. An accompanying booklet sent to 35,000 viewers who requested one took much the same line as Derek Cooper:[8]

An imaginative food scientist with an understanding of the very latest in food technology can create a vast range of textures, shapes, flavours and colours, and produce them to order as cakes, biscuits, snacks, sweets, drinks and sauces. These are made with varying proportions of refined starches, sugars and fats, and a few wholesome ingredients – all blended together with additives.

And on need and safety, the booklet claimed that:

Britain allows more additives and has weaker controls than any other major industrialised country.

This and other public criticism of food additives in the autumn of 1985 amounted, in the view of Mr Jopling and his speechwriters, to:

An unprecedented assault on the integrity of the British food industry. There have been claims that the industry pays little regard to the health of the consumer, and that in this it is aided and abetted by the Government. This is nonsense, as you and I know.

As long as food is safe, he added:[7]

there are, of course, no such things as good foods and bad foods. But there are certainly good diets and bad diets.

Media interest in additives caused similar hyperactivity within the chemical industry in October 1985. The CIA, which in Britain stands for the Chemical Industries Association, called a press conference near the Barbican in London, on the same day as the first Thames Television programme. 'Everything that exists is a chemical,' said John Russell of the CIA.[9] He denounced 'scare stories about chemical additives' that 'confuse, alarm and mislead the public', and promised to 'put this complex subject into perspective'. With his colleagues from the CIA, Mr Russell commended *The Chemistry on Your Table*,[10] a CIA booklet published that day which was being circulated to MPs, health visitors and midwives, health professionals and other opinion-formers, and was given to the journalists at the meeting.

The CIA booklet claimed that additives 'help to provide a balanced and safe diet of great variety', and put them in the perspective of a full-page colour chart of 'some natural toxins in food'. This suggested that tapioca, bananas, cabbage, mustard and carrots might interfere with tissue respiration or cause hallucinations, thyroid insufficiency, dropsy and hallucinations again, respectively. Later, Mr

Alan Hume, a CIA spokesman who is Director of Food and Cosmetic Colours for the Williams division of Morton Thiakol, makers of tartrazine (E102) since the turn of the century, wrote to me saying:[11]

> The current publicity against additives is developing into a neo-religion, similar to the sixteenth century view of witches and Galileo's problems with the round moon [sic].

Mr Hume enclosed a copy of a letter he had sent on behalf of the CIA to all the major British supermarket chains, pointing out that 'your industry is very much dependent on that of the food processing and related manufacturing industries' (such as, for example, the Williams division of Morton Thiakol). He went on:[12]

> As you will be aware, there is a general demand for products which excite the consumer in terms of texture, taste and colour, as the vast majority of our population eat significantly more than is their basic requirement to live healthily. An excellent example is the range of soft drinks and beverages which have grown up to replace water and we feel very strongly that it is our business to help the man in the street by providing colours which are safe and which help to give him a more interesting quality of life.

A letter written on 27 June 1985[13] by Dr Donald Acheson, Chief Medical Officer at the DHSS, to all doctors in England tempered the enthusiasm of government, industry and science for food additives.[13]

> It is known that some individuals may experience allergic or other adverse reactions to food additives, which cannot be reliably predicted by laboratory tests.

Dr Acheson enclosed a MAFF booklet designed to identify additives[14] which he acknowledged 'may on rare occasions' be a problem. The leaflet lists every single regulated additive from E100 to 927!

In December 1985 Derek Cooper of the *Food Programme* interviewed Barrie Williams, then deputy Director-General of the Food and Drink Federation, on the safety of additives.[15] 'I stress again,' he said, 'that these additives go through the most rigorous testing procedure'. But what about those people whom chemical additives make ill? Tsk

tsk, said Mr Williams. Very sad. But very rare. Then he went on:

> We are co-operating with Government and the medical profession to ensure that we can provide the right level of information in terms of additives overall, to ensure that the damage done to the individual in terms of any adverse effect that additives have can be rectified medically.

The message the British food- and chemical-manufacturing industry sends to anyone bothered about dyes and other food additives, can be translated into verse:

> If our brown stain makes you ill
> Go to the quack, and take a pill.

Dr David Snodin, of Tate & Lyle, who is also Chairman of the Food Safety Committee of the Society of Chemical Industry (the trade's professional association) takes a comparable view. So long as the experts of the Committee on Toxicity, the Food Advisory Committee and other government advisory bodies approve chemical additives as safe and necessary, he has put it to me,[16] 'why should we lesser mortals question their judgement?'

BANNED IN AMERICA, APPROVED IN BRITAIN

But foreigners are not always in tune with official British harmony on the safety of food additives. For example, 'Red Dye No 2' is banned in Malaysia. This fact was told to me by the International Organization of Consumers' Unions (IOCU), the worldwide body of national consumer movements, including the Consumers' Association in Britain.

The newsletter of the Consumers' Association of Penang (CAP) explained:[17,18]

> Scientific tests have shown the dye to be carcinogenic (a cancer-causing agent) and also damaging to the liver and sex organs. It has been banned in the United States, Russia and several other countries.

A full account of why Red Dye No 2 is banned both in the USA and in the USSR is given by Samuel Epstein in his book *The Politics of Cancer*.[19] Professor Epstein is Head of the Department of Occupational and Environmental Medicine at the University of Illinois, Chicago and previously was a head of department at the Children's Cancer Research Foundation in Boston.

Red Dye No. 2 is a coal-tar dye, a by-product of the petroleum industry. Coal-tar dyes are used in inks and paints, textiles, and also in cosmetics, food and drink. In the USA, Red Dye No. 2 was provisionally registered as safe under the Food, Drug and Cosmetic (FD&C) Act 1939; between 1960 and 1975, despite doubts about its safety, its provisional clearance was extended fifteen times.[20] Red Dye No. 2 is popular with the food-manufacturing industry, so much so that at one time it was incorporated into $10 billion worth of food every year in the USA.[19]

In 1970 Soviet studies showed that the dye caused birth defects and cancer in laboratory animals. One study concluded that it 'possesses carcinogenic activity of medium strength and should not be used in the food industry'.[21] Accordingly, it was banned in the USSR. Under pressure from consumer groups, the US authorities undertook new tests in the early 1970s. One study showed that the dye was liable to kill rat embryos at a daily dose in excess of 0.0015% of body weight. The usual rule for food is to set a 'safe level' of 1 per cent of the dose that can be toxic − or eventually lethal − in animals. But this would have been equivalent to the amount of Red Dye No. 2 contained in one can of cherry soda.[22] To resolve this problem, the Food and Drug Administration (FDA) initially proposed a unique 'safe level' not of 1 per cent but of 10 per cent of the toxic dose.[20]

Other tests of the carcinogenity of Red Dye No. 2, in which 500 rats were given different doses, started in March 1972 but ran into difficulties. Somehow the rats got muddled up:[19]

There was widespread mixing of animals among assigned dosage groups, and a general neglect of husbandry that had left many rats dead and decomposed in their cages.

However, 198 rats were salvaged, and at the end of the two-year study it was found that at the highest dose the dye caused a large number of malignant tumours in female rats. Accordingly, it was banned in the USA in January 1976. It has now been replaced by 'Red Dye No 40', another coal-tar dye, not allowed in the European Community, which may be just as toxic.[23]

But if you look at a helpful booklet first issued by MAFF in 1982 and called *Look at the Label*,[24] it says:

Manufacturers are allowed to add certain substances to food, when they have been proved to be safe, if they are necessary for colouring, flavouring, preserving or performing various other functions.

After explaining that food additives are now generally listed on food labels with their 'E' (for Europe) number, the booklet lists

E123 Amaranth

which is the E for Europe name for Red Dye No. 2. In the USA, the USSR, Malaysia, Sweden and elsewhere, amaranth is banned in food; its use in food is 'not recommended' in Japan; and in France and Italy it is only used to stain caviar.[25] In Britain, however, amaranth is 'proved to be safe' and is, remember, indispensable in the palette of the modern British 'chocolate' biscuit colourist.[6] A supermarket search done at the end of 1985 showed that amaranth is:[26]

One of the most widely used colourings in the UK for: breadcrumbs, black cherry yoghurt, pickled beetroot, jams, chocolate cakes, swiss rolls, tarts, pot rice, instant soups, raspberry flavour mousses, jellies, quick-set jells, tinned fruit pie fillings, ice cream, ice-pops, tomato ketchup, strawberry flavour syrups, soft drinks including cherryade, blackcurrant drinks, squashes, as well as vitamin C and other so-called 'health' drinks.

COAL-TAR DYES
AND FOOD FOR BABIES

Here is the label of a leading British soft drink, manufactured in 1985 for one large supermarket chain in Britain:

Ingredients: Sugar, concentrated blackcurrant juice, water, citric acid, vitamin C, preservatives E221, E223, flavourings, colours E123, E102, E142.

The other colours listed are tartrazine (E102) and brilliant green (E142), two more coal-tar dyes. A senior food scientist working for one of the major supermarket chains in Britain explained to me why many soft drinks are dyed. During our conversation he asked to remain nameless. Once, he said, a consignment of drink had arrived at the depot of the firm he works for and, on examination, had proved to be faulty. Amaranth had been been left out of the mixture. What did the colour look like? 'Duckham's,' he said, 'Duckham's motor oil'.

Brilliant green (E142) is not only found in soft drinks. A supermarket search[26] showed that it stains a

Variety of jams, e.g. plum, blackcurrant, bramble, tinned soups, peas, broad beans, green beans, range of cakes, gateaux, chocolate covered Swiss rolls, mixed peel, fruit flavoured sweets, soft-centred sweets, chocolate ice cream, ice pops, tinned fruit-pie filling, chocolate flavoured mousses, jellies, gravy granules, mint sauce, soft drinks including bitter lemon, lemon and lime drinks and fruit cocktails

Tartrazine (E102), the best-known coal-tar dye, is found in a vast range of products, including fish fingers, cakes, biscuits, confectionery, soft drinks, party food and 'fun' food, often combined with sunset yellow (E110), an orange/yellow dye.

Why is so much British food dyed, especially food designed to appeal to children? In the case of soft drinks, there is a technical problem. The colour naturally contained in fruit is 'fugitive': put fruit juice in a clear glass bottle, and then in a shop window for a couple of summer months, and it may fade, like all organic colours. But amaranth, like other dyes used to colour ink, paint, textiles and food, is inorganic and 'fast': it is brilliant and does not fade. So in time a skilful mix of dyes looks fresh, whereas the fruit itself, being stale, becomes drab.

Many tinned and bottled vegetables, fruit, pickles and preserves and such-like are brighter than fresh produce, home-grown or bought in a street market, greengrocer or good supermarket. One reason may be that processed vegetables and fruit are dyed to match not their natural colour but the colour of the printer's ink used on labels and in advertisements, which also contain coal-tar dyes. That is to say, foods are dyed to resembled dyed pictures of food, rather than the foods themselves. Check this for yourself by comparing the colour of home-made with mass-manufactured jam; or peas from the pod and the tin; or squeezed orange juice and packaged orange drink. Hand-made food never matches the brilliance of pictures in the cookery-book or the magazine advertisement. Children notice these things.

Colours, together with flavours, are now commonly used to create an illusion of fresh ingredients, such as fruit or vegetables, in products which are in fact entirely processed. Here for example is the ingredients list on a packet containing five sachets of 'raspberry, strawberry, peach, banana, vanilla flavour' blancmange powders:

Raspberry. Cornflour, flavourings, colour E102
Strawberry. Cornflour, flavourings, colours E110, E122, E124
Peach. Cornflour, flavourings, colours E110, E124
Banana. Cornflour, salt, flavourings, colours E102, E110, E124
Vanilla. Cornflour, salt, colours E102, E110, E124, flavourings

The colours are all coal-tar dyes. As well as tartrazine and sunset yellow, they are carmoisine or azorubine (E122) and ponceau 4R (E124), both red dyes. You begin to get the idea: red makes raspberry, two reds and a yellow make strawberry, one yellow and a red make peach, and two yellows and a red make banana or vanilla. Clever stuff.

Women are more aware of chemical additives in food than men, because women do most of the shopping, and therefore most of the looking at the labels. Among women, mothers are most aware of food additives and most worried about them, because manufacturers use additives, colours and flavours especially, to give instant appeal to food designed for children. Take trifle, for instance. The label of a brand of trifle that introduces this chapter, made by a multi-national food-manufacturing company, shows that in one 119-gram (4-ounce) package there are at least thirty-one helpings of additives (flavours do not have to be separately listed), of which a dozen are colours. Of these, all but one are coal-tar dyes: two dustings of tartrazine (E102) and amaranth (E123), and three of sunset yellow (E110); one of azorubine (E122) and of ponceau 4R (E124) and one each again of erythrosine (E127) and indigo carmine (E132), which are red and indigo.

This 'trifle' includes a remarkable number of declared additives, and trifle is a family favourite. In any case, it's easy to find trolley-loads of foods in supermarkets with three or more coal-tar dyes added. In May 1986 *Which?* magazine published a survey of additives.[27] The Consumers' Association's investigators read the labels of almost a thousand packaged foods and counted the additives and declared:

> 85 per cent of the food we found had one or more additives. In fact, though, additives don't tend to come in ones. Of these lines which contained additives, four was not uncommon (not surprising, perhaps, when it took four separate colours alone to make apple and raspberry pie filling).

But why should we worry? One of the experts on the government advisory Committee on Toxicity, to which Mr Jopling[7] and Dr Snodin[16] referred, has been Professor Arnold Bender, who reckons that, if he and his colleagues say additives are safe, then they are safe:[28]

> Altogether several thousand chemical aids are added to food. This may sound alarming, but no one in Britain has ever suffered harm from an intentional additive .... Are artificial colours harmful? So far as we know, none of the food additives – colours, flavours, preservatives and the rest – are harmful otherwise they would not be permitted in food.

So it might seem that Mrs Fenner did know what she was talking about, and that the USA, the USSR, Malaysia and the other countries that are now proceeding to ban more and more chemical food additives, colours and dyes in particular,[25,26] are foreign fuss-pots.

What do the officially appointed experts say about additives, and in particular about food colours and dyes? The latest official advice on colours and dyes until 1987 appeared in a 255-page report by the Food Additives and

Contaminants Committee (FACC) entitled *The Interim Report on the Review of the Colouring Matter in Food Regulations 1973*,[2] which, despite its title, was published in 1979. In 1983 FACC, which advised MAFF, was amalgamated with another body with the relatively reassuring title of the Food Advisory Committee (FAC)[29] which, as Mr Jopling indicated in his joint lunch speech,[7] is now MAFF's official advisory committee on food and health.*

While recommending that colours and dyes should still be permitted in food, FACC declared that 'there is a need for stricter controls on colouring matter'.[2] Within the report, separate documents from the FACC and COT emphasized the formal obligation of Ministers as laid down by the Food and Drugs Act 1955[30] (now updated as the Food Act 1984)[31] to

> have regard for the desirability of restricting, as far as practicable, the use of substances of no nutritional value as foods or as ingredients of foods.

What about children? COT stated that the obligation of Ministers is 'particularly important with foods especially prepared for infants and young children'.[2]

> We are at present carrying out a full review of additives in foods described either directly or by implication as specially prepared for infants and young children and we shall be issuing a full report on the Review in due course.†

The committee was not only concerned about the possible toxicity of colours and dyes. It also stated that:

* More committees! DHSS is advised by COMA (Committee on Medical Aspects of Food Policy), and COMA panels produce what are known as COMA reports. MAFF is advised by the FAC (Food Advisory Committee), and until 1983 by the Food Additives and Contaminants Committee (FACC) and the Food Standards Committee (FSC), which were then amalgamated into the FAC. The Committee on Toxicity (COT) advises both the DHSS and MAFF on the safety of food. MAFF has set up other advisory committees on food research and development (the Priorities Board) and on food quality, safety (of which more later in this chapter) and processing. An account of these and other advisory committees, and an analysis of their members, appears in Document B).

† Yet another MAFF advisory committee, the Steering Group on Food Surveillance, issued a 'progress report' in 1984.[32] This referred to the existence of a 'Working Party' on colours, but made no mention of the promised review of colours and dyes in children's food. So what, if anything, is happening? No information has leaked. Like all DHSS and MAFF advisory committees, the work of the Steering Group on Food Surveillance is covered by the Official Secrets Act.

We are not convinced that the presence of added colours is of any benefit to the infants or young children or that it affects their acceptance of the foods, though it may well, of course, make them more attractive to those who buy them and thus affect their choice .... We recommend therefore that the use of added colouring matter in food described either directly or by implication as having been specially prepared for infants and young children should be prohibited.

So why are coal-tar dyes still found in 'fruit' drinks, 'peach' blancmange, 'raspberry' 'trifle' and other products eaten daily by young children?

The answer is that an advisory committee is just that – advisory. Expert government committees usually have their reports published by HMSO, but that doesn't mean that the government takes any notice of their recommendations. And one reason why you can find tartrazine and plenty of other dyes in products like these is that successive governments have ignored the recommendations of COT and FACC. Instead the food-manufacturing industry, while legally free to add dyes to products 'prepared for infants and young children', has agreed a voluntary ban.

And what do the words 'young child' mean? When does a child stop being 'young'? A DHSS advisory committee on foods for infants and young children stated in a report issued in 1980:[33]

The following definitions will be used:
An infant is a child who has not attained the age of one year.
A young child is a child aged from one to three years.

Over at MAFF, however, kids grow up much faster. COT's recommendation was for a statutory ban on dyes in foods 'specially prepared for infants and young children, under twelve months old'.[2] You may think that a toddler aged eighteen months is a young child. Mr Jopling and Mrs Fenner take the view that children are getting 'old' at about the time they manage their first steps.

But we still haven't got to the bottom of the policy voluntarily agreed between the Ministry and the manufacturers. Plenty of parents feed their infants (under one year old) with fish fingers, say, or biscuits. So what does 'specially prepared' in the phrase 'specially prepared for infants and young children' mean? A Ministry representative explained to me:[34]

> The FACC's recommendation ... refers to those foods which are likely to form the main items in a very young child's diet, e.g. infant formulae, 'junior' foods, and not to foods intended for the general market but which may also be given to babies at an appropriate age.

Of course! The voluntary ban is on baby food! So if a manufacturer sticks a label on a product saying 'baby' or 'junior' food, it won't have coal-tar dyes or other colours in it. Whereas, for any product without the 'baby' label, the manufacturer can bung the dyes in and advertise it on television at kids' viewing time! So now you know. If you don't want to eat food with dyes in it, eat baby food.

In May 1986 three MPs agreed that this was a lot of nonsense, and decided it was time that the advice given to government seven years previously by FACC was implemented. Sir Geoffrey Johnson Smith (Conservative), Michael Meadowcroft (Liberal) and Tony Lloyd (Labour) called on the Minister to:[35]

> prohibit the use of all unnecessary food additives, other than nutrients, in food liable to be eaten by babies and young children under five years of age; this to include food, drink and medicine, claimed or described in advertisements or on labels to be suitable for young children.

By July, 89 MPs of all parties had signed this Early Day Motion. Mr Jopling did not respond.

Mrs Fenner did respond, though, to a half-hour eulogy for the British confectionery industry in the form of a Parliamentary debate, in the House of Commons on 24 May 1985.[36] The main speaker was Conal Gregory, who indicated an interest as Conservative MP for York, headquarters of Rowntree Mackintosh, 'whose sales last year passed the £1,000 million mark for the first time'. Mr Gregory was anxious to protect the interest of British confectionery. He complained about the Japanese:

> The Japanese are extremely fussy about emulsifiers, colours and wrapping materials. I am sure that the Department of Trade and Industry could occasionally discover that the rear axle of a

Japanese car is not exactly the right size and might consider taking action if the Japanese pursue their policy.

He complained about the Greeks:

Greece does not allow food colouring, so all the chocolate exported there is white, and different colour wrappers must be used to show different flavours.

And he complained about the West Europeans:

The usual chocolate sold by Cadbury in the United Kingdom would be considered imitation chocolate in Belgium and the Netherlands, because it does not contain the required amount of cocoa solids. The West Germans say that a minimum of 25 per cent cocoa solids should be used before a product can be called chocolate.

In response, Mrs Fenner reminded the House of Commons that the British confectionery industry was in 1985 worth £2,500,000,000 sales a year and 8 per cent of consumer expenditure on food:

I conclude by congratulating the confectionery industry on its achievements ... and I assure it and the House of our concern to ensure a propitious climate for its continued success.

What was at the root of Mr Gregory's concern and Mrs Fenner's reassuring reply? Additives, for one thing; and colours in particular. Take one very popular line of chocolate sweets:

Ingredients: Milk chocolate, sugar, wheatflour, edible starch; colours E171, E122, E102, E127, 133; flavourings, glazing agent (carnuaba wax), antioxidant E320.

The two colours that haven't already been mentioned in this book are titanium dioxide (E171), a white surface colourant, and brilliant blue FCF (133 – no 'E' number), a coal-tar dye. (The initials 'FCF' stand for 'For Colouring of Food'.)

The next time you are shopping in a supermarket, notice the sweets arranged on the shelves near the floor, below your eye-level but as close as possible to a toddler's gaze; or else heaped in dump bins by the check-out counters. I walked round three shops in September 1986. Three products made by big manufacturers, or else for one of the giant supermarket chains that increased its profits by many million pounds in 1985-86 while boasting about its healthy food, were 'Assorted Sweets: Children's Pack', 'Assorted Fruit Flavour and Toffee Lollies', and 'Dolly Mixtures'. Mixed up in a tot's tummy at party time or over a weekend, these amount to sugar (always the main ingredient), glucose syrup (the next in the list each time), hydrogenated vegetable oils or fat, bicarb (twice) or salt, emulsifiers, gelling agents, an anti-caking agent, an anti-oxidant, dustings of skimmed milk powder, cornflour and fat-reduced cocoa, bits and bobs of other chemicals, an unknown number of flavourings, and colours: E100, E102, E104, E110 (three times), E123 (twice), E124, E127 (twice), E131, E132 (three times), E142, E150, E153, and E171.

The 'new' colours and dyes in this little lot are turmeric (E100), a vegetable dye; quinoline yellow and patent blue V (E104 and E131) two coal-tar dyes; caramel (E150) and carbon black (E153). Of these patent blue V was disliked by the FACC: 'available evidence on all aspects is inadequate' Meanwhile it can be found in dolly mixtures; and indeed in jelly beans, so perhaps it could be advertised as a secret of President Reagan's management style.

SMELLING A RAT

Leaving aside any local ambiguity about the definition of a 'young' child, why shouldn't the major – and the minor – confectionery companies use colours and dyes as a means of turning an honest £2,500,000,000 a year? Why should we pay any attention to the Japanese, the Greeks, the Belgians, the Dutch, the Germans, and all the rest? After all, Mr Jopling, together with Mr Williams of the Food and Drink Federation, have explained that all food additives, colours included, are subject to rigorous testing.

What did FACC have to say in 1979 in their *Interim Report*? For judgements on toxicity (meaning, in this context, whether food colours and dyes can poison vulnerable people), FACC relied on the Committee on Toxicity (COT). In turn, COT relied on 'the available toxicological data': this is the 'rigorous testing' to which Mr Jopling is referring.

COT was not very impressed by some of the available data.[2]

We noted that much of the toxicological data provided was the result of studies carried out many years ago. It does not automatically follow that, merely because a study was conducted some years ago, it can no longer make a contribution to the safety evaluation of a substance today. Nevertheless we considered that certain of the older studies fell so short of present day standards that they should be supplemented with further work.

Of the 346 references to the toxicological data supplied by COT, whose report forms part of the FACC 'Interim Report', some certainly appear somewhat long in the tooth:

176. Hogyes A (1878). *Arch Exp Path Pharm* 9, 117
216. Koschara W (1935). *Hoope-Seylers Z Physiol Chem* 232, 101
246. Muller (1889). *Chem Ber* 22, 856
327. Verady M and Koturuya M (1931). Thesis. University of Sfegedia
329. Vernetti-Blina L (1928). *Rif Med* 47, 1516

were five of the eighty-three studies published 20 years or more before the *Interim Report*. Were these some of the studies that are not up to modern standards? There is no way of telling, since the references are not classified and mostly not referred back to the text, so that only a toxicologist can make sense of them.

Four references to more recent work would have been unremarkable in the mid-1970s. These are:

187. Industrial Bio-Test Laboratories Inc (1972). Report no IBT B700 to Interindustry Colour Committee.
188. Industrial Bio-test Laboratories Inc (1972). Report nos IBT J701 and J1850 to Interindustry Colour Committee
205. Kay JH and Calendra JC (1961). Two unpublished reports by Industrial Bio-Test and Laboratories Inc to Marshall Dairy Laboratory Inc.
206. Kay JH and Calendra JC (1962). Unpublished report of Industrial Bio-test Laboratories Inc.

In the 1970s, Industrial Bio-test, or IBT, which is based near Chicago, was a giant in its field, handling 30 per cent of the world's business of testing the safety of agrichemicals, drugs and food additives for industry. According to Dr Erik Millstone in his book *Additives*,[37] in 1976 a US Environmental Protection Agency inspector who had examined IBT's laboratory notebooks discovered that the initials TBD/TDA stood for 'too badly decomposed/ technician destroyed animal'. Vast numbers of corpses of experimental animals had been left to rot, or else were thrown away and not examined for cause of death. Millstone commented:[37]

> The people at IBT behaved in an irresponsible and illegal manner. They just obtained a new shipment of animals and replaced the dead ones with new ones. By doing so they were entirely invalidating the study, but they were also concealing their actions.

Senior IBT staff were indicted and brought to trial. It turned out that thousands of IBT reports were rubbish, and that IBT staff had frequently faked results, 'which always appeared to confirm the safety of the substances being tested'.[37] At the trial in 1983, three IBT scientists and executives were convicted of fraud. One outcome of this scandal was a review of laboratory practice by the Food and Drug Administration, which concluded that tests for the safety of chemicals, drugs and additives carried out in other laboratories were often incompetent, if not dishonest.

European standards, including those at British toxicity test centres such as the British Industrial Biological Research Association (BIBRA), which tests food additives for government and industry, are high, and there is no evidence of data-faking in Britain. But toxicology is an international trade; and FACC's report on colours cited IBT studies.

The hanky-panky at IBT was bad luck for the rats. Was it bad luck for people, too? Have colours and dyes now used in British food been accepted as a result of IBT reports B700, J701, J1850 and the rest? To what extent did COT and FACC rely on IBT data? I'm sorry, I can't tell you. It's an Official Secret.

On 16 December 1985, I did the democratic thing and wrote to Michael Jopling.[38] In his reply, Mr Jopling said:[39]

> I do recognise that largely because of the detailed, routine nature of toxicology papers, publication may not be easy and does not therefore always happen. I have asked my officials to see whether there are ways of ensuring the greater availability of these references perhaps by lodging copies of such papers with the British Library.

On 11 July 1986, MAFF followed this suggestion up, circulating a paper on 'the Availability of Toxicological Data on Food Additives' to interested parties.[40] In future, the Ministry said to industry, would you consider sending extra copies of your data to Mr J.P. Chillag at the British Library, Boston Spa, Wetherby, West Yorkshire LS23 7BQ? This proposal did not apply to previously published work, however. On trade secrets, the paper said:

> We would also ask that information considered to be commercially sensitive be indicated in some way .... Such information, after discussion and agreement by government departments if necessary, would not be lodged with the British Library.

So there it is. Next time a government advisory committee report on food additives is published, it may or may not include a list of references to toxicity studies. Sometimes it may be possible to work out which references relate to which additives. Many references are likely to be to 'unpublished' work. So, if you are a busy-body bothered about the brilliant green in jelly-babies, you can take yourself off to Boston Spa and ask for Mr J.P. Chillag. The exchange might go something like this:

> Was the toxicological study foreign? 'Sorry, can't help.' Was it completed before 1986 (or whenever industry complies with Mr Jopling's request)? 'Sorry, we don't have it'. Is it commercially sensitive? 'Sorry, you'll have to write off to Unilever, ICI, or whoever owns the data, and ask them if you can take a look.'

I have been able to trace one interesting toxicity study cited in FACC's report on colours: 'Andrianova MM (1970). *Vop Pitan* 29, 61'. This is one of the Russian studies of coal-tar dyes[21] that led to the banning of amaranth in the

USSR and then in the USA. Its title is: Andrianova M. 'Carcinogenic properties of the red food dyes amaranth, ponceau SX, and ponceau 4R'.

In its report, COT cited Andrianova's study as indicating that amaranth caused 'an increased tumour incidence' in laboratory animals, and noted conflicting evidence, some of which suggested that amaranth may be mutagenic (a cause of cell damage) and teratogenic (a cause of damage to babies in the womb – literally, 'a creator of monsters') as well as carcinogenic (a cause of cancer). Of amaranth (E123) COT concluded:

> In view of the uncertainties raised by the results of mutagenicity studies we require the results of a well-conducted study in the rat and metabolism studies within five years.

THE DIRTY DOZEN DYES

So there is evidence that amaranth may cause cell damage, cancer and/or birth defects, when fed in large doses to laboratory animals – and this is why amaranth is banned in the USSR, USA and other countries. Men, women and children are not rats; what harms a rat may not harm humans. But toxicologists have to make do with laboratory animals, and their work has little meaning unless it is assumed that what harms a rat may harm us.

However, in Britain, on the basis of the same evidence, COT took a different view. The system here is to classify additives as 'A', 'B', 'C', 'D', 'E', or 'F'. The full definitions are:[2]

> Group A. Substances that the available evidence suggests are acceptable for use in food.
> Group B. Substances that on the available evidence may be regarded meantime as provisionally acceptable for use in food, but about which further information is necessary and must be reviewed within a specified period of time.
> Group C. Substances for which the available evidence suggests probable toxicity and which ought not to be allowed in food.
> Group D. Substances for which the available evidence suggests possible toxicity, and which ought not to be allowed in food.
> Group E. Substances for which the available evidence was

inadequate to enable an opinion to be expressed as to their suitability for use in food.
Group F. Substances for which no information on toxicity was available.

By any meaningful definition of the word 'toxic', amaranth is obviously either possibly or probably toxic. So did COT classify amaranth as 'D' – probably toxic? No. Did they classify amaranth as 'C' – possibly toxic? No. Amaranth was classified in Group B, as 'provisionally acceptable'. This is why Mrs Fenner said that amaranth, and all the other additives in our food, with or without 'E' numbers, are 'safe'.

What about the other coal-tar dyes to be found in British processed food? COT had this to say about brilliant green (E142):[2]

This colour was previously classified in Group A on the basis of toxicological data, some of which cannot be regarded as adequate by present-day standards .... We therefore require within five years the results of further metabolism studies, short-term oral toxicity studies in the rat, multi-generation and teratology studies in the rat and a long-term carcinogenicity study in a species other than the rat.

Which is more bad luck for rats and for some other laboratory species; and may be more bad luck for us too, because COT did not classify brilliant green in Group E, but once again, like amaranth, in Group B, 'provisionally acceptable'. This is why it remains in products found on every British supermarket shelf. Patent blue V (E131), on the other hand, is classified E, and 'should not be included in any revised permitted list', said the FACC. So why is it in dolly mixtures and jelly beans on sale in September 1986? All will be revealed later in this chapter.

Altogether COT recommended that 17 food colours, including 12 coal-tar dyes, be put on the 'B' list, as provisionally acceptable subject to further tests for possible toxicity. FACC took COT's advice, stating that:[2]

We also recommend that the Group B substances be further reviewed within five years (unless a shorter period is specified in the Committee on Toxicity's Report) .... We would strongly emphasise that if the work required by the Committee on

Toxicity is not carried out on any colouring matter by the time suggested, we will not be prepared to recommend its continued use in food.

FACC was not only concerned about coal-tar dyes in 1979. It also took a special interest in caramel (E150), which is a form of sugar, being 'obtained exclusively by heating sucrose or other edible sugars',[41] on three counts. First, it 'accounts for about 98% by weight of all colouring matter added to food'; average consumption is over 1 lb a person a year, which is a lot of caramel. Second, nobody is really sure what caramel, or rather caramels, amount to, chemically speaking. The FACC welcomed the industry's proposal to classify caramels as follows:[2]

One caustic caramel (CC1), two ammonium caramels (AC1 and AC2) and three ammonium sulphite caramels; of the three ammonium sulphite caramels two would be 'single strength' (SSAS1 and SSAS2) and one 'double strength' (DSAS1).

Industrial caramels have come a long way from sugars heated in saucepans. Third, 'the toxicological studies that have been undertaken had not always allowed no-effect levels to be determined.' This tortuous statement is a reference to the fact that caramel fed in high quantities in test conditions can give animals diarrhoea, swollen guts and swollen kidneys, and can also give human volunteers diarrhoea.[42]

Caramel is used in a vast number of processed products. About two-thirds of world production goes into soft drinks,[6] notably colas; a lot is used in beer, meat products and soups. Why is so much made? Manufacturers like to give us the impression that 'chocolate' biscuits are rich in chocolate — hence the caramel blended with amaranth and the other paints in the food colourists' pots. Likewise, we like to think that sausages are made mostly of meat, so 'sausage casings are often dipped in caramel to obtain the desired colour'[6] and the fatty unmentionables and rusk inside the casing of many 'economy' sausages are stained with the coal-tar dye red 2G (128 — no 'E' number) to give the impression that the sausage is made mostly of meat. Some brown bread is white bread dyed with caramel: look for the tell-tale swirls. A yellow spirit caramel 'gives baked or microwaved poultry an oven-roasted appearance including light and dark highlights'.[6]

AN OMINOUS BROWN STAIN
AND THE FILTHY FIVE

The FACC also felt that the modern kipper is a fishy affair. Kippers nowadays are dyed with brown FK (154 – no 'E' number). The 'FK' stands for 'For Kippers'; and you will be lucky to eat a smoked rather than stained kipper. Brown FK is itself a cocktail of six coal-tar dyes.[2] The FACC disliked it:

> Because the results of bacterial mutagenicity studies indicate that two of the constituents of brown FK are mutagenic, we recommend that the results of a further carcinogenicity study in the rat be made available within five years .... In the meantime we recommend that the use of this colour be restricted.

In 1986 brown FK was to be found not only in kippers, but also in pot noodles, pot rice, preserved meats, crisps, biscuits and sweets.[26] That will have given your immune system something to get its teeth into.

Together with caramel and brown FK, another ominous brown stain is brown HT (155 – no 'E' number), also classified 'B' in 1979. This is the dye favoured by the trade in Britain to colour 'choc'* products such as ice-cream, swiss rolls, cakes and gateaux. It is not used in Europe, where chocolate products are more likely to be made with chocolate.

The reason why the dyes numbered 128 (red 2G), 133 (brilliant blue FCF), 154 and 155 (the brown stains), and also 107 (yellow 2G) have no 'E' numbers, is that they are not authorised in Europe. They are sometimes known as 'the filthy five'. In 1973 Britain insisted on a 'derogation',[2] Eurospeak for going its own way, and continued to use dyes not wanted in other European countries. (Between 1973 and

---

* If a product is called 'chocolate' (as in 'chocolate cake', 'chocolate roll' and so forth), it must by law contain at least 2.5 per cent non-fat cocoa solids. If a product is called 'choc' (as in 'choc-ice' or 'choc roll') its coating must contain at least 2.5 per cent non-fat cocoa solids.[43] This leaves plenty of scope for titillation with colours and flavours.

1976 some other dyes were used in Europe while being banned in Britain.) So in Italy you will not find brilliant blue FCF in your asparagus soup. German sausages are not tinted with red 2G. Sweet and sour flavour pot noodles stained kipper brown have not found favour with the French. And as Conal Gregory MP indicated in the Commons debate on the confectionery industry,[36] you will look in vain for 'chocolate' products painted with chocolate brown HT in Greece, Holland, Belgium or Germany. The fussy foreigners like more vegetables in their soup, more meat in their sausages, and more chocolate in their chocolate.

What is the fate of these 'filthy five' dyes? On 19 September 1985[44] the European Commission proposed to the Council of the European Communities that they be sorted out; 'harmonised', in Eurospeak, in the interests of trade. The proposal, circulated by MAFF to interested parties on 15 November 1985[45] was to 'suppress' yellow 2G, to restrict red 2G to foods not subject to high temperature during processing, to restrict brown FK to kippers and other smoked fish, and apart from yellow 2G, to grant 'E' numbers. So what happened? According to the Ministry of Agriculture a year later in September 1986, the Council had discussed the proposal twice but 'little progress has been made'.[34] A supermarket search made in late 1986 revealed various British-made foods adding 'E's to one or other of the 'filthy five' used in their products. One brand of sausages was found, for example, with added 'E128'. Was this a breach of the law? Yes, said a Ministry representative. 'They're jumping the gun'.[34] Meanwhile, the 'filthy five' are banned in Europe, but used without restriction in Great British food (subject always, of course, to 'good manufacturing practice'). By 1987 British manufacturers, braced for the Euroban on yellow 2G, had stopped using it in food.

RED 2G, BRILLIANT BLUE
AND WHITEWASH

Red 2G is another dye that FACC was not keen on. In 1979 they said, 'we further require the results of teratology studies within two years'. In 1986 red 2G could be found in fish fingers, Scotch eggs, chocolate rolls, chocolate flavour dessert whips and soft drinks, as well as sausages, frankfurters and other meat products.[26] Both caramels and red 2G were on FACC's 'B' list.

FACC took a firm view in 1979: 'We are now satisfied that there is a need for stricter controls on colouring matter.' The report continued:

> It is, of course, one thing for us to recommend that stricter controls are needed. It is yet another to be able to say with certainty how extensive they should be and what form they should take. These are the questions to which we have now turned our attention .... We shall press ahead as quickly as we can with the preparation of our further recommendations.

You will now be wondering what happened to the tests on the five colours and the dozen dyes on the 'provisionally acceptable' 'B' list, which were to check if any cause cell damage, cancer, birth defects and/or other ill effects in laboratory animals. COT's deadlines were 1981, 1983 and 1984. During 1985 and 1986 I contacted MAFF and the DHSS every couple of months or so to ask how things were getting along.

No, the assessment was not complete, I was told at first, 'but there are rather a lot of them'.[34] Then a confidential memorandum written by a MAFF official in July 1985[45] came into my hands. This stated that all seventeen colours and dyes were being discussed in Brussels by the relevant EC expert committee:

> Additional safety studies have been carried out on amaranth and green S and the DHSS Committee on Toxicity has confirmed that both colours are safe and acceptable for use in food and has reclassified them in Group A. In addition, tartrazine has been thoroughly tested for safety and evaluated by committees of independent experts in the UK and the European Community who remain satisfied that the colour is safe and acceptable for use in food.

(There is more about tartrazine and the 'committees of independent experts' later in this chapter.) I telephoned the DHSS and requested confirmation of the COT decision. I was refused: advice given by COT, I was told, is 'confidential and not normally published'.[46] Then Mr Jopling referred to the report that the FACC (now the FAC) was 'pressing ahead with' in 1979 during his joint lunch speech in October 1985; the Committee was, apparently, 'well ahead in its examination of the levels of colours in food, and I await their report with interest'.[7] In March 1986 I wrote again to Mr Jopling, suggesting that 'such delay, given the seventeen colours and dyes on the 'B' list since 1979, is a mounting cause of political embarrassment.'[38] The reply came from Charles Cockbill, a senior official in charge of food standards at MAFF:

> I know that the Food Advisory Committee in their current discussions on colours are concerned that their report should provide sufficient information to explain their recommendations and I hope you will find that report more on the lines you have in mind.

You can make what you like of that.

Are all permitted food colours and dyes safe? It's a matter of opinion. Given the evidence, you can judge as well as any professor of food science. Are colours and dyes needed? It depends on your point of view. Most food manufacturers say yes, most consumers say no. My opinion is that any doubtful additive should not be used in food; that any additive doubtful enough to require special testing for toxicity should be withdrawn immediately; and that safety standards for colours and dyes should be stringent, because these additives are cosmetic and are concentrated in products eaten by little children. Doubtful colours and dyes should not be put on probation but be remanded in custody.

THE TRADE GETS THE BLUES

Worry about food colours and dyes goes back a long way. In 1924 an expert committee set up by the Minister of Health[47] thought that food manufacturers used colours to hoodwink their customers:

> It is evident that colour is frequently used to cover up objectionable or inferior materials, or give a factitious

appearance, so that the articles so coloured masquerade for something which they are not.

In those days manufacturers used any colours and dyes they liked, apart from some on a banned list (such as arsenic and mercury). The committee proposed that this 'negative' list be replaced by a 'positive' list, and that a colour or dye should be permissible in food 'only if the evidence demonstrated its harmless character'. However, the Government of the day 'decided on a different approach',[48] and so this recommendation was rejected.

In the early 1950s Britain still had a Ministry of Health and a Ministry of Food. The central committee advising both Ministries was the Food Standards Committee (FSC). Its brief was to look after the quality of food; it was responsible 'for preventing danger to health, loss of nutritional value or otherwise protecting purchasers'. In 1954 the FSC published a report on 'Colouring Matters'.[48] By this time British manufacturers were already using at least seventy-nine colours in foods, including sixty-three submitted for approval by the Cocoa, Chocolate and Confectionery Alliance, which stated that

a large number of colours was necessary to provide the variety in appearance of confectionery to which the consumer had become accustomed.

The food manufacturers argued for the 'negative' list, which had been operating since the 1920s, saying that they 'have received no complaints of illness due to the consumption of foods containing added colour'.[48] (This is not altogether surprising, since in the 1950s colours were not listed in ingredients lists.)

Another line of argument put to the FSC was that:

The present system gives the necessary freedom of choice to the food manufacturer; and enables foods manufactured for export, which conform to the laws of the importing country in respect of 'coal-tar' colours, to be sold on the home market.

In plainer language, this means that if British manufacturers are free to use almost every food colour and dye ever invented, they may find the crock of gold at the end of the rainbow on the home market, and can also make up special batches of product for export using colour combinations to suit fussy foreigners. But if any colour or dye allowed abroad is banned in Britain, and if a batch of products containing that colour is rejected for export by the fussy foreigners, then the manufacturer will not be able to dump it on the home market. Or, as another report on colours[49] said:

> It will not be possible to sell on the home market the surplus resulting from frustrated exports, over-production and confectionery mis-shapes containing colours not on the recommended list.

It evidently did not occur to the manufacturers that if a colour or dye is banned in Britain it should therefore not be used for products made for export. Business is business.

In 1954 the FSC was not impressed by the trade's arguments:[48]

> We cannot accept the contention that, because 'coal-tar' colours have been used in foods for many years without giving rise to complaint of illness, they are, therefore, harmless substances. Such negative evidence in our view merely illustrates that in the amounts customarily used in food the colours are not acutely toxic but gives no certain indication of any possible chronic effects. Any chronic effects would be insidious and it would be difficult if not impossible to attribute them with certainty to the consumption of food containing colouring matter.

The more the members of the committee looked at the whole issue of toxicity of dyes, the more unhappy they became. 'The possible carcinogenic properties of coal-tar dyes in food cannot be ignored'. An experimental animal may be evidently unharmed when fed or injected with dyes; but this does not mean that humans would therefore also be unharmed. There again, humans may be more vulnerable than animals: 'it is possible that the same dosage of a carcinogen might be as effective in man as in the mouse'. A child is of course more vulnerable than a man or woman. 'In the absence of conclusive evidence we are unable to recommend any colour unreservedly as safe' was another conclusion and:[48]

> We have found the whole subject of food colours so clouded with uncertainty and lack of definition that, with the

safeguarding of the public health as our dominant consideration, we feel that if colours are to be allowed in food at all, the
number permitted should be limited as far as possible. Such a
list should exclude – for the present, at any rate – all dyes
reported to cause toxic effects or tumour formation in any
animal, or which seem likely to be broken down in the body into
substances producing such effects.

Therefore the committee recommended that dyes be
permitted in food only when included in a positive list. Of
the seventy-nine commended by the Association of British
Chemical Manufacturers, the British Baking Industries
Research Association, the British Essence Manufacturers'
Association and Flavouring Compound Manufacturers'
Association, and the Cocoa, Chocolate and Confectionery
Alliance, twelve were accepted and classified 'A' as evidently
not harmful. Thirty-two were classified 'B' ('colours for
which the available evidence is deficient or conflicting') and
thirty-five were rejected ('colours which have been shown or
are suspected, to have harmful effects on health') and
classified 'C'.

As a rule, government advisory committees get around to
publishing reports on specific subjects, like colours, every
ten or fifteen years or so. In this case the FSC published a
'Supplementary Report on Colouring Matters'[49] the very
next year, 1955, the first year of the Ministry of Agriculture,
Fisheries and Food. The trade, having received the 1954
report, had obviously turned various shades of ponceau
cryst 6R, sudan IV, benzyl bordeau B, and methyl violet, to
name just four dyes in the red-purple range now classified
'C'. One protestation was highly revealing:

> The list was weak in blue colours, and that the 'C' classification
> of brilliant blue FCF should be re-examined.

Nothing doing, said the FSC, and confirmed brilliant blue
FCF as 'unsuitable for use in food'. Another nineteen dyes
were commended to the committee by the trade (making a
grand total of ninety-eight): of these, five were classified 'B'
and one 'A'. The trade should be able to paint its
technological masterpieces with the fifty dyes now classified
'A' or 'B', said the FSC, and then made another revealing
statement:[49]

In our earlier deliberations we had in mind that the recommended colours should be confined to those classified 'A'. Such a list would have been unbalanced and in particular would have been overloaded with red colours, some of little utility. To mitigate the difficulties which might have been experienced by the food trade if a colour customarily associated with certain foods were not available it was decided to include some colours of the 'B' class.

The government 'Colouring Matter in Food Regulations 1957'[50] broadly accepted the FSC recommendations and authorised a 'positive' list of thirty dyes: twelve reds, two oranges, eight yellows, one green, one blue (blue VRS, not brilliant blue FCF), one indigo, one violet, three browns and one black. These were all taken from the FSC's 'A' and 'B' lists. The 1957 regulations were reviewed in the next FSC report on 'Colouring Matters'[51] published in 1964.

The 1964 report gave the trade an even bigger shock. Two independent expert panels, one on Pharmacology, the other on Carcinogenic Hazards in Food Additives and Contaminants, were asked to look at the evidence for or against forty-four dyes: the thirty permitted in 1957, plus another nine then used in Europe, and five submitted by the trade – including brilliant blue FCF. Full marks to the Cocoa, Chocolate and Confectionery Alliance for persistence.

But the colours submitted by the trade all got the thumbs down, and four, including brilliant blue FCF, were classified 'D' as 'probably too toxic to be allowed in food'. Of the thirty permitted colours, the FSC, on expert advice, proposed a ban on four – including blue VRS. No blues![51]

We have appreciated that the proposed list of permitted coal-tar colours would not contain any blue colour which would be technically satisfactory for certain requirements of the trade. The evidence available on brilliant blue FCF and blue VRS suggests probable toxicity and as we have already recommended in the report, these colours ought not to be allowed in food. In view of this we are prepared to give immediate consideration to any toxicological evidence which becomes available on any blue colour.

Thirty of the forty-four dyes were rejected and classified

'C', 'D', 'E', or 'F'. Ten got a provisionally acceptable 'B', and only two were classified 'A' as acceptable. These were green S (E142) and amaranth (E123), both of which were demoted to the 'B' list in 1979.

So taking the 1924, 1954, 1955, 1964 and 1979 reports together – and they are all the expert advisory government reports published since the 1920s until 1987 – no coal-tar dye has always been classified 'A' as acceptable. Every coal-tar dye now permitted in our food has at some time been judged by the official government advisory committees as a possible or probable hazard to our health.

Toxicologists who claim that the coal-tar dyes that stain the food in the shops now, are safe, will say that tests on rats and other laboratory animals now, are altogether more accurate than in the 1950s and 1960s. But 142 of the 346 references in the 1979 FACC report are of studies published before the 1964 FSC report was published. The 1964 report, which is helpfully and precisely referenced, lists twelve studies to support its conclusion that brilliant blue is 'probably too toxic to be allowed in food'. Seven of these studies turn up in the 1979 report, evidently as part of the evidence 'sufficient for us to find the use of brilliant blue in food acceptable'[2] and classified 'A' as OK! One committee's poison is another committee's sweet.

Between 1964 and the mid-1970s, it would seem that the boffins at the experimental laboratories, had kept enough rats alive and tumour-free for long enough, to satisfy the Committee on Toxicity that brilliant blue FCF is just the stuff to feed our kids; and the recommendation to ban brilliant blue was ignored. Watch out for a new line in the supermarkets: 'tropical fruit' flavour drink, coloured laser beam blue and smelling of model aeroplane glue. You will find '133' (no 'E' number) in the small print at the end of the ingredients list. The 'Colouring Matter in Food Regulations 1973'[41] with some later amendments, now permits sixteen coal-tar dyes in food: five reds (E122, E123, E124, E127, 128); four yellows (E102, E104, 107, E110); one green (E142); one indigo (E132); two browns (154, 155); one black E151) – and two blues (E131 and 133). Of these tartrazine (E102), sunset yellow (E110), indigo carmine (E132) and brilliant blue FCF (133, no 'E' number, remember) are classified 'A' for acceptable.*

HALF A POUND OF DYE BY AGE 12?

In the mid-1970s, while preparing its *Interim Report*, FACC decided to find out how much colour and dye people in Britain eat in their food. As the report states, there is an obvious way of making this calculation:[2]

> One apparently straightforward approach would be to establish the total annual production of each food-grade colour, divide this by the total population, and again by 365 to give an average daily intake per person.

One quick call to the Chemical Industries Association in London, half a minute on a pocket calculator, and Bob's your uncle. That's what I thought, too, when I attended the CIA's launch of *The Chemistry on Your Table* on 8 October 1985. I asked John Russell of the CIA if he would tell me the annual tonnage of food additives, food colours and food dyes going into consumption in Britain, at five-year intervals from say 1945 to 1985. 'Sorry', said Mr Russell; he didn't have any such figures. So then I asked if he could disclose any information at all about the tonnage of food additives, colours and dyes going into consumption. 'Sorry, no', said Mr Russell, he couldn't help.[9] In October 1986 I repeated my request in a letter to Martin Trowbridge, Director-General of the CIA, which I copied to Mr Russell. He did not reply by letter but, in a telephone call, said that the chemical industry had never got round to collecting comparative data.

Considering that the CIA employs over 70 staff,[9] this seems to me a case of 'won't' rather than 'can't': every industry knows its own production statistics. 'It is a matter of some regret that these figures are not available from the industry itself,'[52] said Professor David Conning of the British Nutrition Foundation in 1986. If Dr Conning, a toxicologist who until 1985 was Director-General of the British Industries Biological Research Association (BIBRA)

---

* In March 1987 the FAC reclassified almost all the 'B' list as 'A' for acceptable. See the concluding chapter.

can't get the chemical industry to cough up its production statistics, then who can?

FACC had been equally out of luck in the mid-1970s:[2]

> We understand from the manufacturers of food colours that it would be difficult to obtain meaningful estimates of probable daily intakes based on total annual production figures. There are many non-food uses of food-grade colours and it is difficult to establish with confidence the proportion of sales destined solely for food use. It is also difficult to take account of imports and exports.

The same considerations do not prevent industry and government agreeing how much sugars go into consumption. However, FACC took the chemical industry's word that the 'apparently straightforward approach' was very, very complicated. So, in 1976 the FACC set up a working party of thirteen men to have a stab at estimating consumption of colours and dyes by other means.

One member of the working party was Jack Philp, the chief environmental officer of Unilever, who, at the time, had an intriguing motto on his office wall: 'LORD deliver thy servant from the hands of EXPERT PANELS'.[53] Mr Philp was also a member of COT, but evidently soldiered on, along with his dozen colleagues.

Using information supplied in confidence by industry (including Unilever), the working party constructed 'average' (i.e. adult's) and 'child's' diets, and also, to be on the safe side, two version of 'extreme' diets containing a lot of highly coloured foods.

Of the 2100 calories liable to be consumed every day by a child weighing 4 stone (25 kg), the working party estimated that over half, about 1200 calories, consists of food containing added colours and dyes. The 'child's' diet contained more colours and dyes than the 'average' diet, because children's food is more highly coloured. If coal-tar dyes are hazardous, any risk will be higher for children, if only because the lighter a body, the greater the toxic load of any given weight of harmful food. A man is unlikely to get drunk on half a bottle of wine, but a woman may feel the effect, and a child will keel over. The same is generally true for drugs and also for food additives that can be toxic. In addition, the immune system of a small child is immature and hence incalculably more vulnerable to any toxic load.

The working party estimates, completed in 1977, showed that chocolate brown HT (155) was then far and away the most common coal-tar dye in children's food, followed by tartrazine (E102), sunset yellow (E110), amaranth (E123), and yellow 2G (107). Adult food contains about two-thirds the amount of dye in children's food.

This does not mean that chocolate brown HT is necessarily the biggest worry, because animal tests indicate that some dyes are more toxic than others. For instance, rats seem to thrive on tartrazine up to quite high levels, whereas their tolerance for brown FK is much lower. Accordingly, expert committees agree what are known as Acceptable Daily Intakes (ADIs) for dyes and also for many other additives.[54] As already mentioned, ADIs are usually set at 1 per cent of the level found to be toxic – or eventually lethal – for laboratory animals. FACC explained:[2]

> The safety factor is intended to allow for any differences in sensitivity between the animal species and man, to allow for wide differences in sensitivity among the human population, and to allow for the fact that the number of animals tested is small compared with the size of the human population that may be exposed.

Official safe daily consumption (ADI) of five coal-tar dyes and estimated actual intake in Britain: 1977.

	'Average' ADI	Intake	Child's ADI	Intake	Extreme(1) ADI	Intake	Extreme(2) ADI	Intake
	mg	mg	mg	mg	mg	mg	mg	mg
Chocolate Brown HT (155)	175	9.76	62.5	14.62	175	19.15	175	13.35
Tartrazine (E102)	525	4.63	187.5	6.69	525	9.07	525	35.93
Sunset Yellow (E110)	175	1.99	62.5	2.40	175	3.90	175	13.67
Amaranth (E123)	52.5	1.44	18.75	1.79	52.5	2.81	52.5	16.59
Yellow 2G (107)	0.7	1.38	0.25	1.39	0.7	2.69	0.7	1.98

All this sounds prudent, bearing in mind that sometimes the rats succeed in clambering out of their cages[19] and sometimes the data have turned out to be faked.[37] Here are the ADIs for the most common coal-tar dyes eaten in mid-1970s Britain, together with the estimates taken from the FACC working party of the amount consumed in the 'average' adult, the 'child's' and the two 'extreme' diets:

On the face of it, these seem reassuring figures; except that children were evidently consuming over five times the acceptable daily intakes of yellow 2G. Perhaps with these figures in mind, the report claimed that 'there are sufficient data to suggest that the metabolism of yellow 2G is similar to that of tartrazine'.[2] In plain language, this means that COT took the view that the ADI for this coal-tar dye is probably far too severe. If yellow 2G is given the same ADI as tartrazine, any public health problem it might represent is solved at the stroke of a pen. Unkind commentators on such manoeuvres call them 'moving the goal posts'. In the event, however, as already mentioned, by the mid 1980s manufacturers decided to stop using yellow 2G.

Brown FK also turned out to be a troublesome dye. It has a particularly low ADI of 3.5 mg a day for an adult and 1.25 mg for a child, which means that it is estimated to be 150 times more toxic than tartrazine. A 4-ounce kipper contains about 2.4 mg of the brown stain. So a 6-ounce kipper would take an adult up to the ADI. Interviewed by the *Sunday Times* in 1976,[53] an unnamed Unilever representative was unimpressed by the ADI system, preferring the view that people need not worry unless they have eaten, not 1 per cent of the dose found to be toxic for rats, but the full toxic dose:

> Unilever ... calculated that a person would have to eat 100 kippers a day for two years or two kippers a day for 100 years before he need be worried.

The working party's 'child's' diet showed that the amount of amaranth consumed is one-tenth the ADI, which indeed seems reassuring. But suppose that a child is an enthusiastic eater or drinker of foods dyed red with amaranth. The fourth column – Extreme (2) – illustrates a diet with an average consumption of coloured foods, all of which are highly coloured, up to the top level used by manufacturers in the mid-1970s. A child following this diet would consume up to the 'acceptable' intake of amaranth every day.

Furthermore, although the acceptable daily intake for a child is 18.75 milligrams a day, for some undisclosed reason, if the US studies cited by Professor Epstein[19] are anything to go by, this ADI has not been fixed at 1 per cent of the level found to be toxic in animal studies, as is customary. Amaranth can kill rat embryos at a dose of 15 mg per kg bodyweight. Therefore a 1 per cent 'safety limit' would be 0.15 mg per kg bodyweight in people, or 3.25 mg for a child weighing 4 stone (25 kg). So why is the ADI used in Britain[54] not 1 per cent but 5 per cent of the dose that can kill rat embryos? If the goal posts were moved back to the 1 per cent safety level at 3.75 milligrams a day, it would be clear that a child who consumes quite a lot of food and drink coloured red could be way over the acceptable daily intake.

The view of the official European Joint Expert Committee on Food Additives (JECFA) is that:[2]

> An ADI provides a sufficiently large safety margin to ensure that there need be no undue concern about occasionally exceeding it provided the average intake over longer periods of time does not exceed it.

So if your child likes red-coloured food, watch out for E123. To be on the safe side, move to Europe.

Eventually, using industry data and a complicated formula involving 'correction factors', the FACC did produce an estimate of the amount of dye contained in British food in the mid-1970s: 29.2 mg a day for children; 20.9 mg a day for adults. For children this amounts to 1/3 ounce of dyes a year, or about 1/4 lb by the age of 12, allowing for wise parents who keep their babies (under one year of age) off dyed foods.

In answer to a Parliamentary Question[55] asked on 18 March 1986, Mrs Peggy Fenner quoted these estimates as current for 1986. The team at the Ministry who briefed Mrs Fenner overlooked the fact that food additives are good business. A reading of two industry sources[56,57] suggests an increase in the tonnage of food colours and dyes in Britain of about 5 per cent a year, which is over 50 per cent a decade.

On this basis, the volume of dyes in children's food in the late 1980s is about 45 mgs a day, or six ounces by the age of 12. Throw in the dyes used in medicines and toothpaste, and a reasonable guess is that a child aged 12 in 1987 will have eaten about 1/2 lb of coal-tar dyes.

In the USA, the Freedom of Information Act has enabled consumer groups and the Food and Drug Administration to ascertain that the use of dyes increased 50 per cent between 1974 and 1984, and that in 1976 4 million American children had eaten more than 1 lb coal-tar dyes by the age of 12, with maximum consumption estimated at 3 lb.[58] Furthermore only seven dyes are now allowed in food in the USA, compared with 16 in Britain.

In Britain information about additives is a trade secret. But both Erik Millstone, who attacks the food additives industry,[37] and David Conning, who defends it,[52] estimate that in the late 1980s 700 tonnes of dyes are used in British food every year. This works out at 35mg per person per day, and therefore at about around 45 to 50 mg a day for children. This is a tiny amount. But some elements in food are very potent. For example, average consumption of vitamin C by 11- and 14-year-olds is 48-49 mg a day.[59]

So it is fair to say that, in Britain today, children eat roughly the same amount of coal-tar dyes as of vitamin C.

'On the whole, we found these statements of colour intake reassuring.'[2] So said COT in the *Interim Report* published in 1979. FACC was rather more enthusiastic: 'On the whole we found the estimates of colour intakes made by the Working Party very reassuring.'[2] One member of COT, Dr A.E.M. McLean of the Laboratory of Toxicology at University College, London, was not so sure. He wrote in 1976:[60]

Food colours in the UK, if permitted, are free of control in respect of how much is added or to what food. As a result an increasing concentration and total intake of colours comes about as competitive marketing leads to deeper coloured soft drinks, sweet and confectionery.

Animal experiments are usually on a small number of healthy animals. But, said Dr McLean:

We have to consider a population of millions, including the old, young, sick and those on the threshold of adaptation, for whom a normally negligible stimulus might lead to breakdown of some physiological system.

The food industry argues that the consumer wants coloured food, but 'demand is not an invariable guide to acceptability of a product, as can be seen from the demand for heroin or cigarettes.' To be acceptable, any risk to life and health should be voluntary and open: people are entitled to know what they are letting themselves in for. But, as Dr McLean pointed out, food additives are:[60]

> not requested by the consumer; are concealed; cannot be avoided by the individual consumer; and are an exploitation of uninformed patterns of taste.

He particularly objected to colours and flavours, the 'cosmetic' additives, and among a list of proposals for 'action to reduce hazards in food to an acceptable level' recommended that production and therefore consumption of food colours and dyes be reduced by 10 per cent a year.

Dr McLean's views contradict those of the Committee on Toxicity as published in 1979, in the FACC 'Interim Report'. Any attempt he may have made to write a minority report did not succeed. Instead, he spoke his piece at a private meeting of the Nutrition Society; his paper was published in the *Proceedings* of the Society, which are distributed exclusively to members and, nowadays, are marked 'Member's Copy. For Personal Use Only'. I found it by chance, in the course of reading through all the *Proceedings* published between 1974 and 1986. It is by such means that conscientious objections made by independent scientists to government and industry food policy are 'kept in the family'.

CORRIDORS OF POWER

There are two opposite views on the nature and workings of the expert advisory committees that serve MAFF and the DHSS. Alan Turner put one of them in the trade magazine *Food Manufacture* in August 1986.[61] Mr Turner is Chief Chemist at Cadbury Schweppes, President of the Institute of

Food Science and Technology, a negotiator with government as a member of various committees of the Food and Drink Federation, and a leading light in the Cake and Biscuit Alliance. He is also a member of MAFF's Food Advisory Committee and was previously a member of the Food Standards Committee. He wrote:

> There is a long tradition of public service in this country and those of us drawn, from whatever background, into advisory committees on the basis of knowledge and experience very quickly find little difficulty in putting to one side our sectoral interests and contributing our experience and expertise in the public interest. But it must be remembered that decisions, at best, are only as good as the known facts allow .... Uncertainties will always exist until knowledge is total.

The alternative point of view was set out by John Rivers and Philip Payne of the Department of Human Nutrition, London University, in the science journal *Nature* in November 1979.[62] In 1987 John Rivers is editor of the Nutrition Society's *Nutrition Notes and News*, and Philip Payne is a member of COMA's Standing Committee on Nutritional Surveillance. They wrote:

> At present where nutrition policies exist at all, they have been evolved by senior administrators in closed counsel with leaders of the health professions. Such cabals will not survive for long .... Once nutritionists recognize the essentially political nature of decisions about food policy, and the necessarily tentative nature of the theories that underpin them, we believe that they will welcome the involvement of consumer organizations and other pressure groups in the consultative process.

In summary, Alan Turner believes that science is a matter of fact and that there should be no conflict among experts and government, science and industry; whereas John Rivers and Philip Payne believe that public health is a matter of judgement, and that there is bound to be conflict between different interest groups. Which of these two sincere views is valid?

John Rivers and Philip Payne have been proved wrong in some respects; in 1987, government advisory committees on food and health remain closed. MAFF committees include advisors such as Alan Turner, who are or were employed by industry. Nor is it true that the advisory reports designed to be the basis for official policy on food and health always make recommendations comfortable to government and industry. Contrary to the impression given by MAFF and the food and chemical manufacturers, every advisory report on food colours from 1924 to date[2,47,48,49,50,51] has expressed anxiety about the use of coal-tar dyes in food.

In Britain, expert reports on food and health have a smooth and polished appearance, like English lawns. But worms lurk under the surface. The case histories of sugars and of food colours, told in Chapter 3 and this chapter, show that, on the main issue, John Rivers and Philip Payne are right. Food policy is political by definition. Food is crucial to health. And so food policy is crucial to public health. Judgements on public health should be well-founded on facts, but also depend on the attitude of the people making the judgement.

Faced with evidence that fats, saturated fats, added sugars, salt or additives, consumed in typical quantities, amount to a public health problem, people employed by the industries whose products depend on those commodities will defend them and seek out counter-evidence. They may do so cynically, but it is more likely that they will do so sincerely, simply because otherwise they could not do their jobs in good faith. Common sense says that the views of senior scientists employed in the food industry will be consistent with the policies of the firms for which they work, otherwise they would not have been employed in the first place and then promoted. Besides which, most food industry personnel who also act as official government advisors are directors of the firms they work for, or else members of national and international trade organizations set up to promote and protect their business interests. In law an interested party may give evidence, but the weight given to such evidence is affected by the degree of interest.[63]

When I started to write this book early in 1985, I decided to find out some facts about the people who advise the British government on food and health. Eventually I selected twenty-seven expert committees working to MAFF or the DHSS between 1974 and 1987 (with one exception which worked to the Cabinet Office). The members of these committees are all listed in Document B.

OFFICIALLY SECRET ADVISORS:
WHO ARE THESE GUYS? (I)

In his book on the contamination of food, *Gluttons for Punishment*,[64] James Erlichman of the *Guardian* writes of government advisors:

> The avenues between academia, industry and government are actually an intricate maze traversed constantly by a relatively small and closely-knit group of men and women. They often perform, interchangeably, all three roles of expert, industrialist and policy-maker. Most of these people see no conflict of interest and believe they can carry out all three jobs with integrity and independence.

Fault can be found with this comment. After eighteen months of research on the twenty-seven committees, it turns out that there are hundreds of advisors. Men outnumber women twelve to one. It is true, though, that since the early 1970s most government advisors on food and health have either worked for, or had other connections with, industry and government. And certain names do occur again and again. Professor Ian Macdonald, for example, served on the FACC between 1977 and 1983, and thus on the panel that produced the *Interim Report* on colours and dyes, before becoming chairman of the food industry-funded British Nutrition Foundation, a member of the BNF Task Force on Sugars and Syrups, and a member of the central Ministry of Agriculture Food Advisory Committee.

Who served on the FACC committee on food colours and dyes, and its supporting working party, and where did they come from? This information is not secret, but it did take some digging out. Because six years elapsed between the formation of the committee and publication of its report in 1979, there was a fair turnover of members. A total of twenty-four experts worked on the main report, together with another thirteen on the working party. Officially described as 'an independent body of experts',[65] FACC was in fact constructed by the civil servants who control the membership of advisory committees to give a rough numerical balance between experts inside and outside the

food industry, with a consumer representative thrown in.
The working party was a special case, being made up only of
people from industry and government.

FACC committee and working party on food colours and
dyes, 1979. Representation from science, industry, government and consumers

	Panel	Working Party	Total
Science	12	—	12
Industry	11	8	19
Government	—	5	5
Consumer	1	—	1

'Science' of course, means scientists not working for
industry at the time they served on the FACC panel. Further
analysis shows that the nineteen industry employees worked
for the firms shown in the table opposite:

The twelve scientists working outside industry included
two food technologists, two public analysts, a government
chemist, and specialists in medicine, physiology (Professor
Macdonald), biochemistry, pharmacology, microbiology and
nutrition. The Chairman of the FACC was Professor Basil
Weedon, Vice-Chancellor of Nottingham University. The
consumer representative was Dr Janet Cockcroft of the
Consumers Committee for Great Britain, a body set up by
MAFF which stated in 1986 that it has no power and little
influence.[66]

The names of certain firms crop up again and again as
employers of government advisors. Every single MAFF
committee on food and health analysed for this book,
includes a man from Unilever. The list opposite includes five
men from the confectionery trade and five from additive
manufacturers. By contrast, there are few farmers, caterers
or retailers (two are unusual in the list opposite), and the
fresh food business is never represented. The great majority
of government advisors from industry work for the giant
manufacturers of highly processed food, who use saturated
fats, added sugars, salt and additives in profusion.

Of the nine giant manufacturers represented in the lists,

FACC committee and working party on food colours and dyes, 1979. Representation from food manufacturers and retailers.

Company	Line of business	Name of committee member
Cadbury Schweppes[a]	confectionery, chocolate, soft drinks	Harry Houghton (WP)[ab]
		Professor John Norris[b]
		William Price-Davies[ab]
ICI[a]	agrichemicals, additives	Dr Peter Brignell
		Dr Geoffrey Davy
Unilever[a]	fats, oils, meat products, soups, additives, etc.	Dr William Fulton[ab]
		Jack Philp (WP)[a]
Ranks Hovis McDougall[a]	bread, salt, additives	John Saunders
Associated British Foods[a]	bread	Dr William Elstow[ab]
Mars[a]	confectionery	Ken Gardner (WP)[b]
Allied Lyons[a]	beer, ice cream, cakes	J. Mears (WP)
Imperial Group[a]	beer	Robert Beedham
Bibby	fats, oils	Dr Harold Jasperson[b]
John F. Renshaw	confectionery supplier	Frank Firth (WP)
Scot Bowyers	meat products	C. T. Ashton (WP)
Marks and Spencer[a]	retailer	Nathan Goldenberg[a]
Sainsbury[a]	retailer	Professor E. Williams[ab]
BIBRA	additive research	Dr R. Crampton (WP)[ab]
CFPRA	agrichemical research	Richard Hinton (WP)[ab]

[a] shows sponsorship of British Nutrition Foundation, or else members of internal BNF committees
[b] shows membership of food industry representative body committees
BIBRA = British Industrial Biological Research Association
CFPRA = Campden Food Preservation Research Association
WP = working party

eight are in 1987 sponsors of the British Nutrition Foundation. In 1977 the BNF produced a booklet called *Why Additives? The Safety of Foods*[67] designed to defend and justify food additives. Two chapters were written by Mr Goldenberg and Dr Crampton. The foreword was by Sir Frank Young, President of the BNF from 1970 to 1979. He wrote:[68]

One can say that food additives may be introduced in order to preserve the quality of the food, and in addition to ensure the maintenance of its appeal and, sometimes, to restore diminished nutritional value .... Let me assure the readers of this booklet that the use of food additives is subject to the most careful government control. Food manufacturers are far from being free to do whatever they like.

Sir Frank Young's name often occurs on government advisory committees. He was Chairman of the DHSS COMA panel on 'Diet and Coronary Heart Disease' (1974);[69] served on two COMA panels on recommended daily amounts of vitamins and minerals (1969 and 1979);[70,71] and was the first Chairman of the COMA panel on 'Nutritional Aspects of Bread and Flour' (1981).*[72]

No doubt, government advisors employed by the manufacturers of highly processed food as a rule give their advice in good faith. But highly processed food depends on the sophisticated use of additives. Anybody worried about food colours and dyes is unlikely to work in a senior position for a firm manufacturing additives or products that cannot be made without additives. In addition, people from industry usually have resources unavailable to independent scientists. They can use the BNF and trade organizations such as the Food and Drink Federation as forums for discussion. They can also rely on support from their firms. Officially, all government advisors 'are appointed in a personal capacity'.[74] In practice, things are different. Sir Kenneth Durham has explained the advantage of working for Unilever while being Chairman of the Priorities Board (another MAFF advisory committee):[75]

> In many ways it's been a help to be Chairman of Unilever. Because I can draw on many resources here – economists, scientists and so on, which have certainly helped me and I think they've helped the Priorities Board.

The dominant voice on MAFF advisory committees is that of the British food manufacturing industry. In the case of FACC's work on food colours and dyes, most of the

---

* This report, the latest official word, has been criticized for recommending white bread as highly as wholemeal bread and for ignoring the chemical additives in white bread. I can explain. Copies of the Officially Secret minutes of the COMA meetings have come into my hands. At the first meeting, held on 6 June 1978, Sir Frank Young 'confirmed that the Panel's Report would not be concerned with such additives as preservatives, bleaching agents, antioxidants or contaminants'.[73] So additives were off the agenda of the most recent government advisory report on the quality of bread. It is not suggested that Sir Frank took this decision himself, but it should be seen in the light of his general commendation of additives published the previous year.

objections made by expert advisors to various colours and dyes in our food have been ignored. Here is the ingredients list of a lead 'chocolate' line made for a major supermarket chain in 1986. I have inserted the relevant comments from FACC's *Interim Report* next to the dyes:

Ingredients: Chocolate flavour* coating (sugar, hydrogenated palm kernel oil, whey powder, wheatflour, fat-reduced cocoa powder, colours E124 ['we require within five years the results of a metabolism study, a carcinogenicity study and a multigeneration study in the rat'], E132 ['some of the available studies fall short of present-day standards'], E153 ['the toxicological evidence is poor']; sugar, animal and vegetable fats, wheatflour, plain chocolate, whole egg; marshmallow (sugar, glucose syrup, starch, egg white); glucose syrup, soya flour, skimmed milk powder, emulsifiers E471, E475, colours 128 ['we further require the results of teratology studies within two years'], E142 ['we therefore require within five years the results of further metabolism studies, short-term oral toxicity studies in the rat, multi-generation and teratology studies in the rat and a long-term/carcinogenicity study in a species other than the rat'], caramel E150 ['we considered the implications to man of the findings of lymphocytopenia, caecal enlargement, growth retardation, renal effects and liver enlargement in animals'], chocolate brown HT† ['we require the results of teratology, multi-generation and metabolism studies to be made available within five years'], flavourings.

Cancer is one possible ill-effect of food additives. MAFF's main concern, in requiring laboratory tests of food additives, is whether or not they can cause tumours in animals. A food additive does not get the thumbs down if it gives a rat a runny muzzle, or asthma, eczema, fits or migraine or makes it hyperactive. These ill-effects can only be properly observed in people, not in animals.

While the toxicologists have been feeding E124, 128, E142, E150 and chocolate brown HT (155) to rats and other laboratory animals, manufacturers have been supplying them to our children.

* 'chocolate flavour' means that there is no chocolate in the coating.

† Chocolate brown HT: manufacturers are coy about listing dyes banned in Europe on food labels, and so sometimes give the name, not the number; 'chocolate' is a warm friendly word too.

CAN ADDITIVES
CAUSE CANCERS?

In heavy doses, a number of additives, including coal-tar dyes, can cause cancers in laboratory animals; and it is prudent to assume that what damages animals may also damage us. The science of toxicology largely depends on this assumption. But how accurate are tests on laboratory animals? According to Dr Erik Millstone,[37] an analysis of long-term feeding studies of animals given chemicals already known to cause cancer in humans has shown that only 37 per cent of animals developed cancers.

> In other words, when it comes to predicting the toxicity of chemicals known to be carcinogenic to humans, the tests are more often wrong than they are right!

Dr Millstone is known as a critic of the food industry. But Dr McLean is not; and he says:[60]

> Toxicity testing using animals is fraught with difficulties .... It is impossible to extrapolate from animals to man with any confidence.

Dr F.J.C. Roe, another member of COT, believes that caged animals fed full of artificial chow 'are hardly suitable for investigating the chronic pharmacological or toxicological effects of exogenous substance'[76] such as food additives.

In their book *The Causes of Cancer*,[77] Sir Richard Doll and his colleague Richard Peto set food additives in the context of other cancer risks. Having identified cancers as largely avoidable diseases, they go on to suggest that perhaps 35 per cent of deaths from cancer are caused by the wrong balance of food (compared with another 30 per cent by smoking, 2 per cent by industrial pollution and maybe a nominal 1 per cent or less by food additives). They also suggest that certain food preservatives may protect against cancers.

This guess is sometimes cited by those who defend food additives as evidence of safety, bearing in mind Sir Richard Doll's reputation as one of the researchers who established beyond reasonable doubt that smoking causes lung cancer. However, a guess is just that – a guess. Doll and Peto themselves point out, and here they agree with Dr McLean and Dr Roe, that studies using laboratory animals are problematic. Taking the chemical sweetener saccharin as an example, they write:[77]

Human exposure to a weak carcinogen may need to be prolonged for several decades before any positive effect can be detected, and no assurances can be given that an effect will not be produced by a lifetime of exposure to the unusually large amounts that are consumed in diet drinks by some children and young adults.

Diet, Nutrition and Cancer, the authoritative report of the American National Academy of Sciences, stresses another objection to the experimental testing of food additives. Like drugs, additives are tested singly. Rats are not given cocktails of additives corresponding to the mixtures typically found in highly processed foods. But two or more additives eaten together may react chemically and become far more toxic as a result:[78]

The possibility that they may act synergistically and may therefore create a greater carcinogenic risk cannot be excluded.

In the USA it is well understood that the main dietary cause of common cancers, notably of the breast (in women) and the colon, is likely to be typical Western food as eaten in the USA and Britain, heavy in fats, poor in fibre; and that fresh vegetables and fruit, rich in essential fats, vitamins and minerals, nourish the immune system and protect against cancers. There is also some evidence that food heavy in added sugars may contribute to colon cancer. It follows that food additives, including those that are innocuous in themselves, are likely to be an indirect cause of cancers and other diseases directly caused by excess fats and sugars, since in highly processed products food manufacturers use sophisticated combinations of additives in order to stick fats and sugars together and make them appear attractive and palatable. If food dyes and flavours were banned, much of this 'sweet fat' in the British food supply could not be marketed.

THE STORY OF E

Faced with the evidence of the ill-effects of food additives, the Commission of the European Communities issued a directive in December 1978[79] requiring member states to list additives on food labels not only by category (such as 'colour') but also by name or number (such as 'tartrazine' or 'E102'). Exemptions included flavours and processing aids. Britain rejected this Directive and insisted on a derogation for five years. As a result the Food Labelling Regulations issued in 1980[80] allowed British manufacturers to continue listing colours, emulsifiers, anti-oxidants, preservatives and stabilizers on labels by category, not by name or number.

The British government's attitude was supported by a report by the Food Standards Committee on *Food Labelling*,[81] published in 1979. FSC reasoned as follows:

> Some people are hypersensitive or allergic to certain foods and ingredients of foods just as much as to certain food additives but serious reactions are experienced only by a very small minority. If a food additive gives rise to widespread hypersensitivity problems, the proper course of action would seem to us to be to ban its use on medical grounds rather than to ensure it is always specifically declared on labels so that it can be avoided by the informed consumer. We cannot recommend the adoption of the proposed EEC labelling requirement for additives.

At first sight this seems a reasonable view. But what is a 'very small minority'? A hundred? A hundred thousand? And when is a 'reaction' 'serious'? When a child has to miss school, or has to be taken to hospital? The FSC experts avoided making such public health judgements. Nor was any reference made to the recommendation of the parallel Food Additives and Contaminants Committee, published the very same year, that seventeen colours and dyes be put on the probationary 'B' list because of possible toxicity. The FSC's attitude seemed to be: 'don't worry; be happy'.

A nationwide Gallup Poll conducted for Tesco in 1984[82] showed that cancer is women's biggest health fear. But despite the toxicological clouds over many chemical food additives – preservatives and sweeteners as well as dyes – there is so far not much evidence of public concern in Britain about food additives as a possibly significant cause of cancer. Most of the disquiet about additives has focused on the evidence that dyes and other additives can be acutely and immediately toxic to vulnerable people, especially young children. And the sharpest focus of all has been on tartrazine (E102), a coal-tar dye scheduled 'A' for acceptable by the FACC in 1979.

What did the *Interim Report*[2] have to say about tartrazine? Citing eleven studies carried out between 1959 and 1977, COT stated:

> There have been a number of reports of hypersensitivity reactions in man following the experimental ingestion of certain food colours, e.g. tartrazine .... The evidence, however, suggests that the occurrence of such reactions is rare ... There is suggestive, but not conclusive, published evidence that idiosyncratic reactions may occur following ingestion of food containing usual amounts of colouring. We are concerned about this situation but, since hypersensitivity to food constituents is a general problem and not one confined to colours, it was felt that useful recommendations could not be made until clear evidence from well controlled studies in man has become available.

Notice the words 'hypersensitive' and 'idiosyncratic': loaded words masquerading as scientific terminology. In plain English, the report is saying that if you suffer as a result of consuming additives, there's something wrong, not with the additives, but with you.

Who served on the FSC at the time of its report on food labelling? An official statement policy[83] said that:

> members are appointed in a personal capacity. Three have a background in the food industry, three in science and three have special interests in matters affecting consumers.

The three with a foreground (rather than background) in industry were Professor Russell Allen of Beecham, the giant drug, food and 'health' drink manufacturer; Dr John

Collingwood of Unilever; and Frank Wood of the UK division of Corn Products Corporation, a manufacturer of glucose syrups. The members of the FSC in 1975, when the food labelling report was commissioned, are listed in Document B.

Like Professor Ian Macdonald and Sir Frank Young, Professor Russell (R.J.L.) Allen has often served on government advisory committees. He was a member of the Food Standards Committee until 1980. He preceded Professor Macdonald as Vice-Chairman and Chairman of the British Nutrition Foundation, and, as already mentioned, in 1987 is Vice-President of the BNF.[84] Beecham was a founder-sponsor of the BNF in 1967, and Dr Allen a BNF founder-committee member.[85] In recent years he has been a colleague of Professor Macdonald as Visiting Professor of Applied Nutrition at Guys Hospital (hence his title); as well as President of the British Dietetic Association, and a Chairman and member of various Food and Drink Federation committees on nutrition and labelling.

In 1975, Dr Allen was not keen on more detailed food labels. Wearing his Beecham hat, he wrote in the BNF's quarterly *Bulletin*:[85]

> I think that the present attitude of most major firms in the industry not to be stampeded by real or supposed external pressure into providing label information for which there is no current demand is perfectly sound. It remains to be seen what official action, if any, may follow from the Food Standards Committee review.

Dr Reg Passmore of Edinburgh University is another regular member of government advisory committes. In the 1970s, he was a member of the DHSS COMA committee as well as the FSC, and served with Sir Frank Young on the 1974 panel on Diet and Coronary Heart Disease[69] and on the 1969 and 1979 panels on recommended daily amounts of vitamins and minerals, acting as Chairman of the 1969 panel.[70,71] In 1984 Dr Passmore too was not keen on more detailed food labels. He wrote in the BNF's quarterly *Bulletin*:[86]

> Providing such information presents many difficulties for manufacturers and would inevitably put up prices; it would

also probably increase the already large number of neurotics who worry unnecessarily about their food.

In 1983, when the five-year derogation ran out, MAFF submitted to the European Directive on food additive labelling. The Food Labelling Regulations issued in 1984[87] require most processed foods made in Britain to follow the same rules that apply in the rest of the EC, with final effect from 1 July 1986. And that is why you will now find 'colour: E102' on many food labels.

You will also find many numbers without an 'E'. No less than 115 additives which have not been granted an 'E' number[88] are used in Britain.

On 15 May 1985, Dr Lesley Yeomans of the Consumers' Association, who was a member of FACC from 1981 to 1983, addressed a meeting of the Society of Chemical Industry on the safety of food additives. By this time Maurice Hanssen was in the best-seller charts with his book *E for Additives*,[89] and food manufacturers were in some disarray. At the meeting Dr Yeomans was asked by a man from Cadbury Schweppes whether consumers were really concerned about food additives. Her reply was revealing:[90]

> You fought for a long time to keep additives off food labels. If you're suffering from a backlash from consumers, you only have yourselves to blame.

NEUROTIC MOTHERS?

NAUGHTY CHILDREN?

The most effective challenge to official British policy on toxicologically dodgy additives has come from two women from West Sussex who are not prepared to wait until all the research results are in, and who in 1977, when their work began, had never heard of tartrazine or the Food Additives and Contaminants Committee. At that time, Mrs Sally Bunday's life, and that of her five-year-old son Miles, was ruined by his unceasing crying, screaming, head-banging, what seemed to be severe catarrh, and generally chaotic behaviour. His G.P. referred Miles to a psychiatrist, who diagnosed 'behaviour problems' and prescribed sedatives, which didn't work. Mrs Bunday then took Miles to a mental hospital where 'mental problems' were diagnosed, and more drugs administered, which didn't work.

Then a friend from the USA sent a press cutting about the work of an American child health specialist, Dr Ben Feingold, who believes that bad food can cause bad behaviour. By this stage Mrs Bunday was prepared to try anything. She threw every item of highly processed food out of the house, and gave Miles, herself, and the rest of her family nothing but whole, fresh food to eat. It worked. In four days, Mrs Bunday told me, Miles was better.[91]

Mrs Bunday had tried out a simplified version of what is known as the 'Feingold Diet'. During many years of practice in California, Dr Feingold had seen many children suffering what appeared to be mental disturbance, resulting in insomnia, aggression, violence and an inability to stay still, to concentrate or to learn. In the 1970s he became convinced that often the 'hyperkinesia' or 'hyperactivity' that he was seeing was not random but a clinical entity, and not a mental disorder, but the ill-effects of specific foods and food additives.[92] He singled out foods containing salicylates, chemical compounds similar to the active ingredient of aspirin, and, among additives, coal-tar dyes, chemical flavours and two preservatives, the anti-oxidants BHA (E320) and BHT (E321), and flavour-enhancers such as monosodium glutamate or MSG (620, 621, 622, 623).

Most of his peers in the medical profession rejected Dr Feingold's thesis as unscientific, but the 'Feingold Diet', which eliminated those foods and additives which he found made children ill, was enthusiastically adopted by vast numbers of parents, at first in the USA and then notably in Canada, Australia and New Zealand. It seemed to work. With her mother, Mrs Vicky Colquhoun, Mrs Bunday founded the Hyperactive Children's Support Group (HACSG) in November 1977, in order to contact other parents and later, as relations with friendly health professionals developed, to offer help. By 1986 Mrs Bunday had received over 100,000 requests for help and advice, and in that year she was receiving 300 to 400 letters a week.[91]

In 1978 Mrs Bunday and Mrs Colquhoun began to write

to MPs. By 1984 they had the support of Professor John Dickerson of the Department of Nutrition at Surrey University and Professor Derek Bryce-Smith of the Department of Organic Chemistry at Reading University, who are not government advisors. By 1984 the HACSG had established a medical panel which included doctors convinced from their own clinical experience that food and food additives do cause disturbances of both mind and body. Not content with a series of reassuring letters from DHSS officials, Mrs Bunday and Mrs Colquhoun were holding meetings up and down the country, had formed 150 local groups, and were contacting manufacturers and retailers, lobbying MPs, and raising money for reliable scientific research. From the point of view of the government, they were making a thorough nuisance of themselves.

On 15 March 1984 Willie Hamilton, Labour MP for Central Fife, asked a Parliamentary Question. Mr Hamilton:[93]

> Asked the Secretary of State for Social Services what representations he has had concerning the problems of hyperactive children; what evidence is available to him about the relationship between this condition and the use of food colourings and other artificial additives in food and drink; and if he will make a statement.

Two weeks later, on 28 March 1984, there was another question, from Andrew Hunter, Conservative MP for Basingstoke, with support from Labour MPs Stuart Randall (Kingston-upon-Hull West) and Robert Wareing (Liverpool, West Derby). Mr Hunter:

> Asked the Secretary of State for Social Services (1) if he will make more funds available (a) for research into the causes of hyperactivity, (b) for the care and treatment of hyperactive children; and if he will make a statement; (2) what support and help is available from his Department to the parents or guardians of hyperactive children; (3) what financial resources are devoted by his Department to the treatment or care of hyperactive children.

In reply to Mr Hamilton, John Patten, then junior Minister at the DHSS, said:[93]

We have received fourteen letters recently from Hon. Members who have apparently had representations made from supporters of the Hyperactive Children's Support Group. The group seeks support from the Government and the DHSS for its objectives. I am advised that, despite a number of studies, mainly in the United States, there is at present no conclusive evidence about the suggested relationship between hyperactivity and the use of additives in food and drink.

In reply to Mr Hunter, Mr Patten said:[94]

The diagnosis of 'hyperkinetic (hyperactive) syndrome' on its own is comparatively rare in the United Kingdom. Many of the children described in lay terms as 'hyperactive' would be regarded as having a conduct disorder. Statistics are not kept on the basis of symptoms treated and information is not available on the number of children displaying hyperactivity who are treated by the NHS, or on the costs involved.

And as a reply to all four MPs, Mr Patten said:[93,94]

The Medical Research Council, which receives its funds as a grant-in-aid under the science budget of the Department of Education and Science, is specifically supporting one trial in this area on oligo-antigenic diet in 3 to 12-year-old hyperactive children; an epidemiological inquiry into hyperactivity in children is also in progress. The results of both studies when available may clarify these problems ... This Department is also prepared to consider soundly based research proposals in this area. Such proposals would be considered by our mental illness research liaison group and would have to compete for funding with others we receive in the mental health field.

Translated from Parliamentary language, Mr Patten seemed to be saying that a bunch of neurotic mothers had been badgering their MPs and asking the DHSS to do something about their fractious children: that the whole thing was probably a fuss about nothing; but that, just in case there was a small problem, the Medical Research Council was funding some research. So Messrs Hamilton, Hunter, Randall and Wareing could rest assured, while Miles Bunday and other hyperactive children were identified as possible cases for psychiatric treatment.

In April 1984, a month after Mr Patten's replies, *Food Intolerance and Food Aversion*[95] was published. This was

was a report of a joint committee set up by the BNF and the Royal College of Physicians. The Chairman was Professor Maurice Lessof of the Department of Medicine at Guys Hospital, some of whose research has been funded by the International Sugar Research Foundation, the Imperial Group, Pfizer, Reckitt and Colman, Unilever, Miles Laboratories and Beecham.[96] The Secretary of the Committee was Dr Juliet Gray, then Science Director of the BNF and also nutritional consultant to numerous firms including McDonalds hamburgers.[97] Members of the committee who were (and are, in 1987) members of BNF internal committees were Sir Douglas Black; Dr Maurice Brook, Dr Russell Allen's successor as head of research at Beecham; Augusta Conry, a dietitian; Professor Jack Edelman of Ranks Hovis McDougall; together with Dr Derek Shrimpton, then Director-General of the BNF. The other members of the committee were Professor Raymond Hoffenberg, Sir Douglas Black's successor as President of the Royal College of Physicians; Dr Anne Ferguson, a gastroenterologist who is also an advisor to the Dairy Trades Federation and to the Milk Marketing Board;[98] Dr Ronald Finn of the Royal Hospital, Liverpool; Dr Hubert Lacey, a psychiatrist; Dr James Leonard of the Institute of Child Health in London; and Dr J.O. Warner, a child health specialist, some of whose research has been funded by Beecham.[99]*

The RCP/BNF report was unenthusiastic about the Feingold diet:

> In 1975, the Nutrition Foundation in the USA examined the claims of Feingold. They concluded that, at that stage, the therapeutic claims were based only on incidental reports and they therefore recommended controlled clinical studies of the diet .... A number of such trials were set up and produced some equivocal results. The Nutrition Foundation reviewed these trials in 1980 and concluded that they provided sufficient evidence to refute the claims that artificial colourings, flavourings and salicylates were responsible for hyperactivity.

* See Document B for more details on the members of this and four other committees set up by the BNF alone or in partnership. It is not suggested that the judgement of members of this committee or of other commentators on food additives and hyperactivity is affected by links they have or may have with industry.

Like the BNF, the Nutrition Foundation in the USA is funded by the food industry.[100] The RCP/BNF report also cited the American Council on Science and Health (ACSH) as:

Unable to find any significant reduction in the incidence of hyperactivity in children on the Feingold diet, which could not be explained by a placebo effect.

ACSH is also funded by the chemical industry; its sponsors in 1984-85[101] included at least fourteen additive manufacturers.

The RCP/BNF report continued on the Feingold diet:[95]

The use of the Feingold diet ... which is essentially free from additives and salicylates, has been extensively encouraged by lay organisations representing the parents of so-called hyperactive children .... It is all too easy to collude with parents, who cannot accept that psychosocial factors are to blame for their child's disruptive behaviour, by accepting that the child is suffering from food intolerance.

HYPERACTIVITY AND BARON MUNCHAUSEN

The RCP/BNF report warns doctors to look out for 'Munchausen's Syndrome By Proxy', a 'bizarre form of child abuse'[102] by the parent. This condition of 'false illness' is named after Baron Munchausen, a fictional compulsive liar. The idea is that if you go to the doctor and say 'food additives are causing my asthma' you may be lying, in which case the doctor may therefore put you down as a case of the Munchausen Syndrome. If a parent goes to a doctor and says 'food additives are causing my child's hyperactivity' it is the parent, not the child, who might be lying, in which case the doctor may put the child down as a case of Munchausen Syndrome By Proxy. This is of course a handy diagnosis for a doctor to make when a parent presents him with a child whose condition does not fit into any conventional classification.

The RCP/BNF report fails to give any advice to doctors on

how to deal with neurotic mothers and monstrous children. But it does comment that:

> In the experience of a number of paediatricians, mood alteration in relation to food never occurs in isolation, but may be prominently associated with other more obvious reactions such as diarrhoea, migraine, urticaria and eczema.

This was a reference to a trial carried out by a team of scientists at the Hospital for Sick Children at Great Ormond Street, London, under the direction of Professor John Soothill. The report of the trial, 'Is Migraine Food Allergy?' was published in the *Lancet* in October 1983.[103]

In all, 88 children, 40 boys and 48 girls, took part; aged between 3 and 16 (mean age 10), all had suffered severe and frequent migraines of unknown cause for periods between 6 months and 11 years (mean period 3.75 years). None of the children had only experienced severe headaches. A majority had also suffered stomach aches, diarrhoea or flatulence (61 out of the 88). A large number were hyperactive (hyperkinetic) (41) or else had fits (14), or aches in their arms or legs (41) or streaming noses (rhinitis) (34). A smaller number suffered from mouth ulcers, eczema, asthma or other ailments. Migraine and hyperactivity typically were part of a disease pattern.

Given a restricted diet, 78 of the 88 children were completely cured of their migraines, and four greatly improved: a remarkable success rate of 93 per cent. Even more remarkable, the other illnesses usually disappeared too. For example, all but five of the hyperactive children recovered, as did all but two of the children who had suffered fits.

Various foods are well known to cause digestive disorders and migraine; and careful testing has established that these foods – notably cows' milk, eggs, wheat, chocolate, oranges and cheese – are indeed common causes of children's illnesses. But the Great Ormond Street trial also found that two of the 'top ten' causes of intractable migraine were the coal-tar dye tartrazine (E102) and the preservative benzoic acid (E210). These, together with the dye sunset yellow (E110), were the only food additives tested.[104] On later analysis, tartrazine turned out to be the second most common single cause of migraine, after cows' milk.[105]

It is commonly thought that bright lights, heat, noise, travel, exercise, trauma and emotion all cause migraine. But given the special diet, all but three out of the 88 children were unaffected by these stresses, which strongly suggests that they are triggers but not causes of migraine. One exception was cigarette smoke and perfume, which affected children both off and on the diet.

In Professor Soothill's opinion, 'migraine is grossly underdiagnosed in children'. And what does he think about the chemical additives that cause migraines in children? 'Dyes and benzoates are so common in factory-processed foods that it's hard to avoid them,'[104] he told me.

What did the RCP/BNF report have to say about migraine and food additives? Referring again to the Great Ormond Street trial, it said:

> There is now evidence from the first double-blind placebo-controlled trial that children with severe migraine are indeed intolerant of certain foods .... There was also a reduction in fits and hyperkinetic behaviour which occurred in a few of the cases .... Foods which provoke migraine include milk and cheese, fish, chocolate, oranges, alcohol, fatty fried food, vegetables (especially onions), tea and coffee .... For the majority of sufferers, the most common precipitating factor is stress.

This is not an accurate summary: there is no mention of chemical additives; the word 'few' is used to describe the 41 out of 88 children who were hyperactive, and the 14 who had fits; and there is no reference to the finding that food and food additives, not stress, appear to cause migraines.

The report's conclusion was that:

> There is no good evidence to implicate intolerance to food additives in hyperactivity.

In this way – as not 'good evidence' – was the work of the Great Ormond Street team, as well as that of Dr Feingold and others, dismissed.

That, however, was not the end of that. For the Medical Research Council evidently did have a good opinion of

Professor Soothill's work and awarded him, together with his colleague Professor Philip Graham, a grant for another trial on the specific relationship between food, food additives and hyperactivity. This was the very research mentioned by John Patten MP in March 1984[93,94] as liable to guide DHSS policy. The report of this 'Controlled Trial of Oligoantigenic Treatment in the Hyperkinetic Syndrome' appeared in the *Lancet* in March 1985.[106]

A total of 76 children, 60 boys and 16 girls, took part in this trial. They were aged between 2 and 15 (mean age 7), and 70 were very difficult or almost impossible to handle at home or at school. As in the previous migraine trial, hyperactivity was part of a pattern. Most of the children suffered headaches (48) and stomach upsets (54); and a large number had aches in their arms or legs (33) or rhinitis (33) or rashes and eczema (28). Others suffered from fits (4) or mouth ulcers (15).

On a special diet, 62 of the 78 hyperactive children improved, and of these 21 recovered completely. As in the 1983 trial, other illnesses also usually disappeared: for example, all but eight of the children with stomach upsets recovered, as did all but nine of those with headaches.

As before, cows' milk, hens' eggs, wheat, chocolate, oranges and cows' cheese were found to be common causes of illness. But this time, tartrazine and benzoic acid, taken together, were the chief causes of hyperactivity: four out of the five children 'challenged' with this additive cocktail became uncontrollable, although no child reacted badly to additives alone. Are tartrazine and benzoic acid uniquely toxic? Not according to Professor Soothill: he said to me that it was logical to assume that all coal-tar dyes, and all benzoates (all E numbers from E210 to E219), are a potential cause of hyperactivity.[104] Referring to dyes, benzoates and hyperactivity, the *Lancet* report concluded:[106]

> More research is needed to explain why these substances, also important in some other allergic diseases, such as angioedema and eczema, are prominent in this syndrome. However, they are particularly readily avoidable, since they have no nutritional value, and our findings strengthen the case for excluding them where possible from factory-processed foods and drugs, and for improved labelling.

Dr Juliet Gray, who as Secretary of the RCP/BNF committee had drafted its report, evidently did not go along with this view. In 1985 she was nutritional advisor to Sutcliffe Catering, whose *Eat Fit* brochure said:[107]

Many people are concerned about the use of a wide range of additives as food processing aids but there are strict laws governing the use of additives in foods. There has been no case so far when an additive has proved dangerous.

What do 'proved' and 'dangerous' mean? The BNF/RCP report accepts that food dyes and preservatives can cause diseases: skin rashes (urticaria and angioedema); asthma; and eczema, especially in children. Of skin rashes the report says:[95]

Reaction to food additives, such as tartrazine, sunset yellow and benzoates, may not be obvious from the clinical history, as they are regularly imbibed in large quantities by children. When no other cause of chronic urticaria can be identified, it is useful to try a diet which is free of azo dyes and preservatives.

Other additives listed in the report as a cause of skin rashes are sulphites (E223 is specifically cited); nitrites (E250); antioxidants (E320 and E321); and flavours (quinine and menthol).

How worrying is all this? Like the Great Ormond Street team, the report recommends much more research:[95]

Research needs to be carried out on both the epidemiology of, and the basic mechanisms concerned in, adverse reactions to food additives. It must be emphasised that there is no suitable experimental model available to assess the allergic potential of new food additives.

In 1984, Dr John Hunter, a specialist in food allergy, published *The Allergy Diet*,[108] a popular book based on his work at the Department of Gastroenterology at Addenbrooke's Hospital, Cambridge; his co-authors were his colleague Dr Virginia Alun Jones and Elizabeth Workman, a dietitian. Dr Hunter and his team have special knowledge of migraine, asthma, rhinitis, urticaria and eczema, together with gut disorders (including the irritable bowel syndrome and the more serious Crohn's Disease). In their book they claim that:

Approximately one-fifth of our patients react to food additives such as preservatives and colourings.

In the opinion of the Addenbrooke's team, how common is adverse reaction to food and food additives? In 1985 a £1 million research appeal was launched with a brochure stating:[109]

> In the last few years one of the most important developments in medical science has been the demonstration that intolerance of everyday foods may be an important factor in a wide range of diseases, including asthma, eczema, urticaria, migraine and hyperactivity in children .... Food intolerance is important in two gastrointestinal conditions, The Irritable Bowel Syndrome and Crohn's Disease. The Irritable Bowel Syndrome is one of the commonest disorders of the Western World with as many as one person in three being affected by recurrent bouts of abdominal pain, wind and diarrhoea .... As many as two-thirds of patients suffering from these conditions can have their symptoms controlled completely by an appropriate diet.

People of all ages suffer from irritable bowel syndrome. Given that one in five react to dyes and preservatives, this means that there are over three and a half million people in a population of 56 million whose digestions could be upset by food additives.

In 1986, Dr Gray published her own popular version of the RCP/BNF report; a paperback book called *Food Intolerance: Fact and Fiction*.[110] She wrote:

> Reactions to additives ... do exist, but probably in very small numbers. Present estimates suggest around 0.03–0.15 per cent (between 3 and 15 people in every 10,000 in the general population).

On food, food additives and hyperactivity, she did not refer to the work of Professor Soothill, Professor Graham and their colleagues at Great Ormond Street, and wrote:

> The evidence linking hyperactivity to diet is quite poor, although every now and again the media make a song and dance about it. It's an idea we have imported from the USA.

In July 1985 a group of researchers at the University of Sydney, Australia, including Professor Stewart Truswell, published their own findings in the *Lancet*[111] of a trial on 140 children which supported the Great Ormond Street findings. As well as coal-tar dyes and benzoates, other chemical additives, including nitrates, a sulphite, antioxidants and also flavour-enhancers (monosodium glutamate) were found to cause behaviour disturbance in children.

Was the DHSS impressed by the Great Ormond Street trial, and by the supporting research from Australia? No, it was not. In December 1985 the Birmingham Daily News[112] reported that a group of Liberal MPs was singing and dancing about additives and hyperactivity. But:

> The Government says that existing research which it funded has proved inconclusive. A DHSS spokesman said 'The research at Great Ormond Street Children's Hospital showed dietary factors may have caused hyperactivity in a few cases, so we have funded more research.'

This 'more research' was an inaccurate reference to the 'epidemiological enquiry' into additives and hyperactivity which, as John Patten stated in 1984,[94] had been commissioned before the results of the Great Ormond Street trial were known. This further research is being carried out by Dr Eric Taylor of the Institute of Psychiatry at the Maudsley Hospital in London.

I spoke to Dr Taylor in September 1986, and he told me that the results of his study would be published in 1987.[113] As a result of screening 3500 seven-year-old boys in East London, he was inclined to agree with the findings of the Great Ormond Street trial. In his judgement, about one in every two hundred young children may suffer from hyperactivity, or from the 'hyperkinetic syndrome'; this is not mere excess energy, but a clinical entity, and a serious condition.

In December 1985 the Birmingham Daily News carried another story headed 'MP TO INVESTIGATE CHILDREN'S FOOD PERIL'. Roger King, Conservative MP for Birmingham, Northfield, was quoted as saying:[114]

> From my personal experience with my eight year-old son James I am satisfied that there may be a link between orange and hyperactivity. James was full of energy and mischievous and was unable to relax but when we cut out orange, which he drank like a fish, he got better.

A week later, on 12 December 1985, FACT (the Food Additives Campaign Team) held its launch conference in the Palace of Westminster, hosted by four MPs, including Barry Sheerman, Labour MP for Huddersfield, who said that his marriage had been threatened by the hyperactivity of his daughter, who had recovered on a diet free from coal-tar dyes and benzoates.[115]

In March 1986 Michael Jopling appeared on *TV-AM* with Mrs Sally Bunday of the Hyperactive Children's Support Group. Obviously unhappy, he said:[116]

> The evidence is very strong, and it's all very distressing .... Some things in foods can affect people .... There's a growing interest in this that I want to respond to .... A good deal of health education needs to be done, and we're going to be doing it in the next year or two.

FOOD TECHNOLOGY TAKES COMMAND

Are some food additives a significant cause of genetic damage, birth defects, and cancers in humans? Nobody really knows. The best available evidence comes from tests in which laboratory animals are given large doses of specific additives. This evidence has led successive groups of scientists appointed to judge the safety of additives to think that the answer is 'yes, probably' or 'yes, possibly'. As a result, some additives have been banned, and others have been allowed pending further tests. Lists of banned additives vary from country to country and from time to time.

Certain additives commonly used in British food today have been repeatedly suspected to be carcinogenic. As listed in *The Causes of Cancer*,[77] *Diet, Nutrition and Cancer*,[78] and in other works,[19,26,37] these include dyes; certain preservatives – especially nitrates and nitrites (E249-252), and the antioxidants BHA and BHT (E320 and E321); and chemical sweeteners, especially saccharin.

But just how dangerous might such additives be? Opinions vary. Some scientists say that animal tests are of doubtful validity and that it's almost anybody's guess whether or not some food additives are carcinogenic. Some experts, notably Sir Richard Doll and Richard Peto,[77] are sure that first smoking and then an unbalanced diet are the main avoidable causes of cancers. Others, notably Dr Samuel Epstein,[19] emphasize the hazards of chemicals in the environment. Since most toxicologically troublesome additives are man-made chemicals contained in food, they could be placed high up on a list of carcinogens according to both these schools of thought. However, smoking usually gets the top billing, certainly as the chief cause of lung cancer.

So there really is no reliable way of grading chemical dyes, preservatives, anti-oxidants and sweeteners as long-term threats to life, compared, say, with emissions from nuclear-processing plants, asbestos, the contraceptive pill and agrichemicals. On the other hand, there is reliable evidence that some additives are significant short-term threats to health.

The official view in Britain and Europe[117] is that some additives uncommonly trigger minor illnesses. This view, convenient to government and industry, is disputed by scientists who say that some additives are a common cause of serious illness. It depends, of course, on what is meant by 'common', 'cause' and 'serious'. But what almost all studies and reports do agree on is the need for more research. Enter the Ministry of Agriculture, Fisheries and Food's Food Priorities Board and its Food Safety Committee.

Since its foundation in 1955, MAFF has been advised by the Food Standards Committee (FSC), and then also by the Food Additives and Contaminants Committee (FACC), which, as already stated, in 1983 were amalgamated into the Food Advisory Committee.

These committees have always been designed to balance the views of scientists inside and outside industry with, as already mentioned, the occasional lay voice. But from the early 1980s, the government started to develop an official policy altogether more favourable to the big food- and chemical-manufacturers through a new and altogether more businesslike structure of advisory committees, whose recommendations have set the style for the British food industry in the late 1980s and the 1990s.

In 1982 the Advisory Council for Applied Research and

Development (ACARD), which reports direct to the Cabinet Office, published a *Report on the Food Industry and Technology*.[118] The document was produced by a Working Group whose brief was to find ways of making British food-manufacturing more competitive.

Its Chairman was Dr Douglas Georgala of Unilever, who in 1982 was Chairman of the Industrial Scientists committee of the BNF.[84] Five of the seven other members were from industry: Professor David Conning, who was then concerned with testing additives on animals at BIBRA, the British Industrial Biological Research Association; Professor Alan Holmes, who develops new technological foods with the help of additives at BFMIRA, the British Food Manufacturing Industries Research Association; Professor Jack Edelman of Ranks Hovis McDougall; Sidney Free of Rowntree Mackintosh; and David Shore of APV Engineering, who is also Chairman of BFMIRA. Unilever and Ranks Hovis McDougall manufacture additives as well as food. There was no consumer representation.*

Dr Georgala's brief included identifying 'new market opportunities that might be exploited with the aid of new technology'. Food technology adds economic value by pulling 'raw materials' (food) apart and then putting them together in novel combinations, with sophisticated machinery. As the report explained:[118]

> The ability to fractionate and recombine food components will create more opportunity for the fashioning of food products in novel ways .... It may take a long time and require considerable expense to obtain safety clearance for foods and additives produced by a novel route. Even when approved they may not be acceptable to the consumer. For innovation to be encouraged, the safety requirements need to be clearly defined in advance and subject to the minimum of change. The benefits to the consumer need to be carefully understood and presented.

In order to compete with 'aggressive, well-organised agri-food industries in France and Germany', a closer

---

* See Document B for more details of the members of this committee. It is not suggested that the judgement of the members of this and the other committees mentioned here is affected by connections they have or may have with industry.

relationship is necessary between government, industry and science, in order to accelerate technological change. 'Centres of excellence' should be established in places of learning:

> Such centres should then also become a magnet to attract research contract funds direct from industry and a training ground for scientists and engineers some of whom could be expected to enter the food industry where they would not only be able to increase the rate of introduction to new technology but, more generally, underpin the industry technically.

Not only are food engineers required to underpin technological acceleration. Additives are needed too. Hundreds of them: whole classes of 'miscellaneous additives' and 'processing aids' to make the product stick together, fill it with water and/or air, and make it hard or soft, thick or thin, damp or dry, crunchy, fizzy, chewy, bouncy or squeezy, and to speed it through the machines. Here's a partial list:[119]

> acid, anti-caking agent, anti-foaming agent, base, buffer, bulking aid, firming agent, flavour modifier, flour bleaching agent, flour improving agent, glazing agent, humectant, liquid freezant, packaging gas, propellant, release agent or sequestrant.

More technology means more additives and new additives. A no-frills approach to safety testing is proposed: what is good for the food-manufacturing industry should be made palatable to the consumer:

> It may cost £0.5 million to satisfy the regulatory procedures for a new additive .... Any new tests devised should, where possible, replace and be more cost-effective than existing procedures so as not to constitute a barrier to innovation .... We believe that the consumer must be better informed about the dietary hazards that result as much from nutritional imbalance and natural foodstuffs as from possibly toxic additives .... In practice this may mean spending less on testing additives and more on educating consumers and food handlers about food hazards.

The ACARD report recommended a new system of 'Requirement Boards'. These would have an executive rather than an advisory role, and would take responsibility for spending on research and development. Their membership would be

> drawn mostly from relevant industries, with minority participation by department officials and representatives from research establishments.

Accordingly, MAFF set up four under-publicized committees. The chairman of these committees, and most of their industrial members, were from the giant food manufacturers.

The Central Priorities Board was chaired by Sir Kenneth Durham, then also Chairman of Unilever.[120] There were three satellite committees: on Food Quality, chaired by Tony Good, then Chairman of Express Dairies;[121] Food Processing, chaired by Dr Tom Gorsuch, Director of Research at Reckitt and Colman;[122] and Food Safety. (A complete analysis of the membership of these committees is included in Document B.)

DANGER! SAFETY COMMITTEE
AT WORK

The Food Safety Committee was chaired by Professor John Norris, Director of Research at Cadbury Schweppes, whose research laboratories, you will recall, are on the campus at Reading University.[123] Professor Norris has also served on committees of the Food and Drink Federation, as a nominee of the Cocoa, Chocolate and Confectionery Alliance,[124] and was a member of the Food Additives and Contaminants Committee that produced the 1979 *Interim Report*[2] on the need for and safety of food colours and dyes. Two members of the Food Safety Committee, Dr Maurice Brook of Beecham, and Dr Barbara MacGibbon of the DHSS, had also sat on the RCP/BNF joint committee that produced the report on *Food Intolerance and Food Aversion*.[95] A further two members were Norman Curtis of Whitbreads Breweries and the inevitable Unilever employee, in this case Dr Anthony Baird-Parker. The four men from industry on this committee of eleven between them had knowledge of drink, drugs, agrichemicals and food, as well as of additives.

Part of the brief of the Food Safety Committee when it was appointed in September 1984 was to advise on 'the significance of allergeinicity and food intolerance in the UK'.[125,126] It was asked to make its recommendations to the Priorities Board by the end of August 1985. What new priority would be given to research into the ill-effects of food additives? From time to time during 1985 I telephoned MAFF and was told that Professor Norris and his colleagues were making progress. August 1985 came and went: no report. It finally surfaced on Monday 14 October.

Or, rather, another Ministry of Agriculture press release dated 7 October arrived on some newspaper news desks on 14 October, headed 'New Objectives and Opportunities for Food Safety Research'.[127] This said that the committee had reported, that its report was available, and that a period for consultation was specified — terminating on 18 October 1985.

So what did the report of the Food Safety Consultative committee say? It was not enclosed with the press release. This seemed rather rum to me, since it left virtually no time at all to get hold of the report, read it, write comments and send them to MAFF.

I was 'consulted' on 17 October, when I obtained my copy of the report. It stated that in 1984-85 total government expenditure on food safety research was £4,781,000, of which £183,000, 3.8 per cent, was for research on 'allergenicity and food intolerance'. This money was being spent on two studies, one on immune response to food chemicals in experimental animals and humans, and another on immune response to food. The report recommended that this 'important work already in progress should continue to be supported'.[125]

A total of £1,527,000, 31.9 per cent, of the budget for food safety research, was allocated to a miscellaneous category called 'Other Aspects of Food Safety Research'. An appendix at the back of the report listed details of various research projects. But £1,396,900 of the 'other' £1,527,000 was merely described as 'in-house work done by the Food Science Division Laboratories'. The very last paragraph of the report explained the nature of this work, and made recommendations:

This is the major area of expenditure and is concerned mainly with work on food additives and contaminants. The subject matter is clearly of great importance, it is research-sensitive, and the possibility of hazards associated with these classes of materials is prominent as a cause of concern for consumers .... The committee notes however that this sector has received substantial attention for many years and that there is no significant evidence of hazard associated with the presence of additives and contaminants in the United Kingdom food supply. We therefore recommend that the pattern of research in this area should be re-examined with a view to effecting a reduction in the level of expenditure in order to liberate funds for use in areas of higher priority.

So the committee recommended that a couple of studies of the ill-effects of food and food additives costing a total of £183,000 be kept going, at least until the results were in; and that other research costing an unspecified proportion of £1,396,000 on all the ill-effects of food additives including those not involving the immune system be cut back, as of low priority. Low priority from whose point of view? Ours, or that of the food and chemical manufacturers? The Committee's policy had obeyed the guidelines set by the ACARD committee three years previously.[118] The justification was as follows:

There is a lack of adequate information with which to estimate the prevalence of food intolerance, including food allergy, in the community at large .... Media comment often assumes that food intolerance and food allergy, especially that induced by food additives, is much more common than can be deduced from the available evidence.

So there you are. No research means no evidence. No evidence means no research. Catch E102!
The editorial comment in the *Lancet* was terse:[128]

Despite growing consumer concern about the potential hazards of food additives the final paragraph of a report from the Food Safety Research Consultative Committee proposes that this area of research be cut back to release more money for 'use in areas of higher priority'.

On 18 October I delivered a letter of complaint to MAFF, proposing that additional funds for research into the ill-effects of food containing additives, and also saturated fats, added sugars and salt, be raised, not from taxation, but from a levy on chemical and food manufacturers who use chemical additives. This levy would enable research to be administered and carried out by institutions wholly independent of government and industry, and would also encourage food manufacturers to make products containing fewer additives.

In a polite reply, a Mr J.B. Hirons wrote to me:[129]

> I have taken note of your criticism of the brief period allowed for comments on the Report and apologise for the difficulties this has caused you. We were delayed by some printing problems outside our control in issuing the Report and the press release. Because of the many sequential steps in the review process, involving some dates which would be extraordinarily difficult to change, we did not wish to defer the date for comments. We do appreciate the importance of this area of our food R & D and we hope to be able to implement recommendations as soon as possible once they are agreed.

Agreed by whom? If my experience was anything to go by, Mr Hirons's problems with his printers meant that consumer representative bodies were granted one day to respond to the report. The food manufacturing industry had rather more time. It turned out that one of the dates Mr Hirons and his colleagues were anxious not to break was a meeting on 7 November between representatives of MAFF, the DHSS and the Agriculture and Food Research council. Professor Norris was at the meeting. So was Dr Peter Russell-Eggitt, who is Chairman of the Scientific and Technical Committee of the Food and Drink Federation.[124,130]

In 1985 Dr Russell-Eggitt's committee of thirty members, all men from the food processing industry, included some familiar names: Professor Russell Allen, Dr Tom Gorsuch, Professor Alan Holmes, Alan Turner and (before his appointment to the BNF) Professor David Conning. The industry position that Dr Russell-Eggitt brought to his negotiations with the Ministry can readily be deduced from the boasting in the annual reports of the Food Manufacturers Federation and the Food and Drink Federation between 1983 and 1985[124] about the achievements of its Scientific and Technical Committee.

In 1983 a triumph was reported. The European Scientific Committee for Food had taken a new look at various food dyes that had been safety-tested 'under the auspices of the food and drink industry-based European Colours Group' at a cost of £1 million, 'the FMF providing the Secretariat and being a major participant' in the seven-year programme. Nine dyes were accepted for use in food throughout Europe as a result of the food industry's own safety-testing: in alphabetical order, amaranth (E123), black PN (E151), brilliant blue FCF (133), brilliant green S (E142), brown HT (155), carmoisine (E122), patent blue V (E131), ponceau 4R (E124) and quinoline yellow (E104). The list includes seven dyes on the Food Additives and Contaminants Committee's 'B' provisional list,[2] one (patent blue V) on its 'E' list, and two (133 and 155) with no 'E' numbers. Dr Russell-Eggitt's committee was able to report, however:[124]

> With the exception of green S, the new recommended ADIs were set up at a higher level than the previous temporary ADIs .... The continued availability to food and drink manufacturers of these nine important colours was a highly satisfactory outcome of this programme of work.

In 1984 the Food and Drink Federation reported that two of Dr Russell-Eggitt's sub-committees, the General Additives Working Group and the Flavourings Working Group, 'continued to work towards the maintenance within the UK of a large range of approved additives to meet the requirements of the whole food chain.' In 1985 the atmosphere changed:[124] 'The General Additives Working Group has been involved in responding to increasing media criticism of the use of food additives': and Sir Derrick Holden-Brown, Chairman of Allied Lyons and FDF President, wrote:[124]

> For 1986 there will be many burning issues, none more so than the extent of feeling running against the industry in relation to dietary health and the safety and quality of processed food. In this specific instance, we intend to make our voice more widely

heard and understood. It would be wrong to entertain any illusions about the scale of the task, but we have made a start.

Indeed so. For in July 1986 MAFF published its 'Food Safety 1985' report,[130] as approved by the food and chemical manufacturing industries but not by you or me. The *Guardian* comment on the report was:[131]

> The Ministry of Agriculture yesterday dismissed growing public concern about the dangers of food additives, saying that its current research into the hazards of adding chemicals to processed foods was adequate .... The Ministry .... now wants to hand over some of the cost (and responsibility) for food safety research to the food manufacturers themselves.

In 1987, the policy of the British government on the safety of food additives has never been stated, but it can be discerned from a reading of the relevant documents, some published, some obscure, some secret. The policy is that what is good for food and chemical manufacturers is good for Britain. Expert government advisory committees with some degree of independence, such as FACC and FAC, are being overlaid by committees controlled by industry with government approval, such as the Food Priorities Board and the Food Safety Committee. Industry will increasingly fund and control safety testing of chemical additives, and expert advisory committees will rely on this research. The general policy of government and industry is to make more and more highly processed food, relying on more and more sophisticated use of food additives. Doubts about the safety of additives are dismissed as hysteria or scaremongering. In Britain in 1987, food technology rules.

Michael Jopling, still Minister of Agriculture and sponsor of the food industry in 1987, addressed the annual luncheon of the Food and Drink Federation at the Dorchester Hotel in London, on 18 September 1986.

BRITAIN'S FOOD INDUSTRY AND THE GOVERNMENT HAVE PROUD RECORD ON FOOD SAFETY AND ADDITIVES, SAYS MICHAEL JOPLING

or, rather, his Ministry scriptwriters[132]

> Government is sometimes accused of being over-secretive about food additives. However, much of this criticism seems to spring from ignorance.

On 10 November Mr Jopling was off to Brighton to open the ninth Fast Food Fair. The Ministry press release was equally enthusiastic:[133]

'FAST FOOD' HAS ITS PLACE IN A HEALTHY, NUTRITIOUS DIET, SAYS MICHAEL JOPLING I would draw attention to a misconception in some quarters that 'fast food' does not provide the consumer with a nutritious meal. The record needs putting straight. The basic ingredients of the fast food meal – beef, chicken, fish, cheese or potato – are all to be found in a normal balanced diet .... Looking about me here today, I am conscious of a distinct wave of optimism for the future of the fast food sector.

CHAPTER 5

Vitamins and Minerals: The Case of the Disappearing (Spinal) Column

The economic importance of nutrition as a discipline rests in Britain today, not in the prevention of beri-beri, scurvy or rickets, but upon the contribution it makes to the prevention of cancer, diabetes, ischaemic heart disease, bronchitis, multiple sclerosis, pregnancy failure, low birth weight, congenital malformations and other disorders costly to the Exchequer and the lives of the nation.

Margaret and Arthur Wynn, Prevention of Handicap and the Health of Women[1], 1977

Much ill-health in Britain today arises from over-indulgence and unwise behaviour ... The standard of nutrition in this country is generally good; where there is under-nutrition it is usually associated with non-nutritional factors such as disease or social inadequacy. The Government believes that its responsibilities should be directed to ensuring that food sold to the public is safe.

Department of Health and Social Security, Prevention and Health[2], 1977

Secrecy – what diplomatically is called 'discretion', as well as the arcana imperii, the mysteries of government – and deception, the deliberate falsehood and the outright lie used as legitimate means to achieve political ends, have been with us since the beginning of recorded history. Truthfulness has never been counted among the political virtues, and lies have always been regarded as justifiable tools in political dealings.

Hannah Arendt, Crises of the Republic[3], 1972

226

Who cares about vitamins and minerals? Food manufacturers certainly do. For, while some products appear to be
chemistry sets, judging by their labels, others seem to be a
kind of bulked-up vitamin and mineral pill. Here, for
instance, is the ingredients list of one leading ready-to-eat
breakfast cereal:

> Ingredients: Wheat flour enriched with wheat bran, maize,
> brown sugar, glucose syrup, oats, malt, honey, salt, vitamin C,
> niacin, vitamin E, zinc oxide, iron, vitamin B6, riboflavin
> (vitamin B2), thiamin (B1), folic acid, vitamin D3, vitamin B12.

'Fortified with vitamins *and iron*' boasts the big print on
the front of another breakfast cereal packet (manufacturer's
emphasis). 'Bread is good for you: eat more bread!' urges the
wrapper of a leading brand of sliced white bread. The claim
is backed up by a drawing of a family in tracksuits and
trainers, standing on top of an Olympic-style podium, on
which is written:

> Iron. Required to keep blood healthy. 6 slices provides 28% of
> the RDA*. Vitamin B1 (thiamin). Gives you energy and keeps
> the nerves and muscles healthy. 6 slices provides 24% of the
> RDA*. Niacin (part of the B Group). Needed for a healthy skin
> and nervous system. 6 slices provides 17% of the RDA*.

The * is translated elsewhere on the label as
'*Recommended Daily Amount'. So it seems that one way to
get your recommended daily amount of niacin, is to eat
thirty-five slices of white bread a day. Since most people eat
ready-to-eat breakfast cereals and white bread, a 'normal,
balanced, varied' diet in Britain today includes foods to
which synthetic vitamins and minerals are added by the
manufacturer. Other products boast about the vitamins or
minerals naturally present in their ingredients.

Another way to have your recommended daily amount of
niacin, it turns out, is to eat a couple of ounces of a
well-known branded savoury spread, whose bottle states
that a 12-gram serving contains:

> Vitamin B1 0.2 mg (1/6 RDA) , vitamin B2 0.81 mg (1/2 RDA),
> niacin 4.5 mg (1/4 RDA), folic acid 50 mcg (1/6 RDA), vitamin
> B12 0.33 mcg (1/6 RDA).

Other processed products continue to stress their nutritional content. For example, 'concentrated health drink with vitamin C. Ascorbic acid (vitamin C) content: not less than 264 mg per 100 ml' says the big print on the front of the blackcurrant 'health' drink listed in chapter 4. Remember the contents?:

Ingredients: Sugar, concentrated blackcurrant juice, water, citric acid, vitamin C, preservatives E211, E223; flavourings; colours E123, E102, E142.

The Government cares about vitamins and minerals too. It is specially anxious that pregnant woman and young children should take them. *Free Milk and Vitamins,*[4] a Department of Health leaflet available at post offices, tells mothers 'Why milk and vitamins are good for you and your baby':

Babies and children need milk, which is an excellent food containing a lot of nourishing ingredients including calcium which is essential for normal healthy growth, especially of bones and teeth .... Food does not always give children enough vitamins A, C and D which they need for good health and growth.

Hence, the manufacturers' health claims for syrupy drinks with added vitamin C.

Here's another product designed to appeal to mothers who have weaned their infants on vitamin drops and picked up a bit of nutrition education from official leaflets: a 'banana flavour milk shake drink' made by a leading company. The legend on the sachet says that in one glassful

Prepared as directed, there are generous amounts of protein and calcium, together with at least one quarter of the recommended daily intake for a child of vitamins A, B1, B2, C and niacin – vitamins essential for healthy growth. Ingredients: Sugar, skim milk powder; flavourings; colours E102, E110; vitamins C, niacin, A, B1.

'Prepared as directed', which suggests some sort of fun medicine, involves mixing up the powder into a glass of milk, which provides much of the 'generous amounts of protein and calcium'. And yes, we have no bananas in this 'banana flavour' product.

The message on the packet, wrapper, bottle and sachet, is that vitamins and minerals are a Good Thing – which indeed they are. But why should we care about the particular vitamins and minerals that the manufacturers boast about?

Take niacin, also known as nicotinic acid, or vitamin B3. Why do cereal-, bread-, spread- and shake-manufacturers make a fuss about it? Vitamins are so called because they are vital to life; we cannot do without them, and severe lack of vitamins causes deficiency diseases. Severe niacin deficiency causes pellagra, a disease once common in some southern states of the USA. According to one textbook'[5]

> The symptoms of pellagra vary considerably and are often summarised in the mnemonic 'diarrhoea, dermatitis and dementia' ... Early mental symptoms include lassitude, apprehension, depression and loss of memory and these may be succeeded by disorientation, confusion, hysteria and sometimes maniacal outbursts.

But is pellagra common in Britain? No, it is not. Has pellagra ever been common in Britain? No, it has not. The only people likely to suffer from gross niacin deficiency are alcoholics.[5] In 1986, the average consumption of niacin in Britain was estimated by MAFF[6] to be almost twice the Recommended Daily Amount (RDA) laid down by the DHSS.[7,8] A recent judgment made for the DHSS by the Committee on Medical Aspects of Food Policy (COMA) is that 'there is no evidence that nicotinic acid deficiency is a problem in this country'.[9] You will not, it seems, lose your marbles if you avoid white bread. Youngsters will not go bananas without banana flavour milk shakes. Why, then, the enthusiasm of government and industry for those vitamins and minerals that we read about on food labels?

The answer to this question, and the key to what is wrong with British food and health policy in the 1980s, lies in events and decisions made half a century or more ago, which shaped the British food supply like that of no other country in the word.

WHAT EVERY ANIMAL BREEDER KNOWS

During the 1920s and the 1930s, scientists in Britain tried to draw the authorities' attention to the appalling state of health of the industrial working classes and, in particular, to the diseases suffered by the young. Poor people crushed into cities as a result of the Industrial Revolution had become diseased. Up to three-quarters of urban working-class children living in cities a century ago suffered from rickets.[10] What motivated the scientists of the 1930s was not simple philanthropy. They thought that they knew the cause and the cure. They had the answers!

Those were heady days for any researcher working in the new science of nutrition. 'Accessory food factors', present in tiny amounts in food, were being identified and isolated in the laboratory, and being shown as vital to health and life. Nobel Prizes were won by the scientists who identified the substances in cereal bran and in citrus fruit that cured beri-beri (a potentially fatal disease of the nervous system common in the East) and scurvy (another deadly disease which had destroyed the health of British sailors). In the 1920s, British working-class children were fed cow's milk and cod liver oil, because experiments with rats and puppies showed that substances in the milk and oil promoted growth and strengthened bones. The experiment worked with humans, too; by the 1930s, poor children were growing taller, and rickets was on the way out.[10,11]

These 'accessory' or 'protective food factors' became known as 'vitamins', and were at first classified 'A', 'B', 'C' and 'D'. Vitamin B was then sub-divided, at first into 'B1', 'B2' and 'B3', as it was found to include substances with different biological activity. For example, in 1937 niacin was extracted from liver and shown to cure black-tongue in dogs and pellagra in humans. It became known as B3; another B vitamin, riboflavin or B2, had already been identified as the growth promoter in milk.[10,12]

During the half century between Pasteur and Fleming, the discovery of the cause and cure of the 'classic' deficiency diseases was the glamour area in the human biological sciences, and British scientists were among the world's leaders. In 1936, John Boyd Orr published his book *Food Health and Income*,[13] writing, in words of utmost confidence:

It has been proved that much of the ill-health which afflicts human populations can be attributed directly to deficiencies in diet.

Boyd Orr was outraged by the ill-health that he and his colleagues from the Rowett Research Institute, Aberdeen, found in their surveys of the food eaten by representative samples of the British population in the mid-1930s. He divided the poorer half of the population into three groups:[13]

The average diet of the poorest group, comprising $4\frac{1}{2}$ million people, is by the standard adopted, deficient in every constituent examined. The second group, comprising 9 million people, is adequate in protein, fat, and carbohydrate, but deficient in all the vitamins and minerals considered. The third group, comprising another 9 million, is deficient in several of the important vitamins and minerals.

In a series of public lectures, also in 1936, Robert McCarrison, another distinguished nutritionist, drew on his life's work in India to describe the effect of bad food.[14] Pallor, stunting, deformity; a scrawny physique and a sluggish and dull temperament; irritation, anxiety and exhaustion. This is what he saw in India, and among the working classes of Britain, too.

Food Health and Income was commissioned by the Agriculture and the Health Ministries of England, Scotland, Wales and Northern Ireland. When Boyd Orr's book was published, some scientists and civil servants questioned his methods and conclusions. Like another great contemporary Scotsman, John Reith of the BBC, Boyd Orr was a man with a mission and without self-doubt. In the second edition of his book, published in 1937,[15] he answered his critics with thunder and lightning:

It has been suggested that the standard adopted, viz, what is needed to enable people to attain their maximum inherited capacity for health and physical fitness, is so high that it is impracticable. One writer terms it 'utopian'. In animal husbandry, an optimum standard, far from being utopian, is regarded as good practice. Every intelligent stock breeder in rearing animals tries to get a minimum diet for maximum health and physical fitness. A suggestion that he should use a lower standard would be regarded as absurd.

The enthusiasm of Boyd Orr and his contemporaries, notably Jack Drummond, Professor of Biochemistry at London University in the 1930s, was generated by the 'new knowledge of nutrition': by their conviction that many of the illnesses they saw in society could be identified, treated, and cured by specific nutrients, and that public health must thereby be transformed. Rickets? Vitamin D, together with calcium. Anaemia? Iron. Stunting? Protein. And the rest? Malaise likely to disappear once people had good food to eat. Drummond quoted a League of Nations expert committee which in 1935 had surveyed the needs of expectant mothers and growing children and shown that these could be met by the vitamins and minerals from specified quantities of milk, cheese, eggs, potatoes and root vegetables, together with greens and salads, fruit, 'and a little cod-liver oil for luck'.[16]

JUST THE STUFF TO GIVE THE TROOPS

Jack Drummond, above all, gave the authorities food for thought. He showed that the German defeat in the First World War had been accelerated by chaotic food supplies, semi-starvation, and a consequent vast black market in food, calamitous to the morale and health of the German civilian population and, eventually, to its armies. He also had a memorable way of saying things. In his book *The Englishman's Food*, first published in 1939 just before he became Chief Scientific Advisor to the wartime Ministry of Food, he wrote:[16]

> It had been stated that in the last year of the War an exceptionally large number of German infantrymen fractured their arms in throwing stick-bombs. As this type of bomb was thrown with a movement of the arm ending in a rather violent jerk it is not unlikely that defects in the bone due to deficiency of vitamin D, and perhaps vitamin A as well, might have led to easy fracture.

Allied troops had also suffered from malnutrition. In Drummond's opinion, the collapse of the Italian armies at Caporetto in October 1917 was because the Italians (who were allies of the British and the French in the First World War) had been on short rations for most of the year; an act of 'inexcusable folly on the part of the authorities, because Italy was not then short of cereal foods'.

Drummond spoke with special authority on the subject of vitamins: it was he who in 1920 had coined the term 'vitamin'.[12] In *The Englishman's Food*, he told the story of the British and Indian expeditionary force in Mesopotamia under General Townsend, besieged in December 1915 at Kut-el-Amara by the Turks. By the spring of 1916 the soldiers were reduced to semi-starvation. The British ate horseflesh, bread and oatmeal; the Indians ate barley flour, butter (ghee) and dates. In April 1916, Townsend capitulated: 'a tragic event, hastened by the ravages of scurvy and beri-beri among the men'. During 1916 11,000 Allied troops were taken out of the war in the Middle East, suffering from scurvy, which incapacitated over 1000 soldiers at Kut, mostly Indians. In addition, 150 of the garrison, mostly British, were suffering from beri-beri. Drummond commented:[16]

> This serious loss of fighting strength might have been prevented had it been possible, as it would be today, to drop from an aeroplane a small packet containing a few ounces of pure vitamins B1 and C. There is a cruel irony in the fact that an aeroplane did drop a small packet to bring relief to the starving garrison; it contained opium to deaden the pangs of hunger.

This obscure siege in Mesopotamia, as commemorated by Jack Drummond in 1939, is the only time in history that beri-beri has been recognized as a disease of any practical significance in Britain. But thus is British national food policy made. Next time somebody you know looks up from reading the side of a cornflakes packet and asks 'what's all this about thiamin?' you can tell them the story of Kut-el-Amara.

Half a century ago, as the Second World War approached, the politicians listened to the scientists and prepared to manipulate the national food supply for the greater good. As the Chief Medical Officer at the Department of Health reported in 1946,[17] 'though the war could be won only by the fighting forces, it might well be lost on the food front'. Vitamins became a weapon of war. If soldiers were to hurl grenades with vigour, and not to languish in the field of battle, they would need strong right arms and constitutions, fortified with vitamins. If women were to keep the home fires burning, raise a new generation, and work effectively in the munitions factories, they and their babies would need fortification too, with vitamins, and with minerals for their blood and bones.

And so standards were set for all those nutrients whose function in the body was well understood. As confirmed after the war in the *Report of the Committee on Nutrition* of the British Medical Association,[18] these, as well as energy (calories), were protein; the vitamins A, B1, B2, B3, C and D; and the minerals iron, calcium and iodine. Cheap foods that supplied these nutrients were emphasized: fatty fish, fish oil and 'vitaminized' margarine for vitamins A and D; the 'National' brown loaf, with some of the B vitamins and minerals lost in milling restored, and calcium added in the form of chalk; potatoes for vitamin C; and above all, cows' milk. In one lecture series given in 1940 and printed the same year in a book called *The Nation's Larder*,[19] Boyd Orr said:

> Every child should have at least 1½ pints of milk per day .... Except for young children, milk is, of course, not an essential food. All that is contained in milk could be obtained from other sources. But it is so rich in first-class protein, minerals and most of the vitamins that it is the most valuable and the cheapest food available for making good the major deficiencies in the diet of the poor.

From the research scientist's point of view, human nutrition became seen as a completed subject. In *The Englishman's Food* Drummond wrote:[16]

> It is fair to say that there is no problem of nutrition in Britain today. So much research has been done in the laboratories and so many precise dietary surveys have been made that we know all we need to know about the food requirements of the people .... The position is perfectly clear-cut.

All that remained, he believed, was to put this perfect knowledge into practice, and feed the people. The great wartime experiment worked. In 1984, in a lecture in honour of Boyd Orr, Dr Donald Acheson, Chief Medical Officer at the Department of Health, claimed that:[20]

The success of the national food policy in the Second World War can probably be counted as the most notably beneficial intervention of government in nutrition so far recorded anywhere.

He then went on to say, of his own days as a medical student in Oxford in 1947:

For most students in Oxford in those days there were no remaining problems in human nutrition. All the accessory food factors had been identified. All that was necessary was to eat a good mixed diet, preferably three square meals daily, avoid obesity and all would be well .... And yet it can be argued that as great a proportion of illnesses and premature deaths have a nutritional factor today as they did 100 years ago.

Being born during the war, this is why I can still hear my mother saying 'Just the stuff to give the troops!' as the spoon hovered near my puckered lips, loaded with foods officially promoted as Body Building, Energy Giving and Protective. Long after the war, the message first sent out by John Boyd Orr, Robert McCarrison and Jack Drummond was still being used by MAFF and the Central Office of Information.[21] Make sure you get enough energy and protein, vitamins and minerals from your food! Score goals with butter and sugar! Emulate Markova with eggs and margarine! Grow up strong and win the war, with chump chops and milk!

We in Britain have been trained to have faith in energy (calories) and protein, in the vitamins A, B1, B2, B3, C and D, and in the minerals calcium and iron, because these are the nutrients that the scientists who became the great social engineers of the 1920s and 1930s believed in, and because the wartime Ministry of Food proclaimed them as vital to national health in newspapers and magazines, on the radio, in cookbooks and nutrition manuals, and in leaflets printed in millions and distributed via schools and colleges, clinics and surgery waiting-rooms. The message has not changed much since the war. In the late 1980s, we live with the shell of a policy designed fifty years ago to make young working-class people grow tall and strong, have bonny bouncing babies and fight bravely.

So, in the late 1980s, manufacturers still boast about the

vitamins and minerals they add in synthetic form to their processed products. You could make an 'balanced' meal as defined by MAFF,[22] breakfast say, starting with a banana flavour milk shake drink (vitamin A), followed by ready-to-eat breakfast cereal (vitamins B1, B2 and B3) sprinkled with sugar (energy), a glass of blackcurrant 'health' drink (vitamin C), and a white bread and margarine sandwich (vitamin D, plus some more vitamin B1 and B3, and also calcium and iron), together with plenty of full-fat cows' milk (protein and energy). There is no official need for any whole vegetables or fruit, or for any fresh food at all, apart from cows' milk.

These official standards are a travesty of the proposals for good food and good health made by John Boyd Orr, Robert McCarrison, Jack Drummond and their colleagues half a century ago. They did the very best they could, using the science of their day. But they went beyond the known facts of science, as those truly committed to public health must always do. Their commitment was above all to whole, fresh food, containing vitamins, minerals and other nourishment, known and unknown, to scientists. Boyd Orr advocated more meat and potatoes, vegetables and fruit.[13] McCarrison championed allotments for growing fresh vegetables:[14]

> in our own country and by our own people .... Surely it is prudent to provide our people with these important foodstuffs in a state as fresh as possible.

Drummond celebrated:[19]

> Those peasant peoples throughout the world whose daily diets are based on these types of food; wholemeal cereals, mixed vegetables and dairy produce. South-eastern Europe provides many striking examples. Little meat is eaten, but the staple diet is a coarse, whole-grain bread, thick vegetable stews and goat's milk cheese. These people are strong and hardy. Their children are rosy-cheeked, sturdy of leg and have fine, firm teeth.

Since the war, government and industry have agreed policies that have degraded the British food supply. This bad work has been done in the name of science and often with the agreement of scientists. The first story is the worst: bread.

USING OUR LOAF

The bran and germ used in wholegrain flour and bread are very nourishing, being rich not only in fibre and essential fats, but also in all the B vitamins and many minerals.[23] By contrast, the inner part of the grain used to make white flour and white bread is poor in vitamins and minerals, being almost entirely protein and starch. A series of experiments done in the 1920s and 1930s, in which animals and children were fed either wholegrain bread or white bread, convinced most experts that white bread is bad food, or at least grossly inferior in comparison with wholegrain bread.[24]

A League of Nations report on nutrition published in 1936 stated that:[25]

> White flour in the process of milling is deprived of important nutritive elements. Its use should be decreased and partial substitution by lightly milled cereals ... is recommended.

An editorial and a long series of letters in the *British Medical Journal* in 1939 were written in support of the following statement:[26]

> It is quite clear that the change over from wholemeal to white flour, that took place when steel roller mills were introduced nearly 70 years ago, has resulted in reduction of the nutritive value of the protein, in serious lowering of the content of calcium, phosphorus, and iron, in reduction of the vitamin B1 and B2 complex content, and carotene content and probably in complete removal of the vitamin E, all representing dead loss nutritionally. In order to change back to wholemeal it is necessary to change the tastes of the people and to overcome the vested interests in the existing milling industry .... The advantages to be gained in national health would make it well worth while to overcome these difficulties.

The milling and baking industry preferred white flour and bread for five different reasons.[24] First, white flour keeps longer. Second, it holds more air and water. Third, bran and germ are valuable sold as animal feed. Fourth, white flour and bread therefore give the trade more turnover. Fifth, wholegrain bread takes more skill and time to make.

In 1940, the trade paper the *Miller* fought back:[27]

> White bread has been a special target for the criticism of every kind of crank, even though it has been proved time and time again that there is no better, cheaper, and more satisfying and sustaining food.

The Medical Research Council was not impressed, and in August 1940 published a 'Memorandum' in the *Lancet*[28] designed to find ways

> in which the health of the people of Great Britain might be benefited by improving the nutritive value of the wheaten bread which they eat.

The first recommendation was that 'Flour for the bread of the people should contain the germ of the wheat grain ... and the finer portions of the bran.' The resulting brown bread, enriched with wheatgerm, 'would benefit greatly the health of adults and children of all classes in Great Britain'. In October 1940 Sir William Bragg, President of the Royal Society, wrote a letter to *The Times* on 'The wartime choice of food',[29] emphasizing the vital importance of milk and vegetables, fruit and wholemeal bread.

There was also a pressing practical argument for wholemeal, or at least brown, bread. In those days Britain depended on wheat imported from Canada to make bread. With the merchant fleet under threat from German U-boats, storage space in ships had to be used to best effect, and Lord Woolton, the Minister of Food, decided that for once human food should have precedence over animal feed. Since white bread uses only 72 per cent of the whole grain, the bran and germ being discarded, he decided in 1942 to stop production of it and require the National Loaf to be brown, made from 85 per cent of the grain. 'Reason has prevailed and the nation's staple food is to be good nutritious stuff,' said the *Lancet*.[30] In another editorial, the *British Medical Journal* was more outspoken:[31]

> There has been a suspicion in more than one quarter that the interests of the millers have been allowed to stand in the way of the nation's health, and that until this moment the Ministry of

Food has shown signs of falling short of wholehearted advocacy of its wheatmeal loaf .... All the evidence goes to show that the human alimentary tract, from the teeth to the colon, rebels against refined foodstuffs, and that in eating a quantity of refined foods people do indeed dig their graves with their teeth. It is a punishable offence to water milk and dilute the solids in it. Why, then, should it be thought praiseworthy to remove from the wheat berry the valuable minerals and vitamins it contains?

In 1945, just before the end of the war, the report of a 'Conference on the Post-War Loaf' was accepted by the Ministers of Food and Health, and presented to Parliament.[32] The scientists attending the conference agreed that the wartime food policy had been a success, and in particular that the brown National Loaf, with its vitamins and minerals, 'must have made a considerable contribution to maintaining and, on average, improving the nation's health'. Should millers and bakers be free after the war to produce whatever bread they chose? Or should the quality of bread continue to be maintained by law? Representatives of the Ministry of Food, including Jack Drummond (now Sir Jack), and of the Ministry of Health, accepted:[32]

the very definite view expressed by the official medical and scientific members of the Conference that a return to white flour, such as was commonly in use before the war, would be thoroughly bad for the nation's health.

They were also guided by a principle: when in doubt, prefer natural, whole food. At that time, the value to human health of three of the vitamins in grain, B1, B2 and B3, was fairly well understood; similarly with two of the minerals, calcium and iron. But in 1945 the government advisors did not believe (as scientists so often arrogantly do believe) that what they don't know wasn't knowledge:[32]

These vitamins, however, are only elements in an organic complex which includes other substances which are known to be physiologically active, though knowledge of them is incomplete .... There is a strong prima facie case for thinking that the vitamins in the wheat berry exist in the form of a balance which has been proved to be conducive to health.

In the same year the Nutrition Society held a meeting to discuss the value of bread as human food. Sir Rudolph Peters, Chairman of the Society, gave the opening address, saying:[33]

> I know that those who have a more purely chemical discipline often feel that it is illogical for biologists to believe in the value of unknown substances but, if you continue to work on these matters for some years ... you become certain that there are valuable substances, present in a complex material such as wheat, of which you do not yet know, and you would prefer to be on the safe side when responsible for advice.

In other words, scientists in a position to influence national policy during and immediately after the War were saying: don't muck about with nature. Their arguments were accepted, those of the millers were rejected, and British bread remained brown until the 1950s.

The millers continued to press their case for white flour and bread. Already in the late 1930s they had developed a new line of argument. Vitamins B1 (thiamin) and B3 (niacin) had now been synthesized by chemists, and were being produced commercially. Charles Dodds, then Professor of Biochemistry at London University, suggested that white flour could be 'fortified' by adding synthetic thiamin. From the trade's point of view, this was a brilliant idea: they could produce white flour and bread, and make health claims for it too. The policy, which the trade enthusiastically adopted, had been satirized by Dorothy L. Sayers in her novel *Murder Must Advertise* as follows:[34]

> By forcing the damn-fool public to pay twice over – once to have its food emasculated and once to have the vitality put back again, we keep the wheels of commerce turning.

The millers pressed their case on the government of the day. One MP who needed no persuasion was Robert Boothby, who was also chairman of a company that manufactured synthetic vitamin B1. In 1940 Mr Boothby was appointed a junior minister at the Ministry of Food. On 18 July he announced the government's intention to add synthetic vitamin B1 to white flour. He declared his interest and said that he had:[24]

resigned my seat on the board immediately I was appointed Parliamentary Secretary, and I have taken all the necessary steps to dispose of all my financial interests in the company.

After a short while, however, the government's decision, described by the trade magazine *Milling* as 'the most productive and economical advertisement that white bread has ever received', was abandoned in favour of the brown National Loaf. Professor Dodds, who had become a consultant to the millers,[35] put their case to the Conference on the Post-War Loaf as an official representative of the National Association of British and Irish Millers (NABIM). It was rejected:[32]

> The Conference is not prepared to differ from the view that natural food is to be preferred to food reinforced with so-called synthetic vitamins.

ORPHANS AS GUINEA-PIGS

The millers ground on and on, seizing a new opportunity in 1954, when the Medical Research Council (MRC) published a report by Dr Elsie Widdowson and Professor Robert McCance.[36] The MRC had commissioned them to carry out research on German orphans aged between three and fifteen in 1947 and 1948. In what became known as the 'Wuppertal Experiments', the children were divided into different groups. They were all given as much as they wanted to eat: bread (lots of it), potatoes, other vegetables, vegetable soup of an unrecorded recipe (lots of it), small amounts of milk and meat, orange juice, and supplements of vitamins A, C and D. Some children were also given measured amounts of fats and sugars. The main difference was in the bread. Some children were given wholemeal bread; some brown; some white; and some were given white bread 'enriched' with vitamins B1, B2, B3, calcium and iron. The experiments lasted a year. The researchers waited to see what happened.

What happened is that all the children grew strong and healthy. With hindsight, we can see that this was unsurprising. All breads contain much the same amount of calories and protein. The children ate their fill. The quality of the food with the supplements was far superior to what other German children, and British children too, were eating. And, as the researchers themselves acknowledged[24] and had good reason to know,[23] vegetables can be good sources of B vitamins. The report concluded that:

> It cannot be emphasised too strongly that the results themselves apply only to the particular conditions under which the investigation was carried out. The diet contained more vegetables, but much less milk and meat, and in one case less fat and sugar, than diets in use at the present time in Britain, so that the conclusions are not in any case directly applicable to this country.

This passage was not quoted by the trade, whose own conclusion was that the Wuppertal Experiments proved that white bread is good stuff, and just as good as brown or wholemeal bread. Two years later, in 1956, Professor McCance and Dr Widdowson themselves decided that their experiments had, after all, been altogether more important than they had previously thought. They published an influential book, *Breads White and Brown*,[24] which concluded:

> Unenriched white flour is *likely* to be as valuable a part of the diets currently used in Europe and America as an enriched flour, an 85 per cent or a 100 per cent wheaten meal .... There is certain to be resistance among the health minded to any evidence that white bread might be as nutritious as brown.

This was what the millers wanted to hear. Professor McCance and Dr Widdowson both gave evidence to a Committee of Enquiry set up in 1955 by MAFF whose department had been created that year by tacking food on to the Ministry of Agriculture and Fisheries. The task of the Committee, which was chaired by Sir Henry Cohen, was to decide once and for all whether there was any significant difference between brown bread, white bread and 'enriched' white bread. (Wholemeal bread was not considered.) Should the government abandon its commitment to, and subsidy of, brown bread? The 'Cohen report', as it became known,[37] recorded that the Medical Research Council and the government's own scientific advisors were unanimous: brown bread must be protected. Pointing to the value of other B vitamins of which brown bread is a good source, and remaining 'health-minded', they

> strongly emphasised the importance of more recently dis-covered vitamins such as pyridoxine, pantothenic acid, biotin and folic acid .... There is no doubt that these factors are essential for man's well-being. Deficiency states in man have been reported for pyridoxine, biotin and folic acid.

Their conclusion was that:

> It is therefore unwise in the present state of knowledge to adopt any measure which would diminish intake of these nutrients.

Pish and tush, said the millers. The public hated brown bread. If brown bread continued to be subsidized, and white bread not, people would stop eating bread altogether, and nobody wanted that. Bread made from 'National Flour'[37]

> is neither white or brown, but tends to be grey. The flour is unpopular with millers, bakers, and the makers of cakes and biscuits.

WHAT WAS IN THE SOUP?

Sir Henry and his colleagues went along with the millers. Their own reading of the scientific literature on the vitamin B complex led them to believe, 'in spite of weighty opinion to the contrary', that there is 'not a great deal to choose' between brown bread and 'enriched' white bread. Besides, 'differences in the nutritive value of flours can be corrected by the adequcy of the rest of the diet'. Which is to say: 'enriched white bread is just as good as brown bread, or practically just as good, and, even if it isn't just as good, you can always eat vegetable soup'. This is a variation of the modern line that 'there is no such thing as good food and bad food, only good and bad diets'.

And that, really, was that. After nearly twenty years of pressure, the millers got what they wanted, which was consent to make a cheap, uniform product. Brown bread was no longer protected. By law, the standard British white loaf was now 'fortified' with vitamins B1 and B3 and with iron, to the levels naturally present not in wholemeal bread, but in brown bread, together with a liberal dose of calcium in the form of chalk. The millers proceeded to take over the bakers, and in 1987 the British milling and baking industry is dominated by two firms, the Canadian-owned Associated British Foods and Ranks Hovis McDougall.[38] The trade maintained that white bread was what the British public wanted. Consumption of white bread dropped steadily from 41 ounces a week in 1957 to 20 ounces a week in 1984.[39]

In 1967 Joseph Rank and various other food manufacturers set up the British Nutrition Foundation (BNF). Charles Dodds (later Sir Charles) was the first Chairman of the BNF in 1967-68, and was succeeded by Mr Rank in 1968-69. In 1985-86 Mr Rank was Vice-President, and in 1986 Dr Widdowson became President of the BNF.[40]

'Fortified' white bread contains about two-thirds of the vitamin B1 and iron, and one-third of the vitamin B3, naturally present in wholegrain bread.[23] Nevertheless, the trade is allowed to boast about the vitamins and minerals present in white bread. The loss of some vitamins and minerals in white bread compared with wholegrain bread has been calculated as follows:[41,42]

Vitamin and mineral losses in 'fortified' white bread compared with wholegrain bread

Vitamins	%	Minerals	%
E (alpha-tocopherol)	86	Potassium (K)	77
B1 (thiamin)	30	Magnesium (Mg)	85
B2 (riboflavin)	80	Zinc (Zn)	78
B3 (niacin)	63		
B6 (pyridoxine)	72		
Folic acid	67		

In 1977, responding to the evidence that fibre, as contained in cereal bran, is vital to health, the Royal College of Physicians commissioned a report on *Medical Aspects of Dietary Fibre*;[43] which, on publication three years later recommended wholegrain bread. In 1978, under pressure the DHSS commissioned a report from COMA on *Nutritional Aspects of Bread and Flour*,[9] which, on publication in 1981 recommended that 'the consumption of all types of bread, whether it be white, brown or wholemeal, should be promoted.'*

What about the 'fortification' of white bread? The experts on the COMA panel, including Dr Widdowson, agreed that the policy was once useful but was now out of date. Official figures suggested that consumption of vitamins B1 and B3 was adequate. There was no point in adding chalk to white bread – and, as it turned out, the iron powder added to white bread did nobody any good: it went straight through. So the COMA report recommended that 'fortification' should no longer be compulsory.

The National Association of British and Irish Millers, representing the trade, protested.[44] Without 'fortification', white bread would be denounced as worthless rubbish. The trade made representations to government. Consequently, MAFF officials told the experts that their advice would be ignored. Dr John Cummings of the Dunn Clinical Nutrition Centre, Cambridge, the Chairman of the COMA panel, was disgusted. He told me that this was an:[45]

> extremely bad precedent, of a decision made on scientific and medical grounds being over-ridden for reasons of political expediency. If there's a public health problem about iron, then the COMA panel should tackle it, instead of going round in circles on the question of whether or not you add iron filings to bread .... Milling has always been a black art, nutritionally.

In 1986 the bread giants promoted two new white breads. Associated British Foods produced 'Mighty White' with the slogan 'Mighty Good For You!' The story on the wrapper went further than the boast on the bread wrapper already mentioned:

* The COMA panel on *Nutritional Aspects of Bread and Flour* had sixteen members. Of these, fourteen, including Dr Widdowson, had BNF connections, including Sir Frank Young (BNF President 1973-75) and Dr Michael Turner (BNF Director-General at the time). The three senior civil servants on the panel also sat on BNF committees: these were Dr Sylvia Darke of the Department of Health; Dr Henry Yellowlees, then Chief Medical Officer at the Department of Health; and Professor George Elton,[40] who before he became Chief Scientist at MAFF was Director of the British Flour Milling and Baking Research Association, where he was jointly credited with the invention of the Chorleywood Bread Process, by which almost all mass produced British sliced wrapped white bread is made. Full details are given in Document B.

Iron. Required to keep blood healthy. 6 slices provides 36% of the RDA. Vitamin B1 (thiamin). Gives you energy and keeps nerves and muscles healthy. 6 slices provides 31% of the RDA. Niacin (part of the B group). Needed for a healthy skin and nervous system. 6 slices provides 17% of the RDA.

Ranks Hovis McDougall's boasts about their 'Champion' loaf went still further:

Iron. For health. Required to keep blood healthy. 6 slices provides 37% of RDA. Vitamin B1 for energy. Needed for energy and keeps nerves and muscles healthy. 6 slices provides 33% of RDA. Calcium. For strength. Essential for strong bones and teeth. 6 slices provides 48% of RDA.

So next time somebody looks up from reading the wrapper of sliced white bread and asks 'what's all this about thiamin, niacin and iron?', you can tell them the story of the Wuppertal orphans. This is how British national food policy is made. The epitaph for British bread was spoken by Sir Rudolph Peters, who maintained that wholemeal bread is best for everybody and that the Wuppertal Experiments were not a good basis for policy. He said: [46]

I would still like to know what was in the soup.

THE JUNK FOOD DISEASE

The cheerful view of the government's advisors in 1981, that the British food supply contains plenty of vitamin B1 and calcium and that we therefore do not need any in our daily bread, was based on national average figures, issued every year by the Ministry of Agriculture. [39] Never mind about averages: what about people? In Chapter 1 I told the story of how the DHSS tried to suppress its own report on *The Diets of British Schoolchildren*. [47] When the report did eventually emerge in 1986, in an obscured form, it nevertheless showed that nowadays schoolchildren are stuffed with processed fats and sugars, and so are correspondingly short of every kind of nourishment, including iron, to mention just one example.

Many children are also short of the official Recommended

Daily Amount (RDA) for vitamin B1 and calcium. Here are the figures:[8,47]

British schoolchildren consuming less than the Department of Health Recommended Daily Amount (RDA) of vitamin B1 and of calcium.

	Boys		Girls	
ages	11	14	11	14
	%	%	%	%
Vitamin B1	18	24	17	38
Calcium	33	53	25	57

Over a quarter of all 14 year olds are short of vitamin B1; over a half are short of calcium. The figures are always worse for girls. Without the vitamin B1 and calcium added to white bread, the figures would be worse still.

But so what? Does it really matter that millions of young people in Britain today consume less vitamin B1 and calcium, not to mention any other vitamins and minerals, than the DHSS recommended intakes? There is evidence that yes, it does matter.

'JUNK FOOD DISEASE' AKIN TO BERI-BERI DISCOVERED AMONG ADOLESCENTS

This was the headline of a *Washington Post* report[48] in 1980 of a study in the *American Journal of Clinical Nutrition*[49] written by Dr Derrick Lonsdale and Dr Raymond Shamberger, two child health experts from Cleveland, Ohio, who had diagnosed 20 apparently neurotic young patients as suffering from disorders of the nervous system caused by vitamin B1 deficiency. Dr Lonsdale described the condition as 'junk food disease':[48]

What these kids were eating was a fairly average American teenage diet. No breakfast. Maybe school lunch maybe not. But lots of doughnuts, snacks, nibbles, washing it down with various colas and such.

Common symptoms included chest and stomach pain; nightmares and sleeplessness; fever, diarrhoea, and lethargy, as well as sudden and puzzling personality shifts. Animals fed carbohydrate such as sugar and white flour, drained of nourishment, often stop eating to protect themselves. Some of the patients were anorexic:[49]

> Access to easily assimilable sweet beverages could represent a modern danger which is insufficiently emphasised in American society and may well be responsible for personality traits and symptomatology that are regularly overlooked and considered to be 'the personality of a growing child or adolescent'.

All the patients improved when they were given vitamin B1 supplements.

What about Britain? A study of 42 adults published in the *Lancet* in 1986[50] identified biochemical abnormalities in 11 of the subjects, all with marginal or deficient vitamin B1 intake. The conclusion of this study was that

> The withdrawal of thiamine fortification of processed cereals would have serious implications for public health.

The researchers also noted that very low vitamin B1 consumption

> caused anorexia and a marked but fluctuating and eventually progressive general impairment of mental and physical health that took three months to respond to oral thiamine replacement. Perhaps thiamine fortification levels of low-extraction bread and flour in the UK (currently less than half US levels) should be raised.

Better still, eat wholegrain bread and cereal.

'Champion' bread wrappers are right: bones are indeed built with calcium. And it may well be that shortage of calcium from food in early life, especially adolescence, together with an inactive life style, causes permanent fragility of bones (osteoporosis). In turn, this may be why bone fractures, of the hip, thigh and back, are now so common in old people. A major review published in the *New England Journal of Medicine* in 1986[51] estimated that osteoporosis causes well over a million bone fractures every year in the USA, at an annual cost of $6000 million. Scaled down for a population one-fifth that of the USA, these figures suggest that weakened bones may be causing over 200,000 fractures a year in Britain, at a cost of perhaps £750 million a year.

What about Britain? A study of 375 11- and 14-year-old children published in the *British Journal of Nutrition* in 1984[52] confirmed that many adolescents are short of calcium, and that if chalk were not added to white bread the situation would be much worse:

> The consequence of the inadequate calcium intake at this critical stage of skeletal development is likely to be less dense bone on maturity, with the prospect of an increased likelihood of skeletal fractures in later life.

The best source of calcium is small fish, eaten bones and all: sardines, sprats, whitebait, for example. In the old days people got much of their calcium from gnawing bones, or cracking them open and rendering them down in stews. Dairy products – milk, cheese and yoghurt – are also good sources of calcium.

There is no Sprat Marketing Board, which is a pity, because sprats, in common with all fatty fish, are altogether nourishing. There is, however, a Milk Marketing Board, which since its foundation in 1933 has monopolized milk-wholesaling in Britain and is subsidized by the government to produce and sell more milk than the consumer wants.[53] In the 1980s the milk industry has been in difficulties. It is now accepted that saturated fats cause heart attacks; and milk, together with cream and cheese, supplies more than a quarter of the saturated fats in the British food supply – and also over half the calcium.[39]

In 1985 the Milk Marketing Board imported an American researcher, Dr David McCarron, who was reported in *Farming News* to be putting the 'CASE FOR FAT'.[54] Pictured holding a milk bottle, Dr McCarron, who believes that heart attacks are caused by lack of calcium, was reported as saying:

> It's dangerous for public health administrators to ignore the risk of heart disease for those who restrict calcium intake due to fear of dairy products.

At the same time, the National Dairy Council launched its 'Everybody's Body Needs Bottle' campaign[55] with this headline:

CALCIUM IS ESSENTIAL IN MAINTAINING STRONG HEALTHY TEETH AND BONES THROUGHOUT YOUR LIFE – AND MILK IS THE MAJOR SOURCE OF CALCIUM IN YOUR DIET.

FAT-FREE DIETS CAN
BREAK YOUR BONES

In the summer of 1986 a *Daily Telegraph* headline jumped off a news page. 'FAT-FREE DIETS CAN BREAK YOUR BONES'.[56] The story described a horrible disease. As it progressed, 'the victim might gradually lose one or two inches in height, and develop a humped back, commonly called "Dowager's Hump".' Bones could break spontaneously. Dr Michael Turner, described as a 'nutritional scientist', was quoted as saying:

Advice to reduce fat intake to prevent coronary artery disease could lead people to reduce their consumption of milk and dairy products, the main sources of dietary calcium.

He went on to claim that one in every four women in the USA now suffers from osteoporosis. The message was – drink milk, or maybe crumble.

The source of this story was a conference organized by the National Dairy Council. Dr Michael Turner, the former Director-General of the British Nutrition Foundation,[40] did also point out (as does the National Dairy Council, rather discreetly), that skimmed milk and semi-skimmed milk contain just as much calcium as full-fat milk. So where did the 'FAT-FREE DIETS CAN BREAK YOUR BONES' horror story come from? In early 1986 I received *Nutrition Briefing*,[57] a newsletter produced by the 'Nutritional Consultative Panel' who would, so the accompanying letter said,[58]

be extremely grateful if on their behalf you could publicise the information contained in this briefing paper in your journal, so that their expert and balanced view on the nutritional aspects of milk and milk products can be made available to your readers.

And indeed, despite its title, the newsletter, published five times between March 1986 and January 1987, was all about milk. It answered various questions. Does school milk make children fat? No. Does milk make children liable to suffer from heart attacks later in life? No. Is milk an important source of calcium, and a protection against osteoporosis? Absolutely.

Before passing on this good news to my readers, I enquired about the 'Nutritional Consultative Panel'. Its Chairman was Professor Ian Macdonald, who was then also Chairman of the BNF. Its ten other members include Dr Richard Cottrell, Science Director of the BNF; Dr David Gammack, Technical Director at St Ivel (a division of the dairy retail giant Unigate); and two members of the main COMA committee, Professor Michael Gurr, who later in 1986 became a full-time employee of the Milk Marketing Board, and Dr Roger Whitehead, head of the Dunn Clinical Nutrition Laboratory in Cambridge.

I was also told that the Panel worked to the 'Joint Committee'. The Joint Committee of what? Although the letter sent on behalf of the Nutritional Consultative Panel shyly didn't say so, it's of the Dairy Trades Federation and the Milk Marketing Board.

We need vitamin B1 and calcium for good health; and both protect against disease. There is good evidence that millions of people in Britain today, perhaps young people especially, are short of these and other vitamins and minerals, and that their health is harmed as a result. Yet the messages we get about vitamin B1 come either from the bread industry, advertising white bread drained of nourishment, or from the breakfast cereal industry, most of whose products are sugared and salted. The messages we get about calcium come from the milk industry, which is intent on denying that the saturated fats in full-fat milk cause heart attacks.

HOW TO TREAT AN OLD SAD SICK SIKH

It's all completely legal, of course. Suppose S. Wizz plc decides to make health claims about Swizzo, a (fictitious, of course) fun food made mostly of fats and sugars stuck together with chemical additives, plus coal-tar dyes for technicolour. All Mr Wizz has to do is to tell his minions in the Wizzo Organoleptics Division to sprinkle some synthetic vitamins, plus iron powder and chalk, on to the product, to specifications sanctioned by the DHSS and MAFF. Swizzo can then boast on the label it contains 'VITAMINS B1, B3 AND C, IRON AND CALCIUM – ESSENTIAL FOR HEALTHY GROWTH', illustrating its claim with pictures of children leaping about full of vim and vigour. In smaller print, the label will make some such statement as 'A serving of Swizzo contains at least one-sixth of the Recommended Daily Amount of thiamin (vitamin B1), niacin (vitamin B3), iron and calcium.'

What does all this mean? What is a Recommended Daily Amount? Here is how the system works.

In so far as Britain has a policy on any aspect of food and health, it depends on government commissioning and then accepting a relevant report of the Committee on Medical Aspects of Food Policy (COMA). The best-known COMA report was the one published in 1984, on *Diet and Cardiovascular Disease*,[59] which identified saturated fats as a cause of heart attacks. How exactly does COMA work? The official word is that:[60]

> COMA is a committee of independent experts chaired by the Chief Medical Officer who appoints the Members who always include the Chief Scientist at MAFF .... Appointment to COMA is considered to be a distinction in scientific circles. But Government looks to COMA for independent scientific advice on matters relating to nutrition, diet and health .... COMA meets twice yearly but operates mainly through a system of Sub-Committees and expert Panels set up to consider and report on particular matters.

So COMA is the central DHSS expert advisory committee, equivalent to MAFF's Food Advisory Committee (FAC), described in chapter 4. COMA panels are set up from time to time to produce reports when civil servants see a need for them. This is typically for one of four reasons.

O Nutritional surveillance. Some groups of the population have special need of good food. These include babies, children, adolescents, pregnant women and the elderly. These 'vulnerable' or 'at-risk' groups are occasionally studied by the COMA Sub-Committee on Nutritional Surveillance or by other COMA panels. Recent reports include *Artificial Feeds for the Young Infant* (1980)[61] and *A Nutrition Survey of Pre-School Children, 1967-68* (1975).[62]

O Reaction to scientific evidence. When the case linking some foodstuff and disease becomes very strong, a COMA panel may be set up. The evidence showing that fibre protects against some diseases led to the COMA report on *Nutritional Aspects of Bread and Flour* (1981),[9] and the evidence linking fats, especially saturated fats, with heart disease led to two COMA reports, *Diet and Coronary Heart Disease* (1974)[63] and the well-known *Diet and Cardiovascular Disease* (1984).[64]

O Reaction to industry developments. When new foodstuffs are invented, the COMA Sub-Committee on Novel Foods or other COMA panels may produce a report. For example, *Foods Which Simulate Meat* (1980)[65] was produced in response to the boom in 'meat' made from soy beans. Likewise, *The Report on the Safety and Wholesomeness of Irradiated Foods* (1986)[66] of which more later in this chapter, was produced in response to plans to expand the food irradiation industry, and nuclear power in general, in Britain.

O Reaction to government decisions. *The Diets of British Schoolchildren* (1986)[47] was commissioned at the insistence of the COMA Nutritional Surveillance Committee, which was anxious about Mrs Thatcher's policy of abandoning nutritional standards for school meals. An earlier Panel, designed to monitor the effects of Mrs Thatcher's decision to abandon free milk for all schoolchildren was set up in 1973; its report surfaced in 1981.[67]

In theory, a COMA report on vitamins and minerals could be set up for any of these reasons. Is lack of vitamin B1 really leading to diseases of the nervous system, and anaemia in British children, and is iron-deficiency anaemia in children increasing? Is it true that deficiency of nutrients whose function was not understood fifty years ago is causing 'new' diseases? For example, is pre-menstrual syndrome caused by lack of vitamin B6? What effect is the boom in fast food having on the quality of the food supply? Are people who eat a lot of cheap food badly nourished? Are there signs that privatized school meals are having ill effects on children who also eat a lot of sweet, fat food away from home and school? The general position of the DHSS on questions such as these is contained in a private document circulated by the DHSS which came into my hands in 1985:[68]

> Malnutrition arising from vitamin/nutrient deficiency is rare in Britain. It is mainly confined to immigrant groups to whom preventive and therapeutic measures are being directed, and the elderly in whom malnutrition, where it exists, occurs almost exclusively in association with medical problems of conditions such as depression following bereavement.

So the DHSS attitude is that if you are a sick Sikh you are probably all right; but if you are an old sad sick Sikh you may be in trouble. The official line is that illness caused by shortage of vitamins and minerals is not a public health problem in Britain today. Don't worry. Be happy. Trust the experts. If little Johnny is acting up, give him some drugs or send him to the psychiatrist.

NO SCURVY, NO PROBLEM – OFFICIAL

Who are the experts on vitamins and minerals? Soon after the Second World War, the BMA set up a 'Committee on Nutrition', whose report was published in 1950.[18] The job of this committee, which was independent of but recognized by government, was to work out how much energy (calories), protein, vitamins and minerals people need from food, in the light of knowledge of nutrition and the wartime experience.

The BMA committee acknowledged that many of the standards laid down in its report were rough and ready: 'that there are gaps and guesses here and there is freely admitted'. It was encouraged and influenced by the evidence that during the war the British people enjoyed good health.

Because of the improvements in the quality of the wartime food supply, the standards set for the well understood vitamins and minerals, which became known as Recommended Daily Amounts (RDAs), were no longer targets, as proposed by John Boyd Orr, but were below the amounts that most people were already consuming. The belief was that Boyd Orr's targets had been reached, and that the job in future would be the relatively humdrum maintenance and surveillance of a generally healthy population.

In one case, vitamin C (ascorbic acid), a highly significant distinction was made between US and British standards. In 1948 the American National Research Council set a standard of 75 to 100 mg of vitamin C a day, on the grounds that this was the amount needed to saturate the blood with vitamin C. The MRC Committee 'was unable to find any trustworthy evidence that maintenance of saturation of the blood with vitamin C was desirable in the interest of health' and instead relied on an MRC study carried out between 1944 and 1946 which showed that 10 mg a day was enough to prevent scurvy. On this basis, a British standard of 20 to 30 mg a day was set: 10 to avoid scurvy and another 10 to 20 to be on the safe side.

This 'minimum plus' standard has been dismissed by Dr Albert Szent-Gyorgyi, who first isolated vitamin C in 1928 and won the Nobel Prize for his work, in the following words:[69]

> The medical profession itself took a very narrow and wrong view. Lack of ascorbic acid caused scurvy, so if there was no scurvy there was no lack of ascorbic acid. Nothing could be clearer than this. The only trouble was that scurvy is not a first symptom of lack but final collapse, a premortal syndrome, and there is a very wide gap between scurvy and full health.

How wide is this gap? There is good evidence that gatherer-hunter peoples, who ate a lot of fresh fruit and vegetables rich in vitamin C, consumed about 400 mg a day.[70] It is probable that vitamin C has other properties than the prevention of scurvy; these include healing powers after trauma such as drugs or surgery, and, with other vitamins and minerals, protection against cancers.[71,72] A review published in the *New England Journal of Medicine* in 1986[73] suggested that optimum consumption of vitamin C is about 100 to 200 mg a day. The current US standard is 60 mg a day.[74]

From the point of view of a Whitehall policy-maker, a standard of 30 mg a day has a great advantage, as the following table demonstrates. It shows MAFF[39] and DHSS[48] estimates of vitamin C consumption in Britain in recent years. The figures for children are taken from *The Diets of British Schoolchildren*.[47]

Vitamin C. Average daily consumption in Britain. All ages (1981–84) and children of 15 years old (1983).

All:	1981 mg	1982 mg	1983 mg	1984 mg	Children:	Boys mg	Girls mg
	59	57	57	55		49	48

If the standard were set at 60 mg a day, these figures would show a worrying situation getting worse: for 'average' figures that come out just below the standard mean that maybe half or more of the population is sub-standard. The lower figures for children show that they are eating even less fresh food than adults. The result of a 60 mg standard? Television programmes identifying a new crisis in British public health; questions in the House of Commons; demand for the reintroduction of nutritional standards for school meals. In other words, trouble. Whereas, with a standard of 30 mg a day, government can say, hand on heart, that everybody (well, nearly everybody) in Britain is consuming more than the officially agreed RDA of vitamin C. No problem.

Nobody in government is going to create a public health problem by proposing a new standard for vitamin C of, say, 60 mg a day. The task of civil servants is to make the life of their masters easier, not more difficult. You can therefore be sure that the British RDA for vitamin C will remain at 30 mg a day for the indefinite future.

In 1950, the BMA issued standards for the other vitamins and minerals it felt able to assess: vitamins A, B1, B2, B3, C

and D, calcium and iron. On 'other B vitamins', the report
said:

> The Committee is of the opinion that it is not yet possible to
> assess human needs for folic acid, pyridoxin, pantothenic acid,
> biotin and other recently discovered components of this group
> of nutrients.

No reference was made to other minerals. Readers were
reminded in the summary that 'Nutrition is a young and
rapidly growing science. Much of the field is still unexplored
or only half explored.'

The DHSS then took over responsibility for setting
standards for vitamins and minerals from the BMA, and in
1969 issued a COMA report on *Recommended Daily Intakes
of Nutrients for the United Kingdom.*[7] Various nutrients
were discussed briefly. Vitamin B6? 'Most diets in this
country provide 1 to 2 mg/day and this appears to be
enough for most people.' Folic acid? 'The vitamin is widely
distributed in foods.' Vitamin B12? 'Dietary vitamin B12
deficiency is exceedingly rare in this country.' Pantothenic
acid? 'Diets in the UK usually provide 10 to 20 mg which is
more than adequate.' Vitamin E? 'There is no evidence upon
which a valid estimate of requirement can be based.' Vitamin
K? 'Under normal conditions a dietary deficiency of vitamin
K is rarely if ever seen.' Essential fats (sometimes classed as a
vitamin)? 'There is no unequivocal evidence that man ever
develops any deficiency disease as a result of a dietary lack;
if such a condition does occur, it must be exceedingly rare.'
Magnesium? 'A dietary deficiency of magnesium is unlikely
to occur in health.' Other minerals? 'Other elements known
to be essential in human metabolism are copper, zinc,
manganese, cobalt, selenium, molybdenum and chromium.
No deficiencies of these elements have been reported among
the UK population, and it must be concluded that our diet
contains adequate amounts.' The general principle was clear.
No signs of deficiency disease: no problem. No problem: no
Recommended Daily Amount.

The scheduled vitamins and minerals remained unchanged from 1950, although the RDAs were adjusted a bit:
vitamin C up to 30 mg a day, for example; calcium and iron
down. The report's short bibliography was not referenced

back to the text, so few readers could have checked the authority on which its judgements were based.

In 1979 another COMA report appeared: *Recommended Daily Amounts of Food Energy and Nutrients for Groups of People in the United Kingdom.*[8] The title was designed to emphasize that RDAs are now officially set for groups of people, not for individuals. So if anybody – you, for example – is consuming less than the RDA, there's (officially) almost certainly nothing to worry about:

> Surveys in this and other developed countries have shown that, although for many nutrients a substantial proportion of people have intakes which are less than those recommended, objective evidence of nutritional deficiency is rare.

What about the vitamins and minerals not scheduled in 1969? One paragraph disposed of 19 of them:[8]

> Other nutrients .... these include the vitamins B6, B12, pantothenic acid, biotin, vitamin E, vitamin K, and the inorganic elements magnesium, potassium, sodium, chloride, chromium, cobalt, copper, iodine, manganese, molybdenum, phosphorus, selenium and zinc, all of which are essential to human health. Deficiency of these vitamins and minerals is either rare, or associated with certain medical conditions, or has not been described or confirmed in man in the United Kingdom. With the exception of vitamin B12, which is found almost entirely only in foods of animal origin, those other nutrients occur in sufficient quantity in a large number of foods. Therefore in the light of present knowledge and in the context of the United Kingdom diet, recommended amounts for these nutrients have not been set.

This report was referenced: a couple of studies on vitamin E were cited, for example, a couple on zinc, and three reviews of trace elements in general, none British. The introduction said that:

> Over the past decade ... there has been relatively little new information on the basis of which the figures should be altered ... The resulting table of recommended daily amounts differs little from Table 1 of the 1969 report.

Indeed so. The list of scheduled vitamins and minerals was the same as in 1950 and 1969, and the standards much the same. Just one new vitamin was scheduled; folic acid, a B vitamin, with an RDA of 300 mg and 500 mcg in pregnancy.

Both the 1969 and the 1979 COMA reports took the view that standards need be set for essential nutrients only when there is accepted evidence of disease in the British population caused by deficiency of that nutrient. But the diseases caused by gross deficiency of energy, protein, vitamins A, B1, B2, B3 and C (marasmus, kwashiorkor, xerophthalmia, beri-beri, riboflavinosis, pellagra and scurvy)[5,10] are officially estimated to be rare or unknown in Britain. In this case, the only possible justification for scheduling these nutrients is inertia – they're there because they're there. Only three deficiency diseases are generally accepted as a public health problem in Britain: rickets and osteomalacia (vitamin D and calcium)[75] and anaemia (iron).[76] So the official COMA line is specious.

Why then was folic acid scheduled in 1979? What was the problem? The only hint the report gave was 'the recommended amount is increased during pregnancy'. Why are British women suffering from shortage of folic acid? The 1979 COMA report wasn't telling. More about folic acid later in this chapter.

BRITISH STANDARDS:
THE WORST IN EUROPE

Governments all over the world regularly issue official reports setting standards for energy (calories) from food, together with protein, vitamins and minerals.[77] These Recommended Daily Amounts (RDAs) of scheduled nutrients are of great importance for public health. In so far as any country has a national food and health policy, it is reflected in its RDAs. Scheduled vitamins and minerals gain an image as 'goodies', and in turn foods claiming to contain relatively large amounts of scheduled nutrients gain a 'goodie' image.

The standards set for vitamins and minerals, energy and

protein, influence government decisions on all aspects of national – and international – food policy. They affect government investment in and subsidy of food production, and therefore they influence official attitudes to the food and farming industries. They determine the way nutrition is taught, and the advice given directly to the public by professionals such as dietitians, health visitors and nurses. Institutional caterers who supply food to schools, hospitals, the armed forces and prisons use RDAs as their guide in buying and preparing food. RDAs also mould consumer choice. In their advertisements, point-of-sale material and food labels, manufacturers can only claim special value for those nutrients allocated RDAs.[78]

All this in turn affects food composition. Only scheduled nutrients can be restored to or added to processed foods. If only for this reason, it is not difficult to construct a 'balanced diet', as officially defined by the DHSS, from highly processed food. For a 'normal, balanced, varied diet' means what the DHSS says it means: a diet supplying the recommended daily amounts of energy, protein, vitamins A, B1, B2, B3, folic acid (maybe – see later), C, D, calcium and iron. The other vitamins and minerals now known to be vital to human health are officially irrelevant. A mother who feeds her child with sugared and salted breakfast cereal fortified with riboflavin (B2) is allowed to believe that she is doing the right thing. A woman who fortifies herself with pyridoxine (B6) has to buy the stuff as pills from a funny food shop and feels like a food faddist.

The quality of any national food and health policy can be judged by the standards set for vitamins and minerals. Britain has the lowest standards in Europe. An analysis done by the International Union of Nutritional Sciences in 1983[77] shows that no European country has lower standards than Britain for vitamins A, C, D and calcium. Only Hungary has lower standards for vitamin B1 and B2; only West Germany and Poland have lower standards for B3; only Finland and Hungary have lower standards for iron. Compared with every country in the world that sets standards for vitamins and minerals, Britain has below-average standards for all vitamins and minerals except iron.

Britain also sets standards for fewer vitamins and minerals

than any other country in Europe with the exception of Portugal (at the last count). Over the last forty years the value of a couple of dozen vitamins and minerals in maintaining health and protecting against disease has become well understood. A number of European countries, notably France, West Germany, East Germany and the Scandinavian nations, have set standards for some of these nutrients. Britain has not done so.

The most remarkable contrast, is between British and US standards for vitamins and minerals. British standards essentially rely on the science of half a century ago; they have not been significantly revised since 1950. They are based on the negative 'minimum plus' principle: enough to prevent clinically observable deficiency disease of a specific nutrient, plus a substantial safety factor.

US standards[74] are based on the state of knowledge in the late 1970s. All the vitamins and minerals now well known to be essential to human health are scheduled in the USA. American standards today are goals that a highly processed food supply will not readily reach. In the USA, it is officially accepted that vitamins and minerals are positively valuable, to maintain good health.

In Britain, the scientists who set standards work to the DHSS, and their reports are effectively instruments of government. In Britain, low standards are set for six vitamins and two minerals. In the USA, the scientists who set standards work to the National Academy of Sciences, a body somewhat like the Royal Society in Britain, independent of but accepted by government. In the USA, high standards are set for thirteen vitamins and twelve minerals. These are not merely differences of scientific judgement. They reveal two completely different attitudes to public health. In Britain, public health problems are obscured; in the USA, they are exposed. In turn, this shows the difference between the national character of Britain and the USA: it is the difference between stagnation and free flow; between a closed and an open society.

This table shows the standards set for vitamins and minerals in Britain (UK RDAs) and the USA (US RDAs). Just in case you think that Americans always overdo things the standards set in the Soviet Union (USSR RDAs) are also given.

Vitamins and Minerals. Standards set in Britain (UK RDAs), in the USA (US RDAs) and in the Soviet Union (USSR RDAs)

		UK RDAs		US RDAs		USSR RDAs	
		Adult[a]	Pregnant Woman	Adult[a]	Pregnant Woman	Adult[a]	Pregnant Woman
Vitamins:							
A (retinol/carotene)	mcg	750	750	1000	1000	1500	1750[b]
D (cholecalciferol)	mcg	2.5	10	5	10	2.5	12.5
E (alpha-tocopherol)	mg	None	None	10	10	15[b]	17.5[b]
K	mcg	None	None	110[b]	110[b]	250[b]	250[b]
C (ascorbic acid)	mg	30	60	60	80	80[b]	150[b]
B1 (thiamin)	mg	1.2	1.0	1.4	1.4	1.8[b]	2.5[b]
B2 (riboflavin)	mg	1.6	1.6	1.6	1.6	2.5[b]	3.25[b]
B3 (niacin)	mg	18	18	18	16	20[b]	20
B6 (pyridoxine)	mg	None	None	2.2	2.6	2	4
B12 (cobalamin)	mcg	2[c]	2[c]	3	4	2	12.5[b]
Folic acid	mcg	300[c]	300[c]	400	800	400	400
Pantothenic acid	mg	None	None	5.5[b]	5.5[b]	10	27.5[b]
Biotin	mcg	None	None	150[b]	150[b]	None	None
Minerals:							
Potassium (K)	mg	None	None	3750[b]	3750[b]	3750[b]	3750[b]
Sodium (Na)	mg	None	None	2200[b]	2200[b]	5000[b]	7500[b]
Chloride (Cl)	mg	None	None	3400[b]	3400[b]	5000[b]	5000[b]
Calcium (Ca)	mg	500	1200	800	1200	800	1500
Phosphorus (P)	mg	None	None	800	1200	1600	2500
Magnesium (Mg)	mg	None	None	350	450	500	925
Iron (Fe)	mg	12	15	10	48[d]	17.5	17.5
Zinc (Zn)	mg	None	None	15	20	12.5	12.5
Copper (Cu)	mg	None	None	2.5[b]	2.5[b]	2.5[b]	2.5[b]
Iodine (I)	mcg	140[c]	140[c]	150	150	150	150
Selenium (Se)	mcg	None	None	125[b]	125[b]	None	None
Chromium (Cr)	mcg	None	None	125[b]	125[b]	None	None

Taken from[77].
a standard for 'moderately active' adult male.
b midpoint of range.
c Not DHSS RDAs, but sanctioned by MAFF for use by food manufacturers.
d supplements recommended in pregnancy.

The differences are the most important thing about this table. First, the USA and USSR set standards for far more vitamins and minerals than Britain does. Second, almost all the standards in those countries are higher than in Britain. Third, the health of pregnant women in the USA and USSR is protected by standards which are mostly much higher than those set for non-pregnant adults.

The job of professionals such as dietitians and caterers, is to translate national standards into food. A number of nutrients scheduled in the USA and USSR but officially ignored in Britain, are found in abundance in whole, fresh food, but are drained from highly processed food. These include the minerals potassium, magnesium and zinc. The implication of the US and Soviet standards is that everybody in those countries, particularly pregnant women, is encouraged to eat whole cereals, and fresh vegetables, fruit and meat. The British standards, by contrast, accommodate a lot more empty calories – processed fats and sugars. In Britain, government sanctions the manufacturers of fatty, sugary processed foods to tout their products to those people most in need of nourishing food – mothers and babies.

The only coherent way to judge the quality of any food supply is to see how it measures up to comprehensive standards set for all the nutrients well-known to be vital to human health. How does the food we eat in Britain today measure up to the goals set by the US RDAs for vitamins and minerals? British food achieves the US goals, or near enough, for those vitamins and minerals scheduled in Britain, with the exceptions of vitamin D and iron. But, by the standards set in the USA, people in Britain are notably short of potassium and zinc, and of two vitamins found in fresh food, vitamin B6 and folic acid.

In Britain we are not encouraged to know or care about these nutrients. The general attitude in Britain is that food fusspots can grow vegetables in their own gardens and bake their own bread if they want to; but it's a free country, and after all, we don't want a nanny state or wartime rations back again, do we?

YOU'D BE BETTER OFF IN RUSSIA

The Americans care. So do the Russians. In December 1985 the *Guardian* published a news story[79] in which Professor Vladimir Spirichev of the Institute of Nutrition in Moscow was quoted as saying, 'we now confront a national problem of partial vitamin deficiency'. Changes in Russian life are having a bad effect on public health, Professor Spirichev explained. People are becoming sedentary and so eating less food – and less food means less nourishment. Wholegrain black rye bread is being replaced by white bread. And 'modern methods of food processing and preservation also destroy the vitamins in natural foods.' There was a plan to add 7000 tonnes of vitamins to the Russian food supply.

I was intrigued, and wrote to Professor Spirichev asking for more details. In his reply, he told me that the plan has been accepted by the Ministry of Public Health in Moscow, having been approved by the State Committee of Science and Technology and the State Committee of Planning. He sent me a copy of an interview he had given to *Izvestia*[80] on which the *Guardian* item had been based. He said, as quoted:

Nowadays people suffer from marginal deficiency of various vitamins. There are no obvious manifestations of deficiency. But people feel unwell, get tired easily, often get colds. The food supply now is up to 30 or 40 per cent short of vitamins. People survive, but are stressed and exhausted. We have examined different groups of people – factory and farm workers, schoolchildren, students, for example. They all suffer from shortage of vitamin C: levels of ascorbic acid in the blood are depleted, down to one third of a healthy level.

Dr Andrei Bogatyrev, Assistant Chief of the Industrial and Agricultural Complex Managing Department added:

Long-term vitamin deficiency is harmful. It affects public health, and industrial productivity. At big factories, the number of days off sick fell by 6 to 7 per cent after we added vitamins to the workers' food. If this policy was carried out nationally it could save 1.5 billion roubles a year.

At the official rate of exchange a rouble is worth a pound, so 1.5 billion roubles is £1.5 billion. In the *Izvestia* interview, Professor Spirichev explained that vitamin C protects against cancers and heart attacks and that vitamin A protects against stomach cancers. He went on to say:

Some studies have shown that 98 per cent of babies born premature or with birth defects, or with various physical or mental subnormalities, had mothers whose food was deficient in

folic acid and other nutrients. Vitamin-rich food is vital for
young people.

OFFICIALLY SECRET ADVISORS:
WHO ARE THESE GUYS? (II)

Professor Spirichev and Dr Bogatyrev would not be welcome
at the DHSS or MAFF. In Britain, scientists who believe that
food technology is or may be a threat to public health are
rarely asked to serve on government advisory committees.
Just as official reports on food and health are effectively
instruments of government, so members of the committees
that produce the reports tend to be drawn from those
advisors whose views are harmonious with government
policy.

This does not mean that when scientists become
government advisors they change their views to suit the
government of the day. A good many members of COMA are
men (they are almost always men) with international
reputations and established views. But most government
advisors on food and health are sure that there is or should
be no conflict between the interests of government, science
and industry or, come to that, of the consumer as well.

Members of the main COMA committee sign the Official
Secrets Act, and members of COMA panels are covered by
the Official Secrets Act.[81] Some academics resent this
arrangement; others enjoy it. It can be thrilling to enter into
the *arcana imperii* – the mysteries of government. Until very
recently government advisors on food and health in Britain
have also been shielded from scrutiny by public ignorance of
and indifference to their work. If you and I, and our elected
representatives in Parliament, do not care about food, and do
not believe that the quality of food has anything to do with
the quality of life, then we are not going to get steamed up
about official reports with dull and boring titles.

Suppose, though, that Britain were bristling with
well-informed journalists and vigorous consumer groups.
Suppose (just to take one example, of which more later) that
well conducted organizations such as the National
Consumer Council shared Professor Spirichev's view that

food rich in folic acid provides vital protection against birth defects. Suppose also, that a major, nationally networked television programme exposed the facts that highly processed food is a very poor source of folic acid; that the rate of spina bifida and other birth defects is higher in Britain than in any other developed country in the world;[82] that the national average consumption of folic acid is far lower than the standards set by the DHSS in 1979;[83] that scientists who have studied the subject for years believe that British women risk having deformed babies because the British food supply is drained of folic acid and other nutrients;[84,85] and produced evidence that government officials were covering these facts up. In such a case, COMA reports setting standards for folic acid would be read with interest, debate about this one example of food and public health would open up, and democracy would be served.

As it is, COMA and such-like committees are private affairs. John Rivers of the Department of Nutrition at London University, whose forthright views have already been quoted in this book, wrote this in the Nutrition Society's own newsletter in 1985:[86]

> We nutritionists are on the whole a sibilant species happiest when breathing our views gently into the official ear. We are a profession dominated by consultants, advisors, and official committee members used always to acting in the acceptable shadows. In relation to our limited numbers, our contacts with the world of industry and of policy are staggering, possibly without parallel amongst the scientific professions. Though whether our influence is in the same proportion depends on how far we are, as a group, puppet masters rather than puppets.

Twenty people served on the COMA panel that produced the 1979 report on standards for vitamins and minerals: eighteen men and two women. Four were government officials: Sir Henry Yellowlees, then Chief Medical Officer at the DHSS; Dr Richard Bevan and Professor Sir John Reid, Sir Henry's Welsh and Scottish equivalents; and Professor George Elton, Chief Scientist at MAFF. Sir Henry and Dr Elton combined their official responsibilities with membership of committees of the BNF, which is funded by the food industry.

The BNF was remarkably well represented. Of the 20 COMA members, 12 also served on BNF committees. The other ten were Professor John Durnin; Dorothy Hollingsworth (BNF Director-General from 1970 to 1977); Dr Egon Kodicek; Dr Reg Passmore; Professor Angus Thomson; Professor Stewart Truswell (Chairman of the BNF Scientific Advisory Committee from 1976 to 1977); Professor John Waterlow (BNF Chairman from 1976 to 1977); Dr Roger Whitehead; Dr Elsie Widdowson (who, as already mentioned, was to become BNF President in 1986); and Sir Frank Young (BNF President from 1973 to 1975).[40]

The remaining six COMA members were Dr Henry Bunjé, from the MRC; Sir John Butterfield of Cambridge University; Professor Arthur Exton-Smith, an expert on the health of old people; Professor Thomas Oppé, an expert on child health; Professor Sir Robert Williams, of the Public Health Laboratory Service; and Professor John Yudkin of the Department of Nutrition at London University.

Professor Yudkin has no-nonsense views about vitamins and minerals. In a popular book *The A-Z of Slimming*[87] published in 1977, he wrote:

Vitamins occur in the food we eat, and if we eat correctly, then we should – with very few exceptions – get all the vitamins we need .... If [vitamins and minerals are] missing, it's your fault! ... any sensible way of eating will give you these nutrients.

In early 1979, Dr Passmore and Miss Hollingsworth collaborated on 'Prescription for a Better British Diet',[88] published in the *British Medical Journal*. They claimed that, with the possible exception of folic acid, British food is 'already well endowed' with vitamins, and that 'diets in Britain already provide more than the present recommended intakes of most nutrients.'

In 1977 Professor Waterlow wrote that:[89]

Once you have decided the calorie (energy) requirements of any group – be they miners, athletes or schoolchildren, the rest will be alright, except for one or two nutrients like ascorbic acid.

In his introduction to the BNF book *Why Additives?*[90] published in 1977, Sir Frank Young wrote that:

Much of the food on the shelves of a supermarket, or of a shop with personal service, has been treated before it is ready for sale in order that its shelf life may be prolonged and its quality retained. With some foods such treatment may cause a small diminution in the amounts present of available protein, vitamins and minerals, but this is not serious and can be easily counterbalanced.

Like his COMA colleagues, Dr Roger Whitehead has strong views about vitamins. He also served on the COMA panel on 'Nutritional Aspects of Bread and Flour'.[9] A set of the Officially Secret minutes of this committee is in my possession. On 9 October 1978, Dr Whitehead is minuted as stating, of bread processing:[91]

> 6.1.11 Dr Whitehead said that since vitamin consumption in this country vastly exceeds prescribed minimum amounts, the consideration of which vitamins are lost in extraction processes was not biologically important.

Professor Exton-Smith, Dr Kodicek, Professor Oppé and Dr Widdowson, together with Miss Hollingsworth, Dr Passmore, Sir Frank Young and Professor Yudkin, were also members of the COMA panel that set standards for vitamins and minerals in 1969. As such, they had put their names to the following statements about the recommendations (RDAs) they made:[7]

> The recommendations can be met by widely varying combinations of foods commonly consumed in the UK, and intakes for which detailed recommendations are given are almost certainly sufficient .... The recommended intakes, which are judged to be sufficient for practically all members of the population, must of necessity be in excess of the requirements of most of them.

So the views – comfortable to both government and the food-manufacturing industry – of 10 of the 20 members of the 1979 COMA panel, expressed before its report was published, were available to DHSS civil servants. The civil servants aside, the remaining six members of the committee are not, to the best of my knowledge, on record as holding uncomfortable views.

What comes out of a committee depends on what is put in; or, rather, on who is put on. If a government believes that lack of vitamins and minerals is or may be causing public health problems and if such a government is committed to public health, then the relevant civil servants will appoint a committee of experts known to be sympathetic with these views. In that case, such a committee would recommend high standards, like those set for vitamins and minerals in the USA.

If, on the other hand, a government does not believe that vitamins and minerals have much relevance to public health, and/or has a greater commitment to the manufacturers of highly processed food than to the nation's health, then the relevant civil servants will appoint a committee of scientists known to be sympathetic with these views. In this case, such a committee will recommend low standards, like those set for vitamins and minerals in Britain.

That's the way it works.

THE CURSE OF THE CELTS

Too many babies are born dead or damaged in Britain. True, infant death, once very common, is now uncommon, and most women no longer fear childbirth. But by the mid-1970s, Britain's record had deteriorated. In 1976 the DHSS acknowledged that 'we had fallen behind other countries'.[92] In 1980 the House of Commons all-party Select Committee on Social Services produced a major report on *Perinatal and Neonatal Mortality*.[93] The report concluded that between 8000 and 10,000 stillbirths and birth defects could and should be prevented in Britain every year.

A stillborn baby is a great sadness for any parent. A baby born deformed but who survives into childhood and even into adult life can be a great disaster: a burden that not all parents can bear. For many years, child health experts have been troubled by the very high numbers of British and Irish babies born with deformities of the central nervous system: in particular spina bifida (damaged spinal column) or anencephaly (no brain).

Spina bifida is sometimes called 'the curse of the Celts', because rates of spina bifida in Scotland, Wales and Ireland have been by far the highest reliably recorded anywhere in the world.[1] In the mid-1970s, one in every 300 babies born in England and Wales was damaged by spina bifida: a higher rate than elsewhere in Europe. But in Scotland, Wales, Northern Ireland and the Republic of Ireland, the rate was up to one in every 100 in some hospitals.[1] It was officially suggested that 'the capacity to produce offspring with central nervous system malformations may be associated with the Celtic race'.[94]

However, the great variation in the number of spina bifida babies both within one country and between different countries has convinced most child health experts that spina bifida is not congenital, 'an act of God', but environmental in origin. Could one cause of spina bifida and similar deformities (also known as neural tube defects, or NTDs) be the food mothers eat? This was thought unlikely in the 1970s, because the idea that Britain has been a well-fed nation since the Second World War was rarely questioned.[84] As Professor Nicholas Wald of the Department of Environmental Medicine at St Bartholomew's Hospital, London, has said – not in the 1970s but in 1986:[95]

> It is quite bizarre that this country has one of the highest frequencies of NTD in the world – but are we most likely to be malnourished? This is quite clearly not so.

But is it true that pregnant women in Britain are well fed? In 1977 Professor Richard Smithells of the Department of Child Health at Leeds University, with co-workers, published the results of a careful study of 195 pregnant women in the *British Journal of Nutrition*.[96] This revealed that the quality of the food many of the women ate fell short of the standards for vitamins and minerals set by the DHSS. And on average the diets of poor and of young women were sub-standard for all but one of the officially scheduled nutrients. Of 27 teenagers:

> Only four mothers prepared and cooked a meal each day and four did so only on Sunday. Few ate fresh fruit and vegetables and in some records the only source of ascorbic acid was chipped potatoes, which together with fried fish, potato crisps and sandwiches formed a major part of the diet.

These results were confirmed in later studies by Professor Michael Crawford and co-workers in London already referred to in chapter 1.[97,98] So if the Leeds study and the DHSS standards are anything to go by, pregnant women in Britain are often not well fed. In addition, poor, lower-class women eat the most highly processed food, with the least vitamins and minerals; and spina bifida babies are most commonly born to women of lower social class.

So perhaps bad food can damage babies growing in the womb. But is the problem bad food in general, or lack of specific nutrients?

In a further trial carried out in London, Belfast, Chester, Leeds and Manchester, Professor Smithells decided to give a large number of women a multi-vitamin and mineral supplement, and see what happened. Mothers who have already borne a baby with spina bifida or another NTD have a high risk (about 1 in 20) of bearing another damaged baby. So a total of 250 women who had already had an NTD baby were given a multi-vitamin and mineral pill (Pregnavite Forte F) containing vitamins A, B1, B2, B3, B6, folic acid, C. D, calcium and iron as soon as they felt ready to have another baby but before they became pregnant. The results (their babies) were compared with those of 300 mothers who were also at high risk, having had a previous spina bifida child, who were given no special treatment.

From the scientific point of view, an ideal trial would have compared the 250 women given the multi-vitamin pill with an equal number of women given a 'dummy' or 'placebo' pill containing nothing of value; this would have made the trial 'controlled'. But Professor Smithells had problems of medical ethics. Pregnant women need additional nourishment,[7,8,74] and for many years have been given vitamin and mineral pills almost as routine. Guidelines laid down by the Medical Research Council (MRC)[99] state that people must always be given the treatment believed to be best or at least believed to be beneficial; and the Hospital Ethical Committees who decide these things refused to believe that a valueless 'dummy' pill could help mothers most at risk of bearing a damaged baby. So permission for dummy pills was refused, and Professor Smithells and his colleagues had to make do with the 300 'uncontrolled' mothers (not under their care) who had not been given pills of any kind.

Professor Smithells published the results of the trial in

1980, in the *Lancet*.[100,101] Of the 250 mothers given the vitamin and mineral supplements, one had a damaged baby. Of the 300 mothers given no treatment, thirteen (4 per cent) had damaged babies or aborted foetuses. These results were of course highly significant: imperfect science perhaps, but good news for mothers. In 1983, the results of a further study were published in the *Lancet*.[102] This time, of 234 mothers given extra nourishment, two had damaged babies, compared with eleven (5.1 per cent) among 210 unsupplemented mothers. These results were also highly significant, and the conclusion of Professor Smithells and nine colleagues, now working from six centres (Liverpool had been added) was that the 'presumptive evidence of a protective effect of vitamin supplementation remains very strong.'[102] In 1982 Professor Smithells addressed a meeting of Link, the association for parents of spina bifida children, and said:[103]

> It is now highly probable that vitamins exert some protective effect: hence more optimism. It is certain that, in proper doses, they do not harm: hence less caution.

But what causes the damage? Is it bad food in general? Or are spina bifida, anencephaly and other similar defects caused at least in part by deficiency of a specific vitamin or mineral? Attention focused on one B vitamin, folic acid, for a number of reasons. First, it has been known since the 1950s that animals deficient in folic acid produce deformed offspring.[104] Second, certain drugs used to treat epilepsy (valproate) and to protect against malaria (pyrimethamine) are teratogenic, meaning that they cause birth defects (literally, 'monsters'), probably because they cause deficiency of folic acid in the body.[105,106] Third, folic acid, together with other nutrients, is necessary for the development and maintenance of the central nervous system.[107]

Fourth, by the standard set by the DHSS in 1979,[8] most people in Britain are short of folic acid. The 1979 Recommended Daily Amount (RDA) was 300 mcg a day for non-pregnant adults and 500 mcg a day for pregnant women. But an analysis of the British food supply by Dr David Buss of MAFF and co-workers published in the *British*

Journal of Nutrition, also in 1979,[108] showed a national average consumption of 190 mcg – less than half the new official standard for pregnancy. Moreover, this study quoted Dr Israel Chanarin, who works at the MRC Centre at Northwick Park Hospital, Harrow and is a world authority on folic acid, as saying that clinical tests showed that three in every ten British pregnant women are deficient in folic acid.[109]

Fifth, it is not surprising that most people in Britain today are short of folic acid. Until 1979 the DHSS regarded it as an irrelevant vitamin, because no scientist had come up with persuasive evidence of any common disease caused by its deficiency. Anybody who eats plenty of whole grain bread and fresh green vegetables and potatoes will be well nourished with folic acid. But most of it is lost in the making of white bread, and, as it is a fragile vitamin, most of it is destroyed by processing and over-cooking.[23]

But what about 'the curse of the Celts'? People in Scotland, Wales and Northern Ireland do indeed eat even smaller amounts of fresh vegetables than people in England[39]. Do they consume even less folic acid than people in England? If so, this would provide a sixth reason to suspect that deficiency of folic acid causes deformities of the cent.al nervous system. In 1979 it looked as if the government would itself provide the answer to this question. When a vitamin or mineral is scheduled by the DHSS with an official Recommended Daily Amount, MAFF is then obliged to give details of the consumption of that nutrient in all regions of Great Britain in *Household Food Consumption and Expenditure*, which is published every year by HMSO.[39] So, by 1983 or 1984 at the latest, the official figures for folic acid consumption in Scotland and Wales would be out in the open for all to see.

Professor Michael Laurence of the Department of Child Health at the Welsh National School of Medicine, Cardiff, has been studying birth defects in South Wales since the 1950s.[110] In 1980, with co-workers, he published a study in the *British Medical Journal* showing that women successfully encouraged to eat more good food are less likely to bear damaged babies. In 1981, impressed by the evidence on folic acid, he published another study[111] in which 44 high-risk women who took folic acid supplements were compared with 61 who did not. Most of them were given a 'dummy' pill, so this was a partially controlled trial. It was a success. None of the supplemented women bore a damaged baby, whereas six of the women given the dummy pill had damaged babies. The women were also classified into those who normally ate 'good', 'fair' and 'inadequate' food. Ten of the women given supplements ate inferior food; all had perfect children. All six of the damaged babies or foetuses were born to unsupplemented women whose food was classified 'inadequate'.

This small trial, which took six years to complete, convinced Professor Laurence that bad food is the key cause of NTDs. In 1984 he went public. The *South Wales Echo* of 13 February 1984 carried the following headline[85]

SOUTH WALES PROJECT TO PREVENT TRAGIC ILLNESS. POP, CHIPS BLAMED FOR SPINA BIFIDA.

The feature article began:

The massive consumption of chips, cakes, sweets and pop has now been pinpointed as the most likely reason for the high rate of spina bifida babies in South Wales.

Professor Laurence was quoted as follows:

For generations women in South Wales have grown up on a poor diet which has included too many buns, chips, sweets and pop, and what vegetables are eaten have had all the goodness boiled out of them. This type of diet which was prompted through necessity has been passed down from mother to daughter until people actually grew to like this sort of food. Strangely the advent of deep frozen vegetables which only need a few minutes cooking has started to change these habits. But you still find people who will cook their vegetables to bits. This destroys the goodness including folic acid.

Results like those of Professor Smithells, Professor Laurence and their colleagues may come only once in the lifetime of research scientists. The results 'were far in excess of what we had dreamed of,' said Mary Seller, head of the London centre at Guys Hospital working with Professor Smithells in an interview with the Roman Catholic newspaper *The Universe* in 1984.[112] The *Daily Telegraph* reported a speech by Dr Chris Schorah, one of the Leeds team, to an international conference held at Innsbruck in 1986:[113]

SPINA BIFIDA BLAMED ON VITAMIN LACK ... Dr C.J. Schorah of Leeds University ... suggested that high-risk women, who had already had a spina bifida baby, should take folic acid supplements, especially in South Wales and Belfast where the condition was more common .... Dr Schorah urged an improvement in diet to include foods with high folic acid content.

Professor John Edwards of the department of Biochemistry at Oxford University, an authority on genetics, claimed that the work of the teams headed by Professor Smithells and Professor Laurence was of historic importance. 'There is compelling evidence of a major effect comparable with that relating cigarette smoking and lung cancer,' he said in the *Lancet* in 1982.[114] Later that year he maintained that NTDs now have 'the status of a deficiency disease'.[84]

The DHSS has always accepted that pregnant women need especially good food, both for themselves and for their growing babies.[7,8] Pregnant women with a low income are entitled to free vitamin pills.[4] Since the 1970s, many health professionals working in the community have suspected that fatty, sugary food does not provide enough nourishment during pregnancy and have encouraged women planning to have children to eat more whole, fresh food, and/or to take multi-vitamin pills.[110,115] By the early 1980s, many child health experts were convinced that good food or supplements consumed in the very first weeks of pregnancy can often prevent spina bifida and other birth defects. In 1982 an Oxford obstetrician gave the following advice in the *British Medical Journal*:[116]

When a woman contemplates becoming pregnant and discontinues contraception, nutrition may become important. For example, vitamin B and folate supplements should be given to any woman with a family or a personal history of a child with spina bifida or anencephaly.

Word got round. While the total number of babies born deformed in Britain has not changed much since the 1970s (the figures are 12,384 in 1976 and 13,347, or about one in every 50 births, in 1985[117]) the number of babies born with deformities of the central nervous system has dropped. One reason is that foetuses with anencephaly or spina bifida are now detected by ultrasound, and then aborted.[118] In addition, the evidence that folic acid and probably other nutrients as well are vital protection against damaged babies has convinced many health professionals working in the field. Above all, GPs and their patients have read all about spina bifida and more and more women preparing for pregnancy are prescribed vitamin pills or get them from 'health food' shops.

PREGNANT WOMEN AS GUINEA-PIGS

Some scientists are not convinced. In October 1982 many of the child-health experts who worked on the trials in which high-risk mothers were given vitamin supplements with such success were invited to a special conference, whose papers and discussions were published as a book, *Prevention of Spina Bifida and Other Neural Tube Defects*, the next year.[84] The chief critic at the conference was Dr Nicholas Wald. Dr Wald said that the trial led by Professor Smithells was big enough, but uncontrolled and biased; and that the trial led by Professor Laurence, while controlled, was not big enough:

> We are left in considerable scientific doubt, as to whether folic acid or other vitamins prevent neural tube defects.

Dr Wald also claimed that the vitamin supplements given in the trials might be harmful:[84]

> The fact that all the vitamins in question, except folic acid in unusual doses, can be obtained without prescription in the UK, does not mean that the regular administration of extra vitamins, even in doses approximating to the recommended daily allowances, will not be associated with some adverse effect.

The case for better nourishment in pregnancy was weak, said Dr Wald. Before any conclusions could properly be reached, or action taken, more and better evidence was needed from another trial. By this time, the DHSS had asked the government-funded Medical Research Council to carry out a new trial, administered by Dr Wald. This was to be immaculately designed. The idea was to find 4000 high-risk women who had already borne a damaged baby and were prepared to have another baby. The women would be randomly divided into four groups. One group would be given the multi-vitamin and mineral pill (Pregnavite Forte F) used in the trial headed by Professor Smithells. A second group would be given the same pill, minus folic acid. A third group would be given folic acid, as in the trial headed by Professor Laurence, plus minerals. And the fourth 'control' group would be given the dummy pill, (which was not inactive, but contained minerals only). The trial would therefore be scientifically immaculate: what is known as randomized and placebo-controlled. With luck, the women would become pregnant, and the scientists would then wait to see what happened. The trial would take five years.[119,120]

Dr Wald was sure that the trial was necessary:[121]

Most senior medical opinion believes the evidence so far is quite inconclusive .... It is possible that the vitamins do no good at all, indeed there is possibly some risk.

He regretted that reports already appearing in the press might discourage women from taking part:[84]

Unfortunately reporting of the subject in the media may have led the public into believing that the vitamins are beneficial.

On 7 December 1982 the Medical Research Council confirmed its decision to go ahead with the trial. According to the MRC press release:[122]

The Council are convinced that the evidence so far obtained, though suggestive, remains so inconclusive that it does not justify offering extra vitamins to all women at risk.

Professor Smithells and his colleagues did not agree, and went public. 'I would not encourage any friend or relative of mine to enter the trial,' said Professor Smithells.[123] Professor Norman Nevin, leader of the Belfast group, said:[124]

> The evidence of a beneficial effect is such that I could not join the trial. I could not, in all conscience, say to a mother who had a spina bifida baby 'Here's a tablet. I do not know whether it is a placebo or whether it has an active ingredient.'

Dr Mary Seller agreed. 'Clinically and morally, we can only give what we know works', she said.[121]

Just before the MRC trial was announced, Arthur Wynn, co-author of the book *Prevention of Handicap and the Health of Women*,[1] claimed in a letter published in the scientific weekly *Nature*[125] that the trial contravened the Helsinki Code of the World Medical Assembly, a statement designed to outlaw unethical experiments on human beings. Dr Wald responded, but withdrew his letter at the last moment, having been pressed to do so by Sir James Gowans, the secretary of the MRC.[126] *Nature* printed a blank space where the letter would have appeared, commenting dryly: 'it would be entirely unworthy to suppose that any component of that pressure is concerned with future research grants.'[127]

Politicians joined in the row. Dr Roger Thomas, Labour MP for Carmarthen, said:[128]

> My message to women is 'sabotage the trial'. Get a prescription for folic acid as soon as you are asked to take part. The whole trial ethically and morally contravenes everything we hold sacred in civilised society.

Frank Dobson, Labour spokesman on health, commented that the trial[129]

> is an example of the pursuit of scientific knowledge losing touch with reality and morality. Recent evidence suggests that the whole thing may be collapsing because so few women are willing to volunteer to be conned.

In April 1984 an all-party group of MPs tabled an Early Day Motion[130] which

> applauds those doctors who have refused to take part in the trials condemning them as ethically unacceptable; and calls on

the Government to abandon the tests, and to ensure that all high-risk women are given proper protection.

Seventy-seven MPs signed the motion, including one energetic Conservative back-bencher, Mrs Edwina Currie. Mr Fowler, Secretary of State for Health and Social Security, did not respond. In 1986 Mrs Currie became Mr Fowler's junior Minister, responsible for public health.

Scientific opinion of the trial was fairly evenly divided. Dr (now Professor) Wald was by no means alone in his view that the trial was necessary. However, many health professionals working in the community agreed with Professor Smithells and his colleagues, and refused to have anything to do with the trial. So did some Ethics Committees, including the one at St Bartholomew's Hospital in London, where Professor Wald had moved. However, the MRC soldiered on. The trial was trimmed to a target of 2000 women. In 1984 it was touch and go whether it would continue; but in June the MRC announced that 16 centres in Britain were collaborating, together with another 11 in Australia, Canada, Israel and Hungary.[131] By the end of 1984, a total of 357 women had been recruited;[132] the total reached 528 in September 1985,[133] and 700 in June 1986.[95]

THE DISAPPEARING (SPINAL) COLUMN

But what was the DHSS doing all these years, having acknowledged in 1976 that birth defects such as spina bifida are a public health problem in Britain?[92] When I started to look into the story of folic acid and NTDs, one point kept puzzling me. As you will remember, in 1979 the DHSS issued its COMA report on standards for vitamins and minerals.[8] And there, on page 7, was the column with the recommended daily amount of folic acid: 300 mcg for everybody above the age of 12, and 500 mcg for pregnant women.

But, as you will also remember, MAFF figures also published in 1979[108] showed that national average consumption of folic acid is 190 mcg. In 1984, (as mentioned in chapter 1) new MAFF figures were published.[83] These squeezed the national average up to 210 to 213 mcg a day: three-quarters of the official standard for non-pregnant people, and still well under half the recommendation for pregnant women. In 1984 I asked Dr Israel Chanarin what he thought, and he told me that 'there is a fair amount of sub-clinical folic acid deficiency' in the British population.[134]

The DHSS and MAFF surveys of the quality of food eaten by 11- and 14-year-olds[47] and 15 to 25-year-olds,[135] which were published in 1986 and 1985 (already discussed in chapter 1), are another source of information. The folic acid consumption of the younger group was not published; so I asked nutritionist Caroline Walker and dietitian Wendy Doyle to make a calculation based on data in the report, using computer facilities at the Nuffield Laboratories of Medicine in London.[136]

Here are the figures assembled in one table. They show consumption by girls or women and the US (1980)[74] and British (1979)[8] Recommended Daily Amounts for pregnant women.

		Consumption	UK RDA	US RDA
			(for pregnant women)	
		mcg	mcg	mcg
MAFF 1979[108]	(all ages)	190	500	800
MAFF 1984[83]	(all ages)	210–213	500	800
DHSS 1986[47]	(11-year-olds)	92–133	500	800
	(14-year-olds)	101–103	500	800
MAFF 1985[135]	(15–18-year-olds)	125	500	800
	(19–21-year-olds)	116	500	800
	(22–25-year-olds)	133	500	800

These figures show that, judged by the government's own standards, young women are grossly deficient in folic acid. Average consumption among 15 to 25-year-old girls and women is one-quarter the recommended amount. If you prefer the US standard, consumption is less than one-sixth of the level set for pregnancy.

Given these statistics, how can the DHSS and the MRC possibly justify witholding folic acid supplements from any pregnant woman, let alone a woman at high risk of bearing a baby with a damaged central nervous system? Why isn't every pregnant woman given a multi-vitamin pill including folic acid for the general protection of herself and her foetus?

Here is how the DHSS got off this hook. In 1982 the Medical Research Council stated in a press release that:[122]

It should be noted that the normal daily requirement for folic acid for normal adults, and more particularly for the developing embryo, is not known.

And in 1983 Peter Brooke, then the Minister at the Department of Education and Science responsible for the Medical Research Council, said it again, in a letter to his fellow Conservative MP Robert Harvey.[137]

The evidence so far obtained ... though suggestive, remains so inconclusive that it does not justify offering extra vitamins to all women at risk. The extra vitamins themselves may not be without risks and some of their functions and actions are still incompletely understood. In this connection I understand from the Council that the normal daily requirement of folic acid for normal adults, and more particularly, for the developing embryo is not known.

How could the MRC and Mr Brooke possibly say this? There, on page 7 of the 1979 COMA report,[8] published by Her Majesty's Stationery Office, ISBN 0 11 320342, price 90p, is the requirement for pregnant women. Folic acid. Pregnant woman. 500 mcg.

One day, when I was in the London HMSO bookshop in High Holborn, I idly picked up another copy of the report. Same ISBN number, with a different price now: £2.70, published in 1981. For no particular reason I turned to the table on page 7. The column giving the recommendations for folic acid had disappeared! On page 14 I found a new paragraph, which says:

The recommendations for healthy people are not yet established firmly enough for a recommended daily amount to be set[!].

So there it is: the mystery of the disappearing (spinal) column.

I then discovered that the 1969 COMA report which set standards for vitamins and minerals[7] and had been superseded by the 1979 report,[8] had also been reissued in 1981: same ISBN number, but with a changed price, this time from 5s 6d to £3.60. This, too, gives no recommendation for folic acid (also known as folate). So are nutritionists and dietitians, school and hospital caterers, and everybody else who needs to know the national standards set for the quality of our food, meant to use ISBN 0 11 320342 price £2.70 as their bible; or ISBN 0 11 320177 X price £3.60? I cannot tell you.

What is certain, though, is that nobody is meant to notice ISBN 0 11 320342 price 90p, in other words, the 1979 COMA report, which did set standards for folic acid and is now a collector's item. In 1984 a justification was given by Dr David Buss, Head of the Nutrition Branch at MAFF, in a nutrition journal.[83]

> The withdrawal was because the recommended amounts of folate were seen to be significantly higher than the intakes estimated from the National Food Survey at the time when there was no widespread folate deficiency in the population.

Another problem remained to be solved in order to ensure the success of the MRC trial as a piece of science. Suppose women recruited for the trial just went ahead and took vitamin supplements? The MRC's *Information for Patients*, issued to their recruits, covered that one in the following question and answer:[138]

> [Question]. If I don't take part in the study can I just buy the vitamins myself and take them? [Answer]. No. The special vitamin capsules used in the study cannot be bought over the counter from a chemist. One of the main constituents (folic acid 4 mg) requires a prescription.

But the MRC trial has outraged many GPs who agree with Dr Roger Thomas and might prescribe vitamin supplements to mothers in their care who had been recruited for the trial. In this case, the doctor and the patient might or might not own up to Professor Wald and his teams; in either case the trial would be screwed up.

In May 1985 the Department of Health banned Pregnavite Forte F: doctors cannot now prescribe it.

ANOREXIA: GOING MENTAL

Spina bifida is not so common in Britain now, no thanks to the DHSS. But it looks as if a new disease of adolescence is becoming more common: anorexia 'nervosa'. The most commonly quoted estimate is that one in every 100 girls over the age of 16 is anorexic.[139]

Why 'nervosa'? The term was coined by Sir William Withey Gull, who found favour with Queen Victoria after treating Prince Edward for typhoid. In 1873 he described the case of the emaciated Miss A of the Clapham Road, whose paradoxical symptoms included starvation, occasional gorging, and incessant activity.

> Various remedies were prescribed – the preparations of conchona, the bichloride of mercury, syrup of the iodine of iron, syrup of the phosphate of iron, citrate of quinine and iron, etc, but no perceptible effect followed their administration.

As a result, Sir William, having exhausted his medicine cabinet, decided that the cause of Miss A's state was morbid and mental. Then as now, doctors enthusiastically labelled women's complaints as 'hysterical' (the word comes from the Latin for 'womb'); but Sir William was aware that males, too, sometimes mysteriously lost their appetite. Sir William named the condition not 'anorexia hysterica' but 'anorexia nervosa'. And, ever since, anorexic adolescents have been the province of psychiatrists.

Is anorexia mental? Psychiatrists say so; but then they would. Anorexics often say so, too; but then, being told you are crackers by teachers, parents, family, friends and doctors tends to make a girl go crackers.

In 1984 I met 'Stephanie', a young teacher who, three years previously, had become one of 10,000 young women in Britain today who are diagnosed as suffering from anorexia nervosa. What happened to Stephanie? Like her parents, with whom she lives harmoniously, she is a vegetarian and favours whole food. At the end of 1980, she was under self-imposed pressure at school; she is an idealist, and 'I couldn't make any lesson an ideal lesson'. She was jogging half an hour a day six days a week, and playing squash as well. 'I felt incredibly fit and proud of my self-discipline,' she told me.

At 5 foot 8 inches and 122 pounds she was on the edge of underweight according to the tables of 'desirable weight'. But she didn't see herself like that, and decided to fine herself down a bit. That was when she lost control. In 1981 she was down to 105 pounds and falling, and refusing to admit that there was anything wrong. Physically and mentally she veered from frantic activity and empty euphoria to 'being sluggish, tired, depressed and terribly moody'. One day in Wallis's, a women's clothes shop,

> I caught sight of myself in the changing room mirror and said O God, that's me. I didn't want to be like that – that awful gauntness.

Now she wanted to stop her self-deception, and to eat more and eat sensibly. But she was already suffering the dark side of anorexia, usually kept secret: bulimia, which in plain language is compulsive gorging followed by vomiting.

> I would pass five shops and go in and buy a chocolate bar in each of them – Galaxy, Yorkie bars, Cadbury's – and then eat bread and peanut butter at home, then put my fingers down my throat. I felt so guilty; it was ugly. I seemed to be some sort of animal.

She learned the language anorexics are taught to use about themselves at meetings of Anorexics Aid, from books, and from a psychiatrist. She adjusted to the knowledge that people were looking at her and talking about her as a type, not a person. But then she decided to trust the family doctor who had delivered her in the spring of 1957. It was a lucky decision. Dr Douglas Latto is one of three brothers originally from Dundee, all doctors, all vegetarians, all committed to the view that the quality of food is of fundamental importance to health. Now in his 70s, Dr Latto has been chairman of the British Safety Council since 1971.

'She was losing weight and ill with it,' he told me, recalling Stephanie's first consultation with him in Harley Street. He gave her a medicine glass containing a mouthful of zinc sulphate; to be exact, an 0.1 per cent solution of zinc sulphate heptahydrate in distilled water, yielding 15 milligrams (mg) of zinc a day, at a cost of a penny a month. Three months later Stephanie had gained 15 pounds in weight. 'Her whole mental pattern changed,' Dr Latto told me. 'I'm relaxed now,' Stephanie said. She was candid with me; her story had been a struggle to tell.

Galvanized into action, so to say, Dr Latto reported this case history in a letter to the *Lancet*, stating also that 20 to 30 of his patients:[141]

> suffering from bouts of unexplained depression, loss of self-confidence, or various phobias, but without marked anorexia ... derived marked benefit from zinc supplementation. We feel therefore that zinc may well have wider applications in psychiatry.

'We' included Professor Derek Bryce-Smith of the organic chemistry department at Reading University and Dr Ian Simpson, a GP. As it turned out, the *Lancet* printed the case history of a patient of Dr Simpson, a 13-year-old girl whose anorexia and acute depression and tearfulness were successfully treated with zinc, but did not print Stephanie's case history and the details of Dr Latto's other patients, evidently finding these less convincing.

I went to see Professor Bryce-Smith, who has crisp views about psychiatrists, seeing them as good customers of drug companies. He told me:

> Mental depression of unknown origin can be a symptom of zinc deficiency. Mental depression is not caused by tranquilliser deficiency. It would be tough for the drug companies if somebody actually found the cause of cancer, or heart disease – or depression.

Dr Simpson felt much the same way.

I had been asked to write a feature on anorexia for the *Observer*. Could it really be caused by zinc deficiency? After talking with Dr Latto, Professor Bryce-Smith, Dr Simpson and Stephanie, the idea still seemed rather wacky to me. It also occurred to me, I confess, that anybody from the sugar industry, say, who wanted evidence that I am wacky might be rather pleased to see me bursting in print on the subject.

What did the DHSS have to say about zinc? Not a lot. The 1969/1981 COMA report stated:[7]

Of the dozen or so minerals known to be essential for man, only three, calcium, iron and iodine, need attention. The others are widely distributed in all diets.

And MAFF? The excellent study by Dr David Buss and his colleagues, published in 1979, stated:[108]

Zn. The average Zn content of the household diet was 9.1 mg/person per day and the value for larger families was 7.9 mg/person per day.

Zinc has never been scheduled and given a Recommended Daily Amount in Britain. But it is scheduled in the USA: the standard is 15 mg a day for adults, and 20 mg a day for pregnant women. So, judged by US standards, most people in Britain are short of zinc.

You will have guessed by now that the story of zinc and anorexia has similarities to that of folic acid and defects of the central nervous system; and so it does.

Since the 1960s, zinc has become the subject of intense interest in medical journals. The 1979/1981 COMA report on vitamins[8] included a couple of specific references to zinc. However, by the 1980s a computer search found that scientific papers on zinc and its function as a nutrient were being published at the rate of a thousand a year.[142] Before committing myself to print, I took the precaution of looking through just over 300 studies of zinc published since the 1950s. They were interesting.

For example, the connection between zinc deficiency, loss of sense of taste (hypogeusia) and the sense that food is disgusting (dysgeusia) was noted in the *Journal of the American Medical Association* in 1973. The investigators reported[143]

A relationship between loss of trace metals, including zinc, and anorexia and hypogeusia ... in man .... Although the mechanism by which zinc loss is related to anorexia, dysgeusia, or hypogeusia is not clear, the presence of these relationships is strongly suggested.

In 1977 Dr Michael Hambidge wrote in an American journal of child health:[144]

The clinical features of zinc deficiency that have been documented in children either in this country or overseas ...

include anorexia, impaired taste perception, failure to thrive in infants and growth retardation in older children, delayed sexual maturation, pica, and lethargy.

('Pica' is the medical term for the craving to eat strange stuff as food, including inorganic matter such as clay and coal. Pregnant women often exhibit pica.)

In a review of the scientific evidence on zinc published in 1983, Dr Peter Aggett, head of the trace elements department at the Rowett Research Institute, Aberdeen, wrote: [145]

Apathy, growth retardation and anorexia are all documented features of, amongst other things, marginal lack of iron, zinc and copper .... Correction of these defects following supplementation with the element is actually rapid in genuine deficiency states.

In a major review published in 1983, Professor Ananda Prasad, who first identified zinc deficiency states in humans, 25 years ago, stated that the condition is common in many countries; that zinc is needed for growth; and that deficiency can be passed from one generation to the next. His list of clinical symptoms included: [146]

increased susceptibility to infections, lethargy and behavioural changes, and a high incidence of congenital malformations of offspring.

And, also, anorexia.

But, having read this far, I was still sceptical. Typically highly processed food and vegetables grown in typically zinc-deficient soil are poor in zinc; fine, I could accept that. Zinc deficiency causes anorexia; very well. But why should anorexics almost always be girls, and most anorexic girls be middle-class? Why the anorexic syndrome of obsessive starving, exercising and gorging? And why is anorexia a potential killer? How could all this be attributed to zinc deficiency? I read on.

Zinc is known to be essential in protein metabolism, or, in plain language, for growth. This is why deficiency symptoms include failure to thrive, slow growth and delayed sexual maturity; and, also, ceased periods in girls and skin that forms stretch marks ('striae') and is slow to heal. So zinc-deficient girls have a practical reason to hate the process of becoming women: as their breasts and hips grow, scars are liable to form under the skin.[146,147]

There are further reasons why girls and young women are much more likely to suffer the consequences of zinc deficiency than males of the same age. Here are four:

First, A high-fat and -protein diet such as we eat in the West, starting with a high consumption of cows' milk in infancy and childhood, accelerates sexual maturity, bringing it on in the period of adolescent growth. This imposes a double extra requirement for zinc, which the body cannot supply at so young an age. Zinc is lost in menses, and so ceased periods are a means whereby the body preserves a balance of zinc in the bloodstream.

Second, The contraceptive pill, and also sex hormones prescribed by doctors for pre-menstrual tension or to bring on periods, raise the level of copper in the blood and so are antagonistic to zinc.[148] Most young women use the pill nowadays, and many young adolescent girls are given hormones. (Incidentally, eating beef and chicken doesn't help either; much meat is injected with hormones.)

Third, Stress sharply increases the excretion of zinc in urine. Stress can take a medical or physical form (an infection or injury) or a mental or emotional form (examinations, young love, trouble at home). Thus referral to a psychiatrist, and being diagnosed as suffering from anorexia nervosa, can only make bad worse. To a significant extent, the condition is therefore iatrogenic (caused by doctors), given the wide use of the pill, the number of female hormones prescribed for non-contraceptive reasons, and the stigma and the diagnosis of anorexia nervosa.

Fourth, Dieting is often the trigger that sets off the self-destructive anorexic syndrome, so hard to reverse and so painful for the sufferer and her family and friends. Doctors, who are usually male and middle-aged, often propose that initially slim girls who diet do so in search of the super-slim ideal, such as Twiggy. This may sometimes be true, but as a general theory is unlikely; you have to be adult to have heard of Twiggy. The severely zinc-deficient girl has reason to fear growth, which will make any deficiency more acute.

It is commonly assumed that the body tissue lost during a diet is unwanted fat. This is not true. Water and glycogen apart, most of the body tissue lost in the first three weeks of a severe diet is lean tissue – muscle and vital organs. Eventually even bone is wasted.[149] Fat is lost too, of course; how much depends to some extent on how much there was to start with. Pathological starvation, as in anorexia 'nervosa', is liable to be life-threatening, because the body eats itself. Meat is muscle. Muscle is a rich source of zinc.

But what causes the bizarre and paradoxically self-destructive behaviour of the anorexic who, like Miss A of the Clapham Road and Stephanie over a century later, gorges food and vomits and exercises fanatically, and whose moods swing from euphoria to despair?

The key lies in the fact that at all times the body will seek, at high cost if necessary, to keep the level of zinc and other trace elements in the bloodstream in balance. In a state of emergency the body will draw zinc from any source, protecting one organ above all others: the brain. Hence the anorexic syndrome:[150]

O In a state of acute deficiency, the body will draw on its own store of zinc and other nutrients.
O Starvation is a fast and efficient means whereby zinc is released from the breakdown of lean tissue.
O Like starvation, continuous vigorous physical activity also breaks down (catabolizes) lean tissue.
O Thus zinc moves sporadically into the brain, causing irrational and uncontrollable mood swings.
O Gorging is another emergency means whereby zinc and other nutrients are gained at the expense of nausea.

The thesis, therefore, is that anorexia is an adaptation to extreme circumstances, but a maladaptation, self-destructive, creating a pattern of behaviour which is likely to be hard to break.

What is Professor Bryce-Smith's view?[151]

The amount of zinc and iron we need is similar. We accept the need for iron supplementation. We should extend this idea to zinc. It is just as essential as iron, and there is better evidence of dietary deficiency of zinc. Nutritionists and doctors –

including psychiatrists – should be alert to the implications of zinc deficiency in our society.

Nobody is seriously suggesting that zinc deficiency is the one and only cause of anorexia 'nervosa', or that anorexics can usually be cured just with doses of zinc. Of course not. Any advanced anorexic suffers from many deficiencies, and zinc should work in balance with iron and copper and in harmony with vitamin B6, B12 and folic acid. But all the scientific research on the biochemistry of zinc points in the same direction. Young women in Britain today are usually short of zinc. Many young women are grossly deficient in zinc. Zinc deficiency causes the anorexic syndrome.

Politics isn't just about politicians. Just as spina bifida is providing employment opportunities for a battalion of research workers in Britain, Australia, Israel and Hungary, the psychiatry business is in good shape thanks in some small part to anorexia 'nervosa'. When my feature appeared in the *Observer* on 2 September 1984,[152] by all accounts it did not go down well at an international conference on anorexia nervosa held at University College, Swansea, the next week. As far as I could judge from the conference programme,[153] perhaps one of the 160 papers presented was concerned with the quality of the food eaten by anorexics. Just like mothers who have had a spina bifida baby, and just like hyperactive children, anorexic adolescents have added value.

ZAP, ZAP; YUM, YUM

'ATOM RAY' SET FOR GO-AHEAD. Revolutionary process is safe, say the experts.

This was the start of an 'exclusive' news feature in the *Daily Express* in February 1985:[154]

Britain's housewives will soon be buying lasting-fresh, germ-free food – which has been bombarded with radiation.

Sure enough, a year later, in April 1986, Barney Hayhoe, then a Minister at the DHSS, celebrated publication of his official expert advisory *Report on the Safety and Wholesomeness of Irradiated Foods.*[155]

My colleagues and I decided that, in order to stimulate public debate on the subject the Report should be published.

So said Mr Hayhoe, which was nice of him.

Interested organisations and individuals wishing to make comments on the Report should send them in writing to my Department to arrive not later than the end of July.

It looked as if the experts from government, science and industry all agreed, and were dead keen on food irradiation. This is how the food technologist Professor Alan Holmes of the government-and industry-funded British Food Manufacturing Industry Research Association (BFMIRA) put it:[154]

I have a dream that for once the public will take the scientists' word and welcome the process as a great step forward.

In 1983, Frank Ley, Technical and Marketing Director of Isotron plc, wrote in the BNF *Bulletin*:[156]

Clearance of food irradiation for wholesomeness is to be expected .... the outcome of deliberations on safety, both nationally and internationally, is awaited eagerly by industry in an atmosphere of reasonable optimism.

And, a year before they were published, Sir Arnold Burgen, Chairman of Mr Hayhoe's irradiation committee, anticipated its findings in May 1985, saying, 'we have no evidence to suggest that irradiation of food is harmful'.[157]

Accordingly, reassuring headlines appeared in the newspapers. 'COMING SOON ... ATOM RAYS THAT KEEP FOODS FRESH', was one.[154] After the press conference held to welcome the prospect of food irradiation, three national newspaper headlines were: 'IRRADIATED FOOD CLEARED FOR SALE;[158] 'FOOD IRRADIATION "POSES NO HEALTH HAZARD"',[159] and 'MEDICAL OFFICER PRAISES FOOD IRRADIATION'.[160] Were there any notes of caution? In 1985 Dr Lesley Yeomans 'of the super-careful Consumers' Association' gave irradiation the green light. 'We think it's completely safe,' she said. 'But we will insist that food which goes through the process must be labelled.'[154] Professor Holmes countered one doubting press story in a letter headed 'GAMMA PIE IS SAFE'.[161]

The process that will be used is so gentle that any change of the chemical composition of the food is so minute as to be within the range of variable composition which is normally encountered .... Certainly less than that caused by cooking.

In the USA, the trade journal *High Technology* has seen the future for food irradiation, and believes it will work. 'Even the seemingly trivial approval of spice irradiation may be a bonanza for food processors,' it wrote in 1984. Frank F. Fraser of Atomic Energy of Canada Ltd, the world's leading supplier of cobalt-60 rods, said, 'I don't see a shortage of isotopes', and declared that irradiation has 'tremendous potential'. Sanford Miller, Director of the Bureau of Foods at the US Food and Drugs Administration, summed up. Irradiation, he said, will become 'a very important part of our entire armamentarium of food processing technology'.[162]

Professor Holmes' dream did not come true straight away. As soon as Sir Arnold's report was published BBC Radio West Midlands summed up the case for and against irradiation on its current affairs show, *John Taynton Today*, which is regularly followed by a computerized poll. On this occasion the question was 'Would you buy food labelled as irradiated?' Of about 400 replies, 96 per cent said 'No'. I asked the producer, Tim Manning, if this was an impressive result. 'Put it this way,' he told me. 'When we asked listeners if they felt safer after the bombing of Tripoli, 93 per cent said "No" '. This was before Chernobyl.

What does the *Report on the Safety and Wholesomeness of Irradiated Food*[163] (which I shall now call 'The Burgen Report', after its Chairman) say? First: 'food like virtually all matter on this planet is radioactive.' That said, though,

Some forms of ionising radiation can cause nuclear reactions which lead to the induction of further radioactivity.

And then:

Even when worst-case assumptions are made about the concentration of certain elements in food and the dose and energy of radiation employed, the estimated induced radio-activity would remain below the level which is of any possible significance to human health or which might be the subject of any regulatory interest.

This sounds like a long-winded way of saying, 'Yes, but there's nothing to worry about.'

At the press conference held to welcome the report, journalists and other interested parties noted that its bibliography of about a hundred items, was not referenced to the text. As a result, it is impossible (taking the extract above) to check out what the report means by 'worst-case assumptions' (how worst-case?) or 'certain elements in food' (heavy metal contamination?) or 'below the level' (how much below, and what level?). Would Sir Arnold agree to publish references together with the evidence submitted to his committee? No, he said, he would not.[164]

What is food irradiation? To quote the press release accompanying the Burgen report:[155]

> Ionising irradiation can be used to destroy or reduce the number of pathogenic or spoilage organisms in food, control insect infestation of grain etc, delay the ripening of fruit, and inhibit sprouting of certain vegetables. The sources of ionising radiation are either radioactive isotopes or machines producing X-rays or electrons, and both can be used for food irradiation.

INSTANT SUNSHINE

Put more plainly, food irradiation is a by-product of the nuclear fuel industry. The source of irradiation is gamma rays from Cobalt-60 or Caesium 137 rods.[165] Of these, Caesium 137 is available in plenty as waste product from the Sellafield (formerly Windscale) plant. Cobalt-60 will become available as radioactive waste if the government builds the new plant at Sizewell. How powerful are food irradiation doses (sometimes known in the trade as 'zaps')? Professor Holmes uses the word 'gentle'. The Burgen report recommends that these kisses be no higher than 10 kGy. The term 'kGy' is short for 'kiloGray'. 'Gray' is a new term; formerly the term was 'Rad'. One 'Rad' is one hundredth of a 'Gray': the zap vocabulary has been devalued 100 times. So, ten kGy is a million Rads. A chest X-ray delivers one hundredth of a Rad. So the dose of radiation proposed for food is up to 100 million times that of an X-ray. Quite a kiss.

Nowadays, prudent nurses back away from chest X-ray

machines, and patients are protected by lead aprons. Can food take it? One way of answering this question is to ask another, which is: can irradiated foods cause cancer? Again, there is no straight answer in the Burgen report, and I had to go to other sources, in particular to Dr Thomas Dormandy of the Whittington Hospital in London, who wrote a paper called 'An Approach to Free Radicals' which appeared in the *Lancet* in 1983.[166] Free radicals are 'an unstable and violently reactive chemical species,' Dr Dormandy explained. They are formed when fats, notably unsaturated fats, oxidize and go rancid. Our immune system protects the unsaturated fats in our bodies against the generation of free radicals. There is good evidence that the maverick activity of free radicals, especially when our immune system is weak, is a key factor in cancer. According to Dr Dormandy:

> That free radical activity is an aetiological factor in malignant change is certain .... The nagging question is not whether free radicals are a cause of cancer but how near they are to the root cause, if such a root cause exists.

What has this got to do with food irradiation? 'Ionising radiation acts on living tissues largely by generating free radicals.' That is how it works.

So, what does the Burgen report have to say about this? Brace yourself for some gorse-bush prose.'[163]

> For some compounds in food, particularly polyunsaturated fats the free radicals formed by irradiation initiate self-perpetuating chain reactions which continue for some weeks after the irradiation has finished and may lead to higher levels of some radiolytic products being present .... It is not possible to exclude the theoretical possibility that unique and potentially toxic substances might be formed in certain irradiated foods .... Some carcinogens are formed in irradiated foods as well as in traditionally processed foods.

The report was anxious to put this in context, and pointed out that some conventional and accepted methods of food preparation and cooking are also problematic. 'The production of potentially toxic substances is not unique to or even a particular feature of food irradiation.' So the answer to the question 'Can irradiated food cause cancer?' is 'Well, it does create carcinogens, but so do other processes. Besides, animals have been fed irradiated food for ages and they seem to be all right.' This of course is still not a straight answer. The straight answer is 'Yes'. But nothing to worry about. Trust us.

Industry representatives such as Professor Holmes are keen on the argument that changes created by irradiation are comparable with those of cooking. There is some hope in industry that irradiated food will be labelled 'pico-waved', which sounds like 'micro-waved'. In South Africa, where irradiation is legal, labels have been devised for irradiated food saying, 'Radura. The Emblem of Quality'.[167] An ideal term for labels, for the irradiators, would be something like 'plus Instant Sunshine', but, failing that, 'pico-waved' would do.

Sir Arnold thought that there is no health reason to label irradiated food.[164] However, at the insistence of the Food Advisory Committee, the Burgen report nevertheless recommended that irradiated food be explicitly labelled.

What else does irradiation do to food? Its main benefit is that it turns perishable foods into better commodities. It slows down the sprouting and rotting of vegetables and fruit. It kills microbes, some of which can cause acute illness, in meat. Irradiation therefore offers the prospect of evidently fresher, safer and cleaner food. From industry's point of view, this means that foods that naturally go bad, will become much more stable; more akin to staples such as saturated fats and processed sugars, the best commodities of all.

Irradiation cannot be used for all foods. Indeed, because it speeds up rancidity, it doesn't work for fatty foods. Irradiated milk tastes burned. Irradiated meat has a 'wet dog' flavour. But it does work for lean meats such as chicken and for white fish. In countries where irradiation is legal, such as the Netherlands, it is used extensively for seafood such as prawns. The fats in irradiated foods can be stopped going rancid by extra special doses of chemical additives that work as anti-oxidants.[168]

Saying that irradiation stops rot and kills bacteria is another way of saying that irradiation kills the life in food. It may (at high doses) kill most known bacteria dead. Does it kill all known nourishment dead, too? What about vitamins?

Depending on the dose and the food, irradiation destroys a proportion of vitamins in fresh food. The amount of vitamin

A, B1, B6 and C destroyed by irradiation is estimated to be between 20 per cent and 80 per cent in various foods. Vitamin E may be completely destroyed. The effect on other vitamins has not been studied. For example, according to the Burgen report:

> Little is known about the effect of food processing including irradiation on folate. Since there are possible problems in the area of public health in relation to the intake of folate this needs further investigation.

It is nice to know that Sir Arnold and his colleagues had noticed the evidence linking folic acid with birth defects.

Does the loss of other vitamins matter? The report estimates that these losses are comparable with those caused by cooking. But irradiation is an additional process. Cooked food will be irradiated as well as cooked, not instead of being cooked. Besides, to take vitamin C, we do not eat much cooked fruit. In general, a judgement about vitamin losses depends on a general judgement about the food supply. An expert who believes that the British food supply is bulging with vitamins is likely to be tolerant of irradiation. Other experts who are aware that vitamins A, C and E protect against cancers, and who are also aware that the most recent surveys show worryingly low vitamin intake, are likely to regard irradiation as an additional threat to public health.

Of course it is good to rid food of microbial contamination. However, in some cases this can only be done by doses of radiation considered too high to be safe. Is it possible that industry would use irradiation as an illegal means of sterilizing food already contaminated with harmful bacteria, such as salmonella or staphylococcus? Perish the thought! But it has been done. A Channel 4 documentary revealed, with hard evidence, that prawns rejected by the Southampton Port Authorities as contaminated with bacteria have been re-exported to the Netherlands, irradiated, and re-imported. The prawns were mostly sold to caterers and to Indian and Chinese restaurants. The company responsible has stated that the incident was a one-off.[169]

One man in the seafood business, Ken Bell of Newcastle, the biggest prawn importer in Europe, believes that his business will be prey to 'irresponsible food processors who use rejected sub-standard food in this way'. (He is not referring to any particular firm.) 'It is quite true that health inspectors or your own biology lab cannot prove that your food has ever been contaminated with filth,' he wrote to his colleagues in the British Frozen Food Federation. 'Is this the business you wish to be in, selling shit?'[170]

Twenty years ago, plans to irradiate food in the USA were dropped like the proverbial hot potato when it was discovered that pigs fed exclusively on irradiated food developed multiple illnesses that looked like radiation sickness. In fact, it is more likely that the pigs were suffering from multiple vitamin deficiency diseases, such as scurvy.[171] 'Twenty years later,' concludes Ken Bell

> The Nuclear Industry and the lobby pushing for irradiation ignore all the previous evidence and carry out different experiments. Like the cluster of cancer around Sellafield, they state there is not enough evidence to say it is harmful; it is an acceptable hazard. I believe that once the public learn what is happening, this problem will not go away.

There are also rumours of a racket in irradiated food. It operates as follows. Contaminated food is shipped to country X, whose port authorities reject it. The shippers collect the insurance money. Then they buy back the contaminated food as a 'reject lot' at maybe a tenth of its market value. It is then shipped to country Y, irradiated, and shipped back to country X. Because the level of contamination is evidently much lower, the port authorities (who of course do not know that they have already inspected the load) accept it. There is no evidence that this great Zap Scam, as it is known, involves any British person or firm.

At the press conference to launch the Burgen Report, Sir Arnold was asked if he was a part-time Director of Amersham International, Britain's leading isotope manu-facturer. He agreed that he was,[164] explaining that the supply of Cobalt-60 isotope (which can be used in food irradiation) accounted for less than 1 per cent of Amersham's business. At the time of his appointment as Chairman of the Irradiation Committee, he explained, he was unaware of any conflict of interest.

On 9 April 1986, six Labour MPs put down a formal Early

Day Motion[172] querying the role of Frank Ley, who was appointed to advise the committee on the technical application of irradiation in August 1983, just after he had featured in the BNF *Bulletin*.[156] Isotron has a virtual monopoly of the British installations capable of irradiating food.[173]

During his press conference, Sir Arnold pointed out that Mr Ley was not a full member of the Burgen committee and that he was appointed after its main recommendations had been agreed.[164]

In the matter of food irradiation, the interests of government, science and industry are not identical with our interests as consumers or citizens. Government wants to develop the nuclear industry. Food scientists will have a new space-age toy, described in Germany many years ago as 'the Sputnik of food technology'. And industry will have a new means of prolonging shelf life.

And us, the consumers? We will get deadened food, which may be hazardous to our health, and which certainly has much of its goodness destroyed. This isn't the official view, of course. The experts say that there's nothing to worry about.

CHAPTER 6

Science, Government and Industry: The System

The dispassionate objectivity of scientists is a myth. No scientist is simply involved in the single-minded pursuit of truth, he is also engaged in the passionate pursuit of research grants and professional success. Nutritionists may wish to attack malnutrition, but they also wish to earn their living in ways they find congenial. Although many people are killed by malnutrition each year, an increasing number of us are kept alive by it.
John Rivers, The Profession of Nutrition,[1] 1979

If I had been as interested then as I am now, I would have discovered who was paying whom, and why it was impossible to produce a government advisory report that came to positive conclusions on food and health ... The experts have at last produced a consensus. When I was Secretary of State, I couldn't get the medics, the nutritionists, the food scientists to agree on anything. I now realise that half the experts on my advisory committees were paid by one side of the food industry or another. So no wonder they didn't agree.
Lord Ennals, Speech to the Institute of Health Food Retailing,[2] 1986

○ *Fat is needed in a balanced diet*
○ *Fat makes meat tender, juicy and flavoursome*
○ *Much fat is left on the side of the plate*
○ *Fat from meat and meat products is falling*
○ *Medical opinion is sharply divided on the cholesterol/fat question*
○ *The meat industry believes in a balanced diet*
   John Locke, Private memorandum to meat manufacturers,[3] 1984

Are the people in government, industry and science who claim to look after our interests as citizens, consumers and patients in fact combined in a plot to poison us? Of course not. Lord Ennals is quoted at the beginning of this chapter.[2] Is he saying that when, as David Ennals, he was Cabinet Minister responsible for the DHSS in the late 1970s, he was hoodwinked by corrupt scientists and businessmen who conspired with civil servants to thwart his plans to improve public health? I am sure the answer is no. That's not the way the system works, in Britain. The question of conspiracy, meaning a secret agreement to gain some end known to be wrong, does not arise. Likewise, the question of corruption, meaning the purchase of support with money, does not arise. As a rule, the people in government, industry and science who create the British food supply act in good faith. They believe that they are right.

NOT THE APPLES, BUT THE BARREL

Take Mrs Thatcher. She is a scientist who worked in industry and then moved into government; and she happens to be a food technologist by training. When she worked for Lyons at Hammersmith in West London in 1950, her speciality was 'fat extension', and she wrote a paper on 'the elasticity of ice-cream', which was admired at the time.[4] The idea was to see how much air can be pumped into ice-cream, through sophisticated use of additives, before it collapses. But there is no reason to suggest she invented Mr Whippy with the intention of defrauding the public, or that she found new ways of making saturated fats palatable in order to degrade the national food supply still further. Of course not. She was earning a living, solving interesting technical problems, and making a little go a long way.

Or take Dr David Owen. He, too, is a scientist who moved into government; his background is as a doctor of medicine. In 1985 he wrote a feature bracing the readers of *The Times* for a new technological Britain in the 1990s. The service sector is where it's at, he said, stating that 'today, McDonald's employs more people than General Motors.'[5] We should go the USA's way, he said, making his point with a table showing predictions for the greatest new job creation in the USA between 1985 and 1995. The top of this table showed:

Estimated new job creations in the USA, 1985-1995

Industry	New jobs	% increase
Medical services	2,929,000	90
Eating and drinking places	2,347,000	84

There will, he said 'be a lot of traditionally low wage jobs in areas such as fast foods, retailing and health care'. But in looking forward to a millenium under the Social Democrats, Dr Owen is not celebrating high-tech food as a boost for high-tech drugs and surgery. Most doctors of medicine are unaware that bad food makes people ill, and, as far as I know, Dr Owen has not made the connection. And then, even if he has, new jobs are new jobs.

Or take Dr John Cunningham. Like Mrs Thatcher, he has a degree in chemistry. He is not in government, but he may be one day; in 1987 he is the Labour Shadow Cabinet Minister who speaks for the Department of the Environment, and as such, is responsible for Labour policy on chemical food additives, announced in August 1986. This states:[6]

It is now recognised that many additives can be harmful. Many children suffer allergic reactions to common colours, anti-oxidants and preservatives. Food workers have experienced ill-health from handling certain additives. The UK controls on additives lag behind those of many European countries.

In opposition, Dr Cunningham is a paid advisor to Albright and Wilson,[7] major manufacturers of the anti-oxidants BHA (E320) and BHT (E321); and also of nitrates, that are used as fertilizer and also as food preservatives (E249-E252).[8] Is Labour's chemical additives policy safe in his hands? Well, first of all, as with Sir Arnold Burgen and Amersham International, it may be that Dr Cunningham has not been aware that Albright and Wilson manufactures chemical food additives. Second, ministers relinquish consultancies with industry once in office. Third, for all I know Dr Cunningham may be using his special relationship with the chemical giants (he is also advisor to Dow Chemicals)[7] as a means of encouraging them to adopt Labour's policies. To point out connections between government, science and industry is not to challenge the personal integrity of the people who have these connections.

Or there again, take Geraint Howells. He is neither a scientist nor in government; he is a sheep farmer[9] who was in 1986 Liberal spokesman on agriculture, and tipped as Minister of Agriculture in any Alliance government. As mentioned in the introduction to this book, in November 1985 the Liberal Party adopted a new policy on food and health. This encourages 'reduced consumption of saturated and hydrogenated fats' and 'halving the total sugar and salt consumption' and calls for:[10]

> A levy on the food processing industry to finance independent research into the relationship between diet and disease.

Mr Howells is also Managing Director of Wilkinson and Steiner, a meat wholesaler,[9] and has been honorary Vice-President of the National Association of Master Bakers, Confectioners and Caterers.[11] Once in office would he pursue Liberal policy with all due zeal? As with Robert Boothby and his synthetic vitamin business, Mr Howells would give up selling meat should he become a minister. Furthermore, his background in farming and his connections with confectioners date back to a time before the ill effects of saturated fats and processed sugars were well known. Third, as it has turned out fellow SDP MP Robert MacLennan has in 1987 taken over responsibility to represent Alliance thinking on agriculture and food.[12]

Back to Mrs Thatcher. As Prime Minister since 1979, she has been responsible for attempts by ministers and government officials to suppress or obscure four expert reports on food and health originally commissioned by the government between 1981 and 1986. These are the NACNE report on dietary goals for everybody in Britain, on which Labour and Liberal thinking is now based,[13] the JACNE booklet on eating for a healthy heart (of which more later),[14] and the two reports on what young people aged 11 to 25 are eating in Britain today.[15,16] Mrs Thatcher is known to take a personal interest in children's food, as well she might given her background; she is also responsible for abolishing nutritional standards in favour of a privatized free-for-all for school meals.[17]

The techniques Mrs Thatcher's government has used to gain its ends are of course contemptible. But this is not to say that Mrs Thatcher herself is bent on the destruction of public health in Britain. Of course not. The sensible explanation is that she believes that there is nothing wrong with the British food supply. That is to be expected, given her background in food technology, mixing fats and sugars up together with additives. Why should she be persuaded by the medical and scientific consensus that the British food supply is unhealthy? She dismisses any views which contradict her own convictions. She is more likely to take advice from her supporters in the food-manufacturing industry, such as chief executives, Sir Hector Laing of United Biscuits, Sir James Cleminson of Reckitt & Colman, Sir Derrick Holden-Brown of Allied-Lyons, Sir Robert Haslam lately of Tate & Lyle, Sir Ronald Halstead lately of Beecham, and Sir Peter Reynolds of Ranks Hovis McDougall, all but one of whom were knighted at her recommendation. These firms contributed a total of £1,110,905 to Conservative Party funds between 1979 and 1984.[18] And if giant manufacturers of fats, sugars, salt and additives believe that their products are good for you, and Mrs Thatcher does too, they are not buying her support: they have it already.

Should Mrs Thatcher, Dr Owen, Dr Cunningham and Mr Howells have responsibility for Conservative, SDP, Labour and Liberal public health policy respectively? I think not. This is not to question their personal integrity. No doubt they all mean what they say. Lack of individual integrity is not the problem – if only it were. The problem is not the individual, but the system; not the apples, but the barrel.

'MPS STIR UP SUGAR WAR'

One of my tasks, in researching this book, was to find out whether or not the food industry has an undue influence on government. It soon became obvious that the term 'the food industry' is not very meaningful. Fruit farmers and deep-sea fishermen have little in common with fat-manufacturers. Vegetables and sugar beet grow in the same land; wholegrain bread and chocolate confectionery compete in the same market. There is antagonism between food manufacturers and retailers. The correct focus of attention is on what in the USA are called the 'food giants': the leading manufacturers of highly processed food, or what might be called the fats, sugars, salt, additives and alcohol business.

One approach is to investigate the links between MPs and that part of the food industry now identified as of public health concern. Some MPs are well known to have such links. Backbench MPs may be employees of or consultants to industry, and are expected to declare their interest. Michael Shersby, Conservative MP for Uxbridge, is often identified as being linked with industry, because he is careful to declare his interest as Director-General of the Sugar Bureau before standing up in the House of Commons and making statements such as:[19]

> Is my right hon and learned Friend ... aware that for many families, especially in Northern Ireland, confectionery is an important part of the diet?

But, like Mrs Thatcher, Mr Shersby is an easy target, and it is wrong – inaccurate, and also somewhat unfair on him – to single him out. The interests of the sugar industry in Parliament are not represented by just one MP who lists his employment by the Sugar Bureau in the *Register of Members' Interests*[7] for all to see. Other links, direct or indirect, present or past, are less obvious or less noticed.

So I spent a year, with four researchers, investigating the links between MPs and the unhealthy food industry. We were often warned that the task would be troublesome. What does 'link' mean? A connection does not of itself mean influence. Should past or indirect links be counted? No list could ever be complete, and every list will be overtaken by deaths, resignations and general elections. Some of the most significant links might be obscure. Some MPs might prove touchy. Some information might be inaccurate. We did our best to address all these problems, and the result, the evidence on which a good judgment can be based, is printed as Document A. As its title, 'Two Hundred and Fifty MPs and the Food Industry', indicates, 250 MPs are listed as having some link with the food industry. Of these, 202 are Conservatives: more than half the parliamentary party in the House of Commons on 1 January 1987.

These are the MPs in Mrs Thatcher's Cabinet who are listed: Paul Channon (Trade and Industry; Guinness,[7] also farmer;[9] Douglas Hurd (Home Office; parents dairy farmers[20]); Michael Jopling (Agriculture; farmer[7]); Tom King (Northern Ireland; shareholder and ex-director food firm, also farmer[9]); Nicholas Ridley (Environment; ex-director Tate & Lyle[9]); Margaret Thatcher (Prime Minister; parents grocers, ex-employee Lyons[21]); Peter Walker (Energy, ex-farmer[9]); George Younger (Defence; beer, also farmer[9]). Also included are two other Cabinet Ministers with influential firms in their constituencies: John Biffen (Leader of the House; Unigate and Express Dairies;[22,23] and John Moore (Transport; Nestlé[24]).

Some of these connections seem slight or insignificant. Are constituency links meaningful? In the opinion of the MPs I have asked, the answer is yes. For instance, one Conservative MP who is not listed because he has a record of speaking up against unhealthy food has a big butter factory in his constituency. Hundreds of his constituents are employed in this factory, whose directors have offered him hospitality and asked him to protect their welfare by speaking up for butter. In response, he has said that he has a more general responsibility to the health of all his constituents – including butter-factory workers. An MP less alert to the evidence against saturated fats might have become an invisible recruit in the House of Commons.

And on the other side? Are there Cabinet Ministers who have links with healthy food? All we found was Kenneth Baker (Education), who once worked for a banana firm, Geest.[9]

Ministers are not expected to have direct links with industry (although they can continue to own farms while in office); so at that level in government, influence is on the whole intangible. What becomes apparent is ambiance:

shared beliefs and feelings. Below ministerial level, links are more direct. It is particularly difficult to obtain information about MPs who are paid by PR companies with food accounts. We have counted 57 Conservative MPs who are or have been consultants to PR companies or such-like organizations representing firms whose products are unhealthy; this list is bound to be incomplete. (Full details are in Document A.)

Some of the more interesting links involve MPs who have been ministers, or who are Parliamentary Private Secretaries (PPS, the level below Ministers), or who serve on Parliamentary committees. In giving some examples here, I am not suggesting that the MPs named put their industry links before their responsibilities as public servants. The list is of Conservative MPs unless otherwise stated.

Graham Bright (PPS, Ex-Vice Chairman Conservative Food and Drink Committee; Director, International Sweeteners[9]); Dr Michael Clark (Secretary All-party Chemical Industries Group; ex-employee ICI[9]); Michael Colvin (PPS, Secretary All-party Licensed Trade Group;[25] Advisor Licensed Victuallers[26]); David Crouch (Ex-Chairman All-party Chemical Industries Group; Director Kingsway PR – sugar, salt, additives etc.[7] Sir Paul Dean (Ex-Chairman Conservative Health and Social Services Committee; Director Watney Mann & Truman – brewers[7]; Rt Hon Edward du Cann (ex-Chairman backbench 1922 Committee; Vice-Chairman Lonrho – sugar etc[9]).

Tim Eggar (Minister; Ex-Parliamentary Advisor Hill and Knowlton PR – Coca-Cola, etc.[27]); Sir Geoffrey Finsberg (Minister Department of Health 1981–83; Ex-Advisor Licensed Victuallers Protection Society 1974–79[9]); Alex Fletcher (Minister Department of Trade –1985; Consultant Argyll Group 1985–[28]); Conal Gregory (Vice Chairman Conservative Food and Drink Committee; Director, Warwick Wintners[7]); Neil Hamilton (PPS, Vice-Chairman Conservative Trade and Industry Committee; Consultant Brewers Society[7]); Alan Haselhurst (All-Party Chemical Industries Group; Consultant Albright and Wilson – additives[7]); Patrick Jenkin (Ex-Cabinet Minister, Environment; previously employees then advisor, Distillers – whisky, gin, drugs[9]).

Mark Lennox Boyd (Minister; family Guinness[7]); Peter Lloyd (Minister; previously employee then advisor, United Biscuits[9]); Richard Luce (Minister; family Nicholson's gin[9]); Sir Peter Mills (Chairman Conservative Agriculture Committee; advisor, ex-employee meat trade[9]); David Mitchell (Minister; shareholder El Vino wine bars[9]); Michael Morris (Treasurer Parliamentary Food and Health Forum; consultant Mars[9]); Hon Colin Moyniham (PPS, Ex-Vice Chairman Conservative Food and Drink Committee; Vice-Chairman Ridgways Tea (Tate & Lyle owned), consultant, ex-employee Tate & Lyle[9]); Chris Murphy (President British Agrichemicals Association[9]); Michael Neubert (Minister; ex-consultant Ranks Hovis McDougall[9]); Barry Porter (Trade and Industry Select Committee; ex-Director Ballantines Whisky[9]); Rt Hon James Prior (Ex-Cabinet Minister, including Agriculture; now Director United Biscuits[9]); Robert Rhodes James (Consultant Allied-Lyons[9]); Brandon Rhys Williams (ex-employee ICI[9]); Giles Shaw (Minister, Trade and Industry; previously employee then advisor, Rowntree Mackintosh[9]); Michael Shersby (Chairman Conservative Food and Drink Committee; Director-General the Sugar Bureau, Secretary UK Sugar Industries Association, Council Food and Drink Federation, Director World Sugar Research Organization[9]); Roger Sims (Vice-Chairman Conservative Health and Social Services Committee; advisor Scotch Whisky Association[9]); Sir Dudley Smith (Consultant Bass, ex-consultant Kingsway PR[7]); Sir John Stradling Thomas (Ex-Minister; ex-consultant Bass[9]).

Donald Thompson (Minister, Agriculture; ex-Director butchers[9]); John Townend (Chairman liquor business[9]); Sir Gerard Vaughan (Ex-Minister Consumer Affairs, Health; family sugar planters[9]); John Watts (Consultant Ranks Hovis McDougall[7]); Bowen Wells (Consultant International Distillers and Vintners[7]); Jerry Wiggin (Ex-Director Manbré Sugars[9]) Dafydd Wigley (Plaid Cymru; ex-employee Mars[9]).

The fifty or so MPs listed so far should not be taken to be the industry's strongest supporters in the House of Commons. I am not saying that just because Nicholas Ridley once worked for Tate & Lyle, Robert Hayward for Coca-Cola, Patrick Jenkin for Distillers, Peter Lloyd for

United Biscuits, Giles Shaw for Rowntree Mackintosh, and Dafydd Wigley for Mars, these firms can count on support. After all, everybody has a living to earn, and ex-employees do not always keep in touch even if their ex-employers would like them to do so. Maybe Dafydd Wigley can't stand the sight of a Mars Bar.

The strength of the industry in Parliament becomes most evident when a big food manufacturer is threatened with a take-over, or else needs support for a take-over. In October 1985 Allied-Lyons was supported in its fight against the Australian firm Elders by an Early Day Motion signed by 16 MPs, mostly with Allied-Lyons factories in their constituencies.[19] Throughout 1986 Tate & Lyle insisted that their attempt to take over British Sugar would not amount to a monopoly, even though the two firms together account for 94 per cent of the British sugar trade. In December 1986 Tate & Lyle showed its strength in the House of Commons. A story in the *Observer* business pages stated:[29]

MPs STIR UP SUGAR WAR. Intense lobbying is building up around the battle for control of British Sugar. In the House of Common 165 MPs have signed an Early Day Motion describing Ferruzzi, the Italian group which has agreed to pay S & W Berisford $425 million for a 70 per cent share in British Sugar, as 'not a suitable owner' .... Tate & Lyle, skilled political lobbyists, can claim strong support in the House of Commons, although Ferruzzi has found its fans among MPs whose constituents include sugar beet farmers.

That's on the one side. And on the other side? A few MPs who represent the interests of the deep-sea fishing fleet or of small farmers. But the Apple and Pear Development Council, the Fresh Fruit and Vegetable Bureau, the Olive Oil Council and the Scottish Fishermen's Federation do not have the clout of the Biscuit, Cake, Chocolate and Confectionery Alliance, The Food and Drink Federation, the Butter Information Council and the Chemical Industries Association. The money is not in whole, fresh food. The money is in processed fats, sugars and additives. The deep-sea fishing fleet is almost destroyed;[30] the prospects are in food technology. A vote in the House of Commons for good food is a principled vote; the expedient votes go to bad food. There are few vested interests in good health.

CARRY ON WITH THE TABLETS

In the same issue of the *Observer* that carried the Tate & Lyle 'sugar war' story in its business section, another story appeared in the main news pages:[31]

> TOP DOCTOR QUITS IN FEES ROW. A world authority on blood pressure has resigned his post with the Medical Research Council after allegations that he accepted thousands of pounds in consultancy fees from the pharmaceutical industry.

The scientist named was Dr Ian Robertson of the Medical Research Council (MRC) Blood Pressure unit in Glasgow. The story went on:

> Dr Robertson, a fellow of the Royal College of Physicians and a former President of the British Hypertension Society, was paid by at least half a dozen leading drug firms to conduct clinical trials, chair conferences and edit sponsored publications .... Among the companies known to have used his services were ICI, Janssen, Sandoz, Pfizer, and Merck Sharp & Dohme .... The market in drugs to control blood pressure is worth millions of pounds a year.

In quoting this story, I am not suggesting that Dr Robertson may have had a uniquely close relationship with the drug industry. By no means. It is common practice for drug companies to fund scientific research.

Indeed, it might well seem excessive for the MRC and thus the *Observer* to single out Dr Robertson for behaviour which is commonplace among research scientists. But in my view Dr Robertson's relationship with drug companies is of public health interest for a reason not mentioned in the *Observer*. The story goes back to August 1984, when the *Lancet* published a letter denying that salt can be said to cause high blood pressure.

Between 1982 and 1984 the World Health Organization,[32] the NACNE report,[33] and the DHSS's own Committee on Medical Aspects of Food Policy,[34] all recommended that national salt consumption be reduced to help to prevent high blood pressure and stroke, as did the British Medical Association in 1986.[35] In May 1984 the Faculty of Community Medicine of the Royal College of Physicians circulated a draft of its report on *Dietary Salt and Health*[36] to research scientists throughout Britain for comments and advice. This also recommended cuts in salt intake 'for the good of the public health.'

Nonsense, said the letter in the *Lancet*,[37] condemning 'dogmatic advice for which there is no scientific evidence'. Furthermore:

> The idea (or likelihood) that salt in the diet has some positive value is totally ignored. Instead, some are even suggesting that this basic substance is a general poison like alcohol or tobacco. The usual scientific standards for weighing evidence and giving advice which are now well established in drug development seem to have been forgotten in an evangelical crusade to present a simplistic view of the evidence which will prove attractive to the media.

In the event, this remarkable diatribe in defence of salt proved most attractive to the media. 'ADVICE TO CUT BACK ON SALT "IRRESPONSIBLE AND POTENTIALLY HARMFUL"' was the story in *The Times*.[38] 'LANCET LETTER PRE-EMPTS FACULTY PLAN FOR SALT' was the title of a well-informed feature in the doctors' journal *General Practitioner*.[39] And, as quoted in one of a series of letters in what became a furious correspondence in the *Lancet*:[40]

> A *Sunday Express* editorial on August 26 told the public that the advice to reduce salt intake is considered by the MRC Blood Pressure Unit in Glasgow to be 'utter twaddle' and told doctors that 'before they next try to scare the nation out of its wits they actually bother to find out what they are talking about.'

The *Lancet* letter from the Medical Research Council Blood Pressure Unit in Glasgow was signed by Dr Ian Robertson, together with three of his colleagues and ten other research scientists from five other centres. In a subsequent letter replying to their critics, they accepted that the evidence against salt is 'plausible, important, and susceptible to evaluation',[41] but stated that more research was needed before any advice could properly be given to the general public.

By then the Faculty of Community Medicine had evidently taken fright. Salt had proved controversial. The report on *Dietary Salt and Health* was never published. 'CARRY ON WITH THE TABLETS',[42] was the *Guardian*'s comment in its headline to an editorial saying that doctors always disagree.

The drug industry will have been delighted with this *Guardian* obituary of the Faculty of Community Medicine's report. The drug industry has a vested interest in high blood pressure; the more people with high blood pressure, the more customers to carry on with the tablets. Antihypertensive drugs are very profitable: a patient may be diagnosed as having high blood pressure and be prescribed antihypertensives to take every day for thirty years or more. Drug industry representatives usually express outrage when it is pointed out that they have a vested interest in disease; well, they would, wouldn't they? As things are, the drug industry is set fair to fulfil Dr Owen's prescription for a flourishing British 'health care' industry.

The food-manufacturing industry reacted enthusiastically to the letters by Dr Robertson and his colleagues. Early in 1986 the Salt Data Centre was set up to shake the cellar for salt. Kingsway Public Relations arranged for Professor John Swales, a co-signatory of the *Lancet* letters, to address efficiently publicized meetings.[43] The resulting press coverage will have pleased not only Ranks Hovis McDougall, who manufacture 70 per cent of the domestic salt consumed in Britain,[44] but all the giant food manufacturers. Like sugar, salt is added systematically to processed food; like sugar, the quantity of salt in the food supply of Britain and other Western countries is now grossly out of balance.[45]

This is not to say that Professor Swales is swayed by invitations from the Salt Data Centre, or that Dr Robertson's scientific judgement has been altered by the funds he has received from the drug industry. Things don't work like that. Typically (as explained by Professor John Reid – see Chapter 3), industry seeks out scientists with useful views, and supports them in coming to useful conclusions – useful to industry, that is. The results are then magnified by conferences, periodicals and publicity controlled by industry. If all then goes well – for industry, that is – more support and more magnification will follow. And the scientists with views unhelpful to industry? They depend on public funds.

The story of Dr Robertson, Professor Swales and the letters in the *Lancet* is of public interest because it shows how scientists whose views are sympathetic to industry are taken up and become part of industry's research, development and publicity machine, which can be and is used to overwhelm the work of scientists whose views are not sympathetic to industry. Most scientists to whom I have spoken about this subject say that they are unaware of this process. When industry's interests are also in the public interest, then no damage is done. But the food-manufacturing industry does not know how to make profits from whole, fresh food, and the drug industry certainly has no use for whole, healthy people. In Britain MAFF protects the food industry; the DHSS depends upon the drug industry. There are no big bucks in prevention.

Another means of influencing government, and thus national policy, is through the expert committees whose reports give official advice to MAFF and the DHSS. Does the food-manufacturing industry have an undue influence on the Food Advisory Committee, the Committee on Medical Aspects of Food Policy, and the numerous other advisory committees concerned with food and health?

The research needed to answer this question also took a year. Investigating scientists is more troublesome than investigating MPs. Politicians are recognized as apt subjects for enquiry, and any research into the links between MPs and industry is given a flying start by the official *Register of Members' Interests*,[7] issued every year in the public interest and published by HMSO; and also by *Parliamentary Profiles*,[9] the unofficial, thorough and entertaining guide to MPs updated regularly by Andrew Roth.[9] By contrast, the work of advisory committees is covered by the Official Secrets Act; there is no *Register of Advisors' Interests*; any files on government advisors kept in Whitehall are not open for inspection; and some scientists are decidedly touchy about their links with industry, seeing these as their personal and private business. The considerations that applied to MPs mentioned above also apply to scientists.

We researched the membership of 27 government advisory

committees, and also five committees set up by the British Nutrition Foundation, whose reports were published between 1974 and 1987. The committees counted include all those whose work has been discussed in the book. We looked into 246 people (almost all men) who occupied a total of 427 seats on the 32 committees.

We did our best to make the information accurate and up-to-date. It was usually not difficult to get information about scientists who work or have worked for industry: this is found in the annual reports of the British Nutrition Foundation[46] and the Food and Drink Federation (and its predecessors).[47] Recent reports give some details of the employment of their advisors; other details came from MAFF and the DHSS; and, as often as not, the firms we contacted were helpful.

Information about the research funding of academic scientists is much harder to find. The details published in two directories, *Research in British Universities, Polytechnics and Colleges*[48] and the *Medical Research Directory*[49] are incomplete. Academic departments are supposed to publish the sources of their staff's research funding: some do, some don't. In the USA, scientific and medical journals require their contributors to acknowledge sources of research funding; this convention is not followed in Britain.[50] And scientists do not publish details of personal consultancies; these occasionally emerge when industry invites its advisors on to public platforms, or boasts about them in print.

So the details of the research funding and personal consultancies of academic scientists given in Document B are certain to be incomplete. This creates an ethical problem, explained privately to me by one scientist who believes that there should be a register of government advisors' interests, as follows:

> It may be very unfair to list the research funding of some people … when you have not sufficient information about others who may be equally or even more involved with industry. If in some way you could be fairly sure you knew everyone whom the sugar industry, for example, had funded in the last five years or so then I think it would be perfectly reasonable to put that in, but just to have partial information is slightly worrying.

However, the purpose of the long lists printed in Document B is not to pick out individuals but to discern patterns. There is nothing wrong in a scientist being funded by industry. However, in my opinion, scientists who are funded by or who represent the interests of industry should be therefore disqualified from sitting on official advisory committees whose subject is of commercial interst to that industry. But the odd case is nothing to worry about. How many is too many; what amounts to 'undue influence'? You can judge for yourself.

We found that of 370 seats on 27 government advisory committees, 100 were occupied by people not known to have connections with industry or government. A total of 270 have (or had) some connection. Of these, 132 work (or worked) for the food industry; 65 are (or were) funded by or advisors to industry; 156 sit (or sat) on committees of the British Nutrition Foundation (BNF), which is funded by the food industry; and 48 are (or were) government officials. These sub-totals add up to more than 270 because many people are connected with industry in more than one way.

It could be said that serving on a BNF committee does not amount to a connection with the food industry. In which case, 144 of the 370 seats were occupied by people not known to have connections with industry or government; whereas 226 were occupied by people who are (or were) employed by, funded by or advisors to the food industry, or else by government officials.

It is safe to say that for every two government advisors on food and health who have no connection with the food industry or with government, three have such connections. If the BNF is counted as an industry connection, advisors independent of industry and government are outnumbered not three to two but five to two.

Of 247 seats on 19 MAFF (and similar) official committees, 116 were occupied by people who work (or worked) for the food industry. Of 123 seats on eight Department of Health official committees, 47 were occupied by people funded by or advisors to the food industry. The ratios are much the same on BNF committees.

When I started to take a sustained interest in food and health policy in Britain in 1983, I was told by a very senior scientist (I paraphrase):

If you want to find out what is wrong with the British food supply, you must find out what is wrong with the structure of British government official advisory committees.

I have already referred to the fact that Professor Maurice Lessof, chairman of the Royal College of Physicians/BNF committee on *Food Intolerance and Food Aversion* (1984), has had some of his research funded by chemical and food manufacturers, three of which (Beecham, Unilever, and Miles Laboratories) manufacture chemical additives. [8,48,51] Again, I have pointed out that Sir Arnold Burgen, chairman of the DHSS/MAFF committee on *The Safety and Wholesomeness of Irradiated Food* (1986), is a part-time director of a firm that supplies isotopes used in the irradiation of food. [52] And, as it turned out, Dr Roger Whitehead, already identified as advisor to the Dairy Trades Federation and the Milk Marketing Board, [53] was in December 1986 appointed chairman of a new COMA panel set up to set standards for energy, protein, vitamins and minerals. [54]

There again, you will recall that between 1976 and 1984, when Professor George Elton and Sir Henry Yellowlees were Chief Scientist at MAFF and Chief Medical Officer at the DHSS respectively, and when Sir Henry was chairman, and Professor Elton a member, of the main DHSS Committee on Medical Aspects of Food Policy (COMA), both were governors of the BNF. [46]

Furthermore, as already mentioned, Professor John Durnin and Professor Harry Keen, both long-standing members of the main COMA committee in 1987, have substantial links with the sugar industry, both having spoken on sugar industry platforms, and Professor Keen having had research funded by the industry. [55,56,57,58] In December 1986 Professor Keen was appointed chairman of the new COMA panel set up to look into sugars and health. Later, Professor Durnin was appointed a member of the panel. [54]

Is the judgement of scientists ever affected by the source of their employment or funding? As a generality, obviously the answer is yes: scientists are human, just like the rest of us. Individual scientists, like those listed here, will say that their own judgement is not affected. I am not doubting their sincerity; after all, if their views always happen to have been in harmony with the interests of industry, which is quite likely in the case of scientists employed or funded by industry, there is no cause for them to change their minds.

Should scientists employed or funded by industry serve on committees whose reports are of commercial interest to that industry? The scientists in question usually see no problem. Again. I am not doubting their sincerity; but they are wrong. And such judgements are not for the scientists themselves to make. However, the responsibility for appointing government advisors rests with government. It is the politicians and the civil servants in MAFF and DHSS who are to blame for appointing advisors who should be disqualified from serving on official committees. And we are responsible too, as are our elected representatives in Parliament.

These issues have been addressed in the USA, where public health policy is debated in public. Here is Republican Senator Charles Percy speaking in 1976 on the subject of a government advisor with industry links:[59]

> He is judge and jury. Regardless of his objectivity and his competence, it appears there is a conflict of interest. Aren't there enough scientists in the United States so that we would be able to select a panel which would render a very important judgment that would be above reproach so far as any lack of objectivity is concerned? I am not impugning his integrity which is of the highest. But it is very hard to justify having people serve on a panel who have been in the employment of the very companies that are making products that they are called forth to judge.

And Senator Sam Ervin, whose commonsense became world famous during Watergate hearings, had a saying about politicians that applies to others too:[59] 'whose bread I eat, his song I sing.'

TRADE SECRETS ARE
OFFICIAL SECRETS – OFFICIAL

In the USA, the Freedom of Information Act enables concerned citizens to keep track of government policy. In Britain we have the Official Secrets Act. In August 1984 I first heard that members of the DHSS COMA committee and the MAFF FAC committee sign the Official Secrets Act. At the time, I found the story hard to believe. Could it really be true that advice on the storage of breast milk,[60] soyburgers,[61] and biscuit labels,[62] (to take some recent examples) is given the same official status as advice on the disposal of nuclear waste, and that any advisor who chats with an interested enquirer – me, for instance – about his work is liable to criminal prosecution? I was intrigued.

Was the story true? I asked some of the government advisors I knew. Their answers seemed rather vague. They changed the subject. I began to wonder whether signing the Official Secrets Act is itself an Official Secret.

Summer 1984 was a time of public debate about where the true loyalty of civil servants should lie, following the prosecutions of Sarah Tisdall and Clive Ponting. Lord Scarman had fulminated against the official abuse of power in a much quoted speech:[63]

> Parliament, politicans in power, and civil servants have established amongst themselves a tightly knit, secretive system for the efficient creation and fulfilment of consistent nationwide policy. The Civil Service, as we know it, fits snugly into this system.

I pursued my enquiries, and one day a note arrived from a DHSS official, saying 'we are now also requiring members of COMA panels to sign the Act.' Word then got out to the *Mail on Sunday*, whose headline and story on 16 September ran:[64]

> DIET THAT'S AN OFFICIAL SECRET. 'Doctors studying how Britain's diet is damaging the nation's health are to be asked to sign the Official Secrets Act. More than twenty doctors and diet experts working on Government research groups will shortly receive copies of the Act to sign.

The *Mail on Sunday*'s leader-writer went into top gear:[65]

> WHEN FREEDOM OF SPEECH MEANS THE PRESS SAYS NOTHING ...
> The Official Secrets Act is mis-used almost daily by this and every Government and it is disgraceful that this should be the case. If the Government decrees that it is an official secret to know about, for example, the incidence of sugar and fat in the

diet, as it is now saying it is, then what else is being kept from us?

Quite. At the Annual General Meeting of the Coronary Prevention Group on 14 May 1985 I raised the subject with John Patten, the guest of honour, then junior Minister at the Department of Health. He seemed a bit surprised at the time, but later rallied with a long and courteous letter suggesting that it was all just a matter of routine:[66]

Under the Official Secrets Act, it is an offence for anyone given Government information in confidence, to disclose that without authority. This applies whether or not they have signed a form; the purpose of the signing is really to ensure that those receiving the information appreciate what the Act says and how it applies to them.

Mr Patten's letter to me was inscribed 'Personal' in his own handwriting. Did this mean that the government information he was giving me was in confidence? Now that I have disclosed it to you, will the boys in plain clothes be knocking at my door?

The Conservative MP Jonathan Aitken also attended the meeting of the Coronary Prevention Group, and a couple of days later addressed a Parliamentary Question to the Minister of Agriculture. He asked:[67]

Will my hon Friend explain why the nutritionists and other experts who serve on committees to do with food labelling, such as the Committee on Medical Aspects of Food Policy, are required to sign the Official Secrets Act? Is food labelling not a subject where maximum publicity is needed, not maximum security?

Mrs Fenner, speaking for MAFF, said she would let Mr Aitken know, and accordingly wrote to him on 23 May as follows:[68]

Food labelling is of course an issue on which the Food Advisory Committee advise the Government rather than the Committee on Medical Aspects of Food Policy. Nevertheless the principle is the same for the membership of both Committees in that members are required to sign the Official Secrets Act.

So it was true! Mrs Fenner continued:

> This is usual procedure and arises because it is necessary from time to time for information on manufacturing processes or other commercially sensitive material to be placed before the members of these Committees in order that they can properly advise Ministers on the subject before them. The signing of the Official Secrets Act by the members of these Committees is the way of ensuring that the integrity of this information is protected from unauthorised disclosure to commercial competitors and I am sure you would agree that it is right that we should do this.

The implication of this answer seemed to be that unless Professor Brainstawme of the COMA committee signed the Official Secrets Act, he would fall into temptation and send microfiches of the formula for Gloppo, disclosed to him during his official duties, to his old chum Stanley Wizz of Wizzo plc. Was this really what Mrs Fenner meant? In any case, Jonathan Aitken, who as a journalist was prosecuted under the Official Secrets Act, (and then acquitted) and is now Chairman of the Campaign for Freedom of Information's Parliamentary Liaison Committee, thought little of Mrs Fenner's letter and disclosed it to me, describing the passages quoted above as 'ludicrous bureaucratic bunkum'.

On 6 March 1986, the Labour MP Tony Lloyd had a go at the Minister of Agriculture, Michael Jopling. Tony Lloyd had heard that representatives of the Food and Drink Federation and the Chemical Industries Association were embarrassed by the shroud of Official Secrecy covering their negotiations with government about food additives. Mr Lloyd's Parliamentary Question was:[69]

> Will the Minister meet representatives of the food industry so that he can discuss this matter with them and tell them when he intends to legislate on the issue, so that the secrecy surrounding the use of additives in food can be broken and the public can have access to and knowledge of what takes place?

Mr Jopling seems to have sighed a tolerant but weary sigh as he got up in order to put Mr Lloyd down:[69]

> I am sorry that the Hon Gentleman is still pursuing a very old story, which I thought had been put to rest. He should know, and I am surprised he has not seen the statements which have

been made, that members of the Committee do not have to sign the Official Secrets Act .... However, certain information is given which is commercially private and the committees are asked to keep it that way.

Judging from the copies of the personal letters written by Mr Jopling's colleagues Mr Patten and Mrs Fenner in my possession, it seemed to me that Mr Jopling was misleading Tony Lloyd and the House of Commons in phrasing his reply as he did; so I sent Mrs Fenner's letter to various MPs. Accordingly, the Liberal MP Michael Meadowcroft asked Mrs Fenner on 10 April exactly what form of words governed the confidentiality of government advisory committees.[70] She replied:

When they are appointed, members of the Food Advisory Committee are informed that under the terms of the Official Secrets Act information give to them in their capacity as members of the committee should not be disclosed outside the committee.

Mr Meadowcroft enjoyed putting his Supplementary Question:[70]

In view of the Minister's reply, why did she write to her Hon Friend the member for Thanet South (Mr Aitken) on 23 May stating categorically that the members of these two committees are required to sign the Official Secrets Act, although her right hon Friend, who is sitting next to her, denied that in March of this year?

'They are not required to sign the Official Secrets Act,' replied Mrs Fenner. But she was in difficulties, and was not helped by Jonathan Aitken (who had been unaware that her note to him had been circulated). He rose and said:[70]

Although I am sure that my hon Friend is almost as surprised as I am that our previous billets doux on the subject of official secrecy have been revealed this afternoon by the Liberal party, will she nevertheless consider the absurdity of the Government's position? Surely it is unrealistic to invoke the criminal law when food advice should be the subject of maximum publicity, rather than maximum secrecy?

Mrs Fenner demurred. But by this time she must have realized that the team of civil servants who brief ministers had given her a bum steer. On 4 June she wrote another personal letter to Jonathan Aitken, and also wrote in similar terms to Tony Lloyd and Michael Meadowcroft and to the Labour MP Barry Sheerman:[71]

> In trying to explain the differences in the responsibilities of the Committee on Medical Aspects of Food Policy and the Food Advisory Committee I have inadvertently told you that members of both Committees were required to sign the Official Secrets Act declaration in order to preserve the confidentiality of certain commercially sensitive information made available to the Committee.

Mrs Fenner then had the task of trying to explain the difference between signing the Official Secrets Act and being covered by the Act:

> Members of COMA which is serviced by DHSS are required to sign the Official Secrets Act declaration and have done so since the Committee's inception in 1957. Members of my Ministry's Food Advisory Committee on the other hand are not required to sign the declaration. Instead they are informed at the time of their appointment that information given to them in their capacity as members of the Committee is subject to the Official Secrets Act .... The necessity to protect unauthorised disclosure of commercially sensitive material is one that is common not only to COMA and the FAC but also to many other Government Committees.

What did government advisors think about the policy that a trade secret is an Official Secret? Professor Philip James, a member of the Food Advisory Committee, said that he had never signed the Act, and 'I would not do so. I am shocked it is even suggested.'[64] What about Mrs Fenner's suggestion that Official Secrecy is really just innocuous traditional routine? In 1985, you will recall, Professor Geoffrey Rose, a member (with Professor James) of the COMA panel whose report on *Diet and Cardiovascular Disease* was published in the summer of 1984,[34] resigned from the government Radioactive Waste Management Advisory Committee, having been (or so it is believed) pressed to agree with politically convenient recommendations which in his view threatened public health.

In June 1986 Professor Rose went public in a story in the *Guardian* by Richard Norton-Taylor headed 'PROFESSOR ACCUSES WHITEHALL OF SECRETS ACT "GAG" ON DOCTORS'.[72] He said:

> There could be a conflict of interests between a duty to be open on matters of public health and the possibility of a prosecution under the Official Secrets Act.

He had been provoked by a statement made in Parliament by the then DHSS Minister, Barney Hayhoe, who disclosed that 43 advisory committees in some way or another concerned with public health are Officially Secret.

And is the Official Secrets Act inconsequential? In contrast with Mr Jopling and Mrs Fenner, Mr Hayhoe evidently did not think so. He emphasized that the Act 'applies to all confidential information whether or not a declaration has been signed',[73] even when no warning to that effect is given.

So the answer to the question 'what is the difference between signing the Official Secrets Act and being covered by the Official Secrets Act?' is that there is no difference.

Professor Rose was infuriated, and published a lead letter in the *British Medical Journal* in June 1986:[74]

> When a Minister announces in Parliament that the Official Secrets Act applies to the Leprosy Opinion Panel, something has gone wrong. The position is clearly crazy and out of control. The British Medical Association should organise pressure on government to exclude from its list all those advisory bodies whose business is not related to national security (which in the case of public health means almost all of them). Meanwhile doctors who are members of government committees ought to inform their chairmen that discretion, not the Official Secrets Act, will be their guide; and that they will not accept secrecy if concern for the public health requires otherwise.

As it turned out, the work done by the Leprosy Opinion Panel is not innocuous, as Professor Rose had assumed. Dr Michael Corcos wrote to the *Guardian* in August 1986[75] explaining that there is a special reason why leprosy research is Officially Secret. In 1968 Dr Corcos had declined an invitation to join the panel. Scientific observations that might help sufferers might also be useful as weapons of war, he said; nowadays much medical research is impounded as it leaves the laboratory bench by defence and security officials. Take leprosy:

> Much current research is pointing to the bacillus not being the direct cause of the condition(s), but rather the carrier of a smaller macromolecular agent which replicates in human nerve fibrils. It does not take anyone with more than a biology A level to understand the significance of this for 'germ warfare': defence researches concerned with the use of molecular mechanisms as a means of killing or disabling potential enemy troops, require a low profile for this type of work, even at the cost of retarding therapy for civilian populations.

So lepers can rest assured that, while research into their disease might do them no good, it might also do the Russians a whole power of no good, too, come the Third World War.

What, though, about the committees in no way concerned with national security? After Professor Rose, there were no more publicly announced resignations. Nor, as far as I know, did any colleagues of Professor James on the Food Advisory Committee voice any protests. Many scientists like the arrangement whereby they are, unobserved, witness, judge and jury, and would dislike being subject to any public scrutiny. Leave it to the experts! In a leading article written for the BNF *Bulletin* in May 1986, Professor David Conning, the BNF Director-General, suspected the motives of 'professional busybodies in pursuit of their vendetta with the food industry'.[76] Professor Conning has, you will recall, been a government advisor, as a member of the Cabinet Office ACARD committee on food technology, while serving on Food and Drink Federation committees. He went on to query 'the current vogue for freedom of information' and 'pompous pronouncements on the "rights" of individuals to govern their own affairs'. For instance:

> Nutrition labelling represents a good example of how 'freedom of information', a noble concept to the addle-brained or cunning, can be more than useless to the ignorant or innocent unless handled with care, insight and sensitivity.

In celebrating the scientist as seigneur, Professor Conning was, I am sure, speaking for a great many of his colleagues, who enjoy their ivory towers of power.

THE BRITISH RAIL BREAKFAST THEORY

You might suppose that nutritionists, above all others, care most about food and public health in Britain, and fight hardest to protect and improve the quality of British food. You would be wrong.

For a start, most nutritionists work with animals or in industry; some may care about human health as individual citizens, but it is not their job to do so. In any case, most nutritionists still think that British food is good. They are trained to believe in a food supply which has been devised, or at least approved of, by an older generation who have advised government and industry, administered university departments, and written textbooks. They believe that food which makes babies and children grow fast is therefore good food. This is the myth with which we in the West have all grown up. And all of us, nutritionists included, have – literally – swallowed the myth; to dispel it, is to repudiate the food that made us bonny bouncing babies, and then made us grow big, strong and tall.

The conventional wisdom of the dominant group of British nutritionists, inside and outside industry, is that high-energy, high-protein food is good food, and that if you look after the energy and the protein, everything else will usually look after itself. This is the British Rail breakfast theory of human nutrition. And British nutritionists put this theory into practice; they can be seen in the early morning in conference centres the world over, tucking into their words in the form of bacon, fried egg and sausage, toast, butter and marmalade, before the day's proceedings.

Many, perhaps most, of the senior British scientists concerned with human nutrition do not worry about food and public health in Britain, and do not exert themselves to improve the quality of the British food supply. This is because they really do not think that there is much of a problem. Britain was the last country in the Western world officially to concede that fats and saturated fats, in the quantities typically present in Western food, are a cause of heart attacks; and, since the publication of the COMA report on *Diet and Cardiovascular Disease* in 1984,[34] it has become clear that some British nutritionists refuse to look at the evidence on fats and heart disease, and that others, unable to refute the evidence, pay a languid lip-service to it.

The British nutritional establishment takes a relaxed attitude to the food-manufacturing industry. Most departments of nutrition and dietetics in universities and other places of learning now provide a support service to the food industry. As a rule, the academics who support food manufacturers and trade associations, as apologists and/or consultants, and who are in turn supported with research grants from the food industry, act in good faith: they do not see any conflict of interests.

After all, anybody who believes that good nutrition is mostly about protein and energy can put in a good word for almost all processed foods, which may well contain little or no protein, but which are very likely to be concentrated sources of energy (calories). And since there is plenty of protein and energy in the British food supply already, other processed foods which are bulked up with water, air or gum can also be recommended, as aids to slimming!

British nutritionists enjoy the highest reputation worldwide, as they have done since the days of the British Empire. It is usually agreed that the most important nutritional problem in the Third World is severe lack of protein and energy; and, indeed, starving and stunted children need food which is concentrated in protein and energy. Because of a tradition of service, particularly in India and Africa, going back half a century and more, many British academic nutritionists with a sense of social responsibility are not very interested in their own country, and are much more concerned with matters of life and death in developing countries.

But going for growth in Africa and Asia does not help us in Britain. It means that some of the most influential British nutritionists, who advise international agencies and governments all over the world, as well as the British government, are liable to encourage the manufacture of dairy products, notably full-fat cows' milk, which supply protein and energy as well as saturated fats, and even of sugar, which supplies energy while being empty calories, devoid of nutrients. This positive approval of fatty, sugary food is a disaster for public health in Britain.

It can also be a disaster for Third World countries. If they become dependent on Western food, their traditional agriculture is liable to disintegrate, causing further famine. And when breast milk is replaced by cows' milk, and indigenous food systems are replaced by sweet fat, in the name of science and progress, Western disease patterns emerge, which create more dependence on Western medicine. The multinational food and drug companies gain; the people lose.

Back home in Britain, nutrition has lost the prestige it enjoyed in the 1930s and 1940s. Why study a solved subject? The title 'nutritionist' does not ring bells, as 'physicist', say, or 'surgeon' does. Nutritionists are commonly confused with dietitians, who are in turn commonly assumed to be some sort of auxiliary nurse or cook. Oxford and Cambridge Universities have never had departments of human nutrition.[77] Complacency about food and health in Britain since the Second World War[78] has meant that few bright science students have chosen to specialize in nutrition, and indeed have had little chance to do so: in 1974 there were only three departments of human nutrition in British universities,[79] and medical students are not taught nutrition.[80] The result? Stagnation.

Academic nutritionists in Britain evidently do not question their associations with the food-manufacturing industry. For example, two government advisory committees, reporting in 1974[79] and 1982,[81] have complained that the Medical Research Council, then responsible for the funding of research into human nutrition, has lost interest in the subject. Yet the appointment of Lord Jellicoe, Director and ex-Chairman of Tate & Lyle, as Chairman of the MRC, is not seen as odd. The Nutrition Society, the forum for people with formal qualifications in nutrition, published a poll of 1257 of its members in 1986,[82] in which some yearning for nutrition to become a profession, designed to exclude outsiders, was expressed. Yet in the same issue of the

Proceedings of the Nutrition Society there appeared a celebration of manufactured salt presented by Ted Druce of Ranks Hovis McDougall,[83] who, you will recall, make most of the salt we eat in Britain.[44] Indeed, the Nutrition Society embraces industry. To give one example, Professor Russell Allen was first the Society's Programmes Secretary, then its Secretary, from 1953 to 1962,[84] before going on to be, simultaneously, Head of Research at Beecham, Chairman of the British Nutrition Foundation, and a member of MAFF's Food Standards Committee. As already mentioned, in 1987 Dr Allen is Vice-President of the BNF and also President of the British Dietetic Association.

This is not intended to show disrespect to Lord Jellicoe, Mr Druce, Professor Allen, or anybody else from the food industry who may influence national food policy. They are entitled to express their views. At the same time, it stands to reason that they will defend their company's product. Since the 1960s, nutrition in Britain has become part of a phenomenon vigorously encouraged by the Conservative government under Mrs Thatcher and which therefore may well become more common in the late 1980s and 1990s: not so much coalition as coalescence between science, government and industry.

FAMINE, FAMINE? RABBIT, RABBIT

Every three or four years, the International Union of Nutritional Sciences (IUNS), a worldwide body, holds a congress in a different country. In 1963 Scotland was the host nation.[85] In 1985 it was England's turn: the Nutrition Society organized the thirteenth congress in Brighton. In the words of Professor John Waterlow of London University, then President of the Nutrition Society, 'it seems unlikely that there will be another one in this country for perhaps half a century.'[86] I attended the congress: it was a unique opportunity to learn from and speak to scientists from all over the world; and also to see the British system in action.

The Chairman of the Executive Committee of the Congress was Professor Donald Naismith of London University, who became well known in 1986 as consultant to the Snack, Nut and Crisp Manufacturers Association and for his view that crisps 'are a very nutritious part of the diet'.[87,88] The Chairman of the Scientific Programmes Committee was Professor Michael Gurr, then of the Food Research Institute at Reading University, who you will again recall, has been a consultant to and funded by the Milk Marketing Board and the Dairy Trades Federation,[48,53] and who in 1987 is employed by the Milk Marketing Board while being a member of the main Department of Health Committee on Medical Aspects of Food Policy.[89]

Over 3000 delegates from 92 countries attended the congress. They participated in 48 symposia and 40 workshops during six days, and presented their work in progress in the form of 1416 'original communications' posted in the conference centres and at the University of Sussex. Among the dignitaries presiding over this gigantic event were Professor Waterlow, Dr R. Buzina from Yugoslavia, then President of the IUNS, and Professor Nevin Scrimshaw from the USA and the United Nations University; he is past President of the IUNS. Both Professor Waterlow and Professor Scrimshaw have for many years advised the World Health Organization on human protein and energy requirements, with special reference to the Third World.[90,91]

In celebration of the Brighton congress, the *British Journal of Nutrition*, the official organ of the Nutrition Society, produced a bumper number, running to 324 pages and containing 28 papers 'of direct relevance to clinical and animal nutrition', together with words of welcome from Professor Waterlow.[86] The subjects of these 28 papers were rats, rats, rats, pigs, rats, rats, rats, rats, rats, rabbits, rats, sheep, sheep, chicks, hamsters, chickens, sheep, sheep, sheep, sheep, sheep, calves, sows, piglets, piglets, rabbits, sheep and pigs. The *Journal*'s editors gave pride of place to two papers from France whose surprising finding was that alcoholic fat rats seem to suffer less from fatty degeneration of the liver than teetotal fat rats: an interesting insight, perhaps, into where French and indeed British nutritionists' heads are at.

Why was there no word about people in this once-in-a-lifetime edition, displaying the latest science to delegates attending the Brighton congress from Africa, India and China, in a year whose main event turned out to be the catastrophic famine in Ethopia? Animals are, of course, not politically problematic.

Referring to the congress, Professor Waterlow suggested that:[86]

> many may feel that we have given too little attention to practical problems, particularly when large numbers of people are facing starvation.

Of the 275 or so formal presentations in Brighton, just 42 were from non-Western countries, including 13 from Central and South America. For the rest, 22 were from Asia and three from the West Indies, and there was a total of four speakers from black Africa. Two other minor 'oral' contributions were on 'Effectiveness of cocoa-pod ash solutions for treating fibrous crop residues' from Nigeria and – the one item from Ethiopia – on 'Molasses urea and legume hay as supplements to poor quality roughage'.[92]

John Rivers, a colleague of Professor Waterlow at London University (School of Hygiene and Tropical Medicine), was appointed press officer for the congress. But, having seen an advance draft of the Brighton programme, he wrote a stinging article in the Nutrition Society's newsletter, which he edits, accusing the organizers of ignoring the famine in Ethiopia and 'the fact that real, human beings are dying of that old cause – filmed, but to a staggering degree, not fed.'[93] Because of this emotional display, he was seen as an untrustworthy spokesman for the congress,[94] and was replaced by Professor Arnold Bender, Professor Naismith's predecessor at London University, who was head of research at Farley's Infant Foods and at Bovril[95] before he became an academic. Questioned about Ethiopia on Radio Brighton at the start of the congress, Professor Bender explained that famine is famine and science is science. Rabbit, rabbit, indeed.

In the programme of the congress, the Executive Committee acknowledged the sponsorship of Cow & Gate baby foods, and Unilever; Associated British Foods, the Cocoa Chocolate and Confectionery Alliance, Kelloggs, the Milk Marketing Board, and the Sugar Bureau; Beecham,

Nestlé, Quaker Oats, Ranks Hovis McDougall, and the Snack Nut and Crisp Manufacturers Association.[92] Every delegate to the Congress found an invitation from the Sugar Bureau to a 'Satellite Symposium' held in the ballroom of the Metropole, the luxury hotel in which the grandest delegates were staying. Remember, said Professor Vincent Marks, in a briefing given away after the 'symposium' at which he spoke, that sugar is a key weapon in the fight against world malnutrition.[96] Suffer little starving children to come to the world sugar trade, was the message.

For me the most remarkable session of the congress was the very last (official) symposium, on 'Contributions of the UN Agencies to Nutrition'. It was organized by Professor Waterlow himself. Dr Buzina was chairman of the session, and Professor Scrimshaw was there to account for the role of the UN University, together with speakers from the World Health Organization, the Food and Agriculture Organization, the World Food Programme, UNICEF and the World Bank. One way and another, the speakers had responsibility for the nature and quality of food grown by and distributed to most of the 92 countries represented at Brighton.

In my dictionary, 'symposium' means 'a collection of views on one topic'. But as the morning wore on, it became clear that there was room only for one view – that the UN agencies are doing a terrific job. Professor Scrimshaw and Dr Buzina both suggested that anybody wanting more information could write in for handouts. At the end of rather a long summing-up, Dr Buzina regretted that no time for questions had been found.

In common with about fifty people in the room, from the USA, Nigeria, Ghana, Kenya, Uganda, Bangladesh, Lesotho, Britain and Europe, I had a question, and stood up and asked for a discussion. After a certain amount of pandemonium, Professor Waterlow, Professor Scrimshaw and Dr Buzina regretted that they could not stay, and walked out, presumably to lunch.

What I wanted, and want, to know, is: why does everybody concerned with food in the Third World confuse malnutrition with severe deficiency only of protein and energy? Certainly, starving children need protein and energy-dense foods. But what about the long term? Surely we know that food high in energy and animal protein, and therefore heavy in saturated fats and sugars, destroys the health of people in middle age all over the Western world? Are the international agencies now part of a process whereby the fats and sugars which we no longer want are being dumped on the Third World, in the name of aid, in what is in fact the most gigantic process of Coca-colonialism yet devised?

Some speakers stayed behind and joined in the discussion initiated by the delegates. But I am still waiting for answers to these questions.

A month later I was in Sri Lanka. 'Taste the superb, natural flavour of lemon in Maliban's marvellous Lemon Puff Biscuits now available in an attractively designed, internationally styled pack,' read a puff in the Colombo Daily News.[97] The headline of a colour advertisement in the Observer was 'MAKE A FUSS'.[98] The picture showed a mother bending over her little boy, who is about to tuck into a 'Little Lion Cake'. 'Pamper the people you love. Give them the best .... They will love you a little more for it,' was the claim.

The policy of President Jawardene's government in Sri Lanka is to open the economic doors to the West: and that means sweet fat. 'Handy Hints' for the readers of the Island included the following:[99]

Leftover sandwiches with firm centres can be made quite appetising. First, cut into quarters then dip in pancake batter. Fry in heated oil or fat and serve hot.

The Observer carried a regular 'Training Your Toddler' comic strip which evidently originated in the West. 'If your five year-old is a little fatty, his school friends may tease. Help him by providing a nourishing, unfattening diet' was the Hint in one strip.[100] The picture shows two (white) parents attacking a breakfast of bacon and eggs, toast and marmalade, while Junior is faced with one boiled egg.

Much of the food advertising in Sri Lanka is aimed at children and young people. 'Write in your own handwriting "I'm a Vegemite Kid",' said an advertisement sponsored by the Island, and enclose an empty packet of Kraft processed cheese, and you might win an electronic game.[101] Hoardings in the villages for Astra margarine, a product with the consistency of lard even in tropical heat, were illustrated by picture of boys playing football. The 'Netball Queen '85' contest for the 'Orange Crush Trophy' was co-sponsored by the *Daily News* and Ceylon Cold Stores.[102] Nestomalt, the Nestlé full-fat milk drink, sponsored the '3rd National Nestomalt Marathon' with heats in Kandy, Ratnapura and Ambalangoda.[103] Lakspray, dried milk 'imported from the finest dairy farms of the world', enticed readers to 'win a car & 165 fabulous prizes worth over Rs 425,000 in the Grand Lakspray Contest', in a full-page *Daily News* colour advertisement.[104]

In Colombo and Kandy supermarkets in October 1985, Puffa Puffa Rice was on sale for the equivalent of £2.00 a packet. Hoardings for Nespray, the Nestlé dried milk, are everywhere. Fly posters promoted a 'Build a Motor Bike Contest with Coca-Cola'.

Doctors in Sri Lanka are not deceived. 'What has happened to mankind?' asked a feature in the *Daily News*,[105] side by side with the ads for Lemon Puffs, Orange Crush, Nestomalt and Lakspray. Dr W.A. Karunaratne, President of the Association of Community Medicine, wrote that

> Cardiovascular and coronary heart diseases are a major public health problem .... The diet should not have excessive calories and saturated fats. It should have less sucrose and salt and more starchy foods, less dairy produce, fat-free milk and more polyunsaturated fats .... For the effective prevention of common diseases the authorities must have a clear and explicit recognition and appreciation of the problem.

Nor are all the people of Sri Lanka deceived. By the bus-stop outside the baby elephant orphanage at the Udawattakelle Forest Reserve, there's a little roadside shop sporting a massive Coca-Cola sign. But 'that's for tourists,' said the owner. He beamed when I asked for a king coconut. 'No chemicals,' he said. 'Natural,' he said, slashing the top off the coconut. But somebody must be buying the Puffa Puffa Rice.

I got back from Sri Lanka to read a *Sunday Times* story headed 'LET A THOUSAND BURGERS BLOSSOM'.[106] Desmond Wong, a Chinese entrepreneur based in New York, was looking for a British partner for a deal already struck with the Chinese government:

> MPs packed meetings in the Commons on Thursday and Friday to hear Wong explain why hamburgers represent the way forward in trade with China. Indeed, Wong's approach may prove to be the most significant breakthrough yet in business relations with China .... He is looking for a British partner to develop a hamburger takeaway opposite the Ming Tombs and Great Wall of China, where some 20,000 tourists flock every day.

Mr Wong was also reported to be looking at other fast-food opportunities and at expanding consumption of dairy food in China. He described the approach of his company, the Good Earth Development Corporation, as 'cultural translation'.

The fourteenth International Congress of Nutrition is scheduled to take place in Seoul, South Korea, in 1989. It remains to be seen what the policy of the International Union of Nutritional Sciences on sponsorship from Little Lion Cakes, Astra margarine, Puffa Puffa Rice, Nespray, Coca-Cola and the Good Earth Development Corporation will be. It is safe to assume that for breakfast delegates from Britain will choose bacon, fried egg and sausage, toast, butter and marmalade.

WHAT DO YOU MEAN, 'PROOF'?

When in June 1984 I published a series of three long features in *The Times* on the medical, commercial and political aspects of food and health in Britain, finishing with some tips for healthy eating,[107] the response, from readers and interested parties, was impressive. Two of the 30 letters printed in *The Times* were from Sir Raymond Hoffenberg, President of the Royal College of Physicians, and Professor Thomas McKeown, advisor on global policy to the World Health Organization. Sir Raymond wrote:[108]

> The average British diet may well be unsatisfactory but there are different views about the relationship of diet to health and it must be said that much of the detailed advice given by Mr

Cannon falls into the category of not yet proved. Many medical institutions in this country and abroad have been concerned about these issues for a long time but have refrained from making categorical statements because of the uncertainty of prevailing knowledge.

In common with Sir Francis Avery Jones, the distinguished gastroenterologist, Professor Jerry Morris of the Department of Epidemiology at London University, and Lord Young, President of the College of Health, Professor McKeown was not happy about Sir Raymond's letter: [108]

I believe that Sir Raymond Hoffenberg will probably agree that (1) On many medical issues, conclusive proof could be obtained only by massive human experiments which are ruled out on ethical or other grounds. (2). It is therefore often necesary to advise action on evidence which is less than complete, having regard for what has been called a 'burden of prudence' rather than a burden of proof. (3). While further experience may lead to a revision of some of the dietary proposals outlined by Geoffrey Cannon ... they are likely to prove broadly correct.

What is the nature of the disagreement between Dr Hoffenberg and Dr McKeown? And given such disagreement, between experts whose credentials are beyond doubt, how can lay people come to any conclusions? Is now the time to change our eating habits and press for changes in the national food supply? Or should we sit tight at table and wait for more research and more evidence, hoping in time for a Great British menu carved in tablets of stone?

Lay people suppose that scientific debates are contests of knowledge in which only experts can take part. You and I, it is supposed, can no more comment meaningfully on expert judgement than we could return the serve of Boris Becker. Scientists are not noted for contradicting this idea; being human, they enjoy their priest-like status. Nowadays we are trained to have faith in science. But what should we do when scientists disagree on issues which vitally affect not just them, but us?

Until very recently, the policy of the British government on food and public health has been to do nothing so long as the experts did not all agree. For example, (as mentioned in chapter 3), when in 1974 the COMA panel on *Diet and*

Coronary Heart Disease[109] recommended that, in order to prevent heart disease, people in Britain should eat less fat, and in particular less hard, saturated fat, Professor John Yudkin, a member of the panel, disagreed, and insisted in writing a minority (of one) report. In July 1984, heart disease prevention was debated in the House of Lords,[110] immediately after the publication of the 1984 COMA report on *Diet and Cardiovascular Disease*,[34] whose conclusions broadly repeated those reached ten years before.

Why, asked Lord Prys-Davies, had little or no positive action been taken by government in the 1970s? In reply Lord Ennals, who as David Ennals was the Labour Cabinet Minister responsible for DHSS between 1976 and 1979, had this to say:[110]

> It was frankly impossible to get an agreed conclusion from the panel of the Committee on Medical Aspects of Food Policy .... They simply did not agree. It was not through any lack of trying on behalf of successive Secretaries of State, and certainly no layman can say 'This is what ought to be done: this is what the experts say' when the experts say different things.

But it is part of the responsibility of politicians, who are elected to represent the interests of citizens, to listen to specialists: and then to make decisions. Why should this responsibility be abdicated, in the case of public health? A politician who has to decide whether or not a nuclear power station should be built, or an inner city area demolished, does not ordinarily quail because expert witnesses disagree. Everybody knows that specialists have different views; and there's nothing necessarily wrong in that. Experts draw different conclusions from the same facts. They may have bees in their bonnets. Besides, knowledge can drive out wisdom; plenty of experts are bad judges of their own learning. Why should a Cabinet Minister be so dependent on expert unanimity that the political process can be paralysed by the dissenting voice of one member of a COMA panel?

The answer, of course, is that lay people, whether politicians, citizens concerned to do their best for themselves and their families, or journalists trying to make sense of a new topic, have been mystified by the scientists. We don't understand what they are saying. But the more we concede our own judgement to that of the experts, the more we are invalidated as citizens; and when our elected representatives make obeisance to science, democracy itself becomes diseased.

While scientists may know more, they may not know better, than lay people. And the fact is that, stripped of jargon and mystique, the work that scientists do, in order to look for links between food, health and disease, is not difficult to understand. Moreover, although scientists seem unaware of the fact, they are as confused as anybody else. The reason is that much of the debate in Britain about food and public health, which persists in the media and in medical journals years after general agreement has been achieved in the USA and other Western countries,[111] depends on a muddled, or deliberately muddled, use of certain key concepts, such as, for example, 'proof'. What does 'proof' mean?

On 15 April 1985 the *Guardian* carried a story with the headline 'CHANNEL 4 ACCUSED OF BIAS AFER PROGRAMME ON FAT AND HEALTH IS BANNED'.[112] Banned? What was the persecuted programme proposing to say? According to the report:

Eating fatty food does not necessarily cause heart disease. Three of seven experts on the programme endorse this view and say that a causal link between fat and coronary heart disease has yet to be conclusively proved. Until it is, the programme suggests, it is wrong for health policy to be based on the supposition that eating fatty foods is dangerous to the heart.

The editorial slant of the Channel 4 programme, which was transmitted in due course, depended on a passage in the 1984 COMA report[34] which, in prefacing its recommendation that the amount of fats and saturated fats in British food be cut, also said:

The Panel, in its consideration of the complex relationship between diet and cardiovascular disease, has acknowledged that the evidence falls short of proof.

This sentence encouraged the fats trade. On 3 April 1985, James Morton, Chairman of the Butter Information Council, introduced a film on fats in food, saying:[113]

We must be clear about this. It is only a matter of opinion that diet change will produce benefit. Proof is lacking as the COMA committee said.

And as a climax to a three-part series with the title 'LIVESTOCK INDUSTRY MUST SPEAK UP',[114] *Farmer's Weekly* averred:

Others will feel that the evidence against animal fat is so tenuous and unproven, that an all-out opposition from the industry would be justified .... After all, there is no proof; only a series of expressions of opinion.

All these statements about food and public health share one concept: that of 'proof'. Other phrases regularly crop up: 'conclusive proof', 'final proof', 'absolute proof' and, most magisterial of all, 'scientific proof'.

There is no one definition of proof. In civil law, proof is 'a preponderance of the evidence';[115] '51 per cent proof will suffice'.[116] Rather like a general practitioner who must decide what to do with a patient, judgement in a civil court is made on the 'balance of probability'. In criminal law, where the stakes are higher, the 'standard of proof' is correspondingly higher, and judgment is made against an accused when the evidence of guilt is 'beyond reasonable doubt'. Hence a dictionary definition of 'proof' as 'evidence such as determines the judgment of a tribunal'. In law, then, 'proof' involves judgement based on evidence; and the better the evidence, the better the proof. In law, there is no such thing as 'absolute' proof. Contrary evidence is always possible. Law, like all human activity, is fallible.

By contrast, mathematical or logical proof, when accurate, is absolute. This is because it is not concerned with evidence or probability, but moves from axiom to theorem by a process of logic using agreed rules.[117] There are no degrees of proof in logic. $1 = 1$, or $1 + 1 = 2$, is true by definition.

How does this apply to medical science? Take two questions that a physician may be asked. First: 'can you prove whether or not John Jones, at this moment, has high blood pressure?' The answer is yes, by definition, because 'high blood pressure' is defined as systolic and/or diastolic pressure above a certain level. So, if John's blood pressure is 120/80, he is proved not to have high blood pressure, simply because, by any definition, 120/80 is normal. The proof that John does not have high blood pressure is syllogistic.

Second, 'can you prove that Jack Smith's death from lung cancer was caused by his smoking habit?' This is a different sort of question. The evidence is that smoking is the main cause of lung cancer. But it is not the sole cause. In a case like this the physician might say, if he chose his words carefully, 'I am sure' or 'there can be no real doubt', making a judgement based on evidence. He is dealing in probabilities. If, after Jack's death, his blackened lungs were extracted at autopsy, as a medical equivalent of the 'smoking gun' the prosecuting counsel longs for in a murder trial, the pathologist might brandish the abused organs and say 'here is the proof!' But, like a lawyer, he is still using the word 'proof' as a judgement based on evidence beyond reasonable doubt; still admitting the possibility of contrary evidence. After all, Jack might have been a coal miner.

So, what about statements such as 'Western food causes Western diseases'; or, more specifically, 'typical Western consumption of saturated fats is a major cause of heart attacks'? These are not, nor ever could be, statements whose truth is self-evident. They cannot be proved in the sense that you can prove that $1 + 1 = 2$ or that John Jones has normal blood pressure. Nor are they statements whose truth derives from agreed laws of nature, such as 'the earth moves round the sun' or 'the moon is not made of green cheese'. That is to say, they are not statements of mathematical or physical science. They are not that type of statement. Medicine, and nutrition, are not branches of mathematics or physics, but of biology; both are sometimes termed 'life sciences'. The meaning of 'proof' in biology is 'a judgement based on evidence': and the better the evidence, and the more impartial the judge, the more reliable the judgement. But, as in the case of Jack Smith, it is in the very nature of medicine that alternative judgements are always possible. 'Proof' in medicine cannot be absolute, and it can only be 'final' or 'conclusive' or 'complete' as a matter of judgement. 'Proof' in medicine is always a matter of judgment.

Two dictionary definitions of 'proof', are 'evidence sufficient (or contributing) to establish a fact or produce a belief', and 'evidence such as determines the judgement of a tribunal'. In these terms, the nature of the disagreement between Sir Raymond Hoffenberg and Professor Thomas McKeown becomes clear. Both can be taken to be impartial judges who have examined the evidence: and Dr Hoffenberg's verdict is 'not proven', whereas Dr McKeown's verdict is 'proved beyond reasonable doubt'. Dr Hoffenberg does not (or did not, in 1984) think that the evidence against Western food is good enough to justify recommendations to the general public. Dr McKeown disagrees, and thinks that the evidence is good enough.*

This does not mean that 'medical opinion is sharply divided on the cholesterol/fat question'[3] (Bacon and Meat Manufacturers): nor that it is 'only a matter of opinion'[113] (Butter Information Council), nor 'supposition'[112] (as quoted in the *Guardian*) that saturated fat is a major cause of heart attacks. Statements such as these, suggesting that 'it's all pretty 50/50' or 'it's anybody's guess' or 'nobody really has any idea' insinuate that the evidence against saturated fat is dubious or flimsy, which of course is not true. But the manufacturers of saturated fat, concerned to protect their product, are able to perpetrate such travesties of reliable scientific judgement because of muddle about the meaning of the word 'proof'.

All expert committees concerned with food and public health both in Britain and other countries, and those that advise international agencies such as the World Health Organization, are judicial: they are, in effect, tribunals, and are established to hear evidence and make judgements. Their reports consistently use language drawn from law. It follows

---

* I have not found any work which usefully defines terms such as 'proof', 'evidence' and 'cause', as used in medical science. Agreement on the meaning of words such as these would help research scientists to stop confusing us and each other. Biological scientists like to aspire to the condition of mathematicians or physicists, and, when philosophically minded, tend to refer to two books written some time ago: Popper's *The Logic of Scientific Discovery*[118] and the probably more helpful and certainly more readable *An Introduction to Logic and Scientific Method* by Cohen and Nagel.[115] My view is that law is a better model for medicine, and certainly for public health, than mathematics or physics: Hart and Honoré's *Causation in the Law*[119] and *Cross on Evidence*[120] should be required reading for members of COMA panels. Dr Lewis Thomas has some wise and witty words to say about the pretensions of medicine as a science in *The Youngest Science*[121] and *Late Night Thoughts*.[122]

that the job of such expert committees is to produce a verdict based either on the standard of proof required in a civil court (balance of probability) or else in a criminal court (beyond reasonable doubt); and that 'proof' in this context cannot be defined in any other way. That is to say, there is of course scientific evidence concerning food and public health, but there is no such thing as 'scientific proof'. It is a meaningless phrase, unless it means 'a judgement based on scientific evidence'.

This is what the Chairman and the members of the American National Institutes of Health Consensus Conference on cholesterol and heart disease had to say, during a debate on these issues in the Lancet in 1985:[123]

> We can never have 100 per cent proof .... We make life-and-death decisions on the basis of 'beyond reasonable doubt', not expecting absolute proof. When physicians make recommendations to the public and to patients based on the best available evidence there will always be some probability that the basis is inadequate and that we are wrong .... Half of the deaths in the United States are attributable to atherosclerosis and its consequences. If we have evidence beyond reasonable doubt and still make no recommendations, then the responsibility for the lives not saved falls squarely on our shoulders. Inaction is not neutral here: we are not dealing with an abstract, ivory tower theorem that can be debated for a decade with no particular human consequence. Furthermore, the kind of diet we are recommending has not been shown to entail any risk. We are personally persuaded that it will save lives.

There is one confusion in this statement. The word 'probability' is used in its technical, statistical sense, and in this context, in ordinary language, means 'possibility'. It is a pity that scientists change the meaning of words. Otherwise, the view of the Consensus Conference, written to justify its recommendation that we in the West should eat less saturated fat in order to prevent heart attacks, is a trenchant declaration of the responsibilities of every scientist who is or should be concerned about public health.

In Britain in 1984, however, the COMA report on heart disease said, of the case against saturated fats, that 'the evidence falls short of proof.'[34] What does this mean? Does it mean that 'the evidence is so conflicting that we can't make up our minds?' No, it doesn't: because with one dissenting voice (Professor Tony Mitchell of the University of Nottingham) the committee did make up its collective mind. Its majority verdict on saturated fat, addressed to the general public, in bold type, is:

> The consumption of saturated fatty acids and of fat in the United Kingdom should be decreased.

And the report then proceeds to make some pretty categorical recommendations, albeit in clumsy language, to doctors, health educators ('if people are to change their diet they must be informed of the need for change'), food manufacturers and government ('consideration should be given to ways and means of encouraging the production of leaner carcasses in sheep, cattle and pigs'). Astonishingly, though, the justification for great changes in public policy turns out, or so it seems, to be the lowest standard of proof:

> Nine of the ten members of the Panel have concluded individually that there is sufficient consistency in this evidence to make it more likely than not that the incidence of coronary heart disease will be reduced, or its age of onset delayed, by decreasing dietary intake of saturated fatty acids and total fat. We are all agreed that the evidence falls short of proof.

And a year later Professor Michael Oliver, a member of the COMA panel, said that the evidence 'falls far short of proof'.[124] So it seems that what the report is actually saying is as follows: 'Professor Mitchell thinks the evidence does not justify any verdict. The rest of us judge that the case against saturated fats, and fats generally, is proved on the balance of probabilities, but not beyond reasonable doubt.'

But that isn't what the report says. And it isn't what it means, either: for two members of the panel, Professor Philip James and Professor Geoffrey Rose, are campaigners against saturated fats which, they are indeed sure beyond reasonable doubt, are a major cause of heart attacks.[125] In any case, no expert report would recommend great changes in public policy on the basis of 51 per cent proof. The idea is absurd.

So when the civil servants who drafted the 1984 COMA report on diet and heart disease obtained agreement from the ten scientists on the panel that the evidence against saturated fats 'falls short of proof', the word 'proof' was being used in a meaning that applies to the physical sciences, not to the biological sciences. The phrase is a meaningless fudge, designed to cover up differences of opinion certainly between Professor Mitchell and Professor Oliver and other members of the panel. Its effect was to give comfort and support to the manufacturers of saturated fats, and to confuse not only readers of the *Guardian* and viewers of Channel 4, but everybody in Britain who is now trying to decide whether or not to eat fewer saturated fats, or who, as a doctor, educator, legislator or indeed manufacturer, is trying to decide what is best for other people.

An accurate and honest conclusion would have been 'Professor Mitchell thinks the evidence does not justify any verdict.* Some of us judge that the case against saturated fats, and fats generally, is proved on the balance of probabilities. Some of us think the case is proved beyond reasonable doubt.' That of course would have given the boys from the butter and sausages trades less room for manoeuvre.

THE ABOMINABLE NO-MEN

Muddle about the meaning of the word 'proof' is matched by misunderstanding about another key word used in medical science: 'evidence'. Like 'proof', 'evidence' is derived from law. Its dictionary definition is clear enough: 'ground for belief: that which tends to prove or disprove any conclusion'. And evidence can only be conclusive in the sense of being judged good enough to support a judgement of 'proved beyond reasonable doubt'. In law, the evidence stops when judgement is given. In science there is never a

---

* Professor Mitchell is one of a small minority of eminent scientists who remains unimpressed by the evidence against saturated fats. His views are well-known.[126] Together with Professor Oliver and Professor Harry Keen (who is unimpressed by the evidence against sugars), Professor Mitchell was invited by the Chief Medical Officer at the DHSS to serve on both the 1974 and the 1984 COMA panels on diet and heart disease. It is fair to say that in inviting Professor Mitchell to serve on the 1984 COMA panel, the civil servants had reason to expect a minority opinion. This is not a reflection on Professor Mitchell.

final judgement, and so evidence is never-ending, interrupted only by a series of provisional judgements.

The Sugar Bureau is fond of the word 'evidence'. In 1983 the Bureau sent a booklet, *Sweet Reason*,[127] to the many thousands of British doctors on its mailing list, with a covering note from Anne-Marie Martin, then its Scientific Officer which remarked, 'I think you will appreciate our "common sense" approach to the subject.' Of sugared food the booklet said:

> There is no evidence to suggest that such foods make any negative contribution to the diet of man.

In 1985, in its sponsored supplement inserted into the *Grocer*,[128] the Bureau carried a contribution from Professor Vincent Marks, who repeated this quote, and went on to say:

> Indeed there is no reliable evidence that any specific nutrient except possibly fat causes obesity, which in the vast majority of cases remains a mystery.

In October 1986, the US Food and Drug Administration produced its Task Force report on sugar and health, mentioned in chapter 3.[129] The World Sugar Research Organization was able to summarize the conclusions of the Task Force in May 1986, five months before publication, courtesy of Dr Allan Forbes of the FDA, who was flown over to London by the sugar industry to present a 'definitive and official progress report'.[130] This, you will recall, included the following statement:

> Atherosclerosis. There is **no** conclusive evidence that dietary sugars are an independent risk factor for coronary artery disease in the general population.

And, among a list of similar such statements:

> Gallstones. There is **no** convincing scientific evidence that sugars consumption is an independent risk factor in the production of gallstones.

The word 'no' in both statements was emphasized in a letter sent by Professor A.J. Vlitos of the WSRO to all doctors in Britain. If, instead, the words 'conclusive', 'convincing', 'independent' and 'general population' had been printed in bold type, the statements would have taken on a rather different meaning. As it was, Professor Vlitos enthused:

> This very important Progress Report by Dr Forbes represents the most substantial and overwhelming evidence to be presented to the effect that sugar is reconfirmed as being safe for human consumption.

When the final report emerged in Britain in October, Charles Runge of the Sugar Bureau, as reported in the *Independent*,[131] was positively effervescent:

> Scientists reviewed ten years research covering almost 1,000 scientific papers from all over the world and came to the conclusion that sugar is not responsible for diseases such as obesity, diabetes, hyperactivity, hypertension or cancer. It will dispel the artificial and unnecessary fear, myths and misinformation promoted by some food faddists.

And on 12 November 1986 the American Sugar Association placed giant advertisements in the *New York Times*, *USA Today* and the *Washington Post* proclaiming 'GOVERNMENT GIVES SUGAR CLEAN BILL OF HEALTH'.[132]

The actual conclusion of the Task Force report was just about capable of this careful misinterpretation. For what it said was:[129]

> Other than the contribution to dental caries, there is no conclusive evidence that demonstrates a hazard to the general public when sugars are consumed at the levels that are now current.

In other words, if you start by assuming that sugars, consumed at the level of about 100 lb per person per year, are harmless until proved harmful, and if you insist that proof requires 'conclusive' evidence, then sugars get a 'not guilty' verdict: a reprieve. But the FDA report includes plenty of evidence against sugars: in its bibliography I have counted over 120 references to the work of scientists whose research provides evidence that sugars are harmful. These include four papers by Dr Kenneth Heaton and co-workers. Interviewed by the *Independent*, Dr Heaton said:[131]

No one is saying that sugar is an *independent* risk factor in causing gallstones. The important question surely is whether sugar contributes to the risk of gallstones and the evidence suggests it does.

'It is unfortunate that the FDA has played into the hands of the junk food manufacturers,' said Dr Michael Jacobson of the Center for Science in the Public Interest.[131]

Medical scientists rarely indicate what they mean by words such as 'proof' and 'evidence' (and another much misunderstood word, 'cause'). The reason is that they themselves do not understand the meaning of the words as applied to their work. With exceptions,[123,133] they do not seem to realize that, unlike mathematicians but like lawyers, the importance of their work is that it is always a matter of judgement, requiring wisdom as well as knowledge. Medicine is a human science.

Almost all discussion about food and public health is muddled right from the start. In Britain until very recently, legislators have taken no action following the recommendations of medical scientists assembled to give advice on public policy. Two reasons for this inertia are, first, that the politicians don't understand what the scientists are saying, partly because the scientists themselves don't know what they are talking about; and, second, that research scientists are in the business of never coming to a conclusion. When researchers are asked to adjudicate, the jury is always out.

Professor Michael Marmot of the University of London, who believes in the need for prevention, put it like this in his inaugural lecture, published in the *Lancet* in 1986:[133]

> This lust for absolute 'proof' represents a view of science that is mistaken, dangerously so, since it interferes with two types of endeavour: translating scientific evidence into public health policy and pursuing research into the social causation of ill-health.

You might suppose that medical researchers, above all others, are most concerned with what causes disease and how to prevent it. You would be wrong. The business of research, is research. There will always be diseases to study. But medical researchers dread solutions. I well remember attending a conference on guar gum as a treatment for diabetes held at the Royal Society of Medicine in December 1985.[134] Dr Hugh Trowell, who spoke at the conference, proposed a theory for both the cause and the cure of adult-onset diabetes. During lunch a young scientist came up to Dr Trowell, and said (I paraphrase) 'I don't want to hear any of this. I've got a career in front of me.' We laughed. It was one of those jokes that went beyond a joke.

Earlier in 1985, Dr E.H. Ahrens of Rockefeller University in New York, who agrees with Professor Mitchell that the evidence against saturated fats is not good enough to justify any judgement, objected in the *Lancet* to the reasonable certainty expressed by the National Institutes of Health's Consensus Conference:[135]

> If this atmosphere prevails, there will be little encouragement for young medical investigators to probe more deeply into the mysteries of nutrition/CHD relations, and there will be increasing resistance by peer reviewers to approve funds for further study of these unsolved questions.

Researchers always believe that more research is always needed. In Britain, this attitude has been institutionalized notably by the two richest medical charities, the British Heart Foundation (BHF) and the Imperial Cancer Research Fund (ICRF), whose combined turnover by the mid-1980s was over £30 million a year.[136,137] 'How the British Heart Foundation is helping to beat heart disease' is the headline of a BHF leaflet.[138] 'Little by little the Imperial Cancer Research Fund is winning the war against cancer' is a slogan the ICRF has used in advertisements.[139] Certainly, many individual lives are saved by scientists funded by the BHF and ICRF. But at the same time as these claims are published in order to gain more funds from legacies and donations, Britain's record for deaths from heart attacks and cancers has become the worst in Europe.[140]

Publicity material issued by the BHF and the ICRF emphasizes pictures of boffins in white coats looking into high-powered microscopes.[136,141] This encourages the idea that heart attacks and cancers have something to do with germs, and that the experts can see something that we can't see. We are given the impression that with more time, and more money, one of these days a scientist will cry 'Ah! There's the little devil!' as his eye alights on a bug with tiny horns and a tail, answering to the name of 'heart disease' or 'cancer', hurrying on down a coronary artery or a lymph gland to do its dirty work. The next day, the news pages of the national press would be filled with 'NEW BREAKTHROUGH IN FIGHT AGAINST' stories, featuring the triumphant research team, still in white coats, with big smiles and a highly technical gizmo, maybe a laser gun designed to target, intercept and zap the little blighters, like some medical equivalent of Star Wars.

Until very recently, the BHF and the ICRF have done almost nothing to encourage people to realize that heart disease and cancers are preventable. Almost all the money they receive from the public, administration costs aside, goes to laboratory work, identifying, classifying and treating heart disease and cancers. Little money goes to prevention; very little goes to work in the community.

In the early 1980s, the BHF established thirteen university departments of cardiology, all with professors. In 1984 it spent £1,500,000 on a Chair of Cardiac Surgery at Hammersmith Hospital and a 'personal Professorship' of Cardiovascular Medicine at St Bartholomew's Hospital.[142,143] In 1982, its biggest single research grant of £70,000 was for a typical research project, at Charing Cross Hospital: 'Mechanical induction of early arrhythmia during myocardial ischaemia: an electro-mechanical study of normal and ischaemic myocardium'. In 1984 I asked the BHF about its policy on prevention and was told: 'there is no known means of preventing heart disease: all you can do is reduce the risk.'[144]

The big news from the ICRF in 1982 was the £3 million it spent on a cyclotron.[137] Its leaflet on cancer epidemiology shows a smiling family together with a dinosaur and an Egyptian mummy.[141] Why? The explanation inside is:

> The dinosaur and the Egyptian pharaohs had at least one important factor in common with modern man. They too contracted cancer.

Is there anything special we can do right now to reduce our risk of cancer? At the back of the leaflet is a large colour photograph of an array of meat and greengrocery, with a heading 'Investigating the food we eat' but without any accompanying text. The explanation is:

It is impossible to mention in a small brochure the amazingly large number of projects carried out by the brilliant pioneering team.

In 1982, the ICRF's Treasurer's Report noted that a further £2,500,000 was spent on its laboratory complex at South Mimms.[137] What about food and cancer, though? An ICRF representative told me that:[145]

The Director's view is that there are lots and lots of indications but not much absolute proof ... we're reluctant to over-emphasise the importance of diet in relation to cancer'.

The policies of the big British health charities infuriate doctors committed to health promotion and disease prevention. One senior community physician, who asked not to be named, told me that in his opinion the BHF and the ICRF set the agenda in their fields: their committees, made up of much of the medical establishment, are as influential as government advisory committees – and indeed many of the BHF and ICRF luminaries are also government advisors. But, he said, the big charities are self-serving; they are 'hoodwinking the general public into giving away money that's frittered away on research'.

Together with industry and government, scientists are also responsible for the fact that British food and British health are now just about the worst in the developed world. The charge is that British research scientists are irresponsible; are refusing to look at the evidence that incriminates typical British food as a major cause of heart attacks, cancers and many other diseases.

By contrast, the American Heart Association and the American Cancer Society are committed to prevention, and are now spending many millions of dollars donated by the public, on campaigns designed to make healthy food big – and good – news.[146,147] Why is there so little action in Britain? In 1983 The Times Health Supplement ran a leader entitled ABOMINABLE NO-MEN.[148] What has gone wrong, it asked:

Another major factor must have been the publicity given by British journalists to the professional 'no-men'. No matter how many doctors recommend a diet low in saturated fat, some academic expert will disagree .... In Britain too, the medical charities which have been given millions of pounds by the public to combat heart disease and cancer, have maintained that their job is research into disease, not prevention .... Could we not have a moratorium on the sort of clever journalism that confuses the public rather than informing and educating it?

But in Britain the abominable no-men remain effective. Tim Fortescue, the genial former Conservative MP and ex-Director General of the Food and Drinks Industries Council (now merged into the Food and Drink Federation), put it to me as follows. 'Any chap,' he said, 'can produce an expert to contradict whatever any other expert has said.'[149]

BIG WHEELS WITHIN WHEELS

This is not to say that academics who give aid and support to government and industry are in it for the money. I am sure that as a rule they act in good faith. But why should a man who has spent his professional life developing increasingly sophisticated methods of examining the mechanisms of heart disease be interested in its prevention? And why should men who have become authorities on fats or carbohydrates metabolism believe that we should eat less of the subjects of their study? As a class, medical research scientists have no more understanding of public health and interest in the prevention of disease than barristers, say, have understanding of public morals and interest in the prevention of crime. There are many people with the title 'Dr'. Only some of these have any knowledge of the cause of disease, and of these only some have insight.

One who has is Professor Henry Blackburn of the Department of Public Health at the University of Minnesota, who believes that there are three ways of looking at disease: the clinical, academic, and the public health points of view:[150]

O Clinical. This is concerned with the treatment of the individual patient in whom 'the hereditary or other non-dietary components of risk may be overwhelmingly strong': for example, in the case of heart disease, a rare inherited disease of the blood, or smoking 40 cigarettes a day.

○ Academic. This is preoccupied with the examination of basic mechanisms at the molecular and cellular levels. 'The academic idea is that specific mechanisms exist and have specific preventatives,' such as a vaccine or drug. 'It is never-ending because "the final evidence" is never in.'

○ Public health. This is concerned with the health of whole populations and looks at disease outside the hospital or laboratory. It tests hypotheses from different disciplines and comes to conclusions based on the evidence, taking social and political as well as scientific factors into account.

Dr Blackburn, who himself takes the public health view, goes on to say:[150]

Academics and clinicians usually have the possibility of temporising and watching the unending unfolding of new knowledge .... The low-key, dispassionate approach to scientific questions ... is reasonable (and comfortable) to the scholar; but public health issues are usually high-key matters involving large sociocultural, economic and political concerns that touch on sensitive personal and national issues.

That is to say, a public health view must be soundly based on science, but goes beyond it. The decision to act on knowledge is not a scientific decision: and is not the type of decision scientists are trained to make.

An exchange between Professor Stewart Truswell and Professor Albert Neuberger in the pages of the *Bulletin* of the British Nutrition Foundation in 1981 illustrates the difference between the public health and the academic/ clinical attitude to food and health. Dr Truswell wrote a review called 'Diet and Coronary Heart Disease. How Much More Evidence Do We Need?',[151] which summarized the findings of 37 expert committees and showed virtual unanimity that saturated fats and fats consumption should be cut in Western countries in order to prevent heart attacks. He said:

I think the time has come to ask ourselves why some people are asking for stronger proof on the benefits of modifying fat intake than they demand on the benefits of most other common contemporary advice for health promotion and disease prevention including coronary heart disease – like not smoking, reducing hypertension, regular exercise, treatment of obesity, reduction of mental stress, good housing and even the National Health Service.

In his reply, Dr Neuberger, who, you will recall, has been President of the BNF, replied:[152]

There is a considerable number of good scientists who feel that the importance of diet is an aetiological factor in heart disease which has been exaggerated .... The whole problem has become too emotive, and I think it is the function of the British Nutrition Foundation to restore a more rational and objective atmosphere into this situation.

In other words, research into the relationship between food and disease should continue, and indeed flourish, but should be detached and value-free: in which case no judgement is ever made, because judgements involve values. From the academic point of view, nobody ever comes to any conclusion willingly.

If you asked an academic medical researcher in the field, 'do you believe as a scientist that the British food supply is a public health problem?', he would be most unlikely to say 'yes', and would probably feel that anybody who said 'yes' was being emotional. (The game often played in medical debates is, in effect, 'I am objective, you are selective, he is emotional'.) He might well say 'I don't know'. More likely than not he would say 'no', meaning 'there is no good/reliable/scientific/convincing/conclusive/final/ absolute evidence to that effect, and until there is, I can only say that things are just fine the way they are.'

This attitude is of course a great comfort to the food-manufacturing industry, and in particular to the Food and Drink Federation (FDF), the trade association set up to protect the interests of the big food-manufacturing companies in Whitehall, Westminster and Brussels. It is officially recognized as the body with which government negotiates. It does not represent the interests of the food industry as a whole any more than that other monolith, the National Farmers Union, represents the interests of the farmers as a whole.[153] It has nothing to do with retailing, which until very recently government has foolishly neglected in its dealings with the food industry.

Formally, as its name implies, the FDF is a federation of trade associations. It has nothing to do with fresh food. It represents, not fresh meat traders, but BMMA and FCA (Bacon and Meat Manufacturers' Association and Food Casings Association); not fruit and vegetables, but BFVCA and VPA (British Fruit and Vegetable Canners' Association, and Vegetable Protein Association; not potatoes, but DPA and PRA (Dehydrated Potato Association and Potato Processors' Association); not fish, but FMSPA (Fish and Meat Spreadable Products Association). Other large associations already mentioned in this book that are members of the FDF include BCCCA (Biscuit, Cake, Chocolate and Confectionery Alliance, itself formed in 1986 from the Cake and Biscuit Alliance and the Cocoa, Chocolate and Confectionery Alliance); NABIM (National Association of British and Irish Millers); SNACMA (Snack, Nut and Crisp Manufacturers Association); and the Sugar Bureau (owned by British Sugar and Tate & Lyle).[47] The FDF does not protect food, but the manufacturers of processed food.

Notwithstanding these acronyms, the FDF is also an association of the giant manufacturers, who dominate its internal committees. The President of the FDF until 1987 was Sir Derrick Holden-Brown, Chairman of Allied-Lyons. The Fair Trading Steering Committee includes Sir Adrian Cadbury, Sir Hector Laing and Sir Peter Reynolds, the chief executives of Cadbury-Schweppes, United Biscuits and Ranks Hovis McDougall.

Other FDF committee chairmen include men (there are no women, as far as I know) from Unilever, Beecham, Kelloggs, Reckitt & Colman, and Tate & Lyle. All these firms are ranked within the top 100 companies in Britain in 1985-86: all individually turn over more than a billion pounds a year.[154]

The most interesting FDF committee is the Scientific and Technical Committee, whose Chairman, Dr Peter Russell-Eggitt, featured in chapter 4 as a champion of chemical food additives. This large committee is remarkable for the number of men who also serve, or have served, on government advisory committees. Here is the list:

Professor Russell Allen (Beecham; MAFF Food Standards Committee)

Gordon Amery (CWS; MAFF Food Processing Committee)

Ron Dicker (Dairy Crest; MAFF Food Processing Committee)

Dr Tom Gorsuch (Reckitt & Colman; MAFF Food Additives and Contaminants Committee, Food Advisory Committee, Chairman Food Processing Committee)

Professor Alan Holmes (British Food Manufacturing Industries Research Association; Cabinet Office Food Processing Committee)

Anthony Skrimshire (Heinz; MAFF Food Processing Committee, Food Advisory Committee)

Geoffrey Telling (Unilever; MAFF Food Additives and Contaminants Committee)

Alan Turner (Cadbury-Schweppes; MAFF Food Standards Committee, Food Advisory Committee).

So it turns out that of the 11 members of the MAFF Food Processing Committee which reported in 1986, four came from the same FDF commitee; as do three of the 15 members of the Food Advisory Committee as set up in 1987. MAFF does not mention the FDF affiliations of members of its committees.

What does the Scientific and Technical Committee do? According to the FDF's Annual Report for 1985,[47] it is made up of 'leading scientists' and has 'established itself as an authoritative forum generating views on a wide range of important issues'. In other words, it is a think-tank for the British food-manufacturing industry. In 1986, its work included helping to set up the FDF's campaign to defend chemical food additives and championing the legalization of food irradiation.

So the Food and Drink Federation protects the interests of the giant manufacturers of processed food, meaning, in effect, processed fats and sugars, salt and additives. Its policy is directed by senior executives from these firms, some of whom also serve on government advisory committees. That's the system, in Britain, and there's nothing quite like it for reaching agreement between government and industry anywhere else in the world.

How does the British Nutrition Foundation fit into this system? Funnily enough, the BNF was described, in an issue of the industry's confidential newsletter, *World Food and Drink Report*,[155] as 'the think tank of Britain's food manufacturing industry'. This will have saddened Professor Ian Macdonald the Chairman of the BNF, who in his 1985–86 report claimed that the BNF is independent, impartial and responsible, despite being wholly funded by the food industry:[46]

> The implication that there must be bias, collusion or downright dishonesty on the premise that he who pays the piper calls the tune is unwarranted and mischievous, and is unsupported by any 'evidence' that can be rated much higher than speculative insinuation. The scientific integrity and impartiality of the Foundation's position on nutritional matters is not in doubt.

The BNF was set up in 1967. Its founding firms included Ranks (now Ranks Hovis McDougall), Beecham and Tate & Lyle, which with Unilever were, and are in the 1980s, the most important individual sources of money and influence within the BNF.[156,157] The first Director-General of the BNF was Dr Alastair Frazer, who was best known as a toxicologist.[158]

After his appointment Dr Frazer drew an animated diagram of his vision for the BNF. Nourished by 'finance from food industry' and 'advice from scientists', it was to be 'the supreme authority on good food habits' and indeed 'The Oracle', concerned with both 'the search for knowledge' and the 'dissemination of knowledge'. It would dangle 'money and prestige bait to attract more scientists to nutrition' and also would assume 'leadership in good habits to all who take part in the growth and preparation of food'.[159] And although government has always been officially chary of the BNF, because of its funding by industry, much of Dr Frazer's plan was achieved.

During the 1970s and the 1980s, the BNF accumulated sponsors: 48 are listed in the 1985-86 Annual Report.[46] These sponsors have been nurtured with great care. The

British food-manufacturing industry is uniquely concentrated. The 22 firms that dominate the market for
biscuits, bread, breakfast cereals, cakes, chocolate confectionery, ice-cream, margarine, milk, pot snacks, ready
meals, savoury snacks, soft drinks, soup and sugar are all
sponsors of the BNF; and all of them are also represented on
the councils of the FDF. All but a handful of BNF sponsors are
manufacturers of processed food, together with half a dozen
trade associations. Three retailers and two fresh food trade
associations are BNF 'member companies'.

The BNF has also accumulated committees with altogether
over a hundred seats for Governors, Scientific Advisors,
Industrial Scientists, Editorial Advisors and so forth. These
committee members have also been chosen with great care.
The BNF has always been keen to attract scientists who are
also members of official government advisory committees. A
count of 32 DHSS, MAFF and such-like committees whose
reports have been published between 1974 and 1987 shows
that of the 427 seats on these committees 191 also are or have
been occupied by members of BNF committees.

So the BNF has become a unique forum for people with
expert knowledge of food and health from industry,
government and the academic world. How does it operate?
Dr Derek Shrimpton was Director-General of the BNF from
1982 to 1984, when he resigned his post. In 1985 he gave a
long interview to Granada Television's *World In Action*
programme 'The Great Food Scandal', transmitted in
October that year. Some of the questions and answers are as
follows.[160]

Q How do you see the BNF .... What's your view of it now?
A In the period I was there the BNF was solely taken up with
   defensive actions for the industry.

This was the time of the NACNE report on dietary goals for
Britain. The BNF was represented on the main committee,
originally set up by government, that oversaw the report and
blocked its progress between 1981 and 1983.[13]

Q What was the BNF's attitude toward NACNE at that time?
A If I could I should kill it but if not it was going to be
   troublesome.

Q Can you just describe why the BNF was so anxious about NACNE?

A If it was an embarrassment to the industry it might indeed result in a reduction of the BNF funding .... If it couldn't be killed it was best to be emasculated. And in all events the BNF must come out of this very white. At no time must the BNF's hand be seen in this .... The tactic was to delay it and delay it again, so that everybody would get fed up and at no point would it see the light of day. If that failed then it was to be published as low key as possible with as little reporting as possible and no official support .... The most important point was to persuade the Department of Health that on no account should it be published as a Department of Health report .... It should be as hard to get at as possible by making a small print run for example of two hundred copies ... And to present the report as a discussion paper by a bunch of scientists who were not even eminent.

This account of nutritional chicanery bemused the interviewer:

Q But the BNF was actually a part of the NACNE committee. This seems to be an absurd situation, here it was trying to kill the committee on which it was a joint member.

A This is the problem of playing both ends against the middle. If you have an organisation that is set up that way, it will get into absurd situations.

Having joined the BNF with high hopes, Dr Shrimpton became completely disillusioned, he explained. What about the BNF's relationship with the DHSS?

Q What impression did you form of the role of Whitehall in relation to NACNE?

A An unhealthy cosy relation. Whitehall didn't want it published either. The BNF was quite clearly a useful tool in fulfilling the aims of Whitehall.

Q Was there a sense of the BNF and Whitehall working together to try and kill and defeat the NACNE report?

A Oh yes, not the slightest doubt.

Q They were both determined to stop it?

A Yes.

It was vital, explained Dr Shrimpton, that the senior civil servants at the DHSS were sympathetic to the BNF line:

A The Chief Medical Officer was a very critical person, to gain his support.

Q Who is the Chief Medical Officer?

A He was Sir Henry Yellowlees; who, when he retired, became Chairman of the BNF Scientific Committee.

Q And he was cultivated through the NACNE period by the BNF?

A He was cultivated throughout the period I was there.

Q Why was it exactly that the BNF wanted to cultivate him?

A In Whitehall terms, the most important professional is the Chief Medical Officer. The BNF needed to have on its side the most senior professional authority.

In 1986 the next BNF Director-General, Professor David Conning, announced a new initiative, the 'BNF Educational Plan', designed 'to teach the concepts of food energy and nutritional balance'.[161] The idea was to test the Plan 'in collaboration with a sizeable health authority', which turned out to be Leeds. The total cost of the Plan, including a booklet and a video, would be £150,000. The money would come from the BNF's sponsors: 'Thus 20 companies each contributing £7,500 each would get the programme off to a good start,' said Dr Conning in his prospectus.[162]

The 'BNF Healthy Eating Plan' was enclosed with the prospectus for consideration by the Leeds Health Authority. The idea was to maintain energy intake while trimming on fat a bit. From the point of view of any of the sponsors asked to stump up £7500, it did not look too alarming. All foods were to be divided into seven groups: starchy foods; fruit and vegetables; meat and such-like; fats and oils; milk and dairy products; sweet and savoury snacks; and soft drinks or alcohol. I worked out a day's menu à la BNF:

Breakfast: two helpings of Sugar Smacks, full-fat milk, white bread plus fatty spread and jam, two cups of sugared tea
Snack: cheesecake and Coca-Cola
Lunch: baked beans, boiled cabbage and peas, chips, large fruit juice
Snack: crisps
Evening meal: sausages and chips, fruit flavour yoghurt, two cups of sugared coffee.

This food makes the grade of the BNF's 'Healthy Eating Plan'. It is, of course, much the same as the food typically made for, supplied to and eaten by people in Britain today. There is goodness in it; but, overall, this is the food, heavy in processed fats and sugars, with salt and additives, which is proved beyond reasonable doubt to be a public health catastrophe. Leeds Health Authority rejected the BNF Plan, having themselves already devised a food policy along NACNE lines, with more whole cereals and fresh vegetables and fruit, and with fewer fats, sugars and processed food generally.

For all practical purposes, the voice of the BNF is the voice of the British food-manufacturing industry. Over the years, it has accumulated staff and officers whose view conform or are sympathetic with those of industry. The pipers play the tune freely: they do not need to be paid. But it has a peculiar influence because it seems to be independent of industry. Granada's interviewer asked Dr Shrimpton about this:

Q The BNF has on its various committees a number of the country's most eminent academics and scientists, doesn't it?

A Partly that's an accident of history .... The scientists remain and undoubtedly they're a convenience to the BNF because they give it a credibility and status which otherwise it would never expect to have.

One scientist who served on BNF committees at the time was Dr John Cummings of the Dunn Clinical Nutrition Centre at Cambridge, who is also a member of the main COMA committee. Granada spoke to him too:[163]

Q Can you describe to us the nature of the BNF Science Committee meetings .... What impression did you get about the general attitude towards the NACNE recommendations?

A The industry representatives were very worried about it. Particularly from the point of view that it might be commercially damaging to them. There was very little concern expressed about the health of the British public and whether they might in fact be dying from food-related diseases. But there was a great deal of talk about whether the proposals might be catastrophic to certain sections of the industry.

Q What is the BNF's actual role?

A Unfortunately it sees itself as defending the interests of industry. And putting what one might call the other side of the case all the time – which in fact tends to be industry's side of the case.

And by 'industry' Dr Cummings does not mean the food industry as a whole. He is not referring to the small farmers, manufacturers and retailers that still flourish in Europe, growing, breeding, making and selling good-quality food. Indeed, he is not referring to farmers or retailers or to caterers at all; nor to the fresh food trade. He means the giant conglomerate manufacturers, often of drink, drugs and chemicals as well as highly processed foods, that dominate the BNF, the FDF, and the system by which science, government and industry meets together in secret to take the decisions that make our food the worst in the developed world.

UNLESS THIS CENSORSHIP
WILL NOW CEASE

In July 1983 I wrote the front-page lead news story for the *Sunday Times* that revealed the existence of the NACNE report, and the facts of its suppression. The headline ran 'CENSORED: A DIET FOR LIFE AND DEATH'.[164] The BNF lost some and won some. On the one hand, the NACNE story became a very high-key affair, still capable of generating major television programmes over two years later; and somehow it put food and public health back on the national agenda after a generation of ignorance. On the other hand, the NACNE report did become a 'discussion paper', published by the Health Education Council in the autumn of 1983,[33] and it was dismissed by the DHSS, whose Chief Medical Officer, Sir Henry Yellowlees, explained to members of the NACNE committee that the whole thing had been a great mistake:[165]

> This document ... went well beyond the remit set out in October 1980. Moreover, there were also numerous objections on scientific grounds and on grounds of balance. DHSS, BNF and MAFF representatives on NACNE were therefore highly critical of this report.

Instead, Sir Henry explained in his confidential memorandum, the forthcoming COMA report on *Diet and Cardiovascular Disease* was the Real Thing. In due course, in the summer of 1984, the COMA report was published. The NACNE committee was abolished, and was replaced by a JACNE committee, whose 'J' signified that it was the joint responsibility of the Health Education Council and the BNF. The main job of JACNE, under the chairmanship of Dr John Garrow, was to 'produce practical guidance for families'[166] based on the recommendation of the COMA report that if you want to reduce the risk of having a heart attack it's probably a good idea to eat less saturated fat and less fat in general.

Was the NACNE story a one-off? Or would any report on food and public health designed to have official status be torpedoed if its findings were disagreeable to the food-manufacturing industry? I watched the progress of JACNE with interest, and was able to make a judgement based on possession of all the minutes and other documents produced by the JACNE committee.

Meetings of the JACNE committee were attended by 'observers' not only from the DHSS, MAFF and the Department of Education, but also from the FDF, in the person of Mr John Wood, head of the FDF secretariat, who circulated summaries of JACNE meetings to the food-manufacturing industry.[167,168]

On 13 March 1985, nine months after the first meeting of the JACNE committee, the first draft of the 'COMA Booklet' was complete.[169] By May it had a name: *Eating for a Healthy Heart*.[170] A further draft produced on June 21 had a new name, which avoided giving readers the impression they might have anything wrong with them: *Eating for a Healthier Heart*.[171] At the seventh JACNE meeting on 23 May 1985, committee members were told that publication could be expected by the end of July, and that the print run would be 500,000 copies.

The June draft included a handy quiz to check whether or not readers were consuming too much saturated fat. The higher your score, the bigger your problem. 'So answer the questions, and be honest with yourself!' said the quiz. The first set of questions ran:

1. What kind of milk do you usually use?
a. Channel Island or gold top   3
b. Ordinary (silver/red top)   2
c. Semi-skimmed   1
d. Skimmed   0
e. I never use milk   0

The meaning of the quiz was clear enough. Best is skimmed milk or no milk; worst is full-fat milk. Of butter, the draft said:

> Butter has a lot of saturated fat. If you don't want to do without butter completely, why not have an alternative handy so you're not using butter all the time?

Of milk, the guide said: 'the trouble is that some types of milk have a lot of saturated fat in them.'

The guide was also rude about typically fatty meat. In stews, 'try using less meat – add more beans and vegetables.' And of burgers:

> Hamburgers and beefburgers tend to be very high in fat – about 20 grams in a quarter pounder. Just look how much comes out when you grill them.

As a courtesy, a copy of the final 21 June draft was sent to Dr Donald Acheson, the new Chief Medical Officer at the DHSS. But at the eighth JACNE meeting on 25 July, Dr Garrow found that Dr Acheson had written him a letter demanding changes in all the passages quoted above. For example, the phrase 'try using less meat' was struck out. A new burger message was proposed:

> Hamburgers and beefburgers tend to be high in fat and contain around 16-20 per cent fat after cooking.

And the milk warning was watered down to:

> The trouble is that because of the amount we drink ordinary milk can provide a lot of saturated fat in the diet.

In response, Dr Garrow, who as a member of the main COMA committee has signed the Official Secrets Act, did something which was certainly not expected of him. He went over the top. On the day of the meeting he wrote a typically stylish letter to Dr Acheson, saying:[172]

We now learn that, without any formal notification or explanation to this committee ... the publication of the leaflet has been countermanded by the DHSS, and we have no assurance that this embargo will be lifted on the publication of any revised version of the leaflet. We resent this treatment by the DHSS which we regard as insulting, and quite contrary to the terms on which members of the committee undertook the work of preparing the leaflet. JACNE (unlike NACNE) was constituted so that it would be seen to operate without pressure from the Government or the food industry. This is not so if the output of JACNE is in effect censored by the Government.

And he concluded:

I see no point in continuing to work with JACNE unless we can be assured that this censorship will now cease.

That did it, of course. 'GUIDE TO HEALTHY EATING BLOCKED' was the *Sunday Times* headline.[173] 'NUTRI- TIONIST'S THREAT TO QUIT OVER "CENSORSHIP"' said the *Guardian* the next day.[174] A copy of the final draft of the JACNE leaflet found its way to Lord Young, President of the College of Health, who threatened to circulate it to the press. And so 'HEALTHY EATING GUIDE BEATS CENSORS' was the *Guardian* headline four days later:[175]

The Guide duly arrived at newspaper offices yesterday and within minutes the Department of Health announced that ministers were approving publication .... Lord Young said 'It was outrageous for the Government to have bowed to the agriculture and food industries and allowed their vested interests to have prevailed over the interests of public health.'

Nothing had changed. And nothing has changed.

Conclusion: Playing the Health Card

A few years hence, when the connection between the poor feeding of mothers and children and subsequent poor physique and ill-health is as clearly recognised as the connection between a contaminated water supply and cholera, the suggestion that a diet fully adequate for health should be available for everyone will be regarded as reasonable and in accordance with common sense, as is the preservation of our domestic water supply from pollution.

John Boyd Orr, Food Health and Income,[1] 1937

The change in the dietary and other medical habits of the human race has been profound and will become more profound with each year ... We must always be on the watch that small quantities of catalysts used in transforming our food oils do not have slow poisonous effects, which it may take a lifetime to show ... Even minute quantities of these and other deleterious products may be fatal after many years of apparently innocuous use, and may contribute to the toll of degenerative disease. It is certain that the processing of foods is subjecting us to many risks universal to the nation if not to the race, which may not show themselves until it is too late to do anything much about them.

Norbert Wiener, The Human Use of Human Beings,[2] 1950

Let me say it now, let me say it clearly, let me say it as clearly as I can, that food additives are already the subject of very careful control in this country. I will state what ought to be obvious. This country's legislation forbids the addition of anything harmful to food.

Agriculture Minister Donald Thompson MP,
Current Ministry of Agriculture Policy,[3] 1986

363

'It looks like June!' said the political commentators, after Chancellor Nigel Lawson's Budget of 17 March 1987; and this book was finished in a pre-General Election atmosphere. What are the prospects for reform of British national food policy, under a new administration headed by Mrs Thatcher, or a new government headed by politicians from other parties?

By the spring of 1987, you could be forgiven for thinking that there was no need for reform.

TREND TOWARDS 'HEALTHIER' DIET CONTINUES, MAFF FOOD SURVEY SHOWS

was the headline of a MAFF press release in October 1986.[4] On 13 March 1987 MAFF boldly took the quote marks off 'healthy':[5]

DONALD THOMPSON WELCOMES CONTINUED TREND TOWARDS HEALTHIER EATING ... The British people are heeding the Government's advice on healthy eating, Mr Donald Thompson, Parliamentary Secretary at the Ministry of Agriculture, said today.

And Mr Thompson, who in 1987 is Mrs Peggy Fenner's successor at MAFF, had some success with the press.

HEALTHIER EATING. The British are adopting a healthier and more nutritious diet, eating extra green vegetables, wholemeal bread and fresh fruits, say government figures published today.

said the *Guardian*.[6] The *Financial Times* had a closer look at Mr Thompson's figures, which compared the results of MAFF's National Food Surveys for 1985 and 1986, and noted that consumption of cakes and biscuits continues to rise (a fact not emphasised by Mr Thompson). In general, though, this story was upbeat too:[7]

HEALTH PUT HIGHER ON THE MENU. The British are remembering to eat up their greens, according to a government survey published yesterday ... More green vegetables, fresh fruit and wholemeal bread were consumed than in 1985. Conversely, the amounts of potatoes, sugar and white bread fell ... Mr Donald Thompson, a junior agriculture minister, said the report was a welcome sign that people were heeding the Government's advice on healthy eating.

The MAFF figures did indeed indicate that in 1986 the British were on average eating about half an ounce more fresh vegetables every day, compared with 1985 (excluding potatoes), and about a quarter of an ounce more fresh fruit. Mr Thompson did not mention that the 'healthy' 1986 figures were, however, much the same as those for 1981.[8] He did not make any comparisons with Europe. Nor did journalists reporting his good news remember to point out that Food Survey figures for 'sugar' refer only to packet sucrose purchased for use in the home, and that the Survey takes no account of confectionery, soft drinks, snacks eaten outside the home, or of alcohol.[8] But then, a story headed

SALES OF BISCUITS, CAKES, CHOCOLATE, SNACKS, SOFT DRINKS SOAR, SAYS DONALD THOMPSON

would not create quite the same impression in the mind of the reader.

By the spring of 1987 you could also be forgiven for thinking that chemical food additives are almost a thing of the past, and that the British food supply has become altogether country-fresh (to coin a phrase). SHOCK HORROR headlines were replaced by good-news stories, as the public relations departments of the food industry cranked into gear. 'SUPERMARKET CHAIN CUTS FOOD ADDITIVES',[9] 'ADDITIVES ARE OUT',[10] 'CUSTOMERS WINNING ADDITIVES BATTLE',[11] 'AS NATURE INTENDED; STORES WORK TO ROOT OUT "RISKY" FOOD ADDITIVES',[12] and 'THUMBS DOWN TO ADDITIVES',[13] were just a few of the hundreds of headlines in the national and regional press published during just one week, in 1986.

Nowadays every manufacturer able to do so, is boasting about additive-free products – including those manu- facturers whose products have always been additive-free. For instance, an advertisement in the *Observer* colour magazine in September 1986[14] showed a picture of a tomato ('the only colouring') and a tin ('the only preservative') and proclaimed

Unlike dried and instant soup, Heinz Tomato contains no artificial colouring or preservative. And, do you know, it never has.

The same day a page advertisement in the *Sunday Times* went one better. Volkswagen boasted about the Polo car, wittily:[15]

> MORE COLOURING (7 lbs of paint). MORE PRESERVATIVES (Injected with 120 litres of wax ...) MORE ADDITIVES (Dual circuit brakes ... Safety cell and crumple zone).

Six months later, in March 1987, Volkswagen was running the same copy lines, reinforced by a picture of the Polo owner emerging from the wholefood warehouse in Neal's Yard, Covent Garden.[16]

My favourite advertisement along these lines was for British Coal: it appeared in the *Observer* in March 1987.[17] Its headline was 'NO ADDITIVES, NO ARTIFICIAL COLOURING. BEST BEFORE DEC 2286'. The copy said:

> Coal is as old as the hills, and just as natural. And it's been going every bit as long as wheatgerm, organic cabbage or juice straight from the fruit.

Three full-page advertisements in just one issue of the trade magazine *The Grocer* in October 1986[18] revealed the name of the new food manufacturing game: 'ROBIRCH BEEF AND KIDNEY PIE. NEW ADDITIVE FREE RECIPE.' 'NEW FLAVOUR WHEAT CRUNCHIES. COUNTRY CHICKEN FLAVOUR. NO ARTIFICIAL COLOURING OR PRESERVATIVES.' And 'MARS. ALWAYS BEST QUALITY, FREE FROM ARTIFICIAL FLAVOURINGS OR COLOURINGS.'

NEW UNIMPROVED GLOBBO

If British food policy were left to us, the consumers, together with the retailers and caterers who pay attention to consumer demand, there would indeed be great changes for the better in the British food supply. Retailers are falling over themselves to kick chemical additives out of their own-label products. 'There is such a groundswell of public opinion now against additives', Tony Combes, Safeway's Public Affairs Manager, told me,[19] explaining his company's policy of removing 51 chemical additives from Safeway foods. Dennis Cumming, Safeway's Head of Quality

Control, commented on 'the level of letters we get from customers',[20] instancing letters from parents whose children suffer from rashes, eczema, asthma, migraine, hyperactivity and other illness caused at least in part by chemical additives.[21,22]

Other retailers have followed Safeway's policy of 'removing all unnecessary ingredients and contentious food additives which are believed to cause unpleasant reactions.'[23] Here is a typical report, from the *Journal* of Newcastle-Upon-Tyne:[24]

> Iceland, the freezer foods store group, is making a bid to tempt the palates of the healthy-eating brigade. 'We're frantically removing artificial additives as fast as possible from our products' revealed chairman and joint managing director Malcolm Walker yesterday, 'and we're alerting customers that we've done so with a special label on the packets.'

Mr Walker also announced that his firm's profits had increased by 29 per cent.

In 1987 it is true that anybody with the knowledge, the freedom and the money to choose and eat well, at home and at work, in friends' houses and in restaurants, can eat better than ever before. It is also true that pressure from well-informed consumers has now pushed bread, milk and fats manufacturers into making and promoting higher-fibre and lower-fat products. And healthy food is making healthy profits, for some manufacturers, and for the giant retail chains.

But this does not mean that the national food supply as a whole, is improving. In 1987 there is little or no evidence that we in Britain are as a nation consuming significantly less fats, saturated fats, added sugar, salt or chemical additives. Manufacturers are moving these unhealthy commodities around, out of some products (for which, often enough, they charge a premium price) and into other products. As a generality, it is probably fair to say that middle-class adults are eating better, whereas children and young people of all classes are eating worse food than a few years ago. And it looks as if the food available in schools and hospitals, and for people living alone, the poor, the unemployed and the elderly, is deteriorating.

Certainly, the food manufacturing giants, as represented by the Food and Drink Federation (FDF) and its predecessor the Food Manufacturers Federation (FMF) are determined to cherish chemical food additives. A confidential memorandum sent by the FMF to its member companies in October 1985 is in my possession. Its headline is:[25]

FOOD INDUSTRY POSITION REGARDING MEDIA ACTIVITY ON ADDITIVES.

But as it turned out, it was not so much the media, as the retailers and manufacturers who were taking chemicals out of their food, that was causing hyperactivity at the FMF. The memorandum continued:

It is not unreasonable for companies to formulate products to meet a genuine or perceived consumer demand for foods without additives. ... [But] if a manufacturer determines to produce a product without the use of food additives – especially as a replacement for the existing product – he should not promote it by stating or suggesting that the new product is thereby inherently safer – or the old one inherently more dangerous.

In other words, if you must kick chemical additives out of your food, keep quiet about it. Imagine the advertisements. NEW UNIMPROVED GLOBBO.

By April 1986 the FMF had turned into the FDF, and launched its public relations campaign to defend the use of chemical additives. The advertising trade magazine *Campaign* reported:[26]

The Federation did consider an advertising campaign but has opted for PR in the short term. This is all important because no matter how much is spent on advertising, additional below-the-line support is required.

SIR DERRICK AND THE GREEN PYGMIES

In other words, creative minds are constantly at work, persuading you that chemical additives are the best thing since mother's milk. By the end of 1986, the food and chemical manufacturers' campaign to clean up the image of chemical additives was having some success in the national press; and a few academics have been prepared to defend additives.

FEARS ABOUT FOOD ADDITIVES 'EXAGGERATED'
FOOD ADDITIVES FEAR 'FABRICATED BY DO-GOODERS'

were two headlines in the *Daily Telegraph* in the same week in autumn 1986.[27,28] Dr Werner Wheelock of Bradford University was quoted as saying that 'consumers need not be concerned about additives'.[29] And Peter King of the Society of Chemical Industry celebrated the contribution of chemicals to the growth and health of children, suggested that additives had a part to play in the success of British athletes in the European Games, and took the view that criticism of additives is the work of 'do-gooders in the social conscience industry' who he also described as the 'Green Pygmy Party'.[28]

On 18 September 1986 the FDF went publicly above the line, and launched its 'Common Sense About Food' campaign. Food executives, scientists and technologists, hurried on down Park Lane, in limos, taxis, and on foot, to have their sinews stiffened and their blood summoned up by their leader, Sir Derrick Holden-Brown, and their sponsor, Michael Jopling, over lunch at the Dorchester.

The assembly did not put its mouth where its £35 billion annual turnover is. The menu was not a mug-a-soup, sweet and sour flavour pot noodles, followed by choc rolls and instant banana flavour topping, washed down with tropical fruitade and with a choc nibble for speechtime. Not a bit of that. Instead, Sir Derrick's captains, foot soldiers and camp followers were fortified with a meal prepared under the direction of Anton Mosimann, enthusiast for healthy food and inventor of that traditional British fare, *cuisine naturelle*.

Sir Derrick announced the FDF's campaign over lunch. This is the line on chemical additives:[30]

The food industry uses additives to provide products with the characteristics that people want. If consumers' attitudes change, the food industry will always adapt accordingly .... No manufacturer uses prohibited additives. The additives, which must by law be listed as ingredients on packets of processed food have been approved as safe by the Government, advised by expert committees.

The FDF is also keen to beat the drum for the products of its member organizations, such as the Bacon and Meat Manufacturers Association and the Biscuit, Cake, Chocolate and Confectionery Alliance:[30]

Some commentators think it is in the public interest to point an accusing finger at particular foods containing fats. But there is no reason why individuals who enjoy sausages, or cream cakes, or chocolate biscuits, should not continue to do so, as long as they accommodate these foods within a diet that, taken as a whole, does not contain excessive fat, especially saturated fat. Some commentators assert that the food industry puts its profits before the nation's health. This is outrageous and untrue.

Without additives, the FDF suggested, we might all be keeling over from deadly food poisons such as salmonella, which are not, said the FDF, caused by bad manufacturing practices but mostly by 'unhygienic food handling in the home'.[30] Mr Jopling, guest of honour at the Dorchester, was duly impressed by the FDF's endeavours and, as reported by the *Guardian*,[31] paid Sir Derrick and his minions an ambiguous compliment:

He admired the tenacity of the food manufacturers in fighting their critics. He acknowledged that public anxiety about food additives and processing now generated a large part of his Ministry's postbag.

We the consumers want additive-free food. But government remains staunch in support of the giant food and chemical manufacturing companies. Behind the scenes, ministers have been pressing the elbows of MPs alarmed by stories from their constituents about the ill-effects of chemical additives. In January 1986 the *Wilmslow World* included the following story:[32]

MP GETS ASSURANCE ON FOOD ADDITIVES. An assurance that strict controls exist on food additives has been given to Tatton MP Neil Hamilton following concern from a constituent that such substances could be harmful. Peggy Fenner, Parliamentary Secretary at the Ministry of Agriculture, Fisheries and Food, said that the Food Act of 1984 prohibited the addition to food of any substance which rendered it injurious to health .... Mrs Fenner said evidence suggested that while some people suffered adverse reactions to food additives, many more people suffered reactions to some of the many chemicals naturally present in food such as milk and eggs.

In February the Southampton *Evening Echo* carried a similar story,[33] in response to a query raised by Sir David Price, MP for Eastleigh. And then in March Conservative MP Peter Thurnham had this to say in his column in the *Bolton Evening News*:[34]

FOOD ADDITIVES AND ALLERGIES ... We are now being urged to check the 'E' numbers (list of additives) on pre-packaged foods. I was intrigued by all this, so investigated further with the Health Minister, Barney Hayhoe. I was told that the Food Act 1984 prohibits the addition to food of any substance that could injure health.

Other MPs needed no Ministerial elbow-pressing. Dr Austin Mitchell, Labour MP for Great Grimsby, spoke up for the fish-processing industry in March 1986. He was reported in the *Grimsby Evening Telegraph*:[35]

GRIMSBY MP SEES RED OVER COLOURLESS KIPPER. A browned-off Austin Mitchell is seeing red because Common Market bureaucrats want to turn the British kipper white .... Those crabby Continentals don't like the way the Brits use dye to turn their kippers into that homely brown colour .... Mr Ivan Jaines-White, head of Grimsby curers F.A. Peterson, said today that fish and food processors were not irresponsible and a lot of money was spent on proving the innocence of Brown FK. 'There has been no link to show that this colourant has any adverse effect on health. Much of the blame for the present anti-colourant lobby must be placed with the media.'

It is no disrespect to Mr Hamilton, Sir David Price, Mr Thurnham and Dr Mitchell to say that they have no special knowledge of chemical additives, and so are liable to accept assurances about their safety from the experts in government and the food manufacturing industry.

DONALD THOMPSON
IS NOT COMPLACENT

In 1987 the ground was prepared: and in February MAFF held a press conference, to which critics of government policy like myself were not invited, to announce the launch of a £100,000 colour booklet, *Food Additives – The Balanced Approach*, which has now been sent free of charge to schools, shops, hospitals and doctors.[36,37] Whole, fresh food has nothing on processed food with its chemical additives, suggests the booklet:

> Remember the benefits they bring – not just longer shelf-life for food, but a greater variety, more convenience and more reliable uniform quality.

Professor Frank Curtis, Chairman of the Food Advisory Committee, was on the platform at the press conference; and James Erlichman of the *Guardian* and Dr Oliver Gillie of the *Independent* took the opportunity to ask when *Review of the Colouring Matter in Food Regulations*,[38] the FAC report awaited since 1982, would be materializing. Soon, said Professor Curtis. Dr Gillie asked whether the FAC would be recommending the banning of any colours or dyes (such as ammonium caramel, tartrazine, amaranth or brown FK). 'Yes,' said Professor Curtis; but then, obviously embarrassed by this revelation, would say nothing more.*

---

* The *Final Report on the Review of the Colouring Matter in Food Regulations 1973* emerged on 30 March 1987. This FAC report recommends the banning of yellow 2G (107). It recommends restricting red 2G to sausages and other processed meats, and brown FK to kippers and other processed fish. Dr Austin Mitchell MP will be pleased. Of the other 'Filthy Five' dyes, brilliant blue FCF (133) and brown HT (155) are passed as safe. All other coal-tar dyes, including the notorious tartrazine (E102), sunset yellow (E110) and amaranth (E123) are passed as safe, with a recommendation that they be classified 'A'. These recommendations merely follow proposals made in Brussels by the Commission of the European Communities.[39] In addition, the report recommends some upper limit on the concentration of colours and dyes, and repeats the recommendation of the 1979 FACC interim report that colours and dyes be banned from baby food. Caramels remain classified 'B' and thus provisionally acceptable, despite mounting evidence that ammonium caramels are a threat to the immune system. Cynics predict that caramels will be classified 'A' in due course (after the appropriate toxicological testing, funded and controlled by industry, is carried out); and point out that manufacturers no longer use yellow 2G in food.

By early 1987 the government had refined its line on additives. On 27 February Donald Thompson addressed the Association of County Councils, giving the MAFF press office the opportunity for a release saying:[40]

FOOD ADDITIVES – WE'RE NOT COMPLACENT ON SAFETY, SAYS DONALD THOMPSON ... Consumers' well-being is at the forefront of Ministers' considerations.

By way of explanation, Mr Thompson announced four 'new government-funded research projects' designed to check out adverse reactions to chemical additives. Did this mean that, after all, there was a problem? Did the food and chemical manufacturing industry have anything to fear? Evidently not; for, as it turned out, he had a pretty good idea what the results of the research would be, even as he announced it. 'Preliminary results suggest that intolerant reactions to food additives are rare' he said. It would seem that politicians can have gifts of prescience not granted to scientists.

As we prepared to vote for a new government in 1987, government and the food industry were putting the same message across to us as consumers and citizens, and to our elected representatives in Parliament, by means of advertising, public relations, press conferences, and those two British standbys, the quiet word and the confidential chat. The official story, promoted by food manufacturers and accepted by food retailers, evidently goes something like this. (1) British food is good – and it's getting better. (2) Maybe some people have problems with too much fat or with a few additives. This is all rather controversial, but it's being sorted out. (3) Be sensible; don't be a fuss-pot, and don't pay any attention to the doom-mongers. (4) If you are a bit of a fuss-pot, though, there are plenty of new products right up your street. (5) But above all, don't worry. Everything is under control.

FLAVOUR OF THE
MILLENIUM: FLAVOURS

Why, though, does government, together with the giant food manufacturers, above all cherish and defend chemical food additives with such zeal, despite reliable doubts about their safety? The answer is not in the value of the additives themselves. The total value of the British additive industry in 1986 is estimated to be about £200 million a year,[41,42] which is better than a slap in the belly with a stained kipper, but a small fraction of the turnover of any leading British food manufacturer or retailer.

The answer is that technological food cannot be made without chemicals, and that technological food is what we are in for, as the millenium approaches.[43]

Take flavours, which remain unregulated despite recommendations for a 'positive' list made by successive government advisory committees.[44,45] Anything between 3000 and 5500 of the chemical additives now used in the British food supply are flavours,[46,47] depending on how the count is done. I have already pointed out (in chapter 2) that the money in flavours is not so much in the flavours themselves, as in what can be done with them. (The same is of course true of colours and dyes, and other classes of additive).

Soon after the Unilever subsidiaries Wall's and Birds Eye announced new, improved additive-free sausages[48] and fish fingers[49], Unilever paid $150 million to take over Naarden, the Dutch chemical food flavour business, so becoming the biggest manufacturer of flavours in Europe, if not the world. Why? *World Food and Drink Report*, the confidential industry newsletter, explained:[50]

> Flavours and fragrances are big business. The market is estimated at $7.4 billion worldwide [with] a growth rate of between 4 and 5 per cent a year. By 1990, it is predicted that the market will be worth more than $10 billion.

According to the *Financial Times*:[51]

> Unilever must want Naarden rather badly. Evidently in flavours and fragrances, there is a lot to be said for a bigger sales base

and marketing efficiencies to support some very expensive research. There may eventually be more bang for Unilever's guilder.

Flavours in particular, and chemical food additives in general, are booming business, because whole, fresh food is being replaced by processed food, the whole world over. In Britain, processed food is becoming more and more sophisticated. And no-additive lines are now accommodated: they are known in the trade as one type of 'NPD', or new product development; a premium product whose extra added value depends on less 'value' being added.

But overall, more and more chemical additives are being pumped into the British food supply. In the five years between 1979 and 1984, according to an industry survey,[52] the 'crisp and snack' market swelled by almost 10 per cent every year. Many of these products (unrecorded in MAFF's National Food Survey) which are 'one of the fastest growing sectors in the total food market',[52] are little more than confections of colours, flavours and/or preservatives, together with processed fats, starches, sugars and/or salt.

You and I may have a steady income, a car, and access to well-stocked supermarkets, fishmongers, greengrocers and butchers; and may eat plenty of whole, fresh food. But as a nation, we British are being supplied with more and more highly processed, cheapened food; and what as a nation we are supplied with, we buy and eat.

SUGAR: A CLEAN BILL OF HEALTH?

So by the spring of 1987, government and the food manufacturing industry in Britain were united in the promotion of food additives in particular and highly processed foods in general. What about sugars, food irradiation, and nutrition education, to take three bits of business discussed in chapters 3, 5 and 6, and unfinished at the end of 1986? What was the news for us, the consumers?

In January 1987, Professor A.J. Vlitos of the World Sugar Research Organization sent copies of the US Food and Drug Administration's Task Force report on sugars[53] to key opinion-formers, such as MPs, with a personalized covering letter.[54] In February the British Nutrition Foundation's Task Force report on sugars and syrups had still not been published, almost a year after its 'conclusions and recommendations' had been released by Professor David Conning, the BNF's Director-General. But a leaked copy of the report found its way to the *Sunday Times*, whose story was headlined:[55]

SUGAR EXPERTS' SOFT LINE SOURS THE HEALTH LOBBY

My own leaked copy of the report[56] (eventually published in April 1987) revealed that Margaret Sanderson's chapter on 'Sugars in the Diet – Practical Aspects', which had originally clearly recommended a halving of consumption of sugars, had been subjected to further changes. Should we all eat less sugars, for the sake of our health? The final version of the text said:

> On the one hand it has been advocated that the average sugar consumption per head of the population should be reduced by roughly 50 per cent (James, 1983) but it has not been claimed that this figure has been based on objective evidence of an optimum level of consumption. Another view (American Council on Science and Health, 1986) does not advocate a general reduction in consumption, but aims to identify those sections of the public at risk of dental caries and/or obesity and then to give advice to those groups.

'James' refers to the NACNE report, published for the National Advisory Committee on Nutrition Education by the Health Education Council.[57] References made by Margaret Sanderson[58] to other reports published by the British Medical Association and the Health Education Council,[59,60] which also recommended a national halving of sugars consumption, were dropped from the BNF report. 'American Council on Science and Health' refers to a booklet *'Sugars and Your Health'*[61] prepared by Dr Elizabeth Whelan's staff at ACSH and published in May 1986, after the publication of the BNF's own 'conclusions and recommendations'! The *Sunday Times*[55] said that the BNF Task Force report

has now gone to the government Committee on Medical
Aspects of Food Policy, which advises the Department of
Health on what to recommend for a good diet.

So, what of the COMA panel on *The Influence of Dietary
Sugars on Human Health and Disease*, whose chairman,
Professor Harry Keen, had been named in December 1986?
It met for the first time on 18 February 1987. During January
and up to mid-February I telephoned the DHSS press office
about twice a week, and asked three questions. First, who
were the members of the COMA panel on sugars? Second,
had the existence of the panel been advertised in any medical
journal, so that interested scientists other than those on the
panel could submit evidence, and if not why not? Third,
how could I, as a researcher in the field, submit evidence?
The courteous DHSS press officers could not answer these
questions. On 19 February I asked another question, which
was: fourth, why were the names of Professor Keen's
colleagues still secret despite the fact that the panel had met
on the previous day? By this time I had found out the
answers to the first three questions by other means.

It is normal for COMA panels to undertake their own
review of the scientific literature. In the case of sugars,
though, a senior MAFF official (who asked not to be
identified) said that in the case of sugars this probably
wouldn't be necessary. In his view, the FDA and BNF Task
Force reports were comprehensive and up-to-date, and
would be all the documents that the COMA panel would
need. This view is shared by Professor Keen, according to a
story published in the trade journal *Chemistry and Industry*
in the week of the first meeting of the COMA panel:[62]

If the panel is put under pressure to produce its review
reasonably quickly, it will have to rely heavily on the FDA
sugars task force report, published last year, and the report of a
British Nutrition Foundation sugars task force, which will be
published shortly. 'I would personally like to use those two
reviews as our jumping off point' Keen says. He believes going
back to review all the papers 'would be a little bit pointless'. 'A
fair amount of the stuff is now open and shut' he says, but adds
that he stands to be corrected if anyone has new evidence.

What about funding provided by the sugar industry for scientific research? Professor Keen confirmed that he has been funded by the sugar industry:

> 'I feel not in the slightest compromised' Keen says of his past support from the sugar industry. 'It will influence me in no way whatsoever'. Keen told C&I he has received no money from any sugar company or association since 1983 ... A source at the DHSS confirmed that Keen had declared his prior funding by the sugar industry, as required, but would not say whether any of the other ten members of the panel 'had declared any matter which could tend to show bias'.

If the COMA panel on *The influence of dietary sugars on human health and disease* follows the lines of the FDA and BNF reports, its conclusions will be that sugars contribute to tooth decay, but so do all carbohydrates; that sugars contribute to overweight, in common with all foods eaten to excess; that otherwise sugars have no role in disease except in so far as obesity increases the risk of disease; and that in general there is no need to recommend any cut in the consumption of sugars. Such conclusions would please both government and the food manufacturing industry.

IRRADIATION: PLAYING
THE EUROCARD

On one issue above all, food technologists faced formidable and united opposition in early 1987: food irradiation. Throughout 1986 the London Food Commission provided a focus for public outcry against irradiated food. According to a summary in the *Guardian* of a Marplan poll of 1486 adults published in February 1987:[63]

> 84 per cent of those questioned were opposed to the ban on food irradiation being lifted. Only two per cent of those questioned thought it was safe to lift the ban before a technique could be developed to test whether foods bought in the shops had been irradiated .... And 99 per cent of respondents said they would choose to buy fresh food which had not been irradiated .... The Marplan poll ... also showed that the public is deeply suspicious of the assurances given by Government and industry. Only 25

per cent said they would buy irradiated foods if the Government said they were safe.

A week later the consumer representatives, trades unionists, environmentalists, retailers and caterers united by the Food Commission's campaign[64] were joined by leaders of the medical profession. The British Medical Association's position was summed up in two headlines in the *Guardian*[65] and the *Times*:[66]

FOOD IRRADIATION 'COULD PUT CHILDREN AT RISK'
FEAR OF HEALTH RISK IF FOODS ARE IRRADIATED

The *Guardian*'s story quoted Dr John Dawson of the BMA as saying that the benefit of food irradiation to the consumer was not established and that there were evident risks:

Irradiation used to sterilise food might cause genetic mutations in children, would destroy some nutrients, and still expose consumers to the risk of food poisoning, the British Medical Association's board of science said yesterday.

It looked as if food irradiation just might become a politically sensitive issue in 1987. The food manufacturers, as represented by the FDF and its new President, Ross Buckland of Kelloggs, were disturbed. As reported in the *Grocer*, Mr Buckland said:[67]

Irradiation suffers from post-Chernobyl connotations. We have a campaign to educate the public about the subject. Manufacturers want to use the technique but believe it should not be introduced until a means of detecting it has been found.

Which is to say, not until after the general election. Meanwhile, however, the food manufacturers had been lobbying in Brussels. Throughout the European Community, national law is being erased in favour of Eurolaw. In February 1987, the Commission of the European Communities issued a proposed Council Directive designed to 'harmonize' Eurofood law, so as to prevent barriers to trade.[68] Harmony can be achieved in different ways. Take chemical additives. If all European countries banned all coal tar dyes, harmony would result: there would be no barriers to trade, because all European countries would be able to export and import unstained food, without impediment from national laws. Take food labelling or food irradiation. If all European countries labelled processed foods with their saturated fats, fats, added sugars and salt content, and also banned food irradiation, harmony would be achieved. In these cases, all European countries would abide by the highest standards, designed to protect the interests of consumers. This can be called the 'levelling up' policy.

There is also the 'levelling down' policy, by which countries abide by the lowest standards, designed to protect the interests of multi-national food manufacturers. Such a policy means that 'E' numbers proliferate, nutritional labelling is blocked, and every European country accepts food irradiation. This is the policy British delegations in Brussels usually favour.[69] Hence a small news item in the *Daily Telegraph* in March 1987:[70]

> IRRADIATED FOOD 'SOON'. Common Market pressure is mounting on the Government to lift the ban on the controversial process of food irradiation .... Ministers are understood to be reluctant to challenge the EEC whose decision to remove the ban is expected after next week's debate in the European Parliament on irradiation. The European Commission is expected to issue a report in the next few weeks criticising the ban as a 'barrier to trade' and recommending its lifting throughout the Common Market.

The prospect, therefore, is that in due course government and the food manufacturers will play the Eurocard, and in response to protests against food irradiation will in effect say 'I do so agree, old boy. You don't like it. We don't like it. But what can we do? We're in the hands of those blasted bureaucrats in Brussels.'

UNCEASING CENSORSHIP

The third item of business unfinished at the end of 1986, was nutrition education. At the end of chapter 6 we left Dr John Garrow, Chairman of JACNE, the one reasonably independent officially sanctioned source of advice about food and health in Britain, threatening to resign unless he could be assured that the DHSS would not censor his work.

His committee was not only concerned with fats and heart disease, but also with obesity, nutrition labelling, and with health education in schools.[71] It had also presided over the Health Education Council's 1986 booklet, *Guide to Healthy Eating*[60] which among other things advises:

> Sugar gives you 'empty calories' – that is calories with no other nutrients: no vitamins, no minerals, no fibre, no protein ... Aim to cut down the amount of sugar you eat by a half.

Norman Fowler, Cabinet Minister responsible for the DHSS, soon sorted Dr Garrow out. In November 1986 Mr Fowler had abolished the HEC, without giving any prior warning to its Director-General, Dr David Player.[72] In March 1987 Mr Fowler abolished JACNE, without warning Dr Garrow.[73] Both bodies were replaced in April by a new Health Education Authority directly controlled by the DHSS and thus by Government.

In February Dr Player went public. As reported in the *Daily Telegraph*:[74]

> He feels the food industry's influence, exercised through the Ministry of Agriculture, Fisheries and Food, will prove too strong for a council wanting to promote a healthier diet. Once the Council is a department of Government, he argues, it would be much harder for it to campaign, for example, for the consumption of less butter and full fat milk.

As Dr Player sees it, the Government had silenced 'the public's only defender against the food, drink and tobacco lobbies'[74] which he went on to describe in the *Guardian*[75] as 'the industries that are antagonistic to health – I call them the enemies of the people.' He explained further:

> The new health authority will be under the direct control of the Secretary of State. We will do what he tells us. Take diet, for example. If the Ministry of Agriculture doesn't want us to say something about fat, then we will not be able to say anything about fat.

In 1983 the NACNE report on dietary goals for everybody in Britain had been published by the Health Education Council, with a preface signed by Professor Jerry Morris, Chairman of NACNE, Dr Player, and Dr Derek Shrimpton, then Director-General of the British Nutrition Foundation.

By 1987 these three men had been removed or had moved from their posts, and the NACNE report was orphaned. A week after the abolition of JACNE, Government made its first move, against the HEC 'Guide to Healthy Eating'. As reported in the *London Daily News*[76]

> WARNING ON SUGAR DROPPED. A warning that people should halve their sugar intake has been removed from a government guide to healthy eating. The move follows discussions between the Department of Health and the Ministry of Agriculture and has angered the Health Education Council which produced the guide ... HEC members believe it has been watered down to placate the powerful sugar lobby ... A Health Department spokesman said: 'We have set up a specialist panel to look at the sugar question. It was felt better not to state how much sugar should be eaten until we had advice from the new panel.'

So in 1987, as it turned out, sugar was given an official clean bill of health, at least until Professor Keen's COMA panel reported. Once again, the sugar industry had gained its ends.

THE HEALTH CARD

What, then, is to be done about food and public health in Britain? There is general agreement among scientists around the world, that in the last few generations the food supplies of Western countries, such as Britain, have become dangerously unbalanced. Western food is becoming more and more processed; heavy in hardened fats, added sugars, salt and chemical additives. Most people come to no harm if they habitually eat small amounts of these deadened commodities; but above a certain level, varying with the individual, they become, singly and in combination, a threat to health. Typical consumption of commercial fats, sugars, salt and additives in Britain is way above this danger level; which is why typical British food is a menace to public health, liable to cause illness in children and young adults, as well as in middle-aged and old people.

In Britain we have special problems. The national palate has been insulted by mass-manufactured 'store' food ever since the Industrial Revolution; corrupted by the confections of fats and sugars available to the middle-classes since Victorian days; and then in the last generation, after the 1939–45 war, degraded by increasingly uniform, cheapened, artificial food.

Successive governments have encouraged a Euroglut of saturated fats and processed sugars, and would if anything like to see more sweet fat poured down the national gullet. The food manufacturing and retailing industries are now concentrated in the hands of fewer firms than in any other country in the developed world.

The British value food less than people on the Continent, because we have been trained to think that food is good just because it is cheap. This nonsensical attitude has been reinforced by industry: food is now the only major commodity usually advertised in terms of its cheapness. As a nation we have learned to value high quality clothes, cars, carpets and computers, but still shop around for 'penny-off' food. As a result, only the food giants can survive and prosper. In Europe, small farmers, manufacturers and retailers still thrive; in Britain, they have been driven out of business. Skilled people who take pride in making and selling good food can find work in Europe; in Britain such craftsmen are often enough on the dole, or else pushing paper or minding machines.

Successive governments in Britain have taken the advice above all of the giant food and chemical manufacturers. This explains British food policy, and also the British farming landscape. Consequently it is now assumed by policy-makers of all political persuasions, that whether we like it or not, the British national economy depends on the development of a highly technological, capital-intensive food manufacturing industry, making 'scientific' food from uniformly processed ingredients by means of highly sophisticated 'processing aids' and other, cosmetic, chemicals. This assumption underlies government policy, and there is little sign that policy will change under a new Conservative administration, or a Labour, Alliance or coalition government.

But a policy of favouring the manufacture of highly processed food can only damage the wealth as well as the health of the nation. Monopoly is the enemy of capitalism as well as of socialism; and the gigantic, semi-monopolistic companies that now dominate food manufacture in Britain are in a position to thwart the proper operation of supply and demand, and continue to make consumer sovereignty an illusion. A rational economic policy is the complete reverse of that adopted by British governments since the 1939–45 war. What we need as a nation is more diversity, more people in work, a food chain which really is demand-led, and above all the re-creation of the infrastructure of small, flourishing food and farming business which have been destroyed in the last generation, and on which the good economic and physical health of the nation depends.

The fact is, though, that personalities aside, no British government during the last generation has paid any real attention to national food policy. Official reports on food and health are used as instruments of government. The evidence is that such policy as we have is controlled by civil servants, working in harmony with the food giants. Many of the scientists who serve on government advisory committees, and who work hard for little reward in good faith, will sincerely deny this view. I think that such honest men are deluded. British food and public health will remain just about the worst in the developed world until a new government commits itself to the transformation of the quality of the food supply.* Without such a policy, the National Health Service is liable to collapse under the weight of patients suffering from illnesses caused by the food with which they are supplied, and therefore buy and eat.

A national policy designed to encourage whole, fresh food, and to discourage processed fats, sugars, salt and chemical additives, will change the shape of British farming and food manufacture. Such a policy will vigorously

---

* What about the national food and health policy documents issued by the major opposition parties in 1985? Labour's *Food Policy: A Priority for Labour*, emerged as a 'consultative paper'[77] and has not been taken on board by the party leadership. A subsequent paper, *A New Vision for Health*,[78] never saw the light of day. The *Guardian*, having uncovered the document in 1986, commented 'Whether Messrs Kinnock and Hattersley will accept that the health gains will be worth the political hassle remains to be seen.'[79] Likewise, while a number of Liberal politicians retain a strong interest, nothing more has been heard of the Liberal Party Assembly Resolution on 'Food and Health'.[80] Food and health is not a party political issue. A Conservative government under new leadership may turn out to be the first administration to make changes for the better.

support the small farmer and the small manufacturer. Overall it will be good for business, creating new jobs and more wealth. We need new priorities: support for small firms and for vegetable and fruit farmers, for the cultivation of low-input and organic produce, and for the fishing fleet.

But nothing will change until politicians realize that we mean business, not just as consumers, but also as citizens and voters.

WISE PLANS FOR HEALTHY
AND WEALTHY FOOD

How can a national good food policy be articulated? Two reforms can be made immediately:

○ The House of Commons Select Committee on Agriculture should change its name and, as the Select Committee on Agriculture, Fisheries and Food, immediately conduct a public enquiry into British food policy since the 1939–45 war.

○ People connected with the food industry should not serve on government advisory committees, and the work of these committees should not be covered by the Official Secrets Act. A 'Register of Advisors' Interests' should be published annually.

Right now, no political party capable of forming a government is planning systematic reform of British food policy. This is because governments almost always take the line of least resistance. Half a century ago, John Boyd Orr wrote:[1]

In a democratic country the necessary legislation must be preceded by an intelligent demand on the part of the people.

In the 1980s we have come full circle. Boyd Orr's views were right in 1937, and they are right in 1987. By the end of the 1930s government realised that good food is a crucial and urgent national priority. What, towards the end of the 1980s, will persuade government to play the health card again? First, and above all, intelligent demand: and this means you, pressing for change as a citizen as well as a consumer. Second, a national plan, which any government can put into action, designed to transform the quality of the national food supply. All the political parties should declare their support for a good food policy, by means such as the following:

○ A new Ministry of Food to be established, incorporating the functions of MAFF, but with over-riding responsibility to ensure a healthy food supply. The Minister to be a senior Cabinet appointment, with powers over the food and farming industry.

○ The first task of the Minister of Food to be to set goals for the quality of the national food supply, for the short-term (within five years) and the long-term (by the end of the century). The NACNE goals to be used until others are devised.

○ The long-term goals to be fulfilled within five years for population groups in special need of good food: notably schoolchildren, people in hospital, and the armed forces. Nutritional standards to be restored to school meals immediately.

○ The Minister of Food to chair a committee of Cabinet colleagues whose support is needed for a coherent national food policy. The committee to include the ministers responsible for the Exchequer, Health, Education, Trade, Scotland, Wales, Northern Ireland.

○ In Europe, the Minister of Food to invoke the Article of the Treaty of Rome which entitles any nation to set its own standards for food for over-riding reasons of public health. The standards set by the Ministry to be the highest within Europe.

○ Industry to be given incentives to breed, grow, make and sell food with low fat, sugar, salt and/or chemical content: vegetables rather than sugar beet, lean instead of fat animals, organic instead of chemicalized produce, wholegrain instead of white bread.

○ Funds for such incentives to be found from a levy on food manufacturers, scaled according to their turnover, and also according to the volume of saturated fats, added sugars, salt and chemical additives used in their products. Small firms not to be taxed.

○ An immediate ban to be imposed on chemical additives in all foods liable to be eaten by babies and young children under five years of age. The use of cosmetic additives to be restricted. All additives under a toxicological cloud to be withdrawn.

○ Compositional standards to be restored for staple foods. High quality staple foods to be subsidised and to sell at the same price as low-quality 'equivalents'. These staples to include wholegrain bread and flour, and other wholegrain cereal products.

○ Official expert advisory committees on all public health issues to be replaced by lay committees of enquiry, briefed to report promptly. Experts representing industrial, medical, consumer and other interests to be free to give evidence.

○ The work of all government advisors to be subject to a Freedom of Information Act. Committee work to include public hearings, and reports to include written and oral evidence, and references. The secretariat to be supplied by an independent professional body.

○ Scientific research into food, health and disease also to be funded from the levy on food manufacturers. The funds to be disbursed by a variety of publicly accountable bodies with no industrial connections, such as a newly constituted Health Education Council.

○ The incidence of diseases believed to be caused by Western food to be monitored permanently, together with the health of vulnerable groups in the population. This work to be done jointly with a new Ministry of Health, in collaboration with the WHO.

○ The educational and medical authorities in Britain to be encouraged to introduce nutrition as a standard subject on the syllabus for schoolchildren and medical students. Food manufacturers to be discouraged from distributing literature to schools and clinics.

Changes such as these will not happen spontaneously. New policies require commitment from politicians, and reliable commitment comes from certain knowledge that such policies are vote-winners. So the first commitment must come from you, the consumer and citizen. Don't wait for somebody else to act. Talk to your supermarket manager. Write to the newspapers. Join local consumer groups. It makes a difference.

And do the democratic thing, and write to your MP. I suggest you say 'My support for you at all times will be influenced by your views on food and health. So please let me have your answers to the following questions. First, do you agree that the quantity of processed fats and sugars, together with salt, chemical additives and alcohol in the British food supply, is a public health problem? Second, will you support the creation of a Ministry of Food, incorporating all the current responsibilities of MAFF, but with the paramount responsibility of improving the quality of our national food supply?'

Alternatively, ask the questions that are most important to you, using this book as a guide. And when you get a reply, please forward it to me care of Century/Hutchinson, and mark your envelope 'Politics of Food'.

Now you are informed, you are responsible for change.

Part Two

DOCUMENT A

Two Hundred and Fifty Politicians and the Food Industry

Many members of Parliament have direct or indirect links with the food industry, or with the associated drink, farming and chemical industries; or, alternatively, have major industry interests situated in their constituencies. As used here, the term 'food industry' includes all stages in the food chain, from growth or manufacture, through sales, marketing and packaging, to advertising and promotion.

This document lists MPs in office on 1 January 1987. It does not include ex-MPs, wives or husbands of MPs, other relatives, members of the House of Lords (even if they are Government ministers), Members of the European Parliament (MEPs), or politicians outside Parliament.

To point out a link between a politician and industry, is not in itself to suggest anything disreputable or inconsistent with public responsibility. Indeed, any MP with factory or farm workers in the constituency has a responsibility to look after their interests.

In this document, four types of link with industry are included:

1. *Consultant* or *advisor*. MPs who are, or were, paid by industry to give expert advice in parliament and elsewhere, or as employees. Some do work for public relations firms who represent the interests of industry.

2. *Director* or *employee*. MPs who combine their parliamentary responsibilities with those of a working director or employer in industry, or else as an employee. *Ex-directors* and *ex-employees* are also included.

3. *Owner* or *shareholder*. MPs who own, or have owned, one or more businesses or shareholdings in business. This may be a big or small business, a farm or a smallholding, a hotel or pub. Also

included are MPs whose *family* business is food.

4. *Constituency* MPs whose constituents include a high percentage of workers (10 per cent or more) in the food industry or farming, or who have major food industry interests in their constituency.

Industry listed is that which is of public health concern: industry using fats and sugars and highly processed food generally; alcohol; meat and dairy farming; agrichemicals and food chemicals. Large food retailers and caterers are also included, as are hotels and pubs.

Relevant offices held by an MP are also listed: ministerial posts, shadow responsibilities, membership of parliamentary committees concerned with food; and the like.

Government posts listed incorporate the reshuffles of 1985 and 1986. MPs who became Ministers after these reshuffles may have divested themselves of any links with industry listed here (from the most recently published sources) by the time this book is published. All details are taken from the most recently published sources, cross-checked wherever possible, as indicated in the references.

MPs who are or who have been associated with those parts of the food industry concerned with food known to be healthy, are not listed. Specifically, MPs with a professional or parliamentary interest in fish, vegetables or fruit are not listed, notwithstanding the fact that much fish is fried in saturated fat, or processed with additives into fingers, and that much fruit is pulped and turned into jam. For example, Sir Walter Clegg is vice-chairman of the Conservative Fisheries sub-committee, and is committed to the interests of the fishing fleet in his Wyre constituency.[1] Sir John Wells, MP for Maidstone, is Chairman of the Conservative Horticulture sub-committee, and has been a fruit farmer and a Director of the Association of Fresh Produce.[2] Kenneth Baker, appointed a Cabinet Minister at the Department of Education and Science in May 1986, was a director of the banana firm Geest from 1974 to 1981.[1] Richard Shepherd is Managing Director and Teddy Taylor a director of Shepherd Foods and Partridges, high-class London grocers specializing in fresh food.[1] These Conservative MPs are not listed.

Special knowledge and experience of the food or farming industry can of course lead people in public life to favour reform; and MPs are not usually listed when they have been identified as consistently favouring policies for a healthier food supply. For example, Sir Richard Body, David Harris, Albert McQuarrie and Jim Spicer are four Conservative MPs for rural constituencies, all of whom are or have been farmers, or have a high proportion of farm workers, or the factories of large food firms, in their constituencies. All of them are members of the Select Committee on Agriculture. At the same time, Sir Richard Body, MP for Holland with Boston (Chairman of the Select Committee as from 1986), is an advocate of low-input, rational, humane farming, and an opponent of the agrichemical industry.[1] Jim Spicer, MP for West Dorset, is a health and fitness enthusiast and advocates explicit food labelling.[3] David Harris and Albert McQuarrie both speak up for the fishermen in their St Ives and Banff & Buchan constituencies,[1] and David Harris has also called for rational milk production and a healthy national food supply.[3]

Robert Adley, Conservative MP for Christchurch, is also a Director of Commonwealth Holiday Inns of Canada, and has called for explicit labelling of the fats content in food.[3] In the Berwick-upon-Tweed constituency of Alan Beith (Liberal deputy leader) 12.9 per cent of the electors are employed in agriculture, and Mr Beith has stated an interest in improving the quality of British food.[3] John Home Robertson, a Labour spokesman on agriculture and MP for East Lothian, owns a farm and wants to see more vigorous government action to promote a healthy diet.[3] Stefan Terlezki, Conservative MP for Cardiff West, was once a baker and now owns a hotel, and advocates explicit sausage labelling.[3] These MPs are not listed.

Inclusion in or exclusion from the list has therefore necessarily had to involve judgement. For example, David Mudd (Conservative) speaks up for the fishing fleet in his Falmouth and Cambourne constituency[1], and is Parliamentary Consultant to the National Federation of Fruit and Potato Traders:[2] his inclusion in the list is not for these reasons, but because he has been advisor to Michael Joyce PR,[1] whose clients include Mitchells Brewery. Similarly, Edward du Cann, Conservative MP for Taunton, is listed as vice-chairman of Lonrho because sugar refining is one of Lonrho's many business interests. Again, this is not to suggest that Mr Mudd or Mr du Cann, or indeed any other MP listed, puts improper pressure on their colleagues, in support of food or farming industry interests.

MPs who have links with the milling and baking industries are included, with apologies to any who speak up for wholemeal bread. Most baking is of white bread and also of cakes and pastries. So, Geraint Howells (Liberal), Jim Lester (Conservative), and Richard Wainwright (Liberal) are listed, as Honorary Vice Presidents (past and present), of the National Association of Master Bakers, Confectioners and Caterers.

The fact that an MP's constituency includes a major food or

farming presence, or that an MP is an advisor to a public relations company with food industry accounts[4], may or may not be reflected in the MP's demeanour in House of Commons debates or elsewhere. It is regarded as normal and reasonable for an MP to press constituency interests, especially when those involve vital matters such as employment. Closure of a large factory, for example, can bring great hardship.

A case in point was the takeover bid for Allied Lyons by the Australian firm Elders IXL, launched in late 1985. Allied Lyons have many large plants, including four in the Ealing North, Barnsley, Brent South and Leicester East constituencies. On 24 October Harry Greenway, Conservative MP for Ealing North, objected to the proposed takeover in an Oral Question.[3] On 7 November Roy Mason, Labour MP for Barnsley Central, tabled an Early Day Motion expressing alarm, supported by twelve other MPs, including Allen McKay, Terry Patchett, Peter Hardy and Walter Harrison, four other Labour MPs for Barnsley and the surrounding area, and Laurie Pavitt, Labour MP for Brent South.[3] On the same day Peter Bruinvels, Conservative MP for Leicester East, tabled another Early Day Motion questioning whether the Elders bid was in the public interest, supported by John Marek and Neil Thorne.[4] So by 7 November 1985 Allied Lyons could count on the support of 16 MPs concerned to protect the interests of Allied Lyons and its shareholders or workers.

A Commons debate on the confectionery industry in May 1985,[3] to which Peggy Fenner replied on behalf of the Ministry of Agriculture, consisted entirely of statements made on behalf of the industry, and of Rowntree Mackintosh and Tate & Lyle in particular, by three MPs who declared their interests: Conal Gregory (Conservative, York, Rowntree Mackintosh); Dr Norman Godman (Labour, Greenock and Port Glasgow, Tate & Lyle) and John Powley (Conservative, Norwich South, Rowntree Mackintosh).[3] Of these Dr Godman and Mr Powley have no other known links with industry, except that Mr Powley is a member of the All-Party retail group.

The food companies whose presence in a constituency is listed, include all those who feature in the top 100 British companies measured by market capitalization[5] and/or among the top 100 British spenders on advertising,[6] in 1984–86. At the last count, five of the top ten and ten of the top twenty British companies are wholly or partly in the food and/or drink trade. The food industry is Britain's biggest industry. In 1982, 2,129,000 people were employed in food processing and distribution (1,478,000) and on farms (651,000).[7] Of the ten top spenders on advertising, seven are food and/or drink firms, with a total spend on food and/or drink in 1984 of £242 million (£267 million if pet food is included). These are Unilever, Mars, Allied Lyons, Imperial Group, Nestlé, Cadbury Schweppes and Rowntree Mackintosh.[6]

The largest British food companies dominate the industry, and are often politically active. For example, in 1985 Allied Lyons was the 19th largest British company[8], and the fifth largest British advertiser, with a total spend on food and drink of £47,000,000.[9] Its Chairman, Sir Derrick Holden-Brown, knighted in Mrs Thatcher's first New Year's honours list in 1979,[10] who was also until 1987 President of the Food and Drink Federation,[11] the representative organization of the food manufacturing industry with which government negotiates. In 1984 and 1985 Allied Lyons headed the table of food industry firms contributing to Conservative party support, with donations of £82,000 in each year.[12] Robert Rhodes James, Conservative MP for Cambridge, is consultant to Allied Lyons.[1] The Prime Minister, Mrs Thatcher, is an ex-employee of Lyons.[13] This is not to suggest that Mrs Thatcher or Conservative government policy is improperly influenced by Allied Lyons.

250 MPs are listed below. Analysed by political party, they are made up as follows:

MPs who are or have been connected with the food industry

	MPs in list	MPs in House of Commons
Conservative	202	391
Labour	35	206
Liberal	7	19
Ulster Unionist	4	10
Plaid Cymru	2	2
rest	0	22
Total	250	650

Of this total of 250, 72 are listed because there is a food or farming interest in their constituency, which they may or may not have represented in the Commons. The remaining 178 have, or have had, further connections with the food industry.

Half of all Conservative MPs have some connection with the food industry; this is true for all Conservative MPs in Parliament (202 of 391) and almost of Ministers and Parliamentary Private Secretaries (PPSs) (65 of 135). Excluding Peers (members of the House of Lords), the totals are as follows. 'Const only' means that only a constituency presence has been identified.

	In list	(of which const only)	Not in list	Total
Cabinet	10	(2)	9	19
Other Ministers	32	(3)	38	70
Total Ministers	42	(5)	47	89
PPSs	23	(8)	23	46
Grand Total	65	(13)	70	135

Of the 35 Labour MPs listed, two are 'shadow' Cabinet Ministers (Peter Archer and Dr John Cunningham). Archer is a consultant to a public relations company with food accounts. Cunningham is advisor to the chemical firm Albright and Wilson, manufacturers of chemical food additives. The other nine senior Labour MPs listed do not currently do work for the food industry.

To understand how the list works, take the Cabinet. Viscount Whitelaw (his farming estates notwithstanding), Lord Hailsham, and Lord Young, are all excluded, since all these are Peers. Of the remaining nineteen members of the Cabinet, nine are not listed. These are Kenneth Baker, Kenneth Clarke, Nicholas Edwards, Norman Fowler, Geoffrey Howe, Nigel Lawson, John MacGregor, Malcolm Rifkind and Norman Tebbit. Two, John Biffen and John Moore, have major food or farming presences in their constituencies.

When appointed, Ministers give up extra-Parliamentary work, which may conflict with their ministerial responsibilities. Consequently, Cabinet Ministers do not have current connections with industry. The other eight Cabinet Ministers in the list are:

PAUL CHANNON. Trade and Industry. *Family* Brewers. *Shareholder* Iveagh Trustees (Guinness) *Ex-Director* Guinness 61–70. *Owner* Farm.

DOUGLAS HURD. Home Secretary. *Family* Farmers (dairy, sheep).

MICHAEL JOPLING. Agriculture, Fisheries and Food. *Owner* Farm.

TOM KING. Northern Ireland. *Shareholder* Sale, Tilney (food and engineering; *ex-Chairman* and *Director*.) *Ex-Director* Peabody Foods. *Owner* Small Farm.

NICHOLAS RIDLEY. Environment. *Ex-Director* Tate & Lyle 74–79.

MARGARET THATCHER. Prime Minister. *Family* Grocers. *Ex-employee* J. Lyons 49–51.

PETER WALKER. Energy. *Ex-Owner* Farm (400 acres) 72–81.

GEORGE YOUNGER. Defence. *Family* Brewers. *Ex-Director* Tennent Caledonian Breweries 77–79; J.G. Thomson (Breweries) 62–66, 74–79; John Fowler (Breweries) 63–67; George Younger (Breweries) 58–68. *Ex-employee* George Younger (Breweries) 54–58. *Family* George Younger (Breweries) (now subsidiary of Bass Charrington). *Owner* Farm (beef) 1000 acres.

So the Cabinet contains six farmers or ex-farmers; two members with a background in alcohol; and one in sugar. Two have a general food industry background, one of whom (Mrs Thatcher) is a food scientist by training. Patrick Jenkin, who left the Cabinet in September 1985, was employed by Distillers, the drug and drinks firm, and was later an advisor, from 1957 to 1970. Michael Heseltine, who left the Cabinet in January 1986, owns a 400 acre farm. Mrs Thatcher's work for Lyons (in the Cadby Hall factory, Hammersmith) included devising fillings for swiss rolls, and aeration of ice cream (Mr Whippy).[13] Mrs Thatcher may be the only MP with a professional background in food additives.

Just because an MP is listed here, it does not of course mean that industry can count on a vote. MPs are responsible to Parliament, not to outside interests. An MP may or may not sympathize with a large food manufacturer in the constituency. The ties of previous employment may or may not be broken. (Previous directorships of Ministers may be more significant). An MP who is advisor or parliamentary consultant to a PR company with food industry clients may or may not represent these accounts actively. An owner of a farm, hotel or pub who is an MP may or may not connect this business with the interests of the industry as a whole. An evidently direct link with industry may have little significance; on the other hand, an MP with a large food manufacturer in the constituency may choose to represent its interests with more energy than a paid consultant.

Take sugar. If the question is asked as narrowly as possible: 'how many MPs are paid by the sugar refiners as expert advisors or employees'? the answer is 'three'. (Colin Moynihan, PPS to Kenneth Clarke at the Department of Health – and, later, Employment – and also advisor to Tate & Lyle; Michael Shersby, who is Director-General of the Sugar Bureau among other sugar industry jobs; and David Crouch, who is a Director of Kingsway PR, whose clients include the Sugar Bureau). If the question is widened, to 'how many MPs are expert advisors to or employed by that section of the food industry which manufactures or uses large amounts of sugars?' the answer is 'at least twenty'. They are

RT. HON. PETER ARCHER QC. Lab Warley West. *Consultant* Good Relations PR (clients inc Cocoa, Chocolate and Confectionery Alliance, Colas Products).

SIR HUMPHREY ATKINS. C Spelthorne. *Consultant* Streets Financial PR (clients inc British Sugar, Rowntree Mackintosh).

DAVID ATKINSON. C Bournemouth E. PPS Paul Channon. *Consultant* Grayling PR (clients inc Burtons Biscuits [Assoc British Foods]).

VIRGINIA BOTTOMLEY. C Surrey SW. PPS Christopher Patten (Foreign Office). *Fellow* Industry and Parliament Trust (United Biscuits).

SIR WILLIAM CLARK. C Croydon S. *Director* Belize Sugar Industries (Tate & Lyle associate).

DAVID CROUCH. C Canterbury. *Director* Kingsway PR (clients inc Sugar Bureau).

EDWARD DU CANN. C Taunton. *Vice-Chairman* Lonrho (sugar-refining etc.)

HUGH DYKES. C Harrow E. *Parl Advisor* Dewe Rogerson PR (clients inc Cadbury Schweppes).

SIR ANTHONY GRANT. C SW Cambridgeshire. *Consultant* Good Relations PR (clients, see Peter Archer).

JIM LESTER. C Broxtowe. *Hon Vice President* Nat Assoc of Master Bakers, Confectioners and Caterers.

MICHAEL MCNAIR WILSON. C Newbury. *Consultant* Extel PR (clients inc J Lyons).

MICHAEL MATES. C Hampshire E. *Consultant* Good Relations PR (clients, see Peter Archer).

MICHAEL MORRIS. C Northampton S. *Owner* AM PR (clients inc Mars). *Consultant* Mars.

HON. COLIN MOYNIHAN. C Lewisham E. PPS Kenneth Clarke (Department of Employment). *Vice Chairman* Ridgways Tea (Tate & Lyle subsidiary). *Consultant* Tate & Lyle. *Ex-employee* Tate & Lyle 78–82.

CHRIS MURPHY. C Welwyn and Hatfield. *Consultant* D'Arcy McManus and Masius PR (clients inc Mars).

RT. HON. REG PRENTICE. C Daventry. *Consultant* Catalyst Communications PR (clients inc Colas Products, Canada Dry).

RT HON JAMES PRIOR. C Waveney. Ex-Minister Ag Fish Food. *Director* United Biscuits, J Sainsbury. *Ex-Director* F Lambert and Son (tobacco, confectionery).

ROBERT RHODES JAMES. C Cambridge. *Consultant* Allied Lyons 82–.

MICHAEL SHERSBY. C Uxbridge. *Director-General* The Sugar Bureau. *Secretary* UK Sugar Ind. Assoc. *Director* World Sugar Research Organization, Sugarmark Holding, Sugarmark International (clients: British Sugar, Tate & Lyle).

RICHARD WAINWRIGHT. Lib Colne Valley. Ex-Spokesman Economic Affairs – 86. *Hon Vice President* Nat Assoc of Master Bakers, Confectioners and Caterers.

If the question is widened to include MPs who have been advisors to or employed by the sugars and associated industries, then another eighteen MPs join the list.

PETER BOTTOMLEY. C Eltham. Minister: DoTransport. *Ex-Personnel Advisor* Cargill-Albion (sugar) 82–83.

TIM EGGAR. C Enfield N. Minister: Foreign Office. *Ex-Parl Advisor* Hill and Knowlton PR (clients inc Coca-Cola, Kelloggs).

NIGEL FORMAN. C Carshalton and Wallington. *Ex-Fellow* Industry and Parliament Trust (United Biscuits). *Ex-Consultant* Lexington PR (clients inc Kelloggs).

GEORGE FOULKES. Lab Carrick, Cumnock and Doon Valley. *Ex-Fellow* Industry and Parliament Trust (United Biscuits).

WILLIAM GARRETT. Lab Wallsend. *Ex-Consultant* Burson-Marsteller PR (clients inc Rowntree Mackintosh).

ROBERT HAYWARD. C Kingswood. *Ex-Employee* Coca-Cola 75–79.

RALPH HOWELL. C Norfolk N. *Ex-Fellow* Industry and Parliament Trust (United Biscuits).

GERAINT HOWELLS. Lib Ceredigion and Pembroke N. Ex-Spokesman Ag Fish Food –86. *Ex Hon Vice President* Nat Assoc of Master Bakers, Confectioners and Caterers.

JOHN HUNT. C Ravensbourne. *Ex-employee* Peek Freans Biscuits 50.[1]

PETER LLOYD. C Fareham. Minister: Whip. *Ex-Consultant* United Biscuits 79–84. *Ex-Employee* United Biscuits 68–79.

CHRIS PATTEN. C Bath. Minister: Foreign Office. *Ex-Consultant* Hill and Knowlton PR (see Tim Eggar).

KEITH RAFFAN. C Delyn. *Ex-Consultant* Hill and Knowlton PR (see Tim Eggar).

RT HON NICHOLAS RIDLEY. C Cirencester and Tewkesbury. Cabinet: Minister of Environment. *Ex-Director* Tate & Lyle 74–79.

GILES SHAW. C Pudsey. Minister: Trade and Industry. *Ex-Consultant* Rowntree Mackintosh 74–79. *Ex-Director* and *Employee* Rowntree Mackintosh (Confectionery Marketing Director 70–74, Advertisement Manager 60–69).

SIR DUDLEY SMITH. C Warwick and Leamington. *Ex-Consultant* Kingsway PR (clients inc Sugar Bureau).

RT HON MARGARET THATCHER. C Finchley. Cabinet: Prime Minister. *Ex-Employee* J Lyons 49–51.

JERRY WIGGIN. C Weston-super-Mare. *Ex-Director* Manbre Sugars 75–77.

DAFYDD WIGLEY. Plaid Cymru Caernarfon. *Ex-Employee* Mars (Financial Planning Manager, Chief Cost Accountant, 67–71).

So this is a list of 38 MPs who are or have been connected with the sugar and associated industries. These do not include Dr Norman Godman, Conal Gregory, and John Powley, who have already been mentioned as having spoken up for the sugar and confectionery interests in their constituencies; nor another 23 MPs with similar constituency interests. So, if the question is: 'how many MPs have or have had connections with the sugars and associated industries, including MPs with such interests in their constituencies?' the answer is 'at least 64'.

Just because a company is listed, this does not imply that it puts improper pressure on MPs or indeed that the MPs yield to any pressure. At the same time, industry will seek to have its interests and those of its shareholders and workers protected. This is normal practice.

A note about referencing: facts about an MP such as constituency, or parliamentary duties, including membership of committees, are not referenced. Four valuable works of reference, are *Parliamentary Profiles* by Andrew Roth, published by Parliamentary Profiles Ltd (Palace Chambers, Bridge Street, Westminster, London SW1A 2JT)[1]; the *Register of Members' Interests between 1983 and 1986* (HMSO)[2]; Hansard, the official record of Parliament[3]; and recent lists of top British companies and advertisers,[5,6] together with directories such as those issued by the Public Relations Consultants Association[4] and the *Times*.[8] Much other information has come from sources within Parliament, local authorities, food firms and elsewhere; this is referenced individually. The list is not complete and I shall be grateful for more information.

TWO HUNDRED AND FIFTY POLITICIANS AND THE FOOD INDUSTRY

RT HON MICHAEL ALISON. C Selby. Minister: PPS Margaret Thatcher. All-party Chem Ind Grp. *Constituency* Northern Foods (Bowyers),[14] Ranks Hovis McDougall (mills).[15]

DAVID AMESS. C Basildon. *Constituency* Gordon's Gin, Distillers.[1]

MICHAEL ANCRAM. C Edinburgh South. Minister: Scotland. *Director* Portzim (ag) 75–.[2] *Owner* Partnership 2 farms (1,500 & 400 acres).[1,2]

RT HON PETER ARCHER QC. Lab Warley West. Shadow Cabinet: Northern Ireland. Ex-Spokesman Trade, Prices & Consumer Protection 82–83. *Consultant* Good Relations PR (clients inc Cocoa, Chocolate and Confectionery Alliance, Colas Products, Freshbake Food Group, Meat and Livestock Commission, Nabisco, Scottish & Newcastle Breweries) 79–.[1,4,16]

TOM ARNOLD. C Hazel Grove. Vice Chairman Conservative Party 83–. *Director* Scotts Restaurant.[2]

JACK ASPINWALL. C Wansdyke. *Director* Sacrum Investments (food shops). *Family* Food shops. *Owner* The Red Lion pub, Bath.[1,2] *Consultant* McAvoy, Wreford Bayley PR (clients inc BAT Industries, ICI, Reckitt & Colman, Trade and Industry Dept).[16]

SIR HUMPHREY ATKINS. C Spelthorne. Ex-Minister Foreign Office 82–83. *Consultant* Streets PR (clients inc Sugar Bureau, Distillers, Grand Metropolitan, Harrisons & Crosfield, Hillsdown Holdings, Iceland Frozen Foods, Rowntree Mackintosh, Imperial Tobacco) (Imperial Group food as well as tobacco).[1,2,16]

ROBERT ATKINS. C South Ribble. PPS Lord Young. (Do Employment) Co-chairman All-party Licensed Trade Grp.[17] *Consultant* Parliamentary Monitoring Services.[2] *Ex-Consultant* MDA PR (clients include Scotch Whisky) 82–83.[1]

DAVID ATKINSON. C Bournemouth E. PPS Paul Channon. (DoTrade) *Consultant* Grayling PR (clients inc Bayer (agrichemicals), Burton's Biscuits (Assoc British Foods)).[16]

NICHOLAS BAKER. C North Dorset. *Constituency* Northern Foods (Dorset Food Products).[18]

TONY BALDRY. C Banbury. PPS Lynda Chalker (Foreign Office). *Constituency* Unilever (Wall's Meat),[19] General Foods (Birds).[20]

ROBERT BANKS. C Harrogate. *Owner* small farm.[1]

ANTHONY BEAUMONT-DARK. C Birmingham Selly Oak. *Director* Cope Allman (Fruit machines).[2] *Constituency* Cadbury Schweppes (Bournville factory).[21]

ROY BEGGS. UUP Antrim E. *Owner* Small farm.[2] *Constituency* Antrim Creameries (Ranks Hovis McDougall).[15]

HARRY BELLINGHAM. C Norfolk NW. *Owner* Farm.[1]

WILLIAM BENYON. C Milton Keynes. *Owner* Farm (2000 acres).[1,2]

DAVID BEVAN. C Yardley. *Parl Advisor* Best Western Hotels.[2]

RT HON JOHN BIFFEN. C Shropshire N. Cabinet: Leader of House. *Constituency* 11% employed in ag.,[22] Unigate: (St Ivel),[14] Express Dairies (food factories).[23]

SIR PETER BLAKER. C Blackpool S. All-party Chem Ind Grp. *Owner* Farm (800 acres).[1,2]

SIR NICHOLAS BONSOR. C Upminster. *Director/Owner* Owner Vending. *Owner* Farm (800 acres).[1,2]

PETER BOTTOMLEY. C Eltham. Minister: DoTransport. Ex-Sec Cons Health and Soc Serv Cttee 77. *Ex-personnel advisor* Cargill-Albion (sugar) 82–83. *Ex-Employee* Wall's 66.[1] *Family* Husband of Virginia Bottomley (below).

VIRGINIA BOTTOMLEY. C Surrey SW. PPS Christopher Patten (Foreign Office). *Fellow* Industry and Parliament Trust (United Biscuits).[24] *Family* Wife of Peter Bottomley (above). *Constituency* ICI (inc. agrichemicals).[25]

RT HON SIR BERNARD BRAINE. C Castle Point. All-party Chem Ind Grp. *Ex-Consultant* Burson-Marsteller PR 68–70.[1] (clients see David Crouch).

MARTIN BRANDON BRAVO. C Nottingham S. PPS John Patten (DoEnviron). *Constituency* Boots,[1] Northern Foods (Pork Farms).[18]

GRAHAM BRIGHT. C Luton S. PPS David Waddington and Douglas Hogg (Home Office). Ex-Vice Chairman Cons Food & Drinks Cttee (Sec 82–83) 83–84. *Chairman & Managing Director* Dietary Foods (diet foods, chemical sweeteners) 70–. *Chairman*

Cumberland Foods 82– and Cumberland Packing Corporation 82–. *Director* International Sweeteners Assoc.[1,2]

TIM BRINTON. C. Gravesham. *Consultant* Communications Strategy PR (clients inc James Buchanan [Black & White Whisky]), British American Tobacco, Huckleberry's, De Vere Hotels, Sheraton Hotels, Showerings Cider).[4,16]

RT HON LEON BRITTAN. C Richmond Yorks. Ex-Cabinet: Trade & Industry Sec –86. All-party Chem Ind. Grp. *Constituency* 11.9% employed in ag.[22]

MICHAEL BROWN. C Brigg & Cleethorpes. *Constituency* British Sugar.[26]

MALCOLM BRUCE. Lib Gordon. *Constituency* Unilever (meat products).[19]

PETER BRUINVELS. C Leicester E. *Constituency* Allied Lyons (foods).[10]

SIR PAUL BRYAN. C Boothferry. *Owner* Farm (200 acres).[1] *Constituency* 11.4% employed in ag.,[22] Northern Foods (Dale Farm Foods).[18]

RT HON ALICK BUCHANAN-SMITH. C Kincardine & Deeside. Minister: DoEnergy. All-party Chem Ind Grp. *Owner* Farm (250 acres, dairy, pigs).[1]

SIR ANTHONY BUCK QC. C Colchester N. All-party Chem Ind Grp. *Director/Shareholder* AF Buck (ag merchants) 70–72, 74–79. *Owner* Farm (30 acres).[1]

NICHOLAS BUDGEN. C Wolverhampton SW. *Owner* Farm.[2]

DESMOND BULMER. C Wyre Forest. *Family* Cider-makers. *Chairman/Shareholder* HP Bulmer (cider) 82– (*Director* 62–82).[2,17] *Ex-Employee* Whitbread 60–61. *Owner* Farm.[1]

ALISTAIR BURT. C Bury N. PPS Kenneth Baker (DoEducation). *Constituency* Benson's Confectionery.[1,15]

RT HON ADAM BUTLER. C Bosworth. Ex-Minister MoDefence –85. *Owner* Farm (200 acres).[1]

RT HON JAMES CALLAGHAN. Lab Cardiff S & Penarth. Prime Minister 76–79. *Owner* Half-share in a farm (200 acres, dairy).[1,2]

IAN CAMPBELL. Lab Dumbarton. Chairman All-party Scotch Whisky Ind Grp 74–. (Sec. 70–74). *Constituency* Barton Distillers.[15]

ALEX CARLILE. Lib Montgomery. Spokesman Home Affairs. *Constituency* 21.3% employed in ag.[22]

JOHN CARLISLE. C Luton N. *Director* Granfin Agriculture (animal feedstuffs).[1]

KENNETH CARLISLE. C Lincoln. PPS Douglas Hurd (Home Secretary). *Ex-employee* Brooke Bond Liebig 66–74. *Owner* farm (700 acres).[1,2]

MRS LYNDA CHALKER. C Wallasey. Minister: Foreign Office. *Ex-employee* Unilever 63–69. *Constituency* Unilever,[27] Cadbury Schweppes (Biscuits),[21] Robertsons (Scotia Barry Foods).[28]

RT HON PAUL CHANNON. C Southend W. Cabinet Minister: DoTrade & Industry. *Family* Brewers. *Shareholder* Iveagh Trustees (Guinness).[2] (See Mark Lennox-Boyd). *Ex-Director* Guinness 61–70. *Owner* Farm.[1]

HON ALAN CLARK. C Plymouth Sutton. Minister: DoTrade. *Owner* Farms.[2] *Constituency* Unigate (Bowyers).[14]

DR MICHAEL CLARK. C Rochford. Sec. All-party Chem Ind Grp. *Ex-employee* ICI (inc agrichemicals) 66–69.[1]

SIR WILLIAM CLARK. C Croydon S. Officer Sugar Cane Parl Cttee (dormant). *Director* Belize Sugar Industries (Tate & Lyle associate) 79–, St Kitts Sugar (plantations) 67–81.[1,2]

ERIC COCKERAM. C Ludlow. Vice Chairman All-party Retail Trade Grp. *Constituency* 12.4% employed in ag.,[22] Unigate (JP Wood poultry).[14]

MICHAEL COLVIN. C Romsey & Waterside. PPS Richard Luce (Arts). Secretary All-party Licensed Trade Group,[29] All-party Chem Ind Grp 84. *Advisor* Licensed Victuallers.[17] *Owner* 'The Cricketer's Arms' pub, farm (600 acres). *Ex-employee* J Walter Thompson ad agency (clients inc Kelloggs, Rowntree Mackintosh,

Associated Dairies Group, Golden Wonder HP, Cadbury Schweppes, Nabisco).[1,2,6]

DEREK CONWAY. C Shrewsbury & Atcham. *Constituency* Express Dairies.[23]

PATRICK CORMACK. C Staffordshire S. *Director* Historic Houses Hotels.[2]

JOHN ALEXANDER CORRIE. C Cunninghame N. Sec. Cons Fish Farming Sub-Cttee. *Tenant farmer* (900 acres).[1]

JAMES COUCHMAN. C Gillingham. PPS Anthony Newton (DoHealth). All-party Chem Ind Grp. Cons Health & Soc Serv Cttee. *Owner/Director* Chiswick Caterers (family firm controlling pubs) 80–, *Manager* 70–80.[1,2]

JIM CRAIGEN. Lab Maryhill. Spokesman, Scotland. Vice Chairman All-party Retail Trade Grp. Sec. Scotch Whisky Grp. *Ex-fellow* Industry and Parliament Trust (Scottish & Newcastle Breweries).[24]

VISCOUNT CRANBOURNE. C Dorset S. *Director* Gascoyne-Cecil Farms (13,000 acre family estate).[1,2]

JULIAN CRITCHLEY. C Aldershot. *Advisor* Lintas ad agency (clients inc Unilever, Van den Berghs, Batchelors Foods etc).[2,30]

DAVID CROUCH. C Canterbury. Ex-Chairman All-party Chem Ind Grp. Ex-Vice Chairman Cons Ind Cttee (Sec. 70–72). *Director* Kingsway PR[2] (clients inc Sugar Bureau, Butter Information Council, Allied Bakeries, Ranks Hovis McDougall (salt), Food and Drink Federation (food additives), UB Frozen Foods, Eggs Authority, Nestlé.[16] *Ex-Director* Burson Marsteller PR (clients inc Allied Bakeries, Cadbury Typhoo, Dow Chemicals, Heinz, McDonalds, Rowntree Mackintosh, Van Den Berghs, British Sugar Bureau 1981)[31] 72–82. *Chairman* and *shareholder* David Crouch & Co 64–. *Consultant* Beecham, David Wedgwood PR (clients inc Lever Bros Home Brewing and Winemaking Trade

Assoc.) *Director* Pfizer (drugs, agrichemicals) *Ex-employee* ICI 50–52.[1,2]

DR JOHN CUNNINGHAM. Lab Copeland. Spokesman Environment. *Advisor* Albright and Wilson (chemical food additives) 80–.[32,33]

ERIC DEAKINS. Lab Walthamstow. Lab Ag Cttee. Ex Spokesman on Ag Fish Food 82–83. Minister DoHealth and Soc Serv 76–79. *Ex-Consultant* FMC (Meat) 71–74. *Ex-Employee* FMC (Pigs Division) 69–71.[1]

SIR PAUL DEAN. C Woodspring. Ex-Chairman Cons Health & Soc Serv Cttee. (Sec. 65–) 79–82. *Director* Watney Mann & Trumans (brewers), 79–[2] *Family* Farm.[2] *Constituency* Lyons bakery.[10]

LORD JAMES DOUGLAS HAMILTON. C Edinburgh W. PPS Malcolm Rifkind (Scotland). *Shareholder* Hamilton & Kinneil (agribusiness) *Owner* Farm.[2]

RT HON EDWARD DU CANN. C Taunton. *Ex-Chairman* 1922 Committee 72–84. *Vice Chairman* Lonrho (sugar etc) *Owner* Farm.[2]

ROBERT DUNN. C Dartford. Minister: DoEducation. *Ex-Consultant* J Sainsbury 79–83. *Ex-Employee* J Sainsbury 73–79.[1]

HUGH DYKES. C Harrow E. Select Cttee European Legislation. *Parl Advisor* British Wine Producers Cttee; Dewe Rogerson PR (clients inc Cadbury Schweppes, J Bibby, Reckitt & Colman).[16]

TIM EGGAR. C Enfield N. Minister: Foreign Office. *Ex-Parl Advisor* Hill & Knowlton PR –86 (clients inc Baxters of Speyside, Burger King, Coca-Cola, English Country Cheese Council,

General Foods, Kelloggs, Lever Bros, McDougalls Catering Foods), Snack Nut and Crisp Manufacturers Association (SNACMA).[2,4]

SIR PETER EMERY. C Honiton. Select Cttee Trade & Ind. All-party Chem Ind Grp. *Constituency* Express Dairies (food factories).[23]

NICHOLAS FAIRBAIRN QC. C Perth & Kinross. *Owner* Farm (450 acres).[1]

SIR JOHN FARR. C Harborough. *Ex-Director* Apollo Products (beer) 50–55. *Shareholder/Family* Beer (Home Brewery). *Owner* Farms (12,000 acres in total) most in Zimbabwe.[1,2] *Constituency* Imperial Foods (Golden Wonder).[34]

TONY FAVELL. C Stockport. PPS John Major (DoHealth) Select Cttee Soc Serv. Hon Sec Cons Health & Soc Serv Cttee. *Constituency* United Biscuits.[15]

TERRY FIELDS. Lab Broadgreen, Liverpool. *Constituency* United Biscuits.[15]

SIR GEOFFREY FINSBERG. C Hampstead & Highgate. Ex-Minister DoHealth 81–83. Chairman All-party retail grp. All-party Chem Ind Group 84. *Ex-Advisor* Licensed Victuallers' Protection Society 74–79.[1]

ALEX FLETCHER. C Edinburgh Central. Ex-Minister DoTrade and Ind until September 1985. *Consultant* Argyll Group.[35] *Ex-Managing Director* Gaskell and Chambers (equipment for licensed trade) 64–71.[1]

NIGEL FORMAN. C Carshalton & Wallington. *Ex-Fellow* Industry & Parliament Trust (United Biscuits)[24] *Ex-Consultant* Lexington PR (clients inc Bread Advertising Grp, Burger King,

General Foods, Kelloggs, Lever Bros, McDougalls Catering Foods, TK Int Foods).[4]

DEREK FOSTER. Lab Bishop Auckland. Chief Whip. Lab Trade & Ind Cttee. *Ex-Fellow* Industry & Parliament Trust (Scottish & Newcastle Breweries).[24]

GEORGE FOULKES. Lab Carrick, Cumnock & Doon Valley. Spokesman, Foreign Affairs. Lab Health Cttee. *Ex-Fellow* Industry & Parliament Trust (United Biscuits).[24]

ROGER FREEMAN. C Kettering. Minister: MoDefence. *Ex-Director* Martini and Rossi.[2]

PETER FRY. C Wellingborough. *Chairman/Shareholder* Political Research & Communications PR (clients inc Kentucky Fried Chicken, Takeaway & Fast Food Federation) *Consultant* Baiden Barron Smith PR (clients inc Balvenie Pure Malt Whisky, Glenfiddich, Grants Scotch Whisky, Takeaway and Fast Food Federation) Carl Byoir PR (clients inc Cinzano, Whitbread).[2,4]

ROY GALLEY. C Halifax. Select Cttee Soc Serv. Hon Sec. Cons Health and Soc Serv Cttee. *Constituency* United Biscuits (Foods).[36] Websters (brewery).[37]

WILLIAM GARRETT. Lab Wallsend. Lab Trade & Ind, and Ag Cttee. Chairman All-Party Chem Ind Group. *Shareholder* Northern Clubs Federation Brewery 40–. *Ex-Consultant* Burson-Marsteller PR (clients see David Crouch).[4] *Ex-employee* ICI (inc agrichemicals).[1]

RT HON SIR IAN GILMOUR. C Chesham & Amersham. *Family* Meux Trust (beer).[1] *Constituency* Unigate (Bowyers).[14]

DR ALAN GLYN. C Windsor & Maidenhead. *Constituency* Ranks Hovis McDougall (HQ).[38]

DR NORMAN GODMAN. Lab Greenock & Port Glasgow. *Constituency* Tate & Lyle refinery.[39]

SIR PHILIP GOODHART. C Beckenham. *Owner* small farm (75 acres).[1,2]

ALISTAIR GOODLAD. C Eddisbury. Minister: DoEnergy. Select Cttee Ag 79–81. All-party Chem Ind Grp 84. *Constituency* Express Dairies.[23]

SIR RAYMOND GOWER. C Vale of Glamorgan. *Director* Airport Hotels.[2]

SIR ANTHONY GRANT. C Cambridgeshire SW. Executive 1922 Cttee 79–. Council of Europe (Chairman Economic Cttee 80) 77–. Ex-Vice Chairman Cons Party 74–76; Chairman Cons Trade Cttee 79-83; *Consultant* Good Relations PR (clients see Peter Archer).[16]

HARRY GREENWAY. C Ealing N. *Constituency* Lyons (HQ).[10]

CONAL GREGORY. C York. Vice Chairman Cons Food and Drink Cttee. *Director* Warwick Vintners. *Wine Consultant*, and writer inc. *Beer of Britain. Ex-employee* wine buyer Reckitt & Colman 73–77. *Consultant* Consort Hotels.[2] *Constituency* Rowntree Mackintosh (HQ),[39] United Biscuits (Terrys).[28]

ELDON GRIFFITHS. C Bury St Edmunds. *Owner* Farm (50 acres, 500 pigs).[1,2] *Constituency* British Sugar.[26]

MICHAEL GRYLLS. C Surrey NW. Chairman Cons Trade & Ind Cttee. All-party Chem Ind Grp. *Consultant* Sterling Winthrop Grp (Chemicals & drugs) 75–. *Ex-Managing Director* Costa Brava Wine 56–74, H & J Wine Agencies 74–76, Edward Butler Wine 76–78.[1]

HON ARCHIE HAMILTON. C Epsom & Ewell. Minister: MoDefence. *Owner* Farm (350 acres).[1,2]

NEIL HAMILTON. C Tatton. PPS David Mitchell (DoTransport). Vice chairman Cons Trade & Indus Cttee. All-party Chem Ind Grp 84. *Consultant* Brewers Society.[2] *Constituency* ICI (inc agrichemicals).[1]

JOHN HANNAM. C Exeter. Ex-Cons Trade Cttee (71–72) and Consumer Protection Cttee (72–74). *Ex-Chairman* John Hannam Motels and other catering interests. *Advisor* Pharmaceutical Society of GB 79–.[1,2]

PETER HARDY. Lab Wentworth. *Constituency* Allied Lyons (foods).[10]

RT HON WALTER HARRISON. Lab Wakefield. *Constituency* Allied Lyons (foods).[10]

ALAN HASELHURST. C Saffron Walden. Select Cttee European Legislation. All-party Chem Ind Grp. *Consultant* Albright &

Wilson (food additives).[2,33] *Ex-employee* ICI (inc agrichemicals) 61–65.[1]

CHRISTOPHER HAWKINS. C High Peak. *Constituency* Rowntree Mackintosh (Sun-Pat).[40]

SIR PAUL HAWKINS. C Norfolk SW. *Ex-Managing Director* West Norfolk Farmers' Auction Company 48–79.[1] *Constituency* 12.2% employed in ag.[22]

BARNEY HAYHOE. C Brentford & Isleworth. Ex-Minister: DoHealth –86. *Constituency* United Biscuits (HQ & Wimpy UK),[36] Beecham (Ribena, Lucozade HQ).[41]

ROBERT HAYWARD. C Kingswood. PPS Michael Howard (DoTrade). *Ex-employee* Coca Cola 75–79.[1]

DAVID HEATHCOAT-AMORY. C Wells. PPS Norman Lamont (Treasury). *Director* Lowman Manufacturing (ag machinery) 80–. *Constituency* Cider-making, Unigate (St. Ivel).[14] *Owner* Farm.[1]

RT HON MICHAEL HESELTINE. C Henley. Ex-Cabinet Minister: MoDefence –86. *Owner* Farm (400 acres).[1] *Constituency* United Biscuits (McVities Frozen Foods).[36]

RICHARD HICKMET. C Glandford & Scunthorpe. Hon Sec Cons Trade & Ind Cttee. *Director/Shareholder* Vurmsol Investments (family hotel group).[2] *Constituency* Rowntree Mackintosh (Sooner Foods).[40]

ROBERT HICKS. C Cornwall SE. Select Cttee European Legislation. Vice Chairman Cons Ag Cttee 74–81. *Advisor* Milk Marketing Board.[2] *Consultant* British Hotels, Restaurants & Caterers Assoc.[1]

RT HON TERENCE HIGGINS. C Worthing. *Ex-Employee* Unilever 59–64. *Lecturer* Unilever Staff College 75–80.[1]

JAMES HILL. C Southampton Test. *Co-owner* Gunsfield Herd Pedigree Piggeries (100 acres, 1500 animals).[1,2]

JAMES HOLT. C Langbaurgh. *Shareholder* Heather Bakeries.[2]

PETER HORDERN. C Horsham. Executive 1922 Cttee. All Party Chem Ind Grp. *Consultant* Fisons (agrichemicals).[2]

RALPH HOWELL. C Norfolk N. All party Chem Ind Grp. *Ex-fellow* Industry & Parliament Trust (United Biscuits)[24] *Ex-Director* Mid-Norfolk Farmers Trading Company 63–80. *Owner* Arable Farm (800 acres).[1] *Constituency* 11.8% employed in ag.[22]

GERAINT HOWELLS. Lib Ceredigion & Pembroke N. Ex-. Spokesman for Ag Fish Food –86. *Managing Director* Wilkinson & Steiner (Meat wholesalers).[1,2] *Ex-Hon Vice President* Nat Assoc of Master Bakers, Confectioners and Caterers.[42] *Owner* hill farm (750 acres, 3000 sheep).[1] *Constituency* 17.6% employed in ag.[22]

JOHN HUNT. C Ravensbourne. *Ex-employee* Peek Freans biscuits 50.[1] *Constituency* Tate & Lyle (agribusiness etc).[39]

RT HON DOUGLAS HURD. C Witney. Cabinet: Home Secretary. *Family* Farmers (dairy, sheep)[43] *Constituency* Northern Foods (Bowyers).[14]

CHARLES IRVING. C Cheltenham. Chairman Commons Catering Cttee. *Director* Irving Hotels (family firm), Norfolk Hotels.[2]

ROBERT JACKSON. C Wantage. Hon Sec Cons Ag, Fish Food Cttee. *Consultant* Brewers Society.[2]

RT HON PATRICK JENKIN. C Wanstead & Woodford. Ex-Cabinet: DoEnvironment –85. *Ex-Advisor* Distillers (whisky, gin, drugs) 66–70. *Ex-employee* Distillers 59–66.[1]

TOBY JESSEL. C Twickenham. *Constituency* United Biscuits (Foods HQ).[36]

RT HON MICHAEL JOPLING. C Westmorland & Lonsdale. Cabinet: Minister Ag Fish & Food. *Owner* Farm (500 acres).[1] *Constituency* Nestlé (Libby's Drinks).[44]

ELAINE KELLET-BOWMAN. C Lancaster. *Owner* Dairy/Arable Farm (149 acres).[1]

RT HON TOM KING. C Bridgewater. Cabinet: Northern Ireland. *Shareholder* Sale Tilney (food & engineering; *Ex-Chairman & Director*). *Ex-Director* Peabody Foods. *Owner* Small farm.[1,2]

ARCHIE KIRKWOOD. Lib Roxburgh & Berwickshire. *Constituency* 15% employed in ag.[22]

DAVID KNOX. C Moorfields. *Ex-Consultant* Gandalf Communication Consortium PR (clients inc Cigogne Cellars (Wine shippers)).[4]

IAN LANG. C Galloway & Upper Nithsdale. Minister: Scotland. *Constituency* 20% employed in ag.[22] Nestlé (Crosse & Blackwell).[44]

MICHAEL LATHAM. C Rutland & Melton. *Constituency* Express Dairies (food),[23] Unigate (St Ivel).[14]

IVAN LAWRENCE QC. C Burton. *Chairman* Burton Breweries Charitable Trust. *Constituency* Burton Breweries,[1] Beecham (Bovril, Marmite).[41]

MARK LENNOX-BOYD. C Morecombe & Lunesdale. Minister: Whip. *Family* Guinness. *Shareholder* Iveagh Trustees (Guinness).[2] (See Paul Channon).

JIM LESTER. C Broxtowe. Ex-Minister DoEmployment 79–81. *Hon Vice President* and *Advisor* Nat Assoc of Master Bakers, Confectioners & Caterers 82–[42] *Constituency* Boots.[2]

SIR KENNETH LEWIS. C Stamford & Spalding. *Constituency* 10.9% employed in ag.[22]

RON LEWIS. Lab Carlisle. Select Cttee Soc Serv. Lab Trade & Indus, & Ag Cttee. All-Party Retail Grp. *Chairman* E. Midlands Co-op Federal Bakery 63–65.[1] *Constituency* United Biscuits (Breweries).[36]

PETER LLOYD. C Fareham. Minister: Whip. *Ex-Consultant* United Biscuits 79–84. *Ex-employee* United Biscuits 68–79.[1]

MICHAEL LORD. C Central Suffolk. PPS John MacGregor (Treasury). *Ex-farmer* 62–66. *Constituency* Fisons (agri-chemicals).[1,20]

RICHARD LUCE. C Shoreham. Minister: Arts. *Ex-Shareholder* Nicholson's Gin (family firm).[1]

NEIL MCFARLANE. C Sutton and Cheam. *Ex-Minister* Do Environment (Sport) –85. *Chairman* Chelsea Restaurant.[2,45]

ALLEN MCKAY. Lab Barnsley West and Penistone. *Constituency* Allied Lyons (foods).[10]

JOHN J MACKAY. C Argyll & Bute. Minister: Scottish Office. *Constituency* 12.1% employed in ag.[22]

DAVID MACLEAN. C Penrith & The Border. PPS Michael Jopling (Ag, Fish, Food) *Constituency* 15.7% employed in ag.[22] Express Dairies (food).[23]

MICHAEL MCNAIR WILSON. C Newbury. Ex PPS Peter Walker (at Ministry of Ag Fish Food, 79–83). *Consultant* Extel PR (clients inc Albright & Wilson (chemical food additives), Courage, Cullen Stores, Imperial Group, Kwik Save Discount Group, J Lyons) *Ex-farmer* Poultry 50–53.[1,4] *Family* Younger brother of Patrick McNair Wilson (below).

PATRICK MCNAIR WILSON. C New Forest. *Consultant, Ex-Director* Consort PR (clients inc Union Carbide (agrichemicals), Re-chem International[1,2] *Family* Older brother of Michael McNair Wilson (above).

KEVIN MCNAMARA. Lab Kingston-upon-Hull N. Spokesman, Defence. Chairman All-party Pharmaceutical Ind Grp 81–. *Constituency* Reckitt & Colman.[1]

JOHN MAREK. Lab Wrexham. *Constituency* Kelloggs, Dairy Crest.[46]

PAUL MARLAND. C Gloucestershire W. Sec. Cons Ag, Fish & Food Cttee. *Owner* Farm 1000 acres (arable) & pigs.[1]

TONY MARLOW. C Northampton N. *Owner* small farm 12 acres.[1]

DAVID MARSHALL. Lab Shettleston. Lab Health Cttee. All-Party Chem Ind Grp. *Constituency* United Biscuits.[36]

RT HON ROY MASON. Lab Barnsley Central. Ex-spokesman Ag Fish Food 79–81. *Consultant* Imperial Tobacco (Imperial Group Food as well as tobacco) *Ex-Consultant* Amalgamated Distilled

Products 71–74; HP Bulmer (cider) 71–74.[1] *Constituency* Allied Lyons (bakery).[10]

MICHAEL MATES. C Hampshire E. *Consultant* Good Relations PR (clients see Peter Archer).[2,16]

CAROL MATHER. C Esher. Minister: Whip. *Shareholder* Hopetown Farmers (Australia, sheep).[1] *Owner* Farm.[2]

DR BRIAN MAWHINNEY. C Peterborough. Minister: Northern Ireland. *Constituency* British Sugar.[26]

ROBERT MAXWELL HYSLOP. C Tiverton. Select Cttee Trade & Ind. *Constituency* 12% employed in ag.[22] Express Dairies (food),[23] Unigate (St Ivel).[14]

SIR PATRICK MAYHEW QC. C Tunbridge Wells. Minister: Solicitor-General. *Owner* Farmland (30 acres)[2] *Constituency* Berisford Foods (HE Daniel).[26]

SIR PETER MILLS. C Devon W & Torridge. Chairman Cons Ag, Fish & Food Cttee. *Advisor* JA Kelly (farmers). *Founder* member North Devon Meat (co-op). *Ex-employee* Slaughterhouse. *Ex-director* W Devon Farmers. *Owner* Farm (230 acres, pigs, sheep, cows).[1,2] *Constituency* 14.8% employed in ag.[22] Express Dairies (food).[23]

NORMAN MISCAMPBELL QC. C Blackpool N. *Constituency* Allied Lyons (Biscuits).[10]

DR AUSTIN MITCHELL. Lab Great Grimsby. Lab Whip 82–. *Ex-employee* Co-op biscuit factory, Crumpsall 53.[1] *Constituency* Nestlé (Findus),[44] British Sugar (beet farming).[26]

DAVID MITCHELL. C Hampshire NW. Minister: DoTransport. All-party Chem Ind Grp. *Shareholder* El Vino Wine bars (family owned), Mitchell Partners (Wine shippers) Ex-farmer 45–50.[1]

SIR HECTOR MUNRO. C Dumfries. Vice Chairman Cons Ag, Fish & Food Cttee. *Owner* Farm (300 acres, sheep).[47]

JOHN MOORE. C Croydon Central. Cabinet Minister: Do Transport. *Constituency* Nestlé (Findus) HQ.[44]

RT HON ALF MORRIS. Lab Wythenshawe. Spokesman, Disabled. *Ex-Employee* Brewery 42–49.[1]

MICHAEL MORRIS. C Northampton S. All-party Chem Ind Grp. Treasurer Parl. Food and Health Forum. *Consultant* Mars, 83–,[1] National Dairy Council.[48] *Owner* AM International PR (clients inc Cttee for Responsible Nutrition, Mars, Reckitt & Colman, Benton & Bowles ad agency (clients inc General Foods, Spillers Foods).[1,2,6] *Ex-Director* Benton & Bowles 71–82. *Ex-Manager* Reckitt & Colman 60–64.[1]

HON CHARLES MORRISON. C Devizes. Vice Chairman 1922 Cttee 74–83. *Director/Shareholder* Islay Estates & CA Morrison Farms (3000 acres).[1,2] *Owner* Fyfield Manor (300 acres, corn, beef).[1] *Family* Older brother of Peter Morrison (below).

HON PETER MORRISON. C Chester. Minister Vice-Chairman Cons Party. *Partner* Bridgend Hotel, Islay, 70–. *Shareholder* Islay House Farming (*Director* 73–79) 73–.[1] *Family* Younger brother of Charles Morrison (above).

HON COLIN MOYNIHAN. C Lewisham E. PPS Kenneth Clarke (DoEmployment, DoHealth –85). Ex-Vice Chairman Cons Food & Drink Cttee. *Vice Chairman* Ridgways Tea (Tate & Lyle subsidiary). *Consultant* Tate & Lyle. *Ex-employee* Tate & Lyle (Marketing Manager, agribusiness 80–82, Personal assistant to Chairman 78–80) 78–82.[1]

DAVID MUDD. C Falmouth & Cambourne. All-party Chem Ind Grp. *Ex-Consultant* Michael Joyce PR (clients inc Mitchells Brewery, Richmond Hill Hotel).[1]

CHRIS MURPHY. C Welwyn & Hatfield. *President* British Agrichemicals Association 83–. *Consultant* D'Arcy MacManus & Masius PR (clients inc Mars, Imperial Tobacco, Brooke Bond Oxo, Co-operative Retail Societies, Lyons Tetley, Weetabix, Allied National Brands, Ranks Hovis McDougall).[1,6] *Constituency* Roche; Smith, Kline & French (chemicals and drugs).[20]

ANTHONY NELSON. C Chichester. *Constituency* Unigate (St Ivel).[14]

MICHAEL NEUBERT. C Romford. Minister: Whip. *Ex-consultant* Ranks Hovis McDougall 81–83.[1]

PATRICK NICHOLLS. C Teignbridge. PPS John Gummer (Min Ag, Fish, Food). *Owner* Agricultural land.[2]

JAMES NICHOLSON. UUP Newry & Armagh. Select Cttee Ag. *Owner* farm.[2]

RT HON GORDON OAKES. Lab Halton. Co-chairman All-party Licensed Trade Group.[17] Vice Chairman All-party Chem Ind Grp. *Consultant* Pharmaceutical Society of GB 79–[2]. *Constituency* ICI-Mond (chemicals) (HQ),[20] Allied Lyons (foods).[10]

MARTIN O'NEILL. Lab Clackmannan. *Constituency* Scotch Green Distillery (whisky).[20]

CRANLEY ONSLOW. C Woking. Chairman 1922 Cttee 84–. *Director* Argyll Group (food) 83–.[2]

PHILIP OPPENHEIM. C Amber Valley. *Owner* Farm (250 acres) and interest in family farm.[2] *Family* Son of Sally Oppenheim (below). *Constituency* Berisford foods (Matthew Walker).[26]

RT HON SALLY OPPENHEIM. C Gloucester. Ex-Minister, Consumer Affairs 79–82. *Director* Boots (drugs, food) 82–. *Shareholder* Farm (275 acres).[1,2] *Family* Mother of Philip Oppenheim (above).

RICHARD OTTAWAY. C Nottingham N. PPS Tim Renton (Foreign Office) *Constituency* Boots, Kimberley Brewery & Mansfield Brewery.[20]

BOB PARRY. Lab Riverside, Liverpool. *Constituency* Unilever (John West foods).[19] Tate & Lyle (refinery) –81.[39]

TERRY PATCHETT. Lab Barnsley East. *Constituency* Allied Lyons (foods).[10]

CHRIS PATTEN. C Bath. Minister: Foreign Office. *Ex-Consultant* Hill and Knowlton PR (clients see Tim Eggar) 81–83.[1,4]

GEOFFREY PATTIE. C Chertsey & Walton. Minister: DoTrade & Ind. *Ex-Director/Shareholder* Collett Dickenson Pearce ad agents (clients inc Grand Metropolitan, Ranks Hovis McDougall) 64–79.[1,6] *Constituency* Unilever (Birds Eye Wall's).[19]

LAURIE PAVITT. Lab Brent S. Lab Health Cttee. Medical Research Council 68–72. *Constituency* Allied Lyons,[10] United Biscuits,[36] Heinz.[49]

JIM PAWSEY. C Rugby and Kenilworth. *Director* Autobar (vending machines for offices, catering) 81–, Autopax Machines 82–. *Ex-Chairman* Machine division of Autobar.[1,2]

ELIZABETH PEACOCK. C Batley & Spen. *Constituency* Northern Foods (Fox's Biscuits).[15]

SIR IAN PERCIVAL QC. C Southport. *Owner* Farms (100 acres).[2]

ALEX POLLOCK. C Moray. PPS George Younger (MoDefence). *Constituency* Scottish Malt Distillers, Glenlivet and Glen Grant Distillers.[20]

BARRY PORTER. C Wirral South. Select Cttee Trade and Ind. Sec All-Party Leisure Ind Grp. *Consultant* Publicity Plus PR (clients inc Truman, Watney Combe Reid, Norwich Brewery). *Ex-Director* Ballantines (whisky).[1] *Constituency* Robertsons (Vista Foods).[28]

RAY POWELL. Lab Ogmore. *Ex-Employee* butcher shop 56–66.[1]

WILLIAM POWELL. C Corby. *Constituency* Assoc British Foods (Chemicals, flour mill).[50]

JOHN POWLEY. C Norwich S. All-party Retail Grp. *Constituency* Rowntree Mackintosh,[40] Reckitt & Colman (Colman's of Norwich).[51]

RT HON REG PRENTICE. C Daventry. *Director* National Agricultural Centres International.[2] *Consultant* Catalyst Communications PR (clients inc Colas Products, Canada Dry).[1,4,16]

SIR DAVID PRICE. C Eastleigh. Select Cttee Soc Serv. All-party Chem Ind Grp. *Consultant* Union International 73–. *Ex-Director* Downs Premier Foods (& other UI subsidiaries) 81–84, Associated British Maltsters 66–70. *Ex-Employee* ICI (inc agrichemicals) 49–62.[1,2]

RT HON JAMES PRIOR. C Waveney. Ex-Cabinet: Northern Ireland 81–84, Leader of the House 72–74, Minister: Min of Ag Fish Food 70–72. *Director* United Biscuits 84– (also 74–79) J Sainsbury 84–. *Owner* Farms: 1700 acres (partner with John

Sainsbury), 380 acres. *Ex-Director* F Lambert & Son (tobacco, confectionery) 58–70. *Ex-consultant* Trust House Forte 74–79.[1]

RT HON FRANCIS PYM. C Cambridgeshire SE. Ex-Cabinet: Foreign Secretary 82–83. *Ex-employee* Merseyside Dairies (general manager) 48–52. *Owner* Partner in two farms (350 acres).[1,2] *Constituency* Cadbury Schweppes (Chivers).[21]

KEITH RAFFAN. C Delyn *Ex-Consultant* Hill and Knowlton PR (clients see Tim Eggar).[2,4]

RT HON TIMOTHY RAISON. C Aylesbury. Ex-Minister: Foreign Office –86. *Constituency* United Biscuits (McVities Foods HQ).[36]

STUART RANDALL. Lab Kingston-upon-Hull West. PPS Roy Hattersley. Lab Trade & Ind Cttee. *Constituency* Northern Foods (HQ), Northern Dairies.[18]

TIM RATHBONE. C Lewes. *Director* Charles Barker City PR (clients inc Allied Lyons, Unilever, Asda, Britvic, Spillers Foods, International Distillers and Vintners, Boots).[2,4]

TIMOTHY RENTON. C Sussex Mid. Minister: Foreign Office. Vice Chairman Cons Trade Cttee 74–79. *Shareholder* Middleton Tea Estates 68–.[1] *Constituency* Express Dairies (Food),[23] Unilever (Van den Berghs, margarine & fats).[19]

ROBERT RHODES JAMES. C Cambridge. *Consultant* Allied Lyons (food & drink) 82–. *Ex-Consultant* Allied Breweries 78–82.[1]

BRANDON RHYS WILLIAMS. C Kensington. *Ex-Employee* ICI (inc agrichemicals) 40–62.[1] *Owner* estate, farmland (1000 acres).[1,2]

RT HON NICHOLAS RIDLEY. C Cirencester & Tewkesbury. Cabinet: Minister, Do Environment. Ex-Cabinet Minister Do Transport –85. Ex-Minister: Treasury 81–83, Foreign Office

79–81, Trade & Ind 70–72. Chairman Cons Finance Cttee 72–73. *Ex-Director* Tate & Lyle 74–79.[1]

ALLAN ROBERTS. Lab Bootle. Chairman Lab Environment Cttee. *Part-owner* the Lord Hood pub, Whitechapel.[17]

STEPHEN ROSS. Lib Isle of Wight. *Owner* Farm (220 acres).[1]

WILLIAM ROSS. UUP Londonderry E. Whip 78–. Spokesman Ag 74–. *Owner* Farm (130 acres).[1]

RICHARD RYDER. C Norfolk Mid. Minister: Whip. Political Secretary to Mrs Thatcher 75–81. *Director/Shareholder* family pig farm.

RT HON TIMOTHY SAINSBURY. C Hove. Minister: Whip. All-party Retail Grp. *Family* Grocers. *Shareholder* J Sainsbury.[2] *Ex-Director* J Sainsbury 62–78.[1] *Owner* two farms.[2]

JONATHAN SAYEED. C Bristol E. *Ex-Employee* Marks & Spencer 72–73.[1]

NICHOLAS SCOTT. C Chelsea. Minister: Northern Ireland. *Ex-Chairman* Mandovi Foods 73.[1]

GILES SHAW. C Pudsey. Minister: Trade and Industry. Ex-Vice Chairman Cons Prices & Consumer Affairs Cttee 75–79. *Ex-Consultant* Rowntree Mackintosh 74–79. *Ex-Director/ Employee* Rowntree Mackintosh (Confectionery Marketing Director 70–74, ad manager 60–69).[1]

COLIN SHEPHERD. C Hereford. Vice Chairman Cons Ag, Fish & Food Cttee. *Constituency* Bulmers (cider), Sun-Valley (poultry processing).[20]

MICHAEL SHERSBY. C Uxbridge. All-party Chem Ind Grp 84. Chairman Cons Food & Drink Cttee. *Director-General* The Sugar Bureau. *Secretary* UK Sugar Ind Assoc. *Council Member* Food & Drink Federation. *Director* World Sugar Research Organisation,

Sugarmark Holding, Sugarmark International (clients: British Sugar, Tate & Lyle).[1,2]

RT HON JOHN SILKIN. Lab Deptford. Ex-Cabinet Min of Ag Fish Food 76–79. Lab Ag Cttee. *Consultant* (arbitrator) Dairy Trades Federation, Milk Marketing Board 84–.[1,2]

FRED SILVESTER. C Withington, Manchester *Director* J Walter Thompson ad agency (clients see Michael Colvin).[1]

ROGER SIMS, C Chislehurst. Vice Chairman Cons Health & Soc Serv Cttee 83–. Sec All-party Scotch Whisky Ind. Grp 77–. *Parl Advisor* Scotch Whisky Assoc 80–.[1,2]

SIR DUDLEY SMITH. C Warwick & Leamington. All-party Chem Ind Grp 84. *Consultant* Bass. *Ex-Consultant* Kingsway PR (clients see David Crouch);[2,4] Bolton Dickinson Associates PR (clients inc Carnation Foods, King Frost, Ross Foods) 81–[31] *Ex-Director* Beecham (drugs, food) 66–70.[1]

NIGEL SPEARING. Lab Newham South. Chairman Select Cttee European Legislation. *Constituency* Unilever (Mattesons Meats),[18] Tate & Lyle (refineries at Silvertown and Plaistow).[15,39]

KEITH SPEED. C Ashford. *Consultant* Murray Evans Associates PR (clients inc Anarkali Restaurants)[16] *Ex-Consultant* Scott Verner Assoc PR (clients inc ASDA food stores, Ranks Hovis McDougall) 74–79. *Ex-Employee* Heinz 56–57.[1]

TONY SPELLER, C Devon N. *Advisor* Catering Equip Mfrs Assoc 84–. Hotel, Catering and Inst. Man. Assoc. 82–[1,2]

ANTHONY STEEN. C South Hams. *Parl Advisor* English Vineyards Assoc.[1]

ANDREW STEWART. C Sherwood. *Owner* Farm (153 acres).[1]

JOHN STOKES. C Halesowen and Stourbridge. *Ex-Employee* ICI (inc agrichemicals) 46–51.[2]

ROGER STOTT. Lab Wigan. Spokesman, Transport. Lab Trade & Ind Cttee. All-party Chem Ind Grp. *Constituency* Heinz.[49]

SIR JOHN STRADLING THOMAS. C Monmouth. Ex-Minister Wales –85. *Ex-Consultant* Bass Charrington 78–79. *Director* Farm

64–70, livestock marketing company 61–64. *Owner* Farm (200 acres).[1]

DAVID SUMBERG. C Bury S. PPS Patrick Mayhew (Law Office). *Constituency* Hall Bros (Confectioners).[15]

SIR PETER TAPSELL. C Lindsey E. *Constituency* 13.1% employed in ag.[22]

JOHN TAYLOR. UUP Strangford. *Director* Bramley Apple Restaurant 74–. West Ulster Hotels 76–.[2]

PETER TEMPLE-MORRIS. C Leominster. *Constituency* Lyons (Jam).[10]

RT HON MARGARET THATCHER. C Finchley. Cabinet: Prime Minister *Family* Grocers. *Ex-employee* J Lyons 49–51.[13]

DAFYDD THOMAS. Plaid Cymru Merioneth. *Constituency* 12.9% employed in ag.[22]

DR ROGER THOMAS. Lab Carmarthen. Lab Ag Cttee. *Constituency* 16.9% employed in ag.[22]

DONALD THOMPSON. C Calder Valley. Minister: Ag, Fish, Food. *Family* Butchers. *Ex-Manufacturer* black puddings. *Ex-Director* Geoff Thompson's Butchers 57–74, Halifax Farmers 52–58. *Owner* Farm 52–60.[1]

PETER THURNHAM. C Bolton NE. Hon Treas All-party Chem Ind Grp. *Owner* Farmland (200 acres).[2]

TOM TORNEY. Lab Bradford S. Select Cttee Ag. Chairman, Lab Ag Cttee, All-party Retail Grp. *Ex-Consultant* Wine and Spirit Assoc of GB 74–76.[1]

JOHN TOWNEND. C Bridlington. *Chairman* J Townend (liquor business) 77–, (Director 59–); *Director* Merchant Vintners 64–; Townend Catering; Willerby Manor Hotels; Townend Wine Bars; Baronoff Vodka, 82–. *Shareholder* in some of these.[1]

NEVILLE TROTTER. C Tynemouth. *Consultant* Biss Lancaster PR (clients inc Kentucky Fried Chicken, St Ivel Gold, Watney Mann & Truman). [4,52] *Constituency* Nestlé (Findus).[44]

DR IAN TWINN. C Edmonton. PPS Peter Morrison (Dept chairman Cons Party). *Hon Sec* Cons Food and Drink Cttee. *Constituency* Coca-Cola, Basildon Dairy Foods.[15]

SIR (DR) GERARD VAUGHAN, C Reading E. Ex-Minister Consumer Affairs 82–83; Ex-Minister DoHealth 79–82; Spokesman Health 75–79, Secretary Cons Health Cttee. *Family* Sugar planters.[1] *Constituency* Imperial Group (Courage brewery).[20]

PETER VIGGERS. C Gosport. Minister: Northern Ireland. *Director* Sweetheart International (food packaging) 81–. *Consultant* Gough Hotels 73–75.[1]

RICHARD WAINWRIGHT. Lib Colne Valley. Ex-Spokesman Economic Affairs –86. All-party Chem Ind Grp 84. *Hon Vice President* Nat Assoc of Master Bakers, Confectioners & Caterers 82.[42]

RT HON JOHN WAKEHAM. C Colchester S and Maldon. Minister: Chief Whip. *Ex-Chairman, Director* Curzon Investments (ag machinery) 73–78. *Owner/Shareholder* Farm (dairy, 66 acres) 72–.[1]

HON WILLIAM WALDEGRAVE. C Bristol West. Minister: DoEnvironment. *Shareholder* Waldegrave Farms 78–.[1]

BILL WALKER. C Tayside N. *Constituency* 12.7% employed in ag.[22]

RT HON PETER WALKER. C Worcester. Cabinet: Minister, DoEnergy. Ex-Minister of Ag Fish Food 79–83. *Ex-Owner* Farm (400 acres) 72–81.[1]

JIM WALLACE. Lib Orkney & Shetland. *Constituency* 14.8% employed in ag.[22]

DENNIS WALTERS. C Westbury. *Constituency* Unigate (St Ivel)[14] Nestlé (Crosse & Blackwell and dairy products).[44]

ROBERT WAREING. Lab Liverpool W Derby. Lab Health Cttee. *Constituency* United Biscuits (Sayers).[36]

JOHN WATTS. C Slough. All-party Chem Ind Grp. *Consultant* Ranks Hovis McDougall 85–.[2] *Constituency* Mars.[20]

JOHN WATSON. C Skipton & Ripon. All-party Chem Ind Grp. *Constituency* 11.4% employed in ag.[22]

BOWEN WELLS. C Hertford & Stortford. Select Cttee European Legislation. Hon Sec Cons Trade & Ind Cttee. *Consultant* International Distillers & Vintners.[2]

RAY WHITNEY. C Wycombe. Ex-Minister DoHealth –86. *Constituency* United Biscuits (Frozen foods HQ).[36]

JERRY WIGGIN. C Weston-super-Mare. *Ex-Director* Manbré Sugars 75–77. *Ex-Farmer* 61–80 (three farms from 250 to 1870 acres).[1]

DAFYDD WIGLEY. Plaid Cymru Caernarfon. *Ex-Employee* Mars (Financial Planning Manager, Chief Cost Accountant), 67–71.[1]

ANN WINTERTON. C Congleton. Treasurer All-Party Licensed Trade Group.[17] *Constituency* Berisford Foods (Haigh, Castle).[26] *Family* Wife of Nicholas Winterton (below).

NICHOLAS WINTERTON. C Macclesfield. Cons Ag Cttee (Sec 74–79). *Ex-Chairman* CAMRA real-ale investments (now Midsummer Inns) 74–84.[1] *Family* Husband of Ann Winterton (above).

RT HON GEORGE YOUNGER. C Ayr. Cabinet Minister: MoDefence. Ex-Cabinet Minister: Scotland –86. *Family* Brewers. *Ex-director* Tennent Caledonian Breweries 77–79; J.G. Thomson (Breweries) 62–66, 74–79; John Fowler (Breweries) 63–67; George Younger (Breweries) 58–68. *Ex-Employee* George Younger (Breweries) 54–58. *Family* George Younger (Breweries) (now subsidiary of Bass Charrington). *Owner* Farm (beef 1000 acres).[1]

DOCUMENT B

Two Hundred and Forty-Six Advisors: Government, Science and the Food Industry

Many scientists have direct or indirect links with the food industry, or with the associated drink, farming and chemical industries. Industry is the chief employer of food scientists and technologists who, as their careers progress, may also move into and between universities, research institutes and government. Alternatively, academic scientists may accept research grants or consultancies from industry, or work for an institution supported by the food industry. The term 'food industry', as used here, is defined in Document A.

The alphabetical lists below after this introduction, are first, of all the scientists (and some lay people) who have served on twenty-seven selected expert government advisory panels whose reports were prepared or published between 1974 and 1987. Of these, all but three work or worked to the Ministry of Agriculture, Fisheries and Food (MAFF) and to the Department of Health and Social Security (DHSS).

The other three worked to the Cabinet Office, the National Economic Development Council (NEDC) and the Agriculture Research Council/Medical Research Council (ARC/MRC).

Expert reports submitted to MAFF, DHSS and other government departments are official, but advisory, and their recommendations may therefore be revised, delayed, overturned or ignored. At the same time, national policy on food and health depends on government acceptance of an expert advisory report. That is the way the system works in Britain. Reports are often more significant for their non-existence than their existence.

The second alphabetical list is of all the members of five expert panels set up solely or jointly by the food industry-funded British

Nutrition Foundation (which is not a government body).

To point out a link between a scientist and industry, is not in itself to suggest anything disreputable or inconsistent with public responsibility. Indeed, any scientist with a background in industry asked to serve on expert committees has a responsibility to give objective advice.

In the alphabetical lists below, three types of link with industry are included:

1. *Director* or *employee*. MAFF panels include people currently employed by the food industry, as a matter of policy. DHSS panels ordinarily do not. *Ex-Directors* and *Ex-employees* are also included.

2. *Consultant* or *advisor*. Scientists who are, or were, paid by industry to give expert advice and/or to represent its interests. Some do work for trade organisations who represent the interests of industry.

3. *Research funding*. Scientists whose own research, and/or that of their department, is funded by the food industry, or who work for an institution supported by the food industry.

Industry listed is that which is of public health concern: the industry using fats and sugars and highly processed food generally; alcohol; meat and dairy farming; agrichemicals and food chemicals. Large food retailers and caterers are also included.

People linked only with those parts of the industry concerned with food known to be healthy, as for example fish, vegetables and fruit, are not listed: or rather, would not be listed – no such people have been found.

Over the years many hundreds of scientists have served on expert advisory panels on food, and this analysis is therefore selective. The principle of selection is different from that used in Document A which lists only those 250 MPs (out of a total of 650) identified as having some link with the food industry. Here, every member of the thirty-two selected panels is listed, whether or not any link with industry has been identified, and the composition of each panel is also analysed.

Special knowledge of the food or farming industries can of course lead people in public life to favour reform; and some scientists, identified here as having a link with industry, consistently favour policies pointed to a healthier food supply. For example, in 1986 Sir Douglas Black, Dr John Cummings, Dr John Garrow and Dorothy Hollingsworth served on internal committees of the food industry-funded British Nutrition Foundation; as did Daphne Grose, Professor Philip James and Professor Jerry Morris before their resignations. Of these, Sir Douglas Black was a member of the ARC/MRC *Food Research* Committee (1974) and of the joint Royal College of Physicians/BNF panel on *Food Intolerance and Food Aversion* (1984); Dr Garrow was Chairman of the joint Health Education Council/BNF JACNE committee until its abolition in 1987, and was a member of the BNF Task Force on *Sugars and Syrups* (1987). Dorothy Hollingsworth was BNF Director-General from 1970 to 1977 and was a member of the joint Department of Health/BNF/Health Education Council panel on *Nutrition Education* (1977); and Professor Morris was a member of the BNF panel on *Dietary Guidelines: Obstacles and Opportunities* (1982). All of these are or have been expert government advisors, and all have made public statements to the effect that there is room to improve British food, as other scientists linked with industry may have done.

In any case, does serving on a British Nutrition Foundation internal committee, or a panel set up by the BNF to produce a report, constitute a link with the food industry? In the sense that the BNF is designed to be a forum for industry, science and government the answer is, of course, yes. But does the BNF speak for industry? This is a matter of dispute.

In 1987, the two best known government advisory committees on food and health whose panels produce reports, are the MAFF Food Advisory Committee (FAC), formed in November 1983 by merging the more explicitly named Food Standards Committee (FSC) and the Food Additives and Contaminants Committee (FACC); and the DHSS Committee on Medical Aspects of Food Policy (COMA).

THE FOOD STANDARDS COMMITTEE

The FSC was itself formed in 1947, to advise government on the composition, description, labelling and advertising of food. Between 1947 and 1983 its panels produced 77 reports. Some of these set standards for specific foods, such as sausages (1956) or soft drinks (1975 and 1976). Others have a broader remit, such as *Bread and Flour* (1960) and *Claims and Misleading Descriptions* (1966). The five FSC reports whose panel members are included in the alphabetical list below, are

Bread and Flour (Second report) (1974)
Water in Food (1978)
Second Report on Food Labelling (1979)
Meat Products (1980)
Second Report on Claims and Misleading Descriptions (1980)

In the 1970s the Food Standards Committee was made up of a Chairman and nine members appointed for three-year terms of office. Official policy was:[1]

> the members are appointed in a personal capacity. Three have a background in the food industry, three in science, and three have special interests in matters affecting consumers.

In the early 1980s the committee was slimmed down to eight members with:[2]

> a background in the food industry, in the enforcement of food standards legislation and special interests in matters affecting consumers.

Membership of the Food Standards Committee, 1975 and 1982

	1975	1982
Chairman	Professor Alan Ward[a] Food Science, Leeds Univ	Professor Frank Curtis[a] Director AFRC Food RI, Norwich
Industry	Professor Russell Allen[ab] Beecham	Dr William Fulton[ab] Unilever
	Dr John Collingwood[a] Unilever	Jasper Grinling[b] Grand Metropolitan
	Frank Wood[a] Corn Products Corp. UK	Alan Turner[b] Cadbury Schweppes
Science	Richard Dalley Public Analyst	Richard Dalley Public Analyst
	Professor Harold Egan[a] The Government Chemist	Professor Philip James[a] Director AFRC RI, Aberdeen
	Dr Reg Passmore[a] Physiology, Glasgow Univ.	
Consumer	J.A. O'Keefe Barrister	Marie Edwards Home Economist
	Mrs G.L.S. Pike[a] Women's Forum	Daphne Grose[a] Consumers' Association
	Rita Stephen Trades Unionist	Roger Manley Trading Standards Officer

[a] Member of one or more internal committees of the British Nutrition Foundation.
[b] Member of one or more committees of representative bodies of the food industry: e.g. Food Manufacturers' Federation; Food and Drink Industries Council; Cocoa, Chocolate and Confectionery Alliance.

Members of the Food Standards Committee in 1975 and 1982 have been categorised in the opposite table. First, those with a foreground (rather than a background) in industry. Second, scientists (including a public analyst). Third, consumer representatives.

In practice, between eleven and fourteen committee members worked on any individual FSC report, simply because the reports usually took around five years to complete, from the date of commissioning to the date of publication. For example, as shown in the full lists below, two other experts who worked on the 1974 *Bread and Flour* report were Colin Dence[b] (who is listed as ex-President of the Food Manufacturers' Federation and ex-Director of Brand and Co (a subsidiary of Ranks Hovis McDougall;[3] and C.C.E. Sopp (a Weights and Measures Inspector).

THE FOOD ADDITIVES AND CONTAMINANTS COMMITTEE

Originally a sub-committee of the FSC, the FACC was established as a full committee in its own right in 1960 to advise government on food additives and contaminants. Between 1960 and 1984 it produced 39 reports, on topics ranging from liquid freezants (1972 and 1974) and sorbic acid (1977) to lead (1975) and beer (1978). The FACC members included in the alphabetical list below are those who worked on the following three reports:

Report of the Review on Flavourings in Food (1976)
Interim Report on the Review of the Colouring Matter in Food Regulations 1973 (1979)
Report of the Working Party on the Dietary Intake of Food Colours (1979)

In the 1970s, the FACC consisted of a Chairman and twelve (sometimes fourteen) members, appointed for a three-year-term. The committee was officially described as 'an independent body of experts'.[4]

Membership of the FACC in 1975 and 1982 is listed overleaf:

Seventeen panel members worked on the report on flavours published in 1976. The report on colours, which took six years to complete, was something of an epic, involving twenty-four panel members. These were everybody on FACC in 1975, (overleaf); Dr Brignell, Dr Elstow,[a] Professor Macdonald,[a] Dr McLaren and Professor Turner, who were appointed to FACC in 1976 or 1977;[5,6] and also Professor Francis Aylward[b] (a food scientist), Nathan

Membership of the Food Additives and Contaminants Committee, 1975 and 1982

	1975	1982
Chairman	Professor Basil Weedon Nottingham Univ	Professor Basil Weedon Nottingham Univ
Industry	Robert Beedham Imperial Group (Smedley)[c]	Dr Peter Brignell ICI
	Geoffrey Davy ICI	Dr John Colquhoun[ab] Rowntree Mackintosh
	Dr William Fulton[ab] Unilever	Dr William Elstow[a] Associated British Foods
	William Price-Davies[ab] Cadbury Schweppes	Dr Thomas Gorsuch[b] Reckitt & Colman
	Professor Ernest Williams[ab] Sainsbury	Geoffrey Telling[b] Unilever
Science	Dr W.R. Bannatyne Food Technology	A.J. Harrison Public Analyst
	A.J. Harrison Public Analyst	Professor June Lloyd[a] Child Health, London
	Professor Maurice Ingram Director AFRC Meat RI	Professor Ian Macdonald[a] Physiology, Guys Hosp.
	Professor Dennis Parke Biochemist	Dr Donald McLaren Medicine, Edinburgh
	R. Sawyer Government chemist	Professor Jeffrey Porter[a] Director, Nat Inst Dairying
	Professor Patricia Scott Nutrition, Royal Free Hosp.	Professor Paul Turner Pharmacology, Barts Hosp.
Consumer	Dr Janet Cockcroft Consumers Cttee for GB	Dr Leslie Yeomans Consumers' Association

[a] Member of one or more internal committees of the British Nutrition Foundation.
[b] Member of one or more committees of representative bodies of the food industry: e.g. Food Manufacturers' Federation; Food and Drink Industries Council; Cocoa, Chocolate and Confectionery Alliance.
[c] Name of firm or controlling firm correct as of 1986.

Goldenberg[a] (Marks and Spencer), Dr J.H. Hamence (a public analyst), Dr Harold Jasperson[b] (Bibby, the edible oils manufacturer), Professor John Norris[b] (Cadbury Schweppes) and John Saunders (Cerebos, a subsidiary of Ranks Hovis McDougall).[3]

The working party on the dietary intake of food colours was set up in 1976 with thirteen members: five from government (MAFF) and eight from industry: C.T. Ashton (Scot Bowyers), Frank Firth (John Renshaw), Ken Gardner[b] (Mars), Harry Houghton[ab] (Cadbury Schweppes), R. Mears[c] (Allied Lyons), Jack Philp[a] (Unilever), together with Dr Reginald Crampton[ab] (British Industrial Biological Research Association) and Richard Hinton[ab] (Campden Food Preservation Research Association).

THE FOOD ADVISORY COMMITTEE

The Food Advisory Committee was formed in 1983, originally from eight members of the FSC, and seven members of the FACC, as shown in the left-hand list overleaf. Of a total of fifteen members, six worked for food manufacturers. In November 1986 the FAC was reformulated: the 'new, improved' committee of fifteen includes seven industry employees, with a broader base: five manufacturers including one biotechnologist, plus an advertising agent and a retailer, as shown in the right-hand list overleaf.

Of the FAC members in 1987 Professor Curtis[a] is a Governor of the BNF, and Professor Macdonald[a] (who retired from the FAC in November 1986) is Chairman of the BNF. Mr Grinling[b] became Chairman of the Apple and Pear Development Council in the summer of 1986 – the one government advisor identified with that part of industry only concerned with healthy food.

The most noticeable change in the composition of the FAC made in 1986, was the doubling of women on the committee, from two to four. Of these, Mrs Mann[a] is a Director of the advertising agency J. Walter Thompson; Dr Ashwell is Principal of the Good Housekeeping Institute, part of whose job is product testing for the food industry; and Ms Ballard is on a committee of the government and industry-funded 'Celebration of British Food and Farming 89', an offshoot of 'Food From Britain'.

Industry employees are in a minority on all the MAFF advisory committees so far analysed with the exception of the FACC working party on food colours. Three out of ten FSC members, five out of thirteen FACC members, and seven out of fifteen FAC members came from industry. If, however, involvement with the British Nutrition Foundation is counted as a link with industry, the numbers rise. For example, in 1981-82 the BNF had fifteen Scientific Governors (excluding two appointed by the Royal Society), of whom seven (Professor Allen, Dr Collingwood, and Professors Curtis, Lloyd, Macdonald, Porter and Ward) are listed above. Another Scientific Governor at this time was Sir Henry

Membership of the Food Advisory Committee, 1983 and 1987

	1983	1987
Chairman	Professor Frank Curtis[a] Director AFRC Food RI, Norwich	Professor Frank Curtis[a] Director AFRC Food RI, Norwich
Industry	Dr Peter Brignell ICI	M.J. Boxall Tesco
	Dr William Elstow[a] Associated British Foods	Dr H.O.W. Eggins Bioquest
	Dr William Fulton[ab] Unilever	Dr William Fulton[ab] Unilever
	Dr Thomas Gorsuch[b] Reckitt & Colman	Dr Thomas Gorsuch[b] Reckitt & Colman
	Jasper Grinling[b] Grand Metropolitan	Mrs Patricia Mann[a] J. Walter Thompson
	Alan Turner[b] Cadbury Schweppes	Anthony Skrimshire[ab] Heinz
		Alan Turner[b] Cadbury Schweppes
Science	A.J. Harrison Public Analyst	A.J. Harrison Public Analyst
	Professor Philip James[a] Director AFRC RI, Aberdeen	Professor Philip James Director AFRC RI, Aberdeen
	Professor Ian Macdonald[a] Physiology, Guys Hosp.	Professor Paul Turner Phamacology, Barts Hosp.
	Dr Donald McLaren Medicine, Edinburgh	Dr Elspeth Young John Radcliffe Hosp, Oxford
	Professor Paul Turner Pharmacology, Barts Hosp.	
Consumer	Marie Edwards Home Economist	Dr Margaret Ashwell Good Housekeeping Inst.
	Daphne Grose[a] Consumers' Association	Anne Ballard Women's Institutes
	Roger Manley Trading Standards Officer	Roger Manley Trading Standards Officer

[a] Member of one or more internal committees of the British Nutrition Foundation
[b] Member of one or more committees of representative bodies of the food industry: e.g. Food Manufacturers' Federation; Food and Drink Industries Council; Cocoa, Chocolate and Confectionery Alliance

Yellowlees, then Chief Medical Officer at the DHSS.[7] (Dr Colquhoun, Dr Elstow, Miss Grose, Professor James, Mrs Mann, Dr Passmore, Mr Price-Davies, Mr Sawyer and Professor Williams also serve or served on BNF committees).[7]

OTHER GOVERNMENT
ADVISORY COMMITTEES

A joint Agriculture Research Council/Medical Research Council committee established government policy on the funding of nutrition research in a report entitled *Food and Nutrition Research*, published in 1974. The chairman of the committee was Professor Albert Neuberger. His views were reflected in what became known as the 'Neuberger report'. The committee included two people from the food industry (Spillers and Unilever) and another eight who are still or have been members of BNF committees. Professor Neuberger himself joined the BNF's Scientific Advisory Committee in 1974 and was President of the BNF from 1982 to 1986.

Members of committees that produced the following seven official advisory reports, all concerned with the future of the British food industry, appear in the alphabetical lists below.

The Food Industry and Technology (Cabinet Office/ACARD 1982)
Review of the Food and Drink Manufacturing Industry (National
    Economic Development Council 1983)
Food Surveillance (1984)
Food Quality (1984)
*Priorities Board for Research and Development in Agriculture and
    Food* (1985)
Food Safety (1985)
Food Processing (1986)

As is normal policy, fifteen of the eighteen members of the NEDC committee were from industry (eight from management, seven from trades unions, plus two from government, and Professor J.S. Marsh, an agriculturist from the University of Aberdeen (who later moved to Reading). The MAFF Food Surveillance Steering Group has fourteen members, ten from government, two from industry, which co-ordinates the work of other MAFF advisory committees and guides, if not sets, their agendas.

The other five reports have a common purpose. The Cabinet Office report, which was produced by the Advisory Council for

Applied Research and Development (ACARD), laid down a strategy for British food science and technology to the turn of the century.[8] In response, The Food Priorities Board for agriculture and food research and development was set up in June 1984,[9] and has been itself advised by the Food Processing, Food Quality and Food Safety committees. The committees that produced these five reports were chaired by Dr Douglas Georgala[a] (Unilever), Sir Kenneth Durham (Unilever), Dr Thomas Gorsuch[b] (Reckitt & Colman) Tony Good[b] (Express Dairies, previously Grand Metropolitan) and Professor John Norris[b] (Cadbury Schweppes).

The membership of the ACARD and the Food Processing committees is listed opposite:

Consumers were not represented on the Food Surveillance Steering Group, nor on the committees that produced the ACARD, Food Processing, Food Priorities and NEDC reports.

A number of British Nutrition Foundation committee members were also on the ACARD committee. In 1987, Dr Georgala is Chairman of the BNF Industrial Scientists committee,[7] and as indicated by[a], Professor Edelman, Professor Holmes, Sir Kenneth Blaxter and Professor Curtis (of FAC) serve on BNF committees. In 1985 Professor Conning, a toxicologist, moved from his post at the British Industrial Biological Research Association, which is jointly funded by industry and government, to become Director-General of the BNF.

MAFF AND OTHER
COMMITTEES ANALYSED

Of the total of 247 seats on the nineteen official advisory panels and committees analysed, 116 were, or are, filled by people employed in the food industry. If the eighteen seats occupied by twelve people employed by the food industry research associations, the BNF and those who have a background in industry are discounted, ninety-eight seats were or are filled by people employed by industry. However, industry as a whole is not evenly represented. There was nobody from the fresh vegetable, fruit, meat or fish trades until Jasper Grinling for a few months in 1986. There is no caterer, unless Grand Metropolitan and Allied-Lyons are counted. There are only seven seats for retailers (Marks and Spencer, Co-operative Wholesale Society, Sainsbury) and two for farmers. Trade unionists (seven) are represented as such only on

Membership of the ACARD Cabinet Office Committee, 1982, and MAFF Food Processing Committee, 1986

	ACARD 1982	Food Processing 1986
Chairman	Dr Douglas Georgala[a] Unilever	Dr Thomas Gorsuch[b] Reckitt & Colman
Industry	Professor David Conning[ab] Director BIBRA	Gordon Amery[b] Co-operative Wholesale Society
	Professor Jack Edelman[ab] Ranks Hovis McDougall	Dr John Cordell Unilever
	Sydney Free[b] Rowntree Mackintosh	Ron Dicker[b] Dairy Crest
	Professor Alan Holmes[ab] Director BFMIRA	Alan Downing Cadbury Schweppes
	David Shore[b] APV Engineering	Dr William Elstow[a] Associated British Foods
		Anthony Skrimshire[b] Heinz
		Dr Alan Whitear Whitbread
Science	Sir Kenneth Blaxter[a] Ex-Director AFRC RI, Aberdeen	Dr Gordon Birch Reading Univ.
	Professor Frank Curtis[a] Director AFRC RI, Norwich	Professor Leo Pyle Reading Univ.
		Dr Andrew Wheatley Cranfield Inst. of Tech.
Consumer	none	none

[a] Member of one or more internal committees of the British Nutrition Foundation.
[b] Member of one or more committees of representative bodies of the food industry: e.g. Food and Drink Federation, Food Manufacturers' Federation; Food and Drink Industries Council; Cocoa, Chocolate and Confectionery Alliance.

one of the committees (Rita Stephen served on the FSC as a consumer representative). There is (as from 1986) one representative from the advertising industry. The great majority of industry seats are filled by the representatives of giant food manufacturers. Most of the firms are conglomerates that may manufacture drink, drugs, additives and/or agrichemicals as well as food. All the managers from the food industry on these committees are men. Unilever is invariably represented.

Analysed by product category, this is how the food manufacturers and retailers represented on these committees break down:

Representation of food manufacturing and retailing companies on nineteen official government advisory committees, 1974–1987

Company	Line of business	People	Seats
Unilever[a]	Margarine, ready meals, soup, ice-cream, meat products, additives, etc	12	20
Cadbury Schweppes[a]	Chocolate, confectionery, soft drinks	6	7
Beecham[a]	Soft drinks, spreads, drugs	3	7
Ranks Hovis McDougall[a]	Bread, cakes, salt, additives	4	5
Grand Metropolitan	Beer, hotels	2	5
ICI[a]	Agrichemicals, additives	2	4
Corn Products Corp. UK	Syrups	1	5
Whitbread[a]	Beer	3	3
Reckitt & Colman[a]	Soft drinks, condiments, drugs	2	4
Marks and Spencer[a]	Retail	2	3
Spillers-Dalgety[a]	Cereals, animal feeds	2	2
Rowntree Mackintosh[a]	Chocolate, confectionery, biscuits	2	2
Associated British Foods[a]	Bread, flour, biscuits	1	3
Heinz[a]	Soup, ready meals	1	2
Express Dairies	Milk, dairy products	1	2
Bibby	Oils	1	2
Sainsbury[a]	Retail	1	2
Imperial Group[a]	Beer	1	1
United Biscuits[a]	Biscuits, cakes, crisps	1	1
CWS[a]	Retail, bread, milk	1	1
Mars[a]	Chocolate, confectionery	1	1
John F. Renshaw	Confectionery supplier	1	1
Dairy Crest	Milk	1	1
Scot Bowyers	Meat Products	1	1
Tesco	Retail	1	1
Allied Lyons[a]	Beer, ice cream, cakes, hotels	1	1
Bioquest	Biotechnology	1	1
Total		56	88

[a] Member company of the British Nutrition Foundation.

Of the twenty-seven companies listed above, eighteen are (or have been) 'member companies', that is sponsors, of the British Nutrition Foundation. Of the 247 seats on the committees already analysed, ninety-three were or are filled by people who were or are also members of BNF committees.

The table opposite summarizes the food industry and government links of the members of the nineteen advisory panels and committees so far analysed, and so also shows the number of advisors with no identified industrial links. Four types of link can be identified: food industry employees, including those with a background in industry and trade unionists; scientists whose work has been funded by the food industry or who have worked as advisors to industry; members of BNF committees; and civil servants (working for government).

Membership of nineteen MAFF and other advisory committees 1974–1987: links with industry and government

	NO	YES	of which			
Seats	Total	Total	Indus staff/backgr.	Indus funds/adv.	BNF	Govt
247	66	181	116	18	93	26

The total number of members identified as having industrial links comes to more than 181 mainly because many industry employees also sit on BNF committees. This analysis includes twenty-six seats occupied by scientists and other advisors whose sole traced link with industry was or is membership of BNF committees; this includes governors of the BNF. If these twenty-six are regarded as not having any links with industry, then ninety-two seats were or are occupied by people with no link with industry or government, compared with 155 occupied by people with such links, some of whom, of course, also belong to BNF committees.

COMMITEE ON MEDICAL
ASPECTS OF FOOD POLICY

The Committee on Medical Aspects of Food Policy (COMA), which reports to the DHSS, was set up in 1957 to provide government with 'independent scientific advice on matters relating to nutrition, diet and health'.[10]. Between 1957 and 1984 it produced twenty-eight reports in the *Health and Social Subjects* series. Some of these were surveys of 'vulnerable' sections of the population: for example, *A Nutrition Survey of Pre-School Children, 1967-1968* (1975). Others examined practical topics: for example *The Collection and Storage of Human Milk* (1981). The five COMA reports whose panel members are included in the alphabetical list below, are

Diet and Coronary Heart Disease (1974)
Recommended Daily Amounts of Food Energy and Nutrients for Groups of People in the United Kingdom (1979, 1981)
Recommended Intakes of Nutrients for the United Kingdom (1969, 1981)
Nutritional Aspects of Bread and Flour (1981)
Diet and Cardiovascular Disease (1984)

In 1987, COMA consists of a chairman and seventeen members appointed for indefinite terms. Official policy is that:[10]

> COMA is a committee of independent experts .... Appointment to COMA is considered to be a distinction in medical/scientific circles.

The main COMA committee meets twice yearly but operates mainly through a system of panels set up to consider and report on particular matters. COMA panels are chaired by a member of the main COMA committee but usually include non-COMA members who are appointed for their particular expertise.[10]

Opposite, as examples, are the members of two COMA panels, set up to report on *Diet and Cardiovascular Disease* (1984) and on *Nutritional Aspects of Bread and Flour* (1981). They have been categorised as follows. First, people employed by industry (the only example being the Director-General of the food industry-funded British Nutrition Foundation). Second, scientists not funded by the food industry (funding from the drug industry is not counted unless the company also manufactures agrichemicals). Third, scientists funded by the food industry, or who have, as advisors, represented the interests of industry. Fourth, civil servants (the DHSS Chief Medical Officer is included, as Chairman of the main COMA panel, while not formally being a member of any COMA panel).

It is worth noting that in the 1980s British government policy is to encourage liaison between science and industry; and the competence of university departments is now judged by their ability to attract money from industry. Scientists must now search out industry money as a necessity if not as a virtue. Senior scientists are not insulated from this process, and so it is not surprising that official government advisors are, or have been, funded by industry.

The table shows that of the sixteen people (including the Chief Medical Officer of the DHSS) who worked on the report on *Bread and Flour*, fourteen also served on British Nutrition Foundation committees. (Dr Cummings succeeded Sir Frank Young as Chairman of the panel in 1980). By contrast, only two of the eleven who worked on the *Diet and Cardiovascular Disease* report also

Membership of COMA panels on Bread and Flour 1981, and Diet and Cardiovascular Disease 1984

	Bread	Cardiovascular Disease
Chairman	Sir Frank Young[a] Biochemistry, Cambridge	Sir Philip Randle Biochemistry, Oxford
Industry	Dr Michael Turner[a] British Nutrition Foundation	
Science not funded	Dr Peter Elwood[a] Epidemiology, Cardiff	Professor Colin Adams Pathology, Guys Hosp.
	Professor June Lloyd[a] Child Health, London	Dr Nicholas Myant Lipid Metabolism, Hamm Hosp.
	Dr Colin Mills AFRC RI, Aberdeen	Professor Michael Oliver Cardiology, Edinburgh
	Professor Jerry Morris[a] Epidemiology, London	Professor Geoffrey Rose Epidemiology, London
	Dr Dennis Parsons Biochemistry, Oxford	
	Dr Elsie Widdowson[a] Medicine, Cambridge	
Science funded/ advisor	Dr John Cummings[a] Nutrition, Cambridge BNF	Professor John Durnin[a] Physiology, Glasgow Sugar, etc.
	Professor John Durnin[a] Physiology, Glasgow Sugar, etc.	Professor Harry Keen[a] Medicine, Guys Hosp. Sugar
	Dr John Garrow[a] MRC CRC, Harrow Sugar	Professor Philip James Director AFRC RI, Aberdeen Milk Products
	Dr David Southgate[a] AFRC RI, Norwich BNF	Dr Jim Mann Medicine, Oxford Sugar, margarine
	Dr Roger Whitehead[a] Nutrition, Cambridge Milk, etc	Professor Tony Mitchell Medicine, Nottingham Agrichemicals
Government	Dr Sylvia Darke[a] DHSS	Sir Donald Acheson CMO DHSS
	Professor George Elton[ab] Chief Scientist, MAFF	
	Sir Henry Yellowlees[a] CMO DHSS	
Consumer	none	none

[a] Member of one or more internal committees of the British Nutrition Foundation.
[b] Member of one or more committees of representative bodies of the food industry: e.g. Food Manufacturers' Federation; Food and Drink Industries Council; Cocoa, Chocolate and Confectionery Alliance.

served on BNF committees. (Professor James had resigned by the time the report was in its final stages and is not counted.)

COMA panel members identified as funded by or advisors to industry are Professor Durnin[a] (advisor to the Sugar Bureau,[11] funding from Nestlé);[12] Dr Garrow[a] (funding from the Sugar Association);[13] Professor James (funding from Nestlé, and the Rank Prize Fund);[12] Professor Keen[a] (advisor to the Sugar Bureau,[14] funding from the Sugar Bureau,[12] the International Sugar Research Foundation,[15] and the World Sugar Research Organization);[16] Dr Mann (funding from Unilever[12] – Flora margarine – and from the World Sugar Research Organization);[16] Professor Mitchell (funding from Pfizer – agrichemicals);[17] Dr Southgate (funding from the British Nutrition Foundation);[7] and Dr Whitehead (advisor to the milk industry,[18] funding from Nestlé).[12]

The pattern of patronage by the sugar industry is apparent. (The Sugar Bureau has stated on behalf of Professor Durnin and Professor Keen that they were not paid for their advice).[20] This does not mean that the COMA panel members funded by or advisors to the sugar industry spoke up on behalf of sugar during COMA meetings. Indeed, neither report, on *Bread and Flour* and *Diet and Cardiovascular Disease*, is enthusiastic about sugar. It may be that other members of these and other COMA panels are funded by or advisors to other sections of the food industry. A 'Register of Advisors' Interests' along the same lines as the 'Register of Members' Interests' for Members of Parliament, published by HMSO, would be enlightening. Given that industry funding is questionable, it is clearly wrong that government advisors who disclose their sources of funding in their published research should be subjects for criticism compared with industry-funded colleagues who choose not to disclose information about their funding.

Membership of the main COMA committee is to some extent predetermined. The Chairman is always the Chief Medical Officer of the DHSS, and it is he who appoints the committee members. Until 1984 the CMO was Sir Henry Yellowlees,[a] and in 1987 is Sir Donald Acheson. The Chief Scientist of MAFF also sits on COMA; until 1985 this post was held by Sir George Elton,[ab] who has a background in industry as former Director of the British Flour Milling and Baking Research Association, where he invented the Chorleywood Bread Process by which almost all mass-produced white bread in Britain is now made. The Chief Medical Officers of Scotland and Wales also sit on COMA. So too do representatives of the Medical Research Council and the Public Health Laboratory Service which, although funded by government, are not counted as government agencies. The remaining ten COMA places as a rule include specialists in child health and geriatrics. Members of the main COMA committee in 1987 are as follows:

Membership of main COMA committee 1987

Chairman	Sir Donald Acheson Chief Medical Officer, DHSS

Industry	Professor Michael Gurr[a] Milk Marketing Board

Science not funded	Dr Enid Bennett Medical Research Council
	Professor Malcolm Hodkinson Geriatrics, London Univ.
	Professor June Lloyd[a] Child Health, St Georges Hosp.
	Dr Tom Meade[a] MRC CRC, Harrow
	Sir Philip Randle Biochemistry, Oxford
	Dr Joe Smith Director, Public Health Lab

Science funded/ advisor	Dr John Cummings[a] Nutrition, Cambridge BNF
	Professor John Durnin[a] Physiology, Glasgow Sugar etc.
	Dr John Garrow[a] MRC CRC, Harrow Sugar
	Professor Harry Keen Medicine, Guys Hosp. Sugar
	Professor Don Naismith[a] Crisps, etc.
	Professor Thomas Oppé Child Health, St Mary's Hosp. Tobacco etc
	Dr Roger Whitehead[a] Nutrition, Cambridge Milk etc

---

continued overleaf

---

continued Membership of main COMA committee 1987

Government	Dr Gareth Crompton CMO Wales
	Dr Tom Crossett Chief Scientist, MAFF
	Dr I.S. Macdonald CMO Scotland

Consumer	none

---

a Member of one or more internal committees of the British Nutrition Foundation.

The other DHSS committee listed here is that on food irradiation, jointly set up with MAFF. Its report, *The Safety and Wholesomeness of Irradiated Foods*, was published in 1986. Controversy about food irradiation increased on publication of the report, partly because Sir Arnold Burgen, Chairman of the Committee, is also a part-time director of Amersham International, the chief supplier of isotope to the food irradiation industry;[21] and partly because Frank Ley, listed as a member of the committee but formally designated as the committee's advisor on the industrial application of food irradiation is also Technical Director of Isotron, the food irradiation business.[22]

DHSS COMMITTEES ANALYSED

There are 123 seats on the eight DHSS panels and committees listed, of which sixty-three were or are filled by people who were or are on BNF committees. The tally of identified links between members and industry and government is as follows:

Membership of eight DHSS advisory committees 1974–1987: links with industry and government

	NO	YES,	of which			
Seats	Total	Total	Indus staff/backgr.	Indus funds/adv.	BNF	Govt
123	34	89	16	47	63	22

For eighteen of the sixty-three scientists concerned, membership of BNF committees is their only industry link. If they are removed to the 'No' column, then fifty-two of the 123 DHSS committee seats were or are occupied by people not linked with industry, seventy-one by people with links.

GOVERNMENT ADVISORY COMMITTEES ANALYSED

The industry and government links of members of the twenty-seven government advisory panels and committees is as follows:

Membership of twenty-seven official advisory committees 1974–1987: links with industry and government

		NO	YES,	of which			
	Seats	Total	Total	Indus Staff/ backgr.	Indus funds/ adv.	BNF	Govt.
Cabinet Office: ACARD 82	8	0	8	7	0	6	0
NEDC: (Food & Drink 83)	18	1	17	15	1	2	1
MAFF: (Food Processing 86)	11	2	9	8	1	1	0
MAFF: (R and D Priorities 85)	8	2	6	4	0	1	2
MAFF: (Food Safety 85)	11	4	7	5	1	2	1
MAFF: (Food Quality 84)	9	3	6	6	0	3	0
MAFF: (Food Surveillance 84)	14	2	12	3	0	1	10
ARC/MRC: (Food Research 74)	14	4	10	3	3	8	2
MAFF: FAC 83–87	22	5	17	11	5	7	0
MAFF: FSC 80–83	7	2	5	4	0	3	0
MAFF: FSC (Claims 80)	14	5	9	4	1	9	1
MAFF: FSC (Meat 80)	14	5	9	4	1	9	1
MAFF: FSC (Labelling 79)	14	5	9	4	1	9	1
MAFF: FSC (Water 78)	11	4	7	3	0	7	1

continued overleaf

continued Membership of twenty-seven official advisory committees 1974–1987: links with industry and government

	Seats	NO Total	YES, Total	Indus Staff/backgr.	Indus funds/adv.	BNF	Govt.
MAFF: FSC (Bread 74)	11	3	8	4	0	7	1
MAFF: FACC 80–83	7	1	6	4	0	3	0
MAFF: FACC (Colours 79)	24	9	15	12	3	7	0
MAFF: FACC (Colours WP 79)	13	0	13	8	0	4	5
MAFF: FACC (Flavours 76)	17	9	8	7	1	4	0
DHSS/MAFF Irrad 86	15	7	8	3	6	3	0
DHSS: COMA (Nutr Surv 86)	9	3	6	0	5	5	0
DHSS: COMA (Main Cttee 84–87)	26	9	17	3	9	11	7
DHSS: COMA (Heart Dis 84)	11	5	6	0	5	4	1
DHSS: COMA (Bread 81)	16	2	14	3	6	14	3
DHSS: COMA (RDAS: 81,79)	20	3	17	3	8	12	5
DHSS: COMA (RDAs 81,69)	12	3	9	2	3	7	3
DHSS: COMA (Heart Dis 74)	14	2	12	2	5	7	3
TOTAL MAFF/DHSS (etc) seats	370	100	270	132	65	156	48
if BNF not counted as industry link	370	144	226				
Total MAFF/DHSS (etc) people	216	63	153	83	34	69	32
if BNF not counted as industry link	216	75	141				

These totals include membership of the main COMA committee in 1984 as well as 1987; and also thirteen seats on the FSC and FACC between 1980 and 1983 whose members were responsible for reports not analysed here.

This analysis shows that of the 370 seats on twenty-seven government advisory panels and committees, 100 were occupied by people without any identified industry or government links, whereas 270 – more than twice as many – were filled by people linked with industry or government. Indeed, the 100 without such links are outnumbered by the 132 seats occupied by people who worked or work for industry, or else have a background in industry.

If membership of BNF committees alone is not counted as a link with industry, then the totals are 144 without links, 226 with links. So, by any reckoning, more people with industry and government links sit on official advisory panels and committees than people without such links.

The analysis also shows that of the 216 people who served on the twenty-seven panels and committees, 63 had no links and 153 had links, with industry or government. Again, if 'BNF-only' people are excluded, the totals still show a minority without links: 75 to 141.

The bottom line is that, more often than not, official advice on food and health in Britain is given by people from industry or government or else linked with industry or government. If officers, governors and committee members of the British Nutrition Foundation, which is funded by the food industry, are counted as having links with industry, advisors without industry or government links are outnumbered by five to two.

Of the 216 people who sat on the twenty-seven panels and committees, nineteen were women.

In Britain, expert advisory reports on food and health, such as FAC, FSC, FACC and COMA reports, are instruments of government. Members of the main COMA committee sign the Official Secrets Act. Members of the other DHSS and MAFF expert panels and committees are covered by the Official Secrets Act.[23]

THE BRITISH NUTRITION FOUNDATION

Reports issued by the British Nutrition Foundation do not have official status. But the composition of the BNF's expert panels is similar to that of government advisory committees. Five BNF reports are analysed overleaf, three of which were jointly compiled with other bodies. In these three cases, the responsibility for appointing panel members will have been shared between the BNF and the collaborating body. BNF committee members who worked on the following five reports are included in the second alphabetical list below.

Nutrition Education (1977) (jointly with the DHSS and the Health
    Education Council)
Dietary Guidelines: Obstacles and Opportunities (1982)
Food Intolerance and Food Aversion (1984) (jointly with the Royal
    College of Physicians)
Eating for a Healthier Heart (1985, the so-called JACNE Report)
    (jointly with the Health Education Council)
Sugars and Syrups (1987).

The table below analyses membership of the panels that
produced the reports on *Dietary Guidelines* and *Sugars and
Syrups*, both of which were the responsibility of the BNF alone.

Professor Waterlow has been funded by Nestlé,[12] Rank Prize
Funds[24] and the BNF.[7] Professor Edgar has been funded by the
Cocoa, Chocolate and Confectionery Alliance,[12] Mars,[25] the Sugar
Association[12] and the World Sugar Research Organization.[16]
Professor Hawthorn has been an advisor to the Food Manu-
facturers Federation.[26] Professor Macdonald has been funded by

Membership of BNF panels on Dietary Guidelines 1982, and Sugars and Syrups 1987

	Dietary Guidelines	Sugars and Syrups
Chairman	Dr Michael Turner[a] British Nutrition Foundation	Sir Cyril Clarke Genetics, Liverpool Hosp.
Industry	Professor Russell Allen[ab] Beecham	Professor David Conning[ab] British Nutrition Foundation
	Professor Jack Edelman[ab] Ranks Hovis McDougall	Dr Richard Cottrell[a] British Nutrition Foundation
	Dr Juliet Gray[a] British Nutrition Foundation	Dr George Greener[a] Mars
	Elizabeth Morse[a] British Nutrition Foundation	Professor A.J. Vlitos[a] World Sugar Research Org.
	Dr Wilson Nicol[a] Tate & Lyle	
	Dr Alan Robertson[a] ICI	
Science not funded	Professor Jerry Morris[a] Epidemiology, London	Dr Tom Meade MRC CRC, Harrow
		Professor Albert Neuberger[a] Pathology, Charing Cross Hosp.
		Dr David Pyke Diabetology, Kings Coll. Hosp.

continued opposite

continued Membership of BNF panels on dietary guidelines 1982, and sugars and syrups 1987

	Dietary Guidelines	Sugars and Syrups
Science funded/ advisor	Dr Roger Whitehead[a] Nutrition, Cambridge Milk, etc	Dr David Booth Psychology, Birmingham Univ. Soft drinks, etc
	Professor John Waterlow[a] Nutrition, London Milk, etc	Professor Michael Edgar Dentistry, Liverpool Hosp. Sugar
		Dr John Garrow[a] MRC CRC, Harrow Sugar
		Professor John Hawthorn[a] FDF/FMF
		Professor Ian Macdonald[a] Physiology, Guys Hosp. Chocolate etc
Government		Dr David Buss[a] Head of nutrition, MAFF
Consumer	Augusta Conry Dietitian	Margaret Sanderson Dietitian

[a] Member of one or more internal committees of the British Nutrition Foundation.
[b] Member of one or more committees of representative bodies of the food industry: e.g. Food and Drink Federation, Food Manufacturers' Federation; Food and Drink Industries Council; Cocoa, Chocolate and Confectionery Alliance

Cadbury,[27] Beecham (soft drinks),[28-36] Glaxo (baby food),[28,29] the Milk Marketing Board[37] and the Lord Rank Trust.[38-40] Professors Allen, Macdonald, Neuberger and Waterlow, and Dr Robertson, have all at some time been President or Chairman of the BNF.[7] The overall summary reckoning for the five BNF committees is as overleaf:

This analysis shows that of the 57 seats on the five BNF and co-BNF committees, 141 were occupied by people without any links with industry or government, whereas 43 had or have links with industry or government. If membership of internal BNF committees is not counted as a link with industry, then the totals are 20 without links, thirty-seven with links.

Of the 51 people who served on these BNF committees, 14 have no links with industry or government, while 37 do have such links.

Membership of five BNF committees 1977–1987: links with industry and government

		NO	YES,	of which			
	Seats	Total	Total	Indus Staff/ backgr.	Indus funds/ adv.	BNF	Govt.
BNF: (Sugars 86)	15	4	11	4	6	9	1
BNF/HEC: (JACNE 85)	9	4	5	1	4	4	0
RCP/BNF: (Food Intol 84)	13	4	9	4	4	6	1
BNF: (Diet 82)	11	0	11	7	4	11	0
DHSS/HEC/BNF: (Nutr Educ 77)	9	2	7	4	0	5	4
Total BNF (etc) seats	57	14	43	20	18	35	6
if BNF not counted as industry link	57	20	37				
Total BNF (etc) people	51	14	37	17	15	29	6
if BNF not counted as industry link	51	17	34				

Again if 'BNF-only' people are excluded, there is still a minority without links: 17 to 34.

The ratios of seats and people without and with industry and government links is much the same on BNF committees as it is on official government advisory panels and committees. One reason is the composition of the BNF committees established jointly with the Health Education Council and the Royal College of Physicians. The RCP, in particular, chooses few people connected with industry for its own panels.

THE BOTTOM LINE

The grand total of the thirty-two MAFF, DHSS, BNF and other committees analysed in this Document is, therefore:

Membership of thirty-two advisory committees: links with industry and government

| | | NO | YES, | of which | | | |
| | | | | Indus Staff/ backgr. | Indus funds/ adv. | BNF | Govt. |
	Seats	Total	Total				
Total seats	427	114	313	152	83	191	54
If BNF not counted as industry link	427	164	263				
Total people	246	75	171	92	41	81	36
If BNF not counted as industry link	246	88	158				

The BNF was set up in 1967 to build bridges between industry, science and government.[41] By 1987 it had done this job effectively.

This analysis inevitably underestimates the number of scientists who receive funds from or act as advisors to the food industry. Since scientists often prefer not to disclose such links, the list is incomplete, and I shall be grateful for additional information.

MEMBERSHIP OF TWENTY-SEVEN GOVERNMENT ADVISORY COMMITTEES 1974–1987

SIR DONALD ACHESON. DHSS: COMA (Chairman, Main Cttee 84–). Chief Medical Officer of Health, DHSS 84–.

PROFESSOR COLIN ADAMS. DHSS: COMA (Heart Disease 84). Dept. Pathology, Guy's Hosp.

PROFESSOR RUSSELL ALLEN. MAFF: FSC –80 (Claims 80, Meat 80, Labelling 79, Water 78, Bread 74). Visiting Professor Applied Nutrition, Guy's Hosp.[42] President British Dietetic Assoc. Ex-Secretary Nutrition Society 57–62. *Ex-Director* Beecham (Head of Research 77–81). *Vice-President* BNF 86–. (*Governor* 78–, *Ex-Chairman* and *Vice-Chairman* 78–81, Industrial Scientists Cttee 67–78).[7] *Committee* FDF (*Ex-Chairman* Nutrition Working Grp 84–85, Nutritional Labelling Support Grp 84, Food Intolerance Working Grp 85, Labelling Panel 84)[43] FDF/FMF (Joint

Scientific Technical Cttee 83–85)[43,44] FMF (Scientific Advisory Cttee 66–78)[45] FDIC (Technical Cttee 80–83, *Ex-Chairman* Nutritional Working Grp 80–83)[44] *Member* BNF Dietary Guidelines Cttee 82.

GORDON AMERY. MAFF: Food Processing 86. *Employee*, Cooperative Wholesale Society (Central Labs.) *Committee* BNF (Industrial Scientists Cttee 84–.)[7] FDF/FMF (Joint Scientific and Technical Cttee 84–85)[43] FMF (Scientific Advisory Cttee 81–82)[45]

C.T. ASHTON. MAFF: FACC (Colours WP 79). *Ex-Employee* Scot Bowyers (cooked meats, sausages and pies).

DR MARGARET ASHWELL. MAFF: FAC 86–. Principal, Good Housekeeping Institute 86–. Secretary Nutrition Society 84–. Ex-Dunn Clinical Nutrition Centre, Cambridge. *Ex-Employee* Consumers' Association.

PROFESSOR FRANCIS AYLWARD. MAFF: FACC (Colours 79, Flavours 76). Emeritus Professor Food Science, Reading Univ. *Ex-Committee* FMF (Scientific Advisory Cttee 66–67).[45]

ALAN AZZARO. MAFF: FACC (Colours WP 79). MAFF.

DR JOYCE BAIRD. DHSS: COMA (Heart Disease 74). Dept. Medicine, Edinburgh Univ.

DR ANTHONY BAIRD-PARKER. MAFF: Food Safety 85, Food Quality 84. *Employee* Unilever Research (Section Manager).

ANNE BALLARD. MAFF: FAC 86–. General Secretary, National Federation of Womens' Institutes. *Committee* Celebration of British Food and Farming 89 (Food from Britain).

DR W.R. BANNATYNE. MAFF: FACC (Colours 79, Flavours 76). Principal, College of Food Technology, Glasgow.

ROBERT BEEDHAM. MAFF: FACC 75–. (Colours 79). *Ex-Director* Imperial Group Foods. *Ex-Employee* Smedley Foods (Chief Chemist).

GRAHAM BELCHAMBER. MAFF: FACC (Chairman Colours WP 79). MAFF.

PROFESSOR E.A. BELL. MAFF: Food Safety 85. Royal Botanic Gardens, Kew.

PROFESSOR RONALD BELL. MAFF: R and D Priorities 85. Chief Scientific Advisor, Ag, MAFF.

PROFESSOR ARNOLD BENDER. DHSS: COMA (Main Cttee –86), DHSS/MAFF: Irrad 86. Emeritus Professor Nutrition London Univ. Ex-Treasurer Nutrition Society 62–67. *Ex-Employee* Farleys Infant Foods (head research 61–64),[47] Bovril (head research 54–61).[46] *Ex-Committee* BNF (Information Cttee 77–80).[7] *Research funding* Bulmer 77–79, Cadbury Schweppes 76–79, Heinz 77–80, Kelloggs 79–80.[47] Ex-DHSS: COT.

DR ENID BENNETT. DHSS: COMA (Main Cttee 85–). Medical Research Council.

DR W.T.C. BERRY. DHSS: COMA (RDAs 81/69). DHSS. *Ex-Committee* BNF (Scientific Advisory Cttee 67–74).[7]

DR RICHARD BEVAN. DHSS: COMA (RDAs 81/79). Ex-Chief Medical Officer Welsh Office.

DR GORDON BIRCH. MAFF. Food Processing 86, National College of Food Technology, Reading Univ. *Research funding* Tate & Lyle (sugar) 75–83.[12]

SIR DOUGLAS BLACK. ARC/MRC: Food Research 74. Ex-Chief Scientist DHSS 73–77. Ex-President Royal College of Physicians 77–83. Ex-President British Medical Assoc. 84–85. Chairman BMA Board of Science and Education 85–. Chairman RCP Obesity Cttee 83, Fibre Cttee 80. *Governor* BNF 83–.[7] *Member* RCP/BNF Food Intolerance Cttee 84.

SIR KENNETH BLAXTER. Cabinet Office: ACARD (Food 82), ARC/MRC: Food Research 74. Ex-Director AFRC Rowett RI Aberdeen. Ex-President Nutrition Society 74–77. *Governor* BNF 73–86 (Editorial Advisory Board 81–), Scientific Advisory Cttee 70–74).

PROFESSOR G.C. BOND. MAFF: Food Surv. 84. Industrial Chemistry Dept, Brunel Univ.

M.J. BOXALL. MAFF: FAC 86–. *Employee* Tesco (company secretary).

PROFESSOR JAMES BRIDGES. DHSS/MAFF: Irrad 86. Director Robens Institute of Industrial Health & Safety, Surrey Univ. *Research funding* Beecham, ICI (agrichemicals) 76–?, Pfizer (agrichemicals) 83–86, Shell (agrichemicals) 82–85.[12]

DR PETER BRIGNELL. MAFF: FAC 83–84 (Colours 87), FACC 77–83 (Colours 79). *Employee* ICI (Manager, Corporate Intelligence).

DR MAURICE BROOK. MAFF: Food Safety 85. *Director* Research Beecham. *Committees* BNF (Industrial Scientists Cttee 79–.),[7] British Food Manufacturing Industries RA (Executive Cttee). *Member* RCP/BNF Food Intolerance Cttee.

PROFESSOR J.D. BU'LOCK. DHSS/MAFF Irrad 86. Dept. Microbiol. Chemistry, Manchester Univ. *Research funding* Pfizer (agrichemicals).[12]

DR HENRY BUNJÉ. DHSS: COMA (RDAs 81/79). Ex-Medical Research Council 57– 83.

DR P.J. BUNYAN. MAFF: Food Surv.84. MAFF.

SIR ARNOLD BURGEN. DHSS: Chairman, Irrad 86. Master Darwin College, Cambridge. *Director* Amersham International (Radio isotope manufacturer).[21]

SIR JOHN BUTTERFIELD. DHSS: COMA (RDAs 81/79, Heart Disease 74). Vice-Chancellor, Cambridge Univ. Master Downing College, Cambridge Univ. Regius Prof. Physic, Cambridge Univ. *Research Funding* Beecham 77-82.[12] National Association of British and Irish Millers.[48]

DR MAURICE CHAPMAN. MAFF: FSC 76–82. (Claims 80, Meat 80, Labelling 79, Water 78). Chief Trading Standards Officer, Gloucestershire.

SIR JAMES CLEMINSON, NEDC: Food and Drink 83. *President* Confederation of British Industries. *Chairman* Reckitt & Colman. *Ex-President* FMF 79–81.[45] *Ex-Chairman* FDF 83–84.[43] *Committees* FDF/FDIC (Executive Cttee 81–84, *Ex-Chairman* Economic Cttee

78, 80, member 78–82, Resource Cttee 80–82, *Ex-Chairman* Fair Trading Sub-Cttee 80).[43,44] *Ex-Governor* BNF 73–82.[7]

CHARLES COCKBILL. MAFF. Food Surv. 84. MAFF.

DR JANET COCKCROFT. MAFF: FACC (Colours 79, Flavours 76). Chairman Consumers Cttee for GB.

DR JOHN COLLINGWOOD. MAFF: FSC 72–79 (Claims 80, Meat 80, Labelling 79, Water 78, Bread 74). *Director* Unilever (Head of Research). Ex-Vice President Brit Assoc. for Advancement of Science. *Governor* BNF (*Ex-Treasurer* 78–82, Industrial Governor 70–77, Scientific Governor 77, 81–86).[7]

DR JOHN COLQUHOUN. MAFF: FACC 80–83. *Ex-Director* Rowntree Mackintosh (Products Research and Development Grp). *Ex-Governor* BNF 81–83.[7] *Vice-President* British Food Manufacturers Industries RA. *Committees* FDF (*Ex-Chairman* Research Working Grp 84),[43] FDIC (*Ex-Chairman* Technical Cttee 79–82, member 79–82, Nutrition Working Grp 80–82. *Ex-Chairman* Research Working Grp 84)[43,44] FMF/FDF (Joint Scientific and Technical Cttee 83–84, nominated by the Cocoa, Chocolate and Confectionery Alliance).[44]

T. COMERFORD. NEDC: Food and Drink 83. *Employee* ASTMS (Assoc of Scientific, Technical and Managerial Staffs).

PROFESSOR DAVID CONNING. Cabinet Office: ACARD (Food 82). *Director-General* BNF 85–. (Scientific Advisory Cttee 79–, Editorial Advisory Board 77–).[7] *Ex-Director* British Industrial Biological RA 78–85. *Ex-Committee* FDF/FMF (Joint Scientific and Technical Cttee 84–85),[45] FDF/FDIC (Technical Cttee 82–83),[43,44] FMF (Scientific Advisory Cttee 78–82).[45] *Member* BNF Sugars and Syrups Task Force 86.

PROFESSOR JOHN COPPOCK. ARC/MRC: Food Research 74. *Ex-Director* Research, Spillers/Dalgety (Flour, bread) 58–76. *Ex-Director* British Baking Industry RA 46–58.[49] *Ex-Committee* BNF (Industrial Scientists Cttee 67–75, Editorial Advisory Board 76–80).[7] Visiting Professor Food, Science and Nutrition, Surrey Univ.

DR JOHN CORDELL. MAFF: Food Processing 86. *Employee* Unilever 69–. (Fats and Bio-Processing).

DR REGINALD CRAMPTON. MAFF: FACC (Colours WP 79). *Ex-Director* British Industrial Biological RA. *Ex-Committee* BNF (Editorial Advisory Board 68–77). Scientific Advisory Cttee 70–77.[7] FMF (Scientific Advisory Cttee 69–77).[45] Working party ARC/MRC: Food Research 74. *Research funding* BNF 70-7[7]

DR GARETH CROMPTON. DHSS: COMA (Main Cttee). Chief Medical Officer, Welsh Office.

DR TOM CROSSETT. DHSS: COMA (Main Cttee). Chief Scientist, MAFF 85–.

DR JOHN CUMMINGS. DHSS: COMA (Main Cttee, Chairman Bread 81). MRC Dunn Clinical Nutrition Centre, Cambridge. *Committees* BNF (Scientific Advisory Cttee 81–.). *Research funding* BNF 72–73.[7]

PROFESSOR FRANK CURTIS. Cabinet Office: ACARD (Food 82). MAFF: Chairman FAC 83– (Colours 87); FSC 83– (Chairman 79–83, Claims 80, Meat 80, Labelling 79). *Director* AFRC Food RI, Norwich. *Ex-Employee* ICI 54–56. *Governor* BNF 80–86.[7] *Committees* British Food Manufacturing Industries RA, Campden Food Preservation RA. Working party ARC/MRC: Food Research 74.

NORMAN CURTIS. MAFF: Food Safety 85. *Director* Whitbread Breweries.

RICHARD DALLEY. MAFF: FSC (Claims 80, Meat 80, Labelling 79, Water 78, Bread 74). Public Analyst, West Yorkshire.

PROFESSOR NORMAN DANIELS. MAFF: Food Quality 84. *Director* Spillers/Dalgety (Head of Basic Research). *Committees* BNF (Industrial Scientists Cttee 82–.).[7]

DR SYLVIA DARKE. DHSS: COMA (Bread 81). DHSS. *Ex-Committee* BNF (Scientific Advisory Cttee 73–80).[7] Working party ARC/MRC: Food Research 74. *Member* DHSS/BNF/HEC Nutrition Education Cttee 77.

DR GEOFFREY DAVY. MAFF: FACC (Colours 79, Flavours 76). *Ex-Employee* ICI (Head Research & Development).

COLIN DENCE. MAFF: FSC 61–72 (Bread 74). *Ex-Director* Brand

and Co. (Ranks Hovis McDougall) *Ex-President* FMF (Scientific Advisory Cttee 67–68).[45]

DR HOWARD DENNER. MAFF: FACC (Colours WP 79). MAFF.

RON DICKER. MAFF: Food Processing 86. *Employee* Dairy Crest Foods. *Committee* FDF (Technical and Scientific Cttee 85–).[43]

ALAN DOWNING. MAFF: Food Processing 86. *Employee* Cadbury-Schweppes (Technical Director).

SIR KENNETH DURHAM. MAFF: Chairman, R and D Priorities 85. *Ex-Chairman* Unilever.

PROFESSOR JOHN DURNIN. DHSS: COMA (Main Cttee, Heart Disease 84, Bread 81, RDAs 81/79). Dept. of Physiology, Glasgow Univ. *Committees* BNF (Editorial Advisory Board 76–). *Advisor* Sugar Bureau.[11] *Research funding* Nestlé 80–85.[12]

PROFESSOR JACK EDELMAN. Cabinet Office: ACARD (Food 82). *Director* Research Ranks Hovis McDougall –86, *Council* Flour Milling and Baking RA. *Vice-Chairman* BNF (Industrial 86–), *Committees* BNF (Scientific Advisory Cttee 86–, Editorial Advisory Board 73–, Industrial Scientists Cttee 73–).[7] FDF (Research Working Grp 84).[43] FDIC (Technical Cttee 80–82).[44] *Advisor* National Association of British and Irish Millers. *Member* RCP/BNF Food Intol Cttee 84, BNF Dietary Guidelines Cttee 82.

MRS MARIE EDWARDS. MAFF: FAC 83–86 (Colours 87), FSC 82–83. Consultant in Home Economics. *Ex-Principal* Gloucestershire College of Higher Education.

PROFESSOR HAROLD EGAN. MAFF: FSC 66–80 (Claims 80, Meat 80, Labelling 79, Water 78, Bread 74). The Government Chemist. *Ex-Governor* BNF (Scientific Advisory Cttee 70–81).[7]

H.O.W. EGGINS. MAFF. FAC 86–. *Director* Bioquest. Editor Industrial Biodeterioration.

PROFESSOR S.R. ELSDON. ARC/MRC: Food Research 74. *Ex-Director* AFRC Food RI, Norwich 65-77.

DR WILLIAM ELSTOW. MAFF: Food Processing 86, FAC 83–85 (Colours 87), FACC 76–83 (Colours 79). *Director* Joint General Manager Weston Research Laboratories (Assoc. British Foods).

Council Flour Milling and Baking RA. *Committees* BNF (Industrial Scientists Cttee 75–).[7]

PROFESSOR GEORGE ELTON. MAFF: Chairman Food Surv. 84. DHSS: COMA (Main Cttee 85–, Bread 81, RDAs 81/79). Ex-Chief Scientist MAFF 70–. *Ex-Director* British Flour Milling and Baking RA 58–70. *Governor* BNF (Editorial Advisory Board 68–84).[7] *Ex-Committee* FMF (Scientific Advisory Cttee 68–69).[45]

DR PETER ELWOOD. DHSS: COMA (Bread 81). MRC Epidemiological Research Unit, Cardiff. *Committee* BNF (Scientific Advisory Cttee 73–77, Editorial Advisory Board 76–).[7]

TONY EMMERSON. NEDC: Food and Drink 83. *Vice-Chairman* UK National Management, Unilever. *Governor* BNF 80–84 (*Ex-Treasurer* –84). *Committee* BNF (Scientific Advisory Cttee 82–84)[7] *Ex-Chairman* FDIC 79–81 (Resources Cttee 75–78, 81–82, Economic Cttee 81–82).[44]

PROFESSOR ARTHUR EXTON-SMITH. DHSS: COMA (RDAs 81/79, 81/69). Geriatric Dept. Univ. College London. Member RCP Fibre Cttee 80.

FRANK FIRTH. MAFF: FACC (Colours WP 79). *Director* John F. Renshaw (Confectionery Supplier).

DR CHRISTOPHER FISHER. MAFF: FACC (Colours WP 79). MAFF.

DR G.I. FORBES. MAFF: Food Surv. 84. DHSS. (Scottish Home and Health Dept.).

SYDNEY FREE. Cabinet Office: ACARD (Food 82). *Ex-Director* Rowntree Mackintosh. *Committee* FDIC (Chairman External Trade Cttee 75–78, member 75–80)[44]

DR WILLIAM FULTON. MAFF: FAC 83–. (Colours 87), FSC 80–83, FACC 80– (Colours 79, Flavours 76). *Employee* Unilever (Senior Technical Member Food & Drink Co-ord). *Governor* BNF 85–.[7] *Committee* FMF (*Ex-Chairman* Scientific Advisory Cttee 73–76, member 66–72,[45] FDIC (*Ex-Chairman* Technical Cttee 75–78, member 75–83).[44]

KEN GARDNER. MAFF: FACC (Colours WP 79). *Employee* Mars (Research). *Committees* Cocoa, Chocolate and Confectionery

Alliance (Labelling Panel), FDF (Additives Working Grp 81–84, Nutrition Labelling Support Grp 83–85, Labelling Panel 83–85).[43]

DR JOHN GARROW. DHSS: COMA (Main Cttee, Bread 81). MRC Clinical Research Centre, Harrow. Member RCP Obesity Cttee 83. *Governor* BNF 83– (Editorial Advisory Board 76–, Scientific Advisory Cttee 77–).[7] *Research funding* Sugar Assoc.[13] Working party ARC/MRC: Food Research 74. *Member* BNF Sugar & Syrups Task Force 87. *Chairman* BNF/HEC NACNE Cttee 84–87.

DR DOUGLAS GEORGALA. Cabinet Office: ACARD (Chairman Food 82). *Employee* Unilever (Head Research). *Committee* BNF (Chairman Industrial Scientists Cttee 79–84),[7] FDF (Research Working Grp 84).[43]

DR R.J. GILBERT. MAFF: Food Safety 85. Public Health Laboratory Service.

SIR GEORGE GODBER. DHSS: COMA (Chairman, Main Cttee 60–73). Ex-Chief Medical Officer of Health DHSS 60–73. *Ex-Governor* BNF 70–76 (Scientific Advisory Cttee 67–76).[7]

MALCOLM GODFREY. DHSS: COMA (Main Cttee –85). Medical Research Council.

NATHAN GOLDENBERG. MAFF: FACC (Colours 79, Flavours 76). *Ex-Employee* Marks & Spencer (Chief Chemist). *Committee* BNF (Industrial Scientists Cttee 73–79, Information Cttee 76–78).[7]

TONY GOOD. NEDC: Food and Drink 83. MAFF: Chairman Food Quality 84. *Ex-Chairman* Express Dairies 84–. *Ex-Director* Grand Metropolitan. *Chairman* Technical Change Centre (*The UK Food Processing Industry*). *Committee* FDIC (Resources Cttee 83–84).[44]

DR THOMAS GORSUCH. MAFF. Chairman Food Processing 86, FAC 83– (Colours 87), FACC 78–83. *Director* Research and Quality Control Reckitt & Colman. *Committees* FDF (Research Working Grp 84),[43] FMF/FDF (Joint Scientific and Tech Cttee 84–85), FMF (Scientific Advisory Cttee 77–83).[45]

DR JAMES GOULD. DHSS/MAFF: Irrad 86. Director Central Microbiological Lab, Edinburgh.

PROFESSOR PAUL GRASSO. MAFF: Food Safety 85. Dept. Experimental Pathology Robens Institute. *Research funding* BP (agrichemicals) 84–87.[12] *Ex-Deputy Director* British Industrial Biological RA.

ALEX GRIFFITHS. MAFF: Food Quality 84. *Employee* Marks & Spencer (Senior Executive, Foods). *Committees* BNF (Industrial Scientists Cttee 79–85).[7]

JASPER GRINLING. NEDC: Food and Drink 83. MAFF: FAC 83–86. (Colours 87), FSC 79–83. Chairman Apple and Pear Development Council 86–. *Ex-Director* Corporate Affairs, Grand Metropolitan (Government and Trade Relations, EEC and UK). *Committees* FDF/FDIC (Chairman European CIAA delegation 75–84, Lomé Working Party 83–84, Resources Cttee 83–84).[43,44]

DAPHNE GROSE. MAFF: FAC 83–86 (Colours 87), Food Safety 85, FSC 80–83. Head of Representation Consumers Assoc. *Committees* BNF (Information Cttee 78–85).[7]

PROFESSOR MICHAEL GURR. DHSS: COMA (Main Cttee 86–). *Employee* Milk Marketing Board (nutritional consultant).[50] *Ex-Director* AFRC Food RI, Reading (previously National Inst for Research in Dairying) 79–86. *Ex-Employee* Unilever 67–79. *Committee* BNF (Scientific Advisory Cttee) 81–. *Consultant* food industry.[51] *Advisor* Dairy Trades Federation/Milk Marketing Board.[18] *Research funding* Dairy Trades Federation/Milk Marketing Board.[12]

SIR RONALD HALSTEAD. MAFF: R and D Priorities 85. *Ex-Chairman* Beecham 84–85. *Ex-Chairman* BNF 70–71, 72–73 (*Governor* 67–80)[7] Executive Cttee 70–78, Information Cttee 71–73)[7] *Ex-President* FMF 73–75.[45] *Governor* National College of Food Technology. Confederation of British Industry (*Chairman* Marketing and Consumer Affairs).

DR J.H. HAMENCE. MAFF: FACC (Colours 79, Flavours 76). Public Analyst, Official Ag. Analyst.

A.J. HARRISON. MAFF: FAC 83–. (Colours 87), FACC (Colours 79, Flavours 76). Chief Public Analyst, Avon and Gloucestershire.

R. HARRISON. NEDC: Food and Drink 83. *Employee* T & GWU (Transport and General Workers' Union).

PROFESSOR JOHN HAWTHORN. DHSS/MAFF: Irrad 86. Dept. Bioscience and Biotechnology, Strathclyde Univ. *Advisor* British

Food Manufacturing Industries RA. *Advisor* FMF.[26] *Committee* BNF (Editorial Advisory Board 73–.)[7] *Member* BNF Sugars & Syrups Task Force 86.

RICHARD HINTON. MAFF (Colours WP 79). *Ex-Director* Campden Food Preservation RA 68–78. *Ex-Committees* BNF (Editorial Advisory Board 68–78).[7] FMF (Scientific Advisory Cttee 68–78).[45]

PROFESSOR MALCOLM HODKINSON. DHSS: COMA (Main Cttee 87–) Dept. Geriatric Medicine, University College London.

DR W HOLLAND. DHSS: COMA (Nutr. Surv. 86). Dept. Social Medicine, St Thomas's Hosp.

DOROTHY HOLLINGSWORTH. DHSS: COMA (RDAs 81/79, 81/69, Heart Disease 74). ARC/MRC: Food Research 74. Ex-Secretary-General International Union of Nutritional Sciences 78–85. MAFF 41–70. Ex-Secretary Nutrition Society 62–65. *Ex-Director-General* BNF 70-77 (Editorial Advisory Board 77–, Scientific Advisory Cttee 74–).[7] *Member* DHSS/BNF/HEC Nutrition Education Cttee 77.

PROFESSOR ALAN HOLMES. Cabinet Office: ACARD (Food 82). Director British Food Manufacturing Industries RA. *Ex-Employee* Unilever.[52] *Committees* BNF (Executive Cttee 76–, Editorial Advisory Board 68–, Scientific Advisory Cttee 83–).[7] *Committees* Cocoa, Chocolate and Confectionery Alliance (Scientific Cttee), FMF/FDF (Joint Scientific and Tech Cttee 83–85),[45] FMF (Scientific Advisory Cttee 66–82).[45] Technical Change Centre (*The UK Food Processing Industry*).

HARRY HOUGHTON. MAFF: FACC (Colours WP 79). *Employee* Cadbury Schweppes (Information Officer). *Committee* BNF (Industrial Scientists Cttee 67–68).[7] *Committee* FDF/FDIC (Nutrition Labelling Support Grp 84, Water Quality Working Grp 80–84),[43,44] FMF (Scientific Advisory Cttee 68–69).[45]

H.W. HUBBARD. MAFF: FACC 69-73 (Flavours 76). Lab of the Govt. Chemist.

DR FRANK HYTTEN. DHSS: COMA (Main Cttee 84–86). Dept of Child Health, MRC Clinical Research Centre, Harrow.

PROFESSOR MAURICE INGRAM. MAFF: FACC (Colours 79, Flavours 760) ARC/MRC: Food Research 74. Dept Applied Microbiology, Bristol Univ. Ex-director AFRC Meat RI.

DR A.T. JAMES. ARC/MRC: Food Research 74. *Employee* Unilever (Manager, Biosciences Grp).

PROFESSOR PHILIP JAMES. DHSS: COMA (Heart Disease 84). DHSS/MAFF: Irrad 86. MAFF: FAC 83– (Colours 87), FSC 78–83 (Claims 80, Meat 80, Labelling 79). Director AFRC Rowett RI[9], Aberdeen. Vice-Chairman NACNE Cttee 79-84. Chairman NACNE Sub-Cttee 80–84. Member RCP Obesity Cttee 83, Fibre Cttee 80. *Ex-Committee* BNF (Scientific Advisory Cttee 77–83, Editorial Advisory Cttee 77–83, resigned).[7] *Research funding* Nestlé,[24] Rank Prize Fund.[24] *Member* BNF/HEC NACNE Cttee 84–87.

DR HAROLD JASPERSON. MAFF: FACC (Colours 79, Flavours 76). *Ex-Employee* Bibby (Edible Oils Manufacturer) (Head Research.) *Ex-Committee* FMF (Scientific Advisory Cttee 66–76).[45]

PROFESSOR J.L. JINKS. MAFF: R and D Priorities 85. Deputy Chairman AFRC.

PROFESSOR HARRY KEEN. DHSS: COMA (Main Cttee; Heart Disease 84, 74). Dept. Medicine Guy's Hosp. Contributor RCP Heart Disease Cttee 76 (Chapter on Diabetes). *Ex-Committee* BNF (Scientific Advisory Cttee 77–83).[7] *Advisor* Sugar Bureau.[14] *Research funding* International Sugar Research Foundation,[15] World Sugar Research Organisation 73–83,[16] British Sugar Bureau 81–83.[12]

DR N.J. KING. MAFF: Food Surv. 84. Dept of Environment.

DR EGON KODICEK. DHSS: COMA (RDAs 81/69, 81/69). ARC/MRC: Food Research 74. *Ex-Director* MRC Dunn Clinical Nutrition Centre, Cambridge 63-73. *Ex-President* Nutrition Society 71–74. *Committee* BNF (Scientific Advisory Cttee) 68–76.[7] *Research funding* BNF 70.[7]

SIR HANS KORNBERG. MAFF: R and D Priorities 85. Dept Biochemistry Cambridge Univ. Member Cabinet Office Advisory Council for Applied Research and Development (ACARD).

SIR HECTOR LAING. NEDC: Food and Drink 83. *Chairman* United Biscuits. *Ex-Chairman* FDIC 77–78 (Resources Cttee

80–82), FDF (Fair Trading Steering Cttee 85). BNF (Industrial Governor 73–76).

PROFESSOR P.J. LAWTHER. MAFF. Food Surv. 84. *Consultant.*

FRANK LEY. DHSS: Irrad 86. *Director* Isotron (Food irradiation).

DR R.C. LITTLE. MAFF. Food Surv. 84. MAFF.

PROFESSOR JUNE LLOYD. DHSS: COMA (Main Cttee, Bread 81, Heart Disease 74). MAFF: FACC 82–83. Dept. Child Health St George's Hosp. Member RCP Heart Disease Cttee 76. *Governor* BNF 73– (Scientific Advisory Cttee 73–77).[7]

PROFESSOR IAN MACDONALD. MAFF: FAC 83–86 (Colours 87), FACC 77–83 (Colours 79). Dept. Applied Physiology Guy's Hosp. Ex-President Nutrition Society 80–83. *Chairman* BNF 85– (*Vice-Chairman* 81–83, *Governor* 73–, Scientific Advisory Cttee 70–, Editorial Advisory Board 81–83).[7] *Advisor* (*Chairman*) Dairy Trades Federation/Milk Marketing Board.[18] *Research funding* Cadbury 69,[27] Beecham 63–66, 73–74,[28-36] Glaxo 65,[28,29] Milk Marketing Board 77,[37] Lord Rank Trust 72–73.[38-40] *Member* BNF Sugars and Syrups Task Force 87.

DR I.S. MACDONALD. DHSS: COMA (Main Cttee). Chief Medical Officer, Scottish Home and Health Dept. 86–.

DR BARBARA MACGIBBON. MAFF: Food Safety 85, Food Surv. 84. DHSS.

DR JOHN MCGUINNESS. MAFF: FACC (Colours WP 79). MAFF.

DR DONALD MCLAREN. MAFF: FAC 83–86. (Colours 87), FACC 77–83 (Colours 79). Reader Dept. Medicine, Royal Infirmary, Edinburgh.

CATHERINE MCMASTER. MAFF: FSC 77–80 (Claims 80, Meat 80, Labelling 79). Senior Lecturer Home Economics, Queen Margaret College, Edinburgh.

ROGER MANLEY. MAFF: FAC 83– (Colours 87), FSC 82–83. Controller Trading Standards, Cheshire.

DR JIM MANN. DHSS: COMA (Heart Disease 84). Dept. Social and Community Medicine Oxford Univ. Member RCP Obesity Cttee 83. *Research Funding* Unilever (Flora margarine) 79–85,[12]

World Sugar Research Organisation 81–83.[16] *Member* BNF/HEC NACNE Cttee 84–87.

J. MARINO. NEDC: Food and Drink 83. *Employee* Bakers', Food and Allied Workers' Union.

PROFESSOR J.S. MARSH. NEDC: Food and Drink 83. Dept of Ag, Reading Univ. *Advisor* British Food Manufacturing Industries RI.

G. MARTIN. NEDC: Food and Drink 83. *Employee* USDAW (Union of Shop, Distributive and Allied Workers).

JOHN MARTIN. MAFF: R and D Priorities 85. *Owner* Farm, Cambridgeshire.

DR TOM MEADE. DHSS: COMA (Main Cttee 86–). Director MRC Clinical Research Centre, Epidemiology Unit, Harrow. *Member* BNF Sugars and Syrups Task Force, 87.

R. MEARS. MAFF: FACC (Colours WP 79). *Ex-Employee* Allied Lyons (Laboratory Manager).

DR COLIN MILLS. DHSS: COMA (Bread 81). AFRC Rowett RI, Aberdeen. Working party ARC/MRC: Food Research 74.

DR R.D.G. MILNER. DHSS: COMA (Nutr Surv. 86). Dept. of Child Health, Sheffield Univ.

PROFESSOR TONY MITCHELL. DHSS: COMA (Heart Disease 84, 74). Dept. of Medicine, Nottingham Univ. *Research funding* Pfizer (agrichemicals).[17]

JOHN MOFFITT. MAFF: R and D Priorities 85. *Owner* Farm, Northumberland.

J. MOORE. NEDC: Food and Drink 83. *Employee* United Road Transport Union.

PROFESSOR JERRY MORRIS. DHSS: COMA (Bread 81, Heart Disease 74). Emeritus Professor Epidemiology London Univ. Chairman NACNE Cttee 79–84. Member RCP Fibre Cttee 80. *Ex-Governor* BNF 71–84 (*Vice-Chairman* 77–78, resigned;

Scientific Advisory Cttee 77–78, Editorial Advisory Board 77–78).[7]
Member BNF Dietary Guidelines Cttee 82.

DR B.E.B. MOSELEY. DHSS/MAFF: Irrad 86. Microbiology Dept. Edinburgh Univ.

PROFESSOR K.A. MUNDAY. ARC/MRC: Food Research 74. Dept. Physiology and Biochemistry, Southampton Univ. *Research funding* ICI (agrichemicals) 81–?[12]

G.J. MURRAY. MAFF: Food Surv. 84. DHSS (Scottish Home and Health Dept.).

DR NICHOLAS MYANT. DHSS: COMA (Heart Disease 84). MRC Lipid Metabolism Unit, Hammersmith Hosp.

G.E. MYERS. NEDC: Food and Drink 83. MAFF.

PROFESSOR DON NAISMITH. DHSS: COMA (Main Cttee 87–) Dept Nutrition London Univ. Ex-Secretary Nutrition Soc 75–80. *Advisor* Snack Nut and Crisp Manufacturers Association.[19] *Committee* BNF (Scientific Advisory Cttee 83–).

PROFESSOR ALBERT NEUBERGER. ARC/MRC: Chairman Food Research 74. Emeritus Professor Chemical Pathology Charing Cross Hosp. *President* BNF 82–86 (Ex-Officio Governor 82–86, Scientific Advisory Cttee 74–82). *Member* BNF Sugars & Syrups Task Force 86.

PROFESSOR JOHN NORRIS. MAFF: Chairman Food Safety 85. FACC 76–83 (Colours 79). *Director* Research Cadbury Schweppes. Ex-Director AFRC Meat RI 76–79, *Advisor* British Food Manufacturing Industries RA (Research Co-ordination Cttee). *Committees* FDF (Biotechnology Working Grp 82–84, Research Working Grp 84, nominated by Cocoa, Chocolate and Confectionery Alliance).[43]

J.A. O'KEEFE. MAFF: FSC 61–76 (Claims 80, Meat 80, Labelling 79, Water 78). *Barrister*.

PROFESSOR MICHAEL OLIVER. DHSS: COMA (Heart Disease 84, 74). Cardiovascular Research Unit Edinburgh Univ. Member RCP Heart Disease Cttee 76.

PROFESSOR THOMAS OPPÉ. DHSS: COMA (Main Cttee, RDAs 81/79, 81/69). Paediatric Unit St. Mary's Hosp. *Research funding* British American Tobacco (inc. International Stores) 81-83.[12]

T.J. ORGAN. NEDC: Food and Drink 83. *Managing Director* Cadbury Schweppes.

DR W.E. PARISH. MAFF. Food Surv. 84. *Employee* Unilever Research 74–.

PROFESSOR DENIS PARKE. MAFF: FACC (Colours 79, Flavours 76). Dept. Biochemistry Surrey Univ. *Ex-Employee* Glaxo 49. *Research Funding* Beecham, British American Tobacco 79–85.[12]

DR DENNIS PARSONS. DHSS: COMA (Bread 81). Dept. Biochemistry Oxford Univ.

DR REG PASSMORE. DHSS: COMA (Chairman RDAs 81/69, RDAs 81/79, Heart Disease 74). MAFF: FSC (Claims 80, Meat 80, Labelling 79, Water 78, Bread 74). Emeritus Reader Physiology Edinburgh Univ. *Committees* BNF (Scientific Advisory Cttee 67–81, Editorial Advisory Board 67–).[7] Working party ARC/MRC: Food Research 74.

PHILIP PAYNE. DHSS: COMA (Nutr. Surv. 86). Dept Human Nutrition London Univ. *Committee* BNF (Scientific Advisory Cttee 77–80) *Research funding*: Nestlé 80–82, Rank Prize Fund 76–?[24]

JACK PHILP. MAFF: FACC (Colours WP 79). *Ex-Employee* Unilever (Environmental Safety Officer). *Committee* BNF (Industrial Scientists' Cttee 67–81)[7] Member MAFF/DHSS: COT.

MRS G.L.S. PIKE. MAFF: FSC 77– (Claims 80, Meat 80, Labelling 79, Water 78, Bread 74). Magistrate. *Ex-Committee* BNF (Information Cttee 72–81).[7]

PROFESSOR B.S. PLATT. DHSS: COMA (RDAs 81/69). Emeritus Professor London Univ.

PROFESSOR JEFFERY PORTER. MAFF: FACC 79–82. *Ex-Director* National Inst for Research in Dairying. *Ex-Governor* BNF 77–83.[7] Working party ARC/MRC: Food Research 74.

WILLIAM PRICE-DAVIES. MAFF: FACC 75–83 (Colours 79). *Ex-Managing Director* Cadbury Schweppes (*Ex-Director* Concentrates and Essences Division). FMF (*Ex-Chairman* Soft Drinks

Section 77–82). (Scientific Advisory Cttee 66–67).[45] *Governor* BNF (Industrial) 67–83.[7]

J.D. PRITCHARD-BARRETT. NEDC: Food and Drink 83. *Director* Whitbread.

PROFESSOR LEO PYLE. MAFF: Food Processing 86. Dept. Food Science and Technology, Reading Univ. 85–.

PROFESSOR SIR PHILIP RANDLE. DHSS: COMA (Main Cttee, Chairman Heart Disease 84). Professor Clinical Biochemistry Oxford Univ. Member RCP Fibre Cttee 80. Working party ARC/MRC: Food Research 74.

ANDREW RAVEN. MAFF: R and D Priorities 85. Scientific Advisor MAFF (Scotland).

PROFESSOR SIR JOHN REID. DHSS: COMA (Main Cttee 86–, RDAs 81/79). Chief Medical Officer, Scottish Home and Health Dept 86–.

SIR PETER REYNOLDS. NEDC: Food and Drink 83. *Chairman* Ranks Hovis McDougall. *Committee* FDF/FDIC. (*Ex-Chairman* Resources Cttee 83–85, *Ex-Chairman* Working Party 83–84 Member 80–85.[43,44]

PROFESSOR GEOFFREY ROSE. DHSS: COMA (Heart Disease 84). Dept. Epidemiology, London Univ. Chairman WHO Heart Disease Cttee 82. Member RCP Heart Disease Cttee 76.

JOHN SAUNDERS. MAFF: FACC (Colours 79, Flavours 76). *Ex-Employee* Cerebos (Rank Hovis McDougall) (Chief Research Chemist).

R. SAWYER. MAFF: FACC (Colours 79, Flavours 76). Ex-Employee Lab Government Chemist (Superintendent Food & Nutrition Division 73–85). *Committee* BNF (Scientific Advisory Cttee 82–85).[7]

PROFESSOR PATRICIA SCOTT. MAFF: FACC (Colours 79, Flavours 76). Dept. Nutrition and Physiology, Royal Free Hosp. *Ex-Treasurer* Nutrition Society.

PROFESSOR JERRY SHAPER. DHSS: COMA (Main Cttee 80–85). Dept. Clinical Epidemiology Royal Free Hosp. Member RCP Heart Disease Cttee 76.

J.B. SHARP. MAFF. Food Surv. 84. DHSS.

DAVID SHORE. Cabinet Office: ACARD (Food 82) *Managing Director* A.P.V. Holdings (Engineering). *Chairman* British Food Manufacturing Industries RA. *Committee* Technical Change Centre (*the UK Food Processing Industry*). FDF/FMF (Joint Scientific and Technical Cttee 83–.)[45]

DR DEREK SHRIMPTON. MAFF: Food Quality 84. *Ex-Director General* BNF 82–84 (resigned). *Ex-Treasurer* Nutrition Society 72–77. *Ex-Employee* Unilever (animal feeds 78–82) *Committee* BNF (Editorial Advisory Board 82–84, Scientific Advisory Cttee 82–84)[7] *Member* RCP/BNF Food Intol Cttee 84. *Observer* BNF Sugars and Syrups Task Force 87.

W.J. SKINNER. NEDC: Food and Drink 83. National Economic Development Office.

ANTHONY SKRIMSHIRE. MAFF: FAC 86 – Food Processing 86. *Employee* Heinz (General Manager, Research Development and Quality Assurance). *Council* BNF 86–.[7] *Committee* FDF (Scientific and Technical Cttee).[43] FMF (Ex-Chairman of Section 71–77, member Sugar Panel 78–81) FDF/FMF (Joint Scientific and Technical Cttee 83–85).[45]

DR H. SMITH. DHSS/MAFF: Irrad 86. Dept. of Biology, National Radiological Protection Board.

DR JOE SMITH. DHSS: COMA (Main Cttee 85–). Director, Public Health Lab Service 86–.

R. SMITH. NEDC: Food and Drink 83. *Employee* GMWU (General and Municipal Workers' Union).

PROFESSOR D.H. SMYTH. ARC/MRC Food Research 74. Dept. of Physiology, Sheffield Univ.

C.C.E. SOPP. MAFF: FSC 67–73 (Bread 74). Chief Weights & Measures Inspector, Berkshire.

DR DAVID SOUTHGATE. DHSS: COMA (Bread 81). Head Nutrition and Food Quality AFRC Food RI, Norwich. Member RCP Fibre Cttee 80. *Committee* BNF (Editorial Advisory Board, 82–.

Scientific Advisory Cttee 82–).[7] Working party ARC/MRC Food Research 74. *Research funding* BNF 70–71.[7]

GEORGE STAINSBURY. MAFF: Food Quality 84. Reader Food Science Leeds Univ.

RITA STEPHEN. NEDC: Food and Drink 83. MAFF: FSC 80– (Claims 80, Meat 80, Labelling 79, Water 78, Bread 74). *Employee* Assoc of Professional, Executive and Computer Staff (APEX).

DR ALEXANDER STOTT. DHSS/MAFF: Irrad 86. Chief Medical Officer, UK Atomic Energy Authority.

DR A.J. SWALLOW. DHSS/MAFF: Irrad 86. Dept. of Oncology, Univ. of Manchester. Patterson Lab. Christie Hosp. and Holt Radium Inst.

J. TANNER. DHSS: COMA (Nutr. Surv. 86). Institute of Child Health, London Univ.

GEOFFREY TELLING. MAFF: FACC 82–83. *Employee* Unilever (Head Trace Analysis Grp). *Committee* FDF/FDIC (Chairman Residues and Contaminants Working Grp 80–85).[43,44]

MALCOLM THAIN. MAFF: Food Quality 84. Director, Tropical Devt. and Research Inst.

PROFESSOR ANGUS THOMSON. DHSS: COMA (RDAs 81/69). Ex-Director MRC Reproduction & Growth Unit Newcastle Upon Tyne. *Governor* BNF 77.[7] Working party ARC/MRC: Food Research 74.

PROFESSOR STEWART TRUSWELL. DHSS: COMA (RDAs 81/69). Professor Human Nutrition Sydney Univ. Ex-Professor Nutrition London Univ. Member RCP Heart Disease Cttee 76. *Governor* BNF 72–77 (Scientific Advisory Cttee 73–77 [Chair 75–76]), Editorial Advisory Board 70–74, 76–77).[7] *Research funding* Bulmer,[48] Heinz,[53] World Sugar Research Organisation 82–85.[16]

ALAN TURNER. MAFF: FAC 83– (Colours 87), FSC 79–83. *Employee* Cadbury Schweppes (Chief Chemist). *Committees* FDF (Additives Working Grp, Nutrition Labelling Support Grp (Labelling Panel),[43] FDF/FMF (Joint Scientific and Tech Cttee 83–85, nominated by Cake and Biscuit Alliance).[45] FMF (Food and Drugs

Act Working Grp, Food Labelling Cttee, Scientific Advisory Cttee 73–82),[45] FDIC (Technical Cttee 80–83, General Additives Working Grp 80–81, 83–84, Nutrition Working Grp 80–83, Labelling Panel 80–85, Weights and Measures Panel 80–85, Food and Drugs Working Party 83–84, Support Grp on Nutritional Labelling 84).[44]

DR MICHAEL TURNER. DHSS: COMA (Bread 81). *Ex-Director General* BNF 77–82. (Editorial Advisory Board 77–82, Scientific Advisory Cttee 77–82).[7] *Advisor* National Dairy Council.[54] *Member* NACNE Cttee 79–82. *Member* BNF Dietary Guidelines Cttee 82.

PROFESSOR PAUL TURNER. MAFF: FAC 83–. (Colours 87), FACC 76–83 (Colours 79). DHSS/MAFF: Irrad 86. Dept. Clinical Pharmacology, Barts Hosp. DHSS: Chairman COT. *Research funding* ICI (agrichemicals) 71–? Hoechst (agrichemicals) 78–?[12]

DR RONALD WALKER. MAFF: Food Safety 85. Reader in Food Science, Surrey Univ.

PROFESSOR ALAN WARD. MAFF: FSC 79– (Chairman Claims 80, Meat 80, Labelling 79, Water 78, Bread 74). ARC/MRC: Food Research 74. Emeritus Professor Food and Leather Science, Leeds Univ. *Governor* BNF 77– (Executive Cttee). *Ex-Chairman* (Scientific Advisory Cttee 80–83; Cttee 67–84).[7]

DAVID WARD. MAFF: FACC 81–82. *Ex-Employee* Unilever/Birds Eye Walls (General Manager Development & Quality).

PROFESSOR JOHN WATERLOW. DHSS: COMA (RDAs 81/79). ARC/MRC: Food Research 74. (Chairman). Emeritus Professor Human Nutrition London Univ. *Ex-chairman* BNF 76–77 (*Vice-Chairman* 75–76, Governor 71–, Editorial Advisory Board 76–, Scientific Advisory Cttee 72– (Chair 77–80)). *Research funding* Nestlé 80–82,[12] Rank Prize Fund 75–,[24] BNF 71–72.[7] *Member* BNF Dietary Guidelines Cttee 82.

PROFESSOR BASIL WEEDON. MAFF: FACC 68–83 (Chairman Colours 79, Flavours 76). Vice-Chancellor, Nottingham Univ.

PROFESSOR B.G.F. WEITZ. ARC/MRC: Food Research 74. *Ex-Director* National Inst for Research in Dairying.

DR ANDREW WHEATLEY. MAFF: Food Processing 86. Dept. Bio-technology, Cranfield Inst. of Tech. 86–.

DR ALAN WHITEAR. MAFF: Food Processing 86. *Employee* Whitbread.

DR JOHN WHITEHEAD. DHSS: COMA (Main Cttee −86), DHSS/MAFF: Irrad 86. Director, Public Health Lab Service 81−85.

DR ROGER WHITEHEAD. DHSS: COMA (Main Cttee, Nutr. Surv. 86, Bread 81, RDAs 81/79). *Head* MRC Dunn Clinical Nutrition Centre, Cambridge 73−. *Governor* BNF 73−. (Scientific Advisory Cttee 73−80).[7] Working party ARC/MRC: Food Research 74. *Advisor* Dairy Trades Federation/Milk Marketing Board.[18] *Research Funding* Nestlé, Rank Prize Fund.[24] *Member* BNF Dietary Guidelines Cttee 82.

DR ELSIE WIDDOWSON. DHSS: COMA (Bread 81, RDAs 81/79, 79/69). Dept. Medicine Cambridge Univ. Ex-President Nutrition Society 77−80. *President* BNF 86−. BNF (Scientific Advisory Cttee 78−, Editorial Advisory Board 86−).[7] Working party ARC/MRC: Food Research 74.

PROFESSOR ERNEST WILLIAMS. MAFF: FACC (Colours 79, Flavours 76). *Ex-Director* Research, Sainsbury. *Committees* BNF (Editorial Advisory Board 73−).[7] Working party ARC/MRC: Food Research 74. FMF (Scientific Advisory Cttee 68−73).[45]

SIR ROBERT WILLIAMS. DHSS: COMA (RDAs 81/79). *Ex-Director* Public Health Lab. Service.

PROFESSOR E.D. WILLS. DHSS/MAFF: Irrad 86. Emeritus Professor, Dept of Biochemistry, Barts Hosp.

DR J.M.G. WILSON. DHSS: COMA (Heart Disease 74). DHSS.

FRANK WOOD. MAFF: FSC −79. (Claims 80, Meat 80, Labelling 79, Water 78, Bread 74). *Director* Corn Products Corp. UK. *Ex-President* International Glucose Federation. *Ex-Committee* BNF (Industrial Scientists Cttee 70−80).[7] FMF (Scientific Advisory Cttee 66−80)[45] FDIC (Technical Cttee 80−81)[44]

PROFESSOR A. WORDEN. MAFF: Food Safety 85. Fellow Wolfson College Cambridge.

DR JOHN WREN. MAFF: Food Surv. 84, Food Quality 84. *Director* Gatehouse (Grand Metropolitan). *Committees* FDF (*Chairman* Working grp on tomorrow's food industry.[55]

DR WYNN GRIFFITH. DHSS: COMA (Heart Disease 74). DHSS.

SIR HENRY YELLOWLEES. DHSS: COMA (Chairman Main Cttee 73–84, Chairman RDAs 81/79). Ex-Chief Medical Officer of Health DHSS 73–84. *Governor* BNF 76– (Chairman Scientific Advisory Cttee) 83–.[7]

DR LESLEY YEOMANS. MAFF: Food Quality 84, FACC 81–83. Research Manager, Consumers' Assoc.

DR ELSPETH YOUNG. MAFF: FAC 86– Senior Registrar Dermatology John Radcliffe Hosp. Oxford.

SIR FRANK YOUNG. DHSS: COMA (Chairman Bread 81; RDAs 81/79, 79/69; Chairman Heart Disease 74). Emeritus Professor Biochemistry Cambridge Univ. Ex-Chairman Smith Kline and French Trustees UK.[46] *Ex-President* BNF 73–75 (Scientific Governor 67–70, 75–80, Scientific Advisory Cttee 74–78, Editorial Advisory Cttee 73–76).[7] *Ex-Scientific Governor* British Industries Biological RA. *Member* DHSS/BNF/HEC Nutrition Education Cttee 77.

PROFESSOR JOHN YUDKIN. DHSS: COMA (RDAs 81/79, 79/69, Heart Disease 74). Emeritus Professor Nutrition, London Univ. *Advisor* Unilever, Ranks Hovis McDougall, Dairy Council, Heinz etc.[56] *Research Funding* Billingtons (sugar).[47]

MEMBERSHIP OF FIVE BRITISH NUTRITION FOUNDATION COMMITTEES 1977-1987.

PROFESSOR RUSSELL ALLEN. BNF: Diet 82. Visiting Professor Applied Nutrition, Guys Hosp.[42] President British Dietetic Assoc. Ex-Secretary Nutrition Society 57–62. *Ex-Director* Beecham (Head of Research 77–81). *Vice-President* BNF 86–. (*Governor* 78–, *Ex-Chairman* and *Vice-Chairman* 78–81, Industrial Scientists Cttee 67–78).[7] *Committees* FDF (*Ex-Chairman*: Nutrition Working Group 84–85, Nutritional Labelling Support Grp 84, Food Intolerance Working Grp 85, Labelling Panel 84).[43] FDF/FMF (Joint Scientific Technical Cttee 83–85,[43,44] FMF (Scientific Advisory Cttee 66–78),[45] FDIC (Technical Cttee 80–83, *Ex-Chairman* Nutritional Working Grp 80–83,[43,44] FMF (Scientific Advisory

Cttee 66–78),[45] FDIC (Technical Cttee 80–83, *Ex-Chairman* Nutritional Working Grp 80–83.[44] Member MAFF: FSC –80 (Claims 80, Meat 80, Labelling 79, Water 78, Bread 74).

SIR DOUGLAS BLACK. RCP/BNF: Food Intol 84. Ex-Chief Scientist DHSS 73–77. *Ex-President* Royal College Physicians 77–83. *Ex-President* British Medical Assoc 84–85. *Chairman* BMA Board of Science and Education 85–. *Chairman* RCP Obesity Cttee 83, Fibre Cttee 80. *Governor* BNF 83–.[7] Member ARC/MRC Food Research 74.

DR DAVID BOOTH. BNF: Sugars 87. Dept. Psychology Birmingham Univ. *Research Funding* Unilever 84–87,[12] Beecham 84–85,[12] British American Tobacco 79–82,[12] BNF 71–72.[7]

PAM BRERETON. BNF/HEC Member NACNE Cttee 79–84. JACNE 85. District Dietician.

DR MAURICE BROOK. RCP/BNF: Food Intol. 84. *Director* Research Beecham. *Committees* BNF (Industrial Scientists Cttee) 79–.[7] British Food Manufacturing Industries RA (Executive Cttee). *Member* MAFF: Food Safety 85.

DR DAVID BUSS. BNF: Sugar 87. Head of Nutrition, MAFF. *Committee* BNF Scientific Advisory Cttee. 77–.[7]

SIR CYRIL CLARKE. BNF: Chairman Sugars 87. *Ex-President* Royal College of Physicians 72–77.

PROFESSOR DAVID CONNING. BNF: Sugars 84. *Director-General* BNF 85– (Scientific Advisory Cttee 79–, Editorial Advisory Board 77–.)[7] *Ex-Director* British Industrial Biological RA 78–85. *Committee* FDF/FMF (Joint Scientific and Technical Cttee 84–85)[45] FDF/FDIC (Technical Cttee 82–83)[43,44] FMF (Scientific Advisory Cttee 78–82).[45] *Member* Cabinet Office: ACARD (Food 82).

AUGUSTA CONRY. RCP/BNF Food Intol 84, BNF: Diet 82. District Dietitian General Infirmary Leeds. *Committees* BNF (Scientific Advisory Cttee 77–).[7]

RICHARD COTTRELL. BNF/HEC: JACNE 85. BNF: Sugars 87. *Science Director* BNF 84–.[7] *Ex-employee* British Industrial Biological RA. *Advisor* Dairy Trades Federation/Milk Marketing Board.[18]

SYLVIA DARKE. DHSS/BNF/HEC Nutr. Educ. 77. DHSS. *Ex-Committee* BNF (Scientific Advisory Cttee 73–80).[7] Member DHSS: COMA (Bread 81). Working party ARC/MRC: Food Research 74.

JASMINE DOWN. BNF/HEC: JACNE 85. Home Economics Advisor. *Member* NACNE Cttee 79–84.

PROFESSOR JACK EDELMAN. RCP/BNF: Food Intol 84. BNF: Diet 82. *Director* research Ranks Hovis McDougall –86 *Council* Flour Milling and Baking RA, *Vice-Chairman* BNF (Industrial 86–). *Committees* BNF (Scientific Advisory Cttee 86–, Editorial Advisory Board 73–, Industrial Scientists Cttee 73–.)[7] FDF (Research Working Grp).[43] FDIC (Technical Cttee 80–82).[44] *Advisor* National Association of British and Irish Millers.[48] *Member* Cabinet Office: ACARD (Food 82).

PROFESSOR MICHAEL EDGAR. BNF: Sugars 87. Dental Dept. Royal Hosp. Liverpool. *Research funding* Mars,[25] World Sugar Research Organisation 82–84,[16] Sugar Assoc, Cocoa Chocolate and Confectionery Alliance.[12]

DR ANNE FERGUSON. RCP/BNF: Food Intol 84. Reader, Medicine, Western General Hosp. Edinburgh. *Advisor* UK Dairy Industry[57] *Advisor* Dairy Trades Federation/Milk Marketing Board.[18]

DR RONALD FINN. RCP/BNF: Food Intol 84. Royal Hosp. Liverpool.

DR JOHN GARROW. BNF: Sugars 87. BNF/HEC: Chairman BNF/HEC: JACNE 84–87. MRC Clinical Research Centre, Harrow. *Member* RCP Obesity Cttee 83. *Governor* BNF 83–. (Editorial Advisory Board 76–, Scientific Advisory Cttee 77–).[7] *Research funding* Sugar Assoc.[13] Member DHSS: COMA (Main Cttee, Bread 81). Working party ARC/MRC: Food Research 74.

DR JULIET GRAY. RCP/BNF: Food Intol 84, BNF: Diet 82. *Ex-Science Director* BNF 81–84.[7] *Consultant* McDonalds (hamburgers).[58] *Member* NACNE Cttee 79–84.

DR GEORGE GREENER. BNF: Sugars 87. *Employee* Mars (General Manager, Netherlands). *Committee* BNF (Industrial Scientists Cttee 82–84).[7]

PROFESSOR JOHN HAWTHORN. BNF: Sugars 87. Dept. Bioscience and Biotechnology, Strathclyde Univ. *Advisor* British Food Manufacturing Industries RA. *Advisor* FMF.[26] *Committee* BNF (Editorial Advisory Board 73–.)[7] *Member* DHSS: Irrad 86.

SIR RAYMOND HOFFENBERG. RCP/BNF: Food Intol 84. Dept. of Medicine, Birmingham Univ. President, Royal College of Physicians, 83–.

DOROTHY HOLLINGSWORTH. BNF/HEC Nutr Educ. 77. Ex-Secretary-General International Union of Nutritional Sciences 78–85. MAFF 41–70. Ex-Secretary Nutrition Society 62–65. *Ex-Director-General* BNF 70–77 (Editorial Advisory Board 77–, Scientific Advisory Cttee 74–.)[7] *Member* ARC/MRC: Food Research 74.

PROFESSOR PHILIP JAMES. BNF/HEC: JACNE 85. Director AFRC Rowett RI, Aberdeen. Vice-Chairman NACNE Cttee 79–84. Chairman NACNE Sub-Cttee 80–84. Member RCP Obesity Cttee 83, Fibre Cttee 80. *Ex-Committee* BNF Scientific Advisory Cttee 77–83. Editorial Advisory Cttee 77–83, resigned.[7] *Research funding* Nestlé,[24] Rank Prize Fund.[24] *Member* DHSS: COMA (Heart Disease 84), DHSS/MAFF (Irradiation 86), MAFF: FAC (Colours 87), FSC 78–83 (Claims 80, Meat 80, Labelling 79).

LESLEY JONES. BNF/HEC: JACNE 85. Health Education Officer. Member NACNE Cttee 79–84.

DR HUBERT LACEY. RCP/BNF: Food Intol 84. Psychiatrist, St Georges Hosp.

DR JAMES LEONARD. BNF/RCP: Food Intol 84. Institute of Child Health, London.

PROFESSOR MAURICE LESSOF. Chairman RCP/BNF: Food Intol 84. Head of Dept. Medicine Guy's Hosp. *Research funding* Intl Sugar Research Foundation 75–82.[59] Beecham 75–82,[59] Imperial Grp 75–82,[59] Pfizer 75–76,[59] Reckitt & Colman 75–76,[59] Unilever 81–82,[59] Miles Laboratories (additives).[12]

PROFESSOR IAN MACDONALD. BNF: Sugars 87. Dept. Applied Physiology Guy's Hosp. Ex-President Nutrition Society 80–83. *Chairman* BNF 85– (*Vice-Chairman* 81–83, Scientific Advisory Cttee 70–, Editorial Advisory Board 81–83)[7] *Advisor* (Chairman) Dairy Trades Federation/Milk Marketing Board.[18]

Research funding Cadbury's 69,[27] Beecham 63–66, 73–74,[28–36] Glaxo 65,[28–29] Milk Marketing Board 77,[37] Lord Rank Trust 72–73.[38–40] *Member* MAFF: FAC 83– (Colours 87), FACC 77–83 (Colours 79).

ALISTAIR MACKIE. DHSS/BNF/HEC: Nutr. Educ. 77. *Director-General* Health Education Council 72–82.

DR JIM MANN. BNF/HEC: JACNE 85. Dept. Social and Community Medicine Oxford Univ. *Member* RCP Obesity Cttee 83. *Research Funding* Unilever (Flora margarine) 79–85,[12] World Sugar Research Organisation 81–83.[16] *Member* DHSS: COMA (Heart Disease 84).

JEAN MARR. BNF/HEC: JACNE 85. Nutritionist, Royal Free Hosp. *Committee* BNF (Scientific Advisory Cttee 79–85).[7] Working party ARC/MRC: Food research 74.

ALAN MARYON-DAVIS. BNF/HEC: Member NACNE Cttee 79–84, JACNE 85. Health Education Council.

DR TOM MEADE. BNF: Sugars 87. Director MRC Clinical Research Centre Epidemiology Unit, Harrow. Member COMA (Main Cttee 86–).

PROFESSOR JERRY MORRIS. BNF: Diet 82. Emeritus Professor Epidemiology London Univ. Chairman NACNE Cttee 79–84. *Ex-Governor* BNF 71–84 (*Vice-Chairman* 77–78, resigned; Scientific Advisory Cttee 77–78, Editorial Advisory Board 77–78).[7] Member RCP Fibre Cttee 80. Member DHSS: COMA (Bread 81, Heart Disease 74).

ELIZABETH MORSE. BNF: Diet 82. BNF/HEC: Nutr. Educ. 77. *Consultant* BNF (Scientific Inf. Officer 76–81).[7] Secretary, BNF: Sugars 87.

PROFESSOR ALBERT NEUBERGER. BNF: Sugars 87. Emeritus Professor Chemical Pathology Charing Cross Hosp. *President* BNF 82–86 (Ex-Officio Governor 82– Scientific Advisory Cttee 74–82)[7] Chairman ARC/MRC Food Research 74.

DR WILSON NICOL. BNF: Diet 82. *Director* Tate & Lyle. *Council* BNF (Industrial Scientists Cttee 77–81).[7]

DR DAVID PYKE. BNF: Sugars 87. Dept. Diabetology, Kings College Hosp.

DR ALAN ROBERTSON. BNF: Diet 82. *Ex-Director* ICI. *Chairman* BNF 81–83 (*Vice-Chairman* 79–81, 83–84, Industrial Governor 75–82, Editorial Advisory Board 79–84, Scientific Advisory Cttee 79–84).[7]

MARGARET SANDERSON. BNF: Sugars 87. Community Dietitian.

J.B. SHARP. *Chairman* DHSS/BNF/HEC: Nutr. Educ. 77. DHSS.

DR DEREK SHRIMPTON. RCP/BNF: Food Intol. 84. *Ex-Director-General* BNF 82–84 (resigned). Ex-Treasurer Nutrition Society 72–77. *Ex-Employee* Unilever (animal feeds, 78–82). *Committee* BNF (Editorial Advisory Board 82–84, Scientific Advisory Cttee 82–84).[7] Member NACNE Cttee 82-84. Member MAFF: Food Quality 84. *Observer* BNF: Sugars 87.

JANE THOMAS. DHSS/BNF/HEC Nutr. Educ. 77. Health Education Council.

MS. PAT TORRENS. DHSS/BNF/HEC Nutr. Educ. 77. DHSS. Member NACNE Cttee 79–84.

DR MICHAEL TURNER. BNF: Diet 82. *Ex-Director-General* BNF 77–82 (Editorial Advisory Board 77–82, Scientific Advisory Cttee 77–82).[7] *Advisor* National Dairy Council.[54] Member NACNE Cttee 79–82. Member DHSS: COMA (Bread 81).

PADDY VICTORY. DHSS/BNF/HEC Nutr. Educ. 77. *Secretary* British Nutrition Foundation 72–85.

PROFESSOR A.J. VLITOS. BNF: Sugars 87. Visiting Professor Reading Univ. *Director-General* World Sugar Research Organisation 84–. *Ex-Director* Tate & Lyle Research & Development 66–84. *Ex-Governor* BNF 79–82 (Industrial Scientists Cttee 67–77).[7]

DR JOHN WARNER. RCP/BNF: Food Intol 84. Paediatrics Dept. Brompton Hosp. *Research funding* Beecham 81–?[24]

PROFESSOR JOHN WATERLOW. BNF Diet 82. Emeritus Professor Human Nutrition London Univ. *Ex-Chairman* BNF 76–77 (*Vice-Chairman* 75–76, Governor 71 –, Editorial Advisory

Board 76–, Scientific Advisory Cttee 72- (Chair 77–80). *Research funding* Nestlé 80–82,[12] Rank Prize Funds 75–,[24] BNF 71–72.[7] *Member* DHSS: COMA (RDAs 81/79). ARC/MRC: Food Research 74.

DR ROGER WHITEHEAD. BNF: Diet 82. Head MRC Dunn Clinical Nutrition Centre, Cambridge 73–. *Governor* BNF 73–. (Scientific Advisory Cttee 73–80),[7] *Advisor* Dairy Trades Federation/Milk Marketing Board.[18] *Research Funding* Nestlé, Rank Prize Funds.[24] Working Party ARC/MRC: Food Research 74. *Member* DHSS: COMA (Main Cttee, Bread 81, RDAs 81/79).

SIR FRANK YOUNG. DHSS/BNF/HEC Nutr. Educ. 77. Emeritus Prof Biochemistry Cambridge Univ. *Ex-Chairman* Smith Kline and French Trustees UK.[46] *Ex-President* BNF 73–75. (Scientific Governor 67–70, 75–80, Scientific Advisory Cttee 74–78, Editorial Advisory Cttee 73–76).[7] *Ex-Scientific Governor* British Industries Biological RA. *Member* DHSS: COMA (Chairman Bread 81, RDAs 81/79, 79/69, Chairman Heart Disease 74.)

DOCUMENT C

Sixty-Five Diseases and British Food

Everybody knows that severe lack of specific nutrients is the direct cause of specific 'deficiency' diseases. Every schoolchild has heard of scurvy and what causes it – eating a diet with no vitamin C. This is because of scurvy's historical role as a scourge of the British navy, and in particular of the famous story of Captain James Cook, who provided his crew with fresh vegetables and fruit, including oranges and lemons, on his voyage round the world in 1772–1775 and so kept them free of scurvy.[1]

In the early years of this century, doctors and researchers compiled a list of vitamins and minerals and their associated deficiency diseases. The list was worked out from observations of and experiments on animals, children, convicts, soldiers, sailors, poor people in America, Africa and Asia, and other unfortunates. The diseases are all listed in standard textbooks:[1,2,3] xerophthalmia (vitamin A deficiency), rickets (D), scurvy (C), beri-beri (B1), hyporiboflavinosis (B2), pellagra (B3), anaemia (folic acid, B12, iron), goitre (iodine), kwashiorkor (protein and energy) and marasmus (energy). Medical students are taught to identify these diseases through textbook descriptions and accompanying photographs of pitiable natives in loincloths.

Deficiency diseases are mostly exotic: uncommon or unknown in Britain, even – so it is sometimes, wrongly, believed[4,5] – extinct. The middle-class, middle-aged men who dominate public policy-making and decision-taking in Britain have grown up believing that problems of food and nutrition are 'solved'.[6] One current official statement runs: 'Nutrition in Britain is generally good.'[7] Given that there is enough to eat, until recently the 'normal' British diet has automatically been characterized as 'balanced and varied'. Overweight and obesity have always been recognized as ill-effects of eating typical food; but the general assumption has been that their cause is over-indulgence – 'too much of a good thing'. As a result doctors have simply dismissed fat people as greedy, and have not seen them as suffering from disease. Another current official statement runs: 'The message is one of moderation. Enough is enough; more is not better and can be harmful.'[8]

Infectious diseases were also mass killers until recently. Cholera ravaged cities throughout Britain little more than a hundred years ago; although many people did survive to old age, life expectancy at birth was not much more than 40 years.[9] During the first half of the twentieth century, every family had reason to fear suffering or death from tuberculosis or poliomyelitis, diphtheria, measles, whooping cough, scarlet fever or infant diarrhoea. Now, thanks to clean water, food and air, enough to eat, decent housing, antiseptics, vaccination and antibiotics – approximately in that order[10] – these and other infectious diseases no longer threaten public health either in Britain or in other developed countries.

Nowadays, most of the diseases we suffer and die from are non-infectious. Of these, the major killers are often still known as 'degenerative' diseases. These, according to another current official statement,[9] are

the problems which are in one sense the consequence of successful prevention in past decades, the diseases and disabilities associated with old age, resulting from the enormous growth in the proportion of the population who are aged.

Doctors are trained to define many non-infectious diseases, as 'degenerative diseases of complex aetiology'. This means that 'there are many causes of these diseases, and they accompany old age.' For example, a *Family Medical Adviser*[11] published in 1983 says of rheumatoid arthritis and heart disease that

there is little that can be done to prevent them – they occur to a greater or lesser extent as part of the natural process of ageing.

And a medical dictionary[12] published in 1981 says 'causes of degeneration are, in many cases, very obscure'.

We have all grown up with the impression that the main diet-related diseases are deficiency diseases caused by gross lack of specific nutrients, and that these are now rare; that infectious diseases, whether caused by dirt or by germs, have mostly been stamped out; and that degenerative diseases, as their name implies, are an inevitable part of the old age that we in the West now enjoy. We have been distanced from disease: it is 'just one of those things' which with luck happens to other people; and, if it does happen to us, with luck again the doctor will 'fix us up'. Middle-aged, middle-class men are given an annual check-up and say 'the quack looked me over, and I'm OK' (or, 'not OK'); they have disowned, medicalized, their own health.

The germ theory of disease promoted by Louis Pasteur makes us think that disease is 'out there' – 'a third party'. A survey of doctors and lay people taken in 1979 showed that: [13]

> The most influential factor in determining whether or not an illness was considered to be a disease was the importance of the doctor in diagnosis and treatment .... To the layman a disease seems to be a living agency that causes illness.

This is the context of the spectacular growth of the drugs industry in the last forty years.

The alternative theory of disease, put forward by Claude Bernard, a contemporary of Pasteur, regards disease as 'in here', part of ourselves. This view emphasizes the importance of the environment, especially the internal environment (*le milieu intérieur*) of our bodies. Disease is not a chance visitor caused by an external agent, but is the result of stresses and imbalances that overwhelm the body's natural defences. Since doctors are not responsible for the environment, health and disease therefore become social rather than medical issues. If Pasteur can be called the father of the treatment of disease, then Bernard is the father of the promotion of health.

Claude Bernard said, 'it is what we think we know that often prevents us from learning'.[14] Because we associate disease with acute illness caused by germs, we tend to think that food can only cause disease if it is acutely toxic – poisonous, like a germ. We tend to overlook the central importance of the environment, and in particular the nourishment of our internal environment. We fear heart *attacks*, which occur suddenly; but remain unaware of heart *disease*, the gradual blocking up of the heart's arteries.

However, we are now in the middle of a revolution in our understanding of food, health and disease. During the last forty years, hundreds of scientists have been accumulating evidence that supports one general conclusion: that the food we in the West typically eat is the main single cause of the diseases we mostly suffer and die from.

This new understanding of the fundamental importance of good food is above all the achievement of original thinkers working independently and often in ignorance of each other, whose ideas are – inevitably – resisted by the established order: [15,16]

> A new scientific truth does not triumph by convincing its opponents and making them see the light, but rather because its opponents eventually die, and a new generation grows up that is familiar with it.

At least seven separate paths of enquiry have led to a broad avenue of agreement. The research has been done all over the world:

1 After the Second World War, the rate of death from heart disease soared in the USA and other Western countries. An increasing number of these deaths were premature, (under the age of 65). By the late 1950s, nearly a million Americans were dying every year from cardiovascular diseases. Doctors in the USA realized that the cause of diseases of the circulation system – angina, atherosclerosis, coronary heart disease, hyperlipidaemia; carotid artery disease, peripheral vascular disease, high blood pressure, stroke – could not merely be the ageing process. In 1959, a group of 114 specialists, led by Paul Dudley White, physician to President Eisenhower, published *A Statement on Arteriosclerosis*.[17] This led to a massive research effort, inspired among many others by the American epidemiologists Ancel Keys and Jeremiah Stamler, which established that Western food is a major cause of circulatory diseases because it is too heavy in total fats and saturated fats.

2 The health of the people of Britain and of other Western European countries improved during wartime, when people had enough to eat. Rates of diabetes, obesity, peptic ulcer, tooth decay and other non-infectious diseases dropped. The food supply also changed: there was more food for the poor, more brown bread and potatoes, less fats and sugars. This 'great experiment' convinced scientists all over the world that the 'normal' Western diet is unhealthy. Above all, T.L. Cleave, Surgeon Captain on board the British warship *King George V*, realized that processed sugars and starches caused an entire pattern of diseases and, after thirty years of research, published *The Saccharine Disease* in 1974.[18] Some of Cleave's work is theoretical. But in the 1980s Kenneth Heaton and Norman Blacklock in Britain have shown likely connections between typical sugars consumption, and gallstones, diseases of the gut and kidney stones. Sheldon Reiser and others in the USA have produced evidence that sugars can increase the risk of diabetes and heart attacks.

3 The belief that high consumption of salt causes high blood pressure and strokes is not new. 'If too much salt is used in food, the pulse hardens,' said the Chinese sage Huang-Ti in about 2300 BC.[19] Salt (sodium chloride) is used all over the world as a preservative. In the West, the salt added in food processing and preparation and at the table amounts to ten or even twenty times more than the body needs.[20] This level of consumption is unbalanced and is now generally agreed to be harmful. In all

societies that consume little salt, high blood pressure is rare or unknown. Conversely, in Japan, where traditional food is very salt, high blood pressure and deaths from stroke and stomach cancer have been very common. However, in recent years Westernization and in particular the use of freezing rather than salt to preserve food, has brought about a dramatic decline in these conditions. In Belgium an impressive national campaign led by Jozef Joossens since 1968 has reduced salt consumption, and the death rate from stroke and stomach cancer.[21]

4 Further evidence that so-called 'degenerative' diseases are wrongly named has come from Africa. Many common Western diseases rarely if ever affect old African people who eat traditional food. But as Africa and other parts of the world have become Westernized, patterns of disease have also changed. Hugh Trowell and Denis Burkitt, a British physician and an Irish surgeon who worked for many years in East Africa, published *Refined Carbohydrate Foods and Disease* in 1975.[22] With evidence from all over the world, they identified over 20 'diseases of civilisation', which Hugh Trowell later correctly termed 'Western diseases'. Their special contribution was to show that dietary fibre, present in all whole vegetable food, but mostly lost in highly processed foods, certainly or probably protects against various diseases of the digestive system, including some common in early life in the West: for example, appendicitis, bowel cancer, constipation, diverticular disease and hiatus hernia.

5 In 1956 Hugh Sinclair, a British nutritionist, wrote a letter entitled 'Deficiency of essential fatty acids and atherosclerosis etc.' to the *Lancet*.[23] It is generally agreed that Western food is short of polyunsaturated fats, which protect against some diseases of the circulation system. Sinclair, a world authority on the subject, took a more precise view. He argued that essential polyunsaturated fats, which are naturally present in wholegrain cereal, free-ranging animals, fatty fish and leafy vegetables but are replaced by saturated fats in modern processed food, also protect against diseases of the immune, locomotor and nervous systems. Like Cleave's writings, Sinclair's work was generally dismissed when it first appeared. It now has many followers, including Michael Crawford and David Horrobin, who have shown that the brain and the nervous system are largely made of and nourished by essential fats. Diseases now associated with lack of essential fats include various cancers, rheumatoid arthritis, and multiple sclerosis.

6 Deficiency diseases are caused by food drained of specific

nutrients. It is now known that vitamins and minerals, singly and in combination, protect against many diseases. A good supply of vitamins A, C and E, together with the trace element selenium (Se), nourishes the immune system and probably protects against some common cancers. Food short of vitamin D and calcium (Ca) increases the risk of diseases of the bones in sedentary people, specifically osteomalacia and osteoporosis. An adequate supply of vitamins B6, B12 and folic acid, together with zinc (Zn), is vital in pregnancy, probably protects against neural tube defects including spina bifida, and possibly against post-natal depression. The trace element zinc has a vital role in growth and healing. The elements potassium (K), magnesium (Mg) and chromium (Cr) probably protect against high blood pressure and heart disease and possibly against diabetes respectively. The common factor is that whole, fresh food is naturally rich in vitamins and minerals.

7 Food is fuel for activity. The more energetic people are, the more energy (calories) they need from food. But food also provides nourishment for all the vital functions of the body; sedentary people and active people need the same amount of many nutrients. During this century the car, central heating and television have all made Western people inactive. As a result, they need 'nutrient-dense' food, rich in nourishment but low in calories. But many Western foods are highly processed and 'energy-dense': heavy in calories, poor in nourishment. The combination of a sedentary life and highly processed food heavy in fats and sugars causes an unknown number of Western diseases. Many specialists overlook this broad view of Western life and death, which has been best expressed by Arvid Wretlind in Sweden[24] and Jean Mayer in the USA,[25] together with the experts who have compiled over 65 reports recommending wiser dietary goals since 1965.

These seven paths of enquiry may seem to diverge, to compete with and contradict each other. In fact they are complementary. Foods heavy in saturated fats are poor in essential polyunsaturated fats. Processed sugars are stripped of fibre. The sodium in salt throws other nutrients out of balance, notably potassium. Saturated fats and processed sugars contain no nourishment, and drive vitamins and minerals out of food. The body has only so much room for food, and sedentary people are most in need of nourishing food.

In 1960, Hugh Trowell compiled a list of 36 diseases uncommon in Africa but common in Europe[26] and in 1981, with Denis Burkitt, published a list of over 30 Western diseases, notably of the circulation and digestive systems. Hugh Sinclair has compiled a list of 45 diseases which are certainly or probably caused at least in part by Western food, including diseases of the immune and nervous systems and of early life and of reproduction.

The list printed here (below) is of 65 diseases now known to have the typical Western diet, as eaten in Britain, as a proven, probable or possible cause. It builds on the research of Hugh Trowell, Denis Burkitt and Hugh Sinclair; on all the expert reports on dietary goals published over the last twenty years; and on recent findings published in leading medical and scientific journals.

The sixty-five diseases are classified, first, into systems of the body. Doctors tend to talk about diseases as if they are all completely separate from each other, whereas many are linked. For example, angina, atherosclerosis, coronary heart disease and hyperlipidaemia are all aspects of disease of the circulation system and have the same dietary causes. Other diseases are classified into stages of life. For instance, asthma, eczema, rhinitis (streaming nose) and urticaria (hives) are all diseases of babies and young children that also have a common dietary cause.

Some of these groupings are arguable. Diabetes (adult-onset, or non-insulin dependent) is classified here as a disease of the vital organs, although it could be classified as a disease of the circulation system, the digestive system or the immune system. Similarly, the immune system protects against cancers, which are here classified according to their location in the body.

Diseases shown in bold type, e.g. **CORONARY HEART DISEASE**, have been proved beyond reasonable doubt to have Western foods as an important cause. Those shown in ordinary type, like APPENDICITIS, are probably (more likely than not) caused by Western food. Where a question mark is added, like CYSTIC FIBROSIS?, the evidence still amounts to possibility rather than probability, but is nevertheless increasing. Question marks are used when the evidence is not very up to date, or has been produced by only a few researchers, or when good evidence is nevertheless questioned.

The same style is used for the Western foods shown which are certain, probable, or possible causes of the disease. Thus tooth decay is certainly a Western disease, and is certainly caused by sugars, and so **TOOTH DECAY** is accompanied by SUGARS. Appendicitis is probably a Western disease, and may be caused by lack of fibre, so APPENDICITIS is accompanied by FIBRES? To take a more complex example, high blood pressure is certainly a Western disease which is certainly caused by too much salt, probably by saturated fats and also probably by imbalance between sodium and potassium (K), and possibly by lack of calcium (Ca). So this entry runs:

SATURATED FATS.[32] SALT[36] HIGH BLOOD PRESSURE[32] Ca?[37] K[38]

The list is also referenced, as this example shows.

In most cases, only a single reference is given. These are the 'best' references I can find, and so are usually to recent leading publications which themselves supply further, more detailed references.

On the whole, scientists disapprove of any claim that a disease has a cause until the evidence amounts to proof beyond reasonable doubt. (In addition, some scientists make incoherent references to a higher form of 'scientific proof'; the notion of proof is discussed in Chapter 6.) Scientists are usually prepared to agree that a disease is caused by Western food (or, in the jargon, is 'diet-related') only after virtually every doubter has been overwhelmed or silenced by a great mass of evidence. This approach effectively excludes non-scientists from the debate, and so is not used here. It is quite justifiable to be extraordinarily cautious before allowing a drug likely to have adverse effects to be used. But, since only good and no harm comes from eating whole, fresh food, and since we all eat and may suffer, it is reasonable to publish evidence that a disease may be caused by typical Western food. For instance, multiple sclerosis is almost certainly a Western disease, and there is evidence that it is caused, at least in part, by food both heavy in saturated fats and poor in essential fats. Hence

SATURATED FATS?[51] MULTIPLE SCLEROSIS[51] ESSENTIAL FATS?[51]

Western food is not the sole cause of the diseases in this list. For instance, it is agreed that smoking is an important cause of disease of the circulation system. Lack of exercise is another cause of a number of Western diseases.[28] Other diseases (like anaemia and birth defects) are also common in non-Western countries. The term 'Western disease' as used here means a disease of which the typical diet as eaten in Britain and other Western countries is an important cause, and which may be prevented by eating more nourishing food. Some Western diseases do not show themselves until late in their development, at which point they may be irreversible: like high blood pressure, multiple sclerosis and cancers. The list consists only of non-infectious diseases. But it is worth knowing that the immune system is strengthened by good food and weakened by bad food.[29,30] There is also some reference in the list to chemical food additives and contaminants, and to toxic elements found in processed food and the environment, notably aluminium (Al) and lead (Pb).

It must be admitted that in one respect the list can be misleading. Scientists are specialists, and in the case of food and disease almost always focus on specific aspects of food (or 'dietary factors') and specific diseases (or 'disease entities'). This can result in a distorted picture. For example, fibre is much studied nowadays as protective against various diseases; but in some cases it may well be the vitamins, minerals and essential polyunsaturated fats in whole fibre-rich food that provide the protection as well as (or rather than) the fibre itself. Again, massive research on the ill-effects of saturated fats has probably in some cases obscured the value of essential polyunsaturated fats. In time research will probably show that it is not only vitamins A, C, E and selenium (Se) that protect or probably protect against cancers. There would be a lot to be said for going beyond current science and including FRESH VEGETABLES AND FRUIT in the right-hand column opposite cancers, rather than merely specific nutrients. Some nutrients, notably zinc (Zn), frequently appear in the list because they are well researched.

A new breed of doctors is now in effect using vitamins and minerals as drugs, in amounts greatly in excess of any found in food, to treat disease. Such work is not referred to here. For instance, while there is reliable evidence that concentrated doses of zinc and other micronutrients in pill form can accelerate wound healing, there is also good evidence that slow wound healing is caused by Western food, which is poor in zinc; hence its inclusion in the list. Vitamin and mineral pills are not a substitute for good food.

The essential cause of many Western diseases may well be the Western diet as a whole, which is heavy in saturated fats, processed starches and sugars, salt, additives and alcohol, and correspondingly poor in fibres, essential fats, vitamins and minerals. Certainly, the best general advice for anyone who wants to stay healthy, and to reduce the risk of suffering from Western diseases, is to eat plenty of whole, fresh food, and to take plenty of exercise.

The key to the abbreviations used here for vitamins and minerals follows the list of diseases and their causes.

Western Diseases and their Dietary Causes

CAUSE: Over-consumption	DISEASE	CAUSE: Under-nutrition
BLOOD (CARDIOVASCULAR SYSTEM)		
	ANAEMIA[31]	Fo B12 Fe[31]
FATS SATURATED FATS[32 33]	ANGINA[32 33]	
FATS SATURATED FATS[32 33]	ATHEROSCLEROSIS[32 33]	ESSENTIAL FATS[32 34]
FATS SATURATED FATS[32 33]	CORONARY HEART DISEASE[32 33]	ESSENTIAL FATS[32 34]
	DEEP VEIN THROMBOSIS[35]	FIBRE?[35]
SATURATED FATS.[32] SALT[36]	HIGH BLOOD PRESSURE[32]	Ca?[37] K[38]
FATS SATURATED FATS[32 33]	HYPERLIPIDAEMIA[32 33]	
SUGARS[39]	HYPO/HYPERGLYCAEMIA[39]	
	PELVIC PHLEBOLITHS[35]	FIBRE?[35]
	PERIPHERAL VASCULAR DISEASE[40]	FIBRE?[40]
	PULMONARY EMBOLISM[35]	FIBRE?[35]
FATS SATURATED FATS.[41] SALT[41]	STROKE (CEREBROVASCULAR DISEASE)[41 42]	
	VARICOSE VEINS[43]	FIBRE?[43]
BONES, JOINTS, MUSCLES (LOCOMOTOR SYSTEM)		
SATURATED FATS?[44]	ARTHRITIS (RHEUMATOID)[40]	ESSENTIAL FATS?[44]
	OSTEOMALACIA[31]	D Ca[31]
	OSTEOPOROSIS[31]	D Ca[31]

CAUSE: Over-consumption	DISEASE	CAUSE: Under-nutrition
BRAIN, NERVOUS SYSTEM		
Al[45]	ALZHEIMER'S DISEASE[46 47]	C?[48] Fo? B12? Fe?[47] Zn.[48] Fe Cu[49]
ADDITIVES[50]	DEPRESSION[48]	
	MIGRAINE[50]	
SATURATED FATS?[51]	MULTIPLE SCLEROSIS[51]	ESSENTIAL FATS?[51]
	POST NATAL DEPRESSION?[52]	B2 B6 Fo Zn?[52]
ALCOHOL[53]	WERNICKE/KORSAKOFF SYNDROME[53]	B1[53]
DIGESTION (GASTROINTESTINAL TRACT)		
	APPENDICITIS[40]	FIBRE?[54]
FATS.[55] SUGARS[56]	BOWEL CANCER, POLYP[55]	FIBRE.[43] A D? E C Ca? Se?[57 58 59]
	CONSTIPATION[43]	FIBRE[43]
SUGARS[60]	CROHN'S DISEASE[60]	
	DIVERTICULAR DISEASE[43]	FIBRE[43]
	HIATUS HERNIA[40]	FIBRE?[40]
	IRRITABLE BOWEL[43]	FIBRE[43]
ALCOHOL[55]	OESOPHAGEAL CANCER[55]	A E C? Se[57 58]
SATURATED FATS?[61] SUGARS?[62]	PEPTIC ULCER?[62]	ESSENTIAL FATS?[61]
	PILES[43]	FIBRE[43]
SALT[55]	STOMACH CANCER[55]	A E C? Se[57 58]
SUGARS[63]	TOOTH DECAY[63]	
SUGARS[60]	ULCERATIVE COLITIS[60]	

continued Western Diseases and their Dietary Causes

CAUSE: Over-consumption	DISEASE	CAUSE: Under-nutrition

IMMUNE SYSTEM

ADDITIVES[64]	ALLERGY (GENERAL)[64]	
ADDITIVES[64]	ASTHMA[64]	
FATS.[55] ALCOHOL[65]	CANCER (GENERAL)[55]	ESSENTIAL FATS[66] A E C? Se[57 58]

Note. Specific allergic reactions also listed under BABIES, CHILDREN. Allergy (and intolerance) also caused by foods. Specific cancers also listed under DIGESTION, SEX, and VITAL ORGANS.

SEX (REPRODUCTIVE SYSTEM)

FATS[55]	BREAST CANCER[55]	ESSENTIAL FATS?[67] A E C? Se[57 58]
	PRE-MENSTRUAL TENSION[68]	B6?[68]
FATS[55]	PROSTATE CANCER[55]	A E C? Se [57 58]

SKIN (EPIDERMIS)

ADDITIVES[64]	ECZEMA[64]	
ADDITIVES?[69]	MOUTH ULCERS?[69]	
	SLOW WOUND HEALING[70]	Zn[70]
ADDITIVES[71]	URTICARIA (HIVES)[71]	

continued Western Diseases and their Dietary Causes

CAUSE: Over-consumption	DISEASE	CAUSE: Under-nutrition
VITAL ORGANS (OTHER THAN HEART)		
	CYSTIC FIBROSIS[72]	E? Se[72]
SUGARS[73]	DIABETES (ADULT/ONSET)[74 75]	FIBRE[43]
SUGARS[76]	GALL STONES[77]	FIBRE[43]
SUGARS[78 79]	KIDNEY STONES[78]	
ALCOHOL[80]	LIVER CIRRHOSIS[80]	
ALCOHOL?[55]	PANCREATIC CANCER[55]	A E C? Se[57 58]
WEIGHT (METABOLISM)		
	ANOREXIA[48]	Zn[48]
FATS,[81] SUGARS[81 82]	OVERWEIGHT, OBESITY[81]	FIBRE[82 83]
BIRTH		
	ANENCEPHALY[84 85]	B6? Fo B12? Zn?[284 85]
ALCOHOL[86]	FETAL ALCOHOL SYNDROME[86]	
ALCOHOL[87]	LOW BIRTH WEIGHT[87]	Zn[88]
Pb[89]	MENTAL RETARDATION[90]	Zn?[91]
	SPINA BIFIDA[84 85]	B6? Fo B12? Zn?[284 85]

Note. These diseases caused by the diet of the mother when pregnant.

continued Western Diseases and their Dietary Causes

CAUSE: Over-consumption	DISEASE	CAUSE: Under-nutrition
BABIES, CHILDREN		
ADDITIVES[92]	ANGIOEDEMA[92]	
ADDITIVES[64 92]	ASTHMA[64 92]	
ADDITIVES[64]	ECZEMA[64]	
ADDITIVES[93]	HYPERACTIVITY[93]	
	KIDNEY FAILURE[94]	Na[94]
Pb[90]	**MENTAL RETARDATION**[90]	Fe?[95] Zn?[96]
ADDITIVES[50]	MIGRAINE[50]	
ADDITIVES[64 92]	RHINITIS[64 92]	
	RICKETS[31]	D[31]
	SLOW GROWTH[96]	Zn[96]
ADDITIVES[64 92]	URTICARIA (HIVES)[64 92]	

Note. General allergic reactions also listed under IMMUNE SYSTEM and SKIN. Allergy (and intolerance) also caused by foods. These diseases, most common in babies and young children, can also affect adults (apart from kidney failure, a problem only in the first few months of life).

	DISEASE	
ADOLESCENTS		
	AMENORRHOEA[48]	Zn[48]
	ANOREXIA[48]	Zn. [48] Fe Cu[96]
	ANOREXIA NERVOSA?[90 97]	K? Ca? Mg?[98] Zn?[90 97]
	DEPRESSION[48 97]	Zn. [48] Fe Cu[49]

List of Abbreviations

Vitamins
A   retinol equivs. or carotene
D   cholecalciferol
E   alpha-tocopherol equivs.
K
C   ascorbic acid
B_1 thiamine
B_2 riboflavin
B_3 niacin
B_6 pyridoxine
B_{12} cobalamin
Fo folic acid, or folate
Pa Pantothenic acid

Minerals and trace elements
K   potassium
Na sodium
Cl chloride
Ca calcium
P   phosphorus
Mg magnesium
Fe iron
Zn zinc
Cu copper
I   iodine
Se selenium
Cr chromium

Toxic elements
Al aluminium
Pb lead
Cd cadmium
Hg mercury
As arsenic

References

INTRODUCTION

1. Popper K. *The Logic of Scientific Discovery*. London: Hutchinson, 1959.
2. Illich I. *Medical Nemesis*. New York: Bantam, 1977.
3. Gillie O, Mercer D (eds). *The Sunday Times Book of Body Maintenance*. London: Michael Joseph, 1978. Updated and revised edition, London: Mermaid Books, 1982.
4. David G. Milk: still a lot of bottle. *Observer*, 30 June 1985.
5. Vaughan J, Fallows S, Wheelock J. Consumer attitudes to liquid milk. Dairy *Industries International* 1985; 50(2):16-19.
6. National Dairy Council. Does everybody's body *really* need bottle? Advertisement. *Observer*, 30 June 1985.
7. Ministry of Food. Manual of nutrition. London: HMSO, 1945, 1953.
8. Select Committee on Nutrition and Human Needs. Dietary Goals for the United States. Washington: US Government Printing Office, 1977, (March), 1977 (December).
9. National Advisory Committee on Nutrition Education. A discussion paper on proposals for nutritional guidelines for health education in Britain. London: Health Education Council, 1983.
10. Hall R. Partnership with responsibility. Talk given to the Coronary Prevention Group AGM, 14 May 1985. Unpublished.
11. 'Super' sausage launched. Wall's press release. 11 February 1985.
12. Wall's. Our new sausages. Advertisement. *Womans Own*, 6 April 1985.
13. Boots. Easy reading for babies. Advertisement, *Radio Times*, 4 April 1985.
14. Malpas D. Tesco points the way to healthy eating. Press conference, 9 January 1985. Unpublished.
15. Tesco. If you're watching what you eat look at our labels. Advertisement. Observer, 20 January 1985.
16. Tesco healthy eating logos. Guidelines. Tesco, doc no 6167A. Unpublished.
17. Mason T. Personal communication.

18. Cornelius A. Joy at Tesco as new 'quality' image emerges. *Guardian*, 29 May 1986.
19. Coronary Prevention Group. Annual Report 1985-86. London: CPG.
20. Ministry of Agriculture, Fisheries and Food. Peggy Fenner MP. The Government's response to the recommendations of the COMA report. Talk given to the Coronary Prevention Group AGM, 13 May 1986. Unpublished.
21. Social Surveys (Gallup Poll). Healthy foods. Survey conducted on behalf of Tesco. London: Gallup, September 1984. Unpublished.
22. British Market Research Bureau. Consumer attitudes to and understanding of nutrition labelling. A research study on behalf of the Consumers' Association, the Ministry of Agriculture, Fisheries and Food, the National Consumer Council. London: BMRB, June 1985.
23. Cannon G. What about sugar and salt? say consumers. *New Health*, August 1985.
24. Stirling Gallacher J. Personal communication.
25. Sutcliffe. Eat fit. Training manual. London: Sutcliffe. Unpublished.
26. Sutcliffe. Eat fit. A guide to healthy eating 1985. Available from Sutcliffe outlets.
27. Tesco guide to healthy eating. 1985. Available from Tesco stores.
28 Wenlock R, Disselduff M, Skinner R, Knight I. The diets of British schoolchildren. April 1986. (Available from the DHSS Leaflets Unit, PO Box 21, Stanmore, Middlesex HA7 1AY).
29. Bull N. Dietary habits of 15 to 25 year olds. *Hum. Nutr. Appl. Nutr.* 1985; 39A (suppl): 1-68.
30. Ministry of Agriculture, Fisheries and Food. Report on meat products. Food Standards Committee. London: HMSO, 1980.
31. Ministry of Agriculture, Fisheries and Food. Report on water in food. Food Standards Committee. London: HMSO, 1978.
32. Ministry of Agriculture, Fisheries and Food. Second report on food labelling. Food Standards Committee. London: HMSO, 1979.
33. Department of Health and Social Security. Nutritional aspects of bread and flour. Committee on Medical Aspects of Food Policy. London: HMSO, 1981.
34. Ministry of Agriculture, Fisheries and Food. Final report on the colouring matter in food regulations 1973. Food Advisory Committee. London: HMSO, 1987.
35. Department of Health and Social Security/Ministry of Agriculture, Fisheries and Food. Report on the safety and wholesomeness of irradiated foods. Advisory Committee on Novel and Irradiated Foods. London: DHSS/MAFF, 1986.
36. Curtis F. 'Calling the tune'. BBC Television: O'Donnell investigates the food business. 29 April 1986.
37. McKeown T. *The Role of Medicine*: dream, mirage or nemesis. Oxford: Blackwell, 1979.
38. Marks J. *A Guide to the Vitamins*. Their role in health and disease. Lancaster: MTP, 1979.
39. Crawford M. Personal communication.
40. Department of Health and Social Security. Recommended intakes of

nutrients for the United Kingdom/Recommended daily amounts of food energy and nutrients for groups of people in the United Kingdom. Committee on Medical Aspects of Food Policy. London: HMSO, 1969, 1981; 1979, 1981.

41. Boyd Orr J. *Food Health and Income*. A survey of adequacy of diet in relation to income. London: Macmillan, 1937.
42. Ministry of Health. On the state of the public health during six years of war. Report of the chief medical officer of the Ministry of Health 1939-45. London: HMSO, 1946.
43. Short R. Personal communication.
44. Society of Flavourists, 6 November 1984. Unpublished.
45. The Labour Party. Food policy: a priority. London: The Labour Party, February 1985.
46. Cannon G. Good food for all. *New Health*, May 1985.
47. The Liberal Party. Food and health. London: The Liberal Party, November 1985.
48. Body R. *Agriculture: The Triumph and the Shame*. London: Temple Smith, 1982.

CHAPTER 1

1. James W., Cummings J., Garrow J., Walker C., Whitney R. Granada Television. *World in Action*, 'The threatened generation'. 14 April 1986. Transcript.
2. Ministry of Agriculture, Fisheries and Food. Second report on claims and misleading descriptions. Food Standards Committee. London: HMSO, 1980.
3. Food Policy Unit, Manchester Polytechnic. Jam Tomorrow? A report of the first findings of a pilot study of the food circumstances, attitudes and consumption of 1000 people on low incomes in the North of England. Manchester: Polytechnic Food Unit, 1984.
4. Smith D. People of the horseradish. *Guardian*, 30 August 1985.
5. Carluccio A. No ceps please, we're British. *Sunday Times Magazine*, 1 September 1985.
6. Dorman C. The very good food guide. *Woman*, 7 September 1985.
7. France C. From an English country kitchen. *Woman's Realm*, 31 August 1985.
8. Anon. Meal in a jacket. *Woman's Own*, 7 September 1985.
9. Batchelor's Foods. New Batchelor's bean cuisine. Advertisement. *Woman*, 7 September 1985.
10. Food from Britain. Try a little tenderness. Advertisement. *Woman*, 7 September 1985.
11. Batchelor's Foods. They don't need calling twice when it's Batchelor's savoury rice. Advertisement. *Woman's Own*, 7 September 1985.
12. Mattesons. New Mattesons salads make every day a Mmm day. Advertisement. *Woman's Own*, 7 September 1985.

13. Weetabix. Healthy eating is a thing of the past. Advertisement. *Woman's Own*, 7 September 1985.
14. Sarson's. Four easy steps to perfect pickled onions. Advertisement. *Woman's Realm*, 30 August 1985.
15. *Woman's Realm*, 30 August 1985.
16. Unilever. Prospectus. The Netherlands: Unilever, 1983.
17. O'Reilly D. 1984: The top 250 spenders. *Campaign*, 7 June 1985.
18. Barker W. (director). Child Development programme. Bristol: Child Development Project (Senate House, University of Bristol), 1984.
19. Barker W. Personal communication.
20. Butler N. McCarrison Society. 14th annual conference. Nutrition and the prevention of physical degeneration. *Nutr and Health* (forthcoming).
21. Taylor B., Wadsworth J., Wadsworth M., Peckham C. Changes in the reported prevalence of childhood eczema since the 1939–45 war. *Lancet* 1984; II: 1255–1257.
22. Royal Society of Medicine. Forum on Food and Health, 11 December 1984. (Proceedings unpublished.)
23. Hencke D. Children 'healthier 35 years ago'. *Guardian*, 10 September 1985.
24. Beardall S. Today's children fatter, sicker and more disturbed. *Times*, 11 September 1985.
25. Department of Health and Social Security. Prevention and health: everybody's business. A reassessment of public and personal health. London: HMSO, 1976, 1981.
26. Black D., Morris J., Smith C., Townsend P. *Inequalities in Health* (the Black report). London: Penguin, 1982.
27. Ministry of Agriculture, Fisheries and Food, Household food consumption and expenditure: 1982, 1983, 1984. Annual report of the national food survey committee. London: HMSO, 1984, 1985, 1986.
28. Catford J., Ford S. On the state of the public ill-health: premature mortality in the United Kingdom and Europe. *Br. Med. J.* 1984; 289: 1668–1670.
29. Hackett A., Rugg-Gunn A., Appleton D., Eastoe J., Jenkins G. 2-year longitudinal survey of 405 Northumberland children initially aged 11.5 years. *Br. J. Nutr.* 1984; 51: 67–75.
30. Hackett A., Rugg-Gunn A., Appleton D., Allinson M., Eastoe J. Sugars-eating habits of 405 11–14-year-old English children. *Br. J. Nutr.*, 1984; 51: 347–356.
31. Whitehead R., Paul A., Cole T. Trends in food energy intakes throughout childhood from one to 18 years. *Hum. Nutr: Appl. Nutr.*, 1982; 36: 57–62.
32. House of Commons, Parliamentary debates. Hansard (official record). Heart disease (School children). Robert Adley MP (Question), Prime Minister (Answer). 21 February 1984.
33. House of Commons, Parliamentary debates. Hansard (official record). School children (Dietary Survey). Gordon Brown MP (Question), John Patten MP (DHSS) (Answer). 17 December 1984.

34. House of Commons, Parliamentary debates. Hansard (official record). School meals (Nutritional Standards). Derek Fatchett MP, Tony Lloyd MP, Robert Adley MP (Questions), Robert Dunn MP (DES) (Answer). 19 March 1985.
35. House of Commons, Parliamentary debates. Hansard (official record). School children (Dietary Survey). Dr John Marek MP (Question), Prime Minister (Answer). 30 January 1986.
36. Wapshott N., Brock G. *Thatcher*: London: Macdonald, 1983.
37. Dixon B. What are Prime Ministers made of? *New Scientist*, 20 February 1986.
38. Wenlock R., Disselduff M., Skinner R., Knight I. The diets of British schoolchildren. Preliminary report of a nutritional analysis of a nationwide dietary survey of British schoolchildren. Department of Health and Social Security/Office of Population Censuses and Surveys, April 1986. (Available from DHSS leaflets unit, PO Box 21, Stanmore, Middlesex HA7 1AY.)
39. Department of Health and Social Security/Office of Population Censuses and Surveys. The diets of British schoolchildren. Committee on Medical Aspects of Food Policy. Unpublished.
40. Parker R. Personal communication.
41. Department of Health and Social Security. Recommended intakes of nutrients for the United Kingdom/Recommended daily amounts of food energy and nutrients for groups of people in the United Kingdom. Committee on Medical Aspects of Food Policy. London: HMSO, 1969, 1981; 1979, 1981.
42. Addy D. Happiness is: iron. *Br. Med. J.*. 1986; 292: 969–970.
43. Cannon G. Happiness is: iron. *Br. Med. J.* 1986; 292: 1599.
44. Fletcher D. Row over teenage diet report. *Daily Telegraph*, 3 April 1986.
45. Veitch A. Survey on 'chips and biscuits' diet to be released. *Guardian*, 4 April 1986.
46. Ministry of Agriculture, Fisheries and Food. Peggy Fenner MP. Letter to Jonathan Aitken MP, Barry Sheerman MP, Tony Lloyd MP, Michael Meadowcroft MP. 4 June 1986.
47. Anon. Children's snack diet criticised. *Times*, 4 April 1986.
48. Department of Health and Social Security. First results of children's dietary survey published. Press release no 86/118. 10 April 1986.
49. Granada Television, *World In Action*. 'The threatened generation'. 14 April 1986.
50. Cummings J. Towards a recommended daily intake of dietary fibre. Paper prepared for the COMA panel on bread, flour and other cereal products. August 1978. Unpublished.
51. Health Education Council. A discussion paper on proposals for nutritional guidelines for health education in Britain. National Advisory Committee on Nutrition Education. London: HEC, 1983.
52. Walker C., Cannon G. *The Food Scandal*. Paperback edition, London: Century, 1985.
53. Department of Health and Social Security. Norman Fowler welcomes experts' report on diet and cardiovascular disease. Press

release no 84/227. 12 July 1984.

54. Gunn S. Free school meals ban gets through. *Times*, 16 July 1986.

55. Black D. Mr Fowler draws up a diet for disaster. Letter. *Guardian*, 14 July 1986.

56. McGhie T., Gibson R. Fight to keep free school nosh. *Star*, 14 July 1986.

57. Brown I. Buck stops. *Guardian*, 29 July 1986.

58. Buss D. Chips with everything. *Nutr. and Food Sc.* 1983; Oct–Nov: 10-11.

59. Bull N. Dietary habits of 15 to 25-year-olds. *Hum. Nutr. Appl. Nutr.* 1985; 39A (suppl): 1–68.

60. Cannon G. Young people: a falling generation? *New Health*, November 1985.

61. Paul A., Southgate D. *The Composition of Foods*. London: HMSO, 1979.

62. National Research Council. Recommended dietary allowances. Ninth revised edition. Washington: National Academy of Sciences, 1980.

63. Statutory Instruments. Food labelling, descriptions etc. The food labelling regulations 1984. No. 1305. London: HMSO, 1984.

64. Smithells R., Seller M., Harris R. *et al.* Further evidence of vitamin supplementation for prevention of neural tube defects. *Lancet* 1983; I: 1027–1031.

65. Smithells R. Prevention of neural tube defects by vitamin supplementation. In *Prevention of Spina Bifida and other Neural Tube Defects*, ed. Dobbing J. London: Academic Press, 1983.

66. Doyle W. Personal communication.

67. Doyle W., Crawford M., Lawrence B., Drury P. Dietary survey during pregnancy in a low socio-economic group. *Hum. Nutr. Appl. Nutr.* 1982; 36A: 95–106.

68. Crawford M., Doyle W., Craft I., Laurence B. A comparison of food intake during pregnancy and birthweight in high and low socio-economic groups. Unpublished.

69. Livingstone R., Galloway D., MacGregor J. *et al.* US poverty impact on brain development. *Int. Brain Res. Organ*, Mono Ser 1, ed. Brazier M. New York: Raven Press, 1975.

70. Cannon G., Walker C. The wheel of health (unpublished).

71. Driver C. How the poor eat. *New Society*, 22 November 1984.

72. Jack I. The best of times .... the worst of times. *Sunday Times Magazine*, 25 August 1985.

73. Organisation for Economic Cooperation and Development. Food consumption statistics 1955–71. Paris: OECD 1973.

74. World Health Organization. Prevention of coronary heart disease. Report of a WHO expert committee, Geneva: WHO, 1982.

75. Marmot M., Adelstein A., Robinson N., Rose G. Changing social-class distribution of heart disease. *Br. Med. J.* 1978; 2: 1109–1112.

76. Marmot M., Shipley M., Rose G. Inequalities in death – specific explanations of a general pattern? *Lancet* 1984; I: 1003–1006.

77. Bender A. Institutional malnutrition. *Br. Med. J.* 1984; 288: 92–9.
78. Herfst H., Nelson M., Woolaway M. The nutritive value of school and hospital meals *Proc. Nutr. Soc.* 398th meeting, 15 May 1984.
79. Schorah C. Inappropriate vitamin C reserves: their frequency and significance in an urban population. In *The Importance of Vitamins to Human Health*, ed. Taylor T. Lancaster: MTP Press, 1979.
80. Anon. Nutritional support, *Lancet* 1983; I: 1025–1026.
81. Shenkin A., Wretlind A. Parental Nutrition, *Wld Rev. Nutr. Diet* 1978; 28: 1–111.
82. Smith E. Report from commissioners 13. Public Health Act, Public records, 1864; XXVIII.
83. Barber T., Oddy D., Yudkin J. *The Dietary Surveys of Dr Edward Smith, 1862–1863.* London: Staples Press/Queen Elizabeth College, 1970.
84. Hughes R., Jones E. *The mid-nineteenth century Welsh diet.* Food education society. Aspects of nutrition in Wales, 1982.
85. Hughes R., Jones E. Holism and reductionism in nutrition: life-span studies with mice. *Nutr. Rep. Int.* 1984; 29: 1009–16.
86. Wretlind A. Nutrition problems in healthy adults with low activity and low caloric consumption. In *Nutrition and Physical Activity*, ed. Blix G. Stockholm: Almqvist & Wiksell, 1967.
87. Hughes R. Personal communication.
88. Poh Tan S., Wenlock R., Buss D. Folic acid content of the diet in various types of British household. *Hum. Nutr: Appl Nutr.* 1984; 38A: 17–22.
89 Burnett J. *Plenty and Want.* London: Methuen, 1983.
90. Geidion S. *Mechanisation Takes Command.* New York: Oxford University Press, 1948.
91. Mintz S. *Sweetness and Power.* London: Viking, 1985.
92. Boyd Orr J. *Food Health and Income. A survey of adequacy of diet in relation to income.* London: Macmillan, 1936, 1937.
93. World Health Organisation. Primary health care. Alma Ata, 1978. WHO: Geneva, 1978.
94. Boyd Orr J. *et al.* Dietary study (the Carnegie survey). Aberdeen: Rowett Research Institute (unpublished).
95. Greaves J., Hollingsworth D. Trends in food consumption in the United Kingdom, *Wld. Rev. Nutr. Diet* 1966; 6: 34–89.
96. Ministry of Food. Manual of Nutrition. London: HMSO, 1945, 1953.
97. Department of Health and Social Security. Diet and cardiovascular disease. Committee on Medical Aspects of Food Policy. London: HMSO, 1984.
98. Marr J. Putting dietary theory into practice. *British Nutrition Foundation Bulletin* 38, 1983; 8(2): 65–72.
99. Taverner J. Talkback: the food scandal. Letter. *Times*, 19 June 1984.
100. Burkitt D. Some diseases characteristic of modern Western civilisation. *Br. Med. J.* 1973; I: 274–278.
101. Sinclair H. Deficiency of essential fatty acids and atherosclerosis, etc. *Lancet* 1956; I: 381–383.
102. Cleave T. *The Saccharine Disease.* Bristol: John Wright, 1974.

103. Trowell H., Burkitt, D. (eds), *Western Diseases: their emergence and prevention*. London: Edward Arnold, 1981.
104. Trowell H., Burkitt D., Heaton K. (eds). *Dietary Fibre, Fibre-Depleted Foods and Disease*. London: Academic Press, 1985.
105. Select Committee on Nutrition and Human Needs. Dietary Goals for the United States. Washington: US Government Printing Office, 1977 (March), 1977 (December).
106. National Research Council, Diet, nutrition and cancer. Assembly of Life Sciences. Washington: National Academy Press, 1982.
107. Turner R. Coronary heart disease. The size and nature of the problem. *Postgrad. Med. J.* 1980; 56: 538–547.
108. Truswell A. The development of dietary guidelines. *Food Technology in Australia* 1983; 35 (11): 498–502.
109. Media Expenditure Analysis Limited. Food company expenditure, 1980 and 1985. London: MEAL, 1986.
110. British Medical Association. Diet, nutrition and health. Report of the Board of Science and Education. London: BMA, 1986.
111. Anon. Britain needs a food and health policy: the government must face its duty. *Lancet* 1986; II: 434–436.
112. Prentice T. Ministers accused of failing in fight against bad-diet deaths. *Times*, 25 August 1986.
113. Anon. Britons 'eat worse than dogs' *Daily Mirror*, 26 August 1986.
114. Joint Advisory Council on Nutrition Education. Eating for a healthier heart. London: British Nutrition Foundation/Health Education Council, 1985.
115. Health Education Council. *Guide to healthy eating*. London: HEC, 1986.
116. Anon. Food for thought. *Daily Mirror*, 27 August 1986.
117. Doll R. Prospects for prevention. *Br. Med. J.* 1983; 286: 445–453.
118. Doll R. Personal communication.
119. Morris J. Personal communication.

CHAPTER 2

1. Nilson B. *The Penguin Cookery Book*. London: Penguin, 1952.
2. Igoe R. *Dictionary of Food Ingredients*. New York: Van Nostrand, 1983.
3. Hanbury-Tenison M. *Soups and Hors d'Oeuvres*. London: Penguin, 1969.
4. Cabinet Office. Advisory Council for Applied Research and Technology. The food industry and technology. London: HMSO, 1982.
5. Cake and Biscuit Alliance. Annual report 1985. London: CBA, 1986.
6. Pragnall G. Flour confectionery. Lecture given to the Society of Chemical Industry (Oils and Fats Group). London, February 1985. Unpublished.
7. Wapshott N, Brock G. *Thatcher*. London: Macdonald, 1983.

8. Ministry of Agriculture, Fisheries and Food. Second report on food labelling. Food Standards Committee. London: HMSO, 1979.
9. Ministry of Agriculture, Fisheries and Food. Household food consumption and expenditure: 1984. Report of the national food survey committee. London: HMSO, 1986.
10. Brasier M. Sainsbury tops £200 million profit mark. *Guardian*, 21 May 1986.
11. Sainsbury. If it isn't better, cheaper or different, it isn't Sainsbury's. Advertisement. *Daily Telegraph*, 8 July 1986.
12. Thames Television. Personal communication.
13. BBC Television (Continuing Education). Personal communication.
14. Thames Television. Good Enough To Eat? London: Thames tv, 1985.
15. BBC Television. Eat your way to health. An introduction to healthy eating. London: BBCtv, 1986.
16. BBC Television. You are what you eat. A practical guide to healthy eating. London: BBCtv, 1986.
17. Moody J. The confectionery battlefield. *Campaign*, 15 June 1984.
18. Huxley J. Bar wars. *Sunday Times*, 6 January 1985.
19. Morris R. Shops threat by animal group. *Times*, 20 November 1984.
20. O'Reilly D. 1983: the top 250 spenders. *Campaign*, 15 June 1984.
21. O'Reilly D. 1984: the top 250 spenders. *Campaign*, 7 June 1985.
22. Maxwell M. Top 40 food accounts. *Media Week*, 30 May 1986.
23. Gee-Smyth A. Wholemeal sets pace as bread buying increases. *Times*, 18 August 1986.
24. Department of Health and Social Security. Ray Whitney MP. Parliamentary written answer, 8 April 1986.
25. Health Education Council. White bread endorsed. HEC press release, April 1985.
26. Department of Health and Social Security. Nutritional aspects of bread and flour. Report of the panel on bread, flour and other cereal products. Committee on Medical Aspects of Food Policy. London: HMSO, 1981.
27. Anon. Bread giant backs marathon fun run. *Marketing*, 14 March 1985.
28. Etherington D. Cricket gives backers healthy sales pitch. *Marketing*, 18 April 1985.
29. Allied Bakeries. Beating heart disease with Allinson Health Education Council, 1985: Little Softie. Unpublished.
30. Pile S. How they scotched the great auk story. *Sunday Times*, 11 May 1986.
31. Butter Information Council. Diet and health. News-sheets. Sevenoaks: BIC 1981–85.
32. Sugar Bureau. Diet and Health. Invitation to meeting. London: Sugar Bureau, 1985.
33. Curzon M. Personal communication.
34. Curzon M. Dental caries. Talk given on 24 April 1985. Unpublished.
35. Sugar Bureau. Dental caries: putting sugar in perspective. London:

Sugar Bureau, 1985.

36. Butter Information Council. Welcome back to butter! *Butter World*, January 1985.

37. Butter Information Council. Facts on fat. Booklet. Sevenoaks: BIC 1985.

38. Ministry of Agriculture, Fisheries and Food. Personal communication.

39. Yallop A. Unmelted by the butter ads. Letter, *Guardian*, July 1985.

40. Wicken G., Byles D. That's the way the money goes. *Media Week*, 30 May 1986.

41. Media Expenditure Analysis Limited. Food company expenditure, 1980 and 1985. London: MEAL, 1986.

42. Walker C., Cannon G. *The Food Scandal*. Paperback edition, London: Century, 1985.

43. Salt Data Centre. Personal communication.

44. Faculty of Community Medicine of the Royal College of Physicians. Dietary salt and health. Report of the Health Promotion Committee. Unpublished.

45. Department of Health and Social Security. Diet and cardiovascular disease. Committee on Medical Aspects of Food Policy. London: HMSO, 1984.

46. Anon. Industry boss slams eat less meat warning. *Meat Trades Journal*, 5 July 1984.

47. Anon. Showdown! *Meat Trades Journal*, 28 June 1984.

48. Ranks Hovis McDougall. The white bread that made the dieticians eat their words. Advertisement. *Radio Times*, 23–29 June 1984.

49. Anon. Food for thought. *Meat Trades Journal*, 28 June 1984.

50. Anon. Now's the time to knock the industry's many critics. *Meat Trades Journal*, 5 July 1984.

51. Anon. Bang goes the MPE. *Farming News*, 3 May 1985.

52. A'Court F. Cancer prevention: new hope in meat. *Meat Trades Journal*, 25 April 1985.

53. Anon. MPE announced campaign for Pork Pie Month. *Meat Trades Journal*, 28 March 1985.

54. Anon. 'Real meat' could be future growth area. *Meat Trades Journal*, 25 April 1985.

55. Scandia. Inject a little advanced engineering. When standards must be high. Advertisements. *Meat Industry*, April 1985.

56. Roberts D. When is a sausage not what it seems? *Municipal Journal*, 16 August 1985.

57. Ministry of Agriculture, Fisheries and Food. Report on meat products. Food Standards Committee. London: HMSO, 1980.

58. Statutory Instruments. Food composition and labelling. The meat products and spreadable fish products regulations 1984. London: HMSO, 1984.

59. Dickinson D. Dispatch the scaremongers. *Meat Trades Journal*, 5 July 1984.

60. Anon. 2,000 sausage jobs cut blamed on media. *Times*, 5 July 1986.

61. Erlichman J. Unilever to shed 2,000 jobs at meat plants. *Guardian*, 5

July 1986.
62. Mintel. Healthy food and health food. London: Mintel, July 1985.
63. MORI. Attitudes towards meat and health. London: MORI, 1985.
64. Cooper D. The Food Programme. BBC Radio 4. 11 April 1986.
65. Seal R. The importance of additives. *Food Manufacture*, August 1985.
66. Cannon G. Trade secrets. In: *Additives: Your Complete Survival Guide*, ed Lawrence F. London: Century, 1986.
67. University of Reading. Undergraduate prospectus 1986. Reading: The University, 1986.
68. Rhodes M. Interviewed on the *Food Programme*. BBC Radio 4, 11 April 1986.
69. RHM Ingredients Supplies. All done in the best possible taste. *Food Manufacture*, February 1985.
70. Ministry of Agriculture, Fisheries and Food. Michael Jopling comments on COMA report. Press release no. 241. London: MAFF, 12 July 1984.
71. Department of Health and Social Security. Chief Medical Officer's Committee on Medical Aspects of Food Policy (COMA). Memorandum. (?) July 1984. Unpublished.
72. Lang T. Presentation at launch of London Food Commission, 23 April 1985. Unpublished.
73. London Food Commission. London Food News no.1. London: LFC, Spring 1985.
74. Luba A. The food labelling debate. London: Food Commission, 1985.
75. Miller M. Danger! Additives at work. A report on food additives: their use and control. London: Food Commission, 1985.
76. Webb T. Food irradiation in Britain? London: Food Commission, 1986.
77. Snell P., Nicol K. Pesticide residues and food. The case for real control. London: Food Commission, 1986.
78. Cole-Hamilton I, Lang T. Tightening belts. A report on the impact of poverty on food. London: Food Commission, 1986.
79. Millstone E. *Food Additives*. London: Penguin, 1986.
80. Lawrence F. (ed). *Food Additives: Your Complete Survival Guide*. London: Century, 1986.
81. Cooper D. The Food Programme. BBC Radio 4. 13 December 1985.
82. Anon. Britain needs a food and health policy: the Government must face its duty. *Lancet* 1986; II: 434–436.
83. Wyatt W. Give this secrecy the bird! *News of the World*, 15 December 1985.
84. Norton-Taylor R. Professor accuses Whitehall of Secrets Act 'gag' on doctors. *Guardian*, 9 June 1986.
85. Rose G. Doctors and the Official Secrets Act. *Br. Med. J.* 1986; 292: 1594.
86. British Dietetic Association. A discussion paper on proposals for nutritional guidelines for health education in Britain. Birmingham: BDA, 1984.

87. Health Education Council. Guide to healthy eating. London: HEC, 1986.

88. British Medical Association. Diet, nutrition and health. London: BMA, 1986.

89. Department of Health and Social Security. Committee on Medical Aspects of Food Policy. Panel on bread, flour and other cereal products. Minutes of meetings. Unpublished.

90. Fortescue T. Nutrition: a new challenge for the food industries of the world. Paper presented at the XIII International Congress of Nutrition, Brighton, 20 August 1985. Unpublished.

91. Angel D. Birds Eye Wall's: annual review. Speech. Unpublished.

92. Hume A. Chemistry on your table. Letter to all major supermarkets. October 1985. Unpublished.

93. Conning D. In: What are they doing to our food? *Sunday Times Magazine*, 20 October 1985.

94. The Sugar Bureau. Food Leninists attacked at sugar conference. News bulletin, London: Sugar Bureau, October 1985.

95. Moore T. Crisps: apple of a dietician's eye. *Sunday Times*, 9 March 1986.

96. Naismith D. Personal communication.

97. Snack, Nut and Crisp Manufacturers Association. News release. London: SNACMA, March 1986.

98. Sanders T. BBCtv *London Plus* interview, 4 March 1986.

99. Allen R. London Food Commission. Letter, 9 February 1986. Unpublished.

100. Erlichman J. Food firms put bite on 'faddists' who are ruining their figures. *Guardian*, 4 July 1986.

101. Drummond J., Wilbraham A. *The Englishman's Food*. London: Jonathan Cape, 1939.

102. Boyd Orr J. *Food Health and Income*. A survey of adequacy of diet in relation to income. London: Macmillan, 1936.

103. Acheson D. Food policy, nutrition and government. Tenth Boyd Orr Memorial Lecture. *Proc. Nutr. Soc.* 1986; 45: 131–138.

104. Ministry of Health. On the state of the public health during six years of war. Report of the chief medical officer of the Ministry of Health. London: HMSO, 1946.

105. Hollingsworth D. 25 years of change: the British diet 1952 to 1977. *British Nutrition Foundation Bulletin* 22, 1978; 4 (4): 264–277.

106. Marsh J. Food policy. Statement prepared for BFMIRA symposium on nutrition and health, 28–29 November 1985. Unpublished.

107. Andriessen M. Stockpiles of food. Answer to question by Bob Cryer. Official journal of the European community, 8 July 1985.

108. Erlichman J. The politics of sugars in Britain and Europe. Talk given to McCarrison Society conference on Sugars: A Menace to Public Health? 4 July 1986. Unpublished.

109. National Economic Development Council. Review of the food and drink manufacturing industry. London: NEDC, 1983.

110. Horsburgh S. Changing levels of concentration in the post farm food chain 1950–82. Manchester Polytechnic, 1985.

111. Unilever. Prospectus. The Netherlands. Unilever, 1983.
112. Body R. *Agriculture: The Triumph and the Shame*. London: Temple Smith, 1983.
113. Dobie C. Unilever joins £1bn profits club after 20 per cent rise. *Independent*, 4 March 1987.
114. ICI. ICI Profits top £1 billion again. Company report. *Guardian*, 27 February 1987.
115. Tyrrell R. Talk given to Food and Drink Federation conference, 25 February 1986. Unpublished.

CHAPTER 3

1. Royal College of Physicians. Obesity. J. Roy. Coll. Phys. London 1983; 17: 3–58.
2. Erlichman J. Tate & Lyle in £35m US expansion. *Guardian*, 13 December 1984.
3. Sprague W. Introductory remarks. World Sugar Research Organisation Symposium, Durban. London: WSRO, 1983.
4. Macdonald I. Medicine and sugar – crystal gazing. As above.
5. British Nutrition Foundation. Annual report 1981–82. London: BNF, 1982.
6. University of Reading. Undergraduate prospectus 1986. Reading: University, 1986.
7. Vlitos A. New products from sugar. World Sugar Research Organisation Symposium, Caracas. London: WSRO, 1981.
8. Vlitos A. WSRO: where do we go from here? World Sugar Research Organisation Symposium, Durban. London: WSRO, 1983.
9. Williams I. Threat to sugar jobs as bid war boils over. *Sunday Times*, 22 June 1986.
10. House of Commons. Register of Members' Interests on 13 January 1986. London: HMSO, 1986.
11. Shaw N., Shersby M. Discussion. World Sugar Research Organisation Symposium, Durban. London: WSRO, 1983.
12. Reid J. The life cycle of funding committees, and the basis of committee decisions. As above.
13. World Sugar Research Organisation. Special bulletin no. 1. Recent research projects sponsored by members of the World Sugar Research Organisation – a global effort. London: WSRO, 1983.
14. Anon. A healthy trend in our eating habits. *Daily Mail*, 27 June 1983.
15. Anon. Households spend more on foods. *Daily Telegraph*, 27 June 1983.
16. Parry B. 'Healthy trend' in food sales. *Daily Telegraph*, 22 October 1984.
17. Anon. 'Danger' meat gets the cold shoulder. *Daily Mail*, 22 October 1984.
18. Anon. Oat cuisine is in. *Daily Mirror*, 22 October 1984.

19. Anon. 'Good health' food is top of the menu. *Sun*, 22 October 1984.
20. Ministry of Agriculture, Fisheries and Food. Household food consumption in the first quarter of 1983. Press release: Food Facts no. 3. National Food Survey.
21. Ministry of Agriculture, Fisheries and Food. Household food consumption in the second quarter of 1984. Press release: Food Facts no.4. National Food Survey.
22. Ministry of Agriculture, Fisheries and Food. Household food consumption and expenditure: 1982. Annual report of the National Food Survey committee. London: HMSO, 1984.
23. Ministry of Agriculture, Fisheries and Food. Household food consumption and expenditure: 1984. Annual report of the National Food Survey Committee. London: HMSO, 1986.
24. National Advisory Committee for Nutrition Education. A discussion paper on proposals for nutritional guidelines for health education in Britain. London: Health Education Council, 1983.
25. Department of Health and Social Security. Diet and cardiovascular disease. Committee on Medical Aspects of Food Policy. London: HMSO, 1984.
26. Department of Health and Social Security. Diet and coronary heart disease. Committee on Medical Aspects of Food Policy. London: HMSO, 1974.
27. Yudkin J. Personal communication.
28. Butter Information Council. Facts on fat. Booklet. Sevenoaks: BIC, 1985.
29. Yudkin J. Letter. *Daily Telegraph*, 24 June 1986.
30. The Sugar Bureau. Sweet news: sugar does not make you fat. News bulletin, 9 May 1986.
31. Kingsway Public Relations. Diet and health. Invitation to meetings. London: Kingsway, 1985.
32. Durnin J. Letter to Daily Telegraph, June 1986. Unpublished.
33. The Sugar Bureau. COMA report clears sugar from CHD implication. Press release. 16 July 1984.
34. Vincent L. Mr Cube from Montreal. *Observer*, 29 July 1984.
35. The Sugar Bureau. The world of sugar. Supplement to *The Grocer*, 9 February 1985.
36. Department of Health and Social Security. Eating for health. A discussion booklet prepared by the Health Departments of Great Britain and Northern Ireland. London: HMSO, 1978.
37. Haslam R. Record profits and dividend after five years' progress. Tate & Lyle annual report. *Guardian*, 2 February 1984.
38. Somerville G. End of static decade for coronary heart disease. *Lancet* 1984; II: 1455.
39. Beckett J., Shersby M. The position in the United Kingdom. World Sugar Research Organisation Symposium, Caracas. London: WSRO, 1979.
40. Buss D. Personal communication.
41. Ministry of Agriculture, Fisheries and Food. John MacGregor MP. Reply to Written Question. House of Commons Official Report

(Hansard), 14 February 1985.

42. Ahlfeld H. Per capita consumption – present and future review of the past ten years and forecast for the next ten. World Sugar Research Organisation Symposium, Caracas. London: WRSO, 1979.

43. Derry B., Buss D. The National Food Survey as a major epidemiological tool. *Br. Med. J.* 1984; 288: 765–767.

44. Paul A., Southgate D (eds). *The Composition of Foods.* London; HMSO, 1979.

45. Department of Health and Social Security. Recommended intakes of nutrients for the United Kingdom. Committee on Medical Aspects of Food Policy. London: HMSO; 1981.

46. Prentice A., Coward W., Davies H., et al. Unexpectedly low levels of energy expenditure in healthy women. *Lancet* 1985; I: 1419–1422.

47. Hentzer P. *A journey into England, 1598.* 1757: Strawberry Hill, England.

48. Hart J. *Klinike, or The Diet of the Diseases.* London: John Beale, 1633.

49. Mintz S. *Sweetness and Power:* The place of sugar in modern history. London: Viking, 1985.

50. Lonrho. Annual report 1985–86. London: Lonrho, 1986.

51. Vlitos A. How sugars and syrups are made. Draft papers for the British Nutrition Foundation Task Force on sugars and syrups. Unpublished.

52. The Sugar Association Inc. and Carl Byoir and Associates. Planning. Undated. Unpublished.

53. Priorities Board for Research and Development in Agriculture and Food. First report to the Agriculture Ministers and the Chairman of the Agriculture and Food Council. London: MAFF, December 1985.

54. Watson-James D. Personal communication.

55. Williams E. *Capitalism and Slavery.* University of North Carolina Press, 1944.

56. Quick A., Sheiham H., Sheiham A. Sweet Nothings. The information the public receives about sugar. London: Health Education Council. Unpublished.

57. Walker C., Cannon G. *The Food Scandal.* Paperback edition. London: Century, 1985.

58. Saatchi and Saatchi. Personal communication.

59. Direction. Supplement to Campaign, July 1984.

60. Harris D. British Sugar plans £2 million sales push. *Times,* 8 May 1984.

61 Anon. £2 million Silver Spoon bid to stem fall. *Marketing,* 4 May 1984.

62. Mackie A. Battle joined by health lobbyists. Letter. The *Sunday Times,* 10 July 1983.

63. Anon. Independence fears for new health council. *Independent,* 22 November 1986.

64. Dufty W. *Sugar Blues.* New York: Warner Books, 1975.

65. Epstein S. *The Politics of Cancer.* New York: Anchor Books, 1979.

66. Ministry of Agriculture, Fisheries and Food. Report on the review of

sweeteners in food. Food Additives and Contaminants Committee. London: HMSO, 1982.

67. Hollie P. Diet Coke claim ignites dispute over no. 3 spot. *New York Times*, 8 March 1984.

68. Marsh P. Secret ingredient at Schweppes. *Financial Times*, 1 May 1985.

69. Anon. The CU cola challenge. *Consumer Reports*, February 1984.

70. Cookson C. New chemical sweeteners set to challenge sugar and saccharin monopolies. *Times*, 3 September 1983.

71. Phillips C. Searle fights to keep red-hot aspartame hot for a long time. *Wall Street Journal*, 18 September 1983.

72. Veitch A. *Guardian*. Feature series, 3–9 September 1983.

73. Wurtman J. *The Carbohydrate Craver's Diet*. London: Arlington Books, 1984.

74. Gelman E. et al. Coke tampers with success. *Newsweek*, 6 May 1985.

75. Royal College of Physicians. *Medical Aspects of Dietary Fibre*. Tunbridge Wells: Pitman, 1980.

76. Heaton K. The sweet road to gall stones. *Lancet* 1984; I: 1103–1104.

77. British Sugar Bureau. Sweet Reason. London: Sugar Bureau, 1983.

78. Papers due to be presented at the International Seminar on Dietary Carbohydrate and Disease, 10 November 1983. Unpublished.

79. Shersby M. Send three and fourpence! Letter to doctors, dentists and medical writers. London: Sugar Bureau, December 1984.

80. Yudkin J. *Pure, White and Deadly*. London: Viking, 1986.

81. Reiser S. Metabolic risk factors associated with heart disease and diabetes in carbohydrate-sensitive humans when consuming sucrose as compared with starch. In: *Metabolic Effects of Utilisable Dietary Carbohydrates*. New York: Marcel Dekker, 1982.

82. Reiser S. Physiological differences between starches and sugars. In Bland J. (ed): *Medical Applications of Clinical Nutrition*. New Canaan, Connecticut: Keats, 1983.

83. Selwyn S. The microbiological background to the use of sugar in wound therapy. World Sugar Research Organisation Symposium, Durban. London: WRSO, 1983.

84. Cannon G. The food scandal. *Times*, 11–13 June 1984.

85. Vlitos A., Selwyn S. Letters to *Times*, 13 and 14 June 1984. Unpublished.

86. Midda M. Talkback: the food scandal. Letter. *Times*, 22 June 1984.

87. Macdonald I. Nutrition in balance – fact and fantasy. *British Nutrition Foundation Bulletin* 1985; 10 (44): 75–89.

88. Anon. Scientist says sugar may prolong life. *Daily Telegraph*, 18 August 1986.

89. Whelan E., Stare F. *The One-Hundred Per-cent Natural, Purely Organic, Cholesterol-Free, Megavitamin, Low-Carbohydrate Nutrition Hoax*. New York: Atheneum, 1983.

90. Stare F. Food faddism. Lecture. The Sugar Research Foundation, 16 May 1951.

91. Center for Science in the Public Interest. Feeding at the Company Trough. Washington: CSPI, 1976.

92. Anon. Too much of a good thing can be dangerous. *Sugar Nutrition Abstracts* no. 8, February 1985.

93. American Diabetes Association. Principles of nutrition and dietary recommendations for individuals with diabetes mellitus: 1979. *Diabetes* 1979; 28: 1027–1030.

94. British Diabetic Association. Dietary recommendations for diabetics in the 1980s – a policy statement by the British Diabetic Association. London: BDA, 1983.

95. Slama G., Jean-Joseph P., Goicolea I., et al. Sucrose taken during mixed meal has no additional hyperglycaemic action over isocaloric starch in well-controlled diabetics. *Lancet* 1984; II: 122–125.

96. Ferner R; also Heaton K., Emmett P., Hartog M. Rice or sucrose in the diabetic diet. *Lancet* 1984; II: 585.

97 Keen H. Sugar and diabetes. Talk given on 15 May 1985. Unpublished.

98. Keen H., Thomas B., Jarrett R., Fuller J. Nutrient intake, adiposity and diabetes. *Br. Med. J.* 1979; I: 655–658.

99. The Sugar Bureau. Putting sugar in perspective. Briefing papers on dental caries, diabetes, diet and behaviour, and obesity. London: The Sugar Bureau, 1985.

100 The Sugar Bureau. Letter from Gerard Bithell to Earl Kitchener. 8 April 1986.

101. The Sugar Bureau. Invitation to 'satellite symposium' at XIII International Congress of Nutrition. 21 August 1985.

102. Marks V. Presentation at Sugar Bureau meeting at XIII International Congress of Nutrition. Unpublished.

103. Clark M., Gosnell M., Katz S., Hager M. The perils of a sweet tooth. *Newsweek*, 25 August 1985.

104 The Sugar Bureau. Food Leninists attacked at sugar conference. News bulletin. 22 October 1985.

105. World Sugar Research Organisation. A progress report on the US Food and Drug Administration Task Force Study on Sugars and Sweeteners. Invitation to meeting. London: WSRO, 1986.

106. World Sugar Research Organisation. Symposium on Sugars and Sweeteners. List of participants and organisations represented. Unpublished.

107. World Sugar Research Organisation. Safety of sugars reconfirmed. News release, 27 May 1986.

108. The Sugar Bureau. Letter from Gerard Bithell to *Homes and Gardens*. Unpublished.

109. Anon. Malnutrition for food faddists' children. *Daily Telegraph*, 2 June 1986.

110. Young J. Professor scolds 'muesli-belt' parents. *Times*, 2 June 1986.

111. Anon. 'Middle-class food fads harm children'. *Daily Mail*, 2 June 1986.

112. Anon. Food fad threat to children's health. *Daily Express*, 2 June 1986.

113. Anon. Kids starve on health foods. *Daily Mirror*, 2 June 1986.

114. Anon. Expert raps the 'muesli menace'. *Today*, 2 June 1986.

115. Anon. An end to the muesli misery. *Today*, 3 June 1986.
116. Norman M. When health food is bad for you. *Daily Telegraph*, 3 June 1986.
117. Grice E. Let them eat cake! *Daily Express*, 4 June 1986.
118. Clough P. Doctors speak in defence of muesli. *Times*, 3 June 1986.
119. House of Commons. Parliamentary debate. Hansard (official record) Simon Coombs MP. Question. 19 November 1984.
120. Department of Health and Social Security. Letter from Jeremy Metters to Advice and Information on Sugar. 24 June 1985.
121 Department of Health and Social Security. Letter from John Patten MP. Unpublished.
122. Department of Health and Social Security. John Patten MP. Answer to Parliamentary Question from Michael Meadowcroft MP. 10 April 1984.
123. British Nutrition Foundation. Task Force on sugars and syrups. Minutes of meetings, internal correspondence, and other papers. Unpublished.
124. As above. Morse E. Recommendations and conclusions. Draft papers.
125. Granada Television. *World in Action*. 'The great food scandal.' Statement by Dr Derek Shrimpton, 7 October 1985.
126. Greener G., Hawthorn J. What are sugars and syrups? Draft papers for the British Nutrition Foundation Task Force on sugars and syrups. Unpublished.
127. As above. Greener G., Hawthorn J. The role of sugars in food and drink. Draft papers. Unpublished.
128. As above. Booth D. How sugars and syrups affect eating habits. Draft papers. Unpublished.
129. As above. Pyke D. Diabetes. Draft papers. Unpublished.
130. Woo R., Garrow J. Pi-Sunyer F-X. Effect of exercise on spontaneous calorie intake in obesity. *Am. J. Clin. Nutr.* 1982; 36: 470–477, 478–484.
131. British Library. Research in British universities, polytechnics and colleges, 1980–85. London: British Library.
132. Cocoa, Chocolate and Confectionery Alliance. Personal communication.
133. Royal Liverpool Hospital. Personal communication.
134. Garrow J. Sugars, energy metabolism and obesity. Draft papers for the British Nutrition Foundation Task Force on sugars and syrups. Unpublished.
135. Hennessy T., Darwen C. Sugar and obesity. Tate & Lyle submission to the British Nutrition Foundation Task Force on sugars and syrups. Unpublished.
136. Righelato R. Letter to Professor A.J. Vlitos. 19 December 1984. Unpublished.
137. Edgar M. Dental health. Draft papers for the British Nutrition Foundation Task Force on sugars and syrups. Unpublished.
138. As above. G. Greener. Commentaries on sugars and dental health draft. Unpublished.

139. Mars. Sugars and dental health. Submission to the British Nutrition Foundation Task Force on sugars and syrups. Unpublished.
140. Department of Health and Social Security. Barney Hayhoe MP: Written Answer, 17 February 1986.
141. Ministry of Agriculture, Fisheries and Food. Peggy Fenner MP: reply to Simon Coombs MP. Meeting of Coronary Prevention Group, 13 May 1986. Unpublished.
142. Shrimpton D. Personal communication.
143. Sanderson M. Towards a sugar health policy. Thesis. Unpublished.
144. Sanderson M: sugars in the diet: practical aspects. Draft papers for the British Nutrition Foundation Task Force on sugars and syrups. Unpublished.
145. Vlitos A. Letter to Elizabeth Morse. 23 January 1986. Unpublished.
146. Greener G. Letter to Sir Cyril Clarke. 28 January 1986. Unpublished.
147. Booth D. Letter to Margaret Sanderson. 31 January 1986. Unpublished.
148. Garrow J. Letter to Sir Cyril Clarke. 4 February 1986. Unpublished.
149. Conning D. Sugars in the diet: practical aspects. Draft papers for the British Nutrition Task Force on sugars and syrups. Unpublished.
150. As above. Cottrell R. Role of sugars in some other disorders. Draft papers. Unpublished.
151. Snodin D. Sucrose and coronary heart disease. Tate & Lyle submission to the British Nutrition Foundation Task Force on sugars and syrups. Unpublished.
152. As above. Meade T. Sugars and coronary heart disease. Draft paper. Unpublished.
153. British Nutrition Foundation. *Bulletin* no. 1, March 1968.
154. British Nutrition Foundation, Annual report 1983–84, London: BNF, 1984.
155. British Medical Association, Diet, nutrition and health. Report of the Board of Science and Education, London: BMA, 1986.
156. Conning D., O'Donnell M. 'Calling the tune.' BBC Television: *O'Donnell Investigates*. 29 April 1986.
157. Conning D. Conclusions and recommendations. Draft paper for the British Nutrition Foundation Task Force on sugars and syrups. Paper TFS/SI/Conc/Rec/10 April 86 – Conning. Unpublished.
158. British Nutrition Foundation. BNF recommends caution on sugars. Press release, 25 April 1986.
159. Conning D., Conclusions and recommendations, London: BNF, April 1986.
160. Illman J. Personal communication.
161. Fletcher D. Doctors in row over 'diluted' sugar report. *Daily Telegraph*, 25 April 1986.
162. Veitch A. Sugar inquiry report released without evidence. *Guardian*, 26 April 1986.
163. Anon. British Nutrition Foundation Task Force on sugars and syrups: a curious press conference. *Lancet*, 3 May 1986.
164. Walker C. Public communication.
165. Alexander D. Time for an inquiry. Letter. *Daily Telegraph*, 1 May

1986.
166. Anon. Effect of sugar in diet. Parliamentary report. *Times*, 11 July 1986.
167. Blackstone T. Battle on for sugar. *Sunday Times*, 20 April 1986.
168. Dover C. Junk Food 'adds spice to your life'. *Daily Express*, 24 April 1986.
169. Anon. The junk food way to keep good health. *Today*, 23 April 1986.
170. Collins R. Warning: food faddists are bad for your health. *Guardian*, 28 April 1986.
171. Hodgkinson L. Truth, myth and a load of sweet talk. *Daily Telegraph*, 25 April 1986.
172. American Council on Science and Health. Annual report 1984–85. New York: ACSH, 1985.
173. Center for Science in the Public Interest. Voodoo science, twisted consumerism. Washington: CSPI, 1983.
174. Whelan E. Personal communication.
175. Medical Research Council. Personal communication.
176. Shamoon S. Coke versus Pepsi: a classic battle. *Observer*, 10 November 1985.

CHAPTER 4

1. Grose D., Our polluted food – fact or fancy? *Royal Society of Health Journal*, October 1977.
2. Ministry of Agriculture, Fisheries and Food. Interim report on the review of the colouring matter in food regulations 1973. Food Additives and Contaminants Committee. London: HMSO, 1979.
3. Ministry of Agriculture, Fisheries and Food. Priorities Board for research and development in agriculture and food. First report. London: MAFF, 1985.
4. Ministry of Agriculture, Fisheries and Food. Priority of fast food industry. Press release no 321. 11 November 1985.
5. Cooper D., The taste of things to come. *Observer Magazine*, 26 February 1984.
6. Anon. Close-up on caramel. *Food Manufacture*, January 1985.
7. Ministry of Agriculture, Fisheries and Food. Michael Jopling calls for food industry's co-operation on COMA report and food additives. Press release no 301. 25 October 1985.
8. Thames Television. Good enough to eat? Booklet. London: Thames TV, 1985.
9. Russell J., The chemistry on your table. Presentation and discussion, 8 October 1985.
10. Chemical Industries Association. The chemistry on your table. Booklet. London: CIA, 1985.
11. Hume A., Personal communication.
12. Hume A., Chemistry on your table. Letter to all major supermarkets. Unpublished.

13. Department of Health and Social Security. Acheson E., Letter to all doctors in England. 27 June 1985.
14. Ministry of Agriculture, Fisheries and Food. Food additives: identification by serial numbers. London: Central Office of Information, 1985.
15. Williams B., The Food Programme. Interview, 13 December 1985.
16. Snodin D., Personal communication.
17. Zaharah A., Ban on UK fruit drink. Malaysia: *The Sunday Mail*, 13 February 1983.
18. Anon. Cancer-causing red dye banned. *Newsletter of the Consumers' Association of Penang*. September 1982.
19. Epstein S., *The Politics of Cancer*. New York: Anchor Books, 1979.
20. Comptroller General of the United States. Need to establish the safety of the colour additive FD&C Red no 2. Report to Senator Gaylord Nelson. MWD-76–40, 1975, Washington DC.
21. Andrianova M., Carcinogenic properties of the red food dyes amaranth, ponceau SX, and ponceau 4R. *Voprosy Pitaniya*, 1970; 29/5.
22. Boffey P., Death of a dye. *New York Times* magazine, 29 February 1976.
23. Moreland G., Warning: Red dye no 40 may be hazardous to your health. *Nutrition Action*, February 1977.
24. Ministry of Agriculture, Fisheries and Food. Look at the label. London: MAFF, 1982.
25. Anon. Snap-fit capsules – all 8836 variants. Capsugel list of approved food dyes (valid for 62 countries and the EEC). 1977: Parke-Davis (circulated to the pharmaceutical industry).
26. Lawrence F(ed)., *Additives: Your Complete Survival Guide*. London: Century, 1986.
27. Consumers' Association. Food additives. 'Which', May 1986.
28. Bender A., *Health or Hoax?* Goring-on-Thames: Elvendon Press, 1985.
29. Ministry of Agriculture, Fisheries and Food. Food Advisory Committee. Press release no 377, 1 November 1984.
30. Statutory Instruments. The Food and Drugs Act 1955. London: HMSO, 1955.
31. Statutory Instruments. The Food Act 1984. London: HMSO, 1984.
32. Ministry of Agriculture, Fisheries and Food. Steering Group on Food Surveillance. Progress report 1984. London: HMSO, 1984.
33. Department of Health and Social Security. Artificial feeds for the young infant. Committee on Medical Aspects of Food Policy. London: HMSO, 1980.
34. Ministry of Agriculture, Fisheries and Food. Personal communication.
35. House of Commons. Hansard (official report). Food additives: protection of children. Early Day Motion, 20 May 1986.
36. House of Commons. Hansard (official report). Confectionery industry. Debate, 24 May 1985.
37. Millstone E., *Additives*. London: Penguin, 1986.

38. Cannon G., Letter to Michael Jopling MP. Unpublished.
39. Ministry of Agriculture, Fisheries and Food. Michael Jopling MP. Personal communication.
40. Ministry of Agriculture, Fisheries and Food. Availability of toxicological data on food additives. Letter to interested parties. 11 July 1986.
41. Statutory Instruments. The colouring matter in food regulations 1973. London: HMSO, 1973.
42. Noltes A., Toxicity of caramel colours. In: *Food Toxicology: Real or Imaginary Problems*. London: Taylor and Francis, 1985.
43. Statutory Instruments. The cocoa and chocolate products regulations, 1976. SI 1976, no 541. London: HMSO, 1976.
44. Commission on the European Communities. Proposal for a Council Directive amending for the eighth time the Directive of 23 October 1962 on colouring matters. Brussels, September 1985.
45. Ministry of Agriculture, Fisheries and Food. Memorandum on the safety of food colours. Unpublished.
46. Department of Health and Social Security. Personal communication.
47. Ministry of Health. Report of the departmental committee on the use of preservatives and colouring matters in food. London: HMSO, 1924.
48. Ministry of Food. Report on colouring matters. Food Standards Committee. London: HMSO, 1954.
49. Ministry of Agriculture, Fisheries and Food. Supplementary report on colouring matters. Food Standards Committee. London: HMSO, 1955.
50. Statutory Instruments. The colouring matter in food regulations 1957. London: HMSO, 1957.
51. Ministry of Agriculture, Fisheries and Food. Report on colouring matters. Food Standards Committee. London: HMSO, 1964.
52. Conning D., Putting additives in perspective. *Food Manufacture*, June 1986.
53. Gillie O., Secrets of Brown FK and the British kipper. *Sunday Times*, 6 June 1986.
54. Food and Agriculture Organisation. FAO/WHO Food Additives Data System. FAO food and nutrition paper 30. Rome: FAO, 1984.
55. House of Commons. Hansard (official report). Simon Coombs MP (Question), Peggy Fenner MP (MAFF) (Answer). 18 March 1986.
56. Seal R., The importance of additives. *Food Manufacture*, August 1985.
57. Key Note Report. Food flavourings and ingredients. An industry sector overview. London: Key Note Publications, 1985.
58. Wolfe S., Lurie P., Letter to Frank D Young, Commissioner, FDA. Washington, DC: *Public Citizen*, 17 December 1984 (unpublished).
59. Wenlock R., Disselduff, M., Skinner, R., Knight, I., The diets of British schoolchildren. London: DHSS, 1986.
60. McLean A., Risk and benefit in food and additives. *Proc. Nutr. Soc.* 1977; 36: 85–90.
61. Turner A., A technologist looks at additives. *Food Manufacture*, August 1986.

62. Rivers J., Payne P., Why eating should carry a government health warning. *Nature* 1979; 291: 98–99.
63. Cross R., *Cross on Evidence*. Fifth edition. London: Butterworths, 1979.
64. Erlichman J., *Gluttons for Punishment*. London: Penguin, 1986.
65. Ministry of Agriculture, Fisheries and Food. Food Additives and Contaminants Committee. Appointment of members. Press notice no 402, 10 November 1982.
66. Consumers Committee for Great Britain. Calls for new consumers' body within MAFF. Press notice, 28 May 1986.
67. British Nutrition Foundation. *Why Additives?* The safety of foods. London: BNF, 1977.
68. Young F., In: *Why Additives?* The safety of foods. London: BNF, 1977.
69. Department of Health and Social Security. Diet and coronary heart disease. Committee on Medical aspects of Food Policy. London: HMSO, 1974.
70. Department of Health and Social Security. Recommended intakes of nutrients for the United Kingdom. Committee on Medical Aspects of Food Policy. London: HMSO, 1969, 1981.
71. Department of Health and Social Security. Recommended daily amounts of food energy and nutrients for groups of people in the United Kingdom. Committee on Medical Aspects of Food Policy. London: HMSO, 1979, 1981.
72. Department of Health and Social Security. Nutritional aspects of bread and flour. Committee on Medical Aspects of Food Policy. London: HMSO, 1981.
73. Department of Health and Social Security. Panel on bread, flour and other cereal products. Minutes of meetings. Unpublished.
74. Ministry of Agriculture, Fisheries and Food. Food Standards Committee. Appointment of members. Press notice no 278, 7 September 1977.
75. Durham K., 'Calling the tune.' BBC Television: O'Donnell investigates the food business. 29 April 1986.
76. Roe F.J.C., Are nutritionists worried about the epidemic of tumours in laboratory animals? *Proc. Nutr. Soc.*, 1981; 40: 57–66
77. Doll R., Peto R. *The Causes of Cancer*, Oxford: University Press, 1981.
78. National Research Council. Diet, Nutrition and Cancer. Committee on Diet, Nutrition and Cancer. Assembly of life sciences. Washington: National Academy Press, 1982.
79. Commission of the European Communities. Council Directive on the approximation of the laws of the Member States relating to the labelling, presentation and advertising of foodstuffs for sale to the ultimate consumer. Brussels: December 1978.
80. Statutory Instruments. The Food Labelling Regulations 1980. London: HMSO, 1980.
81. Ministry of Agriculture, Fisheries and Food. Food Standards Committee. Second report on food labelling. London: HMSO, 1979.

82. Gallup Polls. Health foods. Poll conducted for Tesco. London: Gallup, 1984.
83. Ministry of Agriculture, Fisheries and Food. Food Standards Committee. Appointment of members. Press notice no 278, 7 September 1977.
84. British Nutrition Foundation. Bulletins and annual reports 1967–86. London: BNF, 1968–86.
85. Allen R., Nutritional labelling. *British Nutrition Foundation Bulletin* 14, 1975; 3 (2): 113–119.
86. Passmore R., British Nutrition Foundation Bulletin 40, 1984; 9 (10: 50–51.
87. Statutory Instruments. The Food Labelling Regulations 1984. London: HMSO, 1984.
88. Ministry for Agriculture, Fisheries and Food. Revised proposals for food labelling (amendment) regulations. Circular to interested parties, 2 September 1983.
89. Hanssen M., *E for Additives*. Wellingborough: Thorsons, 1984.
90. Yeomans L., Public communication.
91. Bunday S., Personal communication.
92. Feingold B., *Why Your Child is Hyperactive*. New York: Random House, 1975.
93. House of Commons. Parliamentary debates. Hansard (official record). Willie Hamilton MP (Question), John Patten MP (DHSS) (Answer). 15 March 1984.
94. House of Commons. Parliamentary debates. Hansard (official record). Hyperactive children. Andrew Hunter MP, Stuart Randall MP, Robert Wareing MP (Questions), John Patten MP (DHSS) (Answer). 28 March 1984.
95. Royal College of Physicians/British Nutrition Foundation. Food intolerance and food aversion. A joint report. *J. Roy. Coll. Phys.*, London 1984; 18 (2): 3–41.
96. Guys Hospital Medical School. Annual reports of the Department of Medicine, 1975–82. London: Guys Hospital.
97. McDonald's Hamburgers. Good food, nutrition and McDonald's. Booklet. London: McDonald's, 1984.
98. Milk Marketing Board. Personal communication.
99. *Medical Research Directory*. London: Wiley Medical Publications, 1983.
100. Shrimpton D., Personal communication.
101. American Council on Science and Health. Annual report. 1984–85. New York: ACSH, 1985.
102. Amegavie L., Marzouk O., Mullen J., et al. Munchausen's syndrome by proxy: a warning for health professionals. *Br. Med. J.*, 1986; 293: 855–856.
103. Egger J., Wilson J., Carter C., Turner M., Soothill J., Is migraine food allergy? *Lancet*, 1983; II: 865–869.
104. Soothill J., Personal communication.
105. Egger J., Migraine and food allergy in children. Paper presented to the British Society for Nutritional Medicine, 8 September 1984.

Unpublished.

106. Egger J., Graham P., Carter C., Gumley D., Soothill J., Controlled trial of oligoantigenic treatment in the hyperkinetic syndrome. *Lancet* 1985; I: 540–545.

107. Sutcliffe Catering. Eat Fit. Brochure. London: Sutcliffe, 1985.

108. Hunter J., Alun Jones V., Workman E., *The Allergy Diet*. London: Martin Dunitz, 1984.

109. Addenbrooke's Hospital. Food Intolerance and Disease Research Appeal. Brochure, 1985.

110. Gray J., *Food Intolerance: Fact and Fiction*. London: Grafton, 1986.

111. Swain A., Soutter V., Loblay A., Truswell A., Salicylates, oligoantigenic diets, and behaviour. *Lancet* 1985; II: 41–42.

112. Anon. Top group in new law call. *Birmingham Daily News*, 6 December 1985.

113. Taylor E., Personal communication.

114. Wolfe C., MP to investigate children's food peril. *Birmingham Daily News*, 6 December 1985.

115. Sheerman B., Meeting held to launch FACT, 12 December 1985. Public communication.

116. Ministry of Agriculture, Fisheries and Food. Michael Jopling MP, Interview on TV-AM, 6 March 1986.

117. MacGibbon B., Adverse reactions to food additives. *Proc. Nutr. Soc.*, 1983; 42: 233–240.

118. Advisory Council for Applied Research and Development. Report on the food industry and technology. London: HMSO, 1982.

119. Ministry of Agriculture, Fisheries and Food. Proposals for new bread and flour regulations. Circulated to all interested parties. 5 September 1983.

120. Ministry of Agriculture, Fisheries and Food. Appointments to new Priorities Board for research and development in agriculture and food. Press release no 235, 9 July 1984.

121. Ministry of Agriculture, Fisheries and Food. Food quality. Commission review report. London: MAFF, 1984.

122. Ministry of Agriculture, Fisheries and Food. New consultative committee on food processing R & D. Press release no 58. 6 March 1986.

123. University of Reading. Undergraduate prospectus 1986. Reading: University, 1986.

124. Food and Drink Federation, Food and Drink Industries Council, Food Manufacturers Federation. Annual reports 1983–85. London: FDF, FDF/FMF, FDIC, FMF 1984–86.

125. Ministry of Agriculture, Fisheries and Food. Food Safety Research Consultative Committee. Report to the Priorities Board. London: MAFF, 1985.

126. Ministry of Agriculture, Fisheries and Food. Food safety research committee appointment. Press release no 298. 3 September 1984.

127. Ministry of Agriculture, Fisheries and Food. New objectives and opportunities for food safety research. Press release no. 281. 7 October 1985.

128. Anon. Food safety. *Lancet*, 1985; II: 1198.

129. Ministry of Agriculture, Fisheries and Food. Letter from J.B. Hirons. Unpublished.
130. Ministry of Agriculture, Fisheries and Food. Food safety 1985. Commission review report. London: MAFF, 1986.
131. Erlichman J. Food additive research cash 'is adequate'. *Guardian*, 3 July 1986.
132. Ministry of Agriculture, Fisheries and Food. Press release no 250. 18 September 1986.
133. Ministry of Agriculture, Fisheries and Food. Press release no 310. 10 November 1986.

CHAPTER 5

1. Wynn M., Wynn A., *Prevention of Handicap and the Health of Women*. London: Routledge and Kegan Paul, 1977.
2. Department of Health and Social Security/Department of Education and Science. Prevention and Health. London: HMSO, 1977.
3. Arendt H., *Crises of the Republic*. London: Penguin, 1972.
4. Department of Health and Social Security. Free milk and vitamins. For expectant mothers and children under 5. Leaflet. London: DHSS, 1983.
5. Marks J., *A Guide to the Vitamins. Their role in health and disease*. Lancaster: MTP Press, 1975.
6. Ministry of Agriculture, Fisheries and Food. Trend towards 'healthier' diet continues. Food facts. Press release, 13 October 1986.
7. Department of Health and Social Security. Recommended intakes of nutrients for the United Kingdom. Committee on Medical Aspects of Food Policy. London: HMSO, 1969, 1981.
8. Department of Health and Social Security. Recommended daily amounts of food energy and nutrients for groups of people in the United Kingdom. Committee on Medical Aspects of Food Policy. London: HMSO, 1979, 1981.
9. Department of Health and Social Security. Nutritional aspects of bread and flour. Committee on Medical Aspects of Food Policy. London: HMSO, 1981.
10. Passmore R., Eastwood N., *Human Nutrition and Dietetics*. Eighth edition. Edinburgh: Churchill Livingstone, 1986.
11. Widdowson E., Animals in the service of human nutrition. In: Taylor T., Jenkins N (eds)., *Proceedings of the XIII International Congress of Nutrition 1985*. London: John Libbey, 1986.
12. Yudkin J., *The Penguin Encylopaedia of Nutrition*. London: Viking, 1985.
13. Boyd Orr J., *Food Health and Income*. London: Macmillan, 1936.
14. McCarrison R., *Nutrition and Health*. The Cantor Lectures 1936. London: The McCarrison Society, 1982.
15. Boyd Orr J., *Food Health and Income*. Second edition. London: Macmillan, 1937.

16. Drummond J., Wilbraham A., *The Englishman's Food*. A history of five centuries of British diet. London: Jonathan Cape, 1939.
17. Ministry of Health. On the state of the public health during the six years of war. Report of the chief medical officer of the Ministry of Health 1939–45. London: HMSO, 1946.
18. The British Medical Association. Report of the Committee on Nutrition. London: BMA, 1950.
19. Drummond J., McCarrison R., Boyd Orr J., et al *The Nation's Larder and the housewife's part therein*. London: Bell, 1940.
20. Acheson E., Food policy, nutrition and government. Tenth Boyd Orr lecture. *Proc. Nutr. Soc.*, 1986; 45: 131–138.
21. Ministry of Agriculture, Fisheries and Food. Body building foods. Energy foods. Protective foods 1 and 2. Posters. London: Central Office of Information, 1950s.
22. Ministry of Agriculture, Fisheries and Food. Manual of Nutrition. Eighth edition. London: HMSO, 1976.
23. Paul A., Southgate D., McCance and Widdowson's *The Composition of Foods*. Fourth edition. London: HMSO, 1978.
24. McCance R., Widdowson E., *Breads White and Brown*. Their place in thought and social history. London: Pitman, 1956.
25. League of Nations Health Committee. The problem of nutrition. Report on the physiological bases of nutrition. League of Nations, 1936.
26. Copping A. The nutritive value of wheaten flour and bread. *Nutr. Abstr. Rev.*, 1939; 8: 555.
27. Anon. Nutrition and bread. *Miller* 1940; 66: 433.
28. Medical Research Council. MRC Memorandum on bread. *Lancet* 1940; II: 143.
29. Bragg W., The wartime choice of food. Letter. *Times*, 26 October 1940.
30. Anon. National loaf. *Lancet*, 1942; I: 357.
31. Anon. The national loaf. *Br. Med. J.*, 1942; I: 393.
32. Ministry of Food. Report of the Conference on the Post-War Loaf. London: HMSO, 1945.
33. Sinclair H., Nutritional aspects of high-extraction flour. *Proc. Nutr. Soc.*, 1958; 17: 28–37.
34. Sayers D., *Murder Must Advertise*. London: Gollancz, 1933.
35. Sinclair H. Personal communication.
36. Widdowson E., McCance R., Studies of the nutritive value of bread and on the effect of variations in the extraction rate of flour on the growth of undernourished children. Medical Research Council Special Report series no 287. London: HMSO, 1954.
37. Ministry of Agriculture, Fisheries and Food. Report of the panel on composition and nutritive value of flour. London: HMSO, 1956.
38. British Society for Social Responsibility in Science. Our daily bread: who makes the dough. London: BSSRS, 1978.
39. Ministry of Agriculture, Fisheries and Food. Household food consumption and expenditure 1957–84. Annual report of the National Food Survey Committee. London: HMSO 1959–86.

40. British Nutrition Foundation. Annual Reports 1957–86. London: BNF 1958–1986.
41. Schroeder H., Losses of vitamins and trace minerals resulting from processing and preservation of foods. *Am. J. Clin. Nutr.*, 1971; 24: 467–469.
42. Food and Agriculture Organisation. Wheat in Human Nutrition. Rome: FAO, 1970.
43. Royal College of Physicians. *Medical Aspects of Dietary Fibre.* London: Pitman, 1980.
44. Cannon G., Don't devalue our bread, say millers. *Sunday Times*, 17 July 1983.
45. Cummings J., Personal communication.
46. Greaves J., Personal communication.
47. Wenlock R., Disselduff M., Skinner R., Knight I., The diets of schoolchildren. Preliminary report of a nutritional analysis of a nationwide dietary survey of British schoolchildren. Department of Health and Social Security/Office of Population Censuses and Surveys, April 1986. (Available from DHSS leaflets unit, PO Box 21, Stanmore, Middlesex HA7 1AY).
48. Cohn V., 'Junk food disease' akin to beri-beri discovered among adolescents. *Washington Post*, 20 April 1980.
49. Lonsdale D., Shamberger R., Red cell transketolase as an indicator of nutritional deficiency. *Am. J. Clin. Nutr.* 1980; 33: 205–211.
50. Anderson S., Vickery C., Nicol A., Adult thiamine requirements and the continuing need to fortify processed cereals. *Lancet*, 1986; II: 85–89.
51. Riggs B., Melton L., Involutional osteoporosis. *New Eng. J. Med.*, 1986; 314: 1676–1686.
52. Hackett A., Rugg-Gunn A., Allinson M., et al. The importance of fortification of flour with calcium and the sources of Ca in the diet of 375 English adolescents. *Br. J. Nutr.* 1984; 51: 193–197.
53. The Adam Smith Institute. Milking the consumer. Confusion in the UK dairy industry. London: Adam Smith Institute, 1985.
54. Anon. Case for fat. *Farming News*, 7 June 1985.
55. National Dairy Council. Does everybody's body really need bottle? Advertisement. *Observer Magazine*, 30 June 1985.
56. Hutchin K. Fat-free diets can break your bones. *Daily Telegraph*, 14 July 1986.
57. The Joint Committee (of the Dairy Trades Federation and the Milk Marketing Board). Nutrition briefing. Newsletter no 1–3, March–June 1986.
58. Nutrition briefing. Letter from the Joint Committee (see above). March 1986.
59. Department of Health and Social Security. Diet and Cardiovascular Disease. Committee on Medical Aspects of Food Policy. London: HMSO, 1984.
60. Department of Health and Social Security. Chief Medical Officer's Committee on Medical Aspects of Food Policy (COMA). Briefing document, 1984. Unpublished.

61. Department of Health and Social Security. Artificial feeds for the young infant. Committee on Medical Aspects of Food Policy. London: HMSO, 1980.

62. Department of Health and Social Security. A nutrition survey of pre-school children, 1967–68. Committee on Medical Aspects of Food Policy. London: HMSO, 1975.

63. Department of Health and Social Security. Diet and coronary heart disease. Committee on Medical Aspects of Food Policy. London: HMSO, 1974.

64. Department of Health and Social Security. Diet and cardiovascular disease. Committee on Medical Aspects of Food Policy. London: HMSO, 1984.

65. Department of Health and Social Security. Foods which simulate meat. Committee on Medical Aspects of Food Policy. London: HMSO, 1980.

66. Department of Health and Social Security. Report on the safety and wholesomeness of irradiated foods. Advisory Committee on Irradiated and Novel Foods. London: HMSO, 1986.

67. Department of Health and Social Security. Sub-committee on nutritional surveillance: second report. Committee on Medical Aspects of Food Policy. London: HMSO, 1981.

68. Department of Health and Social Security. Ray Petch: Nutrition: background. DHSS summary fact sheet no. 24. DHSS: July 1984. Unpublished.

69. Szent-Gyorgyi A., Foreward. In Stone I: *The Healing Factor*. New York: Grosset and Dunlap, 1972.

70. Boyd Eaton S., Konner M., Paleolithic nutrition. *New Eng. J. Med.*, 1985; 312: 283–289.

71. National Research Council. Diet, Nutrition and Cancer. Committee on Diet, Nutrition and Cancer. Assembly of life sciences. Washington: National Academy Press, 1982.

72. Willett W., McMahon B., Diet and cancer – an overview. *New Eng. J. Med.* 1984; 310: 633–638, 697–703.

73. Levine M. New concepts in the biology and biochemistry of ascorbic acid. *New Eng. J. Med.*, 1986; 314: 892–902.

74. National Academy of Sciences. Recommended Dietary Allowances. Ninth edition. Washington: National Research Council, 1980.

75. Department of Health and Social Security. Rickets and osteomalacia. Committee on Medical Aspects of Food Policy. London: HMSO, 1980.

76. Addy D., Happiness is: iron. *Br. Med. J.*, 1986; 292: 969–970

77. Truswell A., Irwin T., Beaton G., et al. Recommended dietary intakes round the world. *Nutr. Abst. and Rev.* 1983; 53: 939–1015, 1075–1119.

78. Statutory Instruments. Food. Labelling, descriptions etc. The food labelling regulations 1984. No 1305. London: HMSO, 1984.

79. Walker M., Cure for vitamin deficiency. *Guardian*, 23 December 1985.

80. Anon. What vitamins can do. *Izvestia*, 12 December 1985.

81. Ministry of Agriculture, Fisheries and Food. Peggy Fenner MP. Letters to Jonathan Aitken MP, Tony Lloyd MP, Michael Meadowcroft MP, Barry Sheerman MP. 4 June 1986. Unpublished.

82. Elwood H., Vitamins and neural tube defects. *British Nutrition Foundation Bulletin* 37, 1983; 8 (1): 1–3.

83. Poh Tan S., Wenlock R., Buss D., Folic acid content of the diet in various types of British household. *Hum. Nutr.: Appl. Nutr.*, 1984; 38A: 17–22.

84. Dobbing J (ed)., *Prevention of Spina Bifida and Other Neural Tube Defects.* London: Academic Press, 1983.

85. Tindle G., Pop, chips blamed for spina bifida. *South Wales Echo*, 13 February 1984.

86. Rivers J., The hollow men. Editorial. *Nutrition Notes and News.* 9 August 1985.

87. Yudkin J., *The A–Z of Slimming.* London: Coronet, 1977.

88. Passmore R., Hollingsworth D., Robertson J., Prescription for a better British diet. *Br. Med. J.*, 1979; I: 527-531.

89. Waterlow J., Round table on comparison of dietary recommendations in different European countries. Second European Nutrition Conference, Munich 1976. *Nutr. and Metab.* 1977; 21 (4): 187–280.

90. Young F. In *Why Additives? The safety of foods.* London: Forbes, 1977.

91. Department of Health and Social Security. Panel on bread, flour and other cereal products. Committee on Medical Aspects of Food Policy. Minutes of meeting held on 9 October 1978. Unpublished.

92. Department of Health and Social Security. Prevention and health: everybody's business. London: HMSO, 1976.

93. House of Commons. Second report from the Social Services Committee. Perinatal and neonatal mortality. London: HMSO, 1980.

94. Office of Population Censuses and Surveys. Anencephalus, spina bifida, and congenital hydrocephalus. London: HMSO, 1976.

95. Williamson J., 700 women join MRC's trial of vitamin supplements. *GP*, 6 June 1986.

96. Smithells R., Ankers C., Carver M., et al. Maternal nutrition in early pregnancy. *Br. J. Nutr.*, 1977; 38: 497–506.

97. Doyle W., Crawford M., Laurence B., Drury P., Dietary survey during pregnancy in low socio-economic group. *Hum. Nutr.: Appl. Nutr.*, 1982; 636A: 96–106.

98. Crawford M., Doyle W., Craft I., Laurence B., A comparison of food intake during pregnancy and birthweight in high and low socio-economic groups. Unpublished.

99. Medical Research Council. Responsibility for investigations in human subjects. MRC report 1962–63. London: HMSO, 1963.

100. Smithells R., Sheppard S., Schorah C., et al. Possible prevention of neural tube defects by periconceptual vitamin supplementation. *Lancet*, 1980; I: 339–340.

101. Smithells R., Sheppard S., Schorah C., et al. Apparent prevention of neural tube defects by periconceptual vitamin supplementation.

Arch. Dis. Child., 1981; 56 (12): 911–918.

102. Smithells R., Nevin N., Seller M., et al. Further experience of vitamin supplementation for prevention of neural tube defects recurrences. *Lancet*, 1983; I: 1027–1031.

103. Smithells R., Prevention of spina bifida: more optimism, less caution. *Link* 1982, no 79: 8–9.

104. Giroud A., Lefebvres-Boisselot J., Anomalies provoquées chez le foetus en l'absence d'acide folique. *Arch. Franc. Pediat.*, 1951; 8: 648–656.

105. Lindhour D., Schmidt D., In-utero exposure to valproate and neural tube defects. *Lancet*, 1986; I: 1392–1393.

106. Anon. Pyrimethamine combinations in pregnancy. *Lancet*, 1983; II: 1005–1006.

107. Anon. Folates and foetus. *Lancet*, 1977; I: 462.

108. Spring J., Robertson J., Buss D., Trace nutrients. 3: magnesium, copper, zinc, vitamin B6, vitamin B12 and folic acid in the British household food supply. *Br. J. Nutr.*, 1979; 41: 487–493.

109. Chanarin I., In: Getting the most out of food no 10. Sussex: Van den Berghs and Jurgens, 1975.

110. Laurence K., James N., Miller M., Campbell, H. Increased risk of recurrence of pregnancies complicated by foetal neural tube defects in mothers receiving poor diets and possible benefit of dietary counselling. *Br. Med. J.*, 1980; 281: 1592–1594.

111. Laurence K., James N., Miller M., et al. Double-blind randomised controlled trial of folate treatment before conception to prevent recurrence of neural-tube defects. *Br. Med. J.*, 1981; 282: 1509–1511.

112. Pajak S., Doctors launch fund to fight spina bifida. *The Universe*, 11 May 1984.

113. Hutchin K., Spina bifida blamed on vitamin lack. *Daily Telegraph*, 25 September 1986.

114. Edwards J., Vitamin supplementation and neural tube defects. *Lancet*, 1982; I: 275–276.

115 Walker C., Personal communication.

116. Bull M., Pregnancy. *Br. Med. J.*, 1982; 284: 1611–1612.

117. Office of Population Censuses and Surveys. Congenital malformations 1985. London: OPCS, 1986.

118. Hibbard B., Roberts C., Elder G., et al. Can we afford screening for neural tube defects? The South Wales experience. *Br. Med. J.*, 1985; 290: 293–295.

119. Wald N., Neural-tube defects and vitamins: the need for a randomised clinical trial. *Br. J. Obst and Gynae.*, 1984; 91: 516–523.

120. Anon. Vitamins to prevent neural tube defects. *Lancet*, 1982; II: 1255–1256.

121. Anon. Vitamins for at risk mothers in 'ethics' row. *Medical News*, 29 July 1982.

122. Medical Research Council. The Medical Research Council confirm their decision to conduct a trial to test whether extra vitamins prevent spina bifida. Press release, 7 December 1982.

123. King A., Spina bifida baby project set to start. *Yorkshire Post*, 29 June 1983.
124. Veitch A., Legal doubts over spina bifida trial. *Guardian*, 15 May 1983.
125. Wynn A., Ethics of trials. *Nature*, 1982; 300: 102.
126. Anon. Suppression denied in storm over neural tube defects trial. *Pulse*, 4 December 1982.
127. Anon. Biting off each others' tongues. *Nature*, 1982; 300: 302.
128. Anon. Vitamins Test wins BMA list. *Doctor*, 16 December 1982.
129. Anon. More doctors condemn spina bifida trials. *Human Concern*, January 1984.
130. House of Commons. Hansard (official report). Medical Research Council: spina bifida trials. Early Day Motion, April 1984.
131. Medical Research Council. MRC vitamin study. Press release, 8 June 1984.
132. Anon. Prevention of neural tube defects; Medical Research Council vitamin study. *Lancet*, 1985; I: 535.
133. Anon. Prevention of recurrent neural tube defects: Medical Research Council vitamin study. *Lancet*, 1985; II: 1023.
134. Cannon G., Lawrence F., Do we need vitamins? *New Health*, March 1984.
135. Bull N., Dietary habits of 15 to 25-year-olds. *Hum. Nutr.: Appl. Nutr.*, 1985; 39A (suppl): 1–68.
136. Walker C., Doyle W. Personal communication.
137. Department of Education and Science. Peter Brooke MP. Letter to Robert Harvey MP. 21 February 1984. Unpublished.
138. Medical Research Council. MRC vitamin study. Information for patients. London: MRC, 1983.
139. Crisp, A., Palmer, R., Kalnay, R., How common is anorexia nervosa? *Brit. J. Psychiatr.*, 1979; 128: 549–554.
140. Palmer R., *Anorexia Nervosa*. London: Pelican, 1980.
141. Bryce-Smith D., Latto D., Simpson R., Anorexia nervosa and bulimia nervosa treated by oral zinc sulphate. Letter to the *Lancet*. Full text unpublished.
142. Davies S. Personal communication.
143. Cohen K., Schechter P., Henkin R., Hypogeusia, anorexia, and altered zinc metabolism following thermal burn. *JAMA* 1973; 223: 914–916.
144. Hambidge M. The role of zinc and other trace metals in pediatric nutrition and health. *Pediatr. Clin. of N. Am.*, 1977; 24 (1): 95–106.
145. Aggett P., Harries J., Current status of zinc in health and disease states. *Arch. Dis. Child.*, 1979; 54: 909–917.
146. Prasad A., The role of zinc in gastrointestinal and liver disease. *Clinics in Gastroenterology* 1983; 12 (3): 713–741.
147. Bakan R., Anorexia and zinc. *Lancet*, 1984; II: 874.
148. Bakan R., The role of zinc in anorexia nervosa. *Med. Hypoth.*, 1979; 5 (7): 731–736.
149. Cannon G., Einzig H., *Dieting Makes You Fat*. New York: Simon and Schuster, 1985.
150. Bryce-Smith D., Hodgkinson L., *The Zinc Solution*. London:

Century, 1986.

151. Bryce-Smith D. Personal communication.

152. Cannon G., The zinc solution. *Observer*, 2 September 1984.

153. British Psychological Society. International conference on anorexia nervosa and related diseases. Programme. September 1984.

154. Millar R., 'Atom ray' food set for go-ahead. *Daily Express*, 4 February 1985.

155. Department of Health and Social Security. Safety of irradiated food. Press release. 10 April 1986.

156. Ley F., Food irradiation makes progress. *British Nutrition Foundation Bulletin 37*, 1983; 8 (1): 37–45.

157. Collier S., Gamma pie. *Observer*, 5 May 1985.

158. Erlichman J. Irradiated food cleared for sale. *Guardian*, 11 April 1986.

159. Fletcher D., Food irradiation 'poses no health hazard'. *Daily Telegraph*, 11 April 1986.

160. Fishlock D., Medical Office praises food irradiation. *Financial Times*, 11 April 1986.

161. Holmes A., Gamma pie is safe. Letter. *Observer*, 19 May 1985.

162. Anon. Food irradiation comes down to earth. *High Technology*, March 1984.

163. Department of Health and Social Security/Ministry of Agriculture, Fisheries and Food. Report on the safety and wholesomeness of irradiated foods. Advisory Committee on Irradiated and Novel Foods. London: DHSS/MAFF, 1986.

164. Burgen A. Public communication.

165. Zurer P. Food irradiation. A technology at a turning point. *C&EN*, 5 May 1986.

166. Dormandy T., An approach to free radicals. *Lancet*, 1983; II: 1010–1014.

167. Hodgkinson L., Gamma cuisine? *Times*, 30 July 1986.

168. Webb T. Food irradiation in Britain? London: Food Commission, 1986.

169. Leather S., We broke law with gamma ray prawns says food firm. *Daily Mail*, 3 March 1986.

170. Bell K., Letter to British Frozen Food Federation, 14 April 1986. Unpublished.

171. Martin S., The case against irradiating foods. *Quick Frozen Foods International*, July 1985.

172. House of Commons. Hansard (official report). Irradiated food: conflict of interest. Early Day Motion, 22 April 1986.

173. Isotron. Offer for sale by J. Henry Schroeder Wagg. 27 June 1985.

CHAPTER 6

1. Rivers J., The profession of nutrition – an historical perspective. *Proc. Nutr. Soc.*, 1979; 38: 225–231.

2. Ennals D., Institute of Health Food Retailing. Speech, 4 March 1986. Unpublished.

3. Locke J. COMA report on diet and cardiovascular disease. Confidential memorandum to Bacon and Meat Manufacturers' Association members. London: BMMA, 12 July 1984. Unpublished.
4. Wapshott N. Personal communication.
5. Owen D., *The Times*, 23 May 1985.
6. The Labour Party. Putting people first. Labour's statement on the environment. Policy document, 27 August 1986. London: the Labour Party.
7. Register of Members' Interests 1983–86. London: HMSO, 1984–86.
8. Miller M., Danger! Additives at work. A report on food additives: their use and control. London: Food Commission, 1985.
9. Roth A., *Parliamentary Profiles*. London: Parliamentary Profiles, 1984–85.
10. The Liberal Party. Food and health. Liberal policy document, 23 November 1985. London: the Liberal Party.
11. National Association of Master Bakers, Confectioners and Caterers. Annual reports 1982–84.
12. Liberal Party: personal communication.
13. Walker C., Cannon G., *The Food Scandal*. London: Century, 1985.
14. Gillie O., Guide to health eating blocked. *Sunday Times*, 4 August 1985.
15. Granada Television. *World in Action*. 'The Threatened Generation'. 14 April 1986.
16. Cannon G., Young people: a falling generation: *New Health*, November 1985.
17. Smith P., Is the schoolburger here to stay? *Report*, February 1985.
18. Walker J., *The Queen Has Been Pleased*. London: Secker and Warburg, 1986.
19. House of Commons. Hansard (official report). Debates, Questions, Motions and other business, 1979–86.
20. Coleman T., A man at home with fact and fiction. *Guardian*, 30 November 1985.
21. Wapshott N., Brock G., *Thatcher*. London: Macdonald, 1983.
22. Unigate. Annual reports 1984–86. Additional information from local authorities.
23. Express Dairies. Marketing material. Additional information from local authorities.
24. Nestlé. Personal communication. Additional information from local authorities.
25. Grant-Evans W., MP hosts new pub hours call. *Today*, 4 March 1986.
26. Action on Alcohol Abuse. Personal communication.
27. Public Relations Consultants Association. *The Public Relations Yearbook 1983–1985*. London: Financial Times Business Information, 1984–1986.
28. Fleet K., Is Goldsmith Argyll's secret weapon? *Times*, 5 March 1986.
29. Goodway N., MPs stir up sugar war. *Observer*, 21 December 1986.
30. Stead J., Scotland at nerve-end of EEC cuts in British fishing quotas.

Guardian, 23 December 1985.

31. de Bruxelles S., Wilson B., Top doctor quits in fees row. *Observer*, 21 December 1986.

32. World Health Organisation. Prevention of coronary heart disease. Geneva: WHO, 1982.

33. National Advisory Committee on Nutrition Education. A discussion paper on proposals for nutritional guidlines for health education in Britain. London: Health Education Council, 1983.

34. Department of Health and Social Security. Diet and cardiovascular disease. Committee on Medical Aspects of Food Policy. London: HMSO, 1984.

35. British Medical Association. Diet, nutrition and health. London: BMA, 1986.

36. Faculty of Community Medicine of the Royal College of Physicians. Dietary salt and health. Draft, 1984. Unpublished.

37. Brown J., Lever A., Robertson I., et al., Salt and hypertension. *Lancet* 1984; II: 456.

38. Timmins N., Advice to cut back on salt 'irresponsible and potentially harmful'. *Times*, 25 August 1984.

39. Glynn Owen O., *Lancet* letter pre-empts faculty plan for salt. *GP*, 7 September 1984.

40. de Wardener H., Salt and hypertension. *Lancet* 1984; II: 688.

41 Brown J., Lever A., Robertson I., et al., Salt and hypertension. *Lancet* 1984; II: 1333–1334.

42. Anon. Carry on with the tablets. *Guardian*, 23 August 1984.

43. Salt Data Centre. 'NACNE misinterpreted the salt evidence' says blood pressure expert. Press release, 29 January 1985.

44. Ranks Hovis McDougall. Personal communication.

45. Cannon G., Getting back in balance. Potassium, sodium, chloride. *New Health*, May 1985.

46. British Nutrition Foundation. Annual reports 1967–86. London: BNF, 1968–86.

47. Food and Drink Federation, Food and Drink Industries Council, Food Manufacturers Federation. Annual reports 1966–86. London: FDF, FDIC, FMF, 1967–86.

48. British Library. Research in British universities, polytechnics and colleges, 1980–85. London: British Library.

49. *Medical Research Directory*. London: Wiley Medical Publications, 1983.

50. Cannon G., Taking money from the devil. *Br. Med. J.*, 1986; 292: 270–271.

51. Guys Hospital Medical School. Annual reports of the Department of Medicine 1975–82. London: Guys Hospital.

52. Burgen A., The safety and wholesomeness of irradiated foods. Press conference. Public communication, 10 April 1986.

53. Milk Marketing Board. Personal communication.

54. Department of Health and Social Security. Personal communication.

55. The Sugar Bureau. Sweet news. News bulletin, 9 May 1986. London: Sugar Bureau.

56. Keen H., Sugar and diabetes. Diabetes: putting sugar in perspective. Literature for doctors produced and distributed by the Sugar Bureau. London: Sugar Bureau, May 1985.

57. Keen H., Thomas B., Jarrett R., Fuller J., Nutrient intake, adiposity and diabetes. *Br. Med. J.*, 1979; 1: 655–658.

58. World Sugar Research Organisation. Recent research projects sponsored by members of WSRO: a global effort. Special bulletin no 1. London: WSRO, 1983.

59. US Congressional Record. Feeding at the company trough. 24 August 1976.

60. Department of Health and Social Security. The collection and storage of human milk. Committee on Medical Aspects of Food Policy. London: HMSO, 1981.

61. Department of Health and Social Security. Foods which simulate meat. Committee on Medical Aspects of Food Policy. London: HMSO, 1980.

62. Ministry of Agriculture, Fisheries and Food. Second report on food labelling. Food Standards Committee. London: HMSO, 1979.

63. Dean M., Scarman suggests legal curbs on secrecy. *Guardian*, 15 September 1984.

64. Dobbie P., Diet that's an official secret. *Mail on Sunday*, 16 September 1984.

65. Anon. When freedom of speech means the press says nothing. *Mail on Sunday*, 16 September 1984.

66. Department of Health and Social Security. John Patten MP. Personal communication.

67. House of Commons. Parliamentary debates. Hansard (official record). Nutritional food labelling. Jonathan Aitken MP (Question).

68. Ministry of Agriculture, Fisheries and Food. Peggy Fenner MP. Letter to Jonathan Aitken, 23 May 1985. Unpublished.

69. House of Commons. Hansard (official record). Food manufacturers. Tony Lloyd MP (Question); Michael Jopling MP (MAFF) (Answer). 6 March 1986.

70. House of Commons. Hansard (official record). Food standards (advisory committees). Michael Meadowcroft MP (Question); Peggy Fenner MP (MAFF) (Answer); Jonathan Aitken MP (Question). 10 April 1986.

71. Ministry of Agriculture, Fisheries and Food. Peggy Fenner MP. Letters to Jonathan Aitken MP, Tony Lloyd MP, Michael Meadowcroft MP, Barry Sheerman MP. 4 June 1986. Unpublished.

72. Norton-Taylor R., Professor accuses Whitehall of Secrets Act 'gag' on doctors. *Guardian*, 9 June 1986.

73. Department of Health and Social Security. Barney Hayhoe MP. House of Commons. Hansard (official record). 16 May 1986.

74. Rose G., Doctors and Official Secrets Act. *Br. Med. J.*, 1986; 292: 1594.

75. Corcos M., Secrets Act that kills rather than cures. *Guardian*, 22 August 1986.

76. Conning D., Nutrition labelling and education. *British Nutrition*

Foundation Bulletin 47, 1986; 11 (2): 73–74.

77. Sinclair H. Personal communication.

78. Acheson E., Food policy, nutrition and government. *Proc. Nutr. Soc.*, 1986; 45: 131–138.

79. Agricultural Research Council/Medical Research Council. Food and nutrition research. Report of the ARC/MRC committee. London: HMSO, 1974.

80. British Nutrition Foundation. Nutrition in medical education. Report of the British Nutrition Foundation's Task Force on Clinical Nutrition. London: BNF, 1983.

81. Advisory Council for Applied Research and Development. The food industry and technology. London: HMSO, 1982.

82. Ashwell M., Cole T., The Nutrition Society in the 1980s: the questionnaire analysis. *Proc. Nutr. Soc.*, 1986; 45: 231–252.

83. Druce E., Salt technology and dietary intake. *Proc. Nutr. Soc.*, 1986; 45: 253–257.

84. Copping A., The history of the Nutrition Society. *Proc. Nutr. Soc.*, 1978; 37: 105–139.

85. Cuthbertson D. Personal communication.

86. Waterlow J., Welcome to the XIII International Congress of Nutrition. *Br. J. Nutr.*, 1985; 54: 1–3.

87. Snack, Nut and Crisp Manufacturers Association. Text of remarks by Professor Donald Naismith. London: SNACMA, March 1986.

88. Young R., Food rumpus over 'healthy' crisps. *Times*, 10 March 1986.

89. Anon. MMB appoints a full-time nutritional consultant. *Grocer*, 6 September 1986.

90. Food and Agriculture Organisation/World Health Organisation. Energy and protein requirements. Report of a joint FAO/WHO ad hoc expert committee. Rome: FAO, 1973.

91. Food and Agriculture Organisation/World Health Organisation/ United Nations University. Energy and protein requirements. Geneva: WHO, 1985.

92. International Union of Nutritional Sciences/Nutrition Society. XIII International Congress of Nutrition, Brighton UK. 18–23 August 1985. Programme.

93. Rivers J., Fame and famine. *Nutrition Notes and News*, 1985, 8: 1–2.

94. Rivers J., The hollow men. *Nutrition Notes and News*, 1985, 9: 1–2.

95. *Who's Who in the World*. Chicago: Marquis Who's Who, 1979.

96. The Sugar Bureau. Health hazards associated with the use of sucrose: real and imaginary. Abstract of paper by Vincent Marks. London: Sugar Bureau, 1985.

97. Maliban Biscuit Manufactories. Now! Maliban lemon puff comes to you in a great new pack. Advertisement. *Daily News* (Sri Lanka), 1 October 1985.

98. Little Lion Associaties. Make a fuss. Advertisement. *Observer* (Sri Lanka), 22 September 1985.

99. Anon. Handy hints. Strip cartoon. *Island* (Sri Lanka), 22 September 1985.

100. Anon. Training your toddler. Strip cartoon. *Observer* (Sri Lanka), 22 September 1985.
101. Kraft Foods. Children! Enter the Vegemite follow the path contest of the month. Advertisement. *Island* (Sri Lanka), 22 September 1985.
102. Ceylon Cold Stores. Your choice of the Netball Queen '85 for the Orange Crush trophy. Advertisement. *Daily News* (Sri Lanka), 24 September 1985.
103. Nestlé. 3rd National Nestomalt marathon. Advertisement. *Daily News* (Sri Lanka), 24 September 1985.
104. Lakspray. Win a car & 165 fabulous prizes. Advertisement. *Daily News* (Sri Lanka), 1 October 1985.
105. Karunaratne W., Preventing heart disease ... What has happened to mankind? *Daily News* (Sri Lanka), 30 September 1985.
106. Williams I., Let a thousand burgers blossom. *Sunday Times*, 10 November 1985.
107. Cannon G., The food scandal. *The Times*, 11, 12, 13 June 1984.
108. Hoffenberg R., McKeown T., Talkback: the food scandal. *The Times*, 15, 22 June 1984.
109. Department of Health and Social Security. Diet and coronary heart disease. Committee on Medical Aspects of Food Policy. London: HMSO, 1974.
110. House of Lords. Hansard (official report). Heart disease. Statements by Lord Prys-Davies, Lord Ennals. 25 July 1984.
111. Truswell A., The development of dietary guidelines. *Food Technology in Australia*, 1983; 35(1): 498–502.
112. Chorlton P., Channel 4 is accused of bias after programme on fats and heart disease is banned. *Guardian*, 15 April 1985.
113. Morton J., Facts on fat. Press release. Sevenoaks: Butter Information Council, 3 April 1985.
114. MacDougall A., Livestock industry must speak up. *Farmer's Weekly*, 16 November 1984.
115. Cohen M., Nagel E., *An Introduction to Logic and Scientific Method*. London: Routledge and Kegan Paul, 1934.
116. Robertson G., Nicol A., *Media Law*. The rights of journalists and broadcasters. London: Oyez Longman, 1984.
117. Quine W., *Methods of Logic*. London: Routledge and Kegan Paul, 1952.
118. Popper K., *The Logic of Scientific Discovery*. London: Hutchinson, 1959.
119. Hart H., Honoré, A., *Causation in the Law*. Oxford: University Press, 1959.
120. Cross R., *Cross on Evidence*. Fifth edition. London: Butterworths, 1979.
121. Thomas L., *The Youngest Science*. Oxford: University Press, 1984.
123. Thomas L., *Late Night Thoughts*. Oxford: University Press, 1984.
123. Steinberg D., et al., Consensus conference on cholesterol and heart disease. *Lancet* 1985; II: 205–207.
124. Oliver M. Whose responsibility is medical science? *Chron. Roy. Coll. Phys. Edin.*, 1985; Oct: 245–249.

125. Health Education Council. Coronary Heart Disease: plans for action. (The Canterbury Report). London: Pitman, 1984.

126. Mitchell J., Diet and arterial disease – the myths and the realities. *Proc. Nutr. Soc.*, 1985; 44: 363–367.

127. British Sugar Bureau. Sweet reason. Booklet. London: Sugar Bureau, 1983.

128. Sugar Bureau. The world of sugar. Supplement to *The Grocer*. 9 February 1985.

129. Food and Drug Administration. Evaluation of health aspects of sugars contained in carbohydrate sweeteners. Report of Sugars Task Force. Washington: FDA, 1986.

130. World Sugar Research Organisation. A definitive and official progress report on sugar & health. Letter sent to doctors. London: WSRO, 1986.

131. Gillie O. Sugar report leaves sour taste with diet experts. *Independent*, 22 October 1986.

132. The Sugar Association. Government gives sugar clean bill of health. Advertisement. *New York Times*, 12 November 1986.

133. Marmot M., Epidemiology and the art of the soluble. *Lancet* 1986; I: 897–900.

134. Rybar Laboratories. Guar: where do we go from here? Conference. Royal Society of Medicine, 4 December 1985. Proceedings unpublished.

135. Ahrens E., The diet-heart question in 1985: has it really been settled? *Lancet*, 1985; I: 1085–1087.

136. British Heart Foundation. Annual report and accounts 1982–83. London: BHF, 1983.

137. Imperial Cancer Research Fund. Annual report and accounts 1982. London: ICRF, 1983.

138. British Heart Foundation. How the British Heart Foundation is helping to beat heart disease. London: BHF, undated.

139. Imperial Cancer Research Fund. Help us turn this coupon into the next cutting. Advertisement. *Guardian*, 7 June 1985.

140. Catford J. Fords. On the state of the public ill-health – premature mortality in the United Kingdom and Europe. *Br. Med. J.*, 1984; 289: 1668–1670.

141. Imperial Cancer Research Fund. Cancer epidemiology and clinical trials unit. London: ICRF, undated.

142. British Heart Foundation. Annual report and accounts 1981–82. London: BHF, 1982.

143. British Heart Foundation. County slimmers wooed with Valentine Day proposal. Press release, winter 1983-84.

144. British Heart Foundation. Personal communication.

145. Imperial Cancer Research Fund. Personal communication.

146. Cannon G. Lifestyle with a death knell. *The Times*, 30 March 1984.

147. American Cancer Society. A defense against cancer can be cooked up in your kitchen. Advertisement. *Scientific American*, April 1985.

148. Anon. Abominable no-men. *Times Health Supplement*, February 1983.

149. Fortescue T. Personal communication.
150. Blackburn H., Diet and mass hyperlipidaemia: a public health view. In: *Nutrition, Lipids and Coronary Heart Disease: A Global View*, ed. Levy R., Rifkind B., Dennis B., Ernst N. New York: Raven Press, 1979.
151. Truswell A., Diet and coronary heart disease. How much more evidence do we need? *British Nutrition Foundation Bulletin* 32, 1981; 6(2): 93–107.
152. Neuberger A., More on diet and coronary heart disease. *British Nutrition Foundation Bulletin* 33, 1981; 6(3): 189.
153. Body, R. Personal communication.
154. *The Times 1000 1985–1986*. The world's top companies. London: Times Books, 1986.
155. Fishlock D., British scientist complains about a worldwide decline in agriculture research. *World Food and Drink Report*, 22 December 1986.
156. Sinclair H. Personal communication.
157. Shrimpton D. Personal communication.
158. Anon. Obituary. *British Nutrition Foundation Bulletin* 4, 1970; 2–7.
159. Frazer A., The oracle. BNF vision. Unpublished.
160. Shrimpton D., The great food scandal. Granada Television: *World in Action*. Transcript. 1985. Unpublished.
161. Conning D., Nutrition labelling and education. British Nutrition Foundation Bulletin 47, 1986; 11 (2): 73–74.
162. British Nutrition Foundation. The BNF educational plan. London: BNF, August 1986. Unpublished.
163. Cummings J. The great food scandal. Granada Television: *World in Action*. Transcript. Unpublished.
164. Cannon G., Censored – a diet for life and death. *Sunday Times*, 3 July 1983.
165. Department of Health and Social Security. Letter from the Chief Medical Officer to members of the COMA committee. 25 August 1983. Unpublished.
166. Ministry of Agriculture, Fisheries and Food. Government proposals on the COMA report. Press release no 78, 12 March 1985.
167. Joint Advisory Committee on Nutrition Education. Minutes of meetings, internal correspondence, and other papers. Unpublished.
168. Food and Drink Federation. Notes on meetings of JACNE. Unpublished.
169. Health Education Council/British Nutrition Foundation. COMA booklet. Draft, 13 March 1985. Unpublished.
170. Health Education Council/British Nutrition Foundation. Eating for a healthy heart (COMA booklet). Draft, May 1985. Unpublished.
171. British Nutrition Foundation/Health Education Council. Eating for a healthier heart. Draft, 21 June 1985. Unpublished.
172. Garrow J., Letter to Dr E.D. Acheson. 25 July 1985. Unpublished.
173. Gillie O., Guide to healthy eating blocked. *Sunday Times*, 4 August 1985.
174. Veitch A., Nutritionist's threat to quit over 'censorship'. *Guardian*, 5

August 1985.
175. Veitch A., Healthy eating guide beats censors. *Guardian*, 9 August 1985.

CONCLUSION

1. Boyd Orr J. *Food Health and Income*. London: Macmillan, 1937.
2. Wiener N. *The Human Use of Human Beings*. London: Eyre and Spottiswoode, 1950.
3. Ministry of Agriculture, Fisheries and Food. Donald Thompson MP. Current MAFF policy. Conference on Tomorrow's Food. 21 October 1986.
4. Ministry of Agriculture, Fisheries and Food. Trend towards 'healthier' diet continues, MAFF food survey shows. Press release. 10 October 1986.
5. Ministry of Agriculture, Fisheries and Food. Donald Thompson welcomes continued trend towards healthier eating. Press release. 13 March 1987.
6. Anon. Healthier eating. *Guardian*, 16 March 1987.
7. Wagstyl S. Health put higher on the menu. *Financial Times*, 16 March 1987.
8. Ministry of Agriculture, Fisheries and Food. Household food consumption and expenditure: 1980–84. Annual reports of the National Food Survey committee. London: HMSO, 1982–86.
9. Anon. Supermarket chain cuts food additives. *Wilts and Hants Times*, 10 March 1986.
10. Phillips A. Additives are out! *Basingstoke Gazette*, 14 March 1986.
11. Jeans G. Customers winning additives battle. *Evening Gazette*, Colchester, 7 March 1986.
12. Anon. As nature intended: stores work to root out 'risky' additives. *Oxford Mail*, 6 March 1986.
13. Anon. Thumbs down to additives, *Wiltshire Times*, 14 March 1986.
14. Heinz. The only soup. Advertisement. *Observer Magazine*, 21 September 1986.
15. Volkswagen. More colouring. More preservatives. More additives. Advertisement. *Sunday Times*, 21 September 1986.
16. Volkswagen. More preservatives. More colouring. More additives. Advertisement. *Expression!*, March 1987.
17. British Coal. No additives. Advertisement. *Observer Magazine*, 1 March 1987.
18. Robirch. Sooner Foods. Mars. Advertisements. *Grocer*, 11 October 1986.
19. Combes A. Personal communication.
20. Cumming D. Personal communication.
21. Workman E., Hunter J., Alun Jones V. *The Allergy Diet*. London: Martin Dunitz, 1984.
22. Royal College of Physicians and British Nutrition Foundation. Food

intolerance and food aversion. *J. Roy. Coll. Phys.* 1984; 18: 83–123.
23. Safeway. Food additives. Press release. Maidstone: Safeway, June 1985.
24. Dolan L. Iceland tempts healthy eaters. *The Journal,* Newcastle, 26 March 1986.
25. Food Manufacturers Federation. Food industry position regarding media activity on additives. Memorandum, 10 October 1985. Unpublished.
26. Anon. Birds Eye as a health pioneer. *Campaign,* 25 April 1986.
27. Fletcher D. Fears about food additives 'exaggerated', *Daily Telegraph,* 29 August 1986.
28. Anon. Food additives fear 'fabricated by do-gooders'. *Daily Telegraph,* 4 September 1986.
29. Anon. 'Worries about food additives have been exaggerated.' *The Grocer,* 30 August 1986.
30. Food and Drink Federation. Common sense about food. Booklet. London: FDF, September 1986.
31. Collins R. Food industry defends additives. *Guardian,* 19 September 1986.
32. Anon. MP gets assurance on food additives, *Wilmslow World,* 2 January 1986.
33. Eaton D. Children and additives can mix. *Evening Echo,* Southampton, 26 February 1986.
34. Thurnham P. Food additives and allergies. *Bolton Evening News,* 25 March 1986.
35. Anon. Grimsby MP sees red over colourless kipper. *Grimsby Evening Telegraph,* 20 March 1986.
36. Erlichman J. Curb on food colours urged. *Guardian,* 11 February 1987.
37. Ministry of Agriculture, Fisheries and Food. Food additives – the balanced approach. Booklet. Publications Unit, Lion House, Willowburn Trading Estate, Alnwick, Northumberland NE66 2PF.
38. Ministry of Agriculture, Fisheries and Food. Final report on the Review of the Colouring Matter in Food Regulations. Food Advisory Committee. London: HMSO, 1987.
39. Commission of the European Communities. Proposal for a Council Directive amending for the eighth time the Directive of 23 October 1962 on the approximation of the rules of the Member States concerning the colouring matters authorised for use in foodstuffs intended for human consumption. COM (85) 474. Brussels: September 1985.
40. Ministry of Agriculture, Fisheries and Food. Food additives – we're not complacent on safety, says Donald Thompson. Press release, 27 February 1987.
41. Seal R. The importance of additives. *Food Manufacture,* August 1985.
42. Key Note report. Food flavourings and ingredients. An industry sector overview. London: Key Note Publications, 1985.
43. Advisory Council for Applied Research and Development. Report on the food industry and technology. London: HMSO, 1982.
44. Ministry of Agriculture, Fisheries and Food. Report on flavouring agents. Food Standards Committee. London: HMSO, 1965.

45. Ministry of Agriculture, Fisheries and Food. Report on the review of flavourings in food. Food Additives and Contaminants Committee. London: HMSO, 1974.

46. Lawrence F. (ed). *Food Additives: Your Complete Survival Guide.* London: Century, 1986.

47. Millstone E. *Additives*. London: Penguin, 1986.

48. Wall's. Our new sausages. Advertisement. *Women's Own* 6 April 1985.

49. Levy P. 'Food zealots' force issue. *Observer*, 9 March 1986.

50. King D. Europeans get together to threaten IFF's leadership in flavours. World Food and Drink Report, 15 September 1986.

51. Anon. Unilever. *Financial Times*, 22 August 1986.

52. Allen, Brady and Marsh. Healthy eating: a red herring? London: ABM, 1985. Subscription only.

53. Food and Drug Administration. Evaluation of health aspects of sugars contained in carbohydrate sweeteners. Report from FDA's Sugars Task Force, 1986. Washington: FDA, 1986.

54. World Sugar Research Organisation. Vlitos A. Letter to MPs and others, 29 January 1986. Unpublished.

55. Moore T. Sugar experts' soft line sours the health lobby. *Sunday Times*, 22 February 1987.

56. British Nutrition Foundation. Sugars and syrups. The report of the British Nutrition Foundation's Task Force. February 1987. Page proofs. Unpublished.

57. National Advisory Committee on Nutrition Education. A discussion paper on nutritional guidelines for health education in Britain. London: Health Education Council, 1983.

58. Sanderson M. Sugars in the diet: practical aspects. Draft paper for the British Nutrition Foundation Task Force on sugars and syrups. July 1986. Unpublished.

59. British Medical Association. Diet, nutrition and health. Report of the Board of Science and Education. London: BMA, 1986.

60. Health Education Council. Guide to healthy eating. London: HEC, 1986.

61. American Council on Science and Health. Sugars and your health. New Jersey: ACSH, 1986.

62. Anon. COMA faces sugar mountain? *Chemistry and Industry*, 16 February 1987.

63. Erlichman J. Food lobby backs down on support for irradiation. *Guardian*, 25 February 1987.

64. London Food Commission. Food irradiation: consumers say no! London Food News no 5, Spring 1987.

65. Veitch A. Food irradiation 'could put children at risk'. *Guardian*, 7 March 1987

66. Prentice T. Fear of health risk if foods are irradiated. *Times*, 7 March 1987.

67. Anon. Food industry divided over benefits of irradiation. *Grocer*, 28 February 1987.

68. Commission of the European Communities. Proposal for a Council

Directive, COM (87) 52 final. Brussels, 13 February 1987.
69. Poeton W. Personal communication.
70. Anon. Irradiated food 'soon'. *Daily Telegraph*, 3 March 1987.
71. Ellis M. Britons too fat says Government's key advisor. *Times*, 9 March 1987.
72. Anon. Independence fears for new health council. *Independent*, 22 November 1986.
73. Cannon G. Wanted: a good food policy. *Times*, 5 March 1987.
74. Fletcher D. Unhealthy sound of silence? *Daily Telegraph*, 12 February 1987.
75. Veitch A. Anti-alcohol campaigns 'gagged by ministers'. *Guardian*, 13 February 1987.
76. Anon. Warning on sugar dropped. *London Daily News*, 12 March 1987.
77. The Labour Party. Food policy: a priority. A consultative paper. London: The Labour Party, 1985.
78. The Labour Party. A new vision for health. 1986. Unpublished.
79. Veitch A. A charter for health that could stub out the smokers. *Guardian*, 28 May 1986.
80. The Liberal Party. Food and health. London: The Liberal Party, November 1985.

DOCUMENT A

1. Roth A. *Parliamentary Profiles*. London: Parliamentary Profiles, 1984–85.
2. Register of Members' interests 1983–86. London: HMSO, 1983–86.
3. Hansard (House of Commons Official Report). London: HMSO, 1983–86.
4. Public Relations Consultants Association. The Public Relations Yearbook 1983–85. London: *Financial Times* Business Information, 1984–87.
5. Davis J. Hanson flies high. Top 100 British companies. *Observer*, 28 July 1985.
6. O'Reilly R. 1984: the top 250 spenders. *Campaign*, 7 June 1985.
7. Advisory Council for Applied Research and Development. Report on the food industry and technology. London: HMSO, 1982.
8. *The Times 1000 1984–85*. London: Times Books, 1985.
9. Gibbs G. Elders IXL seeks Allied Lyons. *Guardian*, 6 September 1985.
10. Allied Lyons. Personal communication. Additional information from local authorities.
11. Food and Drink Federation. Annual reports 1984–86. London: FDF, 1984–86.
12. Labour Party Research Department. Company donations to the Tory Party and other political organisations. Labour Party information paper no. 72, July 1985.
13. Wapshott N., Brock G., *Thatcher*. London: Macdonald, 1983.

14. Unigate. Annual reports 1984–86. Additional information from local authorities.
15. Business Statistics Office. Classified list of manufacturing businesses, part 4: Food, Drink and Tobacco, 1984. London: HMSO. Additional information from House of Commons Public Information Office.
16. Public Relations Consultants Association. The Public Relations Yearbook 1986. London: Financial Times Business Information, 1986.
17. Action on Alcohol Abuse. Personal communication.
18. Northern Foods. The world of Northern Foods. Additional information from local authorities.
19. Unilever. Publicity material, 1985–86. Additional information from local authorities.
20. Information from local authorities.
21. Cadbury Schweppes. Information sheets. Additional information from local authorities.
22. Waller R. *The Almanac of British Politics*. London: Croom Helm, 1986. Also OPCS: 1981 census, account taken of 1983 boundary changes.
23. Express Dairies. Marketing material. Additional information from local authorities.
24. Industry and Parliament Trust. Personal communication.
25. ICI. Annual reports 1984–86. Additional information from local authorities.
26. Berisfords. Annual reports 1984–86. Additional information from local authorities.
27. Toynbee P. The other Tory woman. *Guardian*, 20 January 1986.
28. Robertsons. Personal communication. Additional information from local authorities.
29. Grant-Evans W. MP hosts new pub hours call. *Today*, 4 March 1986.
30. Lintas. Personal communication.
31. Public Relations Consultants Association. The Public Relations Yearbook 1981. London: Financial Times Business Information, 1981.
32. Anon. Fall-out over Labour's Green man. *Observer*, 28 September 1986.
33. Albright and Wilson. Review of the year 1985. London: Albright and Wilson, 1986.
34. Imperial Foods. Personal communication. Additional information from local authorities.
35. Fleet K. Is Goldsmith Argyll's secret weapon? *Times*, 5 March 1986.
36. United Biscuits. Annual reports, 1984–86. Additional information from local authorities.
37. Websters. Personal communication. Additional information from local authorities.
38. Ranks Hovis McDougall. Annual reports 1984–86. Additional information from local authorities.
39. Tate & Lyle. Personal communication. Additional information from local authorities.

40. Rowntree Mackintosh. Annual reports, 1984–86. Additional information from local authorities.
41. Beecham. Annual reports, 1984–86. Additional information from local authorities.
42. National Association of Master Bakers, Confectioners and Caterers. Annual reports, 1982–84.
43. Coleman T. A man at home with fact and fiction. *Guardian*, 30 November 1985.
44. Nestlé. Personal communication. Additional information from local authorities.
45. Anon. Art, hotels and restaurants are hungry for cash. *Times*, 9 November 1985.
46. Kelloggs. Personal communication. Additional information from local authorities.
47. Lean G. The last straw. *Observer*, 29 June 1986.
48. National Dairy Council. Personal communication.
49. Heinz. Personal communication. Additional information from local authorities.
50. Associated British Foods. Annual reports, 1984–86. Additional information from local authorities.
51. Reckitt & Colman. Publicity material, 1985. Additional information from local authorities.
52. Jordan G. Parliament under pressure. *Political Quarterly* 1985; 56 (2): 174–182.

DOCUMENT B

1. Ministry of Agriculture, Fisheries and Food. Food Standards Committee. Appointment of members. Press notice no 278, 7 September 1977.
2. Ministry of Agriculture, Fisheries and Food. Food Standards Committee. Appointment of members. Press notice no 317, 1 September 1982.
3. British Society for Social Responsibility in Science. Our daily bread: who makes the dough. London: BSSRS, 1978.
4. Ministry of Agriculture, Fisheries and Food. Food Additives and Contaminants Committee. Appointment of members. Press notice no 402, 10 November 1982.
5. Ministry of Agriculture, Fisheries and Food. Food Advisory Committee. Press release no 377. 1 November 1984.
6. Ministry of Agriculture, Fisheries and Food. Personal communication.
7. British Nutrition Foundation. Annual reports 1967–86. London: BNF. 1968–86.
8. Cabinet Office. Advisory Council for Applied Research and Development. The food industry and technology. London: HMSO, 1982.

9. Ministry of Agriculture, Fisheries and Food. Priorities Board for Research and Development in Agriculture and Food. First report. London: MAFF, 1985.

10 Department of Health and Social Security. Chief Medical Officer's Committee on Medical Aspects of Food Policy (COMA). Briefing document, 1984. Unpublished.

11. The Sugar Bureau. Sweet news. News bulletin, 9 May 1986. London: The Sugar Bureau.

12. British Library. Research in British universities, polytechnics and colleges, 1980–85. London: British Library.

13. Woo R., Garrow J., Pi-Sunyer F-X. Effect of exercise on spontaneous calorie intake in obesity. Am. J. Clin. Nutr. 1982; 36: 470–477, 478–484.

14. Keen H. Sugar and diabetes. Diabetes: putting sugar in perspective. Literature for doctors produced and distributed by the Sugar Bureau. London: Sugar Bureau, May 1985.

15. Keen H., Thomas B., Jarrett R., Fuller J. Nutrient intake, adiposity and diabetes. Br. Med. J. 1979; 1: 655–58.

16. World Sugar Research Organisation. Recent research projects sponsored by members of WSRO: a global effort. Special bulletin no. 1. London: WSRO, 1983.

17. University of Nottingham. Annual report 1984–85.

18. Milk Marketing Board. Personal communication.

19. Young R. Food rumpus over 'healthy' crisps. The Times, 10 March 1986.

20. Somerville G. Statements made at Sugar Bureau presentation, 9 and 15 May 1986.

21. Burgen A. The safety and wholesomeness of irradiated foods. Press conference. Public communication. 10 April 1986.

22. House of Commons. Irradiated food: conflict of interest. Early Day Motion, 2 April 1986.

23. Ministry of Agriculture, Fisheries and Food, Peggy Fenner MP. Letters to Jonathan Aitken MP, Michael Meadowcroft MP, Barry Sheerman MP, Tony Lloyd MP. June 1986.

24. Medical Research Directory. London: Wiley Medical Publications, 1983.

25. Royal Hospital, Liverpool. Personal communication.

26. Thames Television. 'Good Enough To Eat?' Programme transmitted 8 October 1985.

27. Macdonald I, Brice J., Coles B., Jourdan M. The influence of sucrose intake on the concentration of lipids proteins and glucose in the plasma. Proc. Nutr. Soc. 1969; 28: 62A.

28. Stovin V., Macdonald I. Some effects of an oral contraceptive on dietary carbohydrate-lipid inter-relationships in the baboon. Proc. Nutr. Soc. 1974; 34: 55A–56A.

29. Macdonald I., Rebello T., Keyser A. Effects in the rate of early carbohydrate feeding on carbohydrate-lipid relationships. Proc. Nutr. Soc. 1974; 34: 56A–57A.

30. Macdonald I., Taylor J. Differences in body-weight loss on diets

containing either sucrose or glucose syrup. *Guys Hospital Reports,* 1973; 122: 155–159.

31. Macdonald I. Effects of fats and carbohydrates on skin. *Brit. J. Dermatol* 1973; 88: 267–271.

32. Macdonald I. The influence of exercise and dietary carbohydrates on the serum lipids. *Guys Hospital Reports,* 1966; 115: 1–8.

33. Macdonald I. Dietary carbohydrates and serum lipids. *Clin. Sci.* 1965; 29: 193–197.

34. Macdonald I. Dietary fructose and serum lipid levels in man. *Proc. Nutr. Soc.* 1965; 25: iii–iv.

35. Macdonald I. Impact of five-day diets on various carbohydrates on the serum lipids in man. *Proc. Nutr. Soc.* 1964; 24: v–vi.

36. Macdonald I, Braithwaite P. The different lipid response in adult males to dietary starch and sucrose. *Proc. Nutr. Soc.* 1963; 33: i–ii.

37. Phillips T., Macdonald I., Keyser A. Some metabolic effects of ingesting galactose, before and after a high lactose diet. *Proc. Nutr. Soc.* 1977; 37: 24A.

38. Macdonald I. *Proc. Nutr. Soc.* 1973; 33: 51A–52A.

39. Macdonald I. *Proc. Nutr. Soc.* 1972; 32: 33A–34A.

40. Wusteman M., Macdonald I. The effect of intermediates on the incorporation of fructose and glucose into hepatic triglyceride in rats. *Proc. Nutr. Soc.* 1972; 32: 35A.

41. Fraser A. Objectives and programme of activities of the Foundation: *British Nutrition Foundation Bulletin*: 1968; 1: 1–8.

42. Allen R. Nutrition and the food and drink industries. Food and Drink Industries Council Bulletin 1980; 14: 1–5.

43. Food and Drink Federation, Annual reports 1984–86. London: FDF, 1985–86.

44. Food and Drink Industries Council. Annual reports 1980–83, Bulletins 1976–79. London: FDIC, 1976–84.

45. Food Manufacturers Federation. Annual reports 1966–84. London: FMF, 1967–85.

46. Who's Who in the World. Chicago: Marquis Who's Who, 1979.

47. London University. Queen Elizabeth College/Kings College Annual reports 1969–85. London QEC/KC, 1970–86.

48. National Association of British and Irish Millers. Personal communication.

49. Technology Assessment Consumerism Centre. Bread. The TACC report. London: Intermediate Publishing, 1974.

50. Anon. MMB appoints a full-time nutritional consultant. *Grocer,* 6 September 1986.

51. Anon. The Food Research Institute, Reading, looks to the future. *Dairy Industries International,* April 1985.

52. Shrimpton D. Personal communication.

53. Truswell A. Effects of different types of dietary fibre on plasma lipids. In: Hector K. (ed). *Dietary Fibre.* London: John Libbey, 1978.

54. National Dairy Council. Calcium and health. Fact file. London, NDC, 1986.

55. Wren J. The future of food processing. *Chem. and Ind.* 7 April 1986.

56. Yudkin J. Personal communication.
57. Ministry of Agriculture, Fisheries and Food. Food Safety Research Consultative Committee. Report to the Priorities Board. London: MAFF, 1985.
58. McDonalds Hamburgers. Good food, nutrition and McDonalds. Booklet. London: McDonalds, 1984.
59. Guys Hospital Medical School. Annual report of the Dept. of Medicine 1975–82. London: Guys Hospital.

DOCUMENT C

1. Passmore R., Eastwood M. *Human Nutrition and Dietetics*. Eighth edition. Edinburgh: Churchill Livingstone, 1986.
2. McLaren D. *Nutrition and its Disorders*. Edinburgh: Churchill Livingstone, 1981.
3. Pyke M. *Man and Food*. London: World University Library, 1970.
4. Sheiham H., Quick A. The rickets report. Why do British Asians get rickets? London: Haringey CHC, 1982.
5. Barber S., Bull N., Buss D. Low iron intakes among young women in Britain. *Br. Med. J.* 1985; 290: 743–744.
6. Acheson E. Food policy, nutrition and government. Tenth Boyd Orr Memorial Lecture. *Proc. Nutr. Soc.* 1986; 45: 131–138.
7. Department of Health and Social Security. Recommended intakes of nutrients in the United Kingdom. Committee on Medical Aspects of Food Policy. London HMSO, 1969, 1981.
8. Department of Health and Social Security. Eating for health. London: HMSO, 1979.
9. Department of Health and Social Security. Prevention and health: everybody's business. London: HMSO, 1981.
10. McKeown T. *The Role of Medicine*. Dream, mirage or nemesis? Oxford: Blackwell, 1979.
11. Reader's Digest. *Family Medical Adviser*. London: Reader's Digest, 1983.
12. Thomson W. *Black's Medical Dictionary*. Thirty-third edition. London: Adam and Charles Black, 1981.
13. Campbell E., Scadding J., Roberts R. The concept of disease. *Br. Med. J.* 1979; 2: 757–762.
14. Bernard C. *An Introduction to the Study of Experimental Medicine*, 1878. Translated by Greene H. New York: Schuman, 1949.
15. Kuhn T. *The Structure of Scientific Revolutions*. Chicago: University Press, 1970.
16. Planck M. *Scientific Autobiography and Other Papers*. New York: 1949.
17. White P., Sprague H., Stamler J. et al. A statement on arteriosclerosis. Main cause of 'heart attacks' and 'strokes'. New York: National Health Education Committee, 1959.
18. Cleave T. *The Saccharine Disease*. Bristol: John Wright, 1974.

19. Veith I. *The Yellow Emperor's Classic in Internal Medicine.* Berkeley; University of California Press, 1966.
20. Boyd Eaton S., Konner M. Paleolithic nutrition. *New. Eng. J. Med* 1985; 312: 283–289, 1458–1459.
21. Joossens J., Geboers J. Cardiovascular diseases, cancer and nutrition. Acta Cardiologica 1983; 38: 1–12.
22. Burkitt D., Trowell H. (eds). *Refined Carbohydrate Foods and Disease.* Some implications of dietary fibre. London: Academic Press, 1975.
23. Sinclair H. Deficiency of essential fatty acids and atherosclerosis etc. *Lancet* 1956; II: 381–383.
24. Wretlind A. Nutrition problems in healthy adults with low activity and low caloric consumption. In: Blix G. (ed). *Nutrition and Physical Activity,* Stockholm: Almqvist and Wiksell, 1967.
25. Mayer J. Heart disease. Plans for action. In: Mayer J. (ed). *US Nutrition Policies in the 1970s,* San Francisco: W.H. Freeman, 1973.
26. Trowell H. *Non-Infective Diseases in Africa.* London: Edward Arnold, 1960.
27. Sinclair H. Personal communication.
28. The Sports Council. Exercise, health and medicine. London: Sports Council, 1984.
29. Scrimshaw N., Taylor C., Gordon T. *Interactions of Nutrition and Infection.* Geneva: WHO, 1968.
30. Gontzea I. *Nutrition and Anti-Infectious Defence.* Basel: Karger, 1974.
31. National Research Council. Recommended dietary allowances. Committee on dietary allowances, Food and Nutrition Board. Washington: National Academy of Sciences, 1980.
32. World Health Organisation. Prevention of coronary heart disease. Report of a WHO expert committee. Geneva: WHO, 1982.
33. Department of Health and Social Security. Diet and cardiovascular disease. Committee on Medical Aspects of Food Policy. London: HMSO, 1984.
34. Riemersma R., Wood D., Butler S., et al. Linoleic acid content in adipose tissue and coronary heart disease. *Br. Med. J.* 1986; 292: 1423–1427.
35. Burkitt D. Varicose veins, haemorrhoids, deep-vein thrombosis and pelvic phleboliths. In: Trowell H., Burkitt D., Heaton K. *Dietary Fibre, Fibre-Depleted Foods and Disease,* London: Academic Press, 1985.
36. Faculty of Community Medicine of the Royal College of Physicians. Dietary salt and health. In preparation.
37. Ackley S., Barrett-Connor E., Suarez L. Dairy products, calcium and blood pressure. *Am. J. Clin. Nutr.* 1983; 38: 347–361.
38. MacGregor G. Dietary sodium and potassium intake and blood pressure. *Lancet* 1983; I: 750–753.
39. American Heart Association. Rationale of the diet-heart statement of the AHA. Report of Nutrition Committee. Circulation 1982; 65 (4) 839A–854A.

40. Trowell H., Burkitt D. (eds). *Western Diseases. Their emergence and prevention*. London: Edward Arnold, 1981.

41. Marmot M. Diet, hypertension and stroke. In: Turner M. (ed): *Nutrition and Health*, Lancaster: MTP, 1982.

42. Laplan L. Carotid-artery disease. *New Eng. J. Med.* 1986; 315: 886–888.

43. Royal College of Physicians of London. *Medical Aspects of Dietary Fibre*. Tunbridge Wells: Pitman, 1980.

44. Kremer J., Michalek A., Lininger L., et al. Effects of manipulation of dietary fatty acids on clinical manifestations of rheumatoid arthritis. *Lancet* 1985; I: 184–187.

45. Anon. Acid rain and human health. *Lancet* 1985; I: 616–617.

46. Schorah C. Inappropriate vitamin C reserves: their frequency and significance in an urban population. In: *The Importance of Vitamins to Human Health*, ed. Taylor T. Lancaster: MTP, 1979.

47. Craig G., Elliot C., Hughes K. Masked vitamin B12 and folate deficiency in the elderly. *Br. J. Nutr.* 1985; 54: 613–619.

48. Prasad A. The role of zinc in gastrointestinal and liver disease. *Clin. Gastroenterol* 1983; 12: 713–741.

49. Aggett P., Davies N. Some nutritional aspects of trace metals. *J. Inher. Metab. Dis.* 1983; 6(2): 22–30.

50. Egger J., Wilson J., Carter C., Turner M., Soothill J. Is migraine food allergy? *Lancet* 1983: II: 865–869.

51. Shelley E., Dean G. Multiple Sclerosis. In: Trowell H., Burkitt D. (eds). *Western Diseases: their emergence and prevention*. London: Edward Arnold, 1981.

52. Markovits P. Pyridoxine and riboflavin status in mothers suffering from post-natal depression. Study presented to the XIII International Congress of Nutrition, Brighton, 1985. Unpublished.

53. Reuler J., Girard D., Cooney T. Wernicke's encephalopathy. *New Eng. J. Med.* 1985; 312: 1035–1039.

54. Burkitt D. The aetiology of appendicitis. *Br. J. Surg.* 1971; 58: 695–699.

55. National Research Council. Diet, Nutrition and Cancer. Committee on Diet, Nutrition and Cancer. Assembly of life sciences. Washington: National Academy Press, 1982.

56. Bristol J., Emmett P., Heaton K., Williamson R. Sugar, fat, and the risk of colo-rectal cancer. *Br. Med. J.* 1985; 291: 1467–1470.

57. Salonen J., Salonen R., Lappeteläinen R., et al. Risk of cancer in relation to serum concentrations of selenium and vitamins A and E: matched case-control analysis of prospective data. *Br. Med. J.* 1985; 290: 417–420.

58. Willett W., McMahon B. Diet and cancer – an overview. *New Eng. J. Med* 1984; 310: 633–638, 697–703.

59. Garland C., Shekelle R., Barrett-Connor E., et al. Dietary vitamin D and calcium and risk of colorectal cancers: a 19–year prospective study in men. *Lancet* 1985; I: 307.

60. Heaton K. Crohn's disease and ulcerative colitis. In: Trowell H., Burkitt D., Heaton K. (eds). *Dietary Fibre, Fibre-Depleted Foods and*

544   THE POLITICS OF FOOD

Disease. London: Academic Press, 1985.

61. Hollander D., Tarnanski A. Dietary essential fatty acids and the decline in peptic ulcer disease – a hypothesis. *Gut* 1986; 27: 239–242.

62. Cleave T. *Peptic Ulcer.* Bristol: John Wright, 1962.

63. Health Education Council. The scientific basis of dental health education. London: HEC, 1985.

64. Workman E., Hunter J., Alun Jones V. *The Allergy Diet.* London: Martin Dunitz, 1984.

65. American Association for Cancer Research. Alcohol and cancer workshop. *Cancer Research* 1979; 39 (7,2): 2816–2908.

66. Begin M., Das V., Ells G., Horrobin D. Selective killing of human cancer cells by polyunsaturated fatty acids. *Prostaglandins, Leukotrienes and Medicine* 1985; 19: 177–186.

67. Horrobin D. The role of essential fatty acids and prostaglandins in breast cancer. In: Cohen L., Reddy S. (eds). *Diet, Nutrition, and Cancer*: a critical evaluation. Volume I. Boca Raton, Florida: CRC Press, 1 1985.

68. Brush M., Perry M. Pyridoxine and the pre-menstrual syndrome. *Lancet* 1985; I: 1399.

69. Wright A., Ryan F, Willingham S., et al. Food allergy or intolerance in severe recurrent aphthous ulceration of the mouth. *Br. Med. J.* 1986; 292: 1237–1238.

70. Sandstead H., Henriksen L., Greger J., Prasad A., Good R. Zinc nutriture in the elderly in relation to taste acuity, immune response, and wound healing. *Am. J. Clin. Nutr* 1982; 36; 1046–1059.

71. Juhlin L. Recurrent urticaria: clinical investigation of 330 patients. *Br. J. Dermatol* 1981; 104: 369–381.

72. Braganza J. Selenium deficiency, cystic fibrosis, and pancreatic cancer. *Lancet* 1985; II: 1238.

73. Reiser S. Physiological differences between starches and sugars. In: Bland J. (ed). *Medical Applications of Clinical Nutrition,* New Canaan, Connecticut: Keats, 1983.

74. West K. *Epidemiology of Diabetes and its Vascular Lesions.* New York: Elsevier, 1978.

75. Trowell H. Hypertension, obesity, diabetes mellitus and coronary heart disease. In: Trowell H., Burkitt D. (eds). *Western Diseases; their emergence and prevention,* London: Edward Arnold, 1981.

76. Heaton K. Gallstones. In: Trowell H., Burkitt D. (eds). *Western Diseases: their emergence and prevention,* London: Edward Arnold, 1981.

77. Heaton K. The sweet road to gall stones. *Lancet* 1984; I: 1103–1104.

78 Blacklock N. Feast and famine: the chronicle of the stones. *Nutr. and Health* 1982; 2: 89–100.

79. Rao P., Prendiville V., Buxton A., et al. Dietary management of urinary risk factors in renal stone formers. *Br. J. Urol.* 1982; 54: 578–583.

80. Saunders J. Alcoholic liver disease in the 1980s. *Br. Med. J.* 1983; 287: 1919–1921.

81. Royal College of Physicians of London. Obesity. *J. Roy. Coll. Phys.* London 1983; 17: 3–58.

82. Heaton K. Other nutritional implications: energy and micronutrients. In: Trowell H., Burkitt D., Heaton K. (eds). *Dietary Fibre, Fibre-Depleted Foods and Disease*. London: Academic Press, 1985.

83. Van Itallie T. Dietary fiber and obesity. *Am. J. Clin. Nutr.* 1978; 31: 43–52.

84. Smithells R., Seller M., Harris R., et al. Further evidence of vitamin supplementation for prevention of neural tube defects recurrences. *Lancet* 1983; I: 1027–1031.

85. Smithells R. Prevention of neural tube defects by vitamin supplementation. In: Dobbing J. (ed). *Prevention of spina bifida and other neural tube defects*. London: Academic Press, 1983.

86. Beattie J., Day R., Cockburn F., Garg R. Alcohol and the foetus in the west of Scotland. *Br. Med. J.* 1983; 287: 17–20.

87. Wright J., Harrison I., Lewis I., et al. Alcohol consumption, pregnancy and low birth weight. *Lancet* 1983; I: 663–665.

88. Meadows N., Smith M., Keeling P., et al. Zinc and small babies. *Lancet* 1981; II: 1135–1137.

89. Bellinger D., Leviton A., Needleman H., et al. Low-level lead exposure and infant development in the first year. *Neurobehavior Toxicology and Teratology* 1985; 8: 151–61.

90. Bryce-Smith D. Environmental chemical influences on behaviour and mentation. John Jeyes lecture. *Chem. Soc. Rev.* 1986; 15: 93–12.

91. McMichael A., Dresoti I., Gibson G., et al. A prospective study of serial maternal zinc levels and pregnancy outcome. *Early Human Development* 1982 (Elsevier); 7: 59–69.

92. Royal College of Physicians and British Nutrition Foundation. Food intolerance and food aversion. *J. Roy. Coll. Phys* 1984; 18: 83–123.

93. Egger J., Graham P., Carter C., Gumley D., Soothill J. Controlled trial of oligoantigenic treatment in the hyperkinetic syndrome. *Lancet* 1985; I: 540–545.

94. Department of Health and Social Security. Artificial feeds for the young infant. Committee on Medical Aspects of Food Policy. London: HMSO, 1980.

95. Addy D. Happiness is: iron. *Br. Med. J.* 1986; 292: 969–970.

96. Hambidge M. The role of zinc and other trace metals in paediatric nutrition and health. *Paediat. Clin. N. Am.* 1977; 24: 95–106.

97. Bryce-Smith D., Simpson R. Anorexia, depression, and zinc deficiency. *Lancet* 1984; ii: 1162.

98. Fonseca V., Harvard C. Electrolyte disturbances and cardiac failure with hypomagnesaemia in anorexia nervosa. *Br. Med. J.* 1985; 291: 1680–1682.

INDEX